TURKEY

6th Edition

**Where to Stay and Eat
for All Budgets**

**Must-See Sights
and Local Secrets**

Ratings You Can Trust

Fodor's Travel Publications   New York, Toronto, London, Sydney, Auckland
www.fodors.com

FODOR'S TURKEY
Editor: Caroline Trefler

Contributors: Carissa Bluestone, Stephen Brewer, Evin Doğu, Benjamin Harvey, Yeşim Erdem Holland, Gareth Jenkins, Hugh Pope, Yigal Schleifer
Editorial Production: Linda K. Schmidt
Maps: David Lindroth, Inc., *cartographer*; Rebecca Baer and Bob Blake, *map editors*
Design: Fabrizio La Rocca, *creative director*; Guido Caroti, *art director*; Moon Sun Kim, *cover designer*; Melanie Marin, *senior picture editor*
Production/Manufacturing: Robert Shields
Cover Photo (Spice Bazaar, Istanbul): Dennis Cox

SPECIAL SALES
This book is available at special discounts for bulk purchases for sales promotions or premiums. Special editions, including personalized covers, excerpts of existing books, and corporate imprints, can be created in large quantities for special needs. For more information, write to Special Markets/Premium Sales, 1745 Broadway, MD 6-2, New York, New York 10019, or e-mail specialmarkets@randomhouse.com.

AN IMPORTANT TIP & AN INVITATION
Although all prices, opening times, and other details in this book are based on information supplied to us at press time, changes occur all the time in the travel world, and Fodor's cannot accept responsibility for facts that become outdated or for inadvertent errors or omissions. So **always confirm information when it matters,** especially if you're making a detour to visit a specific place. Your experiences—positive and negative—matter to us. If we have missed or misstated something, **please write to us.** We follow up on all suggestions. Contact the Turkey editor at editors@fodors.com or c/o Fodor's at 1745 Broadway, New York, NY 10019.

PRINTED IN THE UNITED STATES OF AMERICA

10 9 8 7 6 5 4 3 2 1

Be a Fodor's Correspondent

Your opinion matters. It matters to us. It matters to your fellow Fodor's travelers, too. And we'd like to hear it. In fact, we *need* to hear it.

When you share your experiences and opinions, you become an active member of the Fodor's community. That means we'll not only use your feedback to make our books better, but we'll publish your name and comments whenever possible. Throughout our guides, look for "Word of Mouth," excerpts of your unvarnished feedback.

Here's how you can help improve Fodor's for all of us.

Tell us when we're right. We rely on local writers to give you an insider's perspective. But our writers and staff editors—who are the best in the business—depend on you. Your positive feedback is a vote to renew our recommendations for the next edition.

Tell us when we're wrong. We're proud that we update most of our guides every year. But we're not perfect. Things change. Hotels cut services. Museums change hours. Charming cafés lose charm. If our writer didn't quite capture the essence of a place, tell us how you'd do it differently. If any of our descriptions are inaccurate or inadequate, we'll incorporate your changes in the next edition and will correct factual errors at fodors.com *immediately.*

Tell us what to include. You probably have had fantastic travel experiences that aren't yet in Fodor's. Why not share them with a community of like-minded travelers? Maybe you chanced upon a beach or bistro or B&B that you don't want to keep to yourself. Tell us why we should include it. And share your discoveries and experiences with everyone directly at fodors.com. Your input may lead us to add a new listing or highlight a place we cover with a "Highly Recommended" star or with our highest rating, "Fodor's Choice."

Give us your opinion instantly at our feedback center at www.fodors.com/feedback. You may also e-mail editors@fodors.com with the subject line "Turkey Editor." Or send your nominations, comments, and complaints by mail to Turkey Editor, Fodor's, 1745 Broadway, New York, NY 10019.

You and travelers like you are the heart of the Fodor's community. Make our community richer by sharing your experiences. Be a Fodor's correspondent.

Iyi yolculuklar! (Or simply: Happy traveling!)

Tim Jarrell, Publisher

CONTENTS

CLOSEUPS

MAPS

ABOUT THIS BOOK

Our Ratings

Sometimes you find terrific travel experiences and sometimes they just find you. But usually the burden is on you to select the right combination of experiences. That's where our ratings come in.

As travelers we've all discovered a place so wonderful that its worthiness is obvious. And sometimes that place is so unique that superlatives don't do it justice: you just have to be there to know. These sights, properties, and experiences get our highest rating, **Fodor's Choice,** indicated by orange stars throughout this book.

Black stars highlight sights and properties we deem **Highly Recommended,** places that our writers, editors, and readers praise again and again for consistency and excellence.

By default, there's another category: any place we include in this book is by definition worth your time, unless we say otherwise. And we will.

Disagree with any of our choices? Care to nominate a place or suggest that we rate one more highly? Visit our feedback center at www.fodors.com/feedback.

Budget Well

Hotel and restaurant price categories from ¢ to $$$$ are defined in the opening pages of each chapter. For attractions, we always give standard adult admission fees; reductions are usually available for children, students, and senior citizens. Want to pay with plastic? **AE, D, DC, MC, V** following restaurant and hotel listings indicate whether American Express, Discover, Diner's Club, MasterCard, and Visa are accepted.

Restaurants

Unless we state otherwise, restaurants are open for lunch and dinner daily. We mention dress only when there's a specific requirement and reservations only when they're essential or not accepted—it's always best to book ahead.

Hotels

Hotels have private bath, phone, TV, and air-conditioning and operate on the European Plan (aka EP, meaning without meals), unless we specify that they use the Continental Plan (CP, with a continental breakfast), Breakfast Plan (BP, with a full breakfast), or Modified American Plan (MAP, with breakfast and dinner) or are all-inclusive (AI, including all meals and most activities). We always list facilities but not whether you'll be charged an extra fee to use them, so when pricing accommodations, find out what's included.

Many Listings

⭐	Fodor's Choice
★	Highly recommended
⊠	Physical address
✛	Directions
⑦	Mailing address
☎	Telephone
🖷	Fax
⊕	On the Web
✆	E-mail
☜	Admission fee
☉	Open/closed times
►	Start of walk/itinerary
Ⓜ	Metro stations
▭	Credit cards

Hotels & Restaurants

🏨	Hotel
⌸	Number of rooms
⌂	Facilities
⏍○⏍	Meal plans
✕	Restaurant
⌂	Reservations
🏛	Dress code
⌇	Smoking
⌾⌾	BYOB
✕🏨	Hotel with restaurant that warrants a visit

Outdoors

⛳	Golf
⛺	Camping

Other

☕	Family-friendly
🎦	Contact information
⇨	See also
⊠	Branch address
☞	Take note

WHAT'S WHERE

ISTANBUL	The undisputed cultural, economic, and historical capital of Turkey, Istanbul has enough monuments and attractions (as well as enticing restaurants and shops) to keep you busy for days. Straddling Europe and Asia, the city once known as Constantinople, capital of the Byzantine and then the Ottoman Empire, has for centuries been a bustling and cosmopolitan crossroads. The Byzantine-built Aya Sofya and the Ottoman-era Blue Mosque and Topkapı Palace are within walking distance of each other, while other historic mosques and churches are sprinkled throughout the city. Wonderful museums, covering the spectrum from archaeology to modern art, are also here. Want to shop? Head for the sprawling Grand Bazaar or trendy new boutiques. Hungry? Istanbul is filled with top-notch restaurants, from simple kebab joints to swank rooftop restaurants and laidback fish restaurants along the shores of the Bosphorus strait, which flows through the middle of the city. Despite its crowds and bustle, this is a city that can work its charms on anyone.
THE SEA OF MARMARA & THE NORTH AEGEAN	This area doesn't have the high-wattage appeal of the Aegean and Mediterranean regions farther south, but that doesn't mean it should be overlooked. If you're searching for an easy and relaxing day trip from Istanbul, try the lakeside town of İznik, an ancient tilemaking center. For history buffs, there's the archaeological site of ancient Troy (complete with a mockup of that famous Trojan horse) and the battlefields of Gallipoli. The beaches here tend to be more pebbly and the water a touch colder than in other regions, but they are also frequently less crowded, since the European package-tour crowd has yet to descend on this part of the Turkish coast. The area around the charming village of Assos, overlooking the Greek island of Lesbos, has several quiet coves and beaches nearby, while the small villages that dot the pine-covered slopes of nearby Mount Ida are some of the most relaxing spots in Turkey.
THE CENTRAL AND SOUTHERN AEGEAN COAST	This is the heart of what was once known by the ancient Greeks as Asia Minor, an area that's been drawing visitors since the time of, well, Homer. İzmir, a busy port town that is Turkey's third-largest city, is a good gateway for exploring the area, with regular flights to and from Istanbul and some European destinations. Near İzmir is the Çeşme peninsula, home to some lovely sandy beaches and the cobblestoned town of Alaçatı. The area's heavyweight attraction, though, is the

WHAT'S WHERE

Roman city of Ephesus, with its well-preserved amphitheater and library. In this region are also the less-visited, though still impressive, ruins of the ancient cities of Didyma, Miletus, and Hierapolis. For a taste of up-to-date Turkey, head to Bodrum, which is getting the reputation of being the St. Tropez of Turkey; the beaches here are not the prettiest and overdevelopment threatens, but with its profusion of seaside restaurants and swank cafés and nightclubs, visitors can get strong doses of sun and (mostly sophisticated) fun.

THE TURQUOISE RIVIERA

Turkey's southern shores—which have been dubbed the Turquoise Riviera—are rapidly becoming one of the country's most popular destinations. It's not surprising. The beaches here, like the long and sandy ones at Patara or İztuzu, are among the best in Turkey and the ruins, such as the grand Roman amphitheater at Aspendos or the cliffside rock tombs in Dalyan, are spectacular. Add to this the chance to visit unspoiled seaside villages with truly charming little hotels and *pansiyons,* and you have something very close to paradise. On the flipside, megaresorts catering to low-budget package tourists have started to invade parts of this area, particularly around Antalya. If you really want to get away from it all, head to the port of Marmaris, where you can charter a boat to take you on a Blue Cruise, a meandering, days-long trip that will bring you to remote coves and beaches where you and your boatmates can swim in splendid isolation.

CAPPADOCIA, ANKARA & THE TURKISH HEARTLAND

It may be far from the beaches of the Aegean and Mediterranean, and the glitter of Istanbul, but central Turkey has charms all its own, especially in magical Cappadocia. Here, wind and rain have over time shaped the area's soft volcanic rock into a kind of fairytale landscape, where conical outcroppings were centuries ago turned into churches and homes. The small towns of Ürgüp, Göreme, and Uçhisar are good spots to visit some of these fascinating structures. Even more amazing is what lies below: underground cities that reached 20 stories beneath the surface and could hold up to 20,000 people. The Ihlara valley, a deep gorge that has ancient churches and villages cut into its cliffs and a green river running through it, is another Cappadocian highlight. Southwest of Cappadocia is Konya, home to a fascinating museum and tomb dedicated to the 13th-century founder of the whirling dervishes. Known as Turkey's most religiously conservative city, Konya

is not a place for those looking for nightlife (alcohol can be difficult to find in the city) or a dining-out scene. This region's other major city is the Turkish capital, Ankara, a mostly characterless city that ranks fairly low on most visitors' itineraries: save for an excellent museum covering Turkey's ancient past and the mausoleum of Atatürk, modern Turkey's founder, there is little here that will help change that.

THE FAR EAST AND THE BLACK SEA COAST

Turkey's eastern half is the place for getting off the beaten path and finding adventure. It may not have the resorts, boutique hotels, and upscale restaurants of western Turkey, but the region makes up for it with its impressive sites—both natural and manmade. In the Black Sea area, rocky beaches are backed by the verdant and majestic Kaçkar mountains—which sometimes look like a little slice of the Alps in Turkey—where you can hike, relax in picturesque mountain villages, or visit the historic city of Trabzon and the nearby cliffside monastery of Sumela. The remote area between the cities of Kars and Van, in Turkey's far east, is home to several wonders: the haunting ancient city of Ani, former capital of an Armenian kingdom; the towering Mt. Ararat, believed by some to be the resting place of Noah's Ark; and the bewitching mountains and historical sites around Lake Van. The walled city of Diyarbakır and beautiful nearby towns of Mardin and Midyat lie in the heart of the ancient region known as Mesopotamia, where you can wander through historic neighborhoods with winding streets and old stone homes and visit churches that date back to the 3rd and 4th centuries AD. The area around the ancient cities of Gaziantep and Şanlıurfa, Turkey's southeast, is steeped in biblical history. Here you can walk through the bustling local bazaars, eat scrumptious local cuisine, and head off for a sunrise visit to fascinating Nemrut Dağı (Mt. Nimrod in English), a mountaintop temple built by a local monarch some 2,000 years ago. In all of these places, you are certain to get a taste of a very different and rewarding Turkey.

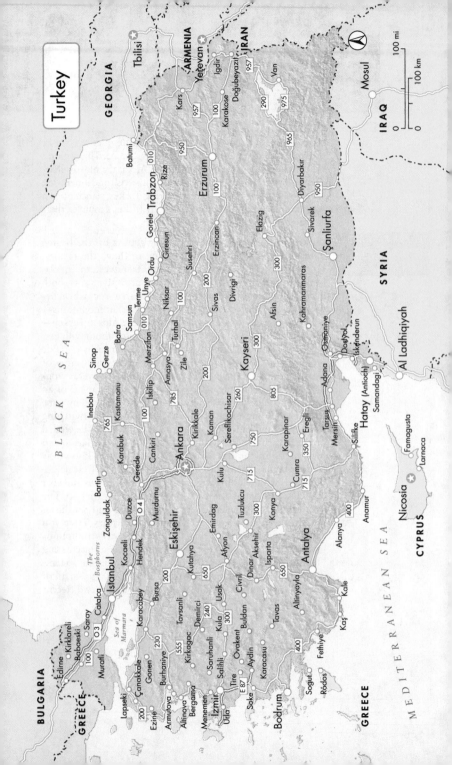

WHEN TO GO

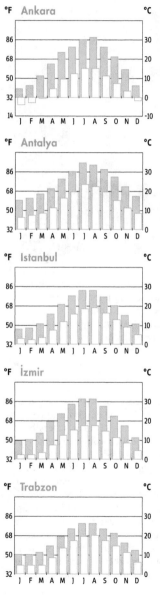

°F Ankara °C

°F Antalya °C

°F Istanbul °C

°F İzmir °C

°F Trabzon °C

Istanbul tends to be hot in summer, cold in winter. The Mediterranean (Turquoise) and Aegean coasts have mild winters and hot summers; you can swim along either coast from late April into October. The Black Sea coast is mild and damp, with a rainfall of 90 inches per year. Central and eastern Anatolia can be extremely cold in winter, and their roads and mountain passes closed by snow; summers bring hot, dry weather, with cool evenings.

Most tourists visit Turkey between April and the end of October. July and August are the busiest months (and the hottest). April through June and September and October offer more temperate weather, smaller crowds, and somewhat lower hotel prices.

🔲 Forecasts **AccuWeather** (⊕ www.accuweather.com). **CNN Weather** (⊕ www.cnn.com/weather). **Weather Channel Connection** (☎ 900/932–8437 95¢ per minute from a Touch-Tone phone ⊕ www.weather.com). **Yahoo Weather** (⊕ weather.yahoo.com).

QUINTESSENTIAL TURKEY

Tea

Visitors who come to Turkey expecting to be served thick Turkish coffee at every turn are in for a surprise—tea is the hot beverage of choice and you'll be offered it wherever you go: when looking at rugs in the Grand Bazaar or when finishing your meal in even the humblest restaurant. Tea, called *çay*, is grown domestically, along the verdant slopes of the Black Sea coast. Flavorful and aromatic, it's not prepared from tea bags, a concept that horrifies most Turks. Rather, it is made in a double boiler that has a larger kettle on the bottom for heating up the water and a smaller kettle on top where a dark concentrate is made using loose tea leaves. The resulting brew—strong and rust-colored—is usually served in a small, tulip-shaped glass, along with two or more cubes of sugar (but never, Allah forbid, with milk or lemon). If you want your tea weak (light), be sure to ask for an *açık çay.*

Most teahouses carry a range of herbal teas, which are also very popular, especially *ada çayı* (sage tea) and *ıhlamur çayı* (linden flower tea). *Elma çayı* (apple tea), usually made from a synthetic powder, is often served to tourists.

Mezes

Good things come in small packages, and the Turkish tradition of serving appetizers known as *mezes*—Turkey's version of tapas—is proof. *Mezes* originated when simple dishes—usually a slice of tangy feta cheese with honeydew melon and fresh bread— were brought out to accompany *rakı*, the anise-flavored spirit that is Turkey national drink. From its humble origins, though, the *meze* tradition has developed into something quite elaborate. Today, in the *meyhanes* (literally "drinking places") of Istanbul and other restaurants throughout Turkey, waiters will approach your

For many Westerners, visiting Turkey is an exotic experience, but it's incredibly easy to get drawn into the everyday rituals that make life here such a pleasure. Eat, drink, shop . . . you'll quickly understand the allure of the country and why the Turks are reknowned for their hospitality.

table with a heavy wooden tray loaded down with sometimes more than 20 different kinds of small dishes—smoky eggplant puree, artichoke hearts braised in olive oil, slices of cured fish, perhaps—for you to choose from. Just point at whatever looks good and the dish will be placed on your table.

Markets and Bargaining

A highlight of any trip to Turkey is a stroll through one of the country's delightful markets; they provide the chance to experience the country at its most vibrant and colorful. The granddaddy of them all is, of course, the Grand Bazaar in Istanbul, a must-see simply because of its sheer size and historical significance. Though touristy, this is the most convenient place to stock up on the souvenirs—inlaid wood backgammon sets, colorful ceramic bowls, and of course, rugs—you'll want to bring back home.

Remember, in all of Turkey's markets, bargaining is the norm. Every vendor (and every buyer, as you will soon discover about yourself) has his or her own style, but some general rules govern the interaction. The seller will undoubtedly offer you a high initial price, so don't feel embarrassed to come back with a price that's much lower—try half, for starters. It's your money that's being spent, so feel free to walk out at any time—although it's both bad manners and bad business to bargain aggressively or to decline to buy once the seller has accepted your offer. Remember, too, don't shop in a rush. Bargaining takes time and good deals rarely come to those in a hurry.

IF YOU LIKE

Ancient Sites

Turkey, a sort of bridge between Europe and Asia, has been a cultural crossroads for thousands of years. Numerous civilizations—Greeks from the west and Mongols from east—settled or moved through the (vast) area at one point or another, leaving lasting and impressive reminders of their sojourns. As a result, virtually every region in Turkey has a bounty of stunning ancient ruins.

Mt. Nemrut: At the top of a desolate mountain, this 2,000-year-old temple—a collection of larger-than-life statues facing the rising and setting sun—is a testament to the vanity of an ancient king.

Ani: The abandoned former capital of a local Armenian kingdom, this haunting city in the middle of nowhere is filled with the ruins of stunning churches.

Ephesus: This remarkably well-preserved Roman city has a colonnaded library that seems like it could still be checking out books and an amphitheater that appears ready for a show.

Termessos: This impregnable ancient city is set dramatically high up in the mountains above Antalya; even Alexander the Great and the Romans found it too difficult to attack.

Cappadocia's underground cities: A marvel of ancient engineering, these subterranean cities—some reaching 20 stories down and holding up to 20,000 people—served as a refuge for Christians under siege from Arab raiders.

Beaches

With 8,000 km (5,000 mi) of coastline, it's no wonder that Turkey is home to several world-famous beaches, and you can find all kinds: from pristine, remote coves to resort hotel beaches with water sports and all sorts of amenities.

With its frigid waters and sometimes rocky shores, the Black Sea is not usually considered a beach destination, but it has some stretches of lovely, sandy shoreline. The beaches at **Kilyos** just outside Istanbul, are among the nicest and are easy to get to, although you may find them crowded on the weekends.

The Aegean has crystal-clear waters and a mix of resorts and quieter seaside spots, although its beaches tend to be pebbly. An exception to that is **Altınkum,** near Çeşme, a series of undeveloped coves with glorious golden sand beaches.

Turkey's Mediterranean coast has turquoise waters that stay warm well into October and an abundance of picture-perfect beaches, although overdevelopment has become a problem in some parts. Thankfully, there are still a good number of unspoiled beaches left. Dalyan's **İztuzu Beach** (a nesting ground for sea turtles) stretches for 5 sandy kilometers (3 mi), with a fresh water lagoon on one side and the Mediterranean on the other. Near Fetiyeh is **Olüdeniz,** a stunning lagoon of azure waters backed by white sand. The beach at **Patara** is one of Turkey's best, an 11-km (7-mi) stretch with little but fine white sand and dunes.

Olympos, near Antalya, is another top spot, with a long crescent-shaped beach that is backed by spectacular mountains and ancient ruins.

Castles

The Byzantine and Ottoman empires may be long gone, but they left behind some truly striking monuments: churches, mosques, and palaces that still hold the power to take your breath away.

As the former capital of both empires, Istanbul has the lion's share of Turkey's most famous structures, but there are also impressive ones to be found in every other part of the country. **Aya Sofya** is the monumental church built by the emperor Justinian some 1,500 years ago continues to be an even more awe-inspiring site—arguably the most impressive one in Istanbul or Turkey. The **Kariye Museum**, in what was the Kariye Cami, is much smaller and not as famous as the Aya Sofya, but this 12th-century Byzantine church, located on the periphery of Istanbul's old city, is filled with glittering mosaics and stunning frescoes that are considered among the finest in the world.

Topkapı Palace, the former home of the Ottoman sultans, is a sumptuous palace with stately buildings, tranquil gardens, and the must-see Harem. Also in Istanbul is the **Blue Mosque:** with its cascading domes and shimmering tiles, this exquisite mosque is one of the Ottomans' finest creations.

Edirne, not far from Istanbul, was the Ottoman capital before Istanbul. It's home to **Selimiye Cami,** the mosque that was the real masterpiece of the sultans' favorite architect, Mimar Sinan. It's massive dome has made many a jaw drop.

In Turkey's far east, near the legendary Mt. Ararat, is **Ishak Paşa Sarayı,** an 18th-century palace that seems like it was transported straight out of a fairy tale.

Museums

The country's wealth and depth of history guarantee that Turkey has lots of artifacts for its museums—even if there has been a problem with other countries shipping the booty off to foreign lands. The best and biggest museums are in Istanbul, where you can spend your days hopping from one fascinating exhibit to the other. The sprawling **Archaeology Museum,** near Topkapı Palace, holds finds from digs throughout the Middle East. Nearby is the excellent **Museum of Turkish and Islamic Art,** housed in an old Ottoman palace, which displays carpets, ceramics, paintings, and folk art. For a taste of something more up-to-date, visit the stylish **Istanbul Modern,** which has a good collection of modern Turkish art and a stunning waterfront location. Also worth visiting is the **Rahmi M Koç Industrial Museum,** an old factory that is now used to display a quirky collection of cars, trains, ships, airplanes, and other industrial artifacts that will pique the interests of children and adults.

Istanbul doesn't have a monopoly on the museum business, though. The **Gaziantep Museum,** in Turkey's southeast, is one of the country's best, with a world-class collection of Roman-era mosaics. Ankara's **Museum of Anatolian Civilizations,** found in a restored 15th-century covered market, holds masterpieces spanning thousands of years of local history. Konya, in central Turkey, is home to the fascinating **Mevlâna Museum,** dedicated to the the founder of the whirling dervishes and located inside what used to be a dervish lodge. The unusual **Museum of Underwater Archaeology,** in a 15th-century castle in Bodrum on the Aegean coast, displays booty found in local shipwrecks.

GREAT ITINERARIES

BEST OF THE BEACHES AND RUINS ON THE AEGEAN AND MEDITERRANEAN COASTS, 10 DAYS

It's fairly safe to say that the main features that attract visitors to Turkey are the beaches and the magnificent archaeological sites. This itinerary covers the best of both, along the two major coastlines. Adding a couple days in Istanbul at the beginning or end would make a perfect trip.

Days 1 and 2: Arrival, Istanbul

Arrive in Istanbul and head to one of the charming small hotels in Sultanahmet (the Empress Zoe and the Sarı Konak Oteli are two favorites). If you have time, go to see the awe-inspiring Aya Sofya and the nearby Blue Mosque.

The next day, visit Topkapı Palace to get a sense of how the Ottoman sultans lived (make sure to take a tour of the Harem). From there, go to the nearby Archaeological Museum, whose collection of Roman and Greek artifacts comes from many of the sites that you'll soon be visiting. In the evening, head to one of the little neighborhoods along the Bosphorus, such as Ortaköy or Arnavutköy, for a fish dinner by the waterside (take a taxi if you're just going for dinner; the Bosphorus ferries are good if you've got time for a leisurely cruise).

Day 3: Ephesus

On the morning of Day 3, take the roughly 1-hr flight to İzmir and rent a car at the airport to make the quick (79-km (50-mi) drive down to the ancient Roman city of Ephesus. If you get an early flight out, you should be here by lunch. The site is one of the most popular tourist attractions in Turkey, and you'll see why: the buildings and monuments here are remarkably well preserved and easily give you the sense of what life must have been like in this important trading city 2,000 years ago. After Ephesus, visit the nearby Meryemana, a pilgrimage site for both Christians and Muslims where the Virgin Mary is believed to have spent her final years. Spend the night in the pleasant town of Selçuk, which is right on the doorstep of Ephesus. Or better yet, head 9 km (5.5 mi) into the mountains above Selçuk and stay in the tranquil village of Şirince, surrounded by fruit orchards and vineyards.

Day 4: Priene, Miletus & Didyma

Start off your day with a visit to Priene, an ancient Greek city that sits on a steep hill looking out on a valley below—it's about 60 km (38 mi) from Şirince. From there continue 16 km (10 mi) south to Miletus, another Greek city, where a spectacular theater is all that remains of its former glory. Twenty km (12 mi) south of here is Didyma and its magnificent Temple of Apollo, its scale as grand as the Parthenon, with 124 well-preserved columns. To keep yourself from burning out on ruins, continue another 5 km (3 mi) to the white-sand beach of Altıkum (NOTE: This is not the same as the similarly named beach near Çeşme) and take a dip in the warm water then have a meal at one of the numerous fish restaurants lining the shore. Drive back to the busy seaside resort town of Kuşadası, where there are several small pansiyons at which you can spend the night.

GREECE

Istanbul

GREECE

İzmir

Aegean Sea

Selçuk
Meryemana ◆ **Ephesus**
Priene
Didyma ○ **Miletus**

Aphrodisias

Gokova ○ **Dalyan**

Kaunos —
İztuzu
Letoön **Kaş**
Patara

Aspendos

Antalya

Olympos

GREECE

MEDITERRANEAN SEA

Day 5: Aphrodisias

Get an early start for the drive to the ruins of Aphrodisias, a Roman city named in honor of the goddess of love, Aphrodite. High up on a plateau and ringed by mountains, Aphrodisias has a spectacular setting and as much to offer as Ephesus, although with significantly fewer crowds. From here work your way down to the coast and the quiet town of Dalyan, where you can spend the next two nights in one of several riverside pansiyons.

Day 6: Dalyan, İztuzu Beach & the Rock Tombs of Kaunos

At Dalyan's riverside quay, you can hire a boat to take you on to the ruins of ancient Kaunos, a city dating back to the 9th century BC and famous for its collection of tombs cut into the surrounding cliffs. Watch for the herons and storks idling in the river's reeds when you stop to take a look at the ruins. Continue your day cruise to the famed İztuzu Beach, a 5-km (3-mile) stretch of undeveloped sand that's also a nesting ground for sea turtles. There are a few snack bars at the beach, but you might want to consider bringing a picnic lunch along.

Day 7: Letoon, Patara & Kaş

The mountainous coastal region south of Dalyan is the home of ancient Lycia. An independent and resourceful people, the Lycians built a series of impressive cities whose ruins are sprinkled throughout the area, today also known as the Turquoise Riviera. To get a good glimpse of one of these Lycian cities, drive from Dalyan to Letoön, a UNESCO World Heritage Site with three fascinating temples dating back to the 2nd century BC. From here continue to Patara, another Lycian ruin that has the added bonus of being right next to one of Turkey's finest and longest beaches. You can spend the night in the relaxing little seaside town of Kaş, which has several good lodging and eating options. ■ TIP➔ **If you have an extra day, take the three-hour boat trip out of Kaş through the beautiful Kekova Sound and its fascinating underwater Greek and Roman ruins.**

Day 8: Olympos

On your 8th day (9th if you spend an extra day in Kaş), drive to the Lycian ruins of Olympos, which have running through them a small river that ends at a beautiful crescent beach backed by mountains. Stay in the lit-

GREAT
ITINERARIES

tle village of Çıralı, a good spot for an evening visit to the legendary Chimaera, small flames of ignited gas that shoot out of the rocks of a nearby mountain.

Day 9: Antalya/Termessos (or Aspendos)

Spend your last night in the rapidly growing resort city of Antalya, but before going there head up into the rugged mountains above the city to visit the dramatic site of Termessos, an impregnable city that both Alexander the Great and the Romans decided not to attack. (Alternatively, continue 54 km [34 mi] past Antalya to visit Aspendos, a spectacular Roman theater that is still in use today.) Return to Antalya in the afternoon and stay in one of the renovated old Ottoman houses in the Kaleıçı, the city's charming old town.

Day 10: Return to Istanbul

If you have time before your flight back to Istanbul, use the morning to walk around the narrow streets of the Kaleıçı and then visit the city's large archaeological museum. If you need to stock up on souvenirs before your return, head to Antalya's bazaar before going to the airport.

TIPS

1. Although the roads here are mostly in good condition, they are rarely wider than two lanes or lighted at night, so do yourself a favor and don't drive after sunset.

2. This trip takes you through some of the most popular spots in Turkey, so book your hotel and pansiyon rooms well in advance.

3. Consider doing this itinerary in the fall: prices will be significantly lower, the crowds will be gone, it won't be baking hot, and the ocean will still be warm enough to swim in.

4. Many of the towns on this itinerary have fabulous weekly markets, when farmers and craftspeople from the surrounding area come in to sell their goods; try to time some of your trip around one of them. Many markets are held on Saturdays, but there are different days in different places so check locally.

5. In Dalyan, use the boats of the local cooperative, Dalyan Kooperatifi, which has set prices.

6. If you really want to get away from it all, hire a boat in Kaş to take you to one of the numerous secluded coves nearby.

CROSSROADS OF FAITH, 9 DAYS

Once home to powerful Christian and Muslim empires, the area that makes up modern Turkey has played a crucial role in the development of both religions. This tour takes you to some of the most important religious sites in Turkey, places that still poignantly convey spirituality.

Days 1 and 2: Istanbul

Arrive in Istanbul and check into a hotel in Sultanahmet. If you have time, visit two of the quintessential Istanbul sites: the Aya Sofya and Blue Mosque.

Start your second day with a visit to the Süleymaniye mosque, one of the greatest achievements of Mimar Sinan, the Ottomans' favorite architect. Then head to the western edge of Istanbul's old city walls, where you'll find the Kariye Museum in what was the Byzantine Chora church. It's filled with glittering mosaics and beautiful frescoes that are considered among the finest in the world. End your day in Eyüp Cami, a historic mosque complex on the Golden Horn that is one of the holiest areas in Istanbul.

Day 3: Konya

Take a morning flight from Istanbul to Konya and pick up a rental car at the airport. In Konya you'll see the magnificent Mevlâna Museum and tomb, dedicated to the life and teachings of Rumi Celaleddin, the 13th-century mystic who founded the order of the whirling dervishes. The city's 13th-century Alaaddin Mosque is also worth a visit. In the evening, catch a live dervish performance at the Cultural Center behind the museum if they're performing. The annual Rumi festival usually takes place in early December. Book well in advance.

Days 4 and 5: Cappadocia

After Konya, head east toward the lunar landscape of Cappadocia, where the volcanic rock outcroppings and cliffs were used by local Christians for centuries as churches, monasteries, and homes. One of the best places to see these unique structures is in the village of Göreme. Spend the night in one of the hotels built into the stone caves. Ürgup has what is regarded by some as the best collection of boutique hotels in Turkey.

The attractions in Cappadocia are above ground and below it. Under siege from Arab invaders in the 7th through 10th centuries, local Christians built a series of underground cities—some going down 20 stories and capable of holding 20,000 people—where they sought refuge. The ruins in Kaymaklı and Derinkuyu are marvels of ancient engineering. Get an early start if you want to beat the summer crowds, and bring a flashlight.

If you have extra time, consider a visit to the Ihlara Valley, a deep gorge that has numerous monasteries and churches cut into its cliffs and a lovely green river running through it.

Days 6 and 7: Cappadocia to Antakya

From landlocked Cappadocia, head south to the Mediterranean Sea and the city of Antakya, formerly known as Antioch, which played an important role in the early days of Christianity. It's a long drive of 472 km (293 mi), so plan on spending most of the day on the road. Fortunately, there's a highway for most of the way. If

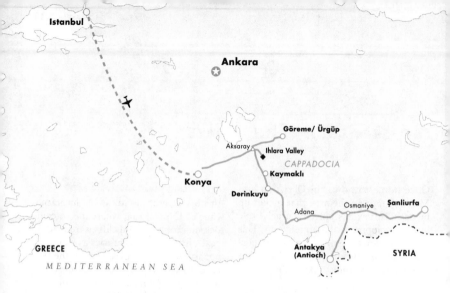

you get to Antakya early enough, head to the Church of St. Peter, in a cave on the outskirts of town. Blackened by 2,000 years' worth of candle smoke, this is perhaps the oldest church in the world, where the apostle Paul preached to his converts.

The next day, spend the morning walking through the narrow lanes and the lively bazaar of Antakya's old town. Then visit the Archaeological Museum, which has an excellent collection of Roman and Byzantine mosaics and other artifacts. Antakya is famous for its Syrian-influenced cooking, so lunch at one of the restaurants serving local dishes (Antik Han and Maison d'Antioch are two good options). After lunch, begin your 333-km (206-mi) drive to Şanliurfa, where you can stay in one of several grand old stone houses that have been converted into small hotels.

Day 8: Şanliurfa

Many Muslims believe the biblical patriarch Abraham was born in Şanliurfa, and a fascinating and peaceful pilgrimage site has developed here, with mosques and a park with spring-fed pools filled with sacred carp. After lunch, make the quick drive to the small village of Harran, 45 km (28 mi) southeast of Şanliurfa. Harran is mentioned in the Bible as a place where Abraham lived for a period, and the village, with its ancient stone walls and unique beehive-shaped houses, has the look of a place that hasn't changed much since biblical times.

Day 9: Şanliurfa and Return to Istanbul

You can fly back to Istanbul from Şanliurfa, or from nearby Gaziantep (138 km or 85 miles away). If you have a flight from Şanliurfa later in the day, take some time to explore Şanliurfa's bustling and authentic bazaar, where coppersmiths hammer and tailors work on foot-powered sewing machines. If your flight is out of Gaziantep, consider driving there in the morning in order to have lunch at one of that city's famous restaurants. Imam Cağdaş, which has great kebabs and heavenly baklava, is your best bet.

Istanbul

WORD OF MOUTH

"You'll love Istanbul! The palaces are grand (Dolmabahçe and Top-kapı), Aya Sofya is magnificent, and the various mosques (Blue Mosque, Suliman, etc.) are quite interesting. Then there's the Grand Bazaar! It's wonderful . . . The people are warm and friendly . . . The merchants will haggle you like crazy but it's all a lot of fun."

—Grcxx3

WELCOME TO ISTANBUL

TOP REASONS TO GO

★ **Explore the exotic monuments** of the Byzantine and Ottoman empires.

★ **Cruise up the Bosphorus,** past waterfront villages and forested slopes topped with fortresses.

★ **Haggle in the Grand Bazaar** and the Egyptian Bazaar, the ultimate shopping experiences.

★ **Sweat in a Hamam,** like an Ottoman sultan, and discover the soothing effects of a Turkish rubdown.

★ **Luxuriate in a palace**— or an Ottoman house, or even a sumptuously outfitted former prison.

★ **Sip a cup of tea** as you watch boats ply the Golden Horn.

★ **Dine in style** on Turkish delights against a backdrop of domes and minarets.

Dolmabahçe Sarayı

1 Old Istanbul. The Blue Mosque's cascading domes are a backdrop to the Roman Hippodrome; the Harem and jewel-filled chambers lie hidden behind the high walls of Topkapı Sarayı; and the dome of Aya Sofya soars above twisting streets lined with woodern Ottoman houses.

dolufeneri

Grand Bazaar

2 The Bazaar area and Environs. Haggle your way through the stalls of the Grand Bazaar and the Egyptian Bazaar, then follow narrow streets crowded with peddlars down to the docks on the Golden Horn.

3 Istanbul's "New Town." See for yourself that new is a relative term in Istanbul. Ornate 19th- and early-20th century apartment houses crowd this hillside neighborhood known both as Pera and Beyoğlu. Beyond is traffic-crowded Taksim Meydanı.

4 Beşiktaş and Beyond. Follow in the footsteps of the last of the Ottoman sultans, who retreated to pleasure palaces and pavilions on the shores of the Bosphorus.

5 The Bosphorus. Board a ferry to zigzag between two continents.

6 Princes' Islands. This nine-island archipelago in the Sea of Marmara has pine forests, gardens, beaches—and a welcome absence of motorized traffic.

7 Edirne This well-preserved Ottoman City is a good side trip from Istanbul.

GETTING ORIENTED

Istanbul is a city divided. The Bosphorus separates the European side from the Asian side, and the European side is itself divided by the Golden Horn, an 8-km (5-mi) long inlet that lies between the Old City to the south and the New Town, known as Beyoğlu, to the north. Many of the acclaimed Byzantine and Ottoman monuments—Topkapı Sarayı, the Blue Mosque and Aya Sofya, the Grand and Egyptian bazaars—are in the Old City. In the so-called New Town, the 14th-century Galata Tower dominates the hillside that rises north of the Golden Horn; just beyond, high-rise hotels and other landmarks of the modern city radiate out from Taksim Meydanı, above the Bosphorus-side neighborhood of Beşiktaş. To the west, the European suburbs line the northern shore of the Bosphorus. The Asian suburbs are on the southern shore.

Cumhuriyet

Kartal

Batı

4 mi

4 km

ISTANBUL PLANNER

Beyoğlu Address Advisory

In late 2006 the Istanbul municipal administration renumbered the buildings in Beyoğlu, the new section of Istanbul. Many people still use the old numbers, though, and some question whether the new system will stick. Even if it does, it will probably take several years for the new numbers to take hold. You'll probably be spending most of your time in Sultanahmet—the old city—but be advised to double check addresses of Beyoğlu destinations.

Mosque Protocol

At the Blue Mosque and other Muslim holy places, you must remove your shoes and leave them at the entrance.

Immodest clothing is not allowed, but an attendant is usually stationed at the door to lend you a robe if he feels you are not dressed appropriately.

Women should cover their heads.

Keep your voice down, don't take photographs of the worshippers, and try to avoid visits during midday prayers on Fridays.

Arresting Antiquities

Many of the antiquities on view in Istanbul have been removed from the archaeological sites of Turkey's ancient cities. Seeing them here, first, will help you visualize what belongs in the empty niches you'll see elsewhere around the country.

Arkeoloji Müzesi/Eski Şark Eserleri Müzesi. Stunning tombs, including one carved with scenes from Alexander the Great's battles, and a 13th-century BC tablet carved with the world's first peace treaty are among the spectacular finds to be enjoyed in these twin collections in a courtyard of Topkapı Sarayı.

Sadberk Hanım Müzesi. Anatolian antiquities, such as Hittite pottery and cuneiform tablets, grace an old waterfront mansion on the Bosphorus.

Magnificent Mosques

There are a lot of mosques in Istanbul. You won't have time to see them all, but you shouldn't leave the city without taking in the beauty and spirituality of at least several that rank as some of the most stunning architectural achievements in the world:

The Blue Mosque, for the sheer spectacle of domes, semi-domes, minarets, and the 20,000 shimmering blue-green İznik tiles that lend the mosque its name.

Rüstem Paşa Cami, for İznik tiles in a magnificient array of colors and patterns.

Süleymaniye Cami, for its size, austere beauty, the emormous dome that seems to be held up principally by divine cooperation, and the tombs of the architect Sinan, his patron Süleyman the Magnificent, and the sultan's wife, Roxelana.

Sokollu Mehmet Paşa Rüstem, for elegance, harmony, and sumptuous tile work.

Getting Around Istanbul

Istanbul is a walker's city, and the best way to experience it is to wander, inevitably getting lost. When your feet get tired, though, it's easy to use public transportation. Don't even think about driving in Istanbul. Traffic is terrible, parking impossible, and signs are in Turkish only.

Bus service is frequent and drivers and riders tend to be helpful, so you should be able to navigate your way to major tourist stops as Sultanahmet, Eminönü, Taksim, and Beşiktaş. Fare is about 70¢. You can purchase tickets at kiosks near major stops or on some buses.

A **dolmus** is a cross between a taxi and a bus—usually a van that picks up passengers heading in more or less the same direction. Fares vary with distance, but are usally about $2 in the city center.

Taxis are an excellent way to get around Istanbul, and they're relatively cheap—a ride from Sultanahmet to Taksim usually costs less than $5. Some tips: Ask your hotel to call a taxi or find a stand in front of a hotel; you'll be more likely to get a driver who won't overcharge. Since most drivers don't speak English, ask the doorman to tell him where you're going and write down the address of your destination.

The **metro** is continually expanding. One handy line links Eminönü and Taksim, and another connects the city center with the airport; fare is about $1 a ride. The historic Tünel, in operation since 1875, is the second-oldest underground in the world, after London's, and connects Karaköy and Tünel Square; the fare is 50¢.

Tramways run on select routes. One runs from Sultanahmet to Eminönü, an easy way to get down to the Grand Bazaar and the Egyptian Bazaar; the fare is about 70¢, and tickets are sold at the stations. A tram also runs along İstiklal Caddesi between Tünel and Taksim; you might want to take the tram up the hill and walk back down. The fare is 50¢, payable on the tram.

Ferries ply the Bosphorus, serving the European and Asian suburbs; Eminönü is a handy departure point. Fares are about $1, payable at booths on the docks.

When in doubt, ask. Even with a good map in hand, it's easy to lose your way on Istanbul's winding streets and alleyways. People are almost always eager to help.

Vintage Views

Istanbul has plenty of hillsides and vantage points from which to take in scenes of the city's busy waterways and exotic skyline. Some of the best views are from:

A Bosphorus ferry. From the water Istanbul looks especially appealing, a millennia-old melange of domes, minarets, and palaces, and beyond, villages of wooden houses tucked between the shore and the forested slopes above.

From the Galata Tower and Bridge. The Genoese built this tower in 1349 as a perch from which to monitor the comings and goings of vessels in the sea lanes below; you can still do so from the viewing gallery.

From the **Mecidiye Pavilion, Topkapı Sarayı.** The former retreat of Sultan Abdül Mecit I (ruled 1839–61), now a restaurant and café, provides magnificent views of the Bosphorus.

GREAT ITINERARIES

IF YOU HAVE 3 DAYS

You will just be immersing yourself when it's time to leave, so make the most of your time and be prepared to feel cheated that you don't have several more days. Turn Day 1 into a head-spinning introduction: make your first stops the Blue Mosque and Aya Sofya to get a sense of the grandeur of the Byzantine and Ottoman empires. In the afternoon venture out of Sultanahmet to the Kariye Müzesi for a look at the finest frescoes and mosaics to come down to us from the Byzantines. One last stop: the Grand Bazaar, where you can wander until closing time at 7 (6:30 in winter). If you're staying in Sultanahmet, take an evening stroll to see the floodlit domes and minarets of the Blue Mosque and Aya Sofya. Spend the next morning at Topkapı Sarayı. Have lunch at one of the cafés in the compound or just outside the gates so you can visit the Arkeoloji Müzesi and Eski Şark Eserleri Müzesi in the palace forecourt in the afternoon. By then you'll probably have reached your quota of looking at treasures and antiquities, so next immerse yourself in Istanbul streetlife. Head to Tünel Square in the New Town, and follow İstiklal Caddesi through Galatasaray Meydanı, stopping at the Fish Market and Flower Arcade, to Taksim Meydanı, the center of the modern city. You'll have seen enough in the past two days to help you decide how to spend your last day. If you want to see more of the Byzantines, descend into the underground cistern, Yerebatan Sarayı, then ogle the exquisite mosaics in the Mozaik Müzesi. If you want to see more evidence of

Ottoman power, head to Beşiktaş to see Domabahçe Sarayı, the naval and military museums, and Yildiz Park and Chalet. However you spend the day, you might want to pop into the Grand Bazaar for one more spurt of shopping and, time permitting, make a quick visit to nearby Rüstem Paşa Cami for a look at one more burst of extravagance: the mesmerizing tile work.

IF YOU HAVE 7 DAYS

A week will give you time to enjoy Istanbul with a little leisure. Think in terms of neighborhoods: You'll want to spend at least three days in the Old City, seeing the Byzantine and Ottoman monuments (see the itinerary above for tips). Plan on a full day in Beşiktaş and one in the New Town. You can spend one day cruising up the Bosphorus, and that still leaves you with the luxury of one day to spend as you'd like in Istanbul—you'll have seen the major sights, so you can go back and spend time in the places that appealed to you most: A morning looking at the mosaics and frescoes at the Kariye Müzesi, then a stop to compare them with those in the Mozaik Müzesi? One more swing through the Grand Bazaar? Maybe a trip to the Princes' Islands? Or maybe just a day of wandering— after all, few cities reward walkers more amply.

Updated by
Gareth Jenkins
and Stephen
Brewer

THOUGH IT IS OFTEN REMARKED THAT TURKEY straddles Europe and Asia, it's really the city of Istanbul that does the straddling. The vast bulk of Turkey resides comfortably on the Asian side, but Istanbul is indeed firmly planted on both continents. European Istanbul is separated from its Asian suburbs by the Bosphorus, the narrow channel of water that connects the Black Sea, north of the city, to the Sea of Marmara in the south.

What will strike you more than the meeting of East and West in Istanbul, though, is the juxtaposition of the old and the new, of tradition and modernity. Brash concrete-and-glass hotels and office towers creep up behind historic old palaces; women in jeans or elegant designer outfits pass others wearing long skirts and head coverings; donkey-drawn carts vie with battered old Fiats and shiny BMWs for dominance of the noisy, narrow streets; and the Grand Bazaar competes with Western-style boutiques and shopping malls. At dawn, when the muezzin's call to prayer rebounds from ancient minarets, there are inevitably a few hearty revelers still making their way home from nightclubs and bars while other residents kneel on their prayer rugs facing Mecca.

Old Istanbul

The old walled city of Stamboul rises on several hills above the port of Eminönü, and an incredible concentration of art and architecture spanning thousands of years is packed into the narrow, winding streets of this part of town. To appreciate the beauty and magic of the Old City, and for a postcard-worthy overview of its main sights, head to the Galata Bridge at the mouth of the Haliç, also known as the Golden Horn, where this inlet meets the Bosphorus. Nowhere else in Istanbul do you get such a rich feel for the magic of this ancient and mysterious place. At the eastern edge of the Old City, Topkapı Sarayı sits perched on the promontory overlooking the Bosphorus and the mouth of the Golden Horn, while behind the palace rise the imposing domes and soaring minarets of the Blue Mosque and Aya Sofya. To the west you can see the sprawl of old buildings that make up Sultanahmet (named after the sultan who built the Blue Mosque), with Yeni Cami close to the waterfront next to the Egyptian Bazaar; to its right is the sprawling Süleymaniye mosque complex. Farther west is the line of the city's ancient land walls. When it comes time to see these sights up close, the best way to get around is on foot, and most of the main sites are within a short distance of each other.

Main Attractions

Numbers in the text correspond to numbers in the margin and on the Istanbul and Bosphorus maps.

> **TIMING YOUR VISIT TO THE OLD CITY**
>
> Check opening times when you plan your outings. Topkapı Sarayı and the Arkeoloji Müzesi are open daily. The Blue Mosque is also open daily, but the Carpet and Kilim museums within are closed on weekends. Aya Sofya and the Ibrahim Paşa Sarayı are closed Monday, the Mozaik Müzesi on Tuesday, and the Kariye Müzesi on Wednesday. It's best not to visit mosques during midday prayers on Friday.

Istanbul: a History in Architecture

THE TOWN OF BYZANTIUM was already 1,000 years old when, in AD 326, Emperor Constantine the Great began to enlarge and rebuild it as the new capital of the Roman Empire. On May 11, 330, the city was officially renamed "New Rome," although it soon became better known as Constantinople, the city of Constantine. The new Byzantine Empire in the East survived long after the Roman Empire had crumbled in the West, and under the Byzantine emperor Justinian (ruled 527–65) Constantine's capital flourished. Constantinople grew to become the largest metropolis the Western world had ever seen. Contemporaries often referred to it simply as the City. Justinian ordered the construction of the magnificent Hagia Sophia, or Church of the Holy Wisdom (known as Aya Sofya in Turkish and referred to as such throughout this book) in 532 on the site of a church originally built for Constantine. This awe-inspiring architectural wonder still dominates Istanbul's skyline.

The Byzantine Empire began to decline toward the end of the 11th century. The first turning point was defeat at the battle of Manzikert in 1071, which seriously weakened the empire in eastern Anatolia and opened up the area to settlement by nomads from Central Asia. A more devastating blow came in 1204 when the western Europeans of the Fourth Crusade, who were supposed to be on their way to recapture Jerusalem, decided that going the extra thousand miles was too much trouble, and sacked and occupied Constantinople instead, forcing the surviving members of the Byzantine dynasty to flee to Trabzon on the Black Sea coast.

The Byzantines eventually regained control, but neither the city nor the Byzantine Empire ever recovered. Constantinople was more of a collection of villages set amongst ruins than a city.

The Ottoman sultan Mehmet II, known as Fatih (the Conqueror), conquered the long-neglected, nearly ruined Constantinople in 1453, rebuilt it, and made the city once again the capital of a great empire. In time it became known as Istanbul—from the Greek *eis tin polin*, meaning "in the city" or "to the city." In 1468 Mehmet II began building a palace on the picturesque hill at the tip of the city where the Golden Horn meets the Bosphorus. Later sultans embellished and extended the building until it grew into the fabulous Topkapı Sarayı. Most of the finest Ottoman buildings in Istanbul, however, date from the time of Süleyman the Magnificent (ruled 1520–1566), who led the Ottoman Empire to its highest achievements in art and architecture, literature, and law. Süleyman commissioned the brilliant architect Sinan (1489–1587) to design buildings that are now recognized as some of the greatest examples of Islamic architecture in the world, including mosques such as the magnificent Süleymaniye, the intimate Sokollu Mehmet Paşa, and the exquisitely tiled Rüstem Paşa. The monuments built by these titans, or in their honor, dominate and define the city and lead you into the arms of the past at every turn.

1

☾ ❷ **Arkeoloji Müzesi** (Archaeology Museum). Step into this vast repository
Fodor'sChoice of spectacular finds, housed in a forecourt of Topkapı Sarayı, for a head-
★ spinning look at the civilizations that have thrived for thousands of years
in Turkey. Many of the treasures were gathered here as long ago as the
1890s, when forward-thinking archaeologist and painter Osman Hamdi
Bey campaigned to keep antiquities in Turkish hands. The most stunning
pieces are tombs that include the so-called Alexander Sarcophagus,
carved with scenes from Alexander the Great's battles and once believed,
wrongly, to be his final resting place. An excellent exhibit on Istanbul
through the ages shows off artifacts from prehistory through the Byzantines and Ottomans and helps put the city's complex past in context.

Another building in the courtyard of Topkapı Sarayı houses the **Eski Şark
Eserleri Müzesi** (Museum of the Ancient Orient), where you will be transported to even earlier times: The vast majority of the panels, mosaics,
obelisks, and other artifacts here, from Anatolia, Mesopotamia, and elsewhere in the Arab world, date from the pre-Christian centuries. A particularly intricate tablet is the Treaty of Kadesh from the 13th century
BC, perhaps the world's earliest known peace treaty, an accord between
the Hittite king Hattusilis III and the Egyptian pharoah Ramses II. The
Çinili Köşkü (Tiled Pavilion) is one of the most visually pleasing sights
in all of Istanbul—a bright profusion of colored tiles covers this onetime hunting lodge of Mehmet the Conqueror, and inside are ceramics
from the early Seljuk and Ottoman empires, as well as tiles from İznik,
the city that produced perhaps the finest ceramics in the world during
the 17th and 18th centuries. In summer, you can mull over these glimpses
into the distant past as you sip coffee or tea at the café in the garden.
✉ *Gülhane Park, next to Topkapı Sarayı* ☎ *212/520–7740* ✍ *$3
(total) for the 3 museums* ☾ *Archaeology Museum: Tues.–Sun. 9:30–5:00,
ticket sales until 4:30; Museum of the Ancient Orient: Tues.–Sun. 1—
5; Tiled Pavilion: Tues.–Sun. 9:30—noon.*

❸ **Aya Sofya** (Hagia Sophia, Church of the Holy Wisdom). This soaring
Fodor'sChoice edifice is perhaps the greatest work of Byzantine architecture and for
★ almost a thousand years, starting from its completion in 537, was the
world's largest and most important religious monument. Only Saint Peter's
in Rome, not completed until the 17th century, surpassed Aya Sofya in
size and grandeur. The Emperor Justinian commissioned the church and,
in response to his dictum that Aya Sofya be the grandest place of worship ever built—far greater than the temples whose columns were incorporated in the church—craftsmen devised a magnificent dome.
Nothing like the dome's construction had ever been attempted before.
New architectural rules were made up as the builders went along and
not all were foolproof, since the dome collapsed during an earthquake
just two years after the church was completed. Subsequent repairs and
such structural innovations as flying buttresses ensured the dome rose
even higher and remained firmly in place, making it the prominent fix-
ture on the Istanbul skyline to this day. Over the centuries Aya Sofya
has survived additional earthquakes, looting crusaders, and the city's
conquest by Mehmet the Conqueror in 1453.

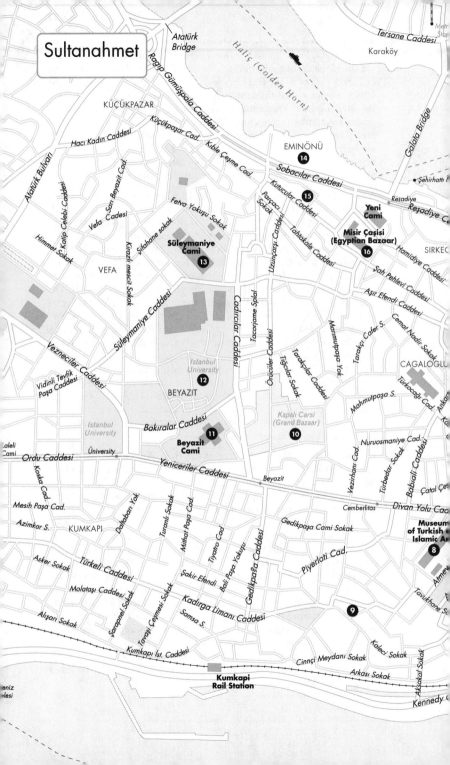

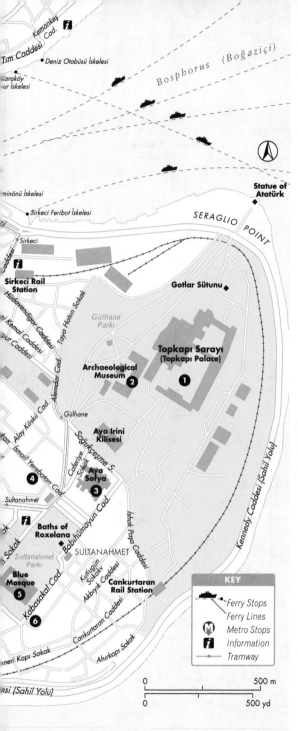

Bosphorus (Boğaziçi)

Kemankeş Cad.
Tim Caddesi
Deniz Otobüsü İskelesi
Karaköy
ur İskelesi
minönü İskelesi
Sirkeci Feribot İskelesi
Statue of
Atatürk
SERAGLIO POINT
Sirkeci
Sirkeci Rail
Station
Hüdavendigar Caddesi
Toya Hatun Sokak
Alemdar Cad.
Gotlar Sütunu
Kemal Caddesi
ut Caddesi
Gülhane
Parkı
Topkapı Sarayı
(Topkapı Palace)
Archaeological
Museum
2
1
Gülhane
Aloy Köşkü Cad.
İsmail Yerebatan Cad.
an
Aya Irini
Kilisesi
Cafariye
Sokak
Soğukçeşme S.
Aya
Sofya
3
Kennedy Caddesi (Sahil Yolu)
4
Sultanahmet
Baths of
Roxelana
Babıhümayun Cad.
İshak Paşa Caddesi
Sokak
Sultanahmet
Parkı
SULTANAHMET
Blue
Mosque
5
6
Kabasakal Cad.
Kutuğun
Sokak
Akbıyık Caddesi
Cankurtaran
Rail Station
Cankurtaran Caddesi
neri Kapı Sokak
Ahırkapı Sokak
esi (Sahil Yolu)

KEY
Ferry Stops
Ferry Lines
Ⓜ Metro Stops
🄸 Information
Tramway

0 ——————— 500 m
0 ——————— 500 yd

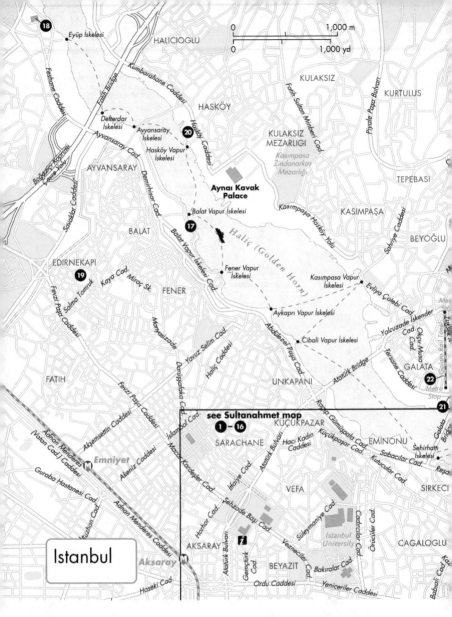

Istanbul

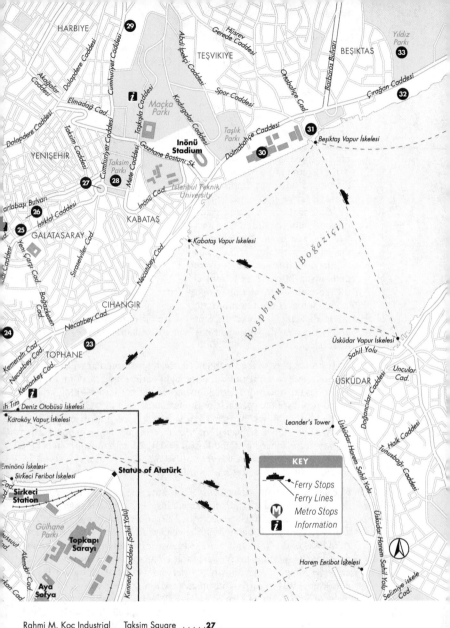

Mehmet converted the church into a mosque, and succeeding sultans added its four minarets. In the 16th century Süleyman the Magnificent ordered the church's Byzantine mosaics to be plastered over in accordance with the Islamic proscription against the portrayal of the human figure in a place of worship. The multicolored tiles that cover parts of the cavernous interior weren't rediscovered until after Atatürk made the Aya Sofya into a museum in 1936. Today, mosaics and frescoes of saints, emperors, and Christ enliven the vast space. A somber Virgin Mary with the infant Jesus, flanked by the severe-looking archangels Michael and Gabriel, fill the wall where the altar once stood. Some of the finest mosaics

---

A COLUMN OF LUCKY CHARMS

The marble-and-brass **Sacred Column,** in the north aisle of Aya Sofya, to the left as you enter through the main door, is laden with legends. It's thought that the column weeps water that can work miracles, and over the centuries believers have worn a hole as they caress the column to come in contact with the miraculous moisture. It's also believed that if you place your thumb in the hole and turn your hand 360 degrees, any wish you make while doing so will come true.

---

are in the gallery, where the Empress Zoe is portrayed with her third and last husband, whose face has been affixed atop those of his predecessors.

As Justinian may well have intended, the impression that will stay with you longest, years after a visit, is the sight of the immense dome, almost 18 stories tall and more than 30 meters (100 feet) across—look up into it and you'll see the spectacle of thousands of gold tiles glittering in the light of 40 windows. In recent years there has been growing pressure for Aya Sofya to be reopened for Muslim worship. Some people gather to pray at the museum at midday on Friday. As with mosques, it is best not to try to visit then. ⊠ *Aya Sofya Sq.* ☎ *212/522–1750* ▨ *$6* ☺ *Tues.–Sun. 9–7, ticket sales until 6:30.*

❺ Blue Mosque (Sultan Ahmet Cami). Only after you enter the Blue Mosque

Fodor'sChoice do you understand why it is so named. Inside, 20,000 shimmering blue-
★ green İznik tiles are interspersed with 260 stained-glass windows; an airy arabesque pattern is painted on the ceiling. After the dark corners and stern faces of the Byzantine mosaics in Aya Sofya, this light-filled mosque is positively uplifting. Such a favorable comparison was the intention of architect Mehmet Aga, known as Sedefkar (Worker of Mother-of-Pearl), whose goal was to surpass Justinian's crowning achievement. At the bequest of Sultan Ahmet I (ruled 1603–17), he spent just eight years creating this masterpiece of Ottoman craftsmanship, beginning in 1609, and many believe he did indeed succeed in outdoing the splendor of Aya Sofya.

Mehmet Aga went a little too far when he surrounded the massive structure, studded with domes and semidomes, with six minarets: this number briefly linked the Blue Mosque with the Elharam Mosque in Mecca—and this could not be allowed. Ahmet I was forced to send

Hamams

ONE OF THE GREAT PLEASURES of a visit to Istanbul is spending a lazy afternoon in one of the city's Turkish baths, known as hamams. Some of the hamams still in use today are exquisite structures more than 500 years old. The hamams were born out of necessity: it was the way people kept clean before the introduction of internal plumbing in homes but, over time, the hamams began to play an important role in Ottoman social life, particularly for women. Men had the coffeehouse and women the hamam, a place to get together, gossip, and relax.

Now that people bathe at home, the hamams have been fading as a central element in Turkish life. There are still bathhouses dotted throughout Istanbul, but many wouldn't survive without steady tourist traffic. Still, going to the hamam is a good opportunity to experience what remains an unbroken link to the Ottoman past.

Most hamams have separate facilities for men and women. Each has a *camekan*, a large domed room with small cubicles where you can undress, wrap yourself in a thin cloth called a *peştemal*, and put on slippers or wooden sandals—all provided. Then you'll continue through a pair of increasingly hotter rooms. The first, known as the *soğukluk*, has showers and toilets and is used for cooling down at the end of your session. Next is the *hararet*, a steamy and softly lit room with marble washbasins along the sides. You can douse yourself by scooping water with a copper bowl. In the middle of the room is the *göbektaşı*, a marble platform heated by furnaces below and usually covered with reclining bodies. This is where, if you decide to take your chances, a

traditional Turkish massage will be "administered."

The masseur will first scrub you down with a rough, loofa-like sponge known as a *kese*. Be prepared to lose several layers of dead skin. Once you're scrubbed, the masseur will soap you up into a frothy lather, rinse you off, and then conduct what will probably be the most vigorous massage you'll ever receive. Speak up if you want your masseuse to ease up.

Once you've been worked over, you can relax (and recover) on the *göbektaşı* or head back to your change cubicle, where you will be wrapped in fresh towels and perhaps massaged a little more, this time with soothing oils. Most cubicles have small beds where you can lie down and sip tea or fresh juice brought by an attendant.

One of the best hamams in Istanbul is **Cağaloğlu Hamamı** (✉ Prof. Kazı Gürkan Cad. 34, Cağaloğlu ☎ 212/522–2424), near Aya Sofya in a magnificent 18th-century building that dates back to 1741. Florence Nightingale and Kaiser Wilhelm II once steamed here; the clientele today remains generally upscale. Self-service baths cost $12; an extra $12 buys you the Turkish massage. It's open daily 8–8 for women and until 10 PM for men.

Also recommended is the even older **Çembrelitas Hamam** (✉ Vezirhan Cad. 8, Çembrelitaş ☎ 212/522–7974) which dates back to 1584.

Both of the above cater primarily to tourists. For a more local flavor, try the **Gedikpaşa Hamam** (✉ Hamam Cad. 65-67, Beyazıt ☎ 212/517–8956), which has been in operation since 1457.

Mehmet Aga down to the Holy City to build a seventh minaret for El-haram and reestablish the eminence of that mosque. Ahmet, his wife, and three sons are interred in the stunningly tiled *türbe* (mausoleum) at a corner of the complex, which at one time also included such traditional Muslim institutions as an almshouse, an infirmary, and a school. From here—or from the Hippodrome or any other good viewpoint—you can see the genius of the Mehmet Aga, who didn't try to surpass the massive dome of Aya Sofya but instead created a secession of domes of varying sizes to cover the massive interior space, creating an effect that is both whimsical and uplifting.

Within the mosque are the **Hünkar Kasrı** (Carpet and Kilim Museums), where rugs are treated as works of art and displayed in suitably grand settings. These are good places to set your standards high when dueling with the modern-day carpet dealers you will confront at every turn in Istanbul. The carpet museum is in the vast, stone-vaulted cellars; the kilims are upstairs at the end of a stone ramp, in a chamber where the sultans rested before and after their prayers. ⊠ *Sultanahmet Sq.* ☎ *212/518–1330 for museum information only* ✆ *Mosque free; museums $2* ☉ *Blue Mosque: daily 9–5, access restricted during prayer times, particularly at midday on Fri.; museums: weekdays 8:30–noon and 1–3:30.*

❶ Topkapı Sarayı (Topkapı Palace). This vast palace on Seraglio Point, above the confluence of the Bosphorus and the Golden Horn, was the residence of sultans and their harems as well as the seat of Ottoman rule from the 1450s until the middle of the 19th century. Few other royal residences can match this hilltop compound when it comes to mystery, intrigue, and the lavishly exotic intricacies of court life

Fodor'sChoice
★

Sultan Mehmet II built the original Topkapı Palace in the 1450s, shortly after his conquest of Constantinople. Over the centuries sultan after sultan added ever more elaborate architectural frills and fantasies, until the palace had acquired four courtyards and quarters for some 5,000 full-time residents, including slaves, concubines, and eunuchs. Many of its inhabitants lived their entire adult lives behind its walls, and the palace was often the scene of intrigues, bloodshed, and drama as members of the sultan's entourage plotted and schemed to advance their favorites, sometimes even deposing and assassinating the sultan himself. Topkapı was finally abandoned in 1853 when Sultan Abdül Mecit I moved his court to the palace at Dolmabahçe on the Bosphorus.

The main entrance, or Imperial Gate, leads to the **Court of the Janissaries,** also known as the First Courtyard. Today, the courtyard where these members of the sultan's guard once assembled is essen-

WORD OF MOUTH

"We toured the Harem and were struck with awe at the wonders inside. From the outside, the palace doesn't look as appealing as the palaces that we find in Europe, however, Topkapı's richness is inside . . . In the Treasury we saw beautiful jewels, exquisite works in diamond and gold with precious stones . . . We were amazed at the size, quantity, and beauty of the exhibits here."   –gabrieltraian

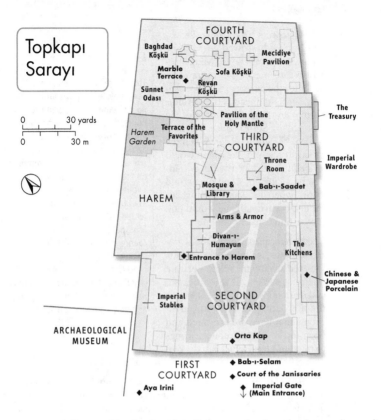

FOURTH
COURTYARD

Baghdad
Köşkü

Mecidiye
Pavilion

Marble
Terrace

Sofa Köşkü

Sünnet
Odası

Revan
Köşkü

The
Treasury

Harem
Garden

Terrace of the
Favorites

Pavilion of the
Holy Mantle

THIRD
COURTYARD

Throne
Room

Imperial
Wardrobe

0   30 yards
0   30 m

HAREM

Mosque &
Library

Bab-ı-Saadet

Arms & Armor

Divan-ı-
Humayun

The
Kitchens

Entrance to Harem

Chinese &
Japanese
Porcelain

ARCHAEOLOGICAL
MUSEUM

Imperial
Stables

SECOND
COURTYARD

Orta Kap

FIRST
COURTYARD

Bab-ı-Selam

Court of the Janissaries

Aya Irini

Imperial Gate
(Main Entrance)

tially a parking lot that does little to evoke the splendors and tragedies of the palace's extraordinary history. Off to one side, though, is the large and modestly beautiful **Aya Irini** (Church of St. Irene, Hagia Eirene in Greek), an unadorned redbrick building that dates from the earliest days of Byzantium.

You will begin to experience the grandeur of the palace when you pass through **Bab-ı-Selam** (Gate of Salutation). Süleyman the Magnificent built the gate in 1524 and was the only person allowed to pass through it on horseback; others had to dismount and enter on foot. Prisoners were kept in the towers on either side of the gate before their executions next to the nearby fountain, a handy arrangement that made it easy for executioners to wash the blood off their hands after carrying out their orders.

The **Second Courtyard** is planted with rose gardens and ornamental trees and filled with a series of ornate *köşks,* pavilions once used for the business of state as well as for more mundane matters, like feeding the hordes of servants. To one side are the palace's kitchens, where more than 1,000 cooks once toiled at the rows of immense ovens to feed the palace residents, whose numbers sometimes swelled to 10,000 or 15,000 during special occasions. The cavernous space now displays one of the world's best collections of porcelain, much of it amassed over years of Ottoman rule as powers from China, Persia, and Europe bestowed gifts on the sultans; the thousands of Ming blue-and-white pieces were made to order for the palace in the 18th century. Straight ahead is the **Divan-ı-Humayun** (Assembly Room of the Council of State), once presided over by the grand vizier. When the mood struck him, the sultan would sit behind a latticed window, hidden by a curtain, so no one would know when he was listening, although occasionally he would pull the curtain aside to comment.

The **Harem**, a maze of 400 halls, terraces, rooms, wings, and apartments grouped around the sultan's private quarters, evokes all the exoticism and mysterious ways of the Ottoman Empire. Seeing the 40 or so Harem rooms that have been restored and open to the public, though, brings to mind not just luxury but the regimentation, and even barbarity, of life in this enclosed enclave.

TIPS FOR A TOPKAPI SARAYI VISIT

The palace gates open at 9; go early, before the bus-tour crowds pour in, and plan to spend several hours. If you go by taxi, be sure to tell the driver you want the Topkapı Sarayı in Sultanahmet, or you could end up at the Topkapı bus terminal on the outskirts of town. There is no English-language written material available, but audio guides can be rented ($8), or you can hire an English-speaking guide—they tend to congregate around the ticket booth. If you visit during busy season, head right to the Harem—you can visit these 40 rooms only on guided, half-hour tours (some in English), and they tend to fill up quickly.

The first Harem compound you see housed about 200 lesser concubines and the palace eunuchs in tiny cubicles, like those in a monastery. As you move into the Harem, the rooms become larger and more opulent. The chief wives of the sultan (Islamic law permitted up to four, though the sultan could consort with as many concubines as he wished) lived in private apartments around a shared courtyard. Beyond are the lavish apartments, courtyard, and marble bath of the *valide* sultan (queen mother), the absolute ruler of the Harem, and finally, the sultan's private rooms—a riot of brocades, murals, colored marble, wildly ornate furniture, gold leaf, and fine carving. The fountains that splash throughout the Harem were not only decorative: they also made it hard to eavesdrop on royal conversations.

Beyond the Harem is **Third Courtyard**, shaded by regal old trees and dotted by some of the most ornate of the palace's pavilions. (From the Harem, you enter to the side of the courtyard, but to see this beautiful space to best advantage, make your way to its main gate, the **Bab-ı-Saadet** (Gate of Felicity), exit and reenter; and consider yourself privileged to do so, because for centuries only the sultan and grand vizier were allowed to pass through the gate.) Foreign ambassadors once groveled in the Arz Odası (Audience Chamber), but access to the courtyard was highly restricted, in part because it housed the **Treasury,** four rooms filled with imperial thrones and lavish gifts bestowed upon generations of sultans, and spoils garnered from centuries of war and invasion (the walls between three of the smaller rooms have been taken down so the Treasury only seems like 2 rooms). The glittering prizes here are the jewels. Two uncut emeralds, each weighing about 8 pounds(!), once hung from the ceiling, but are now displayed behind glass. Other pavilions show off a curious assortment of treasures—Turkish and Persian miniatures; relics of the prophet Muhammad (including hair from his beard); and sultans' robes, from the lavish wardrobes of the first to the last ruler. Some of these robes are bloodstained and torn from assassins' daggers; other garments are stiff with gold and silver thread, tooled leather, and gold, silver, and jewels.

The **Fourth Courtyard** was the private realm of the sultan, and the small, elegant pavilions, mosques, fountains, and reflecting pools are scattered amid the gardens that overlook the Bosphorus and Golden Horn. The octagonal **Revan Köşkü,** built by Murat IV in 1636 to commemorate a military victory in eastern Anatolia and the Caucasus, is often referred to in Ottoman histories as the Turban Room (Sarık Odası) because it is where the sultan used to keep his turbans. In the **İftariye** (Golden Cage), also known as the Sofa Köşkü, the closest relatives of the reigning sultan lived in strict confinement under what amounted to house arrest—superseding an older practice of murdering all possible rivals to the throne. Just off the open terrace with the wishing well is the lavishly tiled **Sünnet Odası** (Circumcision Room), where little princes would be taken for ritual circumcision during their 9th or 10th year. ⊠ *Topkapı Sarayı, Gülhane Park, near Sultanahmet Sq.* ☎ *212/512–0480* ⊕ *www. topkapisarayi.gov.tr* ✍ *$6 for the palace plus another $6 for the Harem tour* ☉ *Wed.–Mon. 9-7 in summer and 9-5 in winter for the palace itself. The Harem is open Wed.–Mon. 9:30-3.30 all year.*

> ## HAREM HIERARCHY
>
> Some of the most beautiful women in the empire were brought to the Harem, having been bought at slave markets, sold by their parents, or carried off during raids. Only the loveliest were presented to the sultan: of the others, some were married off to lesser officials, but most spent their lives as slaves, serving women higher in the social order of the Harem. Eunuchs were captured as boys and castrated before adolescence; they were the only men allowed in the compound and were charged with guarding the Harem. The queen mother, the *valide* sultan, oversaw the Harem.

NEED A BREAK?

Just past the Topkapı Treasury, on the right side of the courtyard, are steps leading to the 19th-century rococo-style Mecidiye Pavilion, also known as the Köşk of Sultan Abdül Mecit I (ruled 1839–61), for whom it was built. It now houses the **Konyalı Restaurant** (☎ 212/513-9696), which serves traditional Turkish dishes—a little overpriced, but you may decide the magnificent view of the Bosphorus is worth the cost. The terrace below has an outdoor café with even better views—without the extravagant prices. Go early to beat the tour-group crush. The restaurant and the café are open for lunch only.

★ ❹ **Yerebatan Sarnıcı** (Basilica Cistern). A slightly creepy journey through this ancient underground waterway takes you along sparsely lit wooden

CLOSE UP

Safety Concerns?

A TRUE STORY: A visitor to Istanbul is approached by a friendly young man who is looking for an opportunity to practice his English and would be happy to show the visitor around. The day extends into night and the friendly young man proposes to take his new friend to a club for a drink. At the end of the night, the young man has disappeared and the hapless visitor is left with a bill totaling several hundred dollars for only a few drinks, and surrounded by bunch of goons who are going to make sure the bill is paid.

Stories like this, fortunately, are the exception, not the rule. Istanbul is, for a city of close to 14 million, very safe, especially in the areas frequented by tourists. Still, like any other big city that attracts hordes of travelers, Istanbul also has its share of unscrupulous touts and shills. The busy and crowded areas around Aya Sofya and Taksim Square seem to especially attract these types. Many of the touts who will approach you, particularly in Sultanahmet, want no more than to steer you toward a harmless carpet shop where they will earn a commission, but the odd few might be less well intentioned. Complicating this is the fact that Turks are by nature exceedingly friendly and will go out of their way to help you—once you approach them. *The key is to be on the lookout for those who approach you first and seem a little too eager to help, and whose English is just a little too polished.* Use your judgment, but don't be embarrassed to say no politely and move on if you feel accosted. You will certainly make many new friends during a visit to Turkey—just make sure you do it on your terms.

walkways that lead between the 336 marble columns that rise 26 feet to support Byzantine arches and domes, from which the water drips unceasingly. Often referred to as the "Sunken Cistern," Yerebatan Sarnıcı is the most impressive part of an underground network of waterways said to have been created at the behest of Emperor Constantine in the 4th century and expanded by Justinian in the 6th century (most of the present structure dates from the Justinian era). The cistern was always kept full as a precaution against long sieges, and fish, presumably descendants of those that arrived in Byzantine times, still flit through the dark waters. So, what's the thrill of visiting what is essentially a municipal waterworks? The cistern is hauntingly beautiful, an oasis of coolness and shadowed, cathedral-like stillness, and a particularly cool and relaxing place to get away from the hubbub of the Old City. ⊠ *Yerebatan Cad. at Divan Yolu* ☎ *212/ 522–1259* ⊕ *www.yerebatan.com* ▧ *$6* ⊙ *Daily 9–4:30.*

TEA HOUSES

Istanbul is filled with teahouses, many with shady gardens, where people spend long hours quietly sipping glass after glass of tea. Sitting down at one of these teahouses, particularly if it has a nice view, such as the one in Eminönü's Gülhane Park, is one of the simple pleasures of Turkish life.

Also Worth Seeing

❼ Hippodrome. It takes a bit of imagination to appreciate the Hippodrome, once a Byzantine stadium with seating for 100,000. There isn't much here anymore, but the shape remains, and hundreds of peddlers selling postcards, nuts, and souvenirs create a hint of the festive atmosphere that must have prevailed during chariot races and circuses. Notably absent are the rows and rows of seats that once surrounded the track and the life-size bronze sculpture of four horses that once adorned the stadium—the Venetians looted the statue, and it now stands above the entrance to the basilica of San Marco in Venice. You can, however, see several other monuments—the **Dikilitaş** (Egyptian Obelisk) from the 15th century BC, the **Örme Sütün** (Column of Constantinos), and the **Yılanlı Sütun** (Serpentine Column), taken from the Temple of Apollo at Delphi in Greece—and you can also enjoy stunning views of the Blue Mosque, with its magical cascade of domes, just across the way. ⊠ *Atmeydanı, Sultanahmet* 🖭 *Free* ☉ *Accessible at all hrs.*

❽ İbrahim Paşa Sarayı (İbrahim Paşa Palace). Süleyman the Magnificent commissioned the great architect Sinan to build this stone palace overlooking the Hippodrome, the most grandiose residence in Istanbul. The sultan's beloved childhood friend, brother-in-law, and grand vizier İbrahim Paşa took up residence here sometime around 1524 with his wife, Süleyman's sister. The men were inseparable, taking all their meals together and watching games in the Hippodrome from the palace balconies. İbrahim Paşa, however, didn't have long to enjoy his new home: Despite his bonds with the sultan, he was executed when he became too powerful for the liking of Süleyman's power-crazed wife, Roxelana. The palace now houses the **Türk Ve İslâm Eserleri Müzesi** (Museum of Turkish and Islamic Arts), where you can learn about the lifestyles of Turks at every level of society, from the 8th century to the present. ⊠ *Atmeydanı 46, Sultanahmet* 🕾 *212/518–1385* 🖭 *$2* ☉ *Tues.–Sun. 9–4:30.*

⓳ Kariye Müzesi. (Kariye Museum) The dazzling mosaics and frescoes in the former Church of the Holy Savior in Chora are considered to be among the finest Byzantine works in the world. Most of the mosaics, in 50 panels, depict scenes from the New Testament and date from the 14th century. They are in splendid condition, largely because they were plastered over when the church became a mosque in the 16th century and were not uncovered until the 1940s. A cluster of Ottoman buildings surrounding the former church have also been restored, making this out-of-the-way corner of the city especially atmospheric. "Chora" comes from the Greek word meaning countryside; the church was originally outside the city walls built by Constantine the Great, but at the beginning of the 5th century AD Theodosius strengthened the city's fortifications and tweaked the line of walls in a few places, which brought the church inside the walls. A tea shop on the garden terrace serves light fare, providing a nice place for lunch here at the western edge of the Old City. ⊠ *1 block north of Fevzi Paşa Cad., by Edirne Gate in city's outer walls* 🕾 *212/631–9241* 🖭 *$6* ☉ *Thurs.–Tues. 9:30–6.30.*

Fodor'sChoice
★

★ **❻ Mozaik Müzesi** (Mosaic Museum). One of Istanbul's more fascinating sights is often overlooked, hidden as it is in the midst of the Arasta Bazaar and overshadowed by such neighbors as the Blue Mosque and Aya Sofya. The Great Palace of Byzantium, the imperial residence of Constantine and other Byzantine emperors when they ruled lands stretching from Iran to Italy and from the Caucasus to North Africa stood here, though only scant ruins remained by 1935. That's when archaeologists began uncovering what is thought to have been the floor of a palace courtyard, paved in some of the most elaborate and delightful mosaics to survive from the era: Scenes of animals, flowers, and trees in many of them depict rural idylls far removed from the pomp and elaborate ritual of the imperial court. ⊠ *Arasta Çarşısı, Kabasakal Cad., Sultanahmet* ☎ *212/518–1205* ⊇ *$3* ⊙ *Tues.–Sun. 9–5.*

> ## SINAN THE ARCHITECT
>
> The master architect Sinan, the greatest of the Ottoman builders, is said to have designed more than 350 buildings and monuments throughout Turkey. His genius as an architect lay in his use of proportion, and as an engineer he mastered the use of buttresses and other elements to create vast, open spaces. Some of the buildings attributed to Sinan are the Sokollu Mehmet Paşa, Süleymaniye, and Rüştem Paşa mosques, parts of the kitchens at Topkapı, two of the minarets at Aya Sofya, and Selimiye Cami in Edirne.

★ ❾ **Sokollu Mehmet Paşa Cami** (Mosque of Mehmet Paşa). This small mosque, built in 1571, is not as grand as Süleymaniye Cami, but many consider it to be the most beautiful of the mosques that the master architect Sinan built under the direction of Süleyman the Magnificent. Sinan chose not to dazzle with size but to create a graceful, harmonious whole, from the courtyard and porticoes outside to the delicately carved *mimber* (pulpit), the gorgeous, well-preserved İznik tiles set off by pure white walls, the and floral-motif stained-glass windows inside. ⊠ *Mehmet Paşa Cad. at Özbekler Sok., Küçük Ayasofya* ☎ *no phone* ⊇ *Free* ⊙ *Daily sunrise–sunset, except during prayer times.*

The Bazaar Area and Environs

The area between the Grand Bazaar and the shore of the Golden Horn teems with people during the day. Even though most of the old Byzantine and Ottoman buildings have long gone, the stalls and peddlars who line the narrow, rather grubby streets winding down the hill from the Grand Bazaar give an impression of how the city must have been like when it was the bustling capital of a vast empire. In addition to the Grand Bazaar and the Egyptian Bazaar, you'll come upon some of the city's most beautiful mosques here.

Main Attractions

⓰ **Egyptian Bazaar** (Mısır Çarşısı). This enticing collection of stalls, also known as the Spice Market, is much smaller than the Grand Bazaar but more crowded and colorful—though not as colorful, perhaps, as it was when built in the 17th century to generate rental income to pay for the upkeep of the **Yeni Cami** (New Mosque), next door. In those earlier days the bazaar was a vast pharmacy filled with burlap bags overflowing with herbs and spices. Even so, today you can wander through stalls chock-ablock with white sacks of spices, as well as bags full of fruit, nuts, and royal jelly from the beehives of the Aegean Sea. ⊠ *Hamidiye Cad., across from Galata Bridge* ⊙ *Mon.–Sat. 8–7.*

NEED A
BREAK?

The **Pandelli,** up two flights of stairs over the arched gateway to the Egyptian Bazaar, is a frenetic Old Istanbul restaurant with impressive tile work. A lunch of typical Turkish fare is served; especially good are the eggplant *börek* (pastry) and the sea bass cooked in paper. ⊠ *Mısır Çarşısı 1, Eminönü* ☎ *212/527-3909* ▭ *AE, MC, V.*

★ ❿ **Grand Bazaar** (Kapalı Çarşısı). Take a deep breath and plunge on into this maze of 65 winding, covered streets crammed with 4,000 tiny shops, cafés, restaurants, mosques, and courtyards. It's said that this early version of a shopping mall is the largest concentration of stores under one roof anywhere in the world, and that's easy to believe; it's also easy to believe that some of the most aggressive salesmanship in the world takes place here, which is why you should take that deep breath and put up your guard before entering. Oddly enough, though, the sales pitches, the crowds, the sheer volumes of junky trinkets on offer can be hypnotizing, and you'll probably find it hard to spend less than a couple of hours wandering through the maze. Originally built by Mehmet II (the Conqueror) in the 1450s, the Grand Bazaar was ravaged twice by fire in relatively recent years—once in 1954 when it was almost destroyed, and once in 1974, in a smaller conflagration. In both cases, the bazaar was quickly rebuilt into something resembling the original style, with its arched passageways and brass-and-tile fountains at regular intervals.

The amazingly polylingual sellers are all anxious to reassure you that you do not have to buy . . . just drink a glass of tea while you browse through leather goods, carpets, fabric, clothing (including counterfeit brand names), brass candelabra, furniture, ceramics, and gold and silver jewelry. A sizable share of the goods are trinkets tailored for the tourist trade, but a separate section for antiques at the very center of the bazaar, called the *bedestan,* always has some beautiful items on offer. Outside the western gate to the bazaar, through a doorway, is the **Sahaflar Çarşısı,** the Old Book Bazaar, where you can buy new editions as well as antique volumes in Turkish and other languages. Remember, whether you are bargaining for a pair of slippers or an antique carpet, the best prices are offered when the would-be seller

IT'S ALL DOWNHILL

When exploring the Bazaar area, start at the Grand Bazaar and work your way downhill to Eminönü—it's a rather stiff climb the other way. From Sultanahmet, you can take a tram partway down the hill to the Grand Bazaar. It's almost impossible to get lost; just keep walking downhill until you reach the water. Take note that the Grand and Egyptian bazaars are closed Sunday. The Beyazıt, Rüstem Paşa, and Süleymaniye mosques are open daily but effectively—if often not officially—closed to non-Muslims at prayer times, particularly Friday midday.

thinks you are about to slip away. ⊠ *Yeniçeriler Cad. and Fuatpaşa Cad.* ⌦ *Free* ⊙ *Apr.–Oct., Mon.–Sat. 8:30–7; Nov.–Mar., Mon.–Sat. 8:30–6:30.*

⑮ **Rüstem Paşa Cami** (Rüstem Paşa Mosque). Take a break from bazaar haggling and step into another Sinan masterpiece, tucked away in the backstreets to the north of the Egyptian Bazaar and built in the 1550s for Süleyman's grand vizier. The mosque is unassuming from the outside, but you're in for a treat when you step into the cool interior, decorated with İznik tiles in a magnificent array of colors and patterns. ⊠ *Hasırcılar Cad., south of Sobacılar Cad.* ⊙ *Daily.*

★ ⑬ **Süleymaniye Cami** (Mosque of Süleyman). Perched on a hilltop near Istanbul University, the largest mosque in Istanbul is less arresting visually than Sokollu Mehmet Paşa Cami and some of the other mosques and monuments the architect Sinan designed, but a masterful achievement and grand presence nonetheless. This mosque houses Sinan's tomb, along with that of his patron, Süleyman the Magnificent, and the sultan's wife, Roxelana. The architectural thrill here is the enormous dome. Supported by four square columns and arches, as well as exterior walls with smaller domes on either side, the soaring space gives the impression that it's held up principally by divine cooperation. Look around the grounds, because the complex still incorporates a hospital, a kervansaray, a huge kitchen, several schools, and other charitable institutions that mosques traditionally operate. ⊠ *Süleymaniye Cad., near Istanbul University's north gate* ⊙ *Daily.*

Also Worth Seeing

⑪ **Beyazıt Cami.** This domed mosque inspired by Aya Sofya isn't really that interesting in itself; its distinction is being the oldest of the Ottoman imperial mosques still standing in the city, dating from 1504. ⊠ *Beyazıt Meyd., Beyazıt* ⌦ *Free* ⊙ *Daily sunrise to sunset; usually closed during prayer times.*

⑭ **Eminönü.** This waterside neighborhood at the south end of the Galata Bridge is the transportation hub of old Istanbul. There are quays for hydrofoil sea buses, the more traditional Bosphorus ferries (including those for the day-long Bosphorus cruises), and the Sirkeci train station and tramway terminal. The main coastal road around the peninsula of the Old City also traverses Eminönü. Thousands of people and vehicles rush through the bustling area, and numerous street traders here sell everything from candles to live animals.

⑱ **Eyüp Cami.** Muslim pilgrims from all over the world make their way to the brightly colored, tile-covered tomb of Eyüp Ensari, the prophet Muhammad's standard-bearer, at this mosque complex on the Golden Horn. Ensari was killed during the first Arab siege, AD 674–78, of what was then Constantinople, and the eternal presence of a man so close to Muhammad makes this the holiest Islamic shrine in Turkey. The mosque, built in the 15th century by Sultan Mehmet the Conqueror and expanded by his successors, is also the final resting place of many other distinguished departed. Despite the numbers of visitors, particularly at Friday midday prayer, the plane-tree-shaded courtyards and hundreds of fluttering pigeons imbue Eyüp Cami with a sense of peace and religious devotion not found in many other parts of this often frenetic city. ✉ *Cami Kebir Caddesi, Eyüp* ☎ *no phone* ☉ *Daily.*

⑫ **Istanbul University.** You won't find much to do here, other than appreciate the open space—the campus, with its long greensward and giant plane trees, originally served as the Ottoman war ministry, which accounts for the magnificent gateway arch facing Beyazıt Square and the grandiose, martial style of the main buildings. In the garden is the white-marble 200-foot **Beyazıt Tower,** the tallest structure in Old Stamboul, built in 1823 by Mahmut II (ruled 1808–39) as a fire-watch station, although you can no longer ascend. ✉ *Fuat Paşa Cad., Beyazıt.*

OFF THE BEATEN PATH

⑰ **SVETI STEFAN BULGAR KILESI** (Bulgarian Church of St. Stefan) – One of the most remarkable structures in Istanbul—and that's saying quite a lot—this neo-Gothic church looks like it's covered with elaborate stone carvings but when you get up close, you realize that it's all cast iron. It was prefabricated in Vienna, shipped down the Danube on barges, and erected on the western shore of the Golden Horn in 1871. The then-flourishing Bulgarian Orthodox community in Istanbul was eager to have an impressive church of its own to back its demand for freedom from the Greek Orthodox patriarchate; ordering this fancy church was a statement of independence. The dwindling numbers of the Bulgarian community in Istanbul today, though, mean that there isn't always someone on hand to unlock the interior, also covered in cast-iron finery, but it's still an impressive structure to look at, even if you can't get inside. The church is set in neatly tended gardens. ✉ *Mürsel Paşa Caddesi, Balat* ☉ *Daily.*

OFF THE BEATEN PATH

YENI CAMI (The New Queen Mother's Mosque) – The most interesting aspect of this mosque is its location, rising out of the Golden Horn on the Eminönü waterfront. The prime location ensures the blockish-looking structure is a dominant feature of the Istanbul skyline—and presented formidable engineering challenges to the student of Sinan who began laying the water-logged foundations in 1597. Queen Mother Turhan Hattice saw the project through to completion in the middle of the 17th century, and is buried here near her son, Sultan Mehmet IV, along with several succeeding sultans. ✉ *Eminönü waterfront* ☉ *Daily.*

> **VIEW FROM THE BRIDGE**
>
> The Galata bridge, or Galata Köprüsü, connects old Istanbul to the so-called New Town on the other side of the Golden Horn. The bridge opened in 1993, replacing the old pontoon bridge that had been around since 1910, in the days when horse-, ox-, or mule-drawn carriages rattled across it for a fee. The bridge itself isn't much to look at, but you can stand for hours watching ferries chug out on the Bosphorus.

Istanbul's "New Town"

The neighborhood that climbs the Galata Hill is known both as Pera and Beyoğlu, and it's often referred to as the "New Town," where the first thing you'll learn is that *new* is a relative term in Istanbul. Much of what you'll see here dates from the nineteenth century. In the early part of the 20th century, Beyoğlu was one of Istanbul's most fashionable areas, home to large numbers of the city's Greeks, Jews, and Armenians and filled with many grand, European-style apartment buildings. As the decades passed, more people started moving to the greener neighborhoods farther up the Bosphorus. What had once been one of Istanbul's most elegant neighborhoods became crime-ridden and filled with crumbling buildings. Gentrification fever has hit the neighborhood recently, and many Istanbulites are rediscovering the splendid old buildings and incredible views. Istanbul's New Town clings to the hillside above Karaköy, a dock area for local fishermen as well as cruise lines. Tünel Square, just north of the docks, is an appealing gathering spot surrounded by shops and cafes. Nearby is the Pera Palace, one of the most famous of Istanbul's hotels, where Agatha Christie wrote *Murder on the Orient Express* and where Mata Hari threw back a few at the bar. From the square, İstiklal Caddesi (Independence Street) climbs uphill through Beyoğlu, past consulates in ornate turn-of-the-century buildings and across Galatasaray Meydanı (Galatasaray Square) to Taksim Meydanı (Taksim Square), the center of modern Istanbul.

NEED A BREAK? Restaurants and cafés line the waterfront by the passenger ferry landing in Karaköy, but you can get a better snack from the fishermen who grill their freshly caught fish on little charcoal barbecues, then stick them in the middle of a half loaf of bread—perhaps with some sliced tomato and onion.

Main Attractions

㉔ Divan Edebiyatı Müzesi (Divan Literature Museum, also called the Galata Mevlevihane). This museum houses a small collection of instruments and other dervish memorabilia, but the best time to come here—and if you're in town then, it's well worth the effort to go out of your way do so—is at 3 PM on the last Sunday of each month, for concerts of Sufi music and dance performances by the Sufi mystics known in the West as the whirling dervishes. ⊠ *Galip Dede Cad. 15, southeast of Tünel Sq., off İstiklal Cad., Beyoğlu* ☎ *212/245–4141* ᳇ *$1, $15 for the monthly dance performances* ⊙ *Wed.–Mon. 9:30–4:30.*

㉒ Galata Tower (Galata Kulesi). The area around the Galata Tower was a thriving Italian settlement both before and after the fall of Constantinople, and the Genoese built this tower as part of their fortifications in 1349, when they controlled the northern shore of the Golden Horn. The hillside location provided good defense, as well as a perch from which to monitor the comings and goings of vessels in the sea lanes below. You can do the same from the viewing gallery, accessible by elevator and open during the day, with panoramic views of the city and across the Golden Horn and Sea of Marmara. The rocket-shaped tower has also served as a jail and, for a time during the 1900s, as a fire lookout. It now also houses a restaurant and nightclub. ⊠ *Galata Tower: Büyük Hendek Cad.* ☎ *212/245–1160* ᳇ *$6* ⊙ *Daily 9–8.*

㉓ Istanbul Modern. A converted warehouse on the shores of the Golden Horn showcases modern painting, sculpture, and photography, from Turkey and around the world. You can wander around by yourself, though you'll learn a lot about the art scene in Turkey if you join one of the free guided tours (in English and Turkish), but you need to call in advance to confirm availability and make a reservation. The gallery also houses a shop, a small cinema, and a restaurant and café with beautiful views toward Topkapı Sarayı and the Sea of Marmara. ⊠ *Meclis-i Mebusan Caddesi Liman İşletmeleri Sahası, Antrepo No. 4, Karaköy* ☎ *212/334–7300, tour reservations 212/334–7322* ⊕ *www.istanbulmodern.org* ✒ *$5, free Thurs.* ☉ *Tues., Wed., Fri., Sat., Sun. 10–6, Thurs. 10–8. Closed Mon.; tours at 1 and 3.*

Also Worth Seeing

㉘ The **Atatürk Cultural Center** (Atatürk Kültür Merkezi), also known as the AKM, is the not very pretty home to Istanbul's major performing arts groups—the State Opera and Ballet, the State Theatre, and the State Symphony Orchestra. Looking lost and grubby in the hubbub of Taksim Square, the modern, 900-seat house is far more attractive at night, when it's beautifully lit. ⊠ *Taksim Sq.* ☎ *0212/251–5600.*

㉕ **Flower Arcade.** (Çiçek Pasajı) Curmudgeons swear this lively warren of flower stalls, tiny restaurants, and bars just off Galatasaray Square is a pale shadow of its former self—its original neo-Baroque home collapsed with a thundering crash one night in 1978, and its redone facade and interior feel too much like a reproduction. You can still get a feel for the arcade's bohemian past, though, especially when street musicians entertain here, as they often do. ⊠ *Along the northernmost stretch of İstiklal Caddesi.*

★ **㉖** **Fish Market** (Balık Pazarı). Behind the Flower Passage a bustling labyrinth of stands peddles fish, fruits, vegetables, and spices—with a couple of pastry shops thrown in—all of which makes for great street theater. Nevizade Soka is a strip of fish restaurants in the market, all with outside tables in the summer. At the end of the market, at Meşrutiyet Caddesi, is the **Üç Horan Armenian Church** (⊠ İstiklal Cad. 288)—with its crosses and haloed Christs, it's an unexpected sight in Muslim Istanbul.

★ **㉑** **Jewish Museum of Turkey.** The history of the Jews in Istanbul and other parts of Turkey is a lot more extensive and colorful than the size of this small museum in the Zulfaris Synagogue might suggest. Even so, the documents and photos here, most of them donated by local Jewish families, provide a fascinating glimpse into the lives of Turkish Jews, who have been traced to Anatolia as early as the 4th century BC. Their numbers became sizeable in the Middle Ages as Jews were expelled from parts of Europe. In 1492, the Spanish Inquisition drove Sephardic Jews from Spain and Portugal, and Sultan Bayazid II welcomed the refugees in the Ottoman Empire. Many settled in Istanbul, and a large Jewish population thrived in the city for centuries. Today, 16 active synagogues, one of which dates from the Byzantine period, serve a Jewish community of 25,000, and some older Turkish Jews still speak a dialect of medieval Spanish called Ladino, or Judeo-Spanish. In the Neve Shalom Synagogue, on Büyük Hendek Sokak near the Galata Tower, 22 Sabbath worshipers were shot by Arabic-speaking gunmen in September 1986. ⊠ *Meydanı*

Perçemil Sok., just off Karaköy Caddesi near the foot of the Galata Bridge ✉ *$1* ⊙ *Mon. and Thurs. 10 AM–4 PM, Fri. and Sun. 10 AM–2 PM.*

NEED A BREAK? The **Patisserie Café Marmara,** in the Marmara Hotel on Taksim Square, serves hot and cold drinks and snacks, ice cream, and excellent homemade cakes. Despite the turbulence and often downright chaos of the square, the café retains an air of unhurried calm. A duo usually plays soothing classical music in the late afternoon and early evening. In summer the shaded terrace is a good place to observe the bustle. ✉ *Marmara Istanbul, Taksim Sq.* ☎ *212/251–4696* ▤ *AE, DC, MC, V.*

㉗ **Taksim Square** (Taksim Meydanı). This square at the north end of İstiklal Caddesi is the not particularly handsome center of the modern city. It's basically a chaotic traffic circle with an entrance to Istanbul's subway system, a bit of grass, and the Monument to the Republic and Independence, featuring Atatürk and his revolutionary cohorts. Around the square are Istanbul's main concert hall (the Atatürk Cultural Center), the high-rise Marmara Hotel, and, on a grassy promenade, the 23-story Ceylan Inter-Continental. On Cumhuriyet Caddesi, the main street heading north from the square, are shops selling carpets and leather goods. Also here are the entrances to the Hyatt, Divan, and Istanbul Hilton hotels; several travel agencies and airline ticket offices; and a few nightclubs. Cumhuriyet turns into Halâskârgazi Caddesi. When this street meets Rumeli Caddesi, you enter the city's high-fashion district, where Turkey's top designers sell their wares.

OFF THE BEATEN PATH

RAHMI M. KOÇ INDUSTRIAL MUSEUM – A foundry that used to cast anchors for the Ottoman fleet, this building is now filled with steam engines, medieval telescopes, planes, boats, a submarine, a tank, trucks, trains, a horse-drawn tram, bicycles, motorbikes, and the great engines that powered the Bosphorus ferries. The wonderful and eclectic collection, on the shore of the Golden Horn, is sponsored by one of Turkey's leading modern industrialists. ✉ *27 Hasköy Cad., Hasköy* ☎ *212/369–6600* 🖷 *212/369–6606* ⊕ *www.rmk-museum.org.tr* ✉ *$4* ⊙ *Tues.–Fri. 10–5, Fri.–Sat. 10–7.*

㉒

Beşiktaş and Beyond

The part of the western shore of the Bosphorus now known as Beşiktaş became the favorite residence of the later Ottoman sultans as they sought to escape overcrowded Old Stamboul. They remained here, in their pleasure palaces and pavilions, until the end of the empire when eventually they, too, were engulfed by the ever-expanding city and, one could argue, by history as well. The big draw here for visitors is Dolmabahçe Sarayı, but the Naval and Military museums and Yıldız Parkı and Şale (chalet) are here, too. When planning your trip, keep in mind that Dolmabahçe Sarayı is closed Monday and Thursday, and the Naval Museum Monday and Thursday. Yıldız Parkı is open daily, but Yıldız Şale is closed Monday and Tuesday.

Main Attractions

32 Çırağan Sarayı (Çırağan Palace). This palace—now Istanbul's most luxurious hotel—was built by Sultan Abdül Aziz (ruled 1861–76), in 1863. Vacuous Abdül Aziz was as extravagant as his brother, Abdül Mecit (who built the nearby Dolmabahçe Sarayı), and was soon attempting to emulate the splendors he had seen on travels in England and France. The Çırağan Sarayı is about a third the size of Dolmabahçe Sarayı, and much less ornate, which says a good deal about the declining state of the Ottoman Empire's coffers.

PARKS AND GREEN SPACES

There isn't much in the way of green parks in the Old City, except for Gülhane Parkı, alongside Topkapı Sarayı. For the most part, you have to head farther out to find tranquil spaces.
The wooded slopes of Yıldız Parkı, just north of the Çırağan Sarayı, are usually blissfully uncrowded. Emirgân Park, in the Bosphorus village of the same name, is noted for its flower gardens and Bosphorus views.

The restored grounds, with a splendid swimming pool, line the shore of the Bosphorus, and the hotel bar provides a plush, cool respite with a view. You won't find much from the original palace, as a major fire gutted the place; the lobby renovations were done with a nod to the palace's original 19th-century design, though the color scheme is decidedly gaudier. ⊠ *Çırağan Cad. 84, Beşiktaş* ☎ *212/326–4646.*

31 Naval Museum (Deniz Müzesi). The flashiest displays here are the sultan's barges: the long, slim boats that served as the primary mode of royal transportation for several hundred years. Elsewhere in these two buildings—one for "sea-going craft" and the other housing artifacts from the maritime history of the Ottoman Empire and Turkish Republic—give a pretty good scope of the Ottoman Empire's onetime supremacy at sea. Unfortunately, most of the labels are in Turkish, but you can still appreciate the standouts, such as cannons that include a 23-ton blaster built for Sultan Selim the Grim and an early Ottoman map of the New World, cribbed from Columbus, dating from 1513. ⊠ *Beşiktaş Cad., Beşiktaş* ☎ *212/327–4346* ⊠ *$2* ⊙ *Wed.–Sun. 9–12:00 and 1:30–5:30.*

30 Dolmabahçe Sarayı (Dolmabahçe Palace). The name means "filled-in garden," from the fact that Sultan Ahmet I (ruled 1603–17) had an imperial garden planted here on land reclaimed from the sea. In 1853, Abdül Mecit, whose free-spending lifestyle (his main distinction) bankrupted the empire, had this palace built as a symbol of Turkey's march away from its past and toward the European mainstream. He gave his Armenian architect, Balian, complete freedom and an unlimited budget. His only demand was that the palace "surpass any other palace of any other potentate anywhere in the world." The result, an extraordinary mixture of Hindu, Turkish, and European styles of architecture and interior design, is a riot of rococo—marble, vast mirrors, stately towers, and formal gardens along a facade stretching nearly ½ km (⅓ mi). Abdül Mecit's bed is solid silver; the tub and basins in his marble-paved bath-

Fodor's Choice
★

room are carved of translucent alabaster. Europe's royalty contributed to the splendor: Queen Victoria sent a chandelier weighing 4½ tons, Czar Nicholas I of Russia provided polar-bear rugs. The result is as gaudy and showy as a palace should be, all gilt and crystal and silk, and every bit as garish as Versailles.

After the establishment of the modern republic in 1923, the palace became the home of Atatürk, who died here in 1938. Abdül Mecit's mother founded the nearby Dolmabahçe Cami (Dolmabahçe Mosque) in 1853. To see the palace you must join a guided tour, which takes about 80 minutes. ⊠ *Dolmabahçe Cad., Beşiktaş* 🕾 *212/258–5544* 🖭 *$12* ⊙ *Tues.–Wed. and Fri.–Sun. 9–4.*

Also Worth Seeing

★ ㉙ **Military Museum** (Askeri Müze). Not surprisingly, given that the Ottoman Empire was built on military might, this collection of swords, armor, and other weaponry is quite fascinating; anyone with an interest in military history will be riveted, while others will find plenty of remarkable tidbits, too. Most showy are the gorgeously embroidered silk tents used by the Ottoman sultans on campaigns, and fragments of the great chain that the last Byzantine rulers stretched across the Golden Horn in a vain attempt to prevent the Turks from gaining access to the city by sea. Atatürk was educated in this former military academy, and his personal effects from the 1915 Gallipoli campaign are touchingly humble. ■ TIP→ **If you're visiting in the summer, try to make sure your visit coincides with the *Mehter* (Janissary) military band as it performs 17th- and 18th-century Ottoman military music in full period costume on the grounds of the museum at 3 PM, Wednesday–Sunday.** ⊠ *Valikonağı Caddesi, Harbiye* 🕾 *212/233–2720* 🖭 *$2* ⊙ *Wed.–Sun. 9–5.*

㉝ **Yıldız Parkı.** The wooded slopes of Yıldız Parkı once formed part of the great forest that covered the European shore of the Bosphorus from the Golden Horn to the Black Sea. In the waning years of the Ottoman Empire, the park was the private garden of Dolmabahçe Sarayı, and the women of the harem would occasionally be allowed to visit. First the gardeners would be removed, then the eunuchs would lead the women across the wooden bridge from the palace and along the avenue to the upper gardens. Secluded from prying eyes, they would sit in the shade or wander beneath the acacias, maples, and cypresses, filling their baskets with flowers and figs. Today the park is still hauntingly beautiful, particularly in spring, when the flowers bloom, and in fall, when the leaves of the deciduous trees change color.

Yıldız Şale (Yıldız Chalet). Sultan Abdül Hamit II, who distinguished himself as the last despot of the Ottoman Empire (ruled 1876–1909) spent most of his time in this relatively modest residence at the top of Yıldız Park; he also lived in the Çırağan and Dolmabahçe palaces. Visiting dignitaries from Kaiser Wilhelm to Charles de Gaulle and Margaret Thatcher have stayed here as well. The chalet is often blissfully empty of other tourists, which makes a visit all the more pleasurable. ⊠ *Çırağan Cad.* 🕾 *212/261–8460 for park, 212/259–4570 for chalet*

Park: 50¢ pedestrians, $1.50 cars; chalet: $1.50 ⊙ Park: daily 9–9; chalet: Wed.–Sun. 9–4.

1

The Bosphorus

One of the most pleasant experiences in Istanbul—and an easy way to escape the chaos of the city—is a trip up the Bosphorus by ferry from the Eminönü docks in the Old Town. Along the way you'll see wooded hills; villages large and small, modern and old-fashioned; and the old wooden summer homes called *yalıs* (waterside houses) that were built for the city's wealthier residents in the Ottoman era—as well as the grand palaces of Beşiktaş.

Bosphorus Sights

After departing from Eminönü, boats head north out of the Golden Horn and past the Dolmabahçe and Çırağan palaces on the European shore, and then under the first **Bosphorus bridge**, a graceful suspension span.

34 As you approach the Bosphorus bridge you'll pass the **Ortaköy** neighborhood on the European shore. It's not far from Beşiktaş, but with its cluster of narrow streets it has the feel of a little village, and is quite charming. There are many cafés and restaurants and, during the day, street stalls selling trinkets and jewelry. An open space faces the Bosphorus and it's a lovely place to spend a summer evening.

34 **Beylerbeyi Sarayı** (Beylerbeyi Palace). Built for Sultan Abdül Aziz in 1865, Beylerbeyi, on the Asian shore, is a mini-Dolmabahçe, though unlike Dolmabahçe, Beylerbeyi is painted a pinkish peach. It's filled with marble and marquetry and gold-encrusted furniture, and the central hall has a white-marble fountain and a stairway wide enough for a regiment. You must join a tour to see the palace, but it's probably more worth your time to visit Dolmabahçe and settle for seeing Beylerbeyi from the ferry. ✉ *Çayıbaşı Durağı, Beylerbeyi* ☎ *216/321–9320* ✉ *$3* ⊙ *Tues.–Wed. and Fri.–Sun. 9:30–5.*

36 **Arnavutköy.** This village on the European side is a pleasant place for a stroll. A row of 19th-century wooden houses lines the waterfront, and up the hill from the water narrow streets are lined with more old wooden houses, some of them with trailing vines.

37 **Bebek.** Also on the European side, Bebek is one of the most fashionable suburbs of Istanbul and is especially popular with an affluent expatriate community. Small rowboats and even sizable cutters with crew can be rented for trips around Bebek Bay. (Bebek is about 20 minutes by taxi from central Istanbul.)

38 **Anadolu Hisarı** (Anatolian Castle). Sultan Beyazıt I built this fortress in 1393 at the mouth of the Göksu stream—known in Ottoman times as one of the "Sweet Waters of Asia"—to cut off Constantinople's access to the Black Sea. The castle looks especially romantic at sunset, when its golden stone blends into the surrounding forest and tiny boats bob beneath its walls (some of which are crumbling, so be careful if you're

CLOSE UP

Planning a Bosphorus Day Cruise

THERE ARE TWO WAYS to take a ferry tour of the Bosphorus: you can take a cruise ferry or a commuter ferry; both leave from Eminönü.

Cruise ferries depart daily from Quay 3 (look for the sign reading BOĞAZ HATTI) at 10:35 and 1:35 (times are subject to change, so check first). The round-trip should cost about $6. These boats zigzag up the Bosphorus with set stops—including for a couple of hours at either **Rumeli Kavağı** or **Anadolu Kavağı**, two fishing villages near the Black Sea, for lunch—then they zigzag back down to Eminönü. (Anadolu Kavağı is particularly fun; its sidewalk vendors sell deep-fried mussels and sweet waffles.)

Taking the commuter ferry allows you to fashion your own tour, hopping on and off wherever you fancy, and then continuing your journey on the next ferry going your way. (Buy a ferry timetable—a *vapur tarifesi*—to figure out your itinerary.) The disadvantage is that you will probably end up spending considerable extra time waiting for the next boat. Note, too, that not all commuter ferries stop at every quay along the Bosphorus, and during the middle of the day schedules can be erratic. When looking at ferry schedules, remember that Rumeli refers to the European side, Anadolu to the Asian.

Whether you take a Bosphorus cruise or make your own way by commuter ferry, you should allow a whole day. The cruises usually take about six hours. If you opt for the commuter ferry, add at least an extra hour (if not longer) for ferry-waiting time, in addition to the time spent at stops along the way. Beylerbeyi Sarayı is closed Monday and Thursday. Rumeli Hisarı is closed Monday. Sadberk Hanım Müzesi is closed Wednesday.

---

walking on them). An unmarked path leads up to the castle ruins; there's no admission fee.

Just beyond the fortress is the second Bosphorus bridge, officially known **③⑨** as **Fatih Sultan Mehmet Bridge. Rumeli Hisarı** (Thracian Castle) is opposite Anadolu Hisarı, on the European shore. Mehmet the Conqueror built this eccentric-looking fortress in 1452, a year before his siege of Constantinople finally succeeded. Its crenellated walls and round towers are popular with photographers, though what you view from the water is about all there is to see. In summer Rumeli Hisarı is sometimes used for Shakespeare performances (usually in Turkish) and music and folk dancing. There are occasionally jazz concerts here, too; it's quite an intimate settting, and doesn't seat many. ✉ *Rumeli Hisarı Cad.* 🖀 *no phone* 🎟 *$1* ☉ *Tues.–Sun. 9:30–5.*

④⓪ **Kanlıca.** This village just north of Fatih Sultan Mehmet Bridge, on the Asian side of the Bosphorus, has been famous for its delicious yogurt for at least 300 years; little restaurants around the plane tree in the square by the quay serve this treat. Nearby, white 19th-century wooden villas line the waterfront.

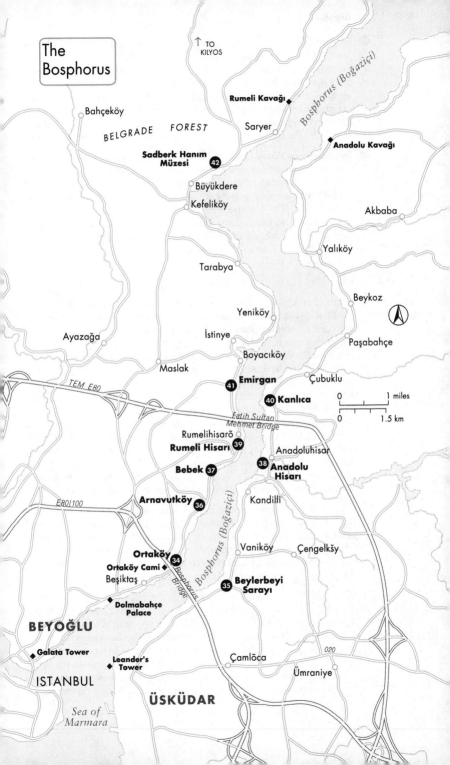

The Bosphorus

TO
KILYOS

Rumeli Kavağı

BELGRADE FOREST

Bahçeköy

Saryer

Bosphorus (Boğaziçi)

Anadolu Kavağı

Sadberk Hanım Müzesi 42

Büyükdere

Kefeliköy

Akbaba

Yalıköy

Tarabya

Beykoz

Yeniköy

İstinye

Ayazağa

Paşabahçe

Boyacıköy

Maslak

Çubuklu

TEM E80

Emirgan 41

Kanlıca 40

0   1 miles

0   1.5 km

Fatih Sultan
Mehmet Bridge

Rumelihisarö

Rumeli Hisarı 39

Anadoluhisar

Bebek 37

38 **Anadolu Hisarı**

E80/100

Kandilli

Arnavutköy 36

Vaniköy

Çengelkšy

Ortaköy 34

Ortaköy Cami

Beşiktaş

Bosphorus Bridge

35 **Beylerbeyi Sarayı**

Dolmabahçe Palace

BEYOĞLU

Galata Tower

Çamlõca

020

Leander's Tower

Ümraniye

ISTANBUL

ÜSKÜDAR

Sea of Marmara

❹ Emirgan. This town on the European shore just across the Bosphorus from Kanlica was named after a 17th-century Persian prince to whom Sultan Murat IV (ruled 1623–40) presented a palace. All that remains are a park with flower gardens and a number of restored Ottoman pavilions. In late April the town stages a Tulip Festival, when many tulips are planted. Tulips take their name from the Turkish *tulbend* (turban); they were originally brought from Mongolia; after their cultivation was refined by the Dutch they were great favorites of the Ottoman sultans.

❹ Sadberk Hanım Müzesi (Sadberk Hanım Museum). An old waterfront mansion on the European side houses this small but stunning collection of İznik tiles, Ottoman embroidery and calligraphy, and other Islamic and Turkish arts, as well such Anatolian antiquities as Hittite pottery and cuneiform tablets. The late billionaire businessman Vehbi Koç amassed the collection and named the museum for his deceased wife. ⊠ *Piyasa Cad. 27–29, Büyükdere* ☎ *212/242–3813* ⊕ *www.sadberkhanimmuzesi. org.tr* ✆ *$3* ☉ *Thurs.–Tues. 10–5.*

WHERE TO EAT

Updated by
Yigal Schleifer

Istanbul is a food lover's town. Restaurants abound, from humble kebab joints to fancy fish restaurants, with lots of excellent options in between. Istanbulites take their food seriously, holding dining establishments to a very high standard: they expect service to be prompt and polite, the restaurant to be spotless, and most importantly, the food to be made with the freshest of ingredients. The places that cater mostly to tourists are the ones that might let their standards slip. Turkish cuisine varies from region to region, and Istanbul, owing to its location on the Bosphorus, which connects the Black Sea to the Sea of Marmara, is famous for seafood. A classic Istanbul meal, usually eaten at one of the city's rollicking *meyhane*s (literally "drinking places"), starts off with a wide selection of tapas-style small appetizers called mezes and then moves on to a main course of grilled fish, all of it accompanied by the anise-flavored spirit rakı, Turkey's national drink. Fish can be expensive, so check prices and ask what's in season before ordering.

While Istanbul's dining scene, though large, was once mostly limited to Turkish cooking, recent years have seen a new generation of chefs successfully fusing local dishes with ingredients and flavors from other parts of the world. Some chefs, trained in the United States and Europe, are bringing contemporary cooking techniques they learned back with them. The result has been a kind of nouvelle Turkish cuisine.

While the Sultanahmet area might have most of the city's major monuments and hotels, it is sorely lacking in good dining options (save for a few standouts). You'll have better luck if you head across the Golden Horn to the lively Beyoğlu district or to some of the charming small neighborhoods along the Bosphorus, famous for their fish restaurants. Beyoğlu, with its small backstreets, has everything from hole-in-the-walls serving delicious homecooking to some of Istanbul's sleekest restaurants. The Bosphorus restaurants tend to be more upscale and expensive.

Since Istanbulites love to go out, reservations are essential at most of the city's better restaurants. In summer, many restaurants move their dining areas outdoors, and reservations become even more important if you want to snag a coveted outside table. Dining, for the most part, is casual, although Istanbulites enjoy dressing smartly when they're out and about. You may feel terribly underdressed if you show up in a restaurant dressed in shorts and a T-shirt, even in summer.

Istanbul has a range of restaurants—and prices to match. Most major hotels serve standard international cuisine, so it's more rewarding to eat in Turkish restaurants. In addition to the ubiquitous kebabs, Istanbul is also famous for its fish, although it is wise to check prices and ask what is in season before ordering. Beer, wine, the local spirit rakı, and sometimes cocktails are widely available, particularly in more upmarket restaurants, despite Muslim proscriptions against alcohol. Dress is casual unless otherwise noted.

> **BEER IN TURKEY**
>
> For years, visitors to Turkey basically had only one choice when ordering beer: Efes, the locally brewed lager. The situation has started to change, though. International brands such as Tuborg and Foster's are now brewed locally, and imports of popular beers such as Corona and Beck's have begun. The most welcome news for beer drinkers, though, may be that Istanbul has entered the microbrew era. Taps (Atiye Sok. 5, Tesçvikiye, 212/269-2020), a brewpub in Istanbul, has started to distribute its well-made beers around the city.

WHAT IT COSTS IN U.S. DOLLARS					
	$$$$	$$$	$$	$	¢
AT DINNER	over $30	$21–$30	$13–$20	$8–$12	under $8

Prices are per person for a main course at dinner, a main course equivalent, or a prix-fixe meal.

Sultanahmet

$$$$ ✕ **Giritli.** Only open since 2005, Giritli has already become an Istanbul
Fodor'sChoice classic, and with a prix-fixe menu that includes a generous four courses
★ and unlimited drink (wine or rakı), it's easy to understand why. Don't come here just to imbibe, though—the food is outstanding, with an enormous selection of delicious appetizers like sea bass ceviche; herb-covered cubes of feta cheese with walnuts and green onion; and perfectly grilled calamari. Appetizers are followed by a choice of freshly caught fish (there aren't any other options), either grilled or fried. The restaurant's garden, with its whitewashed walls with blue trim, feels like a slice of the Greek islands in the middle of Istanbul. ⊠ *Keresteci Hakkı Sokak, Sultanahmet* ☎ *212/458–2270* ⌕ *Reservations essential* ▤ *MC, V.*

$$$$ ✕ **Seasons.** The Istanbul Four Seasons is one of the city's ritziest hotels, and it's also home to one of the city's finest restaurants, in a gazebo-like glass pavilion in the middle of the hotel's manicured garden. The menu is Mediterranean/Italian and features the creations of Italian chef

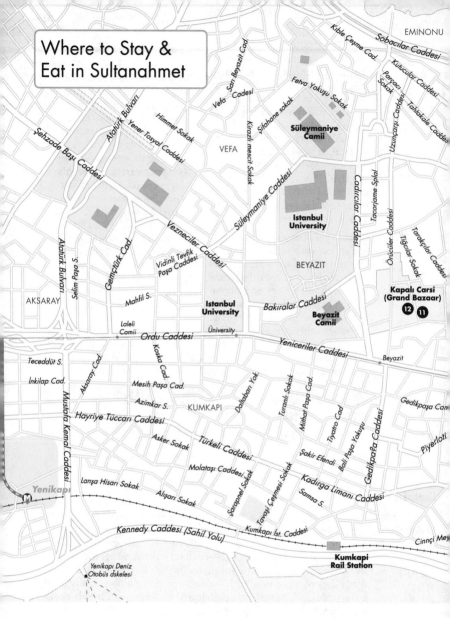

Where to Stay & Eat in Sultanahmet

EMINONU

Kible Çeşme Cad.
Sobacılar Caddesi
Kurucular Caddesi
Poyracı Sokak
Tahtakale Caddesi
Uzunçarşı Caddesi

Fetva Yokuşu Sokak

Süleymaniye Camii

Sarı Beyazıt Cad.
Vefa Cadesi
Şifahane sokak
Kirazlı mescit Sokak

Şehzade Başı Caddesi
Atatürk Bulvarı
Yener Tosyal Caddesi
Himmet Sokak
VEFA

Cadıcılar Caddesi
Tacorjame Splal
Örücüler Caddesi
Tarakçılar Caddesi
Tığcılar Sokak

Süleymaniye Caddesi

Istanbul University

Vezneciler Caddesi

Vidinli Tevfik Paşa Caddesi

BEYAZIT

Gemçtürk Cad.

Atatürk Bulvarı
Selim Paşa S.
Mahfil S.
AKSARAY
Laleli Camii
Istanbul University
Bakıralar Caddesi
Beyazit Camii
Kapalı Carsi (Grand Bazaar)
❶❷ ❶❶

Ordu Caddesi
Üniversity
Yeniceriler Caddesi
Beyazit

Teceddüt S.
İnkilap Cad.
Aksaray Cad.
Koska Cad.
Mesih Paşa Cad.
Azimkar S.
KUMKAPI
Dalbıran Yok.
Turanlı Sokak
Mihat Paşa Cad.
Tiyatro Cad
Bali Paşa Yokuşu
Gedikpaşa Caddesi
Gedikpaşa Can

Hayriye Tüccarı Caddesi
Asker Sokak
Türkeli Caddesi
Şakir Efendi
Piyerloti

Mustafa Kemal Caddesi
Lanşa Hisarı Sokak
Molataşı Caddesi
Alışarı Sokak
Şaraprenel Sokak
Tavaşi Çeşmesi Sokak
Kadırga Limanı Caddesi
Samsa S.

Yenikapı

Kennedy Caddesi (Sahil Yolu)
Kumkapı İst. Caddesi
Cinnçi Mey

Kumkapi Rail Station

Yenikapı Deniz
Otobüs dskelesi

Restaurants

Sultanahmet ▼
Balıkçı Sabahattin **3**
Doy-Doy **4**
Giritli **2**
Konuk Evi **10**

Mozaik **8**
Rami **5**
Rumeli Café Restaurant **9**
Seasons **6**
Tarihi Sultanahmet Köftecisi **7**
Teras **1**

Grand Bazaar ▼
Fes Café **11**
Havuzlu **12**

Eminonu & GH ▼
Borsa Lokantasi . . . **13**
Hamdi Et Lokantsı . . **14**

Hotels

Sultanahmet ▼
Ayasofya Pansiyonları & Konuk Evi **18**
Alzer Hotel **9**
Armada Hotel **1**

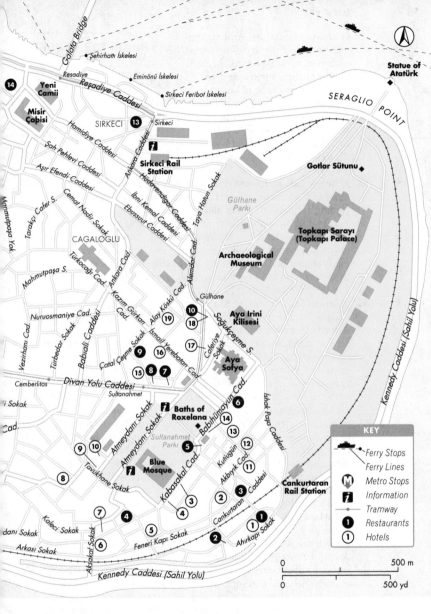

Giancarlo Gottardo. Among the highlights are the saffron risotto with porcini mushrooms, herbed ricotta-arugula ravioli, and basil-parsley crusted rack of lamb. The restaurant's Sunday brunch buffet draws crowds from across Istanbul. ⊠ *Tevkifhane Sokak 1, Sultanahmet* ☎ *212/638–8200* ⌘ *Reservations essential* ⊟ *AE, DC, MC, V.*

BEST BETS FOR BUDGET DINING

- Adem Baba, Bosphorus
- Çiya, Asian Side
- Saray, Beyoğlu
- Tarihi Köftescisi, Sultanahmet

★ $$–$$$ ✕ **Rumeli Café Restaurant.** This little eatery on a quiet side street in Sultanahmet's main tourist area offers good food at reasonable prices, including a range of salads and meat dishes from a menu that spans Turkey and the globe. There are pastas, steaks, and salads, as well as more unusual items like *papaz yahnisi,* a Byzantine stew of lamb, potatoes, and pumpkin cooked in a terra-cotta dish. The cozy interior, formerly the site of a book bindery, has hand-painted frescoes on the walls. In summer you can sit outside at tables on the sidewalk. ⊠ *Ticarethane Sokak 8, Sultanahmet* ☎ *212/512–0008* ⊟ *AE, MC, V.*

★ $$–$$$ ✕ **Teras.** With the Sea of Marmara on one side and the Blue Mosque and the Hagia Sophia on another, this open-air restaurant on top of the Armada Hotel has one of the more romantic locations in Istanbul. The view at night, with the lights of Sultanahmet's historic monuments reflecting off the sea, is especially stunning, and the food, a combination of classic Ottoman and modern Turkish dishes such as grilled lamb with eggplant and phyllo pie stuffed with chard, holds its own against the dramatic setting. ⊠ *Ahırkapı Sokak 24, Sultanahmet* ☎ *212/638–1370* ⌘ *Reservations essential* ⊟ *AE, MC, V* ☉ *No lunch.*

$–$$$ ✕ **Mozaik.** Friendy and accommodating Mozaik is a delightful refuge in the midst of Sultanahmet's bustle. In a restored old house on a quiet corner the charming restaurant's wicker chairs and small, sun-dappled dining rooms give it the feel of a well-worn (and well-loved) bistro. The wide-ranging menu includes Turkish kebabs as well as schnitzel and a T-bone steak. There is also an extensive selection of salads. ⊠ *Incili Çavuş Sokak 1, Sultanahmet* ☎ *212/512–4177* ⊟ *AE, MC, V.*

★ $$ ✕ **Balıkçı Sabahattin.** This Sultanahmet restaurant in a renovated Ottoman house on a quiet backstreet started off more than 40 years ago as a simple fish shack that could barely seat 10 people, but it's now known as one of the best places in Istanbul for seafood. Along with the wide assortment of expertly grilled fish, specialties include a pilaf made with mussels, rice, and currants, and a bouillabaisse-like fish stew. It's an especially appealing spot in summer, when tables are set up outside in a cobblestoned plaza. ⊠ *Seyit Hasan Kuyu Sokak 1, Sultanahmet* ☎ *212/458–1824* ⌘ *Reservations essential* ⊟ *AE, MC, V.*

$$ ✕ **Rami.** The food here is classic Turkish, with dishes like *hünkar beğendi,* roast lamb served over a creamy eggplant puree, but the main attraction is the restaurant's interior: the Ottoman-era wooden house has been restored to its posh late 19th-century likeness, with crystal chandeliers hanging from the ceiling and candle-lit lanterns on the tables.

The food isn't terrible, but not much more than adequate. An upstairs terrace looks out onto the Blue Mosque across the street. ⊠ *Utangaç Sokak 6, Sultanahmet* ☎ *212/517–6593* ▭ *MC, V.*

$–$$ ✕ **Konuk Evi.** A little oasis near Aya Sofya, this inviting restaurant has an outdoor patio with wicker chairs, all shaded by leafy trees. The small menu is comprised of pastas, salads, and grilled meats, as well as an assortment of cakes and Turkish milk puddings. It's a pleasant place to take a break from the hustle and bustle of Sultanahmet. ⊠ *Soğukçeşme Sok., Sultanahmet* ☎ *212/513–3660* ▭ *AE, MC, V.*

¢ ✕ **Doy-Doy.** Unlike many other spots in tourist-filled Sultanahmet, this is a place where locals come to fill up (*doy-doy* is a Turkish expression for "full"), and you can indeed fill up here for a reasonable sum. The restaurant serves simple kebabs, chicken and lamb stews, and *pide* (Turkish pizza) baked in a wood-burning oven. A variety of mezes are also available. The meatless pizzas and salad are excellent options for vegetarians. Service is friendly, and the prices are clearly stated in the menu, sometimes a problem in Istanbul's budget eateries. A pleasant rooftop terrace is open in the summer. ⊠ *Şifa Hamamı Sok. 13, Sultanahmet* ☎ *212/517–1588* ▭ *V.*

¢ ✕ **Tarihi Sultanahmet Köftecisi.** Like pizza for New Yorkers, humble *köfte* (grilled meatballs) inspire countless arguments among Istanbulites about who makes them best. This restaurant has a simple menu— meatballs, *piyaz* (boiled white beans in olive oil), and salad—that has remained virtually unchanged since 1920, and it's one of the best places for *köfte* in the city. With waiters in white coats and marble-topped tables, it also has a surprising amount of class for a budget place that serves essentially nothing but meatballs. Its location, a few minutes' walk from the Blue Mosque and Aya Sofya, makes it ideal for a quick and affordable lunch. ▮ TIP➜ There are several branches of Tarihi Köftecisi throughout Istanbul, but the original is this one, in Sultanahmet. ⊠ *Divany Yolu Caddesi 12, Sultanahmet* ☎ *212/520–0566* ▭ *No credit cards.*

> **WORD OF MOUTH**
>
> "In the old city there is a place that I think is just great: Tarihi Köftecisi. It's a stone's throw from the cistern/ Aya Sofya, etc. . . . someone told me it is one of the oldest köfte cafés in the city. The köfte is delicious! And, it is cheap, cheap, cheap!"   –asa4

Grand Bazaar

¢–$ ✕ **Fes Café.** With funky orange Lucite chairs and fresh flowers on the tables, Fes Café provides a shot of modern style in the heart of the Grand Bazaar. Squeezed into a former market stall, the small kitchen turns out simple sandwiches, salads, fruit shakes, and homemade cakes and pies. It's a great place to sit back and watch the comings and goings of the bazaar. ⊠ *Halıcılar Caddesi 58-62, Kapalıçarşı* ☎ *212/528–1613* ▭ *MC, V* ⊗ *Closed Sun.*

¢ ✕ **Havuzlu.** In need of an escape from the carpet salesmen of the Grand Bazaar? This lunch-only spot, in a quiet corner of the sprawling covered market, offers just that. A large steam table at the front of the restaurant's open kitchen holds a daily assortment of some 25 dishes, including a variety of meat and vegetable stews. The food is homey, well made, and fresh. After you make your selection, waiters in black vests and ties will swiftly bring the food to your table in the

> **BEST BET FISH RESTAURANTS**
>
> ■ Balıkçı Sabahattin, Sultanamet
> ■ Doğa Balık, Beyoğlu
> ■ Giritli, Sultanamet
> ■ Korfez, Bosphorus

impressive 500-year-old dining hall, which has large Ottoman-style blown-glass chandeliers hanging from its vaulted ceilings. It closes at 5 PM. ⊠ *Gani Çelebi Sokak 3, Kapalıçarşı* ☎ *212/527–3346* ⊙ *No dinner, closed Sun.*

Eminönü & the Golden Horn

★ ¢–$ ✕ **Hamdi Et Lokantası.** Among Istanbul food mavens, Hamdi consistently rates as one of the city's top restaurants for grilled meat. Delicious kebabs of minced lamb mixed with pistachios or poppy seeds are among the more unusual items, while the small *lahmacun* (Turkish pizza topped with spiced ground meat) will make your mouth water. Service is impeccable, with white starched tablecloths and waiters in vests and ties. Ask for a table on the restaurant's terrace floor, which has excellent views of the Golden Horn and the Bosphorus. ⊠ *Kalçın Sokak 17, Eminönü* ☎ *212/528–0390* ⌂ *Reservations essential* ⊟ *AE, MC, V.*

★ ¢ ✕ **Borsa Lokantasi.** This unpretentious spot, which has been in business since 1927, attracts a hungry crowd that comes to eat wonderful, reasonably priced food. Among the options—all served cafeteria style—the baked lamb in eggplant puree and the stuffed artichokes are especially good. Borsa is close to the ferry terminals of Eminönü, making it convenient for a quick meal before or after a boat ride on the Bosphorus or across to the Asian side of the city. ⊠ *Yalıköşkü Cad., Yalıköşkü Han 60–62, Eminönü* ☎ *212/511–8079 or 212/527–2350* ⊟ *AE, MC, V.*

Beyoğlu

$$$–$$$$ ✕ **Café du Levant.** Black-and-white floor tiles and turn-of-the century European furnishings give this café next to the Rahmi M. Koç Industrial Museum the feel of a Paris bistro. Chef José Alain Perreau turns out superb classic French cuisine, including fillet of turbot with zucchini and tomatoes, and a fillet of beef in a red wine sauce. For dessert try the crème brûlée or the soufflé au Grand Marnier with ice cream. ⊠ *Kumbarhane Cad. No. 2 27 Hasköy Cad., Hasköy* ☎ *212/369-6607/235–6328* ⌂ *Reservations essential* ⊟ *AE, DC, MC, V* ⊙ *Closed Mon.*

> **BEST BETS FOR KEBABS**
>
> ■ Çiya, Asian Side
> ■ Hamdi, Et Lokantası, Eminönü
> ■ Mabeyin, Asian Side
> ■ Şazeli, Bosphorus

$$$-$$$$ ✕ **Mikla.** Mikla opened its doors in 2006, but it's already made it into the upper echelon of Istanbul restaurants. The location certainly helps: it's on the top floor of the 18-story Marmara Pera hotel and has a stunning 360-degree view of Istanbul. The American-trained chef Mehmet Gürs is responsible for a string of successful restaurants in Istanbul; he creates dishes that balance the classical with the contemporary. Among the mains are sauteed scallops served with vegetable risotto, and a ragu of beef cheeks with root vegetables. An extensive, though expensive, wine list features gems from Turkey and the rest of the world. ⊠ *Meşrutiyet Cad. 167/185 Beyoğlu* ☎ *212/293–5656* ⚸ *Reservations essential* ⊟ *AE, DC, MC, V* ☯ *Closed Sun.*

★ **$$-$$$$** ✕ **Doğa Balık.** Owner and chef Ibrahim Soğukdağ knows fish—he was a fisherman before he got started in the restaurant business—and this is one of the best places in the city for seafood. The friendly restaurant usually offers a wide variety of freshly caught options, most often served grilled. This casual spot is also renowned for its extensive selection of mezes, especially lightly cooked unusual fresh greens, such as beetroot leaves or samphire, a type of seaweed. On the 8th floor of the Villa Zurich hotel, the open-air restaurant has a commanding view of the Bosphorus and the Istanbul rooftops below. ⊠ *Akursu Yokuşu Cad. 46, Cihangir* ☎ *212/293–9144* ⚸ *Reservations essential* ⊟ *AE, MC, V.*

$$-$$$$ ✕ **Rejans.** Established by Russian émigrés who fled the Bolshevik Revolution, Rejans' decor has remained basically unchanged since the restaurant's heyday; the restaurant is now run by their widows. Brass chandeliers hang from the high ceilings and well-polished, dark wood paneling line the walls, which are covered with plaques that bear witness to the famous and infamous who once dined here, from statesmen to World War II spies and diplomats. The decor has remained basically unchanged since the restaurant's heyday. Live Russian music from an accordion-led trio is performed on the balcony Thursday through Saturday evenings. The excellent selection of appetizers includes piroshki and borscht, and main courses include beef Stroganoff, chicken Kiev, and pork chops. ⊠ *Emir Nevrut Sok, Olivo Geçidi 1715, İstiklal Cad., Beyoğlu* ☎ *212/244–1610* ⚸ *Reservations essential* ⊟ *AE, MC, V* ☯ *Closed Sun.*

$-$$$ ✕ **Istanbul Modern Cafe.** With its exquisite waterfront views and stylish industrial-chic décor—exposed airshafts and cement walls—this restaurant has slowly been nudging the exhibits aside as the main attraction of the new Istanbul Museum of Modern Art. It's in a large corner of the repurposed warehouse that is the museum's home, and a sleek, red, rectangular bar dominates the dining room, which looks out onto the busy traffic of Istanbul's harbor. The lunch menu has a variety of pastas, salads, and sandwiches; dinner offers more substantial fare, like thyme-and-rosemary-marinated filet mignon and risotto with grilled shrimp. ⊠ *Meclis-i Mebusan Caddesi, Liman Işletmeleri Sashası, Antrepo 4, Karaköy* ☎ *212/292–2612* ⚸ *Reservations essential* ⊟ *DC, MC, V.*

$$ ✕ **360 Istanbul.** Globe hopping and genre bending, the food at 360 Istanbul tries to take diners to places they've never been to, although the results sometimes fall flat. The location goes for the same effect, with more consistency: at the top of a historic building in the heart of the lively Beyoğlu district, the sleek concrete and glass restaurant has lovely views in all directions. Overseen by chef Mike Norman, who worked for several years in the five-star Çirağan Palace Hotel, the kitchen turns out innovative dishes like shrimp falafel, stuffed sun-dried eggplant with a sour-cherry yogurt sauce, and crabmeat-crusted salmon fillet. ⊠ *İstiklal Caddesi 311, Beyoğlu* ☎ *212/251–1042* ⌒ *Reservations essential* ⊟ *MC, V* ⊘ *No lunch Sat. and Sun.*

$$ ✕ **Leb-i Derya.** It's not easy to find this rooftop restaurant—it's in an apartment building with only a small sign out front—but persevere (ask directions), because the reward is a magnificent view overlooking the Bosphorus and Sultanahmet's historical monuments. The kitchen turns out solid, though unremarkable, versions of international comfort food: cheese nachos, spaghetti carbonara, and schnitzel, as well as desserts like chocolate fondue and cheesecake. The wooden furniture is simple but stylish, and a greenhouse-like glass roof lets the sun, or the stars, peek in. Unlike most places in town the restaurant opens early, at 8:30 AM, on weekends for breakfast. ⊠ *Kumbaracı Yokuşu 115, Beyoğlu* ☎ *212/293–4989* ⊟ *AE, MC, V.*

$-$$ ✕ **Cezayir.** Cezayir serves mostly Turkish dishes, but with an innovative
Fodor'sChoice twist. Chef Dilara Erbay spent several years traveling and working in
★   countries around the world and brings that experience into her kitchen, with delicious results. A South American-style ceviche cleverly uses fresh anchovies from the Black Sea, while Indian spices help turn a bulgur and ground meat patty into a kind of Turkish samosa. The main courses, which include a lamb tagine and several homemade pastas, display the same kind of inventiveness. The restaurant's lounge has wicker chairs, slowly revolving ceiling fans, and pale yellow walls; it's the perfect place to while the night away. ⊠ *Hayriye Cad. 16, Beyoğlu* ☎ *212/ 245–9980* ⌒ *Reservations essential* ⊟ *AE, MC, V.*

$-$$ ✕ **The House Cafe.** This appealing café and restaurant located on a quiet corner serves upscale comfort food that rarely disappoints. The eggs Benedict, pancakes, and other breakfast dishes are superb, and the massive burger is a delicious and juicy mess. The selection of salads is vast; the warm artichoke and prawn combination is a standout. With exposed brick walls and tables of solid oak, the restaurant, in Beyoğlu's charming Asmalımescit area, is an ideal place to linger with coffee and a book. A branch in Ortaköy has a terrace overlooking the Bosphorus and the one in chic Nişantaşı has a shady garden. ⊠ *Sümbül Sokak, Beyoğlu* ☎ *212/245–9515* ⊟ *MC, V* ⊠ *Atiye Sokak 10, Nişantaşı* ☎ *212/ 259–2377* ⊠ *Salhane Sokak 1, Ortaköy* ☎ *212/227–2699.*

¢–$$ ✕ **Hacı Abdullah.** Tracing its roots all the way back to 1888, this Istanbul institution serves authentic, inexpensive traditional, if unexciting, Ottoman and Turkish cuisine, and it's a favorite for locals wishing to enjoy good food in a relaxed atmosphere. Grilled meats, cabbage stuffed with lamb, rice pilaf with pine nuts and currants, and a variety of vegetables stewed in olive oil and served as cold appetizers are among the extensive offerings. The restaurant, which has several ele-

---

BREAKFAST IN ISTANBUL

A Turkish breakfast of fresh bread, *beyaz peynir* (goat cheese), tomatoes, cucumbers, and olives is included at most hotels in Turkey.

gant dining rooms done in dark red, faux-Ottoman style, is especially famous for its seemingly inexhaustible range of pickles and homemade fruit compotes. ⊠ *Ağa Cami Sakızağacı Cad. 17, Beyoğlu* ☎ 212/293–8561 ⊟ *AE, MC, V.*

$ ✕ **Yakup 2.** Thick smoke and nicotine-stained walls; large groups of people sitting at round tables drinking rakı and loudly talking the night away. If you want to experience a Turkish meyhane (literally "drinking place") at its most authentic, this is the place to do it. This cheery hole-in-the-wall is filled with locals rather than tourists. It can get loud, especially if there is a soccer match on the television. The mezes, from the stuffed peppers to the octopus salad, are several notches above average, and the service is friendly. Fun is guaranteed. ⊠ *Asmalı Mescit Cad. 35—37, Beyoğlu* ☎ 212/249-2925 ⊟ *AE, MC, V.*

★ **¢-$** ✕ **Hacı Salih.** You may have to line up for lunch at this tiny, family-run restaurant—it has only 10 tables—but the traditional Turkish fare is worth the wait. Lamb and vegetable dishes, such as eggplant stuffed with ground meat, are specialties. In a quiet arcade off bustling İstiklal Street, it has a warm and inviting atmosphere, and though alcohol is not served, you are welcome to bring your own. ⊠ *Anadolu Han 201/1–2, off Alyon Sok. (off İstiklal Cad.), Beyoğlu* ☎ 212/243-4528 ⊟ *MC, V* ⊘ *Closed Sun. No dinner.*

★ **¢-$** ✕ **Hala Mantı.** As its name suggests, this eatery on busy İstiklal Caddesi specializes in *mantı,* small pockets of pasta filled with ground meat—the Turkish version of ravioli. *Gözleme,* thin pastry shells filled with ingredients such as cheese and spinach, then cooked on huge hot plates as you watch, are also excellent. ⊠ *İstiklal Cad. 211, Beyoğlu* ☎ 212/292-7004 ⊟ *MC, V.*

★ **¢-$** ✕ **İmroz.** Among the mostly identical restaurants along Nevizade Sokak, İmroz stands out for the freshness of its fish and its wide range of tasty mezes such as a creamy and smoky eggplant salad, the spicy cured-meat pastry *pastırmalı böreği,* and the fried cheese dish called *kaşarlı pane.* Presided over by the grandfatherly Yorgi Okumuş, a Greek Turk, the restaurant is crowded and friendly; the cigarette smoke is thick, and the rakı flows freely. One of the few remaining Greek tavernas in Istanbul—albeit with a Turkish menu—İmroz is tucked away in a side street. In summer all the local restaurants have tables outside, which gives the street an almost carnival atmosphere. ⊠ *Nevizade Sokak 24, Beyoğlu* ☎ 212/249-9073 ⊟ *DC, MC, V.*

TURKISH COFFEE

Tea might be the beverage of choice in Turkey these days, but those in need of a coffee fix need not worry. Most teahouses serve Turkish coffee, although you may find a better cup by going to a more upscale café, which will probably use better coffee and take the time to prepare it properly. A well-made cup should be thick and almost chocolaty, with espresso-like foam on top. Turks drink their coffee three ways: *sade* (plain), *orta* (medium sweet), and *şekerli* (extra sweet). It's usually served with a small glass of water and, frequently, a little piece of *lokum* (Turkish delight).

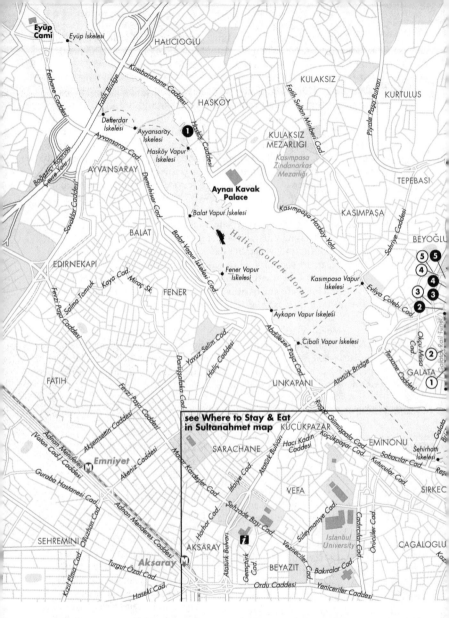

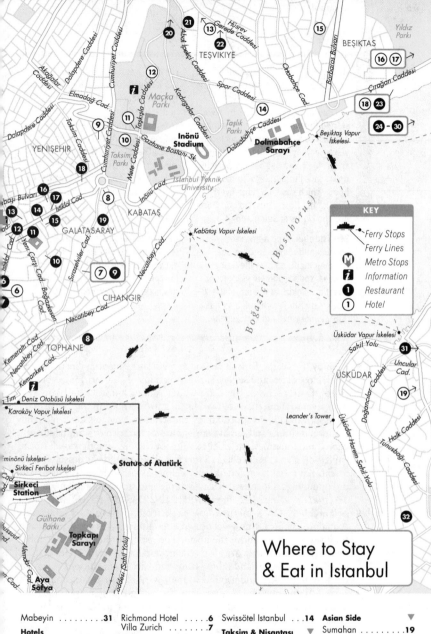

Where to Stay & Eat in Istanbul

Sky-High Dining

IN RECENT YEARS, Istanbul's newest restaurants have been aiming high, literally, as an increasing number of savvy restaurateurs have started to take advantage of Istanbul's greatest natural asset—its spectacular views—and opened rooftop dining spots. The trend has been especially pronounced in the Beyoğlu neighborhood, which sits on a ridge overlooking the Bosphorus, Golden Horn, and the sights of Sultanahmet.

360 Istanbul, atop a historic apartment building, has a globe-hopping menu and, as the name implies, spectacular views in every direction. **Mikla,** at the top of the 18-story Marmara Pera hotel, also has a 360-degree view and features the

cooking of star Turkish chef Mehmet Gürs. (If you're choosing between the two 360-degree views, Mikla is, generally speaking, for an older crowd. 360 Istanbul is a good place to get a glimpse of the city's younger elite.) The open-air **NuTeras** has a chic bar, excellent mezes, and looks out on the Golden Horn. **Leb-i Derya** serves so-so fare on a lovely and breezy terrace where you can watch the sunset over the Bosphorus.

In most of Beyoğlu's rooftop restaurants, you'll have the chance to eat your dinner while looking at both Europe and, across the water, Asia—this is real intercontinental dining.

¢-$ ✕ **Saray.** This is the Turkish version of the classic American diner: it opens early, closes late, and serves Turkish versions of comfort food—but instead of surly service, there are waiters in black aprons and bow ties who seem to think they are working in a five-star restaurant. With marble floors and glass-topped tables, the setting is even less diner-like, but the food is simple and satisfying: eggs are served fried or scrambled with cheese and tomatoes, the chicken soup is delicious, and the *doner* (meat carved off a spit) is excellent. Saray is well known for its desserts, such as the flaky baklava and the marvelous assortment of Turkish-style milk puddings. Open late, it's a great place to stop off after a night out. ⊠ *İstiklal Caddesi 102, Beyoğlu* ☎ *212/292–3434* ▤ *AE, MC, V.*

★ ¢-$ ✕ **Sofyalı 9.** On a picturesque backstreet in Beyoğlu's charming Asmalımescit area, this jewel box of a restaurant takes classic *meyhane* food several levels above the norm. The mezes, brought to your table on a large wooden tray, are all excellent. Standouts include cubes of fried eggplant in a yogurt and tahini sauce and Circassian chicken, a spread made with chicken and ground walnuts. Grilled fish and meat are also served. With Greek music playing in the background and photographs of old Istanbul on the walls, Sofyalı has loads of charm. A limited menu is served during lunch. ⊠ *Sofyalı Sokak 9, Beyoğlu* ☎ *212/245–0362* ⚑ *Reservations essential* ▤ *AE, MC, V* ⊘ *Closed Sun.*

¢ ✕ **Helvetia.** Opened by two 30-something friends in 2004, this affordable, laid-back restaurant serves delicious home-style Turkish food. The menu changes daily but always features a variety of soups and stewed vegetables, as well as more substantial dishes such as zucchini fritters and meatballs in tomato sauce. The red-tiled open kitchen is a hive of constant activity, which occasionally spills into the dining area. Don't be surprised to find one of the cooks shelling peas or peeling an eggplant at the table next to you. The Sunday brunch buffet is an excellent value and highly recommended. ⊠ *General Yazgan Sokak 12, Beyoğlu* ☎ *212/245–8780* ▤ *No credit cards.*

¢ ✕ **Zencefil.** The menu at this pioneering, mostly vegetarian, restaurant (one of the first to open in Istanbul) changes daily, but it usually includes a large assortment of hot dishes such as rice with artichoke or spinach pie, as well as excellent salads and homemade breads. There are also fresh-squeezed juices and cakes baked on the premises. The atmosphere is intimate and cafélike, with exposed brick walls and antique floor tiles. A pleasant garden is open during warm weather. ⊠ *Kurabiye Sok. 38-10, Beyoğlu* ☎ *212/244243–40828234* ▤ *AE, MC, V* ⊗ *Closed Sun.*

Taksim & Nişantaşı

$$-$$$ ✕ **Banyan.** Istanbul's vibrant dining scene is sorely lacking in Asian food, which is why Banyan's arrival in 2003 was so welcome. The restaurant, which has a soothing dining room with long banquettes, serves traditional Asian fare, such as a variety of dim sum and beef in orange sauce, but the kitchen also makes use of regional ingredients to create tantalizing modern dishes such as filet mignon marinated in sake and octopus carpaccio served with a wasabi-ginger sauce. A branch in Ortaköy has a terrace that looks out on the Bosphorus. ⊠ *Abdi İpekçi Caddesi 40/3, Nişantaşı* ☎ *212/219–6011* ⌕ *Reservations essential* ▤ *AE, MC, V.*

$$-$$$ ✕ **Changa.** Opened in 1999, Changa has been blazing a culinary path in Istanbul that others have only recently started to follow. The menu is overseen by award-winning, London-based chef Peter Gordon, and the innovative dishes combine flavors and ingredients from east, west, north, and south. One delicious appetizer has eggplant roasted in a sauce of miso and tahini. Among the mains are tortellini stuffed with wasabi and salmon, served with a grilled porcini and creamed lemongrass sauce, and lamb chops served with *firik,* a type of smoked bulgur wheat. The restaurant is spread out over three floors of an early 20th-century town house, and a large circular "skylight" cut into the ground floor reveals the bustling basement kitchen below. ⊠ *Sıraselviler Caddesi 87/1, Taksim* ☎ *212/249–1348* ⌕ *Reservations essential* ▤ *MC, V* ⊗ *No lunch, Closed Sun.*

$-$$$ ✕ **Mezzaluna.** This is the place to come for what is probably the best Italian cuisine in the city. The pizzas, baked in a brick oven brought over from Italy, are excellent, but chef Rudyl Pellino's kitchen—he, too, was brought over from Italy—also turns out delicious pastas such as ravioli filled with crayfish and spaghetti with clams. The atmosphere is welcoming and lively: the walls are decorated with colorful Italian tile and the tables are filled with chatting locals. ⊠ *Abdi İpekçi Caddesi 38/1, Nişantaşı* ☎ *212/231–3142* ⌕ *Reservations essential* ▤ *AE, MC, V.*

$-$$ ✕ **Hünkar.** Istanbul is full of small, simple, family-run restaurants where a bounty of prepared dishes are served cafeteria-style from a steam table. Hünkar, which has been in business since 1950, is one of them, but it's in a class apart. With its starched white tablecloths, dark wood paneling, and solicitous, hovering waiters, the restaurant almost feels like the dining room of an exclusive club. And the food is excellent. You'll find dishes like zucchini stuffed with ground meat or grilled fish on the menu. Also unlike other similar restaurants, Hünkar serves wine. ⊠ *Mim Kemal Öke Cad. 21, Nişantaşı* ☎ *212/225–4665* ⊟ *AE, MC, V.*

Bosphorus

$$$$ ✕ **Tuğra.** Cookbooks from the Ottoman palace were used to re-create some of the long lost dishes—saffron-marinated turbot with sauteed artichoke and medallions of beef cooked in parchment paper are wonderful options—served at this spacious and luxurious restaurant in the Çırağan Palace. The Bosphorus view is flanked by the palace's marble columns, and ornate glass chandeliers hover above, making you feel like royalty. After dinner, make your way to the hotel's poolside bar and enjoy the breeze. ⊠ *Çırağan Cad. 84 Beşiktaş* ☎ *212/258–3377* ⚭ *Reservations essential* ⓜ *Jacket required* ⊟ *AE, DC, MC, V* ⊗ *No lunch.*

$$-$$$$ ✕ **Körfez.** Call ahead and this restaurant in the picturesque Asian village of Kanlıca can arrange to have you ferried across the Bosphorus from the Rumeli Hisar neighborhood—a 30-minute cab ride from Taksim Square—in its private boat. The look is nautical; the seafood is fresh and superbly cooked to order. The restaurant's signature dish is sea bass cooked in salt, and starters such as flying-fish chowder are worth trying, too. It's a bit of a trek, but it's worth the effort. ⊠ *Körfez Cad. 78, Kanlıca* ☎ *216/413–4314* ⚭ *Reservations essential* ⊟ *AE, DC, MC, V* ⊗ *Closed Mon.*

$$-$$$$ ✕ **Sunset Grill.** On a high hill overlooking the Bosphorus, the Sunset Grill
Fodor'sChoice seems to be flying over the water and the glittering lights below. In warm
★ weather, tables are set in the garden, affording diners an unforgettable view. The menu hops from Japan (there's a terrific sushi bar) to Mexico, Italy, and back to Turkey. The seafood dishes, such as potato-crusted sea bass, are excellent, and the lamb shank wrapped in eggplant, a Turkish classic, is also recommended. The restaurant's interior is elegant yet laid back. There's a large wine and cognac menu that features several outstanding Turkish wines. ⊠ *Yol Sok. Ulus Parkı 2, Ulus* ☎ *212/287–0357* ⚭ *Reservations essential* ⊟ *AE, MC, V.*

$-$$$$ ✕ **İskele.** On a restored historic ferry terminal on the Bosphorus, İskele's romantic setting is more than matched by a fine range of seafood. Ask the waiter to recommend whatever is especially tasty that day. Eating in the restaurant, with its sliding glass doors that look out onto the Bosphorus, will make you feel like you're dining on the deck of a yacht. Phone ahead for a table by the window or, even better, outside on the terrace in warmer weather. ⊠ *Yahya Kemal Caddesi 1, Rumelihisarı* ☎ *212/ 263–2997* ⚭ *Reservations essential* ⊟ *AE, MC, V.*

$$$ ✕ **Feriye Lokantası.** Chef Vedat Başaran's fine restaurant is in a palatial 19th-century building that, believe it or not, was a police station during Ottoman times. The menu, taking a cue from the setting, is inspired by Ottoman cooking. Appetizers include zucchini flowers stuffed with seafood salad and wild fennel, and sea bass with wild herbs and salmon

in a pomegranate sauce are among the main courses. The dining room is elegant, with chandeliers and painted ceilings, but in summer the restaurant sets all the tables outdoors by the edge of the Bosphorus. With the sound of the water flowing by and the picturesque Ortaköy mosque in the background, the romantic setting is hard to beat. ⊠ *Çırağan Caddesi 40, Ortaköy* ☎ *212/227–2216* ⚱ *Reservations essential* ▤ *AE, DC, MC, V.*

★ ¢-$$ ✕ **Adem Baba.** This is the Turkish version of a New England fish shack, with nets and crab traps hanging from the ceiling. They even serve a delicious, thick, fish stew that looks and tastes like clam chowder. Families and large groups come here to enjoy simple, fresh, and perfectly prepared fish, at a fraction of what they would pay at some of the fancier restaurants along the Bosphorus. There's no menu, but a refrigerated display at the entrance holds the day's catch. To start, order the fried calamari and the tasty fish *köfte* (fish cakes). It's in Arnavutköy, a low-key Bosphorus neighborhood with several historic wooden Victorian-style villas—perfect for a stroll before, or after, dinner. ⊠ *Satış Meydanı Sokak 2, Arnavutköy* ☎ *212/263-2933* ▤ *No credit cards.*

¢-$$ ✕ **Cınaraltı.** The neighborhood of Ortaköy is one of the prettier areas along the Bosphorus, with a small waterside square framed by a historic wooden ferry terminal and a pretty Ottoman-era mosque. There are several nearly identical restaurants lining the square, but this one draws a large number of locals. A refrigerated case inside the restaurant holds the catch of the day—go in and pick out your fish. The outside tables look out over a lively scene: vendors selling handicrafts and families strolling, with the Bosphorus behind them. After your meal, you can move to one of the nearby cafés to linger over tea or coffee. ⊠ *Isekele Meydanı 44-46, Ortaköy* ☎ *212/261-4616* ▤ *AE, MC, V.*

¢-$ ✕ **Şazeli.** The specialty at this small, family-run kebab house that turns out very tasty food is *durum,* kebabs wrapped in a soft, tortilla-like flatbread—but make sure you sample some of the delicious appetizers: perhaps the smoky, grilled eggplant spread mixed with walnuts and thick yogurt, or the chopped salad in a tangy pomegranate-molasses dressing. Save room for the "Şazeli special dessert," a baklava-like triangle made out of semolina and ground pistachio and pine nuts and stuffed with butter cream. The restaurant, with an interior dominated by a large cooper charcoal grill, is a good low-cost option in the very pleasant neighborhood of Ortaköy. ⊠ *Muallim Naci Caddesi 76, Ortaköy* ☎ *212/ 260–6969* ▤ *MC, V.*

Asian Side

$ ✕ **Mabeyin.** Though housed in a restored 19th-century pasha's mansion and with an elegant interior that wouldn't seem out of place in an upscale French restaurant, Mabeyin features the earthy but intricately spiced food of Turkey's southeast, which has a strong Middle Eastern influence. Kebabs grilled with quince or loquat—a small, succulent fruit only available in late spring and early summer—are some of the unusual items on the menu, but even more interesting are the stews, such as one made with rice and meat dumplings in a warm yogurt broth or another that has two kinds of bulgur dumplings in a tomato-based sauce. Food is served in a splendid garden during warm weather. Mabeyin is a quick cab ride from the Üsküdar ferry terminal. ⊠ *Eski Kısılı Cad. 129, Kısılı* ☎ *016/422–5580* ⌕ *Reservations essential* ▤ *MC, V.*

¢–$ ✕ **Çiya.** Owner and chef Musa Dağdeviren, who hails from the south-
Fodor'sChoice eastern Turkish city of Gaziantep, is something of a culinary anthropol-
★   ogist, collecting recipes from around Turkey and even publishing a
journal devoted to Turkish food culture. The result is that his no-frills eatery turns out some of Istanbul's most memorable meals, with uniquely seasoned dishes that are hard to find in other restaurants, such as stuffed artichokes in a tangy green plum sauce and rice pilaf with chicken and almonds inside a pastry shell. Çiya's menu changes daily and accord-ing to what's in season, but always features a variety of vegetarian dishes. An annex across the street focuses on kebabs and is also top-notch; it has the same name. ⊠ *Güneşlibahçe Sokak 43, Kadıköy* ☎ *0216/330–3190 or 0216/450–2376* ▤ *MC, V.*

WHERE TO STAY

Updated by
Yigal Schleifer

With the number of visitors to Turkey growing by about 10% every year, Istanbul's hoteliers have been busy keeping up with the increasing de-mand. New lodgings, from full-service hotels to smaller boutique inns, are opening all the time, while older establishments are busy renovat-ing and expanding. This means there are plenty more options than there were in the past, but because Istanbul is such a popular destina-tion, it's not the travel bargain it used to be. It's also worth noting that many hotels have started quoting their rates in euros, which makes what might look like a good deal something less than that when paying in U.S. dollars. Most lodgings, save for the five-star hotels, include a full Turkish breakfast with the room rate.

The majority of visitors to Istanbul stay in the Sultanahmet area—the Aya Sofya, Blue Mosque, Topkapı Palace, and most of Istanbul's major sites are in the neighborhood, which has the city's widest selection of hotels, smaller family-run *pansiyons* (guest houses), and some charm-ing boutique inns. The downside is that at the height of the season, Sul-tanahmet is overrun not only with tourists but touts who will try to steer you to their carpet shop. On the up side, stiff local competition means the Sultanahmet usually has the best deals in town.

For a less touristy taste of Istanbul, try the Beyoğlu area across the water, only a 10-minute cab ride from the sites of Sultanahmet. Once filled with rather grotty low-budget hotels, Beyoğlu has emerged as an attractive option to Sultanahmet, particularly in terms of boutiques and more up-scale hotels. Staying here puts you closer to Istanbul's best restaurants and nightspots and also gives you a chance to stroll through Beyoğlu's lively backstreets. Istanbul's large modern hotels are mostly clustered around Taksim Square and up along the Bosphorus—the latter is where you'll find the luxurious, indulgent options.

No matter where you stay, plan ahead: Istanbul, despite adding so many new lodgings, still has a chronic shortage of beds.

WHAT IT COSTS IN U.S. DOLLARS				
	$$$$	$$$	$$	$	¢
FOR 2 PEOPLE	over $250	$201–$250	$151–$200	$100–$150	under $100

Prices are for two in a standard double in high season, including 18 percent tax.

Sultanahmet

$$$$
Fodor'sChoice
★
⊞ Four Seasons Hotel. What a rehabilitation success story: a former prison, this elegant hotel became one of Istanbul's premier accommodations the instant it opened in 1996. This neoclassical building, painted a buttery yellow and decorated with aqua blue tiles, is steps from Topkapı Palace and Aya Sofya. Rooms and suites overlook either the Sea of Marmara or a manicured interior courtyard and are luxuriously outfitted with reading chairs, original works of art, and bathrooms with deep tubs. The glass-enclosed courtyard restaurant serves international cuisine and local specialties. Service throughout is exceptional. ⊠ *Tevkifhane Sok. 1, Sultanahmet, 34110* ☎ *212/638–8200* 🖷 *212/638–8210* ⊕ *www.fourseasons.com.* ⟿ *65 rooms* ⚏ *Restaurant, room service, health club, bar, business services, cable TV, in-room broadband, laundry, dry cleaning, meeting rooms, minibar, in-room safes, no-smoking rooms* ▤ *AE, DC, MC, V.*

$$–$$$
⊞ Hotel Ibrahim Paşha Oteli. What was once the home of an extended Armenian family has been turned into a stylish and comfortable hotel. The standard rooms are small but bright, with framed reproductions of Ottoman-era artwork and large windows that look out toward the Blue Mosque. Deluxe rooms have a separate seating area with a couch and pillows covered in kilim cloth. The rooftop terrace has glorious views of Sultanahmet and the Blue Mosque. The personable staff helps ensure a relaxing atmosphere. ⊠ *Terzihane Sok. 5, Sultanahmet, 34122* ☎ *212/518–0394 or 212/518–0395* 🖷 *212/518–4457* ⊕ *www.ibrahimpasha .com* ⟿ *16 rooms* ⚏ *Bar, cable TV, Wi-Fi, in-room safes, minibar, no-smoking rooms* ▤ *AE, MC, V* ⑩ *BP.*

★ $$
⊞ Armada Hotel. Only 10 minutes' walk from Istanbul's main tourist sites, the Armada offers spacious, comfortable accommodations with marble-lined bathrooms, lace curtains, and walls painted a soothing shade of green. Rooms look out either to the sea or over the Old City, although one of the best views is at night from the terrace of its rooftop Ahırkapı restaurant, where you can see Aya Sofya and the

WORD OF MOUTH

"We stayed in Sultanahmet and loved it. We had to stay in Taksim the night before we left to go home, and it's a modern, very business type part of the city which made me feel as though I might as well have been in any big city in the USA. Personally, Sultanahmet was wonderful, close to everything that we could walk and enjoy all the history." –dutyfree

Blue Mosque. Despite its large size, the hotel has a friendly, even quirky, feel—how many high-end hotels have a pool full of turtles in the middle of the lobby? ⊠ *Ahırkapı Sokak 24, Sultanahmet 34122* ☎ *212/638–1370* 🖷 *212/518–5060* ⊕ *www.armadahotel.com.tr* 🖙 *110 rooms* ☺ *3 restaurants, room service, bar, meeting rooms, business services, cable TV, Wi-Fi, minibars, in-room safes, no-smoking rooms* ☰ *AE, MC, V* ⦿ *BP.*

$$ 🖻 **Dersaadet Hotel.** Dersaadet means "place of happiness" in Ottoman Turkish and this small hotel lives up to its name. The rooms have an elegant, even plush, feel, with colorful rugs on the floor, solid wood furniture, and ceilings hand painted with swirling Ottoman ornamental motifs. The top two floors of the hotel have rooms with a view, while a cozy terrace, where classical music plays in the background, looks out on the sea. Deniz Duyar, the hotel's young owner and manager, earned his MBA in New York and runs the place with a high level of professionalism. ⊠ *Kuckayasofya Cad. Kapıağası Sokak 5, Sultanahmet 34400* ☎ *212/458–0760* 🖷 *212/518–4918* ⊕ *www.hoteldersaadet. com* 🖙 *14 rooms, 3 suites* ☺ *Café, cable TV, Wi-Fi, minibars* ☰ *MC, V* ⦿ *BP.*

$$ 🖻 **Hotel Empress Zoë.** Opened in 1992, this pioneer of Sultanahmet's
Fodor'sChoice   boutique hotel scene is aging both gracefully and ambitiously. Owner
★   Ann Nevans, an American expat, has in recent years added three new all-suite wings to go along with the hotel's original building, which has small but charming rooms furnished with colorfully canopied four-post beds. The new suites are more spacious, some with marble-lined bathrooms done up to look like mini hamams. A two-floor suite has two balconies, one looking at the sea and one looking at Aya Sofya. The hotel's lush garden, where you can eat breakfast, is one of the most tranquil spots in all of Istanbul. ⊠ *Akbıyık Cad., 4/1, Sultanahmet, 34400* ☎ *212/518–2504* 🖷 *212/518–5699* ⊕ *www.emzoe.com* 🖙 *14 rooms, 12 suites,* ☰ *MC, V* ⦿ *BP .*

$$ 🖻 **Sultanahmet Sarayı.** The sultans meet Las Vegas in this glitzy recreation of an Ottoman palace. The exterior is painted a dusty pink and has faux pink granite columns, the lobby has marble stairways and a stained-glass atrium, and the rooms are opulent, with marble-lined, hamam-style bathrooms, deep red bedspreads, and cushioned divans for reclining and gazing out the windows. Three deluxe rooms have balconies with sea views. A restaurant in back has a terrace looking over the Sea of Marmara. ⊠ *Torun Sok. 19, Sultanahmet 34122* ☎ *212/458–0460* 🖷 *212/518–6224* ⊕ *www.sultanahmetpalace.com* 🖙 *36 rooms* ☺ *restaurant, cable tv, minibar, airport shuttle, parking* ☰ *AE, DC, MC, V* ⦿ *BP.*

★ **$$** 🖻 **Yeşil Ev** (Green House). Another Touring and Automobile Club project, this lovely old mansion is on the edge of a small park between the Blue Mosque and Aya Sofya. It's been meticulously restored and decorated in Ottoman style, with lace curtains and latticed shutters. Rooms aren't large, but have brass beds and carved wooden furniture upholstered in velvet or silk, and small (but modern) baths. The hotel also has a delightful shady garden built around a marble fountain, where guests can have breakfast in warmer weather. ⊠ *Kabasakal Cad. 5, Sultanah-*

met, 34122 ☎ 212/517–6786 ⧉ 212/517–6780 ⊕ *www.istanbulyesilev. com* ⬅ *18 rooms, 1 suite* ♨ *Restaurant, Wi-Fi, minibar, in-room safes, no-smoking rooms; no room TVs, no room phones* ⊟ *AE, MC, V* ⧉ *BP.*

$-$$ ⊡ **Celal Sultan.** With attentive service, a good restaurant, and a delightful lobby bar, this mid-priced option successfully straddles the line between the intimacy of a boutique hotel and the comfort of a full-service one. Created out of three restored town houses that were joined together, the Celal Sultan has compact but thoughtfully decorated rooms. The inviting lobby is decorated with colorful kilims and Turkish rugs. The rooftop terrace provides a fine view of the Blue Mosque and the Sea of Marmara. Unusual for Istanbul, the water in the hotel is filtered. The proprietor, Mr. Selami, and his wife are full of good sightseeing and shopping tips. ☒ *Salkımsöğüt Sok. 16, Yerebatan Cad., Sultanahmet, 34410* ☎ *212/520–9323* ⧉ *212/522–9724* ⬅ *55 rooms, 2 suites* ♨ *Restaurant, 2 bars, cable tv, Wi-Fi, meeting rooms, minibar, no-smoking rooms* ⊟ *AE, MC, V* ⧉ *BP* ⊕ *www.celalsultan.com.*

$-$$ ⊡ **Turkoman Hotel.** This restored Ottoman house on a quiet street not far from the Hippodrome and all the major sites has a spacious lobby and simple, clean rooms with brass beds and attractive antique furniture. Rooms in the new annex are larger, and some look out on Aya Sofya and/or the Blue Mosque. The terrace, where breakfast is served in summer, has a fine view over the Sea of Marmara and a fireplace that's lit in the winter. ☒ *Asmalı Çeşme Sok. 2, Sultanahmet, 34490* ☎ *212/516–2956* ⧉ *212/516–2957* ⬅ *20 rooms* ♨ *Bar, cable TV, Wi-Fi, minibars; no-smoking rooms* ⊟ *AE, MC, V* ⊕ *www.turkomanhotel.com.*

$ ⊡ **Alzer Hotel.** While this hotel may lag behind some of its competitors in terms of style and design, it makes up for it with friendly service, tidy rooms, and a great location right on the Hippodrome. The three rooms with views of the Hippodrome and the Blue Mosque have cozy bay windows with built-in divans, perfect for taking in the action below. At the hotel's entrance is a pleasant sidewalk restaurant; breakfast is served in an enclosed terrace upstairs that has views of the Blue Mosque and the sea. ☒ *At Meydanı 72, Sultanahmet 34400* ☎ *212/516–6262* ⧉ *212/ 516–0000* ⊕ *www.alzerhotel.com* ⬅ *21 rooms, 1 suite* ♨ *2 restaurants, cable TV, in-room safes, minibars, Wi-Fi* ⊟ *MC, V* ⧉ *BP.*

$ ⊡ **Ayasofya Pansiyonları & Konuk Evi.** This group of buildings is part of the project undertaken by Turkey's Touring and Automobile Club to restore a small movie-set-like street of 19th-century wooden houses along the outer wall of Topkapı Palace: one house has been converted into a library and the rest into pansiyons furnished in late Ottoman style. Front rooms have a view of Aya Sofya, but the rest do not, so if you want a view, specify when you reserve. In summer, tea and refreshments are served in the small courtyard throughout the day. The Konuk Evi is a nearby Ottoman-

---

BEST BETS FOR BUDGET SLEEPING

- Galata Residence, Beyoğlu
- Hotel Nomade, Sultanahmet
- Kybele, Sultanahmet
- Sarı Konak Oteli, Sultanahmet
- Şebnem, Sultanahmet

era mansion that has been restored in similar fashion and is run by the same management. ✉ *Soğukçeşme Sok., Sultanahmet, 34122* ☎ *212/513–3660* 🖷 *212/513–3669* ✍ *57 rooms, 6 suites* ⚒ *Restaurant, bar, café, some a/c, Turkish bath; no room TVs* ▤ *AE, DC, MC, V* ⃝◯ *BP* ⊕ *www.ayasofyapensions.com.*

$ 🎬 **Best Western Hotel St. Sophia Hotel.** Why come to Istanbul and stay in a Best Western? For one, the location, only a stone's throw from the glorious Aya Sofya. Two, the hotel's rooms are large by local standards, and tastefully decorated. Ask for a room with a view of Aya Sofya, since some of the others face a busy street. The staff is very helpful. ✉ *Alemdar Caddesi 2, Sultanahmet, 34400* ☎ *212/528–0974* 🖷 *212/511–5491* ✍ *24 rooms, 3 suites* ⚒ *Restaurant, bar, cable TV, Wi-Fi, bicycles, meeting rooms, minibars, in-room safes, no-smoking rooms* ▤ *AE, MC, V* ⃝◯ *BP* ⊕ *www.saintsophiahotel.com.*

★ $ 🎬 **Hotel Nomade.** When twin sisters Esra and Hamra Teker opened the Hotel Nomade in 1984, few tourists stayed in Sultanahmet. Today the area is Istanbul's most popular, and the Hotel Nomade remains one of it's most appealing places to stay. A 2004 renovation saw the hotel redone in a stylish modern-meets-ethnic design: the smallish rooms are painted pastel colors, there are patchwork kilims on the floor, and the bathrooms are lined with mosaic-like tiles. Service is personal and the roof-garden bar and terrace have enchanting views. ✉ *Ticarethane Sok. 15, Sultanahmet, 34410* ☎ *212/513–8172 or* 🖷 *212/513–2404* ✍ *16 rooms* ▤ *AE, DC, MC, V* ⃝◯ *BP* ⊕ *www.hotelnomade.com.*

★ $ 🎬 **Kybele.** Named after an ancient Anatolian fertility goddess, this charming hotel is one of Sultanahamet's most unusual accommodations; its claim to fame is the incredible profusion of antique lamps—3,500 at the latest count—that hang from the ceilings. The lobby, lighted by 1,002 of the lamps, looks like a Victorian parlor, with overstuffed antique furniture, kilims, and calligraphic plates. Rooms are small but imaginatively decorated. A small garden in the back is done up to look like an Anatolian village. Alparslan Akbayrak, the gregarious and helpful owner, is as much of a fixture in the hotel as all the lamps. ✉ *Yerebatan Cad. 35, Sultanahmet, 34410* ☎ *212/511–7766* 🖷 *212/513–4393* ✍ *14 rooms with bath, 2 suites* ⚒ *Restaurant, bar, café, Wi-Fi, shop, minibar, in-room safes; no room TVs* ▤ *AE, DC, MC, V* ⃝◯ *BP* ⊕ *www.kybelehotel.com.*

$ 🎬 **Sari Konak Oteli.** This small, family-run hotel in an Ottoman-style building provides a very comfortable stay. The decor throughout is modern, but thoughtfully done, with Turkish tile-work accents. Bright rooms have brass lamps, antique mirrors, and Ottoman-era etchings. From your room's tiny lattice-shuttered balcony, lean out to hear the call to prayer echoing in Sultanahmet. On the rooftop terrace, you can sip a glass of rakı and contemplate either the Marmara Sea or the spires of the nearby Blue Mosque. If you don't want twin beds, or prefer a bathtub to a shower, request these when making reservations. ✉ *Mimar Mehmet Aga Cad. 42–46, Sultanahmet, 34122* ☎ *212/638–6258* 🖷 *212/517–8635* ✍ *15 rooms, 4 suites* ⚒ *Room service, fans, Cable TV, in-room safes, minibars, some a/c, some in-room TVs, laundry service, no-smoking rooms, travel services* ▤ *AE, MC, V* ⃝◯ *BP* ⊕ *www.sarikonak.com.*

Fodor'sChoice
★

1

¢ ⊞ **Hotel Ararat.** This is a small, homey hotel whose interior is livened up by Byzantine-style wall murals. The location—across the street from the Blue Mosque—is hard to beat, and a cozy upstairs terrace, where breakfast is served, has a nice view of the Sultanahmet area. The rooms tend to be small—some would even qualify as cramped, so be sure to ask for one of the larger ones. A perk is free Wi-Fi. ✉ *Torun Sokak 3, Sultanahmet 34400* ☎ *212/516–0411* 🖷 *212/518–5241* ⊕ *www. ararathotel.com* 🖙 *12 rooms, 1 suite* ☖ *No room TVs* ⊟ *MC, V* †◎† *BP.*

¢ ⊞ **Sarnıç.** This good-value, laid-back hotel is in walking distance to all the major sites of Sultanahmet yet far enough from the hustle and bustle that you won't be overwhelmed when you step out the door. Rooms are spacious and well maintained, with walls painted a warm yellow, and outfitted with comfortable lounge chairs and a small desk. The rooftop terrace has a small restaurant and is a nice place for an evening drink. Sarnıç means "cistern" in Turkish and the hotel sits on top of one that dates back to the 5th century; guests can visit for free. ✉ *Küçük Aya-sofya Caddesi 26, Sultanahmet 34400* ☎ *212/518–2323* 🖷 *212/518–2414* ⊕ *www.sarnichotel.com* 🖙 *16 rooms* ☖ *Restaurant, cable TV, Wi-Fi, meeting rooms, minibars, no-smoking rooms* ⊟ *MC, V* †◎† *BP.*

¢ ⊞ **Şebnem.** With clean, bright rooms that are larger than those found in many of the boutique hotels in the area, this small, family-run hotel is one of Sultanahmet's better values. The rooms are simply decorated, with four-post beds that have embroidered canopies. Two rooms lead out to a small grassy garden with a hammock, while the sought-after room number 18 has a lovely sea view. Breakfast, which includes freshly baked cakes, is served on a pleasant terrace that also has a sea view. ✉ *Adliye Sokak 1, Sultanahmet 34400* ☎ *212/517–6623* 🖷 *212/638–1056* 🖙 *15 rooms* ☖ *Wi-Fi; no TV in some rooms* ⊟ *MC, V* †◎† *BP.*

¢ ⊞ **Sultan's Inn.** This hotel on a quiet backstreet is only a few minutes' walk from the major attractions of Sultanahmet and, with its small but pleasantly decorated rooms, is a good budget option. Some rooms have small balconies with a table and chairs. An upstairs terrace looks out on the Sea of Marmara and the Blue Mosque. ✉ *Mustafapaşa Sokak 50, Sultanahmet 34400* ☎ *212/638–2562* 🖷 *212/518–5453* ⊕ *www. sultansinn.com* 🖙 *17 rooms* ☖ *Cable TV, minibars, no-smoking rooms* ⊟ *MC, V* †◎† *BP.*

Beyoğlu

$$$$ ⊞ **The Marmara Pera.** Opened in 2004, The Marmara Pera has quickly become one of Istanbul's hippest places to stay, combining the luxury of a full-service hotel with the funky decor of a smaller one. The hotel doesn't look like much from the outside, but the interior is a treat; think of it as an 18-story boutique hotel. The lobby is done in floor-to-ceiling brown-and-cream tiles and has vintage 50s and 60s furniture. Rooms have large windows looking over the city. There's a small pool on the roof, and the lobby café has an excellent range of cakes and chocolates. ✉ *Meşrutiyet Cad., Tepebaşı 34430* ☎ *212/251–4646* 🖷 *212/249–8033* ⊕ *www.themarmarahotels.com* 🖙 *200 rooms, 3 suites* ☖ *Restaurant, bar, café, cable TV, in-room safes, minibars, in-room broadband,*

pool, laundry service, dry cleaning, meeting rooms, business services, no-smoking floors ⊟ *AE, DC, MC, V.*

$$$–$$$$ ⊞ **Ansen 130.** Owner Burak Akkok spent several years living in New York and Paris, and the Ansen 130 shows it. Stylish and hip, this small all-suites hotel in a 20th-century building would not seem out of place in either of those cities. The lobby, which doubles as a café and bar, is in an updated Art Deco style, with two-tone wood paneling on the walls and a bar counter topped with dark brown leather. The rooms are smartly decorated and have full kitchens. The staff, though dressed in T-shirts, are attentive and professional. ⊠ *Meşrutiyet Cad. 130, Tepebaşı 34430* ☎ *212/245–8808* 🖷 *212/245–7179* ⊕ *www.ansensuite.com* ⤶ *10 suites* ⚴ *Restaurant, café, bar, cable TV, in-room safes, kitchen, Wi-Fi* ⊟ *AE, MC, V.*

$$–$$$ ⊞ **Villa Zurich.** The quiet Villa Zurich, in the heart of Cihangir, is a good base for exploring this neighborhood, and the rest of Istanbul. The lobby is a little dingy, but the rooms were completely renovated in 2006 (maybe the lobby will be next), with new furniture, carpeting, and bathrooms. The top floor is home to Doğa Balık, one of Istanbul's best fish restaurants. ⊠ *Akarsu Yokuşu Cad. 44, Cihangir* ☎ *212/293–0604* 🖷 *212/249–0232* ⊕ *www.hotelvillazurich.com* ⤶ *41 rooms* ⚴ *Cable TV, in-room safes, minibars, Wi-Fi* ⊟ *AE, MC, V* ⚏ *C P.*

> ### CIHANGIR
>
> Istanbul's Cihangir neighborhood is not on most visitors' maps, but it deserves a look. Long known as a kind of bohemian quarter, it's filled with charming small cafés and restaurants—though not much in the way of historical or cultural sites, or much shopping—and it's far from the bustle of the city, though still walking distance from Beyoğlu's livelier areas. The Villa Zurich hotel, with its Doğa Balık restaurant, are in Cihangir.

$–$$$ ⊞ **Pera Palace.** Currently closed for some much-needed renovations, the Pera Palace was built in 1892 to accommodate guests arriving on the *Orient Express.* Everyone who was anyone in the late 19th and early 20th centuries stayed here, from Mata Hari to numerous heads of state; the rooms once occupied by Kemal Atatürk and Agatha Christie were turned into museums. The hotel has always been full of atmosphere and quirky charm, but although it had been modernized, the facilities and rooms were not in the greatest shape. The Pera is supposed to reopen in late 2008, but check the Web site for updates. ⊠ *Meşrutiyet Cad. 98, Tepebaşı, 80050* ☎ *212/251–4560* ⊕ *www.perapalas.com.*

$$ ⊞ **Anemon Galata.** With winding cobble-stoned streets radiating from a square dominated by a 14th-century Genoese-built tower, the Galata neighborhood is one of Istanbul's most picturesque and least-touristy areas. The Anemon sits in the heart of it, in a meticulously renovated century-old building just across the street from the Galata Tower. The atmosphere is elegant and old world, and rooms are plush and comfortable. An upstairs terrace, where breakfast is served, has a wonderful view of the tower across the street and of the Golden Horn. ⊠ *Büyükhendek Cad. 11, Galata 80020* ☎ *212/293–2343* 🖷 *212/292–2340* ⊕ *www. anemonhotels.com* ↩ *21 room, 7 suites* ⚹ *Restaurant, cable TV, in-room safes, minibars, Wi-Fi, no-smoking rooms* ⊟ *AE, MC, V.*

$$ 🏨 **Richmond Hotel.** Behind the facade of a turn-of-the-century building on lively pedestrian-only İstiklal Caddesi is this modern, comfortable hotel. Rooms are plush, spacious, and clean. Some have views of the Bosphorus, although beware the ones that look out into a dismal inner courtyard. The top floor suites are impressive, with lovely water views, full-size desks, and large flat-screen TVs. The rooftop bar is a great spot for a sunset drink. ⊠ *İstiklal Cad. 445, Tünel 80670* ☎ *212/252–5460* 🖷 *212/252–9707* ↩ *102 rooms, 2 suties* ⚹ *2 restaurants, café, bar, meeting rooms, in-room safes, minibars, cable TV, Wi-Fi, business services, no-smoking rooms, laundry service* ⊟ *AE, MC, V* ⃝ *BP* ⊕ *www. richmondhotels.com.tr.*

★ ¢–$ 🏨 **Galata Residence.** What was originally an apartment building built in 1881 for the Camondos, one of the leading banking families of the late Ottoman Empire, is now a very appealing residence hotel only a few minutes' walk from the Galata Tower. The large one- and two-bedroom lodgings have been carefully decorated with period furniture, but they've also been discreetly supplemented with modern conveniences such as bathtubs, air-conditioning, and full kitchens. The size and price of the apartments make them an especially good value for families or multiple couples. The upper floors and the top-floor restaurant have wonderful views across the Golden Horn to the Old City. ⊠ *Felek Sok. 2, Bankalar Cad., Galata, 80020* ☎ *212/292–4841* 🖷 *212/244–2323* ↩ *22 apartments* ⚹ *Restaurant, café, kitchenettes, cable TV, in-room broadband* ⊟ *MC, V* ⊕ *www.galataresidence.com.*

Taksim & Nişantaşı

$$$$ 🏨 **The Central Palace.** In a clever bit of urban planning, the Istanbul municipality took the area behind Taksim Square, once traffic-choked and filled with car-part shops, and in 2004 turned it into a pedestrian-only zone lined with cobblestones. Since then, a growing number of hotels have sprung up, all with the advantage of being near Taksim but not right in the midst of the noise and commotion. One of the nicer options is The Central Palace, which has large, comfortable rooms—each with a foyer, two closets, a small balcony, and a Jacuzzi tub. ⊠ *Lamartin Cad. 18, Taksim 34437* ☎ *212/313–4040* 🖷 *212/313–4039* ⊕ *www. thecentralpalace.com* ↩ *49 rooms, 6 suites* ⚹ *2 Restaurants, cable TV, in-room safes, minibars, in-room hot tubs, in-room broadband, gym, Turkish bath, business services, meeting rooms, no-smoking floors* ⊟ *AE, DC, MC, V* ⃝ *BP.*

$$$$ 🏨 **Ceylan Inter-Continental.** This plush luxury hotel is one of Turkey's premier accommodations, with a broad range of top-class facilities. The 19-floor building sits on a ridge, looking out on Istanbul and the Bosphorus. All rooms are spacious, with floor-to-ceiling windows; those on the water side have particularly good views. ⊠ *Askerocağı Cad. 1,*

Taksim, 34435 ☎ *212/368–4444, 800/327–0200 in the U.S.,* 🖷 *212/ 368–4499* 🖅 *325 rooms, 55 suites* ⚫ *4 restaurants, 2 bars, pool, health club, hair salon, massage, sauna, Turkish bath, cable TV, in-room safes, minibars, in-room broadband, laundry, dry cleaning, business services, meeting rooms, car rental, no-smoking floors* ▤ *AE, DC, MC, V* ⊕ *www.interconti.com.tr.*

$$$$ ▣ **Hyatt Regency.** This massive but tastefully designed coral-colored building elicits ideas of tasteful Ottoman splendor. Rooms, with fabrics in shades of brown, wood furniture, and glazed ceramic pottery accents, have clean lines that seem more Scandinavian than Ottoman. The lobby is inviting, and the whole place hums with the kind of smooth and classy efficiency that you would expect of a five-star hotel. ✉ *Taşkıla Cad. 1, Taksim, 34437* ☎ *212/368–1234, 800/228–9000 in the U.S.* 🖷 *212/ 368–1000* 🖅 *336 rooms, 28 suites* ⚫ *3 restaurants, café, pool, hair salon, health club, Turkish bath, 4 bars, babysitting, business services, in-room safes, cable TV, in-room broadband, shopping, laundry, dry cleaning, meeting rooms, car rental, travel services, no-smoking rooms* ▤ *AE, DC, MC, V* ⊕ *www.istanbul.hyatt.com.*

$$$$ ▣ **Istanbul Hilton.** Lavishly decorated in white marble, with Turkish rugs and large brass urns, this is arguably one of the best-located Hiltons in the chain, perched on a high hill overlooking the Bosphorus. The extensive grounds, filled with rosebushes, make the hotel a restful haven in a bustling city. Rooms are Hilton standard, with plush carpeting and pastel décor and—unusually for Istanbul hotels—each has a good-sized balcony. ✉ *Cumhuriyet Cad., Harbiye, 34367* ☎ *212/315–6000, 800/ 445–8667 in the U.S.* 🖷 *212/240–4165* 🖅 *484 rooms, 13 suites* ⚫ *2 restaurants, 3 tennis courts, indoor pool, outdoor pool, health club, spa, Turkish bath, squash, 2 bars, shops, cable TV, in-room safes, minibars, Wi-Fi, hair salon, babysitting, laundry, dry cleaning, business services, meeting rooms, car rental, travel services* ▤ *AE, DC, MC, V* ⊕ *www. hilton.com.*

$$$$ ▣ **The Sofa.** The Nişantaşı neighborhood is Istanbul's answer to New York's Upper East Side—an upscale area that has the city's best shopping. It's not an area where tourists usually stay, but The Sofa, a stylish and ambitious hotel that opened in 2006, is starting to change that. The emphasis here is on design, with large rooms that have sleek metal and wood furniture and the eponymous trademark sofa. The lobby has a bookstore and café. The basement has a full-service up-scale spa—a subterranean oasis to unwind in after a hard day of shopping. ✉ *Teşvikiye Cad. 123, Nişantaşı 34367* ☎ *212/247–2889* 🖷 *212/291–9117* ⊕ *www. thesofahotel.com* 🖅 *70 rooms, 12 suites* ⚫ *Restaurant, café, cable TV, indoor pool, in-room safes, minibar, exercise equipment, spa, hot tub, indoor pool, massage, Turkish bath, in-room dataports, business services, meeting rooms, no-smoking floors* ▤ *AE, DC, MC, V.*

$$ ▣ **Taxim Hill Hotel.** A good option of you're looking to stay right on busy Taksim Square, the Taxim has a quiet lobby with comfortable couches and lounge chairs. Rooms are large enough to hold the small dining table and easy chairs they're furnished with. The bathrooms, all with tubs, are also spacious. Some rooms have small balconies looking out onto Taksim—double paned windows help keep out the noise from below. The downstairs Taksimoda restaurant is good for coffee or a light snack, and the rooftop Hill Terrace restaurant has a lovely view of the Bosphorus. ⊠ *Sıraselviler Cad. 9, Taksim 80090* ☎ *212/334–8500* 🖷 *212/334–8598* ⊕ *www.taximhill.com* 🖙 *58 rooms, 12 suites* ⚛ *2 restaurants, cable TV, minibars, Wi-Fi, meeting rooms, no-smoking floors* ⊟ *AE, DC, MC, V* 🍽 *BP.*

Bosphorus

$$$$ ⊡ **Bebek Hotel.** Although it's a bit out of the way from Istanbul's major attractions, this hotel's splendid location and refined elegance make it worth considering. Bebek, one of the Bosphorus's most upscale areas, is filled with delightful small cafés and restaurants that are a short walk from the waterfront hotel. The large rooms—9 have Bosphorus views—have dark wood floors and brass lamps, and each has a seating area with a brown leather couch and easy chair. The downstairs bar, one of Istanbul's best, has a terrace with comfortable wicker chairs and a lovely view of the water. ⊠ *Cevdetpaşa Cad. 34, Bebek 80810* ☎ *212/358–2000* 🖷 *212/263–2636* ⊕ *www.hotelbebek.com* 🖙 *20 rooms* ⚛ *Restaurant, bar, cable TV, in-room safes, minibar, in-room broadband, no-smoking rooms* ⊟ *AE, MC, V.*

★ **$$$$** ⊡ **Çırağan Palace.** This 19th-century Ottoman palace (pronounced shichi-rahn) is Istanbul's most luxurious hotel. There are two buildings: the older palace and a newer addition. The setting is exceptional—right on the Bosphorus—and the outdoor pool seems to hover on the water's edge. The public spaces are done up in cool marble and rich hues, and the rooms have Ottoman-inspired wood furnishings and textiles in warm colors; all have balconies, and the views on the Bosphorus side are exceptional (rooms on the other side look out on a busy road). Most lodgings are in the new wing, though there are 12 suites in the palace, including the $20,000 per night Sultan Suite—start saving now. ⊠ *Çırağan Cad. 8432, Beşiktaş, 34349* ☎ *212/258–3377/326-4646* 🖷 *212/259–6686* 🖙 *304 rooms, 12 suites* ⚛ *4 restaurants, indoor pool, outdoor pool, health club, Turkish bath, bar, in-room safes, minibar, Wi-Fi, hair salon, massage, sauna, spa, babysitting, laundry, dry cleaning, business services, meeting rooms, airport shuttle, no-smoking floors* ⊟ *AE, DC, MC, V* ⊕ *www.ciragan.com.*

$$$$ ⊡ **Conrad International Istanbul.** This modern 14-story tower, catering primarily to business travelers, has spectacular views of the Bosphorus and terraced gardens. The lobby is a gleaming white with furniture covered in golden fabric, and rooms are tastefully furnished and comfortable. The staff is congenial and efficient and can help you navigate the hotel's full range of services. ⊠ *Barbaros Bul. 46, Yildiz Cad., Beşiktaş, 34353* ☎ *212/227–3000* 🖷 *212/259–6667* 🖙 *559 rooms, 31 suites* ⚛ *4 restaurants, 3 tennis courts, indoor pool, outdoor pool, health club, 2 bars, shops, business services, cable TV, in-room safes, minibar, massage, sauna, steam bath, meeting rooms, hair salon, babysitting, car rental, travel services* ⊟ *AE, DC, MC, V* ⊕ *conradhotels1.hilton.com.*

$$$$ ⊡ **Radisson SAS Bosphorus Hotel.** Perched on the water's edge and only a few steps from the cobble-stoned main square of Ortaköy, one of the prettiest Bosphorus neighborhoods, the Radisson's location is unbeatable. Opened at the end of 2005, the hotel also earns high marks for its rooms and full range of services. The lobby has a clean, sleek look, with a large, atrium-like glass entrance; rooms are modern and comfortable. Be sure to ask for a room with a Bosphorus view. The hotel's restaurant has a pleasant open-air terrace looking out on the water. ⊠ *Çirağan Cad. 46, Ortaköy 34349* ☎ *212/310–1500* 🖷 *212/310–1515* ⊕ *www.radissonsas.com* ⇥ *111 rooms, 9 suites ⌂ 2 restaurants, bar, in-room safes, minibars, cable TV, in-room broadband, gym, health club, hair salon, massage, sauna, steam room, Turkish bath, business services, meeting rooms, no-smoking rooms* ▤ *AE, DC, MC, V.*

★ **$$$$**   ☒ **Swissôtel Istanbul.** In a superb spot just above Dolmabahçe Palace, the Swissôtel was controversial when it was built—nobody liked the idea of such a big, modern structure towering over the palace. The views are magnificent, though—from the water all the way to Topkapı Palace across the Golden Horn. The vast, high-ceiling lobby has terraced levels that seem to cascade down to the Bosphorus and is usually filled with the sounds of a tinkling piano. The overall effect is that of a grand and elegant old-world hotel. The occasional Swiss-village mural strikes a jarring note in Istanbul, but service is crisp and efficient. Rooms have contemporary if undistinguished furnishings and original art on the walls. Service is crisp and efficient, with uniformed bellhops swiftly opening doors and summoning taxis. ⊠ *Bayıldım Cad. 2, Maçka, 34357* ☎ *212/326–1100* 🖷 *212/326–1122* ⇥ *600 rooms ⌂ 7 restaurants, indoor pool, outdoor pool, health club, 3 bars, cable TV, in-room safes, minibar, in-room dataport, business services, meeting rooms, sauna, massage, Turkish bath, hair salon, 6 tennis courts* ▤ *AE, DC, MC, V* ⊕ *www.swissotel.com.*

Asian Side

$$$$ ☒ **Sumahan.** Owners Mark and Nedret Butler, both architects, took on
Fodor'sChoice   the challenge of converting a derelict distillery built in 1875 into a lux-
★   ury hotel; the result is one of Istanbul's most chic and original places to stay. On the strait's edge, with an incredible view up the Bosphorus, the hotel—opened in 2005—has comfortable suites, all with water views, and decorated in an unfussy minimalist style. Some rooms have fireplaces, and the ground-level suites open onto a grassy yard. And if you think it'll be inconvenient staying on the Asian side, the hotel has a private launch that makes regular runs across the Bosphorus. ⊠ *Kuleli Cad. 51, Çengelköy 34684* ☎ *216/422–8000* 🖷 *216-422-8008* ⊕ *www. sumahan.com* ⇥ *18 suites ⌂ Café, bar, massage, fitness equipment, Turkish bath, cable TV, in-room safes, 1 tennis court* ▤ *AE, MC, V* ⧈ *BP.*

NIGHTLIFE & THE ARTS

Updated by
Yigal Schleifer

Istanbul's nightlife still revolves, in many ways, around its *meyhanes,* tavern-like restaurants where long nights are spent nibbling on mezes and sipping the anise-flavored spirit rakı. The atmosphere at these places—mostly found in the lively Beyoğlu area—is jovial, friendly, and worth experiencing. There are lots of other options, too, though, again, mostly in Beyoğlu, which has everything from smoky American-style dive bars to sophisticated lounges, performance spaces that host world-class live acts and discos and dance clubs. In warm weather, much of the city's nightlife action shifts to the Bosphorus shore, where chic (and pricey) summer-only nightclubs play host to Istanbul's rich and famous, and those who want to rub shoulders with them.

For upcoming events, reviews, and other information about what to do in Istanbul, pick up a copy of the Istanbul edition of *Time Out*—there's an English version that comes out monthly. Another good option is *The Guide,* a reliable bimonthly English-language publication that has listings of hotels, bars, restaurants, and events, as well as features about Istanbul. The English-language *Turkish Daily News* is another good resource for listings and for keeping abreast of what's happening in Turkish and international politics.

Nightlife

Bars & Lounges

The side streets leading off from İstiklal Caddesi in Beyoğlu are full of small bars. Many cater to a student crowd, with cheap beer and loud music, but there are also several comfortable and inviting lounges. In recent years, the trend in the neighborhood has been literally upward, with the opening of rooftop bars that usually have stunning views and fresh breezes. For more upscale bars, head to the neighborhoods and hotels along the Bosphorus.

BEYOĞLU **5. Kat** (⊠ Soğancı Sok. 7, Cihangir ☎ 212/293–3774) is on the fifth floor of an unassuming building in the quiet Cihangir neighborhood. You'll find an excellent view of the Bosphorus, fabulous cocktails, and comfortable couches and lounge chairs that make it feel like you're passing the time in somebody's living room.

Cezayir (⊠ Hayriye Cad. 16, Beyoğlu ☎ 212/245–9980) is an excellent restaurant that also has a *Casablanca*-ish bar and lounge area—wicker chairs, lazy ceiling fans, and comfortable couches. The bar gets crowded on weekends, when a DJ plays a mix of new and old dance music.

Dulcinea (⊠ Meşelik Sokak 20, Beyoğlu ☎ 212/245–1071) has soft lighting, a long wooden bar, comfortable banquettes and an inviting, arty vibe that quickly seduces you into spending hours here. A downstairs performance space hosts an eclectic variety of DJs and live musicians.

Hayal Kahvesi (⊠ Büyükparmakkapı Sok. 19, Beyoğlu ☎ 212/224–2558) is a smoky, crowded late-night hangout for a mostly young crowd that likes live (and loud) rock and blues. The scuffed wood floors are stained with beer, exactly what you might expect from a classic dive bar.

KeVe (⊠ Tünel Geidi 10, Beyoğlu ☎ 212/251–4338), in a plant-filled late 19th-century open-air arcade, has a distinctly European feel. It's perfect for a quiet drink.

L'Eclipse (⊠ Cezayir Çıkmazı 2, Beyoğlu ☎ 212/245–9066) is a café and bar located along "French Street." It has a rooftop terrace with a nice view of Sultanahmet and the Bosphorus.

NuTeras (⊠ Meşrutiyet Cad. 149, Beyoğlu ☎ 212/245–6070) has a striking location—the rooftop of a historic building looking out on the

Golden Horn—sleek decor to match, and a fashionable crowd. A kitchen turns out mezes and pizzas from a wood-burning oven.

On Numara (✉ Galata Köprüsü, Haliç Tarafı 10, Karaköy ☎ 212/243–9891), in an arcade below the Galata Bridge, is a good perch from which to view the sun as it sets over the Golden Horn and the minarets of Istanbul. There are cushy bean-bag chairs to sit in and a young crowd drinking beer and smoking the water pipes called nargilehs.

The **Orient Express Bar** (✉ Pera Palace Hotel, Meşrutiyet Cad. 98, Beyoğlu ☎ 212/251–4560) is hard to beat for its turn-of-the-century atmosphere. There are stained-glass windows, antique tiles, and elegant furniture; you can't help but sense the ghosts of the various kings, queens, and Hollywood stars who have passed through its doors. Drinks are on the pricey side, but worth every lira.

BOSPHORUS **Bebek Bar,** (✉ Bebek Ambassadeurs Hotel, Cevdet Paşa Cad. 34, Bebek ☎ 212/358–2000) with a breezy terrace on the Bosphorus and a top-notch restaurant next door, attracts a dressed-up crowd. It's the perfect spot for a drink before or after dinner.

SULTANAHMET **Hotel Nomade Bar** (✉ Ticarethane Sok. 15, Sultanahmet ☎ 212/513–8172) is an inviting and laid-back rooftop bar—one of the best options in the Sultanahmet area, not generally known for its nightlife. There are nice views of Aya Sofya and the sea beyond it, and a relaxed vibe.

Live Music Venues

As Istanbul's reputation as a hip city to visit continues to grow, the quality of the live acts that come to town has been rising, too. Established and up-and-coming acts now frequently include Istanbul on their European tours, and the city has become a good place to catch a show for a fraction of what you might pay for the same thing in Paris or London.

Roxy (✉ Aslanyatağı Sok. 9, Taksim ☎ 212/249–1283) is a popular airplane-hangar-like bar with a spirited, young crowd and live music—from experimental rock to acoustic folk. It also serves a good range of tasty food to snack on between drinks and sets.

Babylon (✉ Şehbender Sok. 3, Beyoğlu ☎ 212/292–7368) is Istanbul's best live music space, hosting world-famous jazz, rock, and world music performers. It's in a converted warehouse, and the sound system is excellent. The friendly crowds take their music seriously.

Jazz Clubs

Istanbul may not be a major spot on the world's jazz map, but this has

---

NARGILEHS

Nargilehs (also known as hookahs) and the billowy smoke they produce have been an integral part of Istanbul's coffeehouses for centuries. Although once associated more with older men who would spend their days smoking, sipping Turkish coffee, and playing backgammon, the nargileh is having a renewed popularity with younger Istanbulites. They used to be smoked using strong tobacco, but today they are more often served with a variety of flavored tobaccos, such as apple or strawberry. Because the smoke is filtered through water, it's cool and smooth, though it can make you light-headed if you're not used to it.

been changing in recent years. Several top-notch jazz clubs have opened and, as a result, the number of well-known jazz musicians who come to perform in Istanbul is increasing.

Café Gramofon, (⌗ Tünel Meyd. 3, Tünel ☎ 212/293–0786) looking out over the lively Tünel Square, at the opposite end of Istiklal Caddesi from Taksim Square, is a laid-back café during the day but a lively jazz bar Tuesday to Saturday evenings, featuring mostly Turkish performers.
Istanbul Jazz Center (⌗ Çırağan Caddesi 48, Ortaköy ☎ 212/327–5050), opened in 2005, would not seem out of place in New York or any other big city, with its sophisticated decor, a Steinway concert grand piano on stage, and a program that features well-known musicians from the U.S. and Europe. The club also has a well-regarded restaurant.
Nardis Jazz Club (⌗ Kuledibi Sokak 14, Beyoğlu ☎ 212/244–6327) is a cozy, intimate space that hosts mostly Turkish jazz musicians with the occasional big name from abroad. The club only has room for 120, so reservations are recommended.

Turkish Music

Going out to listen to Turkish music is, for many Istanbulites, a partic-ipatory affair, with many in the crowd clapping and lustily singing along. Live Turkish music in Istanbul can usually be divided into two categories: *fasil*, which is a raucous but melancholy blend of gypsy, Greek, and classical Middle Eastern music; and Anatolian folk music, which is more subdued but as melancholy, and is usually dominated by a lute-like instrument called the *saz*.

Otantik (⌗ Balo Sokak 1, Beyoğlu ☎ 212/293–6515) has kilims on the walls, thick cigarette smoke in the air, and a room filled with Turks singing along to the folk music being played on a small stage at the back.

Andon Meyhane (⌗ Sıraselviler Cad. 89, Taksim ☎ 212–251–0222) is on the 4th floor of a renovated 1920s town house and has live Turkish music every night, played to an appreciative mixed crowd. The build-ing is also home to a café and a rooftop terrace.

Dance Clubs

Istanbul has a vibrant dance club scene, though it's not for the faint of heart. Things typically get rolling at about midnight and usually go until 4 or 5 in the morning. The city's upscale clubs tend to be expensive—admission is generally $20 or more—and there are no guarantees you'll get past the doorman, whose job it is to make sure only Istanbul's best dressed get in. Still, Istanbulites love to party and a good time is assured, if you get in the door.

360 Istanbul (⌗ İstiklal Caddesi 311, Beyoğlu ☎ 212/251–1042) is a swank roof-top restaurant in the early evening, but becomes a fashionable club after 11 PM, when a well-dressed crowd arrives to dance. Music is provided by a DJ who is sometimes joined by a live percussionist.
Crystal (⌗ Muallim Naci Cad. 65, Ortaköy ☎ 212/261–1988) special-izes in techno music, often courtesy of well-known European DJs, and attracts a young, energetic crowd. The club has a nice covered garden and is open only on Friday and Saturday nights.

TURKISH CABARETS

Surviving strictly on the tourist trade, Istanbul's nightclub shows include everything from folk dancers to jugglers, acrobats, belly dancers, and singers. Rather than being authentically Turkish, the shows are a kitschy attempt to provide tourists with something exotic and oriental. Typically, dinner is served at about 8, and floor shows start at around 10. Be aware that these are not inexpensive once you've totaled up drink, food, and cover. Reservations are a good idea; be sure to specify whether you're coming for dinner as well as the show or just for drinks.

You shouldn't feel compelled to go, they're in no way part of a typical Turkish experience. It's sort of like going to the Lido in Paris. If you still want to see for yourself, two of the more reputable places are:

Galata Tower (⊠ Galata ☎ 212/293–8180) is high atop Beyoğlu, in a round room with fabulous views; the ambience, however, is strictly hotel lounge, and the Turkish food is only average. The fixed prices are around $80 for the show and dinner, or $50 for the show and a drink.

Kervansaray (⊠ Cumhuriyet Cad. 30, Harbiye ☎ 212/247–1630) is done up in a style that could be described as Ottoman palace meets wedding hall, with crystal chandeliers, faux-marble columns, and tables that seat 20. It hosts a varied floor show, including belly dancers, folk dances, and medleys of songs from around the world. Dinner and the show will run you about $100; the show and two drinks, about $80.

Laila (⊠ Muallim Naci Caddesi 54, Ortaköy ☎ 212/236–3000) is an open-air, summer-only Bosphorus club where Istanbul's rich and famous come to be seen and where the paparazzi await them. It is, without a doubt, Istanbul's most famous and swank club.

The Arts

Summer is a lively time for the arts in Istanbul. The **Istanbul International Music Festival,** held for the duration of June, attracts renowned artists from around the world performing classical music. Shows take place throughout the city in historic buildings, such as Aya Irini and Rumeli Hisar. In May through early June is the **International Theater Festival,** which attracts major stage talent from across the globe. The **International Istanbul Jazz Festival** takes place early every July and has grown to include much more than just jazz. Recent headliners have included Elvis Costello, the Neville Brothers, and members of the Buena Vista Social Club. Tickets for all of these events can be ordered online through Biletix (www.biletix.com) or by contacting the Istanbul Foundation for Culture and Arts (⊠ Kültür ve Sanat Concer Vakfi, İstiklal Cad. 146, Beyoğlu, 80070 ☎ 212/334-0734).

Concert Venues

Aksanat Cultural Center (⊠ Akbank Bldg., İstiklal Cad. 14-18, Beyoğlu ☎ 212/252–3500) hosts classical and jazz concerts, as well as theater productions and films. It also holds art exhibitions.

Atatürk Kültür Merkezi (⊠ Taksim Sq. ☎ 212/251–5600), in Taksim Square, is Istanbul's main concert hall. The Istanbul State Symphony performs here from October through May, and ballet and dance companies have productions year round. Tickets tend to be almost absurdly cheap.

Cemal Reşit Rey Concert Hall (⊠ Gümüş Sok., Harbiye ☎ 212/232–9830), close to the Istanbul Hilton, has just about every kind of entertainment you could want: from chamber and symphonic music to modern dance, rock, folk, and jazz concerts.

Film

The strip of theaters along İstiklal Caddesi between Taksim and Galatasaray, a square at the midpoint of İstiklal Caddesi, shows the latest from Hollywood, with a few current European or Turkish movies thrown in. There are also plush, modern theaters at the Cevahir mall in Şişli, and at the Akmerkez shopping center, in Levent. Most foreign films are shown with their original soundtrack and Turkish subtitles, although many children's films are dubbed into Turkish. Look for the words *Ingilizce* (English) or *orijinal* (original language). Films in languages other than English will have subtitles in Turkish. When in doubt, ask at the ticket office whether the film is dubbed (*dublaj* in Turkish) or subtitled (*altyazılı* in Turkish).

The annual **Istanbul International Film Festival,** held the first two weeks of April, presents films from around the world; ask for a schedule at any box office and make sure to purchase tickets in advance. Seats are reserved.

SHOPPING

Updated by
Yigal Schleifer

Istanbul has been a shopper's town for, well, centuries—the sprawling Grand Bazaar, open since 1461, could easily be called the world's oldest shopping mall—but this not to say that the city is stuck in the past. Along with its colorful bazaars and outdoor markets, Istanbul also has a wide range of modern options, from large shopping centers (the Cevahir mall in Şişli claims to be the largest in Europe) to small boutiques. Either way, it's almost impossible to leave Istanbul without buying something. Whether you're looking for trinkets and souvenirs, kilims and carpets, brass and silverware, leather goods, old books, prints and maps, or furnishings and clothes (Turkish textiles are among the best in the world), you can find them here. Shopping in Istanbul also provides a snapshot of the city's contrasts and contradictions: from migrants from eastern Turkey selling their wares on the streets to the leisurely, time-honored haggling over endless glasses of tea in the bazaars and back alleys, to the credit cards and bar codes of the plush, upscale Western-style department stores.

İstiklal Caddesi is a pedestrian-only boulevard with everything from stores selling old books and Levi's to the stylish Vakko department store, Turkey's version of Saks Fifth Avenue. The high-fashion district can be found in the upscale **Nişantaşı** neighborhood, 1 km (½ mi) north of İstiklal Caddesi. This is where you'll find the best efforts of Turkish fashion designers, such as Özem Suer or sisters Esra and Tuba Çetin, as well as the flagship stores of international brands such as Armani, DKNY, and Hugo Boss. The **Cevahir** mall, in Şişli, has more than 300 stores selling foreign and local brand-name clothing.

Markets

In addition to the markets listed below, a **flea market** is held every Sunday along Çukurcuma Street in the Beyoğlu area, and along the Bosphorus in the Ortaköy neighborhood is a Sunday crafts market with street entertainment.

Fodor'sChoice
★
The Grand Bazaar (⊠ Yeniçeriler Cad. and Fuatpaşa Cad) is a neighborhood unto itself and a trove of all things Turkish—carpets, brass, copper, jewelry, textiles, and leather goods. Many of the stores have resorted to selling cheap goods aimed at the tourist market, but the bazaar still holds many treasures.

Nuruosmaniye Caddesi (⊠ Grand Bazaar), one of the major streets leading to the Grand Bazaar, is lined with some of Istanbul's most stylish shops, with an emphasis on fine carpets, jewelry, and antiques.

★ **The Arasta Bazaar** (⊠ Sultanahmet) in Sultanahmet is one of few markets open on Sunday; you can get a lot of the same items here as at the Grand Bazaar, but the atmosphere is a lot calmer.

★ **The Egyptian Bazaar** (Eminönü) is definitely worth seeing. Also known as the Spice Market, it has stall after enticing stall filled with mounds of exotic spices and dried fruits.

The Balıkpazarı (Fish Market) (⊠ on Beyoğlu Caddesi off İstiklal Caddesi, Beyoğlu) sells, of course, fish, as well as everything connected with food, from fresh produce to nuts and candies (though it's not cheap); you can buy the makings of a delicious picnic here.

Sahaflar Çarşısı (⊠ Grand Bazaar), just outside the western end of the Grand Bazaar, is home to a bustling book market, with old and new editions; most are in Turkish, but English and other languages are represented, too. The market is open daily, though Sunday has the most vendors.

Specialty Stores

Antiques

These are a surprisingly rare commodity in this antique land, perhaps because the government, to ensure that Turkish culture is not sold off to richer nations, has made it illegal to export most categories of antiques more than 100 years old. The Grand Bazaar, of course, is a good place to go antique hunting, but an even better option is the Çukurcuma area in Beyoğlu, which is filled with small shops carrying everything from small, Ottoman-era knickknacks to outsized antique marble tubs.

Sofa (✉ Nuruosmaniye Cad. 85, Cağaloğlu ☎ 212/520–2850), on a pleasant pedestrian boulevard lined with high-end carpet, jewelry, and antique shops, stocks a fascinating collection of old maps and prints, original İznik (blue and white) and Kütahya (variously colored, and with traditional patterns like tulips, paisleys, or fish) ceramics, vintage jewelry, and assorted other treasures.

Ziya Aykaç Antikaci (✉ Tekkeciler Sok. 68-72, Grand Bazaar ☎ 212/527–6082) has a corner store in the Grand Bazaar filled floor to ceiling with antique fabrics, silverware, ceramics, and other little treasures.

Ala Turca (✉ Faikpaşa Sok. 4, Çukurcuma ☎ 212/245–2933) is more like a grand private home than a store, filled with a carefully selected (and very expensive) collection of antique rugs and artwork.

Çukurcuma Bit Pazarı (✉ Çukurcuma Cad. 45/2 ☎ 212/244–1757) has a delightful jumble of antique rugs, furniture, toys, jewelry, and assorted other dusty treasures.

Artrium (✉ Tünel Geçidi 7, Beyoğlu ☎ 212/251–4302) is a delightful shop located in a historic 19th-century passage. It has a wide range of antiques, especially a fascinating collection of old prints and paintings.

Ottomania (✉ Sofyalı Sok. 30-32, Beyoğlu ☎ 212/243–2157) is a museum-like store that specializes in old maps, engravings, and books.

Levant Koleksiyon (✉ Tünel Meydanı 8, Beyoğlu ☎ 212/293–4394) has very affordable maps, engravings, and charming old postcards with pictures of Ottoman-era Istanbul. Prices are fair and clearly marked.

Clothing

Istanbulites like to dress smartly, and although the city might not be one of Europe's well-known fashion centers, it is certainly not lacking in places to buy clothes, from department stores selling famous international brands to the boutiques of Turkish designers.

Beymen (✉ Abdi Ipekci Cad. 23, Nişantaşı ☎ 212/343–0404) is Istanbul's version of Bloomingdale's, with suited doormen and expensive and up-to-date fashions.

Vakko (✉ Abdi Ipekç i Cad. 38, Nişantaşı) ✉ Akmerkez shopping mall, in Etiler ✉ Bağdat Cad. 422, in Suadiye on the Asian side) is one of Turkey's oldest and most elegant fashion houses, selling high-end fashions and with an excellent fabric department. Former president Bill Clinton could occasionally be seen sporting one of the Vakko ties presented to him by visiting Turkish delegates.

Turkish designer **Zeki Triko** (✉ Tunaman Çarşısı 47-2, Nişantaşı ☎ 212/233–8279) sells his own brand of bathing suits and lingerie, completely up-to-date, at his eponymous boutiques.

WORD OF MOUTH

"My trip to Istanbul was fantastic. Got to see everything I wanted to see and more . . . the highlight of my tour was probably buying a carpet. Went to a good dealer and spent over four hours looking at rugs before finally settling on one that I really loved. Tea, wine, and Turkish coffee (and eventually food) just kept coming. The vendor was determined to make me a rug owner during that visit. No regrets, though! Love my new acquisition."

–tobyandchie

1

CLOSE UP

Carpet-Buying in Istanbul

IF YOU'RE IN TURKEY, you're probably thinking about buying a carpet. It's virtually impossible to visit Istanbul without making a detour into at least one rug shop—though you'll find the best prices and selection in smaller villages. Wherever you end up doing your shopping, you'll undoubtedly be poured a glass of tea (or several) while the salesman rolls out one carpet after another on the floor in front of you. Just remember, regardless of how many cups of tea you drink and how persistent the salesmen, don't be pressured into making a purchase you do not want.

The vivid colors and patterns of Turkish carpets and kilims (kilims are simply flat-woven rugs) are hard to resist—patterns and colors vary by region of origin—and you can find shops at nearly every turn, all stocking rugs for a variety of prices. A visit to the Carpet and Kilim Museums inside Istanbul's Blue Mosque will set you up with valuable information no matter where you do your shopping.

The Grand Bazaar is, without a doubt, the most convenient place in Istanbul to buy a rug. The sheer number of rug dealers means there is a wide selection. That said, don't go to the Grand Bazaar looking for bargains—there are enough tourists coming through every day to keep prices out of the bargain basement. The Arasta Bazaar, near the Blue Mosque, also has several good rug shops in a more relaxed environment. These are a few shops we recommend:

Adnan & Hasan (⊠ Halıcılar Cad. 89-90-92, Grand Bazaar ☎ 212/527-9887) has a large selection of carpets

and kilims, mostly from Turkey's Anatolia region, and a friendly staff.

Şengor (⊠ Takkeciler Sok. 65-83 & 98, Grand Bazaar ☎ 212/527-2192) is a long-standing, family-run shop, with a large inventory.

Ethnicon (⊠ Takkeciler Sok. 58-60, Grand Bazaar ☎ 212/527-6841) sells contemporary kilims made of different-sized squares of fabric reminiscent of American-style quilts.

Galeri Cengiz (⊠ Arasta Bazaar 157, Sultanahmet ☎ 212/518-8882) sells boldly patterned rugs from throughout Turkey and Central Asia.

TIPS

● Look for the store's Certificate of Authenticity.

● Make sure the rug sits flat on the floor when it is laid out, and that its edges are straight and even.

● Look for breaks in color (streaks where the color seems to fade out) as an indication of a poor quality carpet.

● Try to buy the carpet directly from the storeowner, and not a solicitor or third party.

● If you can, take your purchase home with you on the plane. If you've purchased several rugs, consider shipping them yourself, or letting the store do it for you if it has a good reputation. Note, however, that you're taking a risk by shipping your rug and that it will probably take a while to get to you.

Gönül Paksoy (⊠ Atiye Sok. 1/3, Nişantaşı ☎ 212/236–0209) is a designer with an elegant and stunning collection of women's clothes that reinterprets Ottoman design and fabrics. The store also has an outstanding selection of jewelry.

Bahar Korçan (⊠ Abdi Ipekç i Cad. 19/3, Nişantaş ☎ 212/296–9276 ⊠ Serdar Ekrem Sok. 25, Galata) is one of Turkey's most innovative young fashion designers. Her stylish women's clothes, often made using layers of gauzy fabric, have a sense of organic whimsy. The Galata location is a combination store and atelier.

Yargıcı (⊠ Valikonağı Cad. 30, Nişantaş, and 11 other locations in Istanbul ☎ 212/225–2952), the popular Turkish clothing chain, sells moderately priced but attractive women's clothes that veer between preppy and designs with subtle Oriental touches.

The **Mudo** (⊠ Teşvikiye Cad. 143, Nişantaş, and 20 other locations in Istanbul ☎ 212/225–2950) clothing chain is something like Turkey's Banana Republic, selling affordable smart casual clothing for men and women. Some of the Mudo shops also carry housewares.

English-Language Bookstores

Many of the larger hotels and souvenir shops in Sultanahmet stock some English-language newspapers and books, mostly guides to the more famous sights. A more comprehensive range of reading material can be found at specialty bookstores in Beyoğlu and in the fashionable shopping districts of Nişantaşı and Levent. Books originally published outside Turkey are marked up 15%–75%. Many newspaper stands throughout the city carry the *International Herald Tribune*. Some of the larger bookstores carrying English-language books include the following.

Homer (⊠ Yeni Çarşı Cad. 28A, Galatasaray, Beyoğlu ☎ 212/249–5902)is one of Istanbul's best bookstores, carrying an impeccable selection of English-language books, especially ones dealing with the politics and history of Turkey and the Middle East.

Galeri Kayseri (⊠ Divanyolu 58, Sultanahmet 34410 ☎ 212/512–0456) has a large collection of travel books about Turkey, as well as some novels and nonfiction.

Pandora (⊠ Büyük Parmakkapı Sok. 3, Beyoğlu ☎ 212/243–3503) carries books in English and Turkish, with an emphasis on politics and nonfiction.

Robinson Crusoe (⊠ İstiklal Cad. 389 Beyoğlu ☎ 212/293–6968) is as appealing as a bookstore can get, with two cozy levels lined floor to ceiling with a well-chosen selection of English fiction and nonfiction. It also has an excellent collection of magazines and journals.

USED BOOKS A number of stores specialize in secondhand books, many in English, from dog-eared thrillers to rare old texts about the city. These include the following. There is also a cluster of antiquarian booksellers in the Sahaflar Çarsısı just outside the Grand Bazaar.

Aslıhan Sahaflar Çarsısı (⊠ Galatasaray Balık Pazarı, Beyoğlu) is an underground passage near Beyoğlu's fish market filled with small, disorganized shops that sell used books in various languages, as well as old records and posters.

Librairie de Pera (⊠ Galip Dede Sok. 22, Beyoğlu ☎ 212/243–3991) is a small shop filled with countless treasures, including old illustrated travelogues, maps, and engravings as well as antiquarian books in Greek and Armenian.

Jewelry

The most common type of jewelry you'll see for sale in Istanbul are amber necklaces and ethnic Turkish silver jewelry threaded with coral and lapis lazuli. Many jewelers are also taking Ottoman-era charms and tile fragments and setting them in silver or gold.

Urart (⊠ Abdi İpekçi Cad. 18, Nişantaşı) has chic interpretations of ancient Anatolian designs.

Horasan (⊠ Terlikçiler Sok. 37, Grand Bazaar ☎ 212/519–3654) has piles and piles of antique rings, bracelets, and necklaces from Central Asia, as well as walls covered in strands of colorful beads made out of precious and semiprecious stones, from which they will help you create your own jewelry. Prices are very fair.

Bagus (⊠ Cevahir Bedestan 133, Grand Bazaar ☎ 212/528–2519) is located in the Grand Bazaar's Bedestan area and has a large collection of mostly silver handmade jewelry.

Mor (⊠ Turnacıbaşı Sok. 16, Beyoğlu ☎ 212/292–8817) displays the work of a group of young designers who like to make funky and chunky jewelry that incorporates antique elements into modern design.

Handicrafts

While Turkey might be known for rugs, there are plenty of handicrafts to buy that will take up less space in your suitcase and a smaller bite out of your spending budget. Some of the most attractive crafts for sale in Istanbul's bazaars and gift shops are colorful ceramic bowls and plates that are hand decorated with intricate swirling patterns. Wooden objects inlaid with mother of pearl, especially backgammon boards, are another specialty, as are fabrics and embroidered clothes made out of cotton, silk and linen.

Abdulla (⊠ Halıcılar Sok. 62, Grand Bazaar ☎ 212/527–3684) has a simple but immensely appealing and stylish collection of handmade fabrics, tablecloths, and towels made out of all-natural materials, as well as olive-oil soaps and small rugs.

Derviş (⊠ Keseciler Sok. 33-35, Grand Bazaar ☎ 212/514–4525) is run by a former partner at Abdulla and sells similar stock at similar prices.

SıR (⊠ Serdar Ekrem Sok. 66, Beyoğlu ☎ 212/293–3661) is the workshop and showroom of a young craftsman who makes both traditional and modern versions of İznik and Küthaya ceramics and sells them at reasonable rates.

İznik Foundation (⊠ Oksüz Cocük Sok. 14, Kürüçeşme ☎ 212/287–3243), on the Bosphorus, not from the Bebek neighborhood, is the flagship showroom of a non-profit group dedicated to reviving and preserving the classic art of İznik ceramic and tile work. Prices are high, but the quality is outstanding.

SIDE TRIPS

Princes' Islands

20 km (12 mi) off the coast of Istanbul from Sultanahmet.

The nine islands of the Sea of Marmara have provided various use for the people of Istanbul over the years. Back in the days when the city was known as Constantinople, religious undesirables sought refuge here, while in the time of the sultans, the islands provided a convenient place to exile untrustworthy hangers-on. By the turn of the eighteenth century, well-heeled businessmen had staked their claim and built many of the Victorian gingerbread–style houses that lend the islands their charm. In some senses the Princes' Islands remained a place of refuge. In the 1930s, Büyükada, the largest of the islands, was the home for several years of the exiled Leon Trotsky.

Today, the Princes' Islands are just a short ferry ride from Istanbul and provide a relatively quiet, leafy retreat from the heat and chaos of the city. Restrictions on development and a ban on automobiles help maintain the old-fashioned peace and quiet—transportation here is only by horse-drawn carriage or bicycle. There are no real "sights," per se, and populations swell significantly on summer weekends, but the Princes' Islands are perfect for relaxed outings. Of the nine islands, four have regular ferry service, but only the two largest, Büyükada and Heybeliada, are of real interest to the general traveler. Both are hilly and wooded, and the fresh breeze is gently pine scented. Few people actually stay the night, but some Istanbulites rent summer homes here.

Büyükada

Büyükada is the largest of the Princes' Islands and generally the one with the most to offer. To the left as you leave the ferry, you'll see a handful of restaurants. **Yörük Ali Plaj,** the public beach on the west side of the island, is an easy walk from the harbor and also has a little restaurant.

To see the island's splendid old Victorian houses, walk to the clock tower and bear right. Carriages are available at the clock tower square. The carriage tour winds up hilly lanes lined with gardens filled with jasmine, mimosa, and imported palm trees. After all of Istanbul's mosques and palaces, the frilly pastel houses come as something of a surprise. You can have your buggy driver wait while you make the 20–30- minute hike up Yücetepe Hill to the **Greek Monastery of St. George,** where there are three chapels, a sacred fountain believed to have healing waters, and a view that goes on and on. As you walk up the path, notice the pieces of cloth, string, and paper that visitors have tied to the bushes and trees in hope of a wish coming true. This is a popular Orthodox Christian pilgrimage site. If you're lucky, the outdoor restaurant next to the monastery will be serving its homemade wine.

There is little difference from one spot on Büyükada's restaurant row to the next. Generally, the prices are more expensive the closer to the docks. The best bet is to look at a menu and ask to see the dishes on display. Iskele Caddesi, one street behind the shore road, has some cheaper cafés.

$$ ☒ **Splendid Palace Hotel.** For character, it's hard to beat this wooden turn-of-the-century hotel, with its old-fashioned furniture, large rooms, and Ottoman Victorian styling. The building is topped by twin white domes, copies of those at the Hotel Negresco in Nice. It's difficult to get a room on summer weekends unless you book ahead. ☒ *23 Nisan Cad. 71, Büyükada, 34970* ☎ *216/382–6950* ⧉ *216/382–6775* ☞ *70 rooms* ⚏ *Restaurant, pool; no a/c* ☰ *MC, V* ☯ *Closed Oct.–Apr.*

Heybeliada

Heybeliada, the closest island to Büyükada, is similar in appeal, and the quiet, lovely surroundings attract similar boatloads of day-trippers in summer, some hoping to avoid the crowds on the "big island."

The big building to the left of the dock, the **Deniz Kuvvetler** (Turkish Naval Academy), is open to visitors every day except Sunday, though there's not really much to see. To the right of Heybeli's dock are teahouses and cafés stretching along the waterfront. You can take a leisurely carriage ride, stopping, if the mood strikes, at one of the island's several small, sandy, and rarely crowded beaches—the best are on the north shore at the foot of **Değirmen Burnu** (Windmill Point) and **Değirmen Tepesi** (Windmill Hill). You can rent a rowboat for a few dollars at these beaches for the trip out to one of the other Princes' Islands across the way. Carriage rides also pass the ruined monastery of the **Panaghia,** founded in the 15th century. Though damaged by fires and earthquakes, the chapel and several red-tile-roofed buildings remain. Carriages on Heybeliada do not climb the hills above the harbor, where the old mansions and gardens are, but the walk is not that strenuous.

☒ **Merit Halki Palas.** A member of the Merit chain, the Halki Palas was opened in 1994 after its predecessor, which had been built in the 1850s, burned down. The character of the old hotel has been retained, with white-painted wood, ornate eaves, and large, airy rooms. It's one of the most restful hotels in the area of Istanbul, and though the island has few sights of its own, the Old City is only an hour away by ferry. You can dine at the poolside restaurant. ☒ *Refah Şehitleri Cad. 88, 34973, Heybeliada* ☎ *216/351–0025* ⧉ *216/351–8483* ☞ *36 rooms; 9 suites* ⚏ *2 restaurants, bar, pool* ☰ *MC, V* ⊕ *www.merithotels.com.*

Princes' Islands Essentials

Ferries ($1–$2) make the trip from the docks behind Sirkeci train station or from the Bostancı (Asian side) docks in half an hour to an hour, depending on where they depart. Go straight to Büyükada and catch a local ferry to Heybeliada later. You must pay each way to and from Istanbul but can travel for free between the islands themselves. For the return journey you can buy a ticket on the islands, but you must hold on to it and hand it over on disembarkation in Istanbul. In summer the early evening ferries returning to the mainland are often very crowded on weekends.

Much quicker, though less romantic, is the sea bus, departing from Kabataş near the Dolmabahçe Mosque and from Bostancı sea-bus terminals on the Asian side. Buy tokens for the sea bus at the terminals.

GETTING AROUND Since no cars are allowed on the islands, you'll do most of your exploring on foot. Horse-drawn carriage tours cost $10 to $20. You can rent bicycles ($3 per hour) from one of the shops near the clock tower on Büyükada: definitely a more fun (and more strenuous) way to get around. To get from one of the Princes' Islands to the other, hop aboard any of several daily ferries.

Edirne

235 km (146 mi) northwest of Istanbul.

Unlike Istanbul, which every conqueror and pretender within marching distance hoped to have as his capital, Thrace—the area known historically as the territory bounded by the Danube and Nestos rivers, and the Aegean, Marmara, and Black seas—was the sort of region that most warriors passed on through. The climate is harsh—sizzling in summer, bitter in winter—and the landscape unexceptional. But the area does have some worthy sights, particularly Edirne, founded in the 2nd century AD as Hadrianopolis by the Roman emperor Hadrian. This city was fought over by Bulgars, crusaders, Turks, Greeks, and Russians through the centuries, though once the Ottoman capital was moved to Istanbul, it became something of a picturesque backwater.

Edirne is a well-preserved Ottoman city; the overhanging balconies of the traditional Ottoman wooden houses shade Edirne's still-cobbled lanes, and its rich collection of mosques and monuments remains mostly unspoiled by the concrete towers so prevalent in Turkey's boomtowns. Tourists tend to ignore Edirne, but those who visit appreciate its several remarkable mosques and its covered bazaars.

Hürriyet Meydanı (Freedom Square) is Edirne's central square and a good starting point for exploring. Standing in the middle of it is a monument to the city's great passion, wrestling: two enormous wrestlers steal the spotlight from the obligatory Atatürk statue.

Just off the north side of the Hürriyet Meydanı is the **Üç Şerefeli Cami** (Mosque with Three Galleries), built between 1437 and 1447. The galleries circle the tallest of the four minarets, which are notable for their fine brick inlay. On the grounds of the Üç Şerefeli Mosque is the 15th-century Sokurlu Hamam, built by Sinan, and one of the country's more elegant baths. It is open to the public from about 7 AM until 11 PM for men and from 9:30 AM until 6 PM for women and costs $4 for a bath, $7 for a bath with massage.

Walking east from the square along Talat Paşa Caddesi brings you to the **Eski Cami** (Old Mosque). The mosque is appropriately named: completed in 1414, it is the city's oldest. The huge-scale calligraphy presenting quotes from the Koran and naming the prophets is exceptional in its grace and intricacy. Adjoining it is the **Rüstem Paşa Kervansaray**, restored and reopened as a hotel, just as it was in the 16th century. Also alongside the mosque is the 14-domed **bedestan** (market), and one block away, the **Ali Paşa Bazaar.** Both are more authentic than Istanbul's Grand Bazaar, as the wares sold—T-shirts, coffeepots, hats, soap shaped like fruits and vegetables, towels, and household ornaments—are meant for locals rather than tourists. ⊠ *Talat Paşa Cad., east from Hürriyet Meyd.* ☎ *No phone* 💲 *Free* ☉ *Daily 9–7.*

Edirne's **Selimiye Cami** (Selimiye Mosque), not Istanbul's Süleymaniye, is the mosque Sinan described as his masterpiece, and it is certainly one of the most beautiful buildings in Turkey. It stands out from far away on the Thracian plain, virtually a symbol of city. Sinan was 85 years old when it was completed in 1574, and today a statue of the architect stands in front; it's hardly necessary, though—the mosque remains his greatest monument. Outside, four identical and slender minarets rise high, each with three balconies. Inside, the harmony and peacefulness of the space are immediately striking: The central dome, more than 100 feet in diameter and 148 feet high, rests on eight pillars that have been set into the walls so as not to disturb the spacious interior space, and external buttresses help support the weight of 999 windows—legend has it that Sultan Selim thought 1,000 might be a bit greedy. The *medrese* (mosque compound) houses Edirne's **Türk-Islâm Eserleri Müzesi** (Museum of Turkish and Islamic Art), which displays Islamic calligraphy and photos of local wrestlers, as well as collections of weapons and jewelry from ancient Thrace, folk costumes, kilims, and fine embroidery. ⊠ *Hürriyet Meyd.* 💲 *Free* ☉ *Daily sunrise–sunset.*

The other great mosque in Edirne is the striking **Beyazıt Cami** (Beyazıt Mosque), on the outskirts of the city across the Tunca River. The immense complex is about a 20-minute walk northwest from Hürriyet Meydanı via the fine-hewn, six-arched **Beyazıt Bridge,** which dates from the 1480s, as does the mosque. You can also take a *dolmuş* (shared taxi) from the square. The mosque was built by the Sultan Beyazıt, hence its name, at the end of the 15th century, and the complex includes the mosque itself—with a remarkable indented dome and a beautifully fretted mihrab—as well as two schools, a hospital, a kitchen, and storage depots. In recent years the complex has been renovated, and it now has permanent exhibitions in the hospital section using mannequins in period costumes to re-create the different forms of treatment for patients in Ottoman times. The lovely courtyard has benches and tables set in a neatly tended garden. ⊠ *Head northwest from Hürriyet Meydanı, across Beyazıt Bridge* 💲 *$2* ☉ *9 AM–7 AM.*

Sarayiçi, a field with a stadium on one side, is the site of Edirne's famous wrestling tournament. Usually held in June, it is the best known of those held in villages throughout the country: Its burly, olive-oil-coated men have been facing off annually here for more than 600 years, and thousands of spectators still turn out. Sarayiçi is a 20-minute walk up the Tunca River from Benazıt Cami.

Where to Stay & Eat

$ ✕ **The London Cafe.** In the style of a London pub, with dark wood furniture, period wallpaper, and paintings of English rural scenes, this two-story eatery has an excellent range of mains, including Turkish meatballs, *köfte,* grilled meats, and salads. Its air-conditioning and relaxed atmosphere make it a favorite with locals looking to escape the summer heat. ⊠ *Saraçlar Caddesi No. 46* ☎ *284/213–8052* ▤ *AE, M, V.*

$ ✕ **Tunca Cafe** On the edge of the main square opposite Eski Cami, the Tunca Cafe offers a range of snacks, nonalcoholic drinks, and light meals, including the Turkish stuffed filo pastry known as *gözleme,* filled with cheese, spinach, or potato. In summer, the café spreads into a spacious garden with benches and toadstool-shaped tables. ⊠ *Hürriyet Meydanı* ☎ *No phone* ▤ *No credit cards.*

$$ ▦ **Efe Hotel.** Tucked away on a sidestreet just off the main drag, this hotel's bright vermilion exterior belies the muted calm of its interior decor schemes—not that it's going to win any design awards. Rooms are modestly furnished in pastel shades reminiscent of the 1970s but are clean and comfortable. ⊠ *Maarif Caddesi No 13, Kaleiçi, 22100* ☎ *284/213–6166 or 284/213–6466* ☒ *284/213–6080* ⊕ *www.efehotel.com* ⤳ *34 rooms* ☖ *Restaurant, bar, some Wi-Fi; no a/c* ▤ *AE, MC, V.*

$ ▦ **Hotel Rüstem Paşa Kervansaray.** Built in the 1500s, reputedly by the celebrated architect Sinan, today this hotel is the most impressive in Edirne, at least from the outside. The inside is more functional: rooms have high ceilings and decorative fireplaces, plain furniture, and low, single beds; avoid rooms near the nightclub, which are noisy. The building sprawls around a pleasant courtyard full of flowers. ⊠ *İki Kapılı Han Cad. 57, Sabuni Mah., 22100* ☎ *284/225–2195 or 284/225–6119* ☒ *284/212–0462* ⊕ *www.kervansarayhotel.net* ⤳ *79 rooms with bath* ☖ *Restaurant, bar, nightclub, Internet cafe; no a/c* ▤ *AE, MC, V.*

Edirne Essentials

**ARRIVING &
DEPARTING**
Buses headed for Edirne depart frequently from Istanbul's Esenler Terminal. The trip takes three hours and costs $8. If you're going by **car,** take the toll road—the E80 TEM (the toll from Istanbul to Edirne costs $3), which is faster and much easier than Route 100. The trip takes about 2½ hours. Three **trains** leave Istanbul's Sirkeci Station daily for the painfully slow 6- to 10-hour trip—you won't save much money, the cost is about $6, so you're better off taking the bus or driving.

**GETTING
AROUND**
The bus and train stations are on the outskirts of town, too far to walk. Take a taxi into the center, asking for Hürriyet Meydanı. Sights in town can all be reached on foot.

**CONTACTS &
RESOURCES**
Edirne's **tourist information office** (⊠ Talat Paşa Cad., near Hürriyet Meyd. ☎ 284/213–9208) is theoretically open every day in summer, although it sometimes closes on Sundays. It's generally closed in the off-season.

ISTANBUL ESSENTIALS

Transportation

BY AIR

Most international and domestic flights arrive at Istanbul's Atatürk Airport, although some domestic flights and an increasing number of charter airlines, fly into the newer Sabiha Gokçen Airport on the Asian side of the city. Atatürk Airport was upgraded and expanded in the late 1990s, which has greatly reduced waiting times. Exits and taxi stands are well signposted as you emerge from customs. There is a light train directly from Atatürk Airport into the center of Istanbul, although it is usually quicker and easier to take a taxi or one of the shuttle buses operated by the Havaş company ($5). Taxis and the shuttle buses can be found at the main exit from the terminal building. Lines for check-in for Turkish Airlines are often long. Extra security checks for travelers to the U.S. mean that if you are traveling to the U.S., you need to be at the airport three hours before take-off regardless of which airline you are flying. Procedures at Sabiha Gokçen Airport are more straightforward, although at press time all scheduled (i.e. noncharter) international flights currently used Atatürk Airport. There is no rail link to Sabiha Gokçen Airport so take a taxi or a Havaş shuttle bus ($4).

Atatürk Airport ☎ 212/465-5555 ⊕ www.ataturkairport.com. **Sabiha Gokçen Airport** ☎ 216/585-5000 ⊕ www.sgairport.com. **Havaş** ☎ 212/465-5656 ⊕ www.havas.com.tr

BY BOAT & FERRY

You'd expect a sprawling city surrounded by water to be well served by ferries, and Istanbul does not disappoint. The main docks are at Eminönü, on the Old Istanbul side of the Galata Bridge; Karaköy, on the other side of the bridge; Kabataş, near Dolmabahçe Palace; and across the Bosphorus on the Asian shore, at Üsküdar and Kadiköy. Commuter ferries crisscross between these points day and night and provide great views of the city at a most reasonable price (usually $2 round-trip). Information on all city ferries is available between 9 AM and 5 PM from the Istanbul Ferry Lines office (Turkiye Denizcilik İşletmeleri).

One of the most practical and speedy innovations on Istanbul's waterways has been the seabuses or *deniz otobüsü*, which are large, powerful catamarans painted blue, red, and white, operating to and from Karaköy, Kadıköy, Kabataş, Bostancı, Eminönü, the Princes' Islands, Sarıyer, Beykoz, İstinye, Yalova, and Bakırköy. Prices are around $2.50 each way. There are also larger versions, which carry vehicles and passengers on the two-hour journey from Istanbul to Bandırma on the southern coast of the Sea of Marmara. The seabus interiors are air-conditioned and reminiscent of a large aircraft. Schedules are available at docks marked DENIZ OTOBÜSÜ TERMINALI, on a 24-hour Turkish-language telephone service, and on the Internet from İstanbul Deniz Otobüsleri.

Best for sightseeing is the Anadolu Kavağı boat, which makes all the stops on the European and Asian sides of the Bosphorus. It leaves year-round from the Eminönü Docks, Pier 5, next to the Galata Bridge on the Old Stamboul side, at 10:35, 12:00 and 1:35. Unless you speak Turkish, have your hotel call for boat schedules, as English is rarely spoken at the docks. The round-trip fare is $6; the ride each way lasts one hour and 45 minutes. You can disembark at any of the stops and pick up a later boat, or return by taxi, dolmuş, or bus.

İstanbul Deniz Otobüsleri ☎ 212/444-4436 ⊕ www.ido.com.tr **Turkiye Denizcilik İşletmeleri Anadolu Kavağı** ☎ 212/251-5000 ⊕ www.tdi.com.tr

Fishermen on the Bosphorus, Istanbul.

(top left) Turkish delights. (top right) Yerebatan Sarnıcı (Basilica Cistern), Istanbul. (bottom left) A whirling dervish. (bottom right) Inside the Arkeoloji Müzesi (Archaeology Museum), Istanbul.

(top) A Cappadocian landscape. (bottom) Interior of the Blue Mosque, Istanbul.

(top) Ölüdeniz beach, on the Turquoise Riviera. (bottom) Boys in traditional dress.

(top) The white cliffs of Pamukkale. (bottom left) Inside a Turkish bath. (bottom right) The head of Heracles, Mt. Nemrut.

(top) The Grand Bazaar (Kapalı Çarşı), Istanbul. (bottom) The ancient theater in Kaş.
Opposite page: (top left) İznik tiles in the Topkapı Sarayı harem. (top right) An ancient Roman mosaic in a Turkish church. (bottom) The Ortaköy neighborhood on the Bosphorus, Istanbul.

The ruins of the Celsus Library at Ephesus.

1

BY BUS

Istanbul's city's buses (mostly vermilion and blue, although an increasing number are now completely covered in brightly colored advertising) and trams are crowded and slow, but they are useful for getting around the city and—at about $1 per ride—inexpensive. The route name and number are posted on the front of each vehicle; curbside signboards list routes and itineraries. Buy tickets before boarding; they're available individually and in books of 10 from ticket stands near each stop or from newsstands around the city. For a few cents above face value, they can also be purchased from shoeshine boys and men sitting on wooden crates at most bus stops. London-style double-deckers operate between Sultanahmet and Emirgan on the Bosphorus and between Taksim and Bostancı on the Asian side. Unlike the older city buses, these are clean and offer a panoramic ride. A bus attendant collects fares of three individual tickets (totaling $3). Buses become extremely crowed during the rush hours of 7:30–9:30 AM and 5–8 PM. For short trips inside the city it is usually easier, if a little more expensive, to take taxis.

Intercity and international buses arrive and depart from the Esenler Otogar, outside the city near Bayrampaşa. This terminal is accessible by the Hızlı Tren (rapid train) system, which leaves from Aksaray, but the train is often very crowded, particularly at rush hour, and you're often better off taking a taxi. A few buses from Anatolia arrive at the Harem Terminal, on the Asian side of the Bosphorus. Most bus companies have minibus services from the bus terminals to the area around Taksim Square and Aksaray, which is close to many hotels. Private taxis cost about $15 from Esenler Terminal to Taksim or Sultanahmet and about $12 from the Harem Terminal. Note that you'll have to pay the Bosphorus Bridge toll ($2) when crossing from Asia to Europe, or vice versa.
🛈 **Esenler Otogar** ☎ 212/658-1010. **Harem Terminal** ☎ 216/555-3763.

BY CAR

Istanbul is notorious for its congested traffic, often cavalier attitude to traffic regulations, poor signposting, and shortage of parking spaces. It is simply not worth hiring a car to travel anywhere in the city. It's much easier, and ultimately cheaper, to take taxis.

If you're entering or leaving Istanbul by car, E80 runs between Istanbul and central Anatolia to the east; this toll road is the best of several alternatives. You can also enter or leave the city on one of the numerous car ferries that ply the Sea of Marmara from the Kabataş docks. There's an overnight ferry to İzmir from the Eminönü docks. Getting out of the city by car can be a bit of a hassle as the signs aren't always as clear as you would hope. It's always useful to have a driving map.

BY TAXI OR DOLMUŞ

Taxis (*taksi* in Turkish, pronounced as in English), are metered and inexpensive. All registered taxis are painted bright yellow and usually have their registration numbers painted on their doors and roofs to aid identification. Most drivers do not speak English and may not know every street, so write down the name and address of your destination, even those nearby, and the name of the neighborhood you're visiting (staff at your hotel will normally write down names for you and usually call you a taxi for your outward journey). Although tipping is not automatic, it is customary to round off the fare to the nearest 50 kuruş. Fares are 50% more expensive between midnight and 6 AM. Avoid taxi drivers who choose roundabout routes by having your hotel's attendant or a Turkish speaker talk to the driver before you get in. The vast majority of Istanbul taxi drivers are scrupulously honest—but one commonly reported scam is drivers telling foreigner customers that the meter isn't working. It is inadvisable to agree on a set fare unless you know for certain it is cheaper than the metered fare.

The taxi stand at Atatürk airport is outside the arrivals gate, and it's not one company, more like a collective of taxi drivers who work this territory. Much like at an airport such as JFK, there will be a line of cabs, and you get in the first one that is available. There aren't any "pirates" waiting to lure unsuspecting arrivals into what are essentially private cars, mainly because anyone else who tried to muscle in would get beaten up by the taxi drivers in the collective!

Away from the airports, the easiest thing to do is hail a taxi off the street or, if you happen to be close to one, from a taxi stand. Larger hotels have taxi stands outside them, but all staff at even the smallest hotel are usually ready to call a taxi for you. Most can also arrange for one to be waiting for you if, for example, you have an early trip to the airport.

Dolmuşes (shared taxis), many of which are bright yellow minibuses, run along various routes. You can sometimes hail a dolmuş on the street and, as with taxis, dolmuş stands are marked by signs. The destination is shown on either a roof sign or a card in the front window. Dolmuş stands can be found at regular intervals, and the vehicles wait for customers to climb in. Though the savings over a private taxi are significant, you may find the quarters too close for comfort, particularly in summer. Another disadvantage is that as dolmuşes only operate along specific routes, they may not stop very close to your destination. If notified beforehand, drivers will usually try to drop you as close as possible to your destination and will frequently explain how to continue to your destination—although this explanation will almost certanly be in Turkish.

BY TRAIN

Trains from Europe and the west (service is limited) arrive at Sirkeci Station, in Old Istanbul, near the Galata Bridge. Trains from Anatolia and the east currently come into Haydarpaşa Station, on the Asian side, but Haydarpaşa is due to be closed in 2007 as the railtrack is rerouted to link up with a tunnel which is being built under the Bosphorus and will provide the first ever rail link between the two shores of the city. At press time, however, work on the tunnel was progressing slower than anticipated and closure of Haydarpaşa Station could be delayed until late 2007 or early 2008. Turkish trains are operated by the state-owned monopoly Türkiye Cumhuriyeti Devlet Demiryolları (TCDD).

Haydarpaşa Station ☎ 216/336-0475. **Sirkeci Station** ☎ 212/527-0051. **Türkiye Cumhuriyeti Devlet Demiryolları (TCDD)** ☎ 312/311-0602 ⊕ www.tcdd.gov.tr.

Contacts & Resources

BANKS & EXCHANGING SERVICES

There are numerous banks (*banka* in Turkish although signs will usually use the form *bankası*) and foreign exchange offices (*döviz* or *döviz bürosu*) throughout the city. Banks are usually open Mon.–Fri. from 9 AM–5 PM. Some close for lunch. Foreign exchange offices usually provide a slightly better rate of exchange and tend to close later, usually at 6 PM or sometimes 7 PM. Most foreign exchange offices are open Mon.–Sat., although those in the main tourist areas (such as Divan Yolu in the Sultanahmet district) are often open 7 days a week. Almost all hotels will exchange foreign currency, although their rates are usually less attractive than those offered at the foreign exchange offices. Some restaurants and most places frequented by foreign tourists, such as the Grand Bazaar, will accept payment in foreign currency, but this will usually work out to be more expensive than if you change your foreign currency and then pay in Turkish lira.

EMERGENCIES

Most Turkish doctors, particularly the younger generation, will know at least a few basic medical terms in English. The same applies for most pharmacists. There's a pharmacy in every neighborhood, and all Istanbul pharmacies post the name and address of the nearest one open around the clock. The names of 24-hour pharmacies are also available through the directory inquiries service, although it is advisable to ask a Turkish speaker to make the call.

Emergency Contacts Ambulance ☎ 112. **American Hospital** ✉ Güzelbahçe Sok. 20, Nişantaşı ☎ 212/231-4050. **International Hospital (and Ambulance service)** ✉ Istanbul Cad. 82, Yeşilköy ☎ 212/663-3000. **German Hospital** ✉ Siraselviler Cad. 119, Taksim ☎ 212/293-2150. **Tourism police** ☎ 212/527-4503. 24-hour Pharmacies ☎ 111.

INTERNET, MAIL & SHIPPING

If your hotel doesn't have Internet access, the staff will be able to direct you to the nearest Internet café. They tend to be scattered throughout the city, but your best bets are Taksim and Sultahahmet. There is no Turkish phrase for the term "Internet café," so just use the English. It's usually possible to find someone in the Internet café itself, either someone working there or one of the other customers, who has a basic command of computer English and will be able to help you access the Internet.

Post offices have yellow signs with PTT (for the Turkish "Posta ve Telegraf Teşkilatı"). Smaller post offices are usually open Mon.–Fri. 8:30 AM–4:30 PM. The main post office, Büyük Postane, in Istanbul, which is also the destination for anything sent poste restante, is in Sirkeci, several blocks south and west of the Sirkeci Train Station. It's open Mon.–Sat. 8 AM–midnight, and Sun. 9 AM–7 PM. The easiest way to send packages internationally is by courier, although it's not cheap. All the major international companies are represented in Istanbul.

Büyük Postane ✉ Büyük Postane Caddesi, Sirkeci ☎ 212/513-3407. **DHL** ✉ Alemdar Mah. Yerebatan Cad. 15/2, Sultanahmet ☎ 212/512-5452 ⊕ www.dhl.com.tr. **FedEx**

✉ Taşocağı Yolu, Fabrikalar Caddesi 19, Mahmutbey ☎ 212/444-0505 ⊕ www.fedex. com/tr. **UPS** ✉ Kucuk Ayasofya Caddesi Aksakal Sok. 14, Sultanahmet ☎ 212/517-4102 ⊕ www.ups.com/content/tr/en/index.jsx.

TOUR OPTIONS
General Interest

Names of tour companies and their itineraries change so frequently it's best just to make arrangements through a travel agency or your hotel; the offerings are all pretty similar. A "classical tour" of Aya Sofya, the Museum of Turkish and Islamic Arts, the Hippodrome, Yerebatan Sarayı, and the Blue Mosque should cost about $25 for a half-day; the Topkapı Palace, Süleymaniye Cami, the Grand or perhaps the Egyptian Bazaar, and lunch in addition to the above sights would be a full-day and about $50 ($60–$80 by private car). Bosphorus tours often include lunch at Sarıyer and visits to the Dolmabahçe and Beylerbeyi palaces.

VISITOR INFORMATION
There are several branches of the Turkish Ministry of Tourism in Istanbul, including at the airport and in Sultanahmet. Hours are usually from 9 until 5, though some close for an hour around noon.

🚩 **Turkish Ministry of Tourism** ✉ Atatürk Airport ☎ 212/663-0793 ✉ International Maritime Passenger Terminal, Karaköy Meyd. ☎ 212/249-5776 ✉ Istanbul Hilton, Cumhuriyet Cad., Harbiye ☎ 212/233-0592 ✉ In Sultanahmet, Divan Yolu Cad. 3 ☎ 212/518-1802 ✉ In Sirkeci, Sirkeci Garı ☎ 212/511-5888.

The Sea of Marmara & the North Aegean

WORD OF MOUTH

"Behramakale: if you can find this small town you will love it. There are many lovely, inexpensive hotels, and you will have a chance to visit Assos, an important ruin that is still under excavation."

—sinan

WELCOME TO THE NORTH AEGEAN

TOP REASONS TO GO

★ **İznik tiles** Watch the craftswomen engraving on quartz; buy some to take home.

★ **Spend quality time in Bursa** Visit the Yeşil Cami (Green Mosque), stroll the covered bazaar, and make sure to try the local kebab specialty: *İskender kebap*.

★ **Gallipoli** See the battlefields and moving memorials where one of the key campaigns of the First World War was fought.

★ **Explore Mount Ida** Hike among the pine forests and waterfalls, and stay in one of the area's boutique hotels.

★ **Troy** Visit the ruins of this 5,000-year-old city, where more than nine layers of civilization have been uncovered.

★ **Pergamum** Explore this spectacular showcase of the classical period, second in Turkey only to Ephesus.

Ruins of the Temple of Trajan Acropolis of Pergamum Turkey

BLACK SEA

Tekirdag Silivri Mahmutbey Sariyer Sile Agva

Istanbul Sevketpasa Samandira

Kadiköy

MARMARA Sea of Marmara Kartal O 4 Mollareneri Akcaova

Marmara Adasi D 100

Turankoy Gebze

KAPIDAGI YARIMADASI Yalova Kocaeli Sakarya

Bayramdere Armuflu Karamursel

Bugdayli Gemlik Orhangazi Sapanca O 4

Lake Kus Karacabey Mudanya Lake Iznik İznik Haciosman

D 573 Lake Ulubat D 200 Bursa Yenisehir Osmaneli Geyve

Manyas Cali Gursu Golpazari

Susurluk Camamdar Inegol Bilecik

D 565 D 200

Balikesir Bozuyuk

1 Sea of Marmara: You can still feel the Ottoman spirit in this part of Turkey, where you'll find some of the best examples of early Ottoman architecture, faithfully restored old thermal baths, the surviving arts of tile making and silk-weaving, and wonderful old bazaars. This is also where you'll find Mt. Uludağ, the trendiest ski resort in Turkey.

2 The Dardanelles are the straits southwest of Istanbul running between the Aegean and Marmara seas. Most of the sights are on the Gallipoli Peninsula to the north of the straits. Çanakkale is to their south. This windswept peninsula is full of moving historical sites marking the Gallipoli campaign of World War I; beautifully tended cemeteries stretch along the 30 km of land where so many soldiers are buried.

3 North Aegean: The combination of Greek heritage and Turkish rural life, set in an unspoiled natural setting of azure sea, winding coastline, and pine-clad hills, is just starting to attract international tourism. Mount Ida, the home of Greek gods and goddesses, offers a very civilized country experience, and the ruins of Troy, Pergamum, and Behramkale (Assos) aren't far.

GETTING ORIENTED

Tourism to the southern coast of the Sea of Marmara and the North Aegean is taking off as visitors discover some of Turkey's loveliest beaches, best walking country, and an impressive range of historical sites dating from the 3rd millennium BC (Troy) to World War I (Gallipoli). The south coast of the Sea of Marmara is close to Istanbul and where you will find İznik, famed for its beautiful tiles, and the old Ottoman capital of Bursa.

NORTH AEGEAN PLANNER

Getting Here & Around

The best way to explore this area is to rent a car. Intercity buses stop in some spots but it will often require several changes to get from one destination to another; minibuses run between some of the smaller villages and sights, but others are reachable only by taxi.

If you're just planning a day trip or an overnight to the area, though, the ferry from Istanbul's Yenikapi terminal to Yalova takes about an hour, and then you can catch a bus to İznik or Bursa.

When to Go

The Southern Marmara region and the North Aegean are considerably cooler than the South Aegean and Mediterranean coasts, but summer is still very hot. In July or August, the national park at Uludağ, in Bursa, remains refreshingly cool. If you're here in the colder months, Bursa, where you can soak in thermal baths, is a fine antidote to the winter blues.

Mount Ida is lovely all year round but is prettiest in spring when nature is awakening.

Çanakkale, Gallipoli, and Troy can be very windy in late summer and fall. Homer refers to Troy as windy, and some archaeologists argue that the strong gusts are one of the reasons why so many layers of civilization ended up piled on top of one another.

How Much Time Do You Need?

The Sea of Marmara area can be a quick one- or two-day trip from Istanbul. You could just do a day in İznik (make sure you leave Istanbul early), but you'll want to spend an overnight at least in Bursa.

If you have 2 or 3 days in the region, you can visit Gallipoli and Troy, maybe adding a day in the Mt. Ida region. If you have 5 or 6 days, you can pretty much see everything in the area, continuing on to Behramkale (Assos) and Ayvalik, with a visit to Cunda, Ayvalik's main island, and the ruins of Pergamum. Be warned, though: Mt. Ida is lovely and has wonderful hiking. Once you get here, you might want to stay longer.

Gallipoli Tours

Touring the battlefields and memorials with a guide is advisable. Tours are conducted all year, daily between April and November, every other day the rest of the year. They run about 5½ hours, starting at noon in summer, 10:30 AM in winter. In summer bring a hat and water. Good walking shoes or sneakers are advised.

Hassle-Free Travel Agency. This should be your first choice if you're staying in Çanakkale. They also run a hotel and a hostel in town; very practical if you're signed up for the tour. From Çanakkale tours to Gallipoli are about $35 per person including lunch, ferry crossing, and transport. ⊠ Cumhuriyet Meydanı, 61 17100 Çanakkale ☎ 286/213–5969 🖷 286/217–2906 ⊕ www.hasslefreetour.com.

TJ's Tours. TJ's owns a hostel and a hotel in Eceabat. Standard tours to the battlefields cost about $25, including lunch, transport, and admission to the museum. Stay at their hotel and they'll show the film Gallipoli the night before the tour and the documentary The Fatal Shore on their terrace bar in the morning, to set the mood for the visit. ⊠ Kemalpa Şa Mahallesi, Cumhuriyet Cad., 5/A, Eceabat ☎ 286/814-3121 🖷 286/814 3122 ⊕ www.anzacgallipolitours.com.

2

Healthy Aegean Cuisine

Aegean cuisine is in many ways different from Turkish cuisine elsewhere in the country. The shared Turkish and Greek culture of the region's past, the climate and soil suitable for growing a wide range of vegetables, and the prevalence of olive trees and olive-oil production have helped the region develop a much more varied and probably healthier cuisine than elsewhere in Turkey. Olive oil replaces butter and fish replaces meat on most menus. The class of dishes generally called *zeytinyağlı* (literally "with olive oil") mostly comes from this region; it means vegetables cooked in olive oil, mostly with tomatoes and onions, and served cold. If you are a vegetarian, you'll be in heaven.

Local Specialties

İegöl köfte (meatballs) and *İskender kebap* were both invented in Bursa. Most cities in Turkey claim some kind of fame for their köfte, but *İegol köfte*—cooked on charcoal—are especially delicious. *İskender* kebap, tender beef on pita bread, soaked in tomato sauce, and served with yogurt on the side, is a must. And don't let your experience of it elsewhere in Turkey put you off trying it in Bursa, where it's far superior.

In the Mt. Ida region you'll find mezes that are made with wild herbs collected in the area and cooked or dressed in olive oil. Cunda island in Ayvalık has an amazing range of seafood and fish mezes and main dishes, enriched by lesser-known Greek dishes and the restaurants' own creations. Fish is always advisable throughout the region if you stick to local and seasonal catches.

Two Days Around the Sea of Marmara

Leave Istanbul by ferry early enough to be in Yalova by midmorning, then catch a bus or drive to İznik. You can have lunch by the lake and visit the Tiles Foundation by the lakeside road, then head into the center of town to visit Yeşil Cami and Sancta Sophia. If you leave İznik by late afternoon you'll be in Bursa in the early evening. Spend the second day sightseeing in Bursa; don't miss Yeşil Cami, the Covered Bazaar, the Muradiye Tombs, and the city museum. For lunch, make sure to try the *İskender kebap*; it's better in Bursa than anywhere else in Turkey. If you have time, or another day, you can take the cable car to Mt. Uludağ and enjoy the view of its pine-clad hills. Return to Yalova in the early evening and catch the last ferry back to Yenikapı terminal in Istanbul.

WHAT IT COSTS

	$$$$	$$$	$$	$	¢
Restaurants	over $25	$16–25	$11–15	$5–10	under $5
Hotels	over $250	$151–250	$76–150	$51–75	under $50

Restaurant prices are for one main course at dinner or for two mezes (small dishes). Hotel prices are for two people in a double room in high season, including taxes.

Updated by
Yeşim Erdem
Holland

Everyone loves the Mediterranean for its sun and sand; you can't beat the south Aegean for lively nightlife; and yes, there is no other Ephesus. But if you're interested in green landscape, fresh air, a cool sea, unspoiled nature, a region with its fair share of historic sites, sports, little havens in the wilderness, Greek mythology, and generally a less touristy experience, then the north Aegean and the area south of the Marmara Sea is for you. You can see the whole of the region in a week; or if you're based in Istanbul, it can be divided into separate journeys. Spend at least one evening watching the sun go down over Homer's wine-dark sea, and you'll agree that the north Aegean has a little bit of everything–and a lot you won't find anywhere else.

SEA OF MARMARA

Although quite close to Istanbul, the area around the Sea of Marmara is sometimes overlooked by travelers anxious to get to the beaches of the Aegean coast. There is much to attract the traveler interested in both history and beautiful landscape, though, and anyone interested in gorgeous İznik tiles will definitely want to do some shopping.

İznik, a pilgrimage site for Christians and an important city for the Ottomans, offers historical sights from the Roman, Byzantine, Seljuk, and Ottoman periods; the town's beautiful tiles are another reason to visit, and the lake where you can swim is a wonderful bonus. Bursa, the first capital of the Ottoman Empire, boasts some of the finest examples of Ottoman architecture in its mosques and bazaars. Its mountain, Uludağ, is Turkey's most popular skiing resort. You can visit either city as a day trip from Istanbul, though Bursa deserves at least an overnight stay. Both are, more or less, on the way to the Mediterranean, central Anatolia, or even the north Aegean if you're traveling by ferry across the Marmara Sea.

İznik

❶ *190 km from Istanbul via Rte. 100 or E80 to İzmit and Rte. 130 to Yalova; 60 km (37 mi) from Yalova. Or take the ferry from Istanbul's Yenikapı terminal to Yalova (1hour).*

İznik has a distinguished past but a faded present. Nobody knows when the city was actually founded, but it was put on the map in 316 BC when one of Alexander the Great's generals claimed the city. It fell under the rule of many subsequent rulers, including the general Lysimachus, who renamed it Nicaea after his wife. The Seljuks made the city their capital for a brief period in the 11th century, and Byzantine emperors in exile did the same in the 13th century while Constantinople was in the hands of Crusaders. The Ottoman Sultan Orhan Gazi (ruled 1326–61) captured it in 1331.The famous İznik tiles, unequaled even today, were created under Ottoman rule.

İznik reflects little of its former grandeur, although the revival of the tile industry draws many travelers—many of whom end up placing huge orders for delivery overseas. Nature has also been generous to İznik. It is beautifully situated around the east end of İznik Lake (where you can swim, although the water is on the chilly side outside July and August).

İznik's Tiled Beauty

CLOSE UP

İZNİK'S TILE SHOPS are a pleasure to visit even if you don't plan to buy anything (though you'll probably end up buying tiles whether you plan to or not). They are workshops as well as sales points, and you'll usually find one or more women drawing or painting tiles.

İznik tile makers believe that their tiles have magical properties. There is one fairly sound explanation for this (alongside any number of unsound ones): İznik tiles, made from soil that's found only in the area, have a very high level of quartz, an element believed to have soothing effects. It's not just the level of quartz that makes İznik tiles unique, though. The original tiles also have distinctive patterns and colors: predominantly blue, then green and red, reflecting the colors of precious stones. The patterns are inspired by local flora—flowering trees or tulips. These days artists use different colors and designs as well as the traditional ones.

İznik became a center for the ceramics industry after the 15th-century Ottoman conquest of Istanbul. To upgrade the quality of native work, Sultan Selim I (ruled 1512–15) imported 500 potters from Tabriz in Persia. The government-owned kilns were soon turning out exquisite tiles with intricate motifs of circles, stars, and floral and geometric patterns, executed in lush turquoise, green, blue, red, and white. Despite their costliness, their popularity spread through the Islamic world, until the industry went into decline in the 18th century.

İznik tiles are expensive—much more so than those produced in the rival ceramics center of Kütahya, 120 km (72 mi) farther south. A single tile costs about $20, and the price of a plate varies between $30 and $300. İznik tiles are made of better-quality stone, with a higher quartz content, so they are heavier, stronger, and more durable, making them ideal for decorating large spaces, from airports to mosques. They are all hand-made, with no artificial colors, and the designs tend to be more intricate and elegant.

The tile-makers' street, near the city center, has a series of small shops next to each other. Check out **Cengizhan Çini** ⊠ *Mahmut Çelebi Mahallesi, S.Demircan (Çiniciler) sokak, 22* ☎ *224/ 757–6809* ⊙ *10 AM–7 PM.*, which also functions as a Tourist Information Office.

Süleyman Paşa Medresesi ⊠ *Maltepe Caddesi, 29* ⊙ *10 AM–7:30 PM (9 PM in summer)*, the first college of the Ottoman empire, is now a tile workshop with a peaceful courtyard where you can have refreshments.

The İznik Education and Learning Foundation ⊠ *Sahil Yolu, Vakıf sokak, 13* ☎ *224/757–6025* 🖷 *224/ 757–5737* ⊕ *www.İznik.com* ⊙ *8 AM– 6 PM.* is a bit out of town along the lake. It's a pleasant place to wander; the large garden has displays of the quartz stone used to make İznik tiles, and the showrooms are also workshops where you can follow the tile-making process from start to finish—it feels more like a museum than a shop. If you're making a big order for overseas delivery, this is the place to do it; you'll also get a certificate of authencity with the product.

İznik is an easy place to navigate: the town hasn't grown much, so the classical Roman layout still works. You'll almost certainly come across the city's walls as you explore; the four main gates date back to Roman times, and the city's two main streets intersect each other and end at these gates. Running north-south is Kılıçaslan Caddesi; east-west is Atatürk Caddesi. Sancta Sophia Church is at the intersection of these streets.

What to See

Sancta Sophia (Church of the Holy Wisdom) was built in the center of İznik in the 6th century, during the reign of Justinian. Its primitive mosaic floor is believed to date from that time; the wall mosaics were added as part of a reconstruction in the 11th century, after an earthquake toppled the original church. There are some fine fragments of Byzantine fresco and mosaic work, including a mural of Jesus with Mary and St. John the Baptist. ⊠ *Atatürk Cad. and Kılıçaslan Cad.* ☎ *mobile phone 538/854–6966* ▨ *4$* ☾ *Daily 9–noon and 1–6.*

The style of the **Hacı Özbek Cami** is very primitive. It was the first Ottoman monument in İznik and was constructed in 1333 without a minaret, and it lacks the ornamentation seen in later buildings in Bursa and Istanbul. It underwent an extensive restoration in 1959 and has a dome made of tiles. ⊠ *Kılıçaslan Cad., east of the Belediye Sarayı (town hall)* ☎ *no phone* ▨ *Free* ☾ *Daily sunrise–sunset.*

★ The **Yeşil Cami,** a Seljuk-style mosque built in 1392 near İznik's east wall, is known as the Green Mosque because of the color of its minaret, which is overlaid by green bricks and decorated with green-and-blue tiles. The Green Mosque's blue-and-green tiles are not the original İznik work, which was damaged by various earthquakes and replaced during the 19th century. The huge stone columns inside this modest-sized mosque are impressive. Outside are a large garden and courtyard with a *kahvehane,* a Turkish-style café. ■ TIP→ **Don't confuse this with the mosque in Bursa of the same name. The Bursa mosque is the one that's really gorgeous.** ⊠ *Teke Sok., off Kılıçaslan Cad.* ☎ *mobile 0532/440–7336* ▨ *Free* ☾ *Daily sunrise–sunset.*

The building that houses the **İznik Museum** was built in 1388 as a soup kitchen. Such kitchens, serving free food to the poor, were often constructed by the wealthy as demonstrations of Muslim charity. Today the museum contains such artifacts as Greek tombstones, Ottoman weaponry, perfume bottles, and original İznik tiles. If you have time, ask at the museum about a visit to the Byzantine Tomb, the **Yeraltı Mezar,** on the outskirts of town. Discovered in the 1960s, this 5th-century burial place of an unknown family has well-preserved painted murals of peacocks, flowers, and abstract patterns in the Byzantine style. ■ TIP→ **The only way to visit the tomb is by asking at the museum, and they won't take you if they are short of staff.** ⊠ *Kılıçaslan Cad., opposite Yeşil Cami* ☎ *224/757–1027* ▨ *$1.50* ☾ *Daily 8–noon and 1—5, closed Mon.*

The gray-stone **Lefke Gate** (Lefke Kapısı), the eastern gate to the ancient city, was built in honor of a visit by the Roman emperor Hadrian in AD 120. Its old inscriptions, marble reliefs, and friezes remain intact. You can scramble up onto the old city walls for a good view. Thick, sturdy fortifications like these were what saved many a town from ruin. Outside the gate are the city graveyard and Muslim tombs belonging to a nobleman named Hayrettin Paşa and some lesser luminaries. The oldest is 600 years old.

Where to Stay & Eat

¢ ✕ **İmren Köfte Salonu.** Turks love their *köfte* (meatballs), and almost every city in the country makes a claim to fame based on its own way of making them. The locals think İznik *köfte* are, of course, the best around, and fill the large canteen-type tables of this casual place at almost all times of the day. You might not be able to distinguish these *köfte* from any other, but the place is its own sort of treat. Portions are

> ### DINING IN İZNIK
>
> İznik isn't the place for elaborate restaurants: For dinner and drinks, the lakefront hotels with restaurants are your best bet. While touring the sights, eat in the town center, where there are various options for a quick lunch.

big and served with barbecued tomatoes, peppers, and onions. ⊠ *Atatürk Caddesi, opposite İznik Lycee* ☎ *224/757–3597* ▤ *MC, V* ☺ *Open daily 10 AM until midnight.*

¢ ✕ **Kenan Çorba.** Just opposite the Sancta Sophia museum, the locals love this restaurant that specializes in soups and beans. Try the fish or chicken soup. İşkembe (tripe soup) is really for those who are into experimenting. You'll either hate it or love it—although the Turks believe it's the ultimate hangover cure, eaten at the end of a late night of drinking. The beans with sliced Turkish pastrami and rice, accompanied by tiny pickled peppers, is an all-time favorite. The restaurant opens early, at 5:30 AM. ⊠ *Atatürk Caddesi, opposite Sancta Sophia* ☎ *224/ 757–0235* ▤ *No credit cards.*

★ $$ ▦ **İznik Çini Vakfı Konukevi.** Right next to, and owned by, the İznik Tiles Education and Learning Foundation, this small hotel has basic comforts but a nice setting and atmosphere. It's in the remote but still easily reachable part of İznik, at the end of the lakefront and a bit inland. The hotel is built partially from dark wood, unlike the concrete of İznik's other hotels, and its garden and the displays of the quartz stone used to make İznik tiles are a delight. The beach is only a 10-minute walk away. ⊠ *Sahil Yolu, Vakıf sokak, 13* ☎ *224/757–6025* ▧ *224/757–5737* ⊕ *no web* ⇋ *8 rooms* ▤ *MC, V* ¶⊙¶ *BP.*

$ ✕▦ **Çamlık Motel.** This plain but well established hotel is one of the best places to stay in İznik. It's on the quiet end of the lakefront, 100 meters from the beach, and has a large, charming garden. Right behind the nearby beach is a small, shaded area with grass, trees, and picnic tables. Rooms are sparsely furnished. It's also the only remaining nice fish and meat restaurant on the lake front open to nonguests. A variety of tasty mezes and fresh lake fish, *yayın,* caught daily, is served in the garden. ⊠ *Göl Sahil Yolu* ☎ *224/757–1362* ▧ *224/757–1631* ⊕ *www.İznik-camlikmotel.com* ⇋ *24 rooms* ⌂ *Wi-Fi* ▤ *V, MC* ¶⊙¶ *BP.*

$ ✕▦ **Cem Otel & Restaurant.** This hotel has light-filled, spacious rooms, but it's on a loud part of the lakefront, and music from wedding ceremonies is likely to intrude on summer weekends. The restaurant is indoors—a bit dark and gloomy, unlike the rooms—and serves fine but not outstanding food, including local fresh fish, mezes, and meat dishes. As at all the lakefront establishments in İznik, a wide road passes between the hotel and the lake but the beach is only about 150 meters away. ⊠ *Göl Sahil Yolu, Spandau Bul., 34* ☎ *224/757—1687 or 532/481—2511 (mobile)* ⊕ *www.cemotel.com* ➾ *17 rooms* ⚫ *Some a/c, some kitchenettes, minibars, Wi-Fi* ⊟ *MC, V.*

**OFF THE
BEATEN
PATH**

TERMAL (⊠ 12 km [8 mi] southwest of Yalova on the way to Çınarcık; ⊕ www.yalovatermal.com) is an interesting stop if you're enroute between Yalova and either İznik or Bursa. It's been popular as a spa since Roman times. Its springs were used by the Ottomans, refurbished in 1900 by Sultan Abdül Hamid II, and regularly visited by Atatürk in the 1920s and '30s. It's a self-contained resort with two hotels (Çamlık and Çınar), exotic gardens, and three public thermal baths with mineral-rich waters and lockers for clothes. Both hotels also have private baths for guests only. Avoid summer weekends when the area is absolutely packed, and the crowds will probably outweigh any relaxation the baths may do you. The hot baths are more appealing, and the rates cheaper, outside summer, anyway. If you are here when it's overcrowded, consider skipping the soak and opting instead for a walk in the oxygen-rich pine forests, with a packed lunch to eat at the picnic spot.

Bursa

❷ *247 km (153 mi) from Istanbul via Rte. 100 or E80 to İzmit, Rte. 130 to Yalova, and Rte. 575 south from Yalova to Bursa. Or take the ferry from Istanbul's Yenikapı terminal to Yalova. Bursa is 85 km from İznik*

Bursa is one of the rare cities that hasn't ceased being important since early Ottoman times. It became the first capital of the nascent Ottoman Empire after the city was captured in 1326 by Orhan Gazi, the empire's first sultan, and the first five sultans of the Ottoman Empire lived here until Mehmet the Conquerer conquered Istanbul and moved the capital there. Each of the sultans built his own complex on five different hilltops, and each included a mosque, a *medrese* (theological school), a hamam, a kitchen house, kervansaray, and tombs. It was in Bursa that Ottoman architecture blossomed, and where the foundations were laid for the more elaborate works to be found in the later capitals Edirne and Istanbul. More than 125 mosques here are on the list kept by the Turkish Historical Monuments Commission, and their minarets make for a grand skyline.

Present-day Bursa is one of Turkey's more prosperous cities due to its

SPA TIP

Bursa has been a spa town since Roman times. Rich in minerals, the waters are said to cure a variety of ills from rheumatism to nervous complaints. The thermal springs run along the slopes of the Çekirge region, and mineral baths are an amenity at many hotels in this area. If you're not staying in a "thermal hotel," try Yeni Kaplıca or Eski Kaplıca in the eastern side of the region; both are near the Çekirge area.

large automobile and textile industries, and the city is a pleasing mix of bustling modernity, old stone buildings, and wealthy suburbs with vintage wood-frame Ottoman villas. Residents proudly call their city Yeşil Bursa (Green Bursa)—for the green İznik tiles decorating some of its most famous monuments, and also for its parks and gardens and the national forest surrounding nearby Mt. Uludağ, Turkey's most popular ski resort.

The city has history, charming villages, sporting opportunities, good food (two local inventions, *İskender kebap* and *İnegöl köfte,* made significant contributions to Turkish cuisine), good hotels, and shopping opportunities. Many people only spend a half-day here, on the way from Istanbul to the south and west coasts or Cappadocia, but once you're here, there's a good chance you'll want to stay longer, so plan ahead.

What to See

The **Emir Sultan Cami** (Emir Sultan Mosque) was originally built in 1431 by the daughter of Sultan Yıldırım Beyazıt for her husband, Emir Sultan. It was badly damaged in the 1855 earthquake and was almost totally rebuilt by Sultan Abdülaziz. The single-domed mosque with the two cut-stone minarets for which it is famous—they are considered great examples of rococo—is in a courtyard facing the three-domed arcade that houses the tombs of Emir Sultan, his wife, and children. The setting is quite tranquil, on a quiet hilltop next to a large cemetery among cypress and plane trees overlooking the city. ⊠ *Zeytinler Cad.* 🕾 *no phone* 🎟 *Free* 🕓 *Daily sunrise–sunset.*

FodorśChoice ★

A juxtaposition of simple form, inspired stone carving, and spectacular İznik tile work, the **Yeşil Cami** (Green Mosque) is among the finest mosques in Turkey. Work on the mosque began in 1419, during the reign of Mehmet I Çelebi (ruled 1413–21). Its beauty begins in the marble entryway, where complex feathery patterns and calligraphy are carved in the stone. Inside is a sea of blue-and-green İznik tiles. The central hall rests under two shallow domes; in the one near the entrance an oculus sends down a beam of sunlight at midday, illuminating a fountain delicately carved from a single piece of marble. The *mihrab* (prayer niche) towers almost 50 feet, and there are intricate carvings near the top. On a level above the main doorway is the sultan's loge, lavishly decorated and tiled; a caretaker will sometimes take visitors up to see it. ⊠ *Yeşil Cad.* 🎟 *Free* 🕓 *Daily sunrise–sunset.*

The **Yeşil Türbe** (Green Mausoleum) is Mehmet I Çelebi's tomb, built in 1424. The "green" tomb is actually covered in blue tiles, added after an earthquake damaged the originals in the 1800s. Inside, however, are incredible original İznik tiles, including those sheathing Mehmet's immense sarcophagus. The other tombs belong to his children. The tomb was closed for restoration in 2006 but is expected to reopen by 2007. ⊠ *East end of Yeşil Cad., opposite Yeşil Cami.*

The **Türk İslam Eserleri Müzesi** (Turkish Islamic Arts Museum) is on the site of a former theological school that is part of the complex that includes Yeşil Cami and Yeşil Türbe. The collection includes tile work, inlaid wood, jewelry, books and almanacs, calligraphy work, manuscripts, pottery, traditional clothes with colorful embroidery, and bits of Seljuk architectural decoration. ✉ *Yeşil Cad., on west side of Yeşil Cami* ☎ *224/327–7679* 🔒 *$1* 🕐 *Mon–Fri. 8:30–noon and 1–5.*

NEED A BREAK

Several **tea gardens** on the west side of the Yeşil Mosque and Yeşil Tomb are pleasant places to have a sandwich or pastries and take in views of the city. It is a quiet area with restored colorful Bursa houses whose ground floors are either gift shops or cafés.

★ A 10-minute walk from the Yeşil complex, the **Bursa Kent Muzesi** (Bursa City Museum) at Heykel, in the city center right behind the statue, is a showcase for Bursa's history and handicrafts. In the basement are impressive re-creations of antique handicraft bazaars like those of silk weavers and knife makers. The lower floor summarizes the history of Bursa and its first five sultans, and touches on Atatürk during the independence war. The second floor displays past and present Bursa clothes, household tools, and re-creations of life at home and in the hamam. The exhibits are in Turkish, so make sure to get English-language headsets at the entrance. ✉ *Atatürk Cad., 8* ☎ *224/220–2626* ⊕ *www.bursakentmuzesi. gov.tr* 🔒 *$1* 🕐 *Tue–Fri. 9:30–6, Sat. and Sun. 10–6:30, closed Mon.*

Fodor'sChoice The **Kapalı Çarşı** (covered bazaar) is a large area with many adjoining
★ *hans* (kervansarays) and a *bedesten* (the central part of a covered bazaar, vaulted, and fireproofed). The Bursa sultans built their complexes on different hilltops, but they made sure to divert trade to the same place, adding their own bazaars to existing ones, so as to finance the construction or maintenance of their schools, mosques, or kitchen houses. During the reign of Orhan Sultan the area between the hans was loosely covered by roofs, the earliest form of covered bazaar. Then in the late 14th century Yıldırım Beyazıt perfected the concept by building a bedesten with six woven parts connected by arches and topped by 14 domes. It was flattened by a massive earthquake in 1855, and then parts were badly burned by fire in the 1950s, but it has been lovingly restored, and many of the hans inside still provide wonderful flavor of the past. Best buys here include silver and gold jewelry, thick Turkish cotton towels (for which Bursa is famous), and silk goods. ✉ *Between Atatürk and Cumhuriyet Cad. behind Ulu Cami.* 🕐 *Apr.–Oct., daily 9 AM–8 PM; Nov.–Mar., daily 9 AM–7 PM. Closed Sun.*

The striking **Ulu Cami** (Grand Mosque) dates from 1396. Sultan Beyazıt had it built after vowing to build 20 mosques if he was victorious in the battle of Nicopolis in Macedonia; this one mosque with 20 domes was something of a compromise. Its interior is decorated with an elegantly understated display of quotations from the Koran in fine Islamic calligraphy. The fountain, with taps on the sides for ritual washing before prayer, is inside the mosque—an unusual feature. More usual is the fact that the women's section in this huge mosque is rather small and currently also used for other things like dumping construction materials. The sight of several women praying among the men in the main part, rather than in their own designated and inadequate area, is refreshing.
■ TIP➔ **Ulu Cami draws huge crowds during prayer times, which you'll probably want to avoid.** ✉ *On Atatürk Cad. across from Maksem Cad.*

The **Sultan Murat II Cami** (Sultan Murat II Mosque) and surrounding complex around the pleasant little park in Bursa's Muradiye neighborhood were built in 1425–26, during the reign of Mehmet the Conqueror, in honor of Murat, Mehmet's father. The mosque is unexceptional, perhaps because Mehmet's attentions were so firmly focused on Constantinople, which he would soon win. On the right side of the mosque across the street is the kitchen house—once built to give free food to poor people—now the restaurant Darüzziyafe. It was built without windows by Sultan Murad II, so as not to let the poor be embarrassed by being seen from outside. On Tuesdays there is a street market between the mosque and kitchen house.

> **BURSA ORIENTATION**
>
> Bursa is a large city, stretching out along an east–west axis. The town square, at the intersection of Atatürk Caddesi and İnönü Caddesi, is officially called Cumhuriyet Alanı (Republic Square), but is popularly called **Heykel** (Statue), after its imposing equestrian statue of Atatürk. East of Heykel is the Yeşil neighborhood, with Yeşil Cami and Yeşil Türbe.

★ **Muradiye Tombs.** Next to the Sultan Murat mosque, in what is probably the city's most serene resting place, is a fountain ringed by 12 tombs. Among those buried here are Murat himself, Mehmet, and Mustafa, the eldest son of Süleyman the Magnificent, who was strangled in his father's tent. The plainest tomb belongs to Sultan Murad II and was built in accordance with his will, with an open hole in the roof right above the tomb to let the rain in. The most decorated tombs are Celebi Mehmet's and Cem Sultan's (the youngest son of Mehmet the Conquerer), which are kept locked most of the time—ask the caretaker to open them for you. ⊠ *Kaplıca Cad., Osmangazi* ☎ *224/222–0868* ⌂ *Free* ⊙ *Tombs open daily 8—noon and 1 PM-5 PM; mosque open dawn to dusk.*

★ The **Uluumay Müzesi** (Uluumay Ethnography Museum), on the park, opposite the mosque and the tombs, has a fine, though small, collection of Ottoman prêt-a-porter and haute couture costumes along with gorgeous silver jewelry. The building is another *medrese,* built in 1475 by Şair Ahmet Pasha, whose tomb is in its garden. The models displaying the costumes revolve to allow a thorough study. The costumes are full of colorful embroidery and are in very good condition even though some date back to the 15th century. They were worn only on special occasions and preserved meticulously. On the grounds of the museum is a tea house opposite the tomb in the garden, overlooking the city. ⊠ *II. Murad Cad.* ☎ *224/225–4813* ⌂ *$1* ⊙ *May—Oct., Tues.–Sun. 8:30— 8, Mon. 1:30–8; Nov.–Apr. closes one hour earlier.*

Dominating the view on Çekirge Caddesi is the refreshingly green **Kültür Parkı** (Culture Park), with restaurants, tea gardens, a pond with paddleboats, a sports stadium, and a Ferris wheel. This is also where Bursa's **Arkeoloji Müzesi** (Archaeology Museum) is found: It's pleasant enough, with Roman coins and other artifacts, but there are better ones in Is-

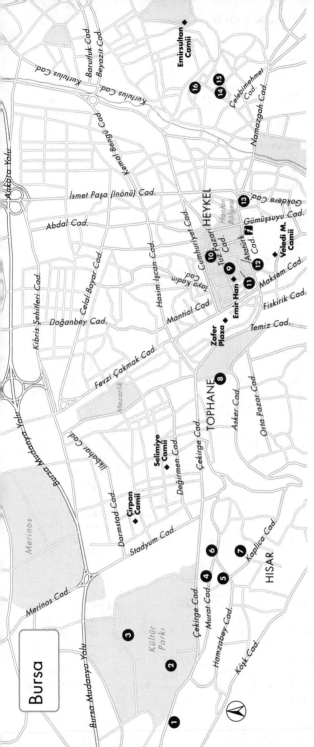

Bursa

Emirsultan Camii

Çelebimehmet Cad.

Namazgah Cad.

Kurtuluş Cad.

Baruthk Cad.

Beyazıt Cad.

Kurtuluş Cad.

Kemal Bengü Cad.

İsmet Paşa (İnönü) Cad.

Abdal Cad.

HEYKEL

Haslar Bölgesi

Gökdere Cad.

Gümüşsuyu Cad.

Cumhuriyet Cad.

Tuz Pazarı Cad.

Atatürk Cad.

Veledi M. Camii

Maksem Cad.

Taya Kadın Cad.

Hasım İşcan Cad.

Ankara Yolu

Kıbrıs Şehitleri Cad.

Celal Bayar Cad.

Doğanbey Cad.

Mantiol Cad.

Emir Han

Fiskirik Cad.

Zafer Plaza

Temiz Cad.

Fevzi Çakmak Cad.

Mezarlik

Çekirge Cad.

TOPHANE

Asker Cad.

Orta Pazar Cad.

Bursa-Mudanya Yolu

İlkbahar Cad.

Darmstad Cad.

Selimiye Camii

Değirmen Cad.

Merinos

Çirpan Camii

Stadyum Cad.

Merinos Cad.

Kültür Parkı

Çekirge Cad.

Murat Cad.

Hamzabey Cad.

HISAR

Kaplıca Cad.

Köşk Cad.

Bursa-Mudanya Yolu

Archaelogy Museum ..**2**
Atatürk Museum **1**
Bursa City Museum ..**13**
Emir Sultan Cami **9**
Kapalı Çarşı (covered bazaar) **10**
Kültür Parkı **3**
Muradiye Tombs **6**

Orhan Gazi Cami ..**12**
Osman Evi **5**
Sultan Murat II Cami ..**7**
Tombs of Osman and Orhan **8**
Turkish Islamic Arts Museum **14**
Ulu Cami **11**

Uluumay Ethnography Museum **4**
Yeşil Cami **16**
Yeşil Türbe **15**

tanbul, Ankara, and elsewhere. The same goes for the nearby **Atatürk Müzesi** (Atatürk Museum), with old-fashioned furniture and a few exhibits on the great leader's life. ⊠ *Kültür Parkı: Çekirge Cad. and Stadyum Cad.* 🕾 *Archaeology Museum 224/234–4918, Atatürk Museum 224/234–7716* 💷 *$2; free for Atatürk museum* ☉ *Archaeology Museum: Tues.–Sun. 8:30–12:30 and 1:30—5; Atatürk museum: Tues-Sat 8-noon and 1-5.*

Rural Ottoman architecture has hardly survived in Turkey, but Bursa has one beautiful example, only 16 km (10 mi) out of town. The village of **Cumalıkızık,** with its well-preserved and colorfully painted houses, narrow cobbled streets, and surrounding green fields, is well worth a visit.

Where to Stay & Eat

★ **$–$$** ✕ **Arap Şükrü Yılmaz.** Food is often a family business in Bursa: it's said that an Arab named Şükrü once opened a fish restaurant on Sakarya Caddesi between the center and Çekirge; now the whole area carries his name, and his sons have filled the street with similarly named restaurants, adding their own names to their father's—in this case Yılmaz. The street is a lively destination with tables outside and wandering musicians serenading diners. ⊠ *Sakarya Cad, 4, Arap Şükrü* 🕾 *224/221–9239 or 224/222–1995* 🚭 *MC, V.*

$ ✕ **Cumurcul.** In the Çekirge section of town, opposite the Çelik Palas Hotel, this old house converted into a restaurant is a local favorite, serving attentatively prepared grilled meats and fish. In addition to the usual cold mezes are hot starters, including the tasty *avcı böreği* (hunter's pie), a deep-fried or oven-baked pastry filled with meat or cheese. Main dishes include international favorites such as filet mignon and chicken Kiev. The upstairs dining room and terrace overlook Kültür Park and the city. ⊠ *Çekirge Cad. 18* 🕾 *224/235 3707* ☉ *No lunch* 🍽 *Reservations essential on weekends* 🚭 *AE, MC, V.*

★ **$** ✕ **Darüzziyafe.** The kitchen house built by Sultan Murad II in the 15th century to help feed the poor is now a restaurant employing old Ottoman recipes as well as Turkish ones. It's no longer a charity, but prices are reasonable. *Hünkar beğendi* (tender beef on grilled eggplant mash with bechamel sauce) literally means "the Sultan liked it," and it's hard not to. The place is also known for its köfte, made with lamb, beef, chicken, and pistachios, and for its Ottoman desserts. The terrace is pleasant, but dine indoors and you'll feel like you're eating in the sultan's quarters. No alcohol is served here. ⊠ *Muradiye Complex II, Murad Cad., 36, Muradiye* 🕾 *224/224–6439* 🍽 *Reservations essential* 🚭 *MC, V.*

$ ✕ **Hacı Bey.** Arguments never end over where to find the best İskender kebap, but this downtown stop is always a contender. The setting is basic cafeteria style, but it's the food that matters. If you want a change from the regular İskender, ask for your kebab to be served with grilled eggplant mash. Just opposite there is another restaurant run by one of the inventor's grandsons, which makes equally good İskender. ⊠ *Ünlü Cad., Yılmaz İş Han 4C* 🕾 *224/221–6440* 🚭 *DC, MC, V.*

★ **$** ✕ **Kebapçı İskender (oğlu Cevat).** This tiny, central restaurant, with lines outside on the pavement most days, is run by a grandson of the inventor of İskender kebap, Mehmet İskenderoğlu—pictured on the wall opposite Atatürk. As is common in the food business in Bursa, more family members opened similar restaurants with similar names all over town, but this one is among the best. ✉ *Atatürk Cad., 60, Heykel* ☎ *224/221–1076* 💳 *MC, V*

★ ¢–$ ✕ **Ömür Köftecisi.** Köfte is the thing to order here, served with grilled peppers and tomatoes; among the salad options, *piyaz* (bean salad with vinegar) accompanies köfte best. In the mornings, the soup is delicious, too. The location is charming, in the covered market by the Ulu Cami—the restaurant has the same architectural features as the hans, with brick and stone walls, and two domes in the ceilings painted in floral patterns. ✉ *Ulu Cami Cad. 7* ☎ *224/ 221 4524* 💳 *MC, V.*

$$$$ FodorśChoice ★ **Çelik Palas.** There are newer, more stylish hotels than the Celik Palas in Bursa, but this one maintains a certain grandeur. The marbled lobby and rooms are old-fashioned but loyally maintained, and the formal service reflects the hotel's pride in its heritage. The Roman-style pool fed by hot springs is a treat—the thermal waters of the Çekirge region were diverted 4 km—and you'll find your fellow guests traipsing through the hallways in their robes, though you can also take the waters in your room. Ask for a room in the historic part overlooking the city; they'll probably oblige, even though it's not supposed to be used unless the newer part is full. ✉ *Çekirge Cad. 79* ☎ *224/233–3800* 📠 *224/236–1910* 🌐 *www.celikpalasotel.com* *156 rooms* *Restaurant, bar, hamam, spa, sauna, fitness equipment, massage, meeting rooms, ball rooms, business room, minibars, Wi-Fi, safe* 💳 *AE, MC, V* 🍽 *BP.*

$$$ FodorśChoice ★ **Hotel Gonluferah.** Ottoman-style decoration is the general rule in most Bursa hotels and this one, recently refurbished, is a good mix of Ottoman and modern: flat-screen TVs and state-of-the-art pressured showers fit in well with the traditional style high beds, velvet curtains and ornamental hanging lamps. The hotel claims to have the city's best baths in terms of water quality and decoration, and they're certainly quite nice, though not included in the room price. The rooftop rooms overlooking the city aren't renovated but are more spacious; the low ceilings and plain wood furniture may remind you of a mountain resort. ✉ *1. Murad Cad. 24, Çekirge, 16090* ☎ *224/233–9210* 📠 *224/233–9218* 🌐 *www.gonluferahhotel.com* *Restaurant, Turkish bath, sauna, massage, Wi-Fi,minibars, safe* 💳 *MC, V* 🍽 *BP.*

$$ **Otel Safran.** The best thing about this hotel is its location: within walking distance of the center and most sights, but on a quiet hilltop outside the bustle of the city center. The street is opposite the tombs of Sultans Osman and Orhan. Rooms are comfortable and decorated partly in line with the Ottoman character; ask for one of the more spacious ones on the upper floors, which also get more light. A restaurant next door with the same name serves Turkish cuisine. ✉ *Ortapazar Cad., Arka Sok., 4, Tophane* ☎ *224/224–7216* 📠 *224/224–7219* *10 rooms* *Restaurant, minibars,* 💳 *MC, V* 🍽 *BP.*

$–$$ **Hotel Dikmen.** Although less grand than the Çekirge-area hotels, the Dikmen (not to be confused with the Dilmen) is conveniently located downtown opposite the Ulu Cami. It has large, plain rooms, a spacious lobby, and a sunny garden with a marble fountain. The rooms and the lobby, where breakfast is served, could use a polish, but it remains a

popular choice. ⊠ *Maksem Cad. 78* ☎ *224/224–1840* 🖷 *224/224–4085*
⊕ *www.hoteldikmen.com* ⇥ *60 rooms* ⚭ *Restaurant, bar, Wi-Fi, mini-bars* ⯃⏘ *BP* ▤ *MC, V.*

$ ⊡ **Atlas Hotel.** Çekirge is Bursa's posh district, but there are some nice hotels where you can take advantage of the spring baths at reasonable prices. This is one of the most inviting with its wood-covered exterior, a small courtyard inside, and cheerful staff. Rooms are basic but have all modern comforts. There are two thermal baths in the hotel, but the rooms do not get thermal waters. ⊠ *Hamamlar Cad., 29, Çekirge* ☎ *224/234–4100* 🖷 *224/236–4605* ⊕ *www.atlashotel.com.tr* ⇥ *40 rooms* ⚭ *Minibars, cable Internet* ⯃⏘ *BP* ▤ *A, DC, MC, V.*

Nightlife

The liveliest time for nightlife around Bursa is winter, and the best place for it is out of town in Uludağ. Istanbul's elite fill the hotels of this ski resort on weekends and on longer holidays. There is popular Turkish and Western music, and lots of dancing.

Bursa itself either imitates the Uludağ nightlife scene or sticks to its Ottoman traditions with Turkish *fasıl*—the latter is traditional Turkish music, which can be found in restaurants such as Cumurcul or Darüzziyafe during weekend dinners or at the **Turistik Fasıl Bar** on Yeşil Caddesi on the way to Yeşil Cami. For nightclubs, try one of the places at the Kültür Park such as **Altın Ceylan** or a place called simply **224. Vici,** 7 km out of town on the way to Mudanya, or **Jaz Bar** on the way to Uludağ are other clubbing options; both are livelier in winter. Near the center, on Sakarya Caddesi (aka Arap Şükrü), past the restaurants is **Café M,** which calls itself a pub; it doesn't look much like one, but its shiny lounge and large terrace are among the nicer places to have a few drinks, if you're not averse to Turkish pop music.

Shopping

In Bursa the **Kapalı Çarşı** (covered bazaar), behind the Ulu Cami, is where the action is from 8:30 to 6:00, Monday through Saturday. As is traditional, each section is dominated by a particular trade: jewelers, silk weavers, antiques dealers. The Koza Han (Cocoon Caravanserai) section behind the Orhan Gazi Mosque by the east entrance is the center of the silk trade. It has a lovely courtyard with a tiny mosque and a 150-year-old linden tree under which you can sip your tea. The Emir Han, behind the Ulu Cami, in the southwest section, is an interesting combination of jewelers and a religious books market and also has a fountain and a courtyard tea garden. Antiques can be

SHOPPING IN BURSA

Bursa has been a center of the silk industry since the coming of the Ottoman sultans and remains a good place to buy silk scarves, raw-silk fabric by the yard, and other silk products. The price of a silk scarf varies between $3 and $60. The same goes for the famed cotton towels, depending on their thickness and density. Bathrobes are a favorite souvenir, as they're higher-quality and cheaper than those found elsewhere in the country, but they might be a bit bulky to carry overseas.

found in the small Eski Aynalı Çarşı section of the bazaar, between Koza Han and Emir Han.

Bursa also has many modern shops. The pyramid-shaped glass mall Zafer Plaza at the east end of the Atatürk Caddesi houses many international brands, and instead of the tea gardens of the old bazaars you'll find a large Starbucks. The food court on the top floor offers choices of American and Turkish fast food. A branch of one of the city's famous İskender restaurants can be found here as well as Burger King and McDonald's.

OFF THE BEATEN PATH

KUŞCENNETI NATIONAL PARK – If you're heading on from Bursa to Çanakkale and the Aegean coast, consider stopping at Kuşcenneti (Bird Paradise) National Park, beside Lake Kuş. There are benches and tables for picnics, a viewing tower for bird-watching, and a small information center with exhibits describing the more than 200 species of birds that visit the park. ⊠ *Take Rte. 200 west about 100 km (62 mi) from Bursa; signs for the park appear before the city of Bandırma.*

Uludağ

➌ *33 km (20 mi) southeast of Bursa.*

Bursa is the jumping-off point for excursions to Uludağ (8,300 ft high), where you will find lush **Uludağ Ulusal Parkı** (Uludağ National Park) and Turkey's most popular ski resort.

To fully appreciate why Bursa is called Green Bursa, take the 30-minute ride up the **teleferik** (cable car) in Bursa to Uludağ's Sarıalan point (5,350 ft) for a panoramic view. This terminus is lively in summer: there are restaurants and picnic areas. In winter, however, the cable car terminus is only a staging point for the hotel area, which is 7 kilometers farther up. In spring or fall, there isn't much activity here, especially when the mist is over the mountain—the cable car runs anyway as the ride itself can be fun. ■ TIP→ **Take a sweater or jacket with you, as temperatures fall dramatically as you climb, even when it's warm downtown.** There are also various walking paths up the mountain from Bursa to Uludağ and Uludağ to Bursa; the hike takes about three hours each way. From Uludağ's hotel area you can reach undeveloped spots for blissfully cool hikes in summer.

Uludağ gets most of its attention for its skiing and, lately, snowboarding. There are 30 intermediate and beginner routes, with five chairlifts, and seven T-bars. The season lasts from November until April, though the best conditions are between mid-December and March. The resort is packed on weekends, school holidays, and religious festivals, when prices increase dramatically.

Where to Stay and Eat

There are 25 hotels in Uludağ. All offer full board and all the modern comforts, and most provide a range of activities and entertainment. Nightlife is becoming almost as important a reason as skiing for the Istanbul elite to go to Uludağ; the more modest hotels do not offer as many amenities but are more likely to attract enthusiastic skiers as opposed to nightclubbers. Akfen Club Hotel, for example, has always been among the favorites. Skiing is a rich man's sport in Turkey, as in the rest of the world, so even the more modest hotels can't really be called budget. Normal winter prices range from $70–$210 for a double room. For information and reservations for all the hotels in the resort, visit ⊕ www.uludaghotels.com or contact **Icem Tourism Travel Agency** (☎ 212/ 516–7553 or 212/638—1986 ⊕ www.icemtour.com/uludag_hotels).

THE DARDANELLES

Dardanelles is the name of the straits that separates Europe from Asia and that connect the Aegean Sea to the Marmara. Controlling these straits meant having substantial commercial and military power, hence its strategic importance. The first historical war took place in the 13th century BC between the Achaeans and Trojans, and the latest was the attack by Anzac (Australian and New Zealand Army Corps), British, and French troops on Gallipoli during the First World War.

There are several places to base yourself for exploring the area; wherever you are, it's best to arrange a guided tour to visit the battlefields, which are spread along a 35-km (58-mi) stretch of the Gallipoli Peninsula. Çanakkale, on the south side of the straits, is convenient; most tourists stay here rather than in Eceabat on the European side of the Dardanelles, even though the latter is actually closer to the battlefields. Çanakkale is livelier, has more options for accommodation and dining, and this is where most of the guided tours start. Ferries making the 25-minute crossing from Çanakkale to Eceabat run every hour until midnight in both directions.

You can visit the region in all times of the year if you're there purely for sightseeing. Spring may be the best time, though, when it's cool enough to walk around the sights, and when the area is at its most colorful, with wildflowers dotting the cemeteries and hillsides. Turks commemorate the war on March 18, and British, Australians, and New Zealanders on April 25. The second, in particular, brings many travelers to the region, and offers the visitor the chance to take part in the emotional memorial services; but this is, of course, when reservations for hotels and guided tours are essential well in advance.

Çanakkale

❹ *320 km (200 mi) southwest of Istanbul; 303 km (186 mi) from Bursa.*

West of Bursa, on the southern shore of the Dardanelles, Çanakkale is the largest city of the north Aegean coast. The city itself doesn't have much to offer, other than a decent selection of hotels and bars, but it's a good base for visiting the memorials and battlefields of Gallipolli, a half-hour's ferry journey across the straits.

The heart of Çanakkale is in the docks area, and you really don't need to go inland. An Ottoman clock tower is located between the two halves of the dock. Head toward the sea from this tower and you'll find the

CLOSE UP

War & Peace

THE DARDANELLES HAVE provided the world with many myths and heroes, romances and tragedies. The most recent, and the main reason the region draws visitors today, was the Gallipoli campaign in the First World War. In this offensive, Britain (with soldiers from Australia and New Zealand, then still British colonies) and France tried to breach Çanakkale's defenses in a campaign devised by the young Winston Churchill, at the time lord of the Admiralty. The goal was to capture Istanbul, control the entire waterway from the Aegean to the Black Sea, open up a supply channel to Russia, and pave the way for an attack on Germany from the south. After nine months of bloody fighting that left more than 50,000 Allied and perhaps twice as many Turks dead, the Allies admitted defeat and evacuated, beaten by the superior strategy of Lieutenant-Colonel Mustafa Kemal—the man who would later be called Atatürk.

Churchill lost his job as a result of the failure in the Dardanelles, and his career suffered until the next world war, two decades later. Mustafa Kemal, on the other hand, became a national hero. He had been an insignificant lieutenant, unpopular among the ruling Committee of Union and Progress, but the fame he earned in this war helped him start and lead the war of independence against the occupying Allies. Soon his enemies were overthrown, and so were the Ottoman sultanate and caliphate. A few years after the Gallipoli campaign, the modern, secular republic of Turkey emerged with Atatürk as president.

For the Australians and New Zealanders, World War I was the first real experience of war overseas, and the shocking losses they sustained left an indelible mark. For the Turks, it was an unexpected defensive victory. It was a war of pride, but also one that left behind many stories of kindness between soldiers on opposing sides. The Anzacs and the Turks came from opposite ends of the earth: there was no history of hostility, or even familiarity between them, until they were told to kill one another, but in some ways the war marked the start of a friendship: Thousands of Anzac pilgrims come to visit the battlefields every year. Atatürk's famous speech, which still moves visitors, engraved on a Turkish monument in Anzac Cove, seemed to foresee this.

"Those heroes that shed their blood and lost their lives! You are now lying in the soil of a friendly country, therefore rest in peace. There is no difference between the Johnnies and the Mehmets to us, where they lie side by side here in this country of ours. You, the mothers who sent their sons from far-away countries, wipe away your tears. Your sons are now lying in our bosom, and are at peace. After having lost their lives on this land, they have become our sons as well."

ferry that departs for historic Gallipoli. Hotels and restaurants are spread on either side of the docks, along the sea front. Most of the budget hotels, cheap dining options, and bars are in the streets behind the seafront to the left of the tower if you're facing the sea.

If you're in Çanakkale, check out the city's **fortress,** which includes the **Askeri Ve Deniz Müzesi** (aka Army and Navy Museum, 286/213–2641). The impressive structure was built in the 15th century under the aegis of Mehmet the Conqueror. Inside the high walls all kinds of weaponry are on display, including dozens of cannons, ancient and modern. The real reason to come here, though, is for the sweeping view of the mouth of the Dardanelles and the Aegean. The fortress grounds are good for a nice stroll among the lawns and gardens. ⊠ *On the waterfront, 3 blocks south of ferry dock* ☎ *286/213—1730* ☯ *Museum: 9–noon and 1:30– 5, except Mon. and Thurs.; fortress grounds daily 9* AM*–10* PM *May–Sept.; daily 9–5 Oct–Apr.* ▨ *2 $.*

Where to Stay & Eat

★ **$$** ✕ **Yalova Liman.** The menu at this waterfront restaurant includes appetizers and grilled fish or meat. Ask the chef which fish is in season and order it grilled or fried. The seafood mezes are all mouthwatering; the grilled octopus in vinegar and the sardines wrapped in vine leaves are especially recommended. One of the perks of eating here is the evocative setting: the photographs of old Çanakkale on the walls and the views across the Dardanelles. ⊠ *Yalı Cad., Gümrük Sok. 7* ☎ *286/217–1045* ▤ *MC, V.*

$–$$ ✕ **Maydos Restaurant.** A few minutes' walk from the ferry port, the Maydos—part of the hotel with the same name—offers more variety than most other Turkish fish restaurants. The menu isn't quite international, but it does include pasta and steak. Ask for a table outside on the terrace, which has fine views across the Dardanelles. There's another branch across the strait in Eceabat, also on the seafront. ⊠ *Yali Cad. 12* ☎ *286/213–5970* ⊕ *www.maydos.com.tr* ▤ *MC, V.*

¢ ✕ **Doyum Pide Kebap Salonu.** If you like *pide* (Turkish pizza) or kebabs, try this casual eatery on the right side of the main street going into town from the ferry dock, past the clock tower. The *pides* are delicious, with mincemeat, cheese, or cubes of lamb as toppings. Try the mixed *pide* if you want to sample them all. Doyum is popular with locals and tourists, though it's better for a quick meal than an extended evening out. ⊠ *Cumhuriyet Meydanı, 13* ☎ *286/217–1866* ▤ *MC, V.*

$$ ▥ **Akol.** If you ask locals to recommend a hotel, most will point you toward the Akol—not because it's spectacular, or even one of the city's best, but because it's the longest-established hotel in town, and inspires the confidence that it knows its business. A modern hotel on the Çanakkale waterfront, it has a bright lobby full of cool white marble and brass fixtures. Rooms are spacious and bright, with light-colored carpets and white furniture. Ask for a room overlooking the Dardanelles; you'll be able to see the war memorials in the distance. ⊠ *Kordonboyu, 17100* ☎ *286/217–9456* ▤ *286/217–2897* ⊕ *www. hotelakol.com.tr* ↩ *138 rooms* ↺ *Restaurant, bar, pool, bar, disco, parking, Wi-Fi, minibars* ▤ *MC, V.*

$–$$ ⌂ **Maydos Hotel.** This is the more upmarket of the Hassle-Free Travel Agency's two hotels. Near the clock tower, it's been thoroughly renovated from a rundown hotel to a glittering modern block without much character. Rooms are shiny and new, though the size and amount of light they get vary dramatically (and so do their prices). Request a room overlooking the water if you want one of the better ones. ⊠ *Yalı Cad. 12, 17100* ☎ *286/213–5970* 📠 *286/217–4090* ⊕ *www.maydos.com.tr/otel* 🛏 *35 rooms* ⌂ *Restaurant, bar, Wi-Fi, broadband, minibars* ▭ *MC, V.*

★ **$**   ⌂ **Kervansaray Hotel.** An old Ottoman house built in 1903 to house the Chief Justice of Çanakkale, the two-story Kervansaray, with its redbrick walls, large bay window, and whitewashed frames and columns, looks very attractive amid the concrete jungle of Çanakkale. In back is a nice courtyard with flowers and a small fountain. The rooms are small but elegantly furnished. On the whole, it's very good value. Eight of the rooms are in the newly built section across the courtyard, but ask for one in the main building, where the original character is more apparent. ⊠*Kemalpaşa mahallesi, Fetvane Sokak, (near the clock tower) 13* ☎ *286/217—9022 or 286/217-8192* 📠 *286/212–9038* ⊕ *www.hotelkervansaray.org* 🛏 *20 rooms* ⌂ *Satellite TV, telephone, Wi-Fi, minibars* ▭ *MC, V* ⓄⓁ *BP.*

¢   ⌂ **Anzac House.** This hostel, near the clock tower, is the Hassle-Free Travel Agency's budget option, and lures many backpackers. There are rooms for 1, 2, 4, 6, or 15 people. As you'd expect from a hostel, the rooms have nothing but beds and small bedside tables, but they're clean, and fans are provided on request. There is Internet in the lobby, and breakfast is available for an extra cost. ⊠ *Cumhuriyet Meydanı, 61, 17100 Çanakkale* ☎ *286/213–5969* 📠 *286/217-2906* ⊕ *www.anzachouse.com* 🛏 *15 rooms* ▭ *A, MC, V.*

Nightlife

Çanakkale doesn't have the liveliest nightlife, but it's the most exciting place in the area. Fetvane Sokak, on the left of the clock tower if you're facing the sea, is the main bar street: you can choose from spacious open-air bars dominated by pop music, or small, dark dives. **Depo** has dancing and a large courtyard with huge cushions and low tables. The historic han at the end of the street called **Tarihi Yalı Hanı** has several bars: you can eat and drink in the ground-floor courtyard and listen to gypsy music on Thursday nights and live rock on Fridays and Saturdays. In winter there's live music every day. On the waterfront is **Lodos,** similar to Depo in terms of music and crowd but with a nicer location.

Gallipoli

★ ❺   The Gallipoli Peninsula lies to the north of the Dardanelles. Turks call it Gelibolu—not to be confused with the town of the same name 40 km (25 mi) east. Thirty-one beautifully tended military cemeteries of the Allied dead from World War I line the Gallipoli battlefields. The major battles were in two main areas—along the coast between Kabatepe and Suvla Bay, and at Cape Helles.

Kabatepe Museum and Information Center is a good place to start your exploration of the area; there's a small but poignant exhibit of photographs of soldiers, their uniforms, weapons, and other findings from the battlefield. There are several cemeteries in this area, all with long, mesmerizing rows of austere white headstones. ✉ *Kabatepe* ☎ *286/862–0082* 🖅 *2$* ☉ *Daily 9–6.*

★

The **Australian Memorial at Lone Pine Cemetery** bears the names of the Australian and New Zealand soldiers with unknown graves killed during the war. Some of the most savage hand-to-hand fighting took place here, and more than 3,000 soldiers died. Seven Victoria crosses, the highest award given by British government for bravery and usually quite sparingly distributed, were awarded after the battle. This is the most affecting of all the Anzac cemeteries, and the epitaphs of the tombstones are very moving.

The name "Lone Pine" comes from a single pine tree which grew on the battlefield. It was destroyed, but the cones were collected and taken to Australia, then sent back to Gallipoli many years later. The lone pine standing there today is the grandson of the original tree.

At the top of the ridge is **Chunk Bair,** which the Allies aimed to occupy because of its strategic location overlooking the peninsula. They failed, and Mustafa Kemal (Atatürk) became a hero. It is here that he told his soldiers, "I order you not just to fight, but to die." All the men of one of his regiments were wiped out, and he himself was saved miraculously when a bullet hit the pocket watch over his heart, but the line held. From this hilltop where there are Turkish trenches, a cemetery, and the New Zealand national memorial, there are good views of the whole peninsula and the strait.

At **Cape Helles,** on the southernmost tip of the peninsula, is a massive, four-pillared memorial to Turkey's war dead. No one knows how many there were; estimates vary from 60,000 to 250,000. When returning on the ferry to Çanakkale, look for the memorials to the campaign carved into the cliffs. The large one at Kilitbahır reads: "Stop, O passerby. This earth you tread unawares is where an age was lost. Bow and listen, for this quiet place is where the heart of a nation throbs."

Where to Stay & Eat

Eceabat, on the Aegean coast, is the closest town to the most-visited battlefields and cemeteries. From where the Eceabat ferry lands on the northern front it's a 20-minute drive east via the single road skirting the coast and then crossing the peninsula.

★ **$–$$** ✕ **Liman Restaurant.** This 35-year-old restaurant is highly respected by locals; there are newer and shinier options on the peninsula but they've failed to tempt the Liman's clientele away. The interior is plain but clean, with white tablecloths and large windows overlooking a small park next to the sea. The fare is fish, meat, and mezes—all are fresh and tasty. ✉ *İsmet Paşa Mahallesi, İstiklal Cad. 67, Eceabat* ☎ *286/814–2755* 🍴 *Reservations essential during anniversaries* 🖃 *MC, V.*

$–$$ 🏨 **Hotel Kum.** On the Aegean coast of the Gallipoli Peninsula, south of the village of Kabatepe, is a beautiful sandy beach, and Hotel Kum is located right in front of it. It's conveniently located for visits to the memorials on both ends of the peninsula. Rooms are plain and functional, but the hotel is surrounded by open space, with the blue sea in front and green land all around. A buffet-style dinner is included, as is breakfast. ✉ *Kapatepe* ☎ *286/814–1455* 📠 *286/814–2665* 🌐 *www.hotelkum.com* 🛏 *72 rooms* 👍 *Swimming pool, volleyball, basketball* 💳 *MC, V* ⏲ *Closed Nov.–Mar.* 🍽 *MAP.*

★ ¢–$ 🏨 **Eceabat Hotel.** From the outside, this is a run-down concrete building, but inside, the rooms are a surprise: Ottoman-style furniture hand-carved from 100-year-old wood—including specially ordered extra-large double beds—and lovely old carpets on the wood-floored corridors. The restoration of the property is ongoing, but not intrusive enough to disrupt your stay. The rooftop bar-restaurant's large windows have good views of the Dardanelles. The Australian-Turkish owners, who also run TJ's Tours, are friendly and helpful and do their best to make your Gallipoli experience special. They run a separate building, in the village itself, as a hostel, but reservations are taken from the same phone number. ✉ *Cumhuriyet Meydanı, near ferry dock, Eceabat* ☎ *286/814–2458* 📠 *286/814–3122* 🌐 *www.anzacgallipolitours.com* 🛏 *24 rooms* 👍 *Satellite TV, broadband* 🍽 *BP* 💳 *MC, V.*

NORTH AEGEAN

The north Aegean offers a different kind of holiday than the south. It's one of the loveliest parts of the Aegean, and in fact of all of Turkey, with unspoiled natural landscapes and activities all year round, from swimming and sea sports to trekking, mountain climbing, and horseback riding. You can soak in hot springs or jump in cool waterfalls in the middle of pine forests, visit sleepy fishing villages, or go on safari to see the region's unique fauna and flora. And it's not a destination for the big agencies which ship tourists in bulk to huge resorts for sun and sea. The towns, or rather villages, are scattered around and so are the sights—they're small, mostly rural, and never totally dedicated to tourism the way they can be in the south. This whole area, so close to Greece, is also where you see what life was like when the area was Greek, while experiencing its rural Turkish present. Ayvalık is the only large town in the region that can't fairly be called unspoiled, but even it has its own rewards.

Troy (Truva)

★ ❻ *32 km (20 mi) south of Çanakkale on Rte. E87.*

The wooden horse that stands outside this magnificent site is a modern addition, there to remind us of Homer's epics, but the city walls, layer upon layer of them, date back several millennia. Troy, known as Truva to the Turks and Ilion to the Greeks, is one of the most evocative place names in literature. Long thought to be a figment of the Greek poet Homer's imagination and depicted in his epic *Iliad*, the site was

WORD OF MOUTH

"Even though there wasn't much in the way of ruins in Troy, I felt the site was very moving. It was so easy to imagine the Greek and Trojan armies in battle there . . . Achilles, Hector, Paris . . . A memorable visit."

–Pegontheroad

Homer's Story

Because the *Iliad* was written 500 years after the war—traditionally believed to have taken place around 1184 BC—it is hard to say how much of it is history and how much is invention. Nonetheless, it makes for a romantic tale: Paris, the son of King Priam, abducted the beautiful Helen, wife of King Menelaus of Sparta, and fled with her to Troy. Menelaus enlisted the aid of his brother, King Agamemnon, and launched a thousand ships to get her back. His siege lasted 10 years and involved such ancient notables as Achilles, Hector, and the crafty Odysseus, king of Ithaca. It was Odysseus who ended the war, after ordering a huge wooden horse to be built and left outside Troy's gates. When it was completed, the Greeks retreated to their ships and pretended to sail away. The Trojans hauled the trophy into their walled city and celebrated their victory. Under cover of darkness, the Greek ships returned, soldiers hidden inside the horse crept out and opened the city's gates, and the attackers at last gained entry to Troy. Hence the saying: "Beware of Greeks bearing gifts."

excavated in the 1870s by Heinrich Schliemann, a German businessman who had struck it rich in California's gold rush. While scholars scoffed, he poured his wealth into the excavations and had the last laugh: He found the remains not only of the fabled Troy but of nine successive civilizations, one on top of the other, dating back 5,000 years (and now known among archaeologists as Troy I–IX). Subsequent excavations during the 1930s revealed 38 additional layers of settlements.

Schliemann found a hoard of jewels that he believed were those of the Trojan War's King Priam, but they have more recently been dated to much earlier. Adding to the controversy that surrounded his discoveries, Schliemann smuggled the jewels out of the country, and his wife was seen wearing them at fashionable social events. Schliemann later donated them to Berlin's Pergamon Museum, but they disappeared during the Red Army's sack of Berlin in World War II. They reappeared in 1993, when Moscow announced that their State Pushkin Museum of Fine Arts housed what they called the lost "Treasure of Priam." Although Germany, Greece, and Turkey have all claimed the treasures, recent custom dictates that archaeological finds belong to the country in which they were originally found. Unfortunately, the treasures have yet to make their way back to Turkey.

What you will see today depends on your imagination. You may find the site highly suggestive, with its remnants of massive, rough-hewn walls, a paved chariot ramp, and strategic views over the coastal plains to the sea. Or you may consider it an unimpressive row of trenches with piles of earth and stone. Considering Troy's fame (and the difficulties involved in conquering it), the city is surprisingly small. The best-preserved features are from the Roman city, with its *bouleuterion* (council chamber), the site's most complete structure, and small theater. A site plan shows the general layout and marks the beginning of a signposted path leading to key features from several historic civilizations. ■ TIP→ **English-speaking guides are often available at the site, but if you don't want to take your chances, arrange a tour in advance from Çanakkale or Istanbul.** ✉ *Follow signs from Rte. E87* 🕾 *no phone* 🎫 *10 YTL, car park: 4YTL* ☉ *Apr.–Oct., daily 8:30–7; Nov.–Mar., daily 8:30–4:30.*

OFF THE BEATEN PATH

If you're heading south from Troy toward Alexandria Troas, you'll pass through Geyikli; there you'll see a signpost for **Bozcaada**, one of the two Aegean islands that belong to Turkey. If you have time, spare a day for this island (though you'll probably then want to spare another) with its unspoiled towns with beautiful old houses, pristine sandy beaches, and lovely country covered with vineyards. The local wine may be the best you'll taste in Turkey without having to spend a fortune. In fact, you can stock up for the rest of your holiday from the island's wineries. There are two very good hotels here. The Rengigül Konukevi (🕾 286/697–8171 ⊕ www.rengigul.com), a small B&B in a Greek-style 19th-century house, is a bit cluttered but has a lot of character. It has a large, lovely garden, and serves delicious breakfasts. Kaikias Hotel (🕾 286/697–0250 ⊕ www.kaikas.com), also a B&B, has elegantly furnished large rooms, a collection of old Greek books and Troy ornaments, and a basement full of wine made by the owners. The ferries (🕾 286/632–0263) run six or seven times a day in summer but only twice daily in winter.

Alexandria Troas

❼ *32 km (20 mi) from Troy off Rte. E87; 10 km (6 mi) south of Geyikli.*

Alexandria Troas was built at the behest of Alexander the Great in approximately 330 BC. It became a wealthy commercial center and the region's main port. The city, called at one point Antigonia, surpassed Troy in its control over the traffic between the Aegean and the Sea of Marmara and was even considered a capital under the Roman and Byzantine empires. The seaside location that won it prosperity also invited plundering by raiders, however, and this led to its demise. St. Paul visited twice on missionary journeys in the middle of the 1st century AD, proceeding by land to Assos at the end of the second trip. In the 16th and 17th centuries, when the city was called Eski Stamboul (Old Istanbul), Ottoman architects had stones hauled from here to Istanbul for use in the building of imperial mosques, the Blue Mosque in particular. Visit today not so much for seeing the scanty remnants of the city's monumental baths and its aqueduct but for the setting: Alexandria Troas is tucked away in a deserted stretch of wilderness that you might very well have all to yourself. The ruins are in the middle of an olive grove, though much of the site itself was damaged by a fire in the summer of 2006, which blackened the stones. Some argue that it was started by villagers to create more space for planting trees.

The ruins are near the village of Dalyan, which can be reached by bus from Çanakkale or minibus from Ezine. The track leading to the ruins is quite bumpy. You can drive most of the way, but leaving your car at the beginning might be best; from the start of the path it's a 15-minute walk.

The Apollo Smintheon

❽ *20 km (12 mi) south of Alexandria Troas via the coast road.*

The Apollo Smintheon is, as the name suggests, a temple dedicated to the god Apollo. It dates from the 2nd century BC. Smintheus—one of the sun god's many names, meaning "killer of mice"—alludes to a problem that Teucer, the town's founder, had with mice eating his soldiers' bowstrings. The temple has no great historical importance, but it does have some interesting carved pillars and is surrounded by wild pomegranate trees. If you arrive before sunset, watching the sun go down behind the three marble columns makes it well worth the trip here. ☾ 8–5 ▨ 5 YTL.

Apollo Smintheon is down the hill from the center of Gülpınar, which can be reached by bus from Çanakkale or by minibus from Ezine.

Babakale

❾ *10 km (6 mi) from the Apollo Smintheon on the coast road, south from Gülpınar.*

Babakale is a small, sleepy fishing village at the southern tip of the Çanakkale Peninsula. It was originally a pirate's lair, and was discovered by Sultan Ahmet III on one of his sea voyages in the 18th century. According to the legend, the villagers complained to the sultan about pirates who were stealing their herds, destroying their crops, and disturbing their peace. The sultan ordered a fortress to be built to keep the pirates out and offered to free all prisoners who helped to build it. Working flat out for three years, the prisoners completed the castle, along with a mosque, hamam, and fountain. It was named "Babakale," or Baba Castle. As for the public fountain, the legend is that they had to build pipelines to carry the water for 5 kilometers. The sultan brought immigrants from Kazakhstan and the Aegean to live in the region; they knew little about fishing, and many died in the course of learning. The tradition of throwing bread into the sea in the wake of the fishing boats is a survival from those years, when so many were killed earning their daily bread. Today, Babakale is wonderfully peaceful and spacious, contrasting dramatically with its turbulent past. Four kilometers (2½ mi) before Babakale village, after a right turn toward Akliman, are a long sandy beach and a café up the hill overlooking the pine trees and the beach.

Behramkale (Assos)

★ *20 km (12 mi) southeast of Gülpınar on coast road; 60 km (36 mi) south of Troy; 40 km (24 mi) to Ayvacık on E87 toward south; 20 km (12 mi) toward southwest to Behramkale on coast road.*

The lofty ruins of Behramkale, known in ancient times as Assos, provide a panoramic view over the Aegean. As you approach, the road forks, one route leading to the ancient, pretty village atop the hill and the other twisting precariously down to the tiny, charming harbor. There's no particularly logical reason, but nowadays the name "Behramkale" is used for the village at the top and "Assos" for the port area.

2

The port is a marvel, pressed against the sheer cliff walls. It's crammed with small hotels that were built of volcanic rock and seem much older than they really are, a fleet of fishing boats, and a small rocky beach at each end. Behramkale village is home to the ruins of Assos, the Acropolis. It has blossomed in recent years and now surpasses the port of Assos in terms of prices—and perhaps in charm as well.

Outside June, July, August, and weekends the rest of the year, the area is less crowded and prices are likely to come down a bit, especially in the port. There are constant minibus services between the port and the village, a five-minute ride. For more spacious and sandier beaches try Kadırga, on the way to Küçükkuyu. The same minibuses will take you there in 15 minutes.

Buses from Çanakkale in the north and Ayvalık or İzmir in the south stop at Ayvacık, which is the closest (19 km) town to Behramkale. From there, minibuses to Behramkale run every hour. Make sure you get one that also goes down to the port, if that's your final destination.

The **Acropolis** lies at the top of a hill, on a site measuring about five square city blocks. Founded about 1000 BC by Aeolian Greeks, the city was successively ruled by Lydians, Persians, Pergamenes, Romans, and Byzantines, until Sultan Orhan Gazi (1288–1360) took it over for the Ottomans in 1330. Aristotle is said to have spent time here in the 4th century BC, and St. Paul stopped en route to Miletus, where he visited church elders in about AD 55. The carpet and trinket sellers along both sides of the road will show you the way from the village. You're best off leaving your car on one of the wider streets and making your way up the steep, cobbled lanes to the top of the Acropolis, where you will be rewarded with a sensational view of the coastline and, in the distance, the Greek island of Lesbos, whose citizens were Assos's original settlers.

At the Acropolis are a gymnasium, theater, *agora* (marketplace), and carved into the hillside below the summit of the Acropolis, the site of the **Temple of Athena** (circa 530 BC), which has splendid sea views and is being restored. A more modern addition to the ruins, right before the entrance is the **Murad Hüdavendigâr Cami,** a mosque built in the late 14th century. The mosque is very simple—a dome atop a square, with little decoration. The Greek crosses carved into the lintel over the door indicate the Ottomans used building material from an earlier church, possibly one on the same site. Back down the slope, on the road to the port, are a parking area for the **necropolis** and city walls stretching 3 km (2 mi). Assos was known for its sarcophagi, made of local limestone, which were shipped throughout the Greek world. Unfortunately, most tombs here are in pieces. ☉ *8–8; closes at 5* PM *in winter* 🖃 *5 YTL.*

Where to Stay & Eat

Most hotels in Assos port include breakfast and dinner, though some will agree on deals for breakfast only. The fish restaurants are not cheap, but the fish will be fresh, the mezes are tasty, and it's all in a beautiful setting.

★ **$–$$** ✕ **Biber Evi.** The small restaurant in the hotel with the same name offers local specialties, international favorites, or fusions like eggplant with tahini sauce, or avocado with chile sauce. The 10 tables are in the hotel courtyard and terrace. The open carafe wine is fine, but there are better (and more expensive) foreign selections. Note that although everything is pretty expensive, the truly shocking surprise is the price of a cup of filter coffee: about $5! Reservations are recommended. ⊠ *Behramkale Village center* ☎ *286/721–7410 or 286/721–7001* 🖷 *286/721–7242* ⊕ *www.biberevi.com* 🖩 *AE, DC, MC, V.*

¢–$ ✕ **Kale Restaurant.** Just a few minutes' walk from the Acropolis, this casual eatery is a welcome stop on the way back from a visit to the ruins, especially on a hot day. The homemade, salted *ayran* (a milky yogurt drink) is thirst-quenching and a great restorative. Try their stuffed vine leaves, or the *gözleme,* thin Turkish pastry filled with minced meat, mashed potato, or cheese and cooked on a Turkish wok. It's open for lunch and dinner. ⊠ *Acropolis road, Behramkale* ☎ *286/721–7439* 🖩 *No credit cards.*

$$ ▦ **Assos Hotel Deluxe.** The harbor's newest hotel was built in 2004 by the Assos Group, and this is the group's deluxe venue: the rooms are elegantly decorated, and there are modern amenities like Jacuzzis in most of the baths. Only seven of the rooms have a sea view, though. Guests can use facilities at the same group's Fenerlihan restaurant and enjoy the beach and beach bar, on the far left end of the harbor—both new additions to the port. Next door is Hotel Assos, less posh than its sister in terms of rooms but offering the same facilities for less money. ⊠ *Assos Liman (Assos Harbour)* ☎ *For both hotels 286/721–7017 or 286/721–7034* 🖷 *286/721–7249* ⊕ *www.assosgroup.com* ⤳ *15 rooms, 1 suite* ⌂ *Minibars, Wi-Fi* 🖩 *A, MC, V* ¦O¦ *MAP.*

$$ ✕▦ **Assos Kervansaray.** The best-located of the Assos hotels, at the far end of the harbor, the Kervansaray has an aura of antiquity, probably because of the gray lava stone from which it was built. Rooms are small and functional, but most are refurbished and have terrific views of the Aegean. The restaurant on the sea serves dressed-up versions of traditional Turkish dishes. There is a swimming pier, though the beach itself is rocky. ⊠ *Assos Liman (Assos Harbor)* ☎ *286/721–7093 or 286/721–7199* 🖷 *286/721–7200* ⊕ *www.assoskervansaray.com* ⤳ *42 rooms, 2 suites* ⌂ *Restaurant, indoor-outdoor pools, windsurfing, sauna, Jacuzzi, Wi-Fi, minibar* 🖩 *MC, V* ¦O¦ *MAP.*

$$ ▦ **Biber Evi.** In the village of Behramakale, a 10-minute walk from the
Fodor'sChoice Acropolis, this is the most exquisite hotel in either the village or the port.
★ Literally "Pepper House," it was named after the several varieties of peppers grown in the small garden and used in their cooking. The hotel is a 150-year-old stone house which once belonged to the village landlord. Each of the six rooms is unique, with Ottoman decoration and modern comforts: old wood furniture, bathrooms with heated floors, and walls tiled with pepper designs. The owner considers himself a whiskey expert and will happily recommend the finest ones in his selection while you sit on the terrace and enjoy the sunset. ⊠ *Behramkale Village center* ☎ *286/721–7410 or 286/721–7001* 🖷 *286/721–7242* ⊕ *www. biberevi.com* ⤳ *6 rooms* ⌂ *Restaurant, bar* 🖩 *AE, DC, MC, V.*

$$ ⌂ **Eris Pansiyon.** The retirement hobby of an American couple who moved to Turkey from New York seven years ago, this 250-year-old stone house is on the edge of Behramkale about 10 minutes' walk from the Acropolis. With bookshelves full of English-language books, homemade cake and tea service in the afternoons, and full cooked breakfasts served around a big table in the kitchen, staying here feels more like you're at a friend's house than in a pansiyon. Rooms are basic, but the warm atmosphere compensates. There is a minimum stay of two days and the pansiyon is open all year, except when the owners visit the U.S. so call ahead. ⊠ *Behramkale Village, 6* ☎ *286/721–7080* 🖷 *286/721–7080* ⊕ *www.assos.de/eris* ⇩ *4 rooms* ▤ *No credit cards.*

★ $ ⌂ **Old Bridge House.** This is one of the most interesting hotels in the region. The large garden is decorated creatively, with recycled materials taken from junkyards and old houses. There are also a small pool to cool off in, a sitting area with kilims and cushions, a bar, and a darts corner. Each room has its own color scheme, and all are furnished with old local furniture. Everything is eclectic and quite eccentric. Cabins are available for a more budget stay, and if you have a tent, you can pitch it on their grounds. They also rent motorbikes and speedboats. Dinner is served on request, but as it is often requested, there is a barbecue in the garden most nights. ⊠ *1 km from Assos, on Ayvacık road, next to Ottoman Bridge* ☎ *286/721–7426* 🖷 *286/721–7044* ⊕ *www.assos. de/obh* ⇩ *4 rooms; 3 cabins* ⚴ *Some A/C, cable Internet* ▤ *No credit cards* ☉ *Closed occasionally in winter.*

Nightlife

You can have drinks at any of the hotel bar-restaurants or check out the only actual bar in the Assos harbor, the **Uzun Ev Bar (Long House Bar).** It might be a bit of a stretch to call the indoor part "long," but the outdoor part is definitely tiny. The music is good: soft jazz during the day, rock and blues at night. It's open until 3 AM on weekends.

The Mount Ida Region (Kaz Dağları)

★ ⓫ *25 km (15 mi) east along the coast from Behramkale, toward Küçükkuyu.*

The area above the Gulf of Edremit is known as Kaz Dağları in Turkish, but to the Greeks it was Mount Ida, home of ancient gods and goddesses. It was here that Paris, son of King Priam of Troy, was given the fateful task of judging the beauty of three goddesses. He chose Aphrodite, the goddess of love, which ultimately caused the Trojan War.

The Turkomans have made their own contribution to the region's mythology. Famous for their skilled woodwork, they migrated here at the request of Mehmet the Conqueror in the 15th century to cut and process wood for the new ships needed to expand Mehmet's navy. According to the Turkomans, these ships were crucial to the conquest of Istanbul.

The 34-km (21-mi) coastal stretch between Küçükkuyu and Edremit is essentially a concrete mess, crammed with holiday homes, and for anyone who doesn't own one, it has little to offer. The mountain area above the coast, however, is a completely different story. Pine trees cover its higher slopes and olive trees predominate lower down, and delightful unspoiled villages are scattered over the hills. Most have managed to keep their original character, with houses made of local stone, narrow cobbled streets, and wide squares in the center, a part of which is usually taken up by the *kahvehane* or coffee house, the heart of village life. Hiking here will take your breath away it's so beautiful. Above the villages is Kaz Dağları National Park.

Yeşilyurt, 4 km (2½ mi) northwest of Küçükkuyu, is one of the most popular villages. It is now largely owned by Istanbulites who love the area and have helped preserve and enhance its beauty, though some degree of local character was inevitably lost along the way. **Adatepe,** 4 km (2½ mi) north of Küçükkuyu, has a site known as the Altar of Zeus, although archaeologists are dubious about its authenticity as there is no reference to it in classical literature—it's a short climb from the village, and the altar itself has splendid views that you'll often have to yourself. Adatepe has been less exposed to the boutique hotel invasion than Yeşilyurt, and so looks more like a real village. A tranquil square at the heart of the Adatepe has chairs and tables under the shade of a giant plane tree. The village is also famous for its olive oil, and down the hill in Küçükkuyu is the **Adatepe Zeytinyaı Müzesi** (Olive Oil Museum), where you can learn how olive oil is made.

Farther east are less prettified villages, some Turkish and some originally Greek, like **Çamlıbel,** a good base for more ambitious walks. **Tahtakuşlar** has an **Etnografya Galerisi** (ethnographic museum; ☎ 266/387–3340 ⊕www.tahtakuslar.8m.com) boasting the biggest Caretta (a Mediterranean sea turtle) in the world as well as traditional Turkoman clothing, tents, and household tools. Both Tahtakuşlar and Çamlıbel are about 2 km (1 mi) inland from the coast road near **Güre,** a hot-spring bath resort.

For those who can't do without the sea, it's nearby, and it's beautiful. The coast between Küçükkuyu and Edremit is highly developed, but between Küçükkuyu and Assos lies one of Turkey's most delightful swimming seas, and it's clean, calm, and refreshing. Most of the good village hotels have their own private beach somewhere on this route. Alternatively, since the whole of the coast is a protected area, you can park your car among the olive trees almost anywhere along the coast road and jump in—there may not be a sandy beach, but you might feel like you're the first to swim in that exact spot. If you'd rather have the sand, Kadırga Beach is on the same coast closer to Assos.

The Kaz Dağları National Park covers 25,000 hectares above the villages, and can only be visited with an official guide—mostly for security purposes, since there are 35 plants and trees unique to the Kaz Dağları and the presence of a guide is a measure against vandalism or smuggling. Make sure you get a guide who speaks English. The Sarıkız peak is 26 km (16 mi) from the entrance: it's a hard day's walk, but most people drive part of the way and walk the rest. There is a series of rivers, pools, and waterfalls, and at the end you'll be rewarded with a magnificent view of the Gulf of Edremit. There are two entrances: one where you can enter with your car and guide; the other is only for special safari tours, as the road is too rough for most cars. You can camp in the park but there's

MOUNT IDA TOURS

There are few designated walking routes in the area, so a guide can be helpful. Tour guides are still a fairly new concept in the region, though, so while your guide will certainly be good with directions, it's less likely he'll be able to tell you much about regional history or botany. A one-day guided tour costs about 40 YTL; some include lunch. Visiting the national park is much cheaper with a tour than on your own, as the 40 YTL will cover entry to the park and the compulsory guide's fee.

Most hotels in the region organize walking tours and arrange transport; others will at least point out the routes and help you hire a guide. Some will take you to Troy, Assos, or Bergama if you ask. İskender Bey, the owner of the İdakoy, wrote a book on the region showing the

various walking routes and the sights to be seen in the park.

There are also several hotels in the area that function as minitravel agencies, helpful for tours but not optimal as places to stay:

Antandros Tourism Agency
(⊠ Atatürk Cad. 9, Sok. 5 Altınoluk ☎ 266/396-5511 or 266/395-2277), in Altınoluk (the largest town between Küçükkuyu and Edremit, though it is not itself worth visiting) has various tours around Mount Ida as well as to Bozcaada, Troy, Assos, and Ayvalık.

Mare & Monte travel agency
(⊠ Fatih Cad. 13, Altınoluk ☎ 266/396-1730 ⊕ www.hotelmaremonte.com) offers tours of Mount Ida and trips to Pergamum (Bergama).

no electricity, toilets, or any other amenities. ⊙ *8–5 daily* 🚗 *17.50 YTL per car, and 40 YTL for the compulsory guide.*

Sports and Outdoors

HIKING Trekking is one of the region's main attractions. There are few designated trails, but people from the villages or at the hotels are well informed about routes and happy to help. Several agencies organize tours. The walks are delightful, and there is usually something to see or do on the way, such as bathing in the Bath of Aphrodite or swimming in the pool under the Başdeğirmen waterfall, where you can also picnic on wooden tables set in the middle of the river and gaze at the Roman bridge that was the only passage to Troy.

Where to Stay & Eat

The villages of Mount Ida are a haven of boutique hotels; in fact, the region helped introduce the idea of the boutique hotel to Turkey, and changed the whole country's tourism culture. Most hotels claim they offer a genuine countryside experience in modern comfort—and they're right. There are no TVs in the rooms, no loud music, and no game rooms, but there's a good chance you'll find poetry-reading nights, or organized courses in cooking, philosophy, or yoga. Most of the people who run these hotels went to Kaz Dağları to find "something a bit different," and they assume that's why you're here, too.

The best place to eat is probably at your hotel, and you're likely to find good international cuisine as well as local specialties. The region is famous for its wild herbs and olive oil; your dinner will probably be cooked with both.

$$$
Fodor'sChoice
★
Manici Kasrı. There's a reason why this was chosen Turkey's best small hotel in 2006 by one of Turkey's most influential newspapers: each room is decorated differently but all are elegant, with four-poster beds and original paintings on the walls. The garden restaurant overlooks the mountains and serves delicious local and international food. Service is flawless. The building is new but it was made from old stones and bricks taken from an old olive oil factory. The hotel has a private beach 5 km (3 mi) down the hill on the Küçükkuyu-Assos road, and a shuttle bus will take you there. The hotel also organizes walking and sightseeing tours. ⊠ *Yeşilyurt village, Küçükkuyu* ☎ *286/752–1731* 🖷 *286/752–1734* ⊕ *www.manicikasri.com* ➫ *7 rooms, 3 suites* ⌂ *Restaurant, bar, Wi-Fi, minibars* ▤ *AE, DC, MC, V* ⑩ *MAP.*

★ **$$**
✕▥ **Ergüvanlı Ev.** Most of the region's hotels overlook mountainous pine forests, but the Erguvanlı Ev is right in the middle of one. The gardens and lawns are beautiful, and the forest beyond keeps the summer heat away. The nonsmoking rooms are plain but pleasant. The owner, Suna, gives yoga lessons in the mornings and also offers massages for a fee. The chef is a village woman assisted by the owners; dinner is tasty, but breakfast is a real feast. Try the *menemen* (egg cooked with tomatoes and peppers) with fresh thyme from the garden. Nonguests can call ahead for dinner reservations. ⊠ *Yeşilyurt village, Küçükkuyu* ☎ *286/752–5676* ⊕ *www.erguvanliev.com* ➫ *7 rooms* ⌂ *Restaurant* ▤ *MC, V* ⑩ *MAP.*

$$
Fodor'sChoice
★
Hünnaphan. This 250-year-old Ottoman mansion has a spacious courtyard and a beautiful large garden. The open buffet dinner has a rich choice of mezes and local specialties. The owner is also a painter and the walls of the rooms and corridors are hung with her pictures. Rooms are spacious, and plainly but elegantly decorated. There is also a private house for large groups, with its own garden. The hotel organizes walking tours and provides guides for its guests. ⊠ *Adatepe, Küçükkuyu* ☎ *286/752–6581* 🖷 *286/752–2066* ⊕ *www.hunnaphan.com* ➫ *22 rooms* ⌂ *Wi-Fi* ▤ *MC, V* ⑩ *MAP.*

$
▥ **Zeushan.** This is one of the few less expensive options that the rather fancy Mount Ida villages have to offer. It's a stone house right on Adatepe's main square; rooms are modestly decorated in village style with old carpets and embroidered curtains. Breakfast and dinner are served in a pleasant courtyard terrace. The pansiyon doesn't organize tours or transport but will help put you in touch with the right people. ⊠ *Adatepe village, Küçükkuyu* ☎ *286/752–54041* ⊕ *www.zeushan.com* ➫ *6 rooms* ▤ *MC, V* ⑩ *MAP.*

$$
▥ **İdakoy.** This homey hotel looks from the distance like the only house on its hillside, outside the village of Çamlıbel. Its chief attractions are the stunning views of the Gulf of Edremit from the terrace, and owner İskender's deep knowledge of the region: he and his wife Suna cowrote a book on Mount Ida describing otherwise undesignated walking routes. After breakfast, İskender will take his guests out for a walk for an hour or the whole day—it's up to you. The rooms vary in size, and there's

no smoking indoors. ✉ *Çamlıbel village, Altınoluk* ☎ 266/3873402
🖷 *266/387–3393* ✍ *6 rooms, 4 with bath* ☰ V ⏇ MAP.

★ ¢ 🖳 **Endes Camping.** Near the entrance to Kaz Dağları National Park, Endes doesn't have much in the way of comforts, but it's a unique and wonderful place to stay. There are three cabins and several tents in this six-acre wilderness, with a terrace restaurant overlooking a small river. Downstream, among the olive, pomegranate, cherry, and walnut trees, is a small, natural pool for swimming. Service is suitably unpretentious. Rooms are basic and so is the food, though it's tasty, and everything from the bread to the butter and olive oil is home-made. Bathrooms are communal. ✉ *Mehmetalan Village, Edremit* ☎ 266/377–1711 ✍ *3 rooms, some tents* ⚭ *Restaurant* ☰ *No credit cards* ☉ *Closed Nov.–mid-Apr.* ⏇ *MAP.*

Ayvalık

⑫ *94 km (58 mi) from Edremit, south on Rte. E87.*

Ayvalık is the biggest holiday resort in the region. Like many Turkish seaside towns, it has been somewhat exploited by package tourism in recent years, but its superb geographical setting, stretching onto a peninsula and surrounded by islands, is hard to beat. The setting is quite lovely, with many bays swirling in and out of its coastline; if you drive up the hill to the Şeytan Sofrası ("the devil's dinner table"), you'll clearly see this. The area also boasts one of Turkey's few blue-flagged (eco-friendly) beaches.

Ayvalık first appears in Ottoman records at the late date of 1770, when an Ottoman naval hero, Gazi Hasan Paşa, was aided by the local Greek community after his ship sank nearby. Soon after, the town was granted autonomy, perhaps as a gesture of gratitude, and the Muslim population was moved to outlying villages, leaving the Greeks to prosper in the olive oil trade. At the close of World War I, the Greeks invaded Turkey and claimed the Aegean coast; in 1922 the Turks ousted the Greek army, and the entire Greek community of Ayvalık was deported. Today the town is mostly Turks, and other than tourism, the main source of income is olive farming and olive oil production.

The old Greek quarter of the town has been neglected for decades, although in the last few years policies of protection and restoration have begun to be enforced. Ayvalık has some of the finest 19th-century Greek-style architecture in Turkey. Unlike the typical Ottoman house (tall, narrow, and built of wood, with an overhanging bay window), Greek buildings are stone, with classic triangular pediments above a square box. The best way to explore is to turn your back to the Aegean and wander the tiny side streets leading up the hill into the heart of the old residential quarter (try Talat Paşa Caddesi and Gümrük Caddesi). Several historic churches in town have been converted into mosques. St.

★ John's is now the **Saatlı Cami** (Clock Mosque). St. George's is now the **Çınarlı Cami** (Plane Tree Mosque). There are many mosques converted from churches in Turkey, but these are among the most striking—the elaborate style of Orthodox churches does not suit the plain minimalist style of mosques, and the unimpressive minaret erected later at the Çınarlı mosque looks almost absurd. The pictures of the saints inside are painted over but can still be seen if you look carefully. The **Taxiarchis Church,** currently closed with no set reopening date, is a museum, with a remarkable series of paintings done on fish skin depicting the life of Christ. Barbaros Caddesi on the south end of the pier will take you to **Phaneromeni Church** (Ayazma Klisesi), displaying beautiful stone craftwork and to **Hayrettin Paşa Cami,** also converted from a church.

In summer, Sarımsaklı Plajı, the 10-km (6-mile) stretch of sandy beach, 7 km (4½ mi) from the center of

> ### A QUICK TRIP TO GREECE
>
> A trip to the Greek island of Lesbos will allow you to see another country and culture with a sea journey of little more than an hour. Ferries depart from Ayvalık pier at 6 PM daily and from Lesbos at 8:30 AM daily between mid-June and mid-November, so a tourist from Ayvalık would need to stay at least two nights. Fares are about $65 return.

town, is a popular destination. It's a crowded resort with a mess of concrete hotels right behind the sea front, and traffic and parking can be a problem, but the beach and sea are lovely.

Day or evening cruises to the bays and islands of Ayvalık are enjoyable. The numerous boats in the harbor with desks in front of them will try and sell you a trip as you walk by, and competition makes prices very reasonable—about 13 YTL for a day trip including a fish meal. The tours are offered from May until the end of October.

Şeytan Sofrası, a hilltop 9 km (5½ mi) from town, on a right turn on the road from Ayvalı to Sarımsaklı, is the place to get a panoramic view of the islands and the bays. It's lovely at sunset, though there's nothing to see on the hilltop itself since a fire in 2006 burned down all the trees and the café closed.

Where to Stay & Eat

★ **$$** ✕ **Canlı Balık.** This fish restaurant at the end of Ayvalık Pier delivers excellent food in a romantic setting. With its starched white tablecloths and weathered decor, the interior has an air of faded grandeur. In fine weather, opt for the terrace at the tip of the pier, where local fishing boats sway in the water a few feet away and the Aegean stretches to the horizon. Start with mezes such as fried squid or mussel salad in local olive oil, then move on to fresh, grilled local fish, perhaps *barbunya* (red mullet), or try *papalina* (small sardines) if you are in town in July and August. ⊠ *South of Atatürk Bulvarı, Cumhuriyet Square, on harbor* ☎ *266/313–0081* ▤ *MC, V.*

¢ ✕ **Fırat Lokantası.** In the heart of Ayvalık, a couple of streets north of Saatlı Mosque, this eatery offers hearty lunches to hardworking street traders; it's tiny but almost always full, and you may have to share one of the half-dozen tables downstairs (there are a few more in the even smaller upstairs section). The decor could not be plainer. Water and bread are served in communal plastic tubs and jugs in the middle of each table. It's typical and delicious Turkish home cooking: rice, beans, eggplant with minced meat, and lamb stew. This is the perfect place for lunch when wandering the historic part of the town. It opens early (6:30 AM) and closes early (4 PM). ⊠ *On the corner of Cumhuriyet and Edremit Caddesi, 25/A* ☎ *266/312–1380* ▭ *No credit cards* ☾ *No dinner; closed Sun.*

★ **$$$** ⌂ **Grand Hotel Temizel.** Away from the other hotels on Sarımsaklı Beach, this fairly luxurious five-star lodging has a private beach, a casino, a small Turkish spa, and an elegant marble-and-gleaming-brass lobby. Rooms are spacious, but the least fancy feature of the hotel, though most have balconies with sea views. The best part is that it's far from the noise and concrete pollution of the rest of the beach. The large common areas and the aqua park make it a good choice for families. ⊠ *Sarmısaklı Plajı, 10425* ☎ *266/324–2000* 🖷 *266/324–1274* ⊕ *www.temizel.com.tr* ⇋ *263 rooms, 12 suites* ⚭ *2 restaurants, tennis court, pool, gym, sauna, massage, Turkish bath, Jacuzzi, windsurfing, soccer, basketball, volleyball, kids playroom, bar, shops, meeting room, dance club, minibars* ⦿⃒ *AP* ▭ *MC, V.*

☾ **$$** ⌂ **Ayvalık Beach Hotel.** This hotel, across a causeway toward Şeytan Sofrası, is actually a cluster of two-story chalets nestled among pine trees on a wooded slope overlooking a sheltered inlet. Wonderful sea views more than compensate for the lack of frills in the clean and comfortable but sparsely furnished rooms. Breakfast and dinner are buffet-style. There are a pool and a park at the edge of the sea. ⊠ *Şeytan Sofrası Yolu, Altınkum Mev., Ayvalık, 10425* ☎ *266/324–5300* 🖷 *266/324–5304* ⊕ *www.ayvalikbeach.com* ⇋ *68 rooms, 2 suites* ⚭ *Restaurant, bar, pool, beach, Wi-Fi, minibars* ▭ *MC, V* ⦿⃒ *MAP.*

$$ ⌂ **Hotel Mare.** One of the many similar hotels at Sarımsaklı Beach, Hotel Mare is at least newer than most. The rooms are standard but comfortable, and all have balconies. It's somewhat surprising that the unimpressive pool, with its clutter of chaise longues and a bar playing loud Turkish pop music, is packed. ⊠ *Sarımsaklı Plajı* ☎ *266/324–1195 or 266/324–1048* 🖷 *266/324–0022* ⊕ *www.hotelmareayvalik.com* ⇋ *103 rooms, 8 suites* ⚭ *Restaurant, café, bar, Wi-Fi, pool, Turkish bath, sauna, fitness minibars, in-room safes* ⦿⃒ *MAP* ▭ *MC, V.*

★ **¢** ⌂ **Taksiyarhis Pansiyon.** This is a very attractive budget option in the old quarter of the city behind the Taxiarchis church. There are large rooms for families, but the place is mostly picked by backpackers. The sitting room, with fireplace, bookshelves, hammock, and sofas, is cluttered but fun. It's a cheerful, communal place, with a kitchen and two balconies for common use. Bathrooms are communal. ⊠ *İsmetpaşa Mahallesi, Maraşal Çakmak Cad. 71* ☎ *266/312–1494* 🖷 *266/312–2661* ⊕ *www.taksiyarhis.com* ⇋ *10 rooms* ▭ *No credit cards.*

Cunda Island (Ali Bey Adası)

⑬ *Just off the coast at Ayvalık (connected by a causeway to mainland).*

Like Ayvalık, Cunda Island was once predominantly Greek, and some Greek is still spoken here. The island has a mix of the two cultures in its food, music, and nightlife, and lately has been deliberately cultivating this, having realized the tourism potential.

This fishing town has good seafood restaurants lining its atmospheric quay; they're noted for their grilled *çipura* (a local fish) and for an amazing variety of Turkish and Greek seafood dishes served grilled, fried, baked, or in a cold seafood salad with interesting dressings.

There are regular buses to Cunda from Ayvalık, but the best way to travel is by boat; they run every hour each way, from 10 AM to midnight in summer (June 15–Sept. 15), and dock at the quay right in the middle of the restaurants in Cunda. In winter, buses are the only option.

The island's Greek houses are well preserved and varied, and the 19th-century **St. Nicholas Church** (better known as Taksiyarhis, or Taxiarchis, Church to the locals) in the middle of town is a must, even though you can only see it from the outside. With its large cracks, caused by an earthquake in 1924, and the birds flying around its airy domes, the whole place has a ghostly air. You can't go inside anymore because of the danger of a collapse, but peep through the glassless windows and you can see some of the frescoes, several of which have been defaced—the eyes of the apostles have been gouged out. On the left side of the church's quiet courtyard is a small café and pansiyon, Zehra Teyze'nin Evi, where you can sit and have a refreshment and enjoy the view of the church.

Where to Stay & Eat

Cunda has recently become a popular place for accommodation and nightlife as well as dining. Unlike mainland Ayvalık, it is purely a tourist resort and also attracts weekend escapers all year around, though it's not as built up, and doesn't (yet, at least), attract the big tour groups. Most of the hotels here are quite expensive for what they offer. Waterfront restaurants, on the other hand, while also expensive, are among the best in Turkey. For cheap eating, try Pizza Uno (it's not the American chain) in the center of town. It's the lunchtime favorite of the local shopkeepers and serves kebabs and *pides* as well as pizza.

$$–$$$ ✕ **Lale Restaurant.** More commonly known as Bay Nihat'ın Yeri (literally "the place of Mr. Nihat"), this is the most popular and probably
FodorśChoice   the most expensive of the waterfront restaurants in Cunda. The meze
★   selection is a feast for the eyes. Quite a few are original creations: fusion dishes based on Greek and Turkish cuisine, like squid eggs with sage, local aquades clams with whiskey sauce, and octopus with thyme and pomegranate extract. All are delicious, and served with hot toast. The seafront part of the restaurant looks similar to its neighbors but a bit sleeker; the indoor winter section is nicely decorated, unlike the scruffy casual interiors of its rivals. ⊠ *The Cunda Quay* ☎ *266/327–1063 or 266/327–1777* ⌦ *Reservations essential* ▤ *MC, V* ☾ *Closed for the month of Ramadan.*

$$ ▦ **Altay Pansiyon.** Among the many centrally located pansiyons with more or less the same prices, this one stands out. In a spacious courtyard with flowers and trees it's a different world from the busy, narrow streets of Cunda's crowded center. French wines with a cheese platter and Italian coffee are served here in the courtyard café, which is also open to nonguests. From the courtyard you can ascend to a quiet terrace overlooking the town; vines hang down from here to the courtyard. The rooms are plain and neat. ⊠ *Namık Kemal Mahallesi, Ayvalık Caddesi, 18, Cunda* ☎ *266/327–1024* ⎙ *266/327–1200* ⊕ *www.*

altaypansiyon.com ➷ *9 rooms with bath* ♿ *Café, Wi-Fi, minibars* ▭ *MC, V* ⊘ *Closed Nov.-Apr.*

$$ ⌨ **Zehra Teyze'nin Evi.** This small pansiyon hidden among the trees in the courtyard of the Taksiyarhis Church is, literally, the House of Aunt Zehra. She's a straightforward lady who talks with her guests if she feels like it; at other times she can be seen sleeping on the sofa of the pansiyon's garden. The location is wonderful, the atmosphere is warm and casual, the garden is cool and quiet, and the rooms are plain and comfortable. ✉ *Cunda center, next to Taksiyarhis Church* ☎ *266/327–2285* ⊕ *www.cundaevi.com* ➷ *5 rooms* ♿ *Café, Wi-Fi, minibars, rooms with A/C, TV* ▭ *No credit cards.*

Nightlife

In Sarımsaklı, the beach area in Ayvalık, you'll find discos and clubs that play pop and electronic techno; Cunda has bars that play Turkish and Greek pop music. There are many, and they're easy to come across while wandering around.

Shaft (✉ Atatürk Bulvarı, 1. Sok. 7 ☎ 266/312–2231 ⊕ www.shatclub. com ⌨ 15 YTL on Fri. and Sat. including one drink ⊘ daily 6 PM–4 AM) is the only rock bar in town. It's at the far end of the Ayvalık pier, one street inland, and plays everything from pop rock to alternative rock. On Fridays and Saturdays there is live music with bands from Istanbul—sometimes famous Turkish rock groups. On other nights a DJ rules.

Mis Kokulu Taverna (✉ Cunda center ☎ 266/327–1545) promises a fun night out with Greek musicians playing songs mostly known to both Turkish and Greek cultures. There is live music every day in summer but some nights are mellower than others. The courtyard is small but cozy, and food is served—mostly snack-type mezes and rakı. Reservations are advisable for the weekends.

Pergamum (Bergama)

⑭ *54 km (33 mi) from Ayvalık; take Rte. E87 south approximately 44 km*
Fodor'sChoice *(27 mi), then follow signs to Bergama.*
★

The windswept ruins of Pergamum, which surround the modern town of Bergama, are among the most spectacular in Turkey. The attractions here are spread out over several square miles, so if you don't have a car, negotiate with a taxi driver in Bergama (you have to pass through the town anyway) to shuttle you from site to site. There is no public transport to the sights and no car rental—or travel agency—in town.

The town itself has no attractions but offers reasonable accommodation and food if you spend the night. The old quarter, on the way to the Acropolis, is pretty run-down but has the most charm.

Pergamum was one of the ancient world's major powers, though it had a relatively brief moment of glory. Led by a dynasty of maverick rulers, it rose to prominence during the 3rd and 2nd centuries BC. Because he was impressed by the city's impregnable fortress, Lysimachus, one of Alexander the Great's generals, decided this was the place to stow the booty he had accumulated while marching through Asia Minor. Then, when Lysimachus was killed, in 281 BC, Philetaerus (circa 343 BC–263 BC), the commander of Pergamum, claimed the fortune and holed up in the city. He established a dynasty known as the Attalids. After defeating the horde of invading Gauls who had been sacking cities up and down the coast in 240 BC, the Pergamenes were celebrated throughout the Hellenic world as saviors. The Attalids ruled until 133 BC, when the mad Attalus III (circa 170 BC–133 BC) died and bequeathed the entire kingdom to Rome. By a liberal interpretation of his ambiguous bequest, his domain became the Roman province of Asia and transformed Rome's economy with its wealth.

The city was a magnificent architectural and artistic center in its heyday—especially under the rule of Eumenes II (197 BC–159 BC). He built Pergamum's famous library, which contained 200,000 books. When it rivaled the great library in Alexandria, Egypt, the Egyptians banned the sale of papyrus to Pergamum, which responded by developing a new paper—parchment, made from animal skins instead of reeds. This *charta pergamena* was more expensive but could be used on both sides; because it was difficult to roll, it was cut into pieces and sewn together, much like today's books. The library of Pergamum was transported to Alexandria by Cleopatra, where it survived until the 7th century AD, when it was destroyed by the fanatical Caliph Omar, who considered the books un-Islamic.

The most dramatic of the remains of Pergamum are at the **acropolis.** Signs point the way to the 6-km (4-mi) road to the top, where you can park in the car park across from the souvenir stand—which sells water, film, and reasonably good picture books containing site maps. Buy your ticket at the gate. Broken but still mighty triple ramparts enclose the **upper town,** with its temples, palaces, private houses, and gymnasia (schools). In later Roman times, the town spread out and down to the plain, where the Byzantines subsequently settled for good.

After entering the acropolis through the Royal Gate, there are several different paths. To start at the top, pick the path to the far right, which takes you past the partially restored **Temple of Trajan,** at the summit. This is the very picture of an ancient ruin, with burnished white-marble pillars high above the valley of the Oç Kemer Çayi (Selinos River). On the terraces just below, you can see the scant remains of the **Temple of Athena** and the **Altar of Zeus.** Once among the grandest monuments in the Greek world, the Altar of Zeus was excavated by German archaeologists who sent Berlin's Pergamon Museum every stone they found, including the frieze, 400 feet long, that vividly depicted the battle of the gods against the giants. Now all that's left is the altar's flat stone foundation. There's much more to see of the **Great Theater,** carved into the steep slope west of the terrace, that holds the Temple of Athena: it can seat some 10,000 spectators and retains its astounding acoustics. You can test them by sitting near the top and having a companion do a reading in the stage area. ☎ 232/631—0778 ✉ $7 ☉ Apr.–Oct., daily 8:30–6:30; Nov.–Mar., daily 8–5.

The **Kızıl Avlu** (Red Courtyard) in Bergama is named for the red bricks from which it's constructed. You'll pass it on the road to and from the acropolis—it's right at the bottom of the hill. This was the last pagan temple constructed in Pergamum before Christianity was declared the state religion in the 4th century. At that time it was converted into a basilica dedicated to St. John. The walls remain, but not the roof. Most interesting are the underground passages, where it is easy to imagine how concealed pagan priests supplied the voices of "spirits" in mystic ceremonies. One of the two towers is closed at the moment for restoration; the other is now used as a mosque. ☎ *232/631–2885* 🎫 *$3.50* ⊙ *Apr.–Oct., daily 8:30–6:30; Nov.–Mar., daily 8–5.*

Bergama's **Arkeoloji Müzesi** (Archaeology Museum) houses a substantial collection of well-presented statues, coins, and other artifacts excavated from the ancient city as well as an ethnography section. The statue of Aphrodite comes from the site of Allianoi, a Roman spa town, which is waiting to be drowned by a dam project. ⊠ *Cumhuriyet Cad., 10* ☎ *232/631–2884* 🎫 *$3.50* ⊙ *Apr.–Oct., Tues.-Sun. 8:30–noon and 1-7; Nov.–Mar., Tues.–Sun. 8–noon and 1–5.*

The **Asklepion** is believed to have been the world's first full-service health clinic. The name is a reference to Asklepios, god of medicine and recovery, whose snake and staff are now the symbol of modern medicine. In the heyday of the Pergamene Asklepion in the 2nd century AD, patients were prescribed such treatments as fasting, colonic irrigation, and running barefoot in cold weather. The nature of the treatment was generally determined by interpretation of the patient's dreams. The entrance to the complex is at the column-lined **Holy Road,** once the main street connecting the Asklepion to Pergamum's acropolis. Follow it for about a city block into a small square and through the Propyleum, the main gate to the temple precinct. Immediately to the right are the **Shrine of Artemis,** devoted to the Greek goddess of chastity, the moon, and hunting, and the **library,** a branch of the one at Pergamum. Patients also received therapy accompanied by music during rites held in the intimate theater, which is now used each May for performances of the Bergama Arts Festival. Nearby are pools that were used for mud and sacred water baths. A subterranean passageway leads down to the sacred cellar of the **Temple of Telesphorus,** where the devout would pray themselves into a trance and record their dreams upon waking; later, the dreams would be interpreted by a resident priest. ⊠ *Follow Cumhuriyet Cad. west to Rte. E87; near tourist information office, follow sign pointing off to right 1½ km (1 mi)* ☎ *232/631–2886* 🎫 *$7* ⊙ *Apr.–Oct. daily 8:30–6:30; Nov.–Mar. daily 8–5.*

Where to Stay & Eat

$ 🏨 **Akropolis Guest House.** In the old city on the way to Acropolis and just 200 yards up from the Basilica, this is a good base for touring. The pool in the middle of the courtyard is attractive on a hot day, although it's not big enough for much swimming. The rooms are a bit dark but comfortable. Dinner is served on request; you must notify them in the morning. Meals are good Turkish home cooking, with options such as zucchini stuffed with minced meat. ⊠ *Kurtuluş mahallesi, Kayalık Sok.,*

5 ☎ 232/631–2621 ⊕ *www.akropolisguesthouse.com* ⇲ 8 rooms △ *Some a/c, some satellite TV, Wi-Fi* ⊟ *MC, V.*

$ ⊡ **Berksoy Hotel.** This hotel is just outside the town center. Rooms are large, plainly furnished, and have balconies. There's a pool, an attractive feature in Bergama, where the nearest beach is 30 km (19 mi) away. There are two restaurants to choose from, one a farmhouse restaurant featuring local specialties. ⊠ *İzmir Yolu (İzmir road), 19* ☎ *232/633–2595* 🖷 *232/633–5346* ⊕ *www.berksoyhotel.com* ⇲ *57* △ *2 restaurants, bar, pool, tennis court, table tennis, Wi-Fi* ⊟ *AE, DC, MC, V* ⭘| *BP.*

$ ✕ **Sağlam Restaurant.** This restaurant in the center of town, near the museum and tourist information office, is popular, despite the premises' being a bit run-down. There are three large sitting areas inside, a garden, and an Ottoman dining room with low stools—all this space is necessary since it's the lunch stop for almost all tour buses to Bergama. The selection of food is also large, from *pides* to kebabs to stews. Everything is good, though not exceptional. ⊠ *Cumhuriyet Meydanı, 47* ☎ *232/632–8897* ⊟ *AE, MC, V.*

$ ✕ **Ticaret Odası Lokali.** This 150-year-old Greek building in a tranquil part of town is owned by the Bergama Chamber of Trade. The restaurant overlooks the town and has views of the acropolis and basilica from some of its tables. Tables are set in the terrace and in the garden in summer. Meze, kebab, and steaks are on the menu, and like all other restaurants of such official institutions in Turkey, prices are more reasonable than what the somewhat fancy and formal decor and the serious service might lead you to expect. ⊠ *Ulucami Mahalesi, Büyükalan mevkii* ☎ *232/632–9641* ⊟ *MC, V* ⭘ *Closed for a month in Ramadan.*

THE SEA OF MARMARA & NORTH AEGEAN ESSENTIALS

Transportation

BY AIR

Bursa and Çanakkale, the two biggest cities in the region, have non-operating airports. Every year the possibility of opening them is discussed and then the issue is postponed for another year. They may be operating by the summer of 2007, but check first. Turkish Airlines or private airlines such as Atlas Jet will have the latest information.

Edremit, 55 km north of Ayvalık on the tip of the Gulf of Edremit, has a new airport. Atlas flies to Edremit, but only from Istanbul and only three or four times a week. Edremit is a convenient place to fly to if your destination is Ayvalık, the Mount Ida region, or Assos.

BY BOAT & FERRY

Fast ferries operate daily between Istanbul's Yenikapı terminal and Yalova and are the quickest way to get to Bursa or İznik. They run every two hours each way between 7:30 AM and 9:30 PM, though on weekends sailings may start later and finish later. The journey takes just over an hour and costs about $8 for passengers and about $35 for a car including driver. They also operate daily to Bandırma, a good way to get to the Mount Ida region, Assos, or Ayvalık. Since the Bandırma–Çanakkale road is normally less crowded than Istanbul–Çanakkale, you may want to choose this route when traveling to Gallipoli, though it's not much shorter. Ferries to/from Bandırma run three times daily, take two hours and cost about $17 per passenger and about $70 for a car including driver. For both ferries reservations are essential during religious holidays and summer weekends, and advisable generally for weekends and between June and August.

⧉ IDO (Istanbul sea bus and fast Ferry) ☎ 212/444–4436 ⊕ www.ido.com.tr. **Yalova dock** ☎ 226/812–0499.

BY BUS

Buses are a frequently used form of transport in this region. They are usually new vehicles, and on many routes run what is effectively an inter-city shuttle. There is no smoking in the buses, and most offer complimentaries like tea, Coke, and biscuits. It is normally a comfortable way to travel and quite inexpensive, although the frequent stops on some routes, such as between Çanakkale and Edremit, can be frustrating.

There are no central telephone numbers for the main bus terminals in the small towns in this area, and in any case there would probably be no English-speakers available to help. Most bus companies, though, in particular Truva and Kamil Koç, have branches both in the terminal and the center of the towns and they're usually easy to spot: in Çanakkale, the station is right on the harbor, and the same in Ayvalık. In Bursa, the terminal is a bit out of town, but the bus company has branches both in the city center and in the Çekirge region.

The major bus companies in the region are Atan Kardeşler, Kamil Koç, and Truva Tourism. Several buses daily make the trip from Istanbul's terminal at Esenler to Yalova and Bursa. The journey takes about four hours to Yalova and five to Bursa, including the ferry trip from Darıca to Yalova, and costs about $12. A better option is to take the sea bus to Yalova; near the sea-bus quay in Yalova are buses to Bursa that cost about $5 and take one hour. The trip from Istanbul to Çanakkale is about 6 hours and costs $20. From Bursa to Çanakkale is 4½ hours and costs about $14.

From Çanakkale buses run almost every hour to İzmir, passing Ezine, Ayvacık, Küçükkuyu, Edremit, Ayvalık, and Bergama on the way. Fares are usually about $10.

⧉ Bus stations Bursa bus station ☎ 224/261–5400. **İznik bus station** ☎ 224/757–1418.
⧉ Atan Kardeşler ☎ 224/261–5090 for Bursa, 224/ 757–2583 for İznik. **Kamil Koç** ☎ 286/752–6261 in Küçükkuyu, 266/373–4446 in Edremit, 266/312–2279 in Ayvalık ⊕ www.kamilkoc.kom.tr. **Truva Tourism** ☎ 224/261–5068 in Bursa, 212/444–0017 in Istanbul, 286/212–2764 in Çanakkale, 286/814–1110 in Eceabat.

BY CAR

Renting a car is a good idea if you're planning to do a lot of traveling, though as elsewhere in Turkey, drive carefully. Cars are useful for a trip to historic Gallipoli, where the memorials are well signposted, roads are quite good, and parking is available.

There are several options for getting out of Istanbul: one is to take the E80 headed for Ankara. At İzmit take Route 130 to Yalova; Route 575 connects Yalova and Bursa. For İznik, at the Orhangazi turning of Route 575 between Yalova and Bursa, turn east on the Route 595 to İznik, which goes along the north coast of the lake.

Another option is to take Route 100 or E80 out of Istanbul to Yalova. The ferry trip lops 140 km (87 mi) off the journey, but the quickest, though also most expensive, alternative is to take the fast ferry from Yenikapı terminal in central Istanbul, which takes just over an hour. After that, Bursa and İznik are only a one-hour drive.

From Yalova, Bursa is 60 km (37 mi) south via Route 575; İznik is 62 km (38 mi) southeast via Route 595. From Bursa, Route 200 (which becomes E90) runs west toward Çanakkale; the trip is 303 kms and takes about 3.5 hours.

If you're heading for Çanakkale from İstanbul, take E80 west to Tekirdă, the E84 to Keşan, and the E87 to Eceabat.

From Çanakkale, the E87 goes through Troy, Ezine, Ayvacık, Küçükkuyu, Edremit, and Ayvalık. Ezine is 50 km from Çanakkale, and from there you can take the coast road west to Geyikli, where ferries run to Boz- caada, or to Alexandra Trois, Apollon Smintheion, Babakale, and Assos, all further south. This is a coastal road that runs through villages; it's a bit rough and winding, but quite scenic and enjoyable. Ayvacık is 75 km from Çanakkale on E87, and from here you can turn off onto the 19-km road to Assos. Küçükkuyu, which is 25km from Ayvacık and 100 km from Çanakkale, is the setting-off point for the villages of Mount Ida, where a car is especially handy as there is no public transport to some of these villages, which lie to the north of the coastal towns.

Edremit is on the eastern stretch of the Mount Ida region: it's the biggest transport hub after Çanakkale in the north Aegean region and it also has an airport. It is 25 km from Küçükkuyu and 125 km from Çanakkale on E87. Ayvalı is 94 km south from Edremit, also on E87.

Bergama is about 54 km southeast of Ayvalık. Travel about 44 km south on the E87 and then turn off following the signs to Bergama, a further 10 km.

🚗 Local rental car companies **Duke Tour (in Ayvalık)** ☎ 266/373–5807. **Gezgin Oto (in Çanakkale)** ☎ 286/212–2892.

BY TAXI AND DOLMUŞ

As in most of Turkey, taxis are yellow and very easy to spot. You can hail them on the streets.

The fares in cities and towns are metered, with daytime and nighttime tariffs, the latter about 50 percent more expensive and running from midnight to 6am. Make sure that the driver doesn't switch to nighttime tariff (in which case the word "gece" appears on the meter) if you are traveling during the day. There is a separate luggage fee if your luggage is big, but most taxi drivers do not apply it, especially if you are going a good distance. In smaller towns, the meter system is often replaced by fixed tariffs for destination. Drivers should keep a sheet that shows the prices of each destination. Bargaining is not common for taxis operating meters, nor for fixed prices for documented destinations, but if you are going a long way, you can try.

BY TRAIN
Train journey in this region is not advisable. The trains (and the tracks) are very old, and painfully slow. Train travel is also often more expensive than the bus.

Contacts & Resources

BANKS & EXCHANGING SERVICES
Exchange bureaus are found only in big cities, usually in the center, so if you are heading to small towns make sure you change your money before leaving. İş Bankası is Turkey's largest bank, with many branches in the cities and at least one in each town.

EMERGENCIES
Ambulance (☎ 112). **Police** (☎ 155). **Tourism police** (☎ 286/217—5260 or 286/217–5376 in Çanakkale, 224/364—1855 in Bursa).
🏥 Hospitals **Bergama Hospital** ☎ 232/631–2894. **Bursa State Hospital** ☎ 224/220–0020. **Çanakkale State Hospital** ☎ 286/217–1098.

INTERNET, MAIL & SHIPPING
Most hotels referred to in this chapter have some type of Internet access, usually Wi-Fi. Some also have a computer reserved for guests. There are also internet cafes in larger towns, usually centrally located. And since they're also called internet cafes in Turkish, you'll have no trouble asking locals about the nearest ones. Most charge less than a dollar per hour.

Post offices are easily recognized in Turkey—they're bright yellow and marked PTT. Hours vary, but most are open from about 9 AM to early evening.

There are Fed Ex branches in Bursa, Çanakkale, and Edremit.
📮 Post Offices **Ayvalık** ⊠ Atatürk Bulvarı, 49 ☎ 266/ 312 1003. **Bergama** ⊠ Ertuğrul Sokak, 1 ☎ 232/632 3990. **Bursa** ⊠ Atatürk caddesi, 79, Heykel ☎ 224/224–1717. **Çanakkale** ⊠ İnönü caddesi, 78 ☎ 286/217 1022. **Eceabat** ⊠ Cumhuriyet Caddesi, 40 ☎ 286/ 814 1419. **Edremit** ⊠ Menderes Bulvarı ☎ 266/373 1039. **İznik** ⊠ Kılıçaslant caddesi, 46 ☎ 224/757–3261.

TOUR OPTIONS
Tours are a good way to see many of the sites in this area, especially Gallipoli. For the most part, we don't recommend taking tours to Gallipoli from anywhere other than Çanakkale or Gallipoli itself, they're just not as good. The same usally applies to Ephesus, where local guides will be better informed.

There are many companies that offer guided tours of Gallipoli, including Hassle-Free Travel Agency and TJ's Tours. Yöntur Turizm arranges tours of Bursa and İznik.

Hassle Free Tourism ☎ 286/213-5969 ⊕ www.hasslefreetour.com **TJ's Tours** ☎ 286/814-3121 ⊕ www.anzacgallipolitours.com **Yöntur Turizm** ✉ İnönü Cad., Hüzmen Plaza Çarsısı 29 B 15, Bursa ☎ 224/220-9132

VISITOR INFORMATION

Ayvalık ✉ harbour ☎ 266/312 2122. **Bergama** ✉ Hükümet Konağı, B Blok, Ground Floor ☎ 232/631 2851. **Bursa** ✉ Ulu Cami park, next to Orhan Gazi underpass, No:1, Heykel ☎ 224/220 1848. **Çanakkale** ✉ İskele Meydanı, No: 67 ☎ 286/217 1187. **İznik** ✉ Mahmut Çelebi Mahallesi, S.Demircan (Çiniciler) sokak, 22. ☎ 224/ 757 6809.

The Central & South Aegean Coast

WORD OF MOUTH

"We had a good tip to visit the Ephesus museum in Selçuk first, so when we visited Ephesus, we had more than ruins to picture. It really did help, and, anyway, the museum had air-conditioning!"

—christycruz

WELCOME TO THE CENTRAL & SOUTHERN AEGEAN COAST

TOP REASONS TO GO

★ **Sailing on a Blue Cruise** Gulets, converted wooden fishing boats, take off from the coastal towns of Çeşme and Bodrum.

★ **Visit Ephesus** This ancient city still has many impressive features from over 2,000 years ago.

★ **Wandering through Şirince** This lovely village has preserved its culture, and its homes, and the villagers create beautiful crafts.

★ **Swimming and scuba diving in Çeşme and Bodrum** Some of the brightest and bluest water in the country can be found here.

★ **Feasting on fish in Gümüşlük** The best part of this attractive, nontouristy Bodrum town is its string of waterside restaurants.

1 Izmir & Çeşme: İzmir, in the middle of the Aegean coast, is the region's largest city. Çeşme, a peninsula, is the westernmost tip of the region, and has some of the region's most pristine water. Some of the best beaches are located in Altınkum, southwest of Çeşme.

2 Selçuk, Ephesus & Şirince: Selçuk is the town nearest to the archaeological ruins at Ephesus and the old hill village of Şirince. The slower pace and authentic Turkish feel of both Selçuk and Şirince are a refreshing change from the region's more touristy areas.

3 Kuşadası & Environs: Kuşadası, although not very interesting in itself, is the most geographically practical place from which to tour the ancient Greek and Ionian ruins of Didyma, Miletus, and Priene to the south. The ancient Roman city of Aphrodisias and the layered limestone-travertine terraces and hot springs of Pamukkale, both to the east of Kuşadası, make worthwhile side trips.

4 Bodrum Peninsula: Bodrum is the southern Aegean coast's other peninsula—its towns are smaller, and its coves and bays are great for swimming. Most travelers start at the northeastern tip at the popular town of Gölköy-Türkbükkü and continue counterclockwise along the coast. Bodrum shares an airport with Milas, to its north.

GETTING ORIENTED

Although it's the country's most touristy and developed region, the central and southern Aegean also holds some of Turkey's most fascinating and diverse treasures, from gorgeous white-sand beaches to the ruins of Ephesus. To get a good sense of the region, travel to the smaller, outlying villages and towns, where much of the Aegean's character lives on.

Cine Bozdogan

550

Yatagan

Mugla D 330

Yerkesik Gericam

Lake Köyceğiz Koycegiz
Marmaris
Kaunos ◆
Marmaris Limani Dalaman
D 400
Fethiye

St. John's Basillica, Selçuk

CENTRAL & SOUTH AEGEAN COAST PLANNER

Getting Here

The quickest way to get to the central and southern Aegean is by plane. There are daily flights leaving Istanbul to airports in İzmir and Milas/Bodrum. There are direct flights to İzmir and Bodrum from Turkey's other major airport hubs: Ankara, Adana, Trabzon, Dalaman, and Antalya.

There are a number of bus lines serving the Aegean coast. The ride from Istanbul to İzmir takes around 12 hours, and from Istanbul to Bodrum takes 16.

Having your own car will save you a lot of time between sights and allow you to explore some of the neat places that are inaccessible by bus. There are car rental agencies in all of the major towns, but be sure to check their conditions as some have more liberal drop-off policies than others.

When to Go

July and August are the region's most crowded months. You'll have the beaches pretty much to yourself in June and September, although the water is much cooler than during high season. If you're interested in touring the villages and historic sites—and if you've never been to a camel-wrestling match—plan your trip from December through March, when flights and accommodations are inexpensive and camels are competing throughout the region.

How Much Time Do You Need?

Given the distances involved and the wealth of alluring sights, ideally, you would need 10 to 12 days to thoroughly explore the region. As a general rule of thumb, if you want to make a lot of stops, it makes more sense to tour as you go along, as driving back and forth between base cities and sights can be tiring. If you are pressed for time, it is best to head straight for İzmir or Selçuk—making either city the base from which you can take in some of the main sights nearby. If you're traveling by car, be sure to leave time to stop and stay in the smaller towns along the coast.

Blue Cruises

Blue Cruises were originally inexpensive boat tours taken by Turkish intellectuals in the 1970s, and they're still one of the most enjoyable and low-key ways to see the coast. Trips can last 2 to 14 days between April and October. Most voyages are on *gulets*, converted wooden fishing craft with full crew. The boats' amenities range from modest to luxurious, and prices fluctuate accordingly. You can arrange your trip before you leave home or on the spot at the docks. Ask a travel agent or someone at your hotel to recommend a reputable company with a good boat and crew. On the Aegean coast, voyages depart from İzmir, Çeşme, Kuşadası, and Bodrum.

For information try these contacts: **Cano Yachting** (☎ 252/385–3740 ⊕ www.canoyachting.com); **Era Tourism** (☎ 252/316–2310 ⊕ www.erayachting.com); **Neyzen Tours** (☎ 252/316–7204); **Borda Yachting** (☎ 252/316–6252 in Bodrum, 216/313–7764 in Istanbul); **Motif Travel** (☎ 252/316–1536 ⊕ www.motifyachting.com).

Aegean Seafood

Eating along the Aegean coast is a pleasure, especially if you like seafood. The main course is often the fresh catch of the day, though meat lovers can rest assured that there are always beef and lamb kebabs.

Some of the more common fish you'll find are *palamut* (baby tuna), *lüfer* (bluefish), *levrek* (sea bass), *çupra* (sea bream), and *kalkan* (turbot).

TIPS FOR SEAFOOD RESTAURANTS:

■ Fish is often sold whole (as opposed to fillets) and priced by the kilo. The price and weight are often not listed, so don't hesitate to ask. For example, 1 kilo of sea bream may be equal to two whole fish, and cost $30.

■ Don't be afraid to bargain for your fish. Many restaurants in touristy areas tend to mark up their prices significantly. Check out the prices offered elsewhere and use those as a reference point. Remember that bargaining is part of Turkish culture!

■ Don't feel awkward about sharing a main course. This is always acceptable, especially when ordering a large-sized fish.

■ Make a point of letting your server know if you don't want the fixed-menu option that many restaurants offer. Also, be specific about the exact quantity of the meze, or appetizer, you would like—sometimes waiters will bring you more than one serving of a dish and charge you extra.

■ Note that there is often an obligatory service charge added to your bill. Some restaurants, regardless of the number of people in your party, also add a gratuity of 10%. Always look at your check to see if it's been added before you leave a tip. The check will say *servis* or *servis ucreti dahildir* if a gratuity has been added.

WHAT IT COSTS

	$$$$	$$$	$$	$	¢
Restaurants	over $25	$16–25	$11–15	$5–10	under $5
Hotels	over $250	$151–250	$76–150	$51–75	under $50

Restaurant prices are for one main course at dinner or for two mezes (small dishes). Hotel prices are for two people in a double room in high season, including taxes.

Off the Beaten Path

Undeveloped areas exist even in this region full of beaten paths. If you want to get away from the hubbub, Lake Bafa would be a good place to start. One hour north of popular Bodrum, the lake offers a more peaceful place to swim and to spend time outdoors. There's a beautiful nature resort here, the ruins at Heraklia are across the lake, and if you start to get bored, Bodrum is just a short bus ride away. Also near Bodrum, Çomakdā is a beautiful village accessible by car. Although group tours do go there, it has only recently been discovered by locals and tourists, so you should have a pretty authentic experience. Milas and its neighboring sights would also make an enriching trip.

Don't Forget to Bring. . .

1. **Sunscreen.** It's very expensive in the resort towns.

2. **A towel for sunbathing.** Hotels don't like it when you use the in-room towels on the beach.

3. **A hat.** In the summer, temperatures often rise into the 90s. It's amazing what a little shade will do!

4. **Mosquito repellent.** They're fast and furious on the coast!

5. **Your camera.** There are some truly great viewpoints along the coast.

6. **Sporting gear.** Rental costs can be high, so if you have room in your luggage, try to bring snorkeling gear, wetsuits, etc. with you.

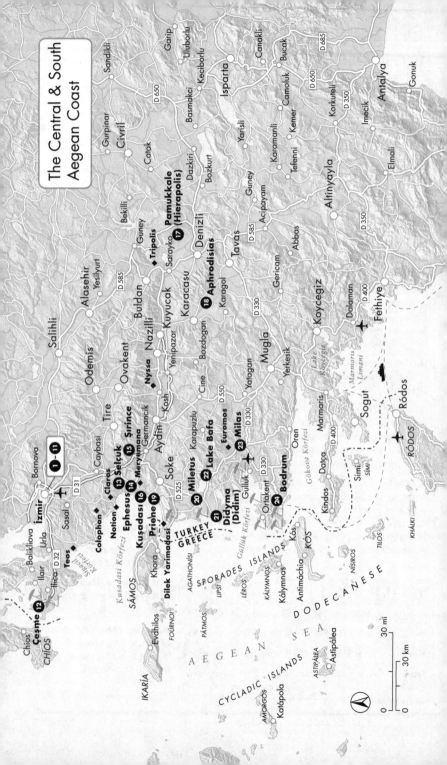

The Central & South Aegean Coast

Updated by
Evin Doğu

The central and southern Aegean is probably the most developed area of Turkey, and the rolling hills, mountains surrounded by clear blue seas, and glorious white-sand beaches are just a few of the reasons why. Wandering through historic ruins, boating, scuba diving, basking in the Anatolian sun, and eating fresh fish are just some of the ways you can fill your days. While it's true that some of the bigger resort areas like Kuşadası and Bodrum proper attract multitudes of package tourists in the busy summer months—this is also where you'll find most of the booming nightlife that the area is becoming known for—there are certainly lots of more tranquil spots to be found. Head out to some of the smaller villages, and you'll be amply rewarded.

İZMIR & ÇEŞME

İzmir

565 km (351 mi) south of Istanbul; 156 km (97 mi) south of Ayvaık.

At first glance, Turkey's third-largest city, though set on the Gulf of İzmir and surrounded by mountains, seems very modern and industrial—it's the site of many trade expositions and home to NATO's Southeast headquarters, and definitely appears to be more of a hub than a vacation destination. Indeed, shoddy overdevelopment along some of the city's slopes does detract from the natural beauty of its surroundings, and the palm trees that line the major streets do little to compensate.

İzmir may not have immediate appeal, but it's a great starting point and/or base for exploring the southern Aegean region. Even if the city itself doesn't interest you, there are many outdoor activities nearby like bird-watching, skiing, and trekking, and if you take a few days to explore, you'll come to appreciate the diverse architecture, fascinating ruins, and interesting museums that give the city its edge. Despite the rapid growth of the past few decades, navigating İzmir is still manageable and pleasant. Interconnected piazzas and pedestrian-friendly walkways help ease your travels around the city. Walking along the waterfront promenade, taking time to learn about the city's 7,000-year history, shopping in the outdoor bazaar, or discovering the old churches, synagogues, and other buildings scattered throughout the city are some worthwhile ways to spend your time. There are enough historical points of interest to pique one's curiosity, and there is a lively café culture.

What to See

The sweeping view of the city and its harbor from the windy restored ❶ ramparts of the **Kadifekale** (Velvet Fortress), built by Alexander the Great, make it a good spot to orient yourself to İzmir. The name, according to romantics (if not to scholars), alludes to the resemblance of the present-day citadel's walls to rubbed velvet. Rebuilt after various mishaps, and enlarged and strengthened by successive conquerors, the structure looks like a childhood fantasy of a medieval castle, with solid stone blocks (some dating from Alexander's day), Byzantine cisterns, and Ottoman buttresses jutting out to support the walls. ⚠ **Locals will warn you (especially women) against going to the Kadifekale alone for fear of**

CLOSE UP

History of İzmir

TURKEY'S THIRD-LARGEST CITY, with a population of 2 million, İzmir was called Smyrna until 1923. A vital trading port, though one often ravaged by wars and earthquakes, it also had its share of glory. Many believe that Homer was born in Old Smyrna sometime around 850 BC. Alexander the Great favored this city with a citadel atop its highest hill.

İzmir fell into assorted hands after the Romans, starting with the Byzantines and Arabs. From 1097 on, it was a battlefield in the Crusades, passing back and forth between Muslims and Christians. Destroyed and restored successively by Byzantines and Seljuks, Smyrna was held by the Knights of Rhodes in 1402 when the Mongol raider Tamerlane came along, sacked it yet again, and slaughtered its inhabitants. Thirteen years later Sultan Mehmet I Çelebi incorporated it into the Ottoman Empire.

Toward the end of the 15th century, Jews driven from Spain settled in Smyrna, forming a lasting Sephardic community. By the 18th and 19th centuries Smyrna had become a successful, sophisticated commercial port with an international flavor. Its business community included a sizable number of Jews, Italians, Greeks, Armenians, British, and French. This era came to an end with World War I, when Ottoman Turkey allied itself with Germany. In 1918 the Greek army, encouraged by the British and French, landed at the harbor and claimed the city. The occupation lasted until 1922, when Turkish troops under Atatürk defeated the Greek forces and forced them to evacuate. On September 9, 1922, Atatürk made a triumphant entry into the port. The joy of the local Turks was short-lived; a fire shortly thereafter blazed through the city. Fanned by the wind, it burned wooden houses like matches while hidden stores of munitions exploded.

The city was quickly rebuilt—and given the Turkish name İzmir. Like the name, much of the city dates from the '20s, from its wide boulevards to the office buildings and apartment houses painted in bright white or soft pastels. This important industrial center is not particularly pretty, though it has a harbor-front promenade and peaceful green Kültür Parkı at its center.

---

being hassled or harassed. The site is near a run-down neighborhood, so to be on the safe side, you may want to go with a guide.

 The **agora** at the foot of Kadifekale Hill, just off 816 Sokak (816 Street), was the Roman city's market. The present site is a large, dusty, open space surrounded by ancient columns and foundations. Part of it has been closed off for excavations, but there's still much to see. There are well-preserved Roman statues of Poseidon, Artemis, and Demeter in the northwest corner. To get there from Kadifekale, exit from the fortress's main gate and take the road that descends to the left; when you see steps built into the sidewalk, turn right and go down. ⊠ *Namazgah, Anafartalar Cad.* ☜ *$1.50* ☉ *Daily 8:30–noon and 1–5.*

 Konak Meydanı (Konak Square), at the water's edge, is one of the city's two main squares (the other, Cumhuriyet Meydanı, or Republic Square, is to the north along Atatürk Cad.). The **Saat Kulesi** (clock tower) stands out at the center of the plaza, with its ornate, late-Ottoman design. The tower was built in honor of Sultan Abdulhamid in 1901, and the clock itself was sent as a gift from Kaiser Wilhelm II. The small, 18th-century single-domed **Konak Yalı**

PLANNING AHEAD

Museum opening hours in İzmir can vary depending on the season. Always confirm a museum's hours beforehand.

Mosque, set back from the clock tower, is decorated with colorful tiles and was built by Mehmet Paça's daughter, Ayçe.

❹ Konak Meydanı marks the start of the modern-day marketplace, **Kemeraltı**, a maze of tiny streets filled with shops and covered stalls. Unlike Istanbul's Grand Bazaar, İzmir's is not indoors. Anafartalar Caddesi is the bazaar's principal thoroughfare, but try the smaller side streets, too, where you'll find minimarkets dedicated to musical instruments, songbirds, leather, beads, jewelry, and many other treats. Go farther into Kemeraltı, and you'll wind up at the **Kestane Pazarı**, a miniature version of Istanbul's Spice Bazaar, which has a decent selection of spices, tea and coffee, fabric stores, and a whole slew of confectioners.

Enter Kemeraltı from Fevzipaşa Bulvarı and you'll be surrounded by the cafés and eateries of the Hisar Camii area. The Hisar Mosque, the largest and oldest in İzmir, is worth a look inside. Past Kemeraltı, near the Hisar Cami is the **Kızlarāası Hanı**, an 18th-century, recenty restored Ottoman kervansaray with lots of vaulted shops inside. The shops offer quality, although sometimes expensive, Turkish goods like purses, jewelry, miniatures, and rugs. ■ TIP→ **For a reliable carpet store, check out Gallery Cetiz. For three generations, the Cetiz family has been selling carpets. The storeowners, father and son, work together and have a wide selection of Turkish kilims, antique and modern Turkish carpets, complete with their own certificate of authenticity.** Many of the store's workshops are located on the top floor, where you can sit and have a well-prepared cup of Turkish coffee at Acı Kahve overlooking the kervansaray's courtyard.

NEED A BREAK? **Making your way through Kemeraltı can be exhausting. Stop by Ömer Usta Kahveci (⊠ 905 Sok. No. 15, Hisar Cami Back Entrance ☎ 232/425–4706) for a shot of Turkish coffee brewed in the cup. The atmosphere is pleasant and lively, and if you're traveling during the summer, there are plenty of shaded areas to keep you cool. Be aware that the cups can be scalding hot!**

❺ The **Arkeoloji Müzesi** (Archaeology Museum) contains the 2nd-century statues of Demeter and Poseidon found when the agora was excavated, as well as an impressive collection of tombs and friezes and the memorable, colossal statue of the Roman emperor Domitian (AD 51–96, ruled 81–96). ⊠ *Cumhuriyet Bul., Bahribaba Parkı* ☎*232/489–0796* ✆*$2.50* ☉ *Tues.–Sun. 8:30–5:30.*

❻ The **İzmir Etnoğrafya Müzesi** (İzmir Ethnographic Museum), across the street from the Archaeology Museum, focuses on folk arts and daily life,

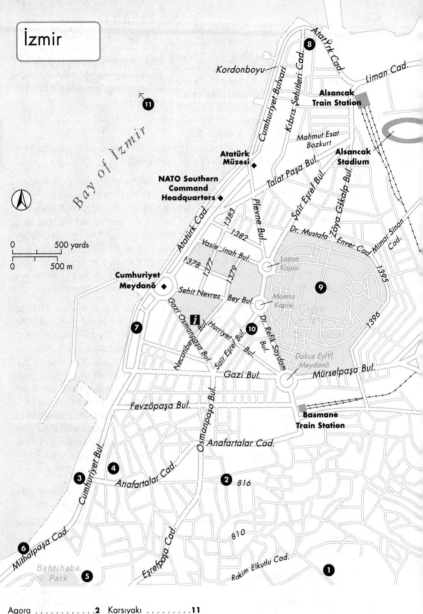

İzmir

Kordonboyu

Bay of İzmir

0   500 yards
0   500 m

Cumhuriyet Bulvari

Kıbrıs Şehitleri Cad.

Atatürk Cad.

Liman Cad.

Alsancak Train Station

Mahmut Esat Bozkurt

Atatürk Müzesi

Talat Paşa Bul.

Şair Eşref Bul.

Alsancak Stadium

Zöya Gökalp Bul.

NATO Southern Command Headquarters

Pleyne Bul.

1383

1382

Atatürk Cad.

Dr. Mustafa

Enver Cad.

Mimar Sinan Cad.

Vasie -inah Bul.

1378

1377

1379

Lozan Kapısı

Cumhuriyet Meydanō

Şehit Nevres

Bey Bul.

Montro Kapısı

1395

1396

Gazi Osmanpaşa Bul.

Hürriyet Bul.

Necatibegaşa Bul.

Şair Eşref Bul.

Dr. Refik Saydam Bul.

Dokuz EylŶl Meydanō

Mürselpaşa Bul.

Gazi Bul.

Fevzōpaşa Bul.

Osmanpaşa Bul.

Basmane Train Station

Anafartalar Cad.

Anafartalar Cad.

Cumhuriyet Bul.

816

Eşrefpaşa Cad.

810

Mithalpaşa Cad.

Bahribaba Park

Rakim Elkutlu Cad.

housing everything from period bedrooms to a reconstruction of İzmir's first pharmacy. ⊠ *Cumhuriyet Bul., Bahribaba Parkı* ☎ *232/489–0796* 🖭 *$2.50* ⊙ *Tues.–Sun. 8:30–5:30.*

❼ The **Kordonboyu** (Cordon), the waterfront promenade, is the most fashionable section of town. It starts at the museum complex in **Bahribaba Parkı** and stretches north along the busy harbor, past Konak Meydanı, NATO's Southern Command headquarters, and the small **Atatürk Müzesi** (Atatürk Museum; ⊠ Atatürk Cad., Alsancak 248 ☎ 232/421–7026 ⊙ Tues.–Sun. 8:30–noon and 1–5), housed in a pale yellow Levantine building that was originally a house presented to Atatürk as a gift. Along the strip are several good seafood restaurants, all with a few tables outside overlooking the water. You can tour the area ($15 per ride) by *fayton* (horse-drawn carriages); carriages are stationed in the Cumhuriyet Meydanı area of the Kordon.

❽ South of the museum is the neighborhood of **Alsancak.** Now a trendy spot for İzmir's "high society," during Ottoman times, the neighborhood was predominantly Jewish and Christian, and there are still a number of synagogues and churches in the area. The pretty two- and three-story Levantine houses with bay windows are tucked away in some of the back streets, which perk up at night with the influx of young İzmirians drawn to the quaint cafes, bars, and restaurants.

❾ **Kültür Parkı** (Culture Park), İzmir's central park, has gardens, a zoo (which they will be moving to another area soon), amusement rides, and nightclubs. It is the site of a major industrial fair from late August to late September. You'll also find **Izmir Tarih ve Sanat Müzesi** (İzmir's History and Art Museum) in the Kültür Parkı, a modern compound made up of three buildings showcasing stone objects, ceramic objects, and precious artifacts. The jewelry in the precious artifacts exhibit dates from Hellenistic, Roman, and Byzantine periods. ⊠ *Museum: East of Lozan and Montrö Meyds.* ☎ *232/445–7876* 🖭 *$3* ⊙ *Tues.–Sun. 8:30–5:30.*

❿ Just South of the Kültür Parkı is the **İzmir Ahmet Piristina City Archive and Museum,** a 7,000-year chronicle of the city's history through colorful posters with informative descriptions in English and Turkish. The museum, housed in the old fire station, has a special section dedicated to the history of İzmir's multiple fires and its fire brigade. ⊠ *Şair Eref Bul. 1/A Çankaya* ☎ *232/441–6178* 🖭 *Free* ⊙ *Daily 9–6.*

⓫ **Karsıyakı,** the area known as "Opposite Shore" in Turkish, is the purported birthplace of the poet Homer, and was the residence of one of Turkey's most famous contemporary poets, Attila Ilhan. For years, it was a tranquil summer resort for İzmir high society, but now the area has expanded to make room for the suburbs that have sprung up to accommodate İzmir's growing population. On a hot summer day, the 20-minute ferry from Konak to Karsıyakı is a great way to cool off, and once you're here, you can walk along the commercial strip, İzmir's version of Istanbul's İstiklal Caddesi in Taksim. Try some İzmir *lokma* (sweet Turkish donut holes) for which the district is famous. You can catch the ferry at Konak's quay; tickets cost around $1.

**OFF THE
BEATEN
PATH**

The **Homa Lagoon (Homa Dalyani)** (☎ 232/482–1218), also known as kuş cenneti (bird heaven), is nestled in the Gediz Delta on the north shore of İzmir Bay in Çamaltı. It's a great day trip out of the city. The delta itself is made up of lagoons, mudflats, salt marshes, reed beds, and farmland, which provide diverse habitats to more than 230 species of birds, mammals, reptiles, and fish. Tours of the lagoon, which is a nature reserve protected by the Ministry of Culture, can be taken by car or by foot—all tours start at the visitor center and are free. Unfortunately, few of the staff members at the visitor center speak English, but the Web site, www.izmirkuscenneti.org, has an English link and is pretty informative. You'll need a car to get here, or you might be able to hire a taxi for the trip.

Where to Stay & Eat

$$ ✕ **Ömür Balık Lokantası.** Open only at lunchtime, this pleasant restaurant in a restored Ottoman building serves all sorts of seafood, including fresh fish, octopus, and shrimp. ⊠ *902 Sok. 44, Hisarönü* ☎ *232/425–6839* 🖃 *No credit cards.*

★ **$-$$** ✕ **Koşebaşı.** At this large kebab house, you can savor your kebab from one of the many tables overlooking İzmir's expansive gulf and cascade of mountains. To begin, choose from one of the tray full of mezes or start with a warm, mini *lahmacun* (a thin, Turkish pizza). Entrées come in generous portions and are consistently well prepared. The Beyti kebab, ground beef and lamb wrapped in thin lavash served with yogurt, is hearty and tasty. The tender cubes of meat in the Şaşlık kebab are also particularly flavorful. If you'd like something lighter, go for the eggplant kebab. Note that it'll take a rental car or very expensive taxi ride to get here. ⊠ *Çeşme Çevreyolu, Limontepe Mevkii, Balçova* ☎ *232/ 278–2806* ⊕ *www.kosebasi.com* 🖃 *AE, MC, V.*

$ ✕ **Altınkapı.** Probably the best of the many kebab houses on 1444 Sokak, this is the only one to have received the Turkish Standards Institute seal of approval. Its specialties include excellent *İnegöl köfte* (grilled beef-lamb patties) and a fine selection of *pide* (Turkish pizza). ⊠ *1444 Sok. 9, Alsancak* ☎ *232/422–5687* 🖃 *MC, V.*

$ ✕ **Deniz.** Befitting its bayside location, the main event in this attractive spot on the ground floor of the İzmir Palas Hotel is the seafood. *Kılıç şiş* (grilled swordfish kebab) is a house specialty. ⊠ *Atatürk Cad. 188, Alsancak* ☎ *232/422–0601* 🖃 *DC, MC, V.*

$ ✕ **Tarihi Kemeraltı Lokantası.** This small, inexpensive eatery is a great place to stop for lunch after exploring the Kemeraltı bazaar. Its main draws are delicious, coal-fired döner (gyro meat) and traditional Turkish daily specials. If the weather is nice, the outside tables are a great place to people-watch. ⊠ *Anafartalar Cad. No. 47/A Veysel Çıkmaz Kemeraltı* ☎ *232/425–5393* 🖃 *AE, MC, V.*

¢ ✕ **Geçit Pide Salonu.** If you find yourself on the "opposite shore," this little *pide* restaurant at the end of the main drag in Karşıyakı is your best bet. The traditional Turkish building is a blast from the (recent) past: the great glass doors and black-and-white-tiled floors give the place a decidedly 1950s feel. Crispy dough is cooked in a wood-fire brick oven and comes with your choice of ingredients. The classic kaşar cheese *pide* is a delicious and reliable choice. Geçit also has great homemade soup; the red lentil and tripe is particularly recommended. ⊠ *1713 Sokak No.74/ B, Karşıyakı* ☎ *232/368–9516* ▤ *No credit cards.*

¢ ✕ **Reyhan Pastanesi.** This patisserie and café in the heart of Alsancak is a favorite among İzmir's denizens. Reyhan is a great place to go for breakfast or dessert—traditional Turkish baked treats and chocolates are available as well as Western-style sweets like cheesecake and an excellent carrot cake. ⊠ *Mustafa Bey Cad. No. 24* ☎ *232/422–2802* ▤ *AE, MC, V.*

$$$ ▦ **Best Western Konak Hotel.** This waterfront hotel has lots of cool marble and greenery. Guest rooms have full-size beds, plush carpeting, and big windows with views. The city's museums are within easy walking distance. ⊠ *Mithatpasa Cad. 128, 35210* ☎ *232/489–1500* 🖷 *232/489–1709* ⊕ *www.bestwesternturkey.com* ⤳ *82 rooms* ⌂ *Safe, ethernet, restaurant, room service, bar, laundry service, concierge* ▤ *AE, MC, V.*

$$–$$$ ▦ **İzmir Hilton.** At 34 stories, the Hilton is one of the tallest buildings on the Aegean coast. From the 10-story atrium to the elegant rooftop restaurant, the public spaces are suitably grand. Guest rooms are plush, with thick floral comforters and matching drapes. About the only complaint you could make is that there's nothing particularly Turkish about the place. ⊠ *Gazi Osman Paşa Bul. 7, 35210* ☎ *232/441–6060* 🖷 *232/441–2277* ⊕ *www.hilton.com* ⤳ *381 rooms* ⌂ *Ethernet, 2 restaurants, room service, 2 bars, 2 tennis courts, pool, gym, concierge, executive floor* ▤ *AE, DC, MC, V* ⊕ *www.hilton.com.*

$$ ▦ **Hotel Baylan.** This four-story property with a shiny marble facade is a good value. Its bright and pleasant rooms, on the small side, have nondescript Scandinavian-style furniture. ⊠ *Anafartalar Cad., Basmane, 1299 Sok. 8, 35240* ☎ *232/483–1426* 🖷 *232/483–3844* ⊕ *www.hotelbaylan. com* ⤳ *36 rooms* ⌂ *Restaurant, bar* ▤ *AE, MC, V.*

$$ ▦ **Hotel Kilim.** The Hotel Kilim is centrally located in the fashionable Kordon neighborhood. The rooms here are very comfortable, but those close to the street can be noisy, so ask for one on a higher floor. Be sure to also ask for a room with a bay and harbor view—they're the same price as the other rooms. There is a somewhat nondescript restaurant in the hotel that serves seafood and traditional Turkish lamb dishes—wait for good weather to eat here, when you can enjoy the sidewalk tables overlooking the harbor. ⊠ *Kazim Dirik Cad. 1, 35210* ☎ *232/484–5340* 🖷 *232/489–5070* ⊕ *www.kilimotel.com.tr* ⤳ *75 rooms* ⌂ *Safe, restaurant, bar* ▤ *MC, V.*

$$ ▦ **Kısmet.** The public spaces and guest rooms at this comfortable hotel are tastefully decorated, but since it doesn't have a great view and is an older property, you'll pay less. What's more, the sidestreet location makes it quieter than the places on the main drag. The staff is very friendly. ⊠ *1377 Sok. 9, 35210* ☎ *232/463–3850* 🖷 *232/421–4856* ⤳ *62 rooms* ⌂ *Restaurant* ▤ *AE, MC, V.*

Nightlife & The Arts

The **State Ballet and Opera House** (⊠ Milli Kütüphane Cad. ☎ 232/484–3692) offers dance performances, chamber music, and pop and jazz concerts. Tickets can be purchased at the theater on the day of the performance. For outdoor classical music concerts, check out the open-air theater in **Kültür Parkı.**

The International İzmir Film Festival takes place in June and July, however, many of the screenings are actually held at Ephesus or Çeşme Castle. The İzmir Foundation for Culture and Arts has festival information on their web site (www.iksv.org). Tickets are usually available at the İzmir Hilton and the State Ballet and Opera House box office.

Rain (⊠ 1649 Sokak No. 79, Karşıyakı ☎ 232/372–2929 ⊕ www.rain-club.com) is İzmir's new seaside dining-and-entertainment complex—it has four restaurants (each with its own bar and cuisine), a coffee house, and a glamorous nightclub called **En Velo** with a dance floor and DJs that spin club music. The complex is open 24/7, but food service doesn't begin until 6 PM; En Velo doesn't get going until around 11 PM. There is an entrance fee for the complex of $22 on weekends, which includes one drink.

Alsancak has a colorful, lively nightlife and an assortment of bars. **Eko Pub** (⊠ Plevne Bul., No.1, Alsancak ☎ 232/421–4459) is popular with the expatriate and twenty-something crowd. Try **Rena** (⊠ 1453 Gazi Kadınlar Sokağı No.11, Alsancak ☎ 536/324–6310) on Thursday night for tango and live music on the terrace. Rena is located on the Gazi Kadınlar Sokağı, a great street to check out in general, full of cafés and attractive Levantine homes. For a good beer and a more alternative crowd, head to **Sardunya** (⊠ Muzaffer Izgü Sok. 11, Alsancak ☎ 232/464–4664) on one of Alsancak's popular streets, Kıbrıs Şehitleri.

Sports & the Outdoors

The most well-known area for hiking and skiing is the 120-km (75-mi) stretch between the Gediz and the Küçük Menderes rivers. **Mount Bozdağ** is 45 km (28 mi) from İzmir. You'll need a car to get there, but the trip is well worth it.

HIKING   Summer is a great time for hiking Mount Bozdağ's slopes, with cool, crisp air providing refuge from the city's suffocating heat.

For a less strenuous trip, set out to Gölcük, where there are smaller hills and a beautiful lake ideal for picnics. To get to Gölcük via public transportation, take a bus from İzmir's terminal to Ödemiş; the trip takes about three hours. From Ödemiş, you can get a dolmuş to Gölcük from the corner of Hatay and Namik Kemal streets, near the Ödemiş bus terminal.

SKIING   For ski enthusiasts, Mount Bozdağ's 2159-meter-high summit is a good place to start. Take the chairlift to the top and ski or trek back down (a 2½-hour journey). For less expe-

> ## THE WRATH OF ARTEMIS
>
> When Ares' son, Tmolos, fell in love with the water nymph Arriepe, Artemis, goddess of fertility, was furious. Angered that a mortal would have the audacity to set his sights this high and blemish the human-divine divide, Artemis sent a bull to trample him to death, with success. Tmolos's son buried his father on the summit of Bozdağ, which subsequently became known as Tmolos.

rienced skiers, there are two shorter slopes as well. The pistes are ready for skiers as early as November, when they're covered with artificial snow. The ski resort at Büyük Çavdar, 7 km (4 mi) from the village, has two hotels, as well as bungalows for rent.

Shopping

For high-end, brand-name, and designer clothing, the Alsancak neighborhood has it all. In addition, check out the Wednesday **Bostanlı bazaar** in Karşıyakı. It's known for its good-quality, inexpensive clothes. The earlier you go, the better the selection. There's rumor that it might close down, so check before you go.

Dösim (✉ Cumhuriyet Bulvarı, No.115, Alsancak ☎ 232/483–0789) is run by Turkey's Ministry of Culture. In addition to selling Turkish handicrafts, Dösim preserves and promotes Turkish heritage by maintaining traditional art forms and practices. The fixed prices are very reasonable, and the quality is top notch.

Çeşme

⓬ *81 km (50 mi) west of İzmir on Rte. 300.*

Çeşme, originally a local beach getaway for İzmirians, has now also become a popular summer destination for Istanbul's elite. It's Turkey's westernmost point after Çanakkale. Despite rapid development, much of the town retains its provincial feel, even if you have to sometimes travel off the beaten path to find it. Its location leaves it exposed to constant winds, making it a hot spot for windsurfing. In fact, one of the nearby beaches, Alaçatı, was recently chosen as the second most ideal windsurfing destination in the world.

What to See

The 14th-century **Genoese castle** is very picturesque, with its stone walls lined with sun-basking lizards and its keep often deep in wildflowers. The castle's museum displays weaponry from the glory days of the Ottoman Empire. 🎟 *$2* ☉ *Daily 8:30–11:45 and 1–5:15.*

Ayios Haralambos is a large old Greek basilica named after a patron saint. It's worth taking a look at the facade as you stroll down the main street of Çeşme's shopping district. The space is now used as a cultural center that hosts art exhibitions and chess tournaments. ✉ *Inkilap Cad.*

Beaches

The beaches that span 29 km (18 mi) of Çeşme's coastline are the main reason people come here. Each beach has its own distinctive ambiance, and you can access most by minibus or dolmuş (to get out to

> **TRANSPORTATION AROUND THE PENINSULA**
>
> Most of the coves and bays are accessible by dolmuş, which depart near the entrance of Çeşme's main street and from the tourist office every thirty minutes or when full. Çeşme serves as the main hub, and you may have to make a transfer here if you're traveling from one outlying cove to the other. Dolmuşes cost around $1 per ride. Note that they run less frequently during the off-season.

more secluded areas, it helps to have a car). Despite high winds, the aqua-marine water is often still and calm, and it's often easy to see to the bottom. The public beach areas are more crowded and unkempt, so it is often worth paying the $5–$10 per person to secure a spot with a chaise longue and umbrella. Swimming season starts in April and continues until mid-November—the most popular months are July and August.

Ilıca is one of the peninsula's most popular beaches, with crystal-clear water and white sand. Originally, the town served as a summer retreat for İzmir's wealthy. It's only 5 km (3 mi) from Çeşme, and dolmuşes leave every half hour or when full. There are public and private beach areas here, and many hotels lined up along the shore. The town has a lot of shops, and is known for its *kumru*, (literally translated as "dove" in Turkish), a Turkish-style panini of grilled kaşar cheese, sucuk (a spicy, Turkish beef sausage), and salami stuffed inside a sesame-seed bread made with chickpea yeast.

Slightly west of Ilıca is **Boyalık bay.** The popular Ayayorgi beach is at the center of Boyalık and for those who like the beach bar scene, but the rest of Boyalık bay is calmer. You'll have to take a minibus or cab to get from Ayayorgi to the other areas of the bay.

Alaçatı is a pretty village 2 km (1 mi) south of Ilıca. It has become a very popular day trip for locals and tourists alike, and buses serving the town leave every half hour from both Ilıca and Çeşme. People flock to Alaçatı in the evening, when its cosmopolitan cafés, restaurants, boutiques, and high-end pansiyons awake to serve the hip, urbanite crowd. To avoid the hubbub, spend an afternoon in Alaçatı, when only locals and store-owners are around.

The beach at Alaçatı is 2 km (1 mi) south of town, and a prime wind-surfing spot, with strong winds and few waves. Disappointingly, there is only a small, public beach here. The water is cooler compared to the other beaches, and the attitude is also a bit frostier. Go for the dozen or so water sports available, including water-skiing, banana boat rides, and windsurfing. Babylon, a popular jazz club, has its beach branch here in the summer, where you can lay out on wooden decks that extend out over the water during the day, and attend concerts at night.

Dalyanköy, 5 km (3 mi) north of Çeşme, is a small fishing village, known for the excellent seafood restaurants that line the small harbor. The beaches are not that noteworthy, so save your trip out here for the evening, when you can wine and dine by the water.

About 5 km (3 mi) south of Çeşme, out along Akburun (White Cape) near the village of Çiflikköy, are several nice stretches and numerous unnamed coves. For lots of waves and wind, try **Piçrlantı** beach, just out-side of Çiflik to the southwest. The beach has a small section reserved for kite-boarding. There's a small section for the public, which is, un-fortunately, usually littered with cigarette butts. For a cleaner space, you can rent two chaises and an umbrella for around $7. For lunch, your options are limited to a few beachside cafés. **Altınkum** is a bit farther south of Çiflik, and has calmer, gorgeous water. There are a campsite, and a

Fun Club, where you can rent kayaks and windsurfers. To steer clear from the crowds, head east along the sand.

Where to Eat

★ $$$ ✕ **Cevat'ın Yeri.** An upscale, elegant fish restaurant overlooking Dalyan Bay's marina, Cevat'ın Yeri (Cevat's Place), is an ideal place to spend a summer evening. The menu includes traditional mezes and fresh fish, and all dishes are prepared with attention to taste and presentation. The *gevurdağ* salad, a spicy mix of tomato and onion, whets the appetite, and the fresh, crispy calamari with homemade tartar sauce is perfectly cooked. You can order the fresh catch of the day, and if you want, select the exact fish you want from the glass display case. ⊠ *Liman Cad., Dalyanköy* ☎ 232/724–7045 ▭ *AE, MC, V.*

$$ ✕ **Cafe Agrilia.** This Italian restaurant was around long before the rest of Alaçatı's trendy restaurant scene. It's in old tobacco warehouse, and the excellent food makes up for the fact that it's a bit secluded from the scene. The homemade tagliatelle with shrimp in a light, garlic sauce is fantastic, and the ravioli with *lor* cheese is a good option for all. Agrilia also makes creative fresh fruit juice concoctions. ⊠ *Kemal Paşa Cad. No.75, Alaçatı* ☎ 232/716–8594 ▭ *AE, MC, V.*

Fodor'sChoice
★

$$ ✕ **Sahil.** A waterfront eatery across from the Ertan Hotel, Sahil serves fresh, tasty appetizers like eggplant salad, and typical Turkish dishes, such as lamb kebabs and grilled fish. There's a terrace for al fresco dining, with a pleasant but unremarkable view of the Bay of Çeşme and promenading vacationers. Reservations are essential in summer. ⊠ *Cumhuriyet Meyd. 12, Çeşme* ☎ 232/712–8294 ▭ *V, MC.*

$ ✕ **Sevim Café.** Despite its location on an awkward corner at the edge of the main square by the sea, this establishment is charming, and the owner, Ms. Zehra, hand-prepares the *mantı* (meat-filled ravioli topped with garlicky yogurt). Grilled meats are served with salads on the side. Come early for a good seat. ⊠ *Hal Binası 5, opposite Kervansaray* ☎ 232/712-9647 ▭ *AE, MC, V.*

$ ✕ **Yıldız Restaurant.** In Alaçatı, where prices are skyrocketing, Yıldız is a good option for a good and reasonably priced lunch. The family-owned spot serves homemade mantı, Turkish meatballs, and other daily specials. The cool breeze and friendly service are also a plus. ⊠ *Kemalpaşa Cad., No. 51, Alaçatı* ☎ 232/716–8090 ▭ *AE, MC, V.*

¢ ✕ **Dost Pide.** This local favorite lunch spot has been open for over 30 years and specializes in super-long, closed *pides* (Turkish-style calzones), a specialty of the Black Sea Region. ⊠ *Şifne Cad. No.27, Ilıca* ☎ 232/ 723–2059 ▭ *AE, MC, V.*

¢ ✕ **Kumrucu Sevki.** Ilıca has the best *kumru* (Turkish-style panini) around and Kumrucu Sevki has the best reputation of all restaurants serving the dish. The sandwich goes well with a bottle of Eker ayran, a refreshing yogurt drink that tones

SWEET SPOT

For dessert, try local favorite **Imren** (⊠ Tokoğlu Mah. Kemalpaşa Cad., Alaçatı ☎ 232/716–8356). Ice cream is available in many flavors, and the local mastic tree is used for *sakız muhallebe,* a Turkish gumdrop pudding.

down the spicy kumru. This bustling beachside joint has its sister branch in Ilıca's center. ⊠ *Çeşme Ilıca Merkez* ☎ *232/723–2392* ⊟ *AE, D, MC, V.*

★ ¢ ✕**L'Apero.** This café, set on a hill right above Cevat'ın Yeri (the stairs behind the restaurant lead up to the café), is the perfect place to watch the sun set over an aperitif and a serene view of the Dalyan harbor. It's run by a friendly, Belgian woman who speaks very good English, and you might find yourself back at this charming little spot for after-dinner drinks. Light sandwiches and tasty desserts are served also. ⊠ *4227 Sokak, Dalyankoy* ☎ *232/724–7034* ⊟ *AE, MC, V.*

Where to Stay

The prices of most hotels in beach towns peak during the busy summer months of July and August. Prices drop before and after this time, and hotels will usually adjust prices for guests staying longer than one week.

ÇEŞME ✕⌂ **Kervansaray.** Built in 1528 during the reign of Süleyman the Mag-
★ $$$ nificent, this old property in the town center, next to Çeşme's medieval castle, is largely decorated in traditional Turkish style, with kilims and low wooden furniture. Good choices for lunch or dinner in the excellent restaurant include lamb kebabs with yogurt, cold eggplant salad, and *börek* (deep-fried pastry shells, here filled with goat cheese). In pleasant weather, you can dine outdoors in a courtyard surrounded by the ancient stone walls of the Kervansaray. ⊠ *Kale Yanı* ☎ *232/712–7177 or 232/712–6491* 🖶 *232/712–2906* ⇗ *34 rooms* ♨ *Restaurant, bar* ⊟ *AE, DC, MC, V* ☾ *Closed Nov.–Mar.*

$$ ⌂ **Pasifik.** This four-story hotel on Çeşme's waterfront has clean bright rooms with sea views. It's the last hotel along the harbor—about a 15-minute walk from the town's square—which means it's quiet at night. It's next to Çeşme's small public beach, which seems convenient, but be aware that this particular beach can get very crowded in July and August and the main beach club plays loud music in the afternoon, so you'll probably want to head to one of the other coves during the day. ⊠ *3264 Sol.Tekke Plajı Mevkii, No.16* ☎ *232/712–2700* ⇗ *16 rooms* ⊟ *AE, MC, V.*

$ ⌂ **Ertan Oteli.** This five-story white-stucco hotel on the water is modern and efficient. Many rooms have views of the Aegean, as does the terrace restaurant. The hotel has its own private beach at Ayayorgi, and provides shuttle bus service to and from the beach. ⊠ *Cumhuriyet Meyd. 12* ☎ *232/712–6795* 🖶 *232/712–7852* ⇗ *67 rooms* ♨ *Restaurant, bar* ⊟ *MC, V.*

$ ⌂ **Tani Pansiyon.** A friendly retired couple run this modest pansiyon. The simple rooms have low wooden beds and views of the bay through handmade crocheted lace curtains. Be sure to ask for one facing the bay. Bathrooms and showers are shared, as is a lace-decked kitchen upstairs on the terrace, where breakfast is served. ⊠ *Çarşı Sok. 5, Musalla Mah.* ☎ *232/712–6238* ⇗ *8 rooms* ⊟ *No credit cards.*

ILICA ⌂ **Sheraton Çeşme.** The Sheraton looms over the rapidly changing Ilıca
$$$$ skyline—another mega-resort hotel with its own private beach. There's nothing particularly noteworthy about the rooms, but they are clean and provide reliable Sheraton quality and comfort. Ask for one with a bal-

cony and ocean view. The hotel is farther removed from Ilica's town square than the other big resorts, but it's still within walking distance. ☒ *Şifne Cad., No. 35* ☎ *232/723–1240* 🖷 *232/723–1856* ⊕ *www.sheratoncesme. com* 🖙 *367 rooms, 11 suites* ⚒ *Safe, ethernet, 2 restaurants, room service, 3 bars, tennis court, 2 pools, gym, spa, executive floor, public Internet* 🖃 *AE, DC, MC, V.*

⏱ **$$$** 🎫 **Ilıca Hotel.** Ilica's newest five-star hotel has a spa and wellness cen-
Fodor'sChoice ter and its own private beach. The beach has wooden sunbathing plat-
★ forms that extend out over the water, with chaises and plush pillows. There are several thermal water pools to choose from, too, and one seawater pool. Many of the chic rooms have beautiful sea views, and they are all decorated elegantly with attractive, dark-wood furniture and handsomely framed paintings and photographs. Family rooms have upper floors for parents and separate downstairs sleeping area for kids. If you're looking for more privacy, you can opt for one of bungalows a short walk from the main hotel area. ☒ *Boyalk Mevkii* ☎ *232/723–3131* 🖷 *232/ 723–3484* ⊕ *www.ilicahotel.com* 🖙 *237 rooms, 12 suites, 11 family rooms* ⚒ *Ethernet, 2 restaurants, 9 bars, tennis court, 7 pools, gym, spa, beachfront, kids' programs* 🖃 *AE, D, MC, V.*

⏱ **$$** 🎫 **Altın Yunus Tatilköyü.** The low, bright white cuboid buildings of this big resort—whose name translates as "golden dolphin"—curve along an attractive white-sand beach edging a cove dotted with sailboats. Rooms are done in Mediterranean style, with lots of white and pale ocean-blue. Here you'll find thicker carpets, bigger beds, and a plusher feel than is usual for Turkey. With almost every imaginable recreational facility, the resort is a destination unto itself. ☒ *Kalemburnu Boyalık Mev., Ilıca* ☎ *232/723–1250* 🖷 *232/723–2252* ⊕ *www.altinyunus.com.tr* 🖙 *517 rooms* ⚒ *6 restaurants, 2 bars, 5 tennis courts, 4 pools, gym, beachfront, watersports, public Internet* 🖃 *AE, MC, V.*

¢ 🎫 **Karabina Pansiyon.** This small, modest pansiyon is in a century-old house. The building is a bit run down and the rooms are small, but restoration began in fall 2006, so things should look much better by summer 2007. On a positive note, the tall ceilings and bay windows make the rooms feel more spacious than they actually are. Rooms come with private or shared bathrooms. The hotel is in the center of Ilica's main thoroughfare, so you'll hear the hustle and bustle until well past midnight. ☒ *İzmir Cad. No. 59, Ilıca* ☎ *232/723–1007* 🖷 *232/484–8663* 🖙 *40 rooms* 🖃 *No credit cards.*

DALYANKÖY ✕🎫 **Dalyan Plaza Hotel.** If you're looking for a more secluded spot, this
$$$$ boutique hotel is ideal. Rooms are full of light and spacious, with cool
Fodor'sChoice tile floors instead of the wall-to-wall carpeting that seems to be popu-
★ lar in many of the beachside hotels. There's a pleasant reception area that leads out to a small bar and outdoor terrace where guests can relax, and the hotel has its own private beach with wooden sunbathing platforms. They are several restaurants on-site, featuring Aegean, French, and Italian cuisines, and Dalyan's seafood restaurants are within walking distance. ☒ *Dalyan Mahallesi, 4227 Sokak, No. 26* ☎ *232/724– 8000* 🖷 *232/724–9252* ⊕ *www.dalyanplaza.com.tr* 🖙 *46 rooms, 10 suites* ⚒ *3 restaurants, bar, pool, gym* 🖃 *AE, MC, V.*

$ ⊞ **L'Apero.** This small pansiyon is run by a friendly Belgian woman who rents out two double rooms in her house. The rooms are large and tastefully decorated, and one has a kitchen attached. The best part about the pansiyon, aside from the wonderful view, is the great company. There is a café attached to the pansiyon. ⊠ *4227 Sokak* ☎ *232/724–7034* ⌂ *2 rooms* ⌂ *No a/c, restaurant, pool* ⊟ *AE, MC, V.*

ALAÇATI ⊞ **Sailors.** This bright bed-and-breakfast has sunny rooms that smell of
$$$ fresh pine. Breakfast, complete with homemade jams, is enjoyed in the garden restaurant, underneath pomegranate and jasmine trees. The restaurant also has an excellent lunch and dinner menu that includes brick-oven pizzas. Note that only one room has air-conditioning, but all rooms have their own TVs and phones. ⊠ *75. Yıl Cad. Esen Sok., No. 3* ☎ *232/716–8822* ⊕ *www.sailorsotel.com* ⌂ *6 rooms* ⌂ *Restaurant* ⊟ *AE, MC, V.*

$$ ⊞ **Fesleğen Hanım.** Right in the center of Alaçatı's square, this unique hotel is owned by an İzmirian artist, who has decorated the rooms with a lot of character—and a lot of red accents. The hotel is in a restored stone house, and the two rooms (one with air-conditioning) are on the top floor. Ask about the interesting story behind the name, Fesleğen Hanım, which means "Basil Woman." ⊠ *Kemalpaşa Cad., No. 96* ☎ *232/716–6551* ⊕ *www.kirmiziardic.com* ⌂ *2 rooms* ⊟ *AE, D, MC, V* ⊘ *Closed Oct.–May.*

$$ ⊞ **Sakızlı Han.** The restored stone house of a wealthy 19th-century family, this pansiyon offers all of the modern amenities with a country-style ambiance. The reception area is set up like a living room. Most rooms have air-conditioning. ⊠ *Yeni Mecidiye Mah. Kemalpaşa Cad., No.114* ☎ *232/716–6108* 🖷 *232/716–6109* ⊕ *www.sakizlihan.com* ⌂ *8 rooms* ⌂ *a/c in some rooms* ⊟ *MC, V.*

Nightlife & the Arts

Açık Hava Teyatrosu, Çeşme's open-air theater, hosts a series of Turkish concerts in summer, and the peninsula has a very active nightlife. Many of its small eateries stay open 24 hours to accommodate the late-night munchies. The bar and club scene has moved out of Çeşme proper and into the neighboring towns of Ilıca and Alaçatı.

Yıldız Burnu (⊠ 5253 Sokak, No. 1, Yıldızburnu ☎ 232/723–4642), a trendy part of Ilıca, is made up of fancy waterfront bars and lounges that cater to a young crowd. The entrance is free—the cost is built into the overly expensive drinks. **Rouge**, with its lounge and Latin music, is a hot spot in the complex.

Ayayorgi's clubs and discos are quite popular with night owls. The 22-year-old **Paparazzi** (⊠ Sakara Mah., Ayayorgi ☎ 232/712–6767) is still at the top of many people's lists.

The popular Istanbul jazz club **Babylon** (⊠ Çark Plajı, Liman Mevkii, Alaçatı ☎ 232/716–6707) spends its summer season seaside in Alaçatı. Many weeknight concerts are free, and the club brings in an excellent selection of local and international musicians, covering traditional and pop Turkish music, and jazz.

Sports & the Outdoors

BOAT TOURS During high season, daily boat tours leave from the main harbor in Çeşme and from Ilıca. They cost around $15 per person, including lunch, and stop at several different islands. One of the most popular stops is Donkey Island, where dozens of donkeys will greet you upon arrival. Although a great way to explore Çeşme's waters, many of the boat tours tend to play loud pop music and can sometimes be overcrowded. *Benta,* a smaller boat, is known for being calmer and quieter, whereas *Nirvana* is known as the party boat. The boats operate on a less frequent basis in the spring and fall and won't take off unless their minimum quota is filled. You can just go to the harbor and choose a tour on the day you wish to travel.

KITESURFING Piçrlantı Beach has a small kitesurfing site. If you don't have any experience in the sport, you can enroll in a three-day course from the beach's **Kiteschool** (☎ 536/458–8494 ⊕ www.kitesurfbeach.com) for $270. Experienced kitesurfers can simply rent equipment for $75 per day. Use of Kiteschool's facilities (changing rooms, showers, and beach umbrellas) is included in the price of rental or instruction.

Shopping

The main street in Çeşme has many gift shops selling trinkets and souvenirs, beachwear, carpets, and leather items. There are also many jewelry stores selling silver and gold, which are marked up a lot, so be sure to bargain. During high season, Ilıca has a weekly antique bazaar Monday through Friday. You can find old furniture, swords, guns, paintings, and dish and glassware from the Ottoman and Selçuk periods. Alaçatı also has an antique bazaar on weekends in summer. Alaçatı's main strip has many little boutiques nestled in between cafés and stone houses.

SELÇUK, EPHESUS & ŞIRINCE

You can easily spend several days wandering around these three towns. Staying in Selçuk is a convenient, practical, and comfortable way to tour the area. Between the open-air museum of Ephesus and the Archaeology Museum in Selçuk, you'll surely get your share of history, but if you need a break, Şirince is the place to go, with its bucolic views, charming village homes, and deliciously fresh food.

Selçuk

⑬ *79 km (49 mi) south of İzmir on Rte. E87.*

Selçuk, the closest city to the archaelogical site of Ephesus, lies beneath an ancient fortress and is unfortunately, often overlooked. The former farming town has interesting sights of its own to offer—St. John the Evangelist was purportedly buried here, and the city has one of the oldest mosques in Turkey. It's also a practical place to base yourself, as it's close to many of the area's attractions. The city is easy to navigate, and there are many friendly, well-run pansiyons in the area. The town also hosts an annual camel-wrestling festival every January.

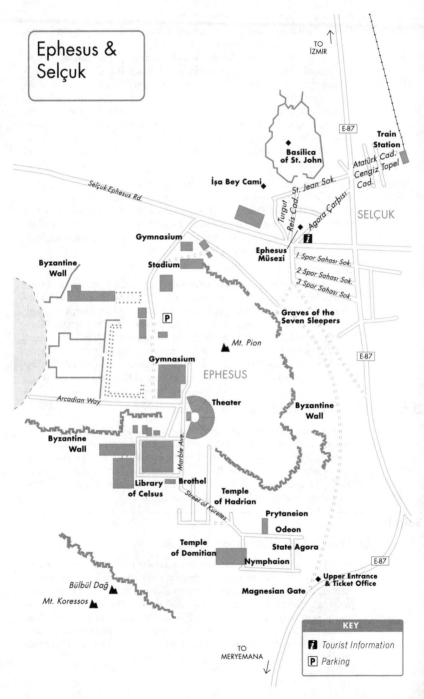

Ephesus & Selçuk

TO
İZMIR

E-87

Train Station

Atatürk Cad.
Cengiz Topel
Cad.

Basilica of St. John

İşa Bey Cami

St. Jean Sok.

Turgut Reis Cad.

Agora Çarşısı

SELÇUK

Selçuk-Ephesus Rd.

Gymnasium

Stadium

Ephesus Müzezi

🛈

1 Spor Sahası Sok.

2 Spor Sahası Sok.

3 Spor Sahası Sok.

Byzantine Wall

P

Graves of the Seven Sleepers

Mt. Pion

E-87

Gymnasium

EPHESUS

Arcadian Way

Theater

Byzantine Wall

Byzantine Wall

Marble Ave.

Library of Celsus

Brothel

Street of Kuretes

Temple of Hadrian

Prytaneion

Odeon

Temple of Domitian

State Agora

Nymphaion

E-87

Upper Entrance & Ticket Office

Magnesian Gate

Bülbül Dağ

Mt. Koressos

TO
MERYEMANA

KEY
🛈 Tourist Information
P Parking

What to See

★ The small **Ephesus Müzesi** (Ephesus Museum) has one of the best collections of Roman and Greek artifacts found anywhere in Turkey. Along with some fine frescoes and mosaics are two white statues of Artemis. In each she is portrayed with several rows of what are alternatively described as breasts or a belt of eggs; in either case, they symbolize fertility. ⊠ *Agora Çarsısı, opposite visitor center* ☎ *232/892–6010* ⌂ *$2* ☉ *Daily 8:30–noon and 1–7.*

İsa Bey Cami (İsa Bey Mosque) is one of the oldest mosques in Turkey, dating from 1375. Its jumble of architectural styles suggests a transition between Seljuk and Ottoman design: Like later Ottoman mosques, this one has a courtyard, something not found in Seljuk mosques. The structure is built out of "borrowed" stone: marble blocks with Latin inscriptions, Corinthian columns, black-granite columns from the baths at Ephesus, and pieces from the altar of the Temple of Artemis. ⊠ *St. Jean Sok.* ☉ *Daily 9–6.*

The fragments of the **Temple of Artemis** on display at the İsa Bey Mosque are about all you will see of the holy site that drew pilgrims from around the ancient world and was one of its Seven Wonders. Begun in the 7th century BC, greatly expanded by the wealthy Lydian king Croesus, and redone in marble in the 6th century BC, the temple was burned down by a disgruntled worshiper in 356 BC. Rebuilt by Alexander the Great, it was sacked by Goths in AD 263 and later stripped for materials to build Istanbul's Aya Sofya and Selçuk's St. John Basilica. Today a lone column towering over a scattering of fallen stones in a green field on the Selçuk–Ephesus road is all that remains of a temple that was once four times larger than the Parthenon in Athens.

The emperor Justinian built the **St. John Basilica** over a 2nd-century tomb on Ayasoluk Hill, believed by many to have once held the body of St. John the Evangelist. Eleven domes formerly topped the basilica, which rivaled Istanbul's Aya Sofya in scale. The barrel-vaulted roof collapsed after a long-ago earthquake, but the church is still an incredible sight, with its labyrinth of halls and marble courtyards. It provides beautiful views both of Selçuk's castle and the Plain of Ephesus. ⊠ *Entrance off St. Jean Sok., just east of İsa Bey Cami* ☎ *no phone* ⌂ *$2* ☉ *Daily 8–5.*

NEED A BREAK? Tea and a wide selection of excellent *lokum* (Turkish delight candies) are sold at tiny **Tadım** (⊠ In Emlak Bankası arcade). Hikmet Çeliker's family has been making the confection for the last 250 years and shipping it the world over.

Meryemana, the House of the Virgin Mary, is becoming an increasingly popular pilgrimage for Catholics. A small church was built above a leafy gully on what had been the site of an ancient house believed by many to have been the place where St. John took the mother of Jesus after the crucifixion and from which she ascended to heaven. You'll need a private car or taxi to get there, and you should probably go on the same day you're touring Ephesus. For around $35 a cab will take you to the church, wait for you for about 30 minutes, and then drop you off at the entrance to Ephesus. ⊠ *Off Rte. E87, 5 km (3 mi) south of Ephesus* ☉ *Daily 7:30–sunset.*

Camel Wrestling

WHILE AMERICANS ARE BUSY stuffing turkeys and stocking up on Christmas trees, Turkish camels and their owners prepare for an intense season of travel, confrontation, and competition. Every year, around 100 male camels tour the Marmara, Mediterranean, and the Aegean to compete in more than 30 wrestling festivals. Their primary motivation: get the girl. Camels will wrestle only during their mating season, which lasts from November to March, and a female camel is paraded around to provoke them into these contests. The camels' mouths are tied during the match so that they can do no real harm to each other, and between the judges, separaters (urgancı), and commentators (cazgirs), there are 21 officials (not including the camel owners) moderating the events.

A wrestling camel can expect to compete in 10 to 14 matches per year. The camels begin their wrestling "career" at age 4, when they are purchased from Iran. They train for the next four years and spend years 8 through 10 coming of age and developing their own strategies. Their right of passage, much like that of Turkish boys, occurs at this age, when the camels receive *havuts*, decorative cloths with their name and the word *maşallah* (may God protect him) sewn on the inside. According to camel owners and those familiar with the sport, wrestling is not a foreign, inhumane practice being imposed on the camels. On the contrary, these *dayluk* (as they're called until age 7, when they become *tülü* or hairy) begin wrestling naturally in the wild during their first years out of the womb, and if trained, can continue until age 25.

People have different theories about camel-wrestling's origins, although many argue it was a nomadic practice and part of the competition between caravan owners. Nomadic or not, these festivals have become a deep-rooted cultural pasttime in Turkey. Celebratory events actually begin the day before, during *halı gecesi*, or carpet night, when camels are flaunted around to percussive music, their bells jingling as they amble along. The camel owners, who often get to know one another during the prefestivities, are also dolled up in cornered caps, traditional neck scarves, and accordion-like boots.

To prevent wearing out the camels, the matches last no more than 10 minutes, and camels compete only once a day. The victor, the camel who gets the most points for outsmarting his rival by swiftly maneuvering and having the most control over the match (which might simply mean not running away), can win anywhere from $2,500–$25,000, depending on the competition. There's usually a wrestling World Cup of sorts at the culmination of the festivals, in which the top camels compete.

The exact dates, times, and locations of the festivals change from year to year, but competitions are always held every Sunday from December to March. The central and southern Aegean cities of Selçuk, İzmir, Bodrum, and Kuşadası host camel-wrestling festivals. Local tourism offices will have specific information about that year's festivals. Tickets cost around $7 per match and can be purchased on site.

—Evin Dogu

Where to Stay & Eat

$ ✕ **Eski Ev.** A wide selection of Turkish dishes, including vegetarian meals, is served on fancy copper plates. Their Eski Ev meat stew is unique but a bit on the salty side. They also have a wide variety of mezes. The Ottoman motifs may feel a bit touristy, but the place is done up nicely, with a peaceful, shaded courtyard for outdoor dining attached to an old house. ⊠ *Cengiz Topel Cad.* ▭ *AE, MC, V.*

¢ ✕ **Ejder Restaurant.** A middle-aged Turkish couple run this restaurant on the lively Cengiz Topel Street. There's a grand view of the Selçuk aqueduct from the outdoor tables. Mehmet, the owner, manages the place, and his wife is the sole cook. Because of this, it may sometimes take a while for you to get your food. Dishes include traditional kebabs and Turkish specials of the day, all very tasty. There's a guestbook for customers' comments that the owner, Mehmet, takes much pride in. ⊠ *Cengiz Topel Cad. No. 9/E* ☎ *232/892–3296* ▭ *AE, MC, V.*

$ ▦ **Kale Han.** A friendly family runs this hotel built around a walled garden. Rooms are simple, with bare whitewashed walls and dark timber beams. Ask for one facing the castle behind the hotel. One of the buildings in the garden has a four-bed suite. Simple grilled meats and fish are served in the airy dining room, which has a big fireplace. ⊠ *Atatürk Cad. 49, Selçuk* ☎ *232/892–6154* ▤ *232/892–2169* ⊕ *www.kalehan. com* ⤳ *54 rooms, 1 suite* ⚭ *Restaurant, pool* ▭ *MC, V.*

¢ ▦ **Hotel Akay.** This hotel, set in a quiet residential neighborhood by the İsa Bey Mosque, has old-Ottoman flourishes—whitewashed walls inside and out, latticed balconies, arched windows and doors, kilims on the floor, and copper and brass pots here and there. The newest rooms (with TVs) are near the pool, and cost $15 more than the standard rooms. ⊠ *İsa Bey Cami Kar., Serin Sok. 3, Selçuk* ☎ *232/892–3172* ▤ *232/ 892–3009* ⊕ *www.hotelakay.com* ⤳ *23 rooms* ⚭ *Restaurant, bar, pool, laundry service, public Internet, airport shuttle* ▭ *AE, MC, V.*

★ ¢ ▦ **Hotel Bella.** This attractive hotel, painted a cheerful yellow, is right by the St. John Basilica. A spacious terrace has a small library with books in English, backgammon boards, and a large-screen TV. Some rooms have balconies and wood floors with Turkish carpets; walls are adorned with colorful kilims. There's a carpet store attached to the hotel. ⊠ *Ataturk Mah. St. John St. No.7* ☎ *232/892–3944* ▤ *232/892–0344* ⊕ *www.hotelbella.com* ⤳ *12 rooms* ⚭ *Laundry service, public Internet; no a/c in some rooms* ▭ *AE, MC, V.*

¢ ▦ **Wallabies Victoria Hotel.** The name of this four-story hostelry in the heart of Selçuk recalls the owners' time in England. It's a tidy, cheerful place, with a comfortable lobby and whitewashed walls set off by honey-colored wood trim throughout. Rooms have delightful views of storks nesting on the ancient columns of an aqueduct. ⊠ *Cengiz Topel Cad. 4, Selçuk* ☎ *232/892–3204* ▤ *232/892 9406* ⤳ *24 rooms* ▭ *No credit cards.*

Shopping

Selçuk's weekly bazaar is held on Wednesday and Saturday in the main square from 9–6. There's also a daily, open market by the İsa Bey Mosque that sells souvenirs and Turkish-themed gifts.

Ephesus Archaeological Site

14 *4 km (2½ mi) west of Selçuk*

Ephesus (Efes in Turkish), the showpiece of Aegean archaeology, is probably the most evocative ancient city in the eastern Mediterranean, and one of the grandest reconstructed ancient sites in the world. The remarkably preserved ruins were rediscovered in the late 1800s; excavations have been going on for nearly a century. The site is a pleasure to explore: marble-paved streets with grooves made by chariot wheels lead past partially reconstructed buildings and monuments. The remains are especially appealing off-season, when the place can seem deserted. In the summer it's packed with tourists, many of whom pour off the Greek ships that cruise the Aegean and call at Kuşadası, 20 km (12 mi) to the south. Go early or late in the day, if possible. ■ TIP→ **Guides are available at the trinket stands ringing the parking lot.**

Ancient Ephesus grew from a seaside settlement to a powerful trading port and sacred center for the cult of Artemis. Its fame drew the attention of a series of conquerors, among them Croesus of Lydia and 6th-century BC Cyrus of Persia. After a Greek uprising against the Persians failed, the people of Ephesus, exercising effective diplomacy, managed to avoid conflict by appeasing each side, both of whom took turns controlling the city until Hellenistic times. The city was visited by powerful leaders such as Alexander the Great, who aided the city in its efforts to rebuild. After he died, his lieutenant moved the city to its current location.

Like most Ionian cities in Asia Minor, Ephesus was conquered by the Romans, and eventually became Christian. St. Paul is believed to have written some of his Epistles here and was later driven out by the city's silversmiths for preaching that their models of Diana were not divine. The artisans were "full of wrath, and cried out, saying 'Great is Diana of the Ephesians' " (Acts 19:24–40). St. John visited Ephesus between 37 and 48 AD, perhaps with the Virgin Mary, and again in 95, when he ostensibly wrote his gospel and then died. In 431 Ephesus was the scene of the Third Ecumenical Council, during which Mary was proclaimed the Mother of God.

Ephesus was doomed by the silting in its harbor. By the 6th century the port had become useless, and the population had shifted to what is now Selçuk; today Ephesus is 5 km (about 3 mi) from the sea. The new

THE IONIAN LEGEND

According to legend, the Delphic oracle, who led the Ionian Greeks to the Ephesus region from their home in central Greece in the 11th century BC, advised Androkles, the Ionian leader, to follow a boar, while claiming that "The new town will be shown . . . by a fish." Androkles and his men came across some people ready to cook a fish that suddenly jumped and knocked embers into nearby brush. The fire spread, and Androkles followed the boar fleeing the flames to Mt. Koressos, later called Bülbül Dağ, or Mount of the Nightingale. This is where the Ionians settled.

city was surrounded by ramparts, and a citadel was built. In the year 1000, crusaders came from the west, Turks from the east. The first Seljuk invaders were fought off in 1090, and the Byzantines held out until 1304. The town was incorporated into the Ottoman Empire at the beginning of the 15th century.

What to See

The Site. The road leading to the site parking lot passes a 1st-century AD **stadium,** where chariot and horse races were held on a track 712 ft long and where gladiators and wild beasts met in combat before 70,000 spectators. On your left after you enter the site is the 25,000-seat **theater,** backed by the western slope of Mt. Pion. A huge semicircle, with row upon row of curved benches, it was begun by Alexander's general Lysimachus and completed by emperors Claudius and Trajan in the 2nd century AD. There is a fine view from the top of the steps; higher still, near the top of Mt. Pion, are vestiges of the city's Byzantine walls. The theater is used for music and dance performances each May during the Selçuk Ephesus Festival of Culture and Art. Leading away from the theater toward the ancient port, now a marsh, is the **Arcadian Way.** This 1,710-foot-long street was once lined with shops and covered archways. Only a long line of slender marble columns remains.

In front of the theater is Marble Avenue. Follow it to the beautiful, two-story **Library of Celsus.** The courtyard of this much-photographed building is backed by wide steps that climb to the reading room, where you can still see rolls of papyrus. The library is near Marble Avenue's intersection with the **Street of Kuretes,** a still-impressive thoroughfare named for the college of priests once located there. At this corner is a large house believed to have been a **brothel.** Look for the floor mosaics of three women. To the right along the street are the multistoried houses of the nobility, with terraces and courtyards. To the left are public buildings. A block from the brothel is the facade of the **Temple of Hadrian,** with four Corinthian columns and a serpent-headed hydra above the door to keep out evil spirits; beyond is a partially restored fountain dedicated to the emperor Trajan. The street then forks and opens into a central square that once held the **Prytaneion,** or town hall; the **Nymphaion,** a small temple decked with fountains; and the **Temple of Domitian,** on the south side of the square, which was once a vast sanctuary with a colossal statue of the emperor for whom it was named. All are now a jumble of collapsed walls and columns.

Returning to the Street of Kuretes, turn right to reach the **odeon,** an intimate semicircle with just a few rows of seats, where spectators would listen to poetry readings and music. Columns mark the northern edge of the state **agora** (market). Beyond, the **Magnesian Gate** (also known as the Manisa Gate), at the end of the street, was the starting point for a caravan trail and a colonnaded road to the Temple of Artemis. ⊠ *Site entry 4 km (2½ mi) west of Selçuk on Selçuk–Ephesus Rd.* ☎ *232/892–6402 or 232/892–6940* ⊑ *$10* ☉ *Daily 8–5:30.*

According to the legend attached to the **Graves of the Seven Sleepers,** seven young Christian men hid in a cave to avoid persecution by the Romans in the 3rd century AD. They fell into a sleep that lasted 200 years, waking only after the Byzantine Empire had made Christianity the official state religion. When they died, they were buried here, and the church that you see was built over them. The tombs in the large cemetery are largely from the Byzantine era. ⊠ *South of Sor Sahasi Sok. 3* 🕭 *Free.*

Where to Eat

$ ✕ **Günhan Restaurant.** One of the few places to eat at the Ephesus ruins, this restaurant serves a variety of foods, from sandwiches to traditional stewed Turkish dishes, kebabs, and grilled lamb chops. Shaded by awnings, it's perfect for a rest and cool drink before or after a trip to the ruins. ⊠ *Ephesus Ruins* 🕾 *232/892–2291* ⊟ *MC, V* ☽ *No dinner.*

$ ✕ **Tusan Efes Restaurant.** This restaurant next to the Ephesus archaeological site feels blissfully removed from the action—it's surrounded by eucalyptus trees and next to a campground. The restaurant prepares delicious Turkish foods, specializing in shish kebabs, fish, and soups. Their *ezogelin* (wedding soup) is especially popular. ⊠ *Ephesus* 🕾 *232/892–6060* ⊟ *AE, MC, V.*

> ### EPHESUS TOURS
>
> There are several travel agencies in Selçuk that can arrange daily tours to Ephesus and other nearby attractions. Some offer small, private tours as well as group tours. Below are a few of the most reliable agencies:
>
> ■ **Grand Wonders** (⊠ Atatürk Mah. 1019 Sok.6, Selçuk 🕾 232/892-7364).
>
> ■ **Helios Turizm** (⊠ Atatürk Mah. 1019 Sok. 6, Selçuk 🕾 232/892-6717).
>
> ■ **Peron Tour** (⊠ Atatürk Mah. 1006 Sok. 4, Selçuk 🕾 232/892-9547).

Şirince

🔟 *8 km (5 mi) east of Selçuk*

Şirince, one of Turkey's wealthiest villages, is another worthwhile excursion from Selçuk. Its picturesque cluster of two-story houses is set on a lush hill; the rows of houses create a long string of windows, which have decorative eaves with nature motifs. A former Greek enclave, Şirince has a 19th-century church and a stone basilica, also 19th-century, which has been restored and turned into an art gallery.

The village women's handiwork has become quite popular, and they sell their work along the village paths, in front of Şirince's pretty homes. Locals also sell fruit wine like mulberry, quince, and melon, which you can sample over a friendly conversation. Village food is delicious, and there are several inexpensive restaurants scattered around town.

Şrinice attracts many local and foreign visitors, but it is never deluged with tourists. To get to Şirince, take one of the dolmuşes that leave periodically from Selçuk from 8:30 AM to 5 PM.

Where to Stay & Eat

★ $ ✕ **Ocakbaş.** This restaurant serves excellent homemade Turkish food and specialties of the region, like zucchini flowers stuffed with rice, grilled peppers stuffed with seasoned cheese, and *gözleme,* a Turkish-style crepe. The large outdoor space offers a scenic view of the Şirince landscape. To get here follow the road that winds past the town's two churches. ⊠ *Iki Kilisinin Arasinda, Şirince* ☏ *232/898–3094* ▤ *AE, MC, V.*

$ ✕ **Artemis.** Artemis's superb setting overlooking a verdant valley and its excellent range of appetizers and meat dishes, particularly its baked lamb, are reason enough to make the trip here from Selçuk. It's also a great place to try the local wine, which is produced by the villagers in their homes. ⊠ *Şirince* ☏ *232/898–3201 or 232/898–3202* ▤ *MC, V.*

¢ ✕ **Köy.** One of the first restaurants in town. Köy is right in the main square. The menu covers everything from grilled meats to mezes, local cuisine, and *gözleme.* ⊠ *Across from the bus terminal* ☏ *232/898–3120* ▤ *AE, MC, V.*

$$–$$$ 🏠 **Kırkınca Pansiyon B&B.** The cleanliness and elegant simplicity of the rooms, named after flowers, and the early morning quiet of its terrace shaded by vines make the Kırkınca charming and romantic. In addition to the standard rooms, there are five restored Greek houses perfect for larger groups. The pansiyon also offers free hiking and orientation tours; horseback riding costs more. The restaurant serves local traditional dishes, kebabs, grilled items, Ottoman meat sautés, and a highly recommended eggplant soup. During special occasions, live piano music fills the reception area. ⊠ *Şirince* ☏ *232/898–3133 or 232/898 3140* 🖷 *232/898–3140* ⊕ *www.kirkinca.com* ➘ *7 rooms, 5 houses* ⚹ *Restaurant; no a/c in some rooms; no phone in some rooms, no TV in some rooms* ▤ *AE, MC, V.*

$$–$$$ 🏠 **Nişanyan Evleri.** Nişanyan is the last name of the owners, whose
Fodor'sChoice background in architecture is evident in the beautiful remodeling and
★ layout of the rooms they rent. You can rent standard rooms in the inn, a restored mansion; one of five independent stone cottages on the outskirts of the village (a few minutes' walk from the inn); or one of three houses in the village proper. All properties are furnished with stunning Ottoman antiques. There is a small book and CD collection in the welcoming reception area, and an upscale restaurant opens up at night and takes advantage of a lovely terrace. The cottages are short on modern conveniences inside but share a swimming pool and a lovely garden. ⌖ *At the entrance to Şirince, turn right at the hotel's sign and drive 1.2 km (¾ mi)* ☏ *232/898–3208* 🖷 *232/898–3209* ⊕ *www.nisanyan.com* ➘ *5 rooms, 5 cottages, 3 houses* ⚹ *Restaurant, pool, public Internet; no a/c, some phones, some TVs* ▤ *MC, V.*

$ 🏠 **Şirince Pansiyon.** Four rooms, each with antique furniture, make up this pansiyon. Standard room prices include a village breakfast (bread, homemade jam, Turkish cheese, olives, tomatoes, and cucumbers) and dinner at the owners' restaurant at the top of the hill by the church. ⊠ *Şirince* ☎ *232/898–3163 or 232/898–3090* ⊕ *www.sirincepansiyon.com* ⇩ *5 rooms* ⊟ *No credit cards.*

¢ ▦ **Alis Pansiyon.** Follow the red-and-white dove emblem from the main square to get to this cozy and tranquil bed-and-breakfast on the outskirts of the village. One room has its own private fireplace. There's a relaxing garden where you can sit with the owners, a friendly couple who perform music for their guests on the *ud,* a traditional Turkish instrument. ☎ *232/898–3212 or 505/232–2476 (cellphone)* ⊕ *www. sirincealispansiyon.com* ⇩ *3 rooms* ⊟ *No credit cards.*

KUŞADASI & ENVIRONS

One of Kuşadası's attractions is that it serves as a good base from which to explore Pamukkale and Aphrodisias. The town itself is a brash, highly touristy place replete with pubs, fish-and-chips restaurants, and souvenir shops. On a positive note, Kuşadası is near one of Turkey's most beautiful national parks, as well as two amazing historic and natural sights.

Kuşadası

16 *20 km (12 mi) southwest of Selçuk on Rte. 515.*

One of the most popular resort towns in the southern Aegean, Kuşadası is an ideal base, geographically, from which to explore the surrounding area. Unfortunately, being popular isn't always easy, and Kuşadası long ago lost its local charm to invasive, sterile buildings and overpopulation. The huge yacht marina, the largest in the region, has only exacerbated the situation. What was a small fishing village up until the 1970s is now a sprawling, hyperactive town packed with curio shops and a year-round population of around 60,000, which swells several times over in summer with the influx of tourists and Turks with vacation homes.

If you're looking for beaches, either head north from Kuşadası to Pamucak or travel 33 km (20 mi) south to lovely, wooded **Samsundağ Milli Parkı** (Samsundağ National Park, also known as Dilek Peninsula National Park), which has good hiking trails and several quiet stretches of sandy beach. The İçmeler beach, closest to the entrance, is also the most crowded. Travel 15 minutes to Karaburun for a more low-key atmosphere. To get to the park, take the coast road, marked Güzelçamlı or Devutlar, for about 10 km (6 mi) south of Kuşadası. If you're taking a dolmuş, expect to pay $4 for transportation and entrance into the park. ▧ *Park $2* ☉ *Apr.–Dec.*

There aren't many sights in Kuşadası proper, but the causeway off Kadınlar Denizi, just south of the harbor, connects the town to an old **Genoese castle** on Güvercin Adası (Pigeon Island). Today the site of a popular disco and several teahouses with gardens and sea views, the fortress was home to three Turkish brothers in the 16th century. These infamous pirates—Barbarossa, Oruc, and Hayrettin—pillaged the coasts of Spain and Italy and sold passengers and crews from captured ships into slavery in Algiers and Constantinople. Rather than fight them, Süleyman the Magnificent (ruled 1520–66) hired Hayrettin as his grand admiral and set him loose on enemies in the Mediterranean. The strategy worked: Hayrettin won victory after victory and was heaped with honors and riches.

Kuşadası's 300-year-old **kervansaray** (⊠ Atatürk Bul. 1), now the Club Kervansaray, is loaded with Ottoman atmosphere. Its public areas are worth a look even if you're not staying here.

Where to Stay & Eat

$$$$ ✕ **Kazim Usta Restaurant.** Open since 1956, this upscale restaurant made its reputation on its fish dishes, and now serves international cuisine as well. It's on the water, and there are a nice lounge and bar inside. ⊠ *Scalanuova AVM, Kuşadası* ☎ *256/612–2566* ▤ *AE, MC, V.*

$$–$$$ ✕ **Ali Baba Restaurant.** An appetizing and colorful display of the day's catch meets you at the entrance to this waterside fish restaurant. The decor is simple, the view over the bay is soothing, and the food is fabulous. For starters, try the cold black-eyed pea salad, the marinated octopus salad, or the fried calamari. ⊠ *Belediye Turistik Çarşısı 5* ☎ *256/614–1551* ⚲ *Reservations essential* ▤ *MC, V.*

$ ✕ **Özurfa.** The focus at this Turkish fast-food spot is kebabs. The Urfa kebab—spicy, grilled slices of lamb on pita bread—is the house specialty, and the fish kebabs are tasty, too. The location just off Barbaros Hayrettin Caddesi is convenient to the market and a step away from the crowds. ⊠ *Cephane Sok. No 9* ☎ *256/614–6070* ▤ *AE, MC, V.*

$ ✕ **Tarihi Çınar Et.** This popular eatery on the outskirts of town takes its name from the 800-year-old Oriental plane tree (*çınar* in Turkish), whose spreading branches shade its tables. House specialties are lamb and chicken cooked on a spit. There is also a wide range of *mezes* and superb ice cream. ⊠ *Davutlar Yolu, Saraydamlı* ☎ *256/681–1177* ▤ *AE, MC, V.*

$ ✕ **Yuvam.** Yuvam or "My Nest/Home" is truly that—it offers food you'd find in a Turkish home. During lunch hour the food runs out quickly, so get there early! Some of their specials include mantı, okra in a tomato-olive oil sauce, meat stew, and baked chicken with rice. ⊠ *Kaleici Yedieylül Sokak No 4* ☎ *256/614–9460* ▤ *MC, V.*

¢ ✕ **Cosgun Abi.** A younger mix of locals and tourists come to Cosgun Abi's, a café and nargileh (water-pipe) salon, and the atmosphere is very congenial. *Gözleme,* a Turkish-style crepe, is the thing to get here, with fillings of either cheese, spinach, or *ot* (Aegean wild plants). ⊠ *Belediye Dugun Salonu Karsisi, Kuşadası* ☎ *256/612–8258* ▤ *No credit cards.*

$$ ▥ **Club Kervansaray.** A refurbished 300-year-old inn that was once a way station for camel caravans, this hotel in the center of town is decorated in Ottoman style. The central courtyard—where the camels once were kept—is paved with marble and planted with palm trees. Rooms are decorated with kilims and Turkish folk art. In the dressy Turkish restaurant, there's live entertainment: singers, perhaps a belly dancer, and later, a pop band. ⊠ *Atatürk Bul. 2, 09400* ☎ *256/614–4115* 🖷 *256/614–2423* ⊕ *www.kusadasihotels.com/caravanserail* ⇴ *26 rooms* ⌂ *Wi-Fi, restaurant, bar* ▤ *AE, MC, V.*

★ $$ ⊞ **Kismet.** Surrounded by beautifully maintained gardens, the Kismet is set on a promontory overlooking the marina on one side and the Aegean on the other, and feels almost like a private Mediterranean villa. Each room has a private balcony, most with sea views. Kismet's popularity makes reservations a must. ⊠ *Akyar Mev., Türkmen Mah., 09400* ☎ *256/618–1290* 🖷 *256/618–1295* ⊕ *www.kismet.com.tr* ⏎ *107 rooms* ⚴ *Restaurant, 2 bars, tennis court, beachfront* ▤ *AE, D, MC, V* ⊘ *Closed Nov.–Mar.*

> **WORD OF MOUTH**
>
> "Sit in the garden of the Kismet, the western end overlooking the sea, order a drink, and watch the sun go down! Great memories."
> —Marko

$ ⊞ **Atınç Otel.** The Atınç, a mid-rise hotel, is in a good location: just a 5- to 10-minute walk from the center of town. Pluses include the Aegean views from the front rooms and the rooftop pool that looks out over the town. Guest rooms have balconies but not much style. ⊠ *Atatürk Bul. 42, 09400* ☎ *256/614–7608* 🖷 *256/614–4967* ⏎ *75 rooms* ⚴ *2 restaurants, 2 bars, pool* ▤ *AE, MC, V.*

¢ ⊞ **Bahar Pansiyon.** This cozy hotel is a block from Hayrettin Barbaros Caddesi. Front rooms have balconies, and all are quiet, affordable, and simply furnished. ⊠ *Cephane Sok. 12, 09400* ☎ *256/614–1191* 🖷 *256/614–9359* ⏎ *16 rooms* ⚴ *Restaurant, bar* ▤ *No credit cards.*

¢ ⊞ **Efe Otel.** This mid-price hotel sits on the waterfront a little beyond the path to Pigeon Island. A four-story whitewashed box with dark-wood trim, it's small and unremarkable, but it has a personable staff. ⊠ *Güvercin Ada Cad. 37, 09400* ☎ *256/614–3661* 🖷 *256/614–3662* ⊕ *www.hotelefe.com.tr* ⏎ *84 rooms* ⚴ *2 restaurants, room service, bar, pool, laundry service* ▤ *MC, V.*

Nightlife

The **Club Kervansaray** (⊠ Atatürk Bul. 2 ☎ 256/614–4115) has dining, dancing, and a show on most nights, but a younger crowd heads to the vast **Ecstasy Bar** (⊠ Sakarya Sok. 22 ☎ 256/613–1391), which plays the latest chart-topping sounds and has an official capacity of 1,000 spread over two floors. On Barlar Sokak, Kuşadası's loud, abrasive bar strip, the spacious and popular **Queen Victoria** (☎ no phone) has live music in summer. There are several Irish and British-style pubs farther along **Barlar Sokak.** For a lively night of dancing, young Turks and energetic tourists walk across the causeway to **Pigeon Island** to the "Disco"—there's no other name on the sign, but you can hear its music almost everywhere on this minuscule island.

Pamukkale (Hierapolis)

🅱 *170 km (105 mi) from Selçuk on Rte. E87 (follow road signs after Sarayköy); 200 km (124 mi) from Kuşadası.*

Pamukkale (pronounced pam-*uck*-al-lay) first appears as an enormous, chalky white cliff rising 330 ft from the plains. Mineral-rich volcanic spring water cascades over basins and natural terraces, crystallizing into white curtains of solidified water seemingly suspended in air. These hot springs are believed to cure rheumatism and other ailments. In the mid-1990s, the diversion of water from the springs to fill **thermal pools** in nearby luxury hotels reduced the volume of water reaching the site to a trickle; that, combined with a huge increase in the number of visitors, discolored the water's once-pristine whiteness. Large sections of the site are now cordoned off as authorities strive to conserve and restore a still-striking natural wonder to its former magnificence. Be forewarned that the surrounding area is very commercialized.

If you have time, spend the night here, as the one-day bus tours from the coast are exhausting and limiting: You'll end up spending more time on the bus than you do at the actual site. One full day at Pamukkale will give you enough time to explore the area.

Hierapolis is an example of how long the magical springs of Pamukkale have cast their spell. The ruins that can be seen today date from the time of the Roman Empire, but there are references to a settlement here as far back as the 5th century BC. Because the sights are spread over about ½ km (¼ mi), prepare for some walking. Between the theater and the Pamukkale Motel are the ruins of a **Temple of Apollo** and a bulky **Byzantine church.** The monumental fountain known as the **Nymphaion,** just north of the Apollo Temple, dates from the 4th century AD. Near the northern city gates is another indication of the town's former popularity, a vast **necropolis** (cemetery) with more than 1,000 cut-stone sarcophagi spilling all the way down to the base of the hill.

The stone building that enclosed Hierapolis's baths is now the **Pamukkale Müzesi,** a museum with a fine display of marble statues found at the site. ☎ *258/272–2077 for visitor center (for information), 258/272–2034 for museum* ⌨ *$1* ⊙ *Tues.–Sun. 8–noon and 12:30–6.*

Where to Stay & Eat

Most of the restaurants in town are touristy and don't have much to offer. You may want to eat at your hotel, or if you have a car and are feeling ambitious, head to the nearby town of Denizli.

$$ **Colossae Hotel Thermal.** More of a health resort than a hotel, the Colossae offers thermal and mud baths and has its own masseurs, beauticians, and health consultants. The low-rise complex is set among well-tended gardens around an Olympic-size pool. The rooms are plush and tastefully decorated, and many have shaded terraces overlooking the gardens. ⊠ *Karahayıt, Denizli 20227,* ☎ *258/271–4156* 🖷 *258/271–4250* ⊕ *www.colossae.com.tr* 🛏 *230 rooms with bath* ♿ *4 restaurants, 2 tennis courts, 2 pools, gym, spa* ⊟ *AE, MC, V.*

$ **Polat Thermal Hotel.** Clean and spacious, with a full range of facilities, the Polat Thermal is almost a thermal resort in itself, consisting of one- and two-story buildings around a large outdoor pool. The rooms are comfortable, although plain, with functional furnishings and whitewashed walls. ⊠ *Karahayıt, Denizli 20227* ☎ *258/271–4110* 🖷 *258/271–4092* ⊕ *www.polatthermalhotel.com* 🛏 *296 rooms* ♿ *2 restaurants, 2 pools, sauna* ⊟ *AE, MC, V.*

¢ **Koray Hotel.** This hotel is in the village, at the foot of the falls, which are a five-minute walk, but it has its own thermal pool. Rooms are attractive, with simple pine furnishings and whitewashed walls. ⊠ *Karahayıt, Denizli* ☎ *258/272–2300, 258/272–2222 for reservations* 🖷 *258/272–2095* ⊕ *www.hotelkoray.com* 🖙 *35 rooms* ⌂ *Restaurant, pool* ⊟ *AE, MC, V.*

Aphrodisias

★ ⑱ *80 km (50 mi) from Pamukkale, west on E87 and south on Rte. 585 at town of Kuyucak.*

The city of Aphrodite, goddess of love, is one of the largest and best-preserved archaeological sites in Turkey. Though most of what you see today dates from the 1st and 2nd centuries AD, archaeological evidence indicates the local dedication to Aphrodite follows a long history of veneration of pre-Hellenic goddesses, such as the Anatolian mother goddess and the Babylonian god Ishtar. Only about half the site has been excavated to date.

Aphrodisias, which was granted autonomy by the Roman Empire in the late 1st century BC, prospered as a significant center for religion, arts, and literature in the early 1st century AD. Imposing Christianity on its citizens proved far more difficult than granting autonomy to the pagan city, however, because of Aphrodite's large following. One method used to eradicate remnants of paganism was renaming the city, first Stavropolis (City of the Cross), then simply Caria, which archaeologists believe is the origin of the name of the present-day village of Geyre, which contains Aphrodisias in its borders.

The excavations here have led archaeologists to believe Aphrodisias was a thriving sculpture center, with patrons beyond the borders of the city. The signatures of Aphrodisian artists on statues, fragments, and bases as far away as Greece and Italy attest to this. The towering Babadağ range of mountains, east of the city, offered ancient sculptors a copious supply of white and delicately veined blue-gray marble, which has been used to stunning effect in the statues in the site museum, in the spiral, fluted, and other columns that sprout throughout, and in the delicate reliefs of gods and men, vines, and acanthus leaves on decorative friezes.

You can easily reach Aphrodisias on the way to Pamukkale, or from İzmir, Çeşme, and Selçuk, but the most direct route is from Kuşadası, which is why you'll that find a large number of daily tours head here. Many of the tours include Pamukkale as well, since these two sights are only 50 miles apart. You'll need a full day to get a true taste of Aphrodisias, and it may save you much time and energy to rent a car and visit these towns on your own.

The beauty of Aphrodisias rests in its details, and a good place to start absorbing them is the **site museum,** just past the ticket booth. The museum's collection includes several impressive statues from the site, including Aphrodite herself. ■ TIP➔ **Pick up a guide and a map—you'll need them, as the signage is poor.**

From the museum, follow the footpath to the right, which makes a circuit around the site and ends up back at the museum. The **Tetrapylon** is a monumental gateway with four rows of columns and some of the better remaining friezes. The **Temple of Aphrodite** was built in the 1st century BC on the model of the great temples at Ephesus. Its gate and many of its columns are still standing; some bear inscriptions naming the donor of the column. Next to the temple is the fine **Odeon,** an intimate, semicircular concert hall and public meeting room. Farther on is the **stadium,** which once was the scene of footraces, boxing and wrestling matches, and other competitions. One of the best preserved of its kind anywhere, the stadium could seat up to 30,000 spectators. The **theater,** built into the side of a small hill, is still being excavated. Its 5,000 white-marble seats are simply dazzling on a bright day. The adjacent **School of Philosophy** has a colonnaded courtyard with chambers lining both sides where teachers would work with small groups of students. 🕮 *Site $2.50, museum $2.50* ⊘ *Site and museum daily 8:30–5.*

Priene, Miletus, and Didyma

These three towns make up part of Ancient Ionia. They're all within 40 km (25 mi) of each another, and if you get an early enough start, you can visit them all in one day. There are many tours available to the three cities from İzmir, Çeşme, Kuşadası, Selçuk, and Bodrum. ■ TIP→ **If you have more time, and want some time away from the commotion of the Aegean coast, consider staying in Priene, where there's a lovely little pansiyon.**

★ ⑲ **Priene** sits spectacularly atop a steep hill above the flat valley of the Büyük Menderes (Maeander River). Dating from about 350 BC, the present-day remains of the city were still under construction in 334, when Alexander the Great liberated the Ionian settlements from Persian rule. At that time it was a thriving port, but as in Ephesus, the harbor silted over, commerce moved to neighboring Miletus, and the city's prosperity waned. As a result, the Romans never rebuilt Priene, and the simpler Greek style predominates as in few other ancient cities in Turkey. Excavated by British archaeologists in 1868–69, it's smaller than Ephesus and far less grandiose.

From the parking area, the walk up to the Priene ruins is fairly steep; because the routes through it are well marked, you won't need a map. After passing through the old city walls, you follow the city's original main thoroughfare; note the drainage gutters and the grooves worn into the marble paving stones by the wheels of 4th-century BC chariots. Continuing west, you come to the well-preserved *bouleterion* (council chamber) on the left. Its 10 rows of seats flank an orchestra pit with a little altar, decorated with bulls' heads and laurel leaves, at the center. Passing through the doors on the opposite side of the council chamber takes you to the

> WORD OF MOUTH
>
> "Priene, a short drive to the south of Kuşadası, is a neat city ruin on the terrace of a pine-covered mountain. The ruins of Miletus (a mammoth theater, but not as impressive as Ephesus) and the temple of Apollo at Didyma are all within an easy day trip to the south. The usual circuit is Priene–Miletus–Didyma."   –jeffergray

Sacred Stoa, a colonnaded civic center, and the edge of the **agora,** the marketplace. Farther west along the broad promenade are the remains of a row of **private houses,** each of which typically has two or three rooms on two floors; of the upper stories, only traces of a few stairwells remain. In the largest house a statue of Alexander was found.

A block or so farther along the main street is the **Temple of Athena.** Its design—the work of Pytheos, architect of the Mausoleum of Halicarnassus (one of the Seven Wonders of the Ancient World)—was repeatedly copied at other sites in the Greek empire. Alexander apparently chipped in on construction costs. The temple was a dwelling for the goddess Athena rather than a place for worshipers to gather; only priests could enter. Earthquakes have toppled the columns; the five that have been reerected evoke the former appearance of the temple, which once had a stunning view over the Menderes Valley. A walk north and then east along the track leads to the well-preserved little **theater,** sheltered on all sides by pine trees. Enter through the stage door into the orchestra section; note the five front-row VIP seats, carved thrones with lions' feet. If you scramble up a huge rock known as Samsun Dağı (behind the theater and to your left as you face the seats), you will find the scanty remains of the **Sanctuary of Demeter,** goddess of the harvest; a few bits of columns and walls remain, as well as a big hole through which blood of sacrificial victims was poured as a gift to the deities of the underworld. Since few people make it up here, it is an incredibly peaceful spot, with a terrific view over Priene and the plains. Above this, should you care to go farther, are the remnants of a Hellenistic fortress. *37 km (23 mi) from Kuşadası, southeast on Rte. 515, south on Rte. 525, west on Rte. 09–55 (follow signs)* 📞 *no phone* 💲 *$1.50* 🕒 *Daily 8:30–6.*

⑳ Miletus was one of the greatest commercial centers of the Greek world before its harbor silted over. The first settlers were Minoan Greeks from Crete, who arrived between 1400 BC and 1200 BC. The Ionians, who arrived 200 years later, slaughtered the male population and married the widows. The philosopher Thales was born here in the early 6th century BC; he calculated the height of the pyramids at Giza, suggested that the universe was actually a rational place despite its apparent disorder, and coined the phrase "Know thyself." An intellectual center, the city was also home to the mathematicians Anaximenes, who held that air was the single element behind the diversity of nature, and Anaximander, whose ideas anticipated the theory of evolution and the concept of the indestructibility of matter. Like the other Ionian cities, Miletus was passed from one ruling empire to another and was successively governed by Alexander's generals Antigonus and Lysimachus and Pergamum's Attalids, among others. Under the Romans the town finally regained some control over its own affairs and shared in the prosperity of the region. St. Paul preached here before the harbor became impassable and the city had to be abandoned once and for all.

The archaeological site is sprawled out along a desolate plain. Well-marked trails make a guide or map unnecessary. The parking lot is right outside the city's most magnificent building—the **Great Theater,** a remarkably intact 25,000-seat amphitheater built by the Ionians and kept up by the Romans. Along the third to sixth rows some inscriptions reserving seats for notables are still visible, and the vaulted passages leading to the seats have the feel of a modern sporting arena. Climb to the top of the theater for a look at the defensive walls built by the Byzantines and a view across the ancient city.

To see the rest of the ruins, follow the dirt track to the right of the theater. A stand of buildings marks what was once a broad processional avenue. The series begins with the **Delphinion,** a sanctuary of Apollo; a **Seljuk hammam** added to the site in the 15th century, with pipes for hot and cold water still visible; a **stoa** (colonnaded porch) with several reerected Ionic columns; the foundations of a **Roman bath** and **gymnasium;** and the first story of the **Nymphaion,** all that remains of the once highly ornate three-story structure, resembling the Library of Celsus at Ephesus, that once distributed water to the rest of the city.

To the south, the dirt track becomes a tree-lined lane that leads to the **İlyas Bey Cami,** a mosque built in 1404 in celebration of its builder and namesake's escape from Tamerlane, the Mongol terror. The mosque is now a romantic ruin: The ceiling is cracked, dust covers the tiles, and birds roost inside. The path from the mosque back to the parking lot passes a small museum, the **Miletus Müzesi,** containing some finds from the site and the surrounding area. *22 km (14 mi) south of Priene on Rte. 09–55* ☎ *no phone* ✉ *Ruins $1.50, museum $2* ☾ *Tues.–Sun. 8:30–6.*

㉑ Didyma (Didim in Turkish), a resort town on the rise, was an important sacred site connected to Miletus by a road of statues. The temple of Apollo is here, as well as some beaches, which are increasingly frequented by Brits who have bought real estate in the area.

Didyma is famous for its magnificent **Temple of Apollo.** As grand in scale as the Parthenon—measuring 623 ft by 167 ft—the temple has 124 well-preserved columns, some still supporting their architraves. Started in 300 BC and under construction for five centuries, it was never completed, and some of the columns remain unfluted. The temple's oracles rivaled those of Delphi. Beneath the courtyard is a network of underground corridors where the temple priests would consult the oracle. The corridor walls would throw the oracle's voice into deep and ghostly echoes, which the priests would interpret. The tradition of seeking advice from sacred oracles probably started long before the arrival of the Greeks; in all likelihood, the Greeks converted an older Anatolian cult based at the site into their own religion. The Greek oracle had a good track record, and at the birth of Alexander the Great (356 BC), predicted that he would be victorious over the Persians, that his general Seleucus would later become king, and that Trajan would become an emperor.

The popularity of the oracle dwindled with the rise of Christianity, around AD 385. The temple was later excavated by French and German archaeologists; its statues are long gone, hauled back to England by Sir Charles Newton in 1858. Fragments of bas-reliefs on display by the entrance to the site include a gigantic head of Medusa and a small statue of Poseidon and his wife, Amphitrite. *22 km (14 mi) south of Priene on Rte. 09–55* ☏ *No phone* 💲 *$1.50* ☉ *Daily 8:30–6.*

For a rest after all this history, continue another 5 km (3 mi) south to **Altınkum.** The white-sand beach, which stretches for a bit less than 1 km (½ mi), is bordered by a row of decent seafood restaurants, all facing the water, and some small hotels.

Where to Stay & Eat

$$–$$$ ✕ **Kamacı 2.** This is the best restaurant you'll find in Altınkum, located right on the water at the end of the pier away from the noise of Didyma's touristy bars. The evenings are very romantic, with the moon often in full view, and the selection and price of fresh fish standard for a Turkish seafood restaurant. The fresh prawns, seasoned and cooked to perfection, are a great appetizer to share. ⊠ *Yali Cad. Iskele Karsisi, Altınkum-Didim* ☎ *256/813–2349* ▤ *AE, MC, V.*

$ ✕ **Didim Şehir Lokantası.** This restaurant is in one of Didyma's residential neighborhoods, Yenihisar, where you'll find the food to be cheaper and better in general. It's worth walking the mile or taking the bus out here, although the restaurant does have its own, complimentary shuttle service. You can order a homemade dish from the buffet or try one of their grilled items. The İskender, thin strips of gyro over pita chips, served with a tomato sauce and yogurt, is especially good. ⊠ *Off of Cumhuriyet Cad., next to Tedaş, Didyma* ☎ *256/811–4488 or 256/811–4499* ▤ *AE, MC, V.*

$ ▥ **Medusa House Pansiyon.** This small, unassuming restored stone house is made for relaxation—the garden and the terrace have plenty of spots for quiet contemplation. It's next to the Temple of Apollo and is one of the nicest accommodations Didyma has to offer. ⊠ *Next to the Temple of Apollo* ☎ *256/811–0063* ⊕ *www.medusahouse.com* ▨ *7 rooms, 2 houses* ⚸ *No a/c, no phones, no TVs* ▤ *AE, MC, V.*

¢   ▥ **Priene Pansiyon.** This pansiyon is a pleasant getaway and a retreat from the resort towns. Tidy, bright rooms are centered around a rectangular courtyard. Güllübahçe, the village near the ruins of Priene, is a nice town to stroll through. Book in advance in August, when archaeology students fill up the place. ⊠ *Turunçlar Mh., Güllübahçe* ☎ *256/547–1725 or 256/547–1009* ▨ *16 rooms* ⚸ *No a/c* ▤ *No credit cards.*

Lake Bafa

㉒ *30 km (19 mi) north of Bodrum.*

Shortly before you reach Milas, along the road to Bodrum, Route 525 skirts the south shore of **Çamiçi Gölü** (Bafa Gölü, or Lake Bafa). The lake is relatively small and undeveloped, especially away from the main road.

For a real change of pace, rent a boat (which will cost you around $45 round-trip) to go across the lake, or drive the rough 10-km (6-mi) road along the eastern shore, to the village of Kapıkiri and the ancient ruins of **Heracleia.** Though a minor town in antiquity, Heracleia has a wonderful setting, surrounded by high mountains. The villagers are Türkmen, descended from the Turkish tribes that settled Anatolia in the 13th and 14th centuries. The ruins, a Temple of Athena and some city walls, are also unusual: They were left by Carians, a native Asian people who adopted the Greek language and culture. On an islet facing the village are the remains of a Byzantine monastery, and huge volcanic boulders are scattered about. The combination of elements is incredibly atmospheric.

Where to Stay & Eat

$ ✕ **Çeri Cafe and Restaurant.** Fresh fish from the lake is served up at Çeri. Because the lake is so salty, you can find sea bream, sea bass, and eel, all fresh from the lake. You can also just stop by for a drink or snack on the lake, which is beautiful at dusk. The café will also be offering boat tours beginning in the summer of 2007 ($25 for a small group, $65 for a large group). ⊠ *Off the İzmir-Bodrum road at Lafe Bafa* ☎ 252/519–1011 ▤ AE, MC, V.

¢ 🖼 **Club Natura Oliva.** If you're looking for a nature resort, this is your place. There are 24 rooms in several two-story houses, with fireplaces and views of Heracleia, the lake, and the Latmos Mountains. Bird-watching is an option, with flamingos and pelicans stopping by, and hiking trails abound. Spring is the ideal time to come, when the flowers are in bloom. You can go swimming from the club's dock, but make sure you bring swimming shoes during the summer, when there's lots of seaweed and mussel shells. Club Natura also functions as a travel agency and can arrange tours to places like Bodrum, Pamukkale, and Iassos. Breakfast and dinner are included. ⊠ *Bafa Gölü* ☎ 252/519–1072 ⊕ *www.clubnatura.com* ⇥ 24 rooms ⌂ Restaurant, bar, watersports, public Internet; no a/c in some rooms, no TV in some rooms ▤ AE, MC, V.

FodorśChoice
★

Milas

㉓ *50 km (31 mi) north of Bodrum*

The city of Milas, rich in history and charm, is often considered a connecting hub rather than a destination in itself. It's on the way to Bodrum, though, and if you're already flying into the Milas airport (the closest one to Bodrum), the town, with its 27 archaeological sites, deserves a peek.

What to See

The **Archaeological Museum,** south of the Dolmuş terminal, and the city's newly opened tourism bureau are side by side and would be a good place to start. The staff at the tourism office are friendly and helpful. The Ulu Cami (The Great Mosque), the largest one in Milas, is made of pillaged material from antiquity and dates from 1378.

From the mosque, make your way up to the Baltalı Kapı, or Axed Gate, which dates back to the 1st century BC, and is named after the double-headed ax located on the gate's keystone. The Gümüşkesen Tomb, from the 2nd century AD, is still in good shape and resembles the Mausoleum in Bodrum.

Before heading to the city's old kervansaray, tour the old Milas houses built in the 19th and early 20th century. Entering the houses from their courtyards, you'll notice that many have bay windows that jut out into the street. There are also a slew of republican houses built by architects who were influenced by European architecture.

The Turkish era has left many interesting sights to explore as well. The Çöllüölu Hanı is an 18th-century kervansaray where locals continue to keep workshops and storage for the items they sell near the kervansaray. They'll let you walk around up top, which feels a bit precarious, as the building has

> ### MILAS RUGS
>
> Milas rugs, woven out of wool, are internationally famous—there is one on display at the Metropolitan Museum of Art in New York City. They are currently no longer produced in Milas, but in the dozen villages around Milas. The entire Milas district includes up to 7,000 weavers, some of whom work full-time and others who work only during periods of high demand.

not been restored (although there is talk of restoration projects starting soon). One artisan makes 100% goat-hair doormats with colorful animal motifs or geometric patterns. If you continue to head west, you'll end up at one of the most important Menteşoğulları remains, the 14th century Firuz Āa Cami, built of gray marble.

Where to Eat

There's not much of a dining scene in Milas, but eateries in the Arasta Park neighborhood serve inexpensive local dishes. Note that many are only open for lunch. There's not much in terms of noteworthy accommodations, either, so you're better off spending the night elsewhere.

Shopping

The city's **bazaar,** open Tuesday and Friday, stretches along the western part of Hisarbaşı hill. You could easily spend half the day sorting through the clothes, household goods, carpets, leather goods, jewelry, and other handicrafts. The bazaar receives many visitors from nearby towns, including Bodrum.

There's also a very interesting antique shop, **Antik Eşya** (⊠ Hisarbaşı Mah. Belediye Cad., No. 20 ☎ 252/512–6898), across from the tourist office that specializes in restoring antique guns. In addition to weaponry, they have an extensive collection of antiques, some purportedly dating back to pre-Ottoman times.

BODRUM & THE BODRUM PENINSULA

㉔ *161 km (100 mi) from Kuşadası, southeast on Rte. 515 to Rte. 525, south to Rte. 330 heading southwest; 125 km (78 mi) from Didyma, northeast on town road to Rte. 525 south to Rte. 330 southwest.*

Bodrum, known as Halicarnassus in antiquity, is one of Turkey's leading resorts. The modern town stretches along the shores of two crescent-shape bays and has for years been the favorite haunt of the Turkish upper classes. Today thousands of foreign visitors come here, too, and the area is bursting with hotels, guest houses, cafés, restaurants, and dis-

Bodrum Peninsula

Küçük Tavsan Island

Güllük Korfezi

Salih Adasi Island

Türkbükü

Gündoğan

Gölköy (Göltürkbükkü)

İkiz Island

Yalıkavak

Geriş

Torba Bay

Pazar Mountain

Torba

390

BODRUM PENINSULA

Karakaya

Ortakent

Yahşi

Agacli

Bodrum

Gümüşlük

Bitez

Gümbet

Kadikalesi

Çiftlik

Turgutreis

Kargi Bay

Bagla

Bagla Bay

İc Ada Island

Bodrum Korfezi

Kara Ada Island

Akyarlar

Karaincir Bay

Akyar Point

Koca Point

TO KOS, GREECE

TO DATÇA

TO KORMEN

0   2 mi

0   2 km

cos. It's still beautiful, though, with gleaming whitewashed buildings covered in bougainvillea and unfettered vistas of the sparkling bays.

Founded around 1000 BC, Halicarnassus was one of the first Greek colonies in Asia. The northern cities of the Aegean formed the Ionian League, but those farther south—Halicarnassus, Kos, Rhodes, Knidos, Lalysos, Lindos, Camiros—joined the Dorian Federation. Halicarnassus reached its height under Mausolus, who ruled from 377 BC to 353 BC as a *satrap* (governor) of what was then a distant outpost of the far-flung Persian Empire. After his death, his wife (who was also his sister), Artemisia, succeeded him. On learning that a woman ruled Halicarnassus, Rhodes sent its fleet to seize the city, only to be promptly—and soundly—defeated.

Artemisia ordered the construction of the great white-marble tomb for Mausolus at Halicarnassus that made the Seven Wonders list and gave us the word *mausoleum*. The **mausoleum** consisted of a solid rectangular base topped by 36 Ionic columns, surmounted by a pyramid, and crowned with a massive statue of Mausolus and Artemisia riding a chariot. The mausoleum has been dismantled, and the site—two blocks north of the bay and indicated by signs on Neyzen Tevfik Cad., the shore road ringing the west bay—is not worth the price of admission. ☎ *252/316–1095* ✉ *$4* ☉ *Tues.–Sun. 8:30–noon and 1–5.*

GETTING AROUND BODRUM

Renting a car is only a good idea if you plan on making many day trips outside of the city. Roads are worn out, not labeled very well, and probably not worth the trouble. Instead, hop on one of the minibuses (on average $1.50 per ride) that run all day and, in the summer, practically all night.

The ancient **theater** is one of the few surviving pre-Hellenic theaters in Asia Minor and thus one of the oldest; it's a popular place to take in a sunset. ✉ *North of mausoleum* ✉ *Free.*

The **Petronion** (Castle of St. Peter) is the most outstanding historic site in modern Bodrum and one of the great showpieces of late-medieval military architecture. The European crusaders known as the Knights of St. John seized Bodrum in 1402 and dismantled the mausoleum, using many of the stones to build the Petronion. The castle and its beautiful gardens, visible from every part of town, look as if they belong in a fairy tale. On the ramparts, you may recognize prominent coats of arms—those of the Plantagenets, d'Aubussons, and others. The five turrets are named after the homelands of the knights, who came from England, France, Germany, Italy, and Spain. Inside is an unusual and interesting **Museum of Underwater Archaeology,** with treasures recovered from historic wrecks discovered off the Aegean coast. Many artists set up little stands throughout the fortress, including the museum area, where they sell their work. Although some people complain about this addition, the artists have very interesting pieces. One artist, Cem Özakman, has won several awards for his jewelry. ✉ *Kale Cad.* ☎ *252/316–2516* ✉ *$7* ☉ *Tues.–Sun. 8:30–noon and 1–5.*

Where to Stay and Eat

Bodrum's city center has a large marina and is on the water, but there's really nowhere to swim. Many daily boat tours leave from the marina and take guests to various coves around the peninsula, which is optimal for swimming. Gümbet, 2 km away from Bodrum, is pretty much considered Bodrum's beach, and as a result, is full of restaurants, bars, and shops, as well as surf schools.

$$ ✕ **Club Pirinç.** This restaurant, which somewhat resembles an American-style steakhouse, is notable for its fish and meat. Steaks come with their own unique sauces. ✉ *Yeni Çarşi 8* ☎ *252/316–2902* ▭ *MC, V.*

★ **$$** ✕ **Kortan Restaurant.** This seaside fish house has outdoor seating with views of Bodrum's castle and of Chios, off the coast. The better dishes include fish kebabs, octopus salad, and whatever the catch of the day happens to be, usually served grilled. Reservations are essential in summer. ⊠ *Cumhuriyet Cad. 32* ☎ *252/316–1241* ▤ *AE, MC, V.*

$ ✕ **Sünger Pizza.** A cheap, cheerful, and central spot, Sünger is popular with the locals. In addition to their coal-fired, stone-oven pizza, they're known for the Bodrum specialty *Çökertme* kebab, finely grated French fries topped with thin slices of sirloin and garlicky yogurt and garnished with lettuce and a few slices of tomato. ⊠ *Neyzen Tevfik Cad.* ☎ *252/316–0854* ▤ *MC, V.*

$$ ▥ **Manastir Hotel Bodrum.** This comfortable Mediterranean-style hotel was once a monastery. Front rooms have balconies; all are cool and spacious, with whitewashed walls and tasteful, modern furnishings. ⊠ *Barış Sitesi Mev., Kumbahçe, 48400* ☎ *252/316–2854* 🖷 *252/316–2112* ⊕ *www.cande.com.tr* ⤵ *59 rooms* ♨ *2 restaurants, bar, tennis court, 2 pools* ▤ *AE, DC, MC, V.*

$ ▥ **Ayaz Hotel.** This hotel is on a small bay just east of the Bodrum harbor, away from the noise and bustle of town, yet less than a five-minute drive from the center. It has its own gardens and a beach with a bar, where you can listen to the waves and while away the hours. The guest rooms are done in contemporary style and have balconies and sea views. ⊠ *On Gümbet Bay, 48400* ☎ *252/316–1174 or 252/316–2956* 🖷 *252/ 316–4751* ⊕ *www.ayazhotels.com* ⤵ *96 rooms* ♨ *Restaurant, bar, pool, beachfront, watersports; no TV in some rooms* ▤ *MC, V.*

$ ▥ **Mylasa Pansiyon.** An Australian archaeologist who found it hard to leave Bodrum runs this pansiyon, which is in an attractive white stucco building in the center of town. It has a comfortable lounge and a roof deck with a view of the Aegean. Rooms are just what you find in most pansiyons—the beds are low, with simple wooden frames, and the decor isn't noteworthy. ⊠ *Cumhuriyet Cad. 34, 48400* ☎ *252/316–1846* 🖷 *252/316–1254* ⊕ *www.mylasapansiyon.com* ⤵ *16 rooms* ♨ *Restaurant, room service, bar* ▤ *MC, V.*

Nightlife

The scene in Bodrum is more sophisticated than anywhere else along the Aegean. The **Halikarnas Disco** (⊠ Cumhuriyet Cad. 178 ☎ 252/ 316–8000) bills itself as "probably the most amazing nightclub in the world." It is, in fact, rather like discos more commonly found in western Mediterranean resorts, complete with fog machines and laser lights. Locals claim the quality has gone down. **Hadigari** (⊠ Dr. Alım Bey Cad. 37 ☎ 252/313–1960) is one of Bodrum's long-time discos that still draws a big crowd. They bring in DJs from Germany and play everything from Turkish and international pop to techno, house, and Latin beats. On the weekends, they have female showdancers, and a live act featuring a bellydancer with a snake.

The **Marina Yacht Club** (⊠ Bodrum Marina, Neyzen Tevfik Caddesi No. 5 ☎ 252/316–1228) is the first place both Bodrum locals and Turkish tourists will recommend for a good night out. The live music is as diverse as the age groups that come to listen, and the dining area on the second floor has a long bar with a terrific view of the marina. Drinks are pricey, but there's no cover charge.

Fink and Küba (⊠ Fink: Neyzan Tefvik Cad., No. 32; Küba: Neyzan Tefvık Cad.), two upscale lounges within earshot of each other on Bodrum's harbor, are practically carbon copies of one another and both are popular with the young, hip crowd. Music ranges from pop-techno to jazz and world. **Mavi Bar** (⊠ Cumhuriyet Cad. 175 ☎ 252/316–3932) is a venerable mecca in Bodrum drinking circles, attracting Turkish artists, writers, and their numerous hangers-on. **Marine Club Catamaran** (⊠ Next to the Bodrum castle ☎ 252/313–3600 ⊕ www.clubcatamaran.com) is a full-fledged sea party. The Catamaran, a floating disco with a transparent, glass-floor disco, sails out to sea after 1 AM, when other nightclubs are required by law to turn the volume down or close up altogether. The catamaran has two resident DJs and a choice of five bars.

Each Bodrum "neighborhood" or cove has its own nightlife, Türkbükkü being the most renowned. The whole quay is covered with lounges, bars, and clubs, each sporting its own deck stretching out over the sea. The place to see and be seen is **Ship Ahoy**, (⊠ Türkbükkü ☎ 252/377–5070), and it's the most crowded spot on any given night. The chic and sleek **Supper Club** (⊠ Yalı Mevkii, Gölköy- Türkbükkü ⊕ www.supperclub. com) is the new kid on the block, one of the many bars on the dimly lit slope in Gölköy (coming from Bodrum, it's the neighborhood before you get to Türkbükkü). You'll probably have to ask around to find it.

Sports & the Outdoors
The Bodrum Peninsula has tons of outdoor activities, including scuba diving, sponge diving, horseback riding, hiking, waterskiing, wakeboarding, and windsurfing.

DIVING The sea around Bodrum provides some of the best diving in the Aegean. There are sixteen dive spots, with Geriş being the best for sponge divers. At least ten schools are registered with PADI, the worldwide diving organization. The **Diving Center** in Aktur/Bitez (☎ 252/343–1032) is one of the most reliable PADI-certified dive operators. Also check out **Motif Diving** (⊠ Eski Hukumet Sok.112/C, Bodrum ☎ 252/316–6252 ⊕ www. motifdiving.com). The **Erman Dive Center** (☎ 252/368–9594 or 532/ 213–5989 ⊕ www.ermandive.com) has two locations in Bodrum, in the Hapimag Resort Sea Garden and at the Karada Marina.

HIKING Yalıkavak, with its mountainous terrain, is the most ideal hiking area. Contact **Bodrum Nature Sport Club** (☎ 252/313–2159) for more information.

HORSEBACK RIDING Gündoğan is the best place for horseback riding, with its nice forest trails, although Ortakent and Turgutreis are also good alternatives. Contact **Farilya Farm** (☎ 532/355–9170) in Gündoğan, **Country Ranch** (☎ 252/ 382–5654 or 533/654–9586 for English) in Turgutreis, and **Yahşi Riding** (☎ 252/358–6526) in Yahşi for horseback riding packages.

> ### THE GREAT INDOORS
>
> If you'd rather just sit back and relax or if you're recovering from an intensive workout, Bodrum's recently opened **hamam** (⊠ Opposite the bus station on Cevat Şakir Rd. ☎ 252/313–4129) is a welcoming, tidy place. There are separate facilities for men and women.

WINDSURFING Fener, in the Turgutreis area, is great for windsurfing. **Kempinski Hotel** in Bodrum (☎ 252/311–0303) has windsurfing rentals and instruction.

Shopping

There is a bazaar every day of the week in Bodrum and in the surrounding towns, the most popular being in Turgutreis. The Turgutreis bazaar, held on Saturday, has everything under the Bodrum sun, including leather goods and jewelry. The rest of the bazaars are as follows: Türkbükkü on Monday, Bodrum and Gölköy on Tuesday, Ortakent and Gündoğan on Wednesday, Yalıkavak on Thursday, and Bodrum's fruit, vegetable, and food bazaar on Thursday and Friday.

Bodrum's handmade sandals are renowned. **Ali Güven** (✉ Bodrum Sq.), who once made sandals for Mick Jagger, is the most trusted and well-established of the cobblers; he's been in business for over 40 years. His lightweight designs are made from specially worked leather, very comfortable for the Mediterranean summer, and aesthetically pleasing as well.

Bodrum's Beach Towns

Visitors flock to the peninsula for its numerous coves, bays, and multi-toned water. Each beach has its own style and ambiance, so choose accordingly. You can access many by land, and even more by water, which is why taking a day-long boat trip is especially a good idea in Bodrum. With competition on the rise, there are many different options available.

Bitez

The village of Bitez lies 8 km (5 mi) west of Bodrum, and its beach, the longest in Bodrum, is another 2 km (1 mi) to the south. The stone houses in the village were built right on the road to make room for mandarin trees in the backyard. Until several decades ago, residents picked and packed the mandarins onto camels, who then carried them to the nearby ports. Walk along the backroads of Bitez to take in the fresh, citric scent of the mandarins, intermingled with 500-year-old olive trees. The village also has a *kahve* (traditionally, a Turkish café where only men socialize and play backgammon) for women, propped up by the Bitez municipality. The kahve is on Atatürk Caddesi. Most of the sand in this semicircle cove is covered by chaises or plush pillows set up in little, enclosed enclaves. A pedestrian walkway leads through the 2-km (1-mi) stretch of beach, dividing the cafés and hotels from the shore.

WHERE TO STAY & EAT ✕**Daphne.** A garden and a fireplace **$$** make this spot ideal in either summer or winter. The fusion menu combines international favorites and seafood. One of the best parts of the meal is the complimentary eggplant, sundried tomato, and olive oil spreads you get, served with homemade bread. ✉ *Bitez Yalısı, Bitez* ☎ *252/363–7722* ▭ *MC, V.*

SWEET SPOT

People travel in from outside of Bitez just to have some of **Bitez Dondurması's** (✉ Atatürk Cad. Bitez) delicious ice cream, which has fresh fruit like mulberries—hand-picked in the mountains—mixed in. It's a bit overpriced but very satisfying on a hot summer's day.

$ ✕ **Café Sarnıç.** This trendy beach club has a full-service restaurant. The outstanding homemade mantı, Turkish ravioli topped with a tomato-yogurt sauce (as opposed to just yogurt, which is what you get at most restaurants), and the stuffed grape leaves make it worth bearing the loud club music that often plays during the day. The best time to come here is when everyone leaves—after dusk. ⊠ *Aktur entrance, Bitez* ☎ *252/ 343–1433* ▭ *MC, V.*

¢ ✕ **Bitez Pidesi.** The *pides* here have been written up in the local papers, and it's no wonder. The crusts are crispy, the fillings delicious, and the prices unbeatable. ⊠ *Atatürk Cad., No. 98, Bitez* ☎ *252/363–7925* ▭ *no credit cards.*

$$ 🏨 **Toloman Hotel.** This hotel is actually a complex of white, two-story town-house-like buildings. Rooms are airy with small balconies. A large outdoor dining area allows you to look out onto the water over your Turkish breakfast. The beachfront is dotted with chaises and wicker umbrellas.The hotel is calm and attracts an older crowd, and the only real distraction, if you could call it that, is the constant buzzing of the cicadas in summer. ⊠ *Bitez Yalısı, Bitez* ☎ *252/363–7751* 🖷 *252/363–7822* ⊕ *www.toloman.com* ➦ *33 rooms* ⌂ *Restaurant, bar, pool* ▭ *AE, MC, V.*

Yalıkavak

This town is 20 km (12 mi) outside of Bodrum, and is easily identified by the beautiful windmills atop its hill. Once a tiny cluster of houses on the quay, Yalıkavak has recently added a spiffy yacht marina, the peninsula's third. The newly remodeled tourist office is also cheerful and welcoming, and has a number of informative brochures. There are numerous coves to explore around Yalıkavak, and the strong wind makes it ideal for windsurfing. The two most popular beaches here, Dodo and Camel, tend to be overcrowded thanks to a lively beach club scene. There are also quieter, unnamed stretches of beach. The town is more of a car place, and you'll see a lot more if you have your own transporation.

WHERE TO STAY ✕ **Ali Baba.** Open for breakfast, lunch, and dinner, Ali Baba caters to
AND EAT all tastes. The restaurant features fish and meat dishes like sirloin steak
$$ and lamb, and their specialty, the Amphora kebab. ⊠ *Atatürk Cad., No. 42E* ☎ *252/385–3194* ▭ *AE, DC, MC, V.*

$ ✕ **Kavaklı Köfeteci.** For $6, you get a serving of Turkish meatballs, piyaz (a cold bean dish), and ayran. The köfte is a little on the greasy side, but very tasty nonetheless. ⊠ *Çarşı Içi No. 24* ☎ *252/385–4748* ▭ *no credit cards.*

★ $$ 🏨 **Lavanta Hotel.** Surrounded by well-maintained grounds on a hillside overlooking Bodrum Peninsula just outside the village of Yalıkavak, the Lavanta is a tranquil retreat in an area where many hotels are bland and geared toward package tourism. All of the attractive rooms overlook the sea from private terraces and are furnished with tasteful traditional pieces and antiques. Dinner, served to hotel guests only, features traditional Turkish home cooking. ⊠ *Yalikavak-Bodrum, 48430* ☎ *252/385– 2167* 🖷 *252/385–2290* ⊕ *www.lavanta.com* ➦ *11 apartment units and 8 rooms* ⌂ *Restaurant, bar, pool, laundry service, public Internet* ▭ *DC, MC, V.*

$$ ⚹ **Yalıkavak Marina Hotel.** Many of the beautiful rooms in this stone build-ing have palm trees right outside their windows. Bamboo chairs, ham-mocks, and large cushions in the garden invite a lazy afternoon. Rooms are tastefully decorated, but the dark paint on the walls makes them a bit dim. The hotel caters especially to guests docking at the marina, but all are welcome. ✉ *Çokertme Mevkii, Yalikavak* ☎ *252/385–3872* 🖷 *252/385–3281* ⊕ *www.portbodrum.com* ⤴ *17 rooms* ⚹ *Laundry service* ⊟ *AE, DC, MC, V.*

$$ ⚹ **Maya Hotel and Pansiyon.** Though it's in the center of town, this hotel feels secluded, with its private garden and swimming pool bor-dered by flowers. Rooms, in low white-stucco buildings, are utilitarian, with Scandinavian-style furniture. In the associated pansiyon, on a tiny side street behind the marina, rooms are smaller, and you have to walk over to the hotel for a dip in the pool, but the prices are lower. ✉ *Ger-ence Sok. 32, Gümbet, 48400* ☎ *252/316–4741* 🖷 *252/316–4745* ⤴ *72 rooms* ⚹ *Restaurant, bar, pool, gym* ⊟ *MC, V.*

Akyarlar/Karaincir/Turgutreis

Akyarlar and Karaincir, opposite bays, are on the way to Turgutreis near the Aspat Mountains. Some of the peninsula's most picture-postcard wa-ters make up these two beaches. Turgutreis has a more developed coast, with a very popular and lively bazaar. Its marina attracts the yachting crowd and is a bit more touristy than the other bays. After swimming in the pristine sea at Akyarlar and Karaincir, the beaches of Turgutreis don't seem all that enticing.

WHERE TO STAY   ⚹ **Hotel Balkız & Ali.** This beachfront hotel consists of a restored stone
$$ house with a view of Kos Island. The intimate beach area is lined with chaises. The hotel itself is laid-back, and blends in well with the natu-ral area surrounding it. The kitchen serves Italian food, as well as home-made Turkish dishes. ✉ *Akyarlar No. 87, Akyarlar* ☎ *252/393–6025* 🖷 *252/393–6233* ⊕ *www.balkizali.com* ⤴ *18 rooms* ⚹ *Restaurant, beachfront* ⊟ *AE, MC, V.*

$ ⚹ **Hotel Kortan.** Kortan is a simple but elegant hotel in the heart of Turgutreis. Two fancy, red swings add flair to the reception area. Rooms are tasteful and some have sea views. The hotel has its own private beach with the requisite chaises. ✉ *Atatürk Meydanı, Sabancı Cad. No.5, Turgutreis* ☎ *252/382–2932* 🖷 *252/382–4797* ⊕ *www.kortanotel. com* ⤴ *25 rooms* ⚹ *Restaurant, room service, bar, Wi-Fi, laundry service* ⊟ *AE, MC, V.*

Göltürkbükkü

The two coastal towns Gölköy and Türkbükkü, 20 km (12 mi) north of Bodrum, recently merged to become Göltürkbükkü, the most glam-orous part of the Bodrum peninsula. Türkbükkü, which has been called the "St. Tropez of Turkey," is the summer playground of jet-setting, high-society Turks and foreigners, and its coastline is jam-packed with bars, cafés, restaurants, and boutiques. Gölköy is probably the better place to stay, as it has a slower pace and more stretches of undeveloped wa-terfront—and you can always head into Türkbükkü to socialize and party. Note that there's not much more to do in Gölköy besides sunbathe, as its layout makes it pretty difficult to walk around. Neither beach has sand, but the water is accessible from wooden decks.

✕ **Mey.** A Türkbükkü favorite, this fish restaurant is fixed-menu only. They have a rich selection of mezes, like Swiss chard dolma, lightly marinated smoked salmon, rice mixed with octopus, and their special *tarama* (olive oil- and lemon-infused caviar). Leave room for some baklava. Reservations are recommended in summer. ⊠ *Atatürk Cad. Yalı Mevkii No. 61* ☎ *252/377–5118 or 252/377–5464* ▭ *AE, MC, V.*

★ **$$$** ✕ **Atılay.** Atılay is one of the best seaside restaurants, with white-clothed tables arranged on the wooden sunbathing decks in the summer. Fish— always fresh and grilled or fried just right—is the thing, and the catches of the day are neatly displayed. You can't go wrong with any meze you choose, but the melon and feta cheese is always a great starter. Make sure to put in your chocolate soufflé order ahead of time. Service is friendly, and there are fixed-menu and à la carte options. ⊠ *Türkbükkü Yalı Mevkii* ☎ *252/377–5095* ▭ *AE, MC, V.*

$$$$ ⌸ **Maça Kızı.** Türkbükkü is the perfect nook for the Queen of Spades, or Maça Kızı. Ayla, the owner, has moved the well-established hotel around a lot, finally settling on the Göltürk quay. The rooms, which have either bay or garden views, are stylish and sophisticated, with wood floors and pretty kilims. Plush pillows are set out on the hotel's long deck, which is part of its private bay. The restaurant specializes in Mediterranean nouveau cuisine. ⊠ *Kesireburnu Mevkii, Türkbükkü* ☎ *252/377–6272* 🖶 *252/377–6287* ⊕ *www.macakizi.com* ➷ *37 rooms* ⌂ *Restaurant, bar, pool, beachfront* ▭ *AE, MC, V.*

✕⌸ **Karianda B&B.** A small red sign marks the spot for this small family-run boutique hotel tucked among the trees. Natives of Gölköy, Karianda's father-and-daughter team built and expanded this place from the ground up. Rooms are modestly decorated, spic and span, and very functional. Karianda focuses just as much on food as it does on comfort. The B&B has its own wood-fire brick oven—at the small crescent-shape bar you can order delectable *pide*s and *lahmacun* (Turkish pizzas) and wash them down with creative and flavorful cocktails. During teatime, guests are treated to complimentary Turkish baked goods. The hotel has its own private bay with a wooden deck from which to sunbathe or plunge into the sea. In the evening, the deck transforms into a restaurant that serves well-prepared fish and mezes. The hotel is generally quiet, but the peace is occasionally disturbed by loud music from the neighboring, trendier hotel. ⊠ *Cumhuriyet Cad. No. 104–106, Gölköy* ☎ *252/357– 7303 or 252/357–7819* 🖶 *252/357–7819* ⊕ *www.karianda.com* ➷ *25 rooms* ⌂ *No room TVs, restaurant, bar, beachfront* ▭ *AE, MC, V.*

Gümüşlük

Gümüşlük, 25 km (15½ mi) from Bodrum, is one of the peninsula's more authentic, slower-paced, less-developed villages. It's built on the ancient ruins of Myndos—much of the ruins are submerged underwater, but major land excavations are taking place to recover the ancient city, and an ancient drainage system dating to Myndos's Roman civilization period has already been discovered. The town is popular for its fish restaurants on the water. Its restored church is now a site for cultural and artistic events, including an international classical music festival in August.

There are also lots of water sports and easy outdoor adventures. One of the popular things to do is walk through the shallow water to Tavşan Adasıı, Rabbit Island. Glassmakers and other artists reside and keep shop here, and sometimes you can see them at work.

If you have the time, and a car, visit Karakaya, a village of stone houses perched up on the hillside above Gümüşlük. Development is restricted in this town—no highrises or large hotels are allowed.

WHERE TO EAT ✕**Gusta.** This Italian-inspired seafood, meat, and pizza restaurant offers
$$ more than the typical grilled and fried fish. The large space has a classy beach-themed decor, and of course, there are tables on the expansive deck for waterfront dining. Attention is given to detail—even the coffee comes in a copper, Ottoman-style cup. The white chocolate cake is a great finish to an excellent meal. ⊠ *Gümüşlük* ☎ *252/394–4228* ⊟ *AE, MC, V.*

$ ✕**Dalgıç.** If you're tired of fish, this restaurant offers a refreshing alternative—homemade, traditional Turkish dishes. The owner is friendly and welcoming, and prices very reasonable. ⊠ *Across from the pier, Gümüşlük* ☎ *252/394–4229* ⊟ *AE, MC, V.*

THE CENTRAL AND SOUTHERN AEGEAN COAST ESSENTIALS

Transportation

BY AIR

The major airports serving the region are Adnan Menderes Airport, 25 km (16 mi) south of İzmir, and the Bodrum-Milas Airport, 40 km (25 mi) north of Bodrum.

Turkish Airlines and Atlas Jet make the hour-long flight from Istanbul to İzmir a few times daily. Turkish Airlines also flies to Bodrum up to six times daily in summer, and twice daily off-season. Atlas Jet flies to Bodrum five to six times daily in summer and once or twice daily off-season. One of Turkey's domestic airlines, Onur Air, also has direct flights from Istanbul to İzmir or Milas-Bodrum several times daily throughout the year, often at cheaper prices.

One of the most comfortable and economical ways to get to and from the İzmir and Bodrum airports to their respective downtown areas is Havaş, a modern, spacious shuttle bus service with air-conditioning. The Havaş bus leaves İzmir's airport every 20, 35, or 60 minutes, depending on the time of day. It returns to the airport from Mavi Şehir in Karşıyakı and the Grand Efes Hotel in Alsancak every hour. The İzmir Havas bus tickets cost about $6.50 one-way. The Havaş Bodrum bus schedule is aligned with the schedules of Turkish Airlines, Onur Air, Atlas Jet, and FLYAIR; they usually leave Bodrum's bus terminal two hours before a flight departure. The cost is about $9 one-way. All Havaş tickets cost 25% more from midnight to 6 AM.

In İzmir, you can also get downtown via train; the station is next to the International Terminal, connected by a covered walkway. Trains depart every hour for Alsancak Gar (Alsancak station), but note that this will leave you to the north of the city. Trains from the airport to Basmane train station (south of İzmir's Kültürpark) in the city proper run mostly in the afternoons. The trains are rickety but very cheap.

Taxis serve the İzmir and Bodrum airports. Bodrum's fares are known as the most expensive in Turkey, and İzmir is up there as well, so you might want to bargain before agreeing to a ride. Prices go up even more from midnight to 6 AM.

Airports **Adnan Menderes Airport** ✉ 35510 Gaziemir, İzmir ☎ 232/274-2626. **Bodrum-Milas Airport** ✉ A.O. Milas Havaalanı 48200, Milas-Mūla ☎ 252/523-0101.

Taxis and Shuttles **Bodrum Tour** ☎ 252/313-3009. **Havaş** ☎ 212/465-5656 general, 252/444-0487 for Bodrum 🌐 www.havas.net/ or http://www.havas.com.tr/en/otobus.asp. **Havalimanı Taksi (İzmir Adnan Airport Taxi)** ☎ 232/274-2075. **Proper Car Rental (and Airport Transfers)** ✉ Bodrum ☎ 252/316-9540 🌐 www.propercar.com/bodrum-airport-transfer.htm.

BY BOAT & FERRY

Turkish Maritime Lines operates passenger and car ferry services to İzmir from Istanbul once a week from May through October. Boats leave in the afternoon and arrive the next morning. Fares range from $50 for a single seat to $133 for a suite accommodating up to four people. In summer there is also service between İzmir and Marseille, Genoa, Venice, and Piraeus, the port for Athens.

The Bodrum Ferryboat Assosication has ferries from Bodrum to Kos and Datça, which are right off its shores. The Bodrum Express Lines Hydrofoil and Ferryboat Services also has ferries from Bodrum to Kos, and they've recently added ferries to Rhodes, Marmaris, and Cleopatra Island from June through August. All trips run about $40 one-way. Reservations are recommended if you're bringing your car. Make sure you bring your passport for ferries to Greece.

Bodrum Express Lines ☎ 252/316-2309 🌐 www.bodrumexpresslines.com. **Bodrum Ferryboat Association** ☎ 252/316-0882 🌐 www.bodrumferryboat.com. **Turkish Maritime Lines** ✉ Rıhtım Cad. 1 ☎ 212/244-0207 for information 🌐 www.tdi.com.tr/eng/denizyollari.shtml.

BY BUS

Though it's slower and more restrictive than traveling by car, bus travel is a viable option if you don't want to drive. It can be exceptionally inexpensive, and all the towns and attractions are well served by bus. When you arrive at the main bus station for one town, simply ask about connecting service to the next town along the line.

Buses, typically modern and air-conditioned, operate between the larger and smaller towns and from there depart for the major archaeological sites. Typical travel times are: Istanbul to İzmir, 12 hours; Istanbul to Bodrum, 12 hours; İzmir to Bodrum, 3½ hours, İzmir to Çeşme, 1½ hours; İzmir to Selçuk, 1½ hours; İzmir to Kuşadası, 80 minutes; and Çeşme to Bodrum, 4½ hours.

In general, buses are a reliable and very popular way to get around the Southern Aegean. For 10-hour-plus journeys, Varan, by far the most luxurious company, and Ulusoy are at the high end, and often make these long trips at night. Kamil Koç and Boss are some other good choices. Bus companies offer more trips per day for shorter routes and during high season (e.g., eight times a day from İzmir to Bodrum).

Major bus lines travel between İzmir, Selçuk, Kuşadaş, Didyma, Milas, and Bodrum, but you'll have to rely on local, often smaller buses to travel shorter distances to and between smaller towns. Çeşme Seyhat Bus Company is the sole bus company for traveling between İzmir and Çeşme. During the summer, buses leave every 20–45 minutes or so, often until around 9 PM. Reservations are recommended and especially important for the return trip to İzmir. Tickets cost around $8 one way and can be bought either at the otogar stand or on the bus, in cash.

📘 **Boss** ☎ 212/444-0562 Istanbul, 232/464-4170 İzmir, 252/382-5841 Bodrum, 232/712-1242 Çeşme ⊕ www.bossturizm.com. **Çeşme Seyhat Bus Company** ☎ 232/712-6499. **Kamil Koç** ☎ 212/444-0562 general inquiries, 212/658-2000 Istanbul, 232/472-0099 İzmir ⊕ www.kamilkoc.com.tr. **Ulusoy** ☎ 212/444-1888 general reservations ⊕ www.ulusoy.com.tr. **Varan** ☎ 212/444-8999 reservations, 232/472-0389 İzmir office ⊕ www.varan.com.tr.

BY CAR

A car is a plus for exploring this region, since it allows you to stop at will at picturesque towns and track down lesser-known ruins and less-crowded beaches. Except around İzmir, where heavy and hectic traffic requires serious concentration to keep you from getting lost, the highways are generally in good condition, the traffic fairly light, and the main attractions relatively close together. Distances are: Çanakkale to Bergama, 245 km (152 mi); Bergama to İzmir, 98 km (61 mi); İzmir to Ephesus, 79 km (49 mi); Ephesus to Bodrum, 172 km (107 mi).

Portions of the highway that runs down the Aegean coast can be beautiful, especially as you're approaching Çeşme and Bodrum. Sometimes driving within the cities themselves can be tricky, especially in Bodrum, where many important turn-offs are unmarked and many winding roads are still very undeveloped. There is a long stretch of multilane highway as you head south toward Bodrum, including the toll highway from İzmir to Çeşme, but by the time you're within 100 miles of the city, single lanes going in every direction take over. Unfortunately, many people still drive as if this weren't the case, and it's common for drivers to pass, even during risky moments and around blind curves.

You're best off picking up a car once you get to the region. It's a long haul from Istanbul to İzmir—565 km (350 mi), an exhausting seven- or eight-hour drive. To make this trip, pick up Route 200 heading west toward Çanakkale. From there the E87 follows the coast south all the way to Kuşadası, where it turns inland toward Antalya. Route 525 continues along the coast, past Priene and Miletus; Route 330 branches off in Bodrum and connects with the main Mediterranean highways.

BY TAXI AND DOLMUŞ

Taxi stands, or *taksi durāı,* can be found in every major city and town. Taxis can be hailed on the street or called ahead of time; doing the latter is generally more reliable. Cab fares start at around $1 and the rates increase based on distance covered, as well as idle time spent in traffic. They're very expensive in resort towns like Çeşme and Bodrum. In areas with high taxi-to-customer ratios, or when you're traveling long distances, you should definitely use your bargaining skills. In these cases, agree to a fare ahead of time and try to give the driver the exact fare at the end of the trip (in the off chance that he'll try to renege on your agreement and keep the change). Metered cab prices are fixed and shouldn't change based on number of passengers or pieces of luggage.

The dolmuş is a much more economical way to travel, especially in the resort towns. Fares range from $1–$2 per ride and you can get dropped off anywhere along the driver's route (just say the magic words "*eenejek var*").

🚖 **29 Aûustos Taksi (İzmir)** ☎ 232/422–1958. **Bostanlı Taksi (İzmir)** ☎ 232/336–7094. **Çeşme Taksi** ☎ 232/712–6690. **Garaj Taksi (Bodrum)** ☎ 252/316–1515. **Ückuyular Terminal Taksi** (İzmir) ☎ 232/278–1538.

BY TRAIN

Trains to İzmir from Istanbul take a good 10 to 12 hours, and you must first take a four-hour boat ride across the Sea of Marmara then connect with a train at Bandırma. Opt for the morning departure rather than the night one if you want to enjoy the scenery of the cruise and the ride ride along the northern Aegean coast. Contact Turkish Maritime Lines in Istanbul for schedules and fares.

You can take the train from İzmir's Basmane Station to Selçuk in less than two hours (six departures daily).

🚂 **Turkish Maritime Lines** ✉ Rıhtım Cad. 1 ☎ 212/244–0207 for information ⊕ www. tdi.com.tr/eng/denizyollari.shtml.

Contacts & Resources

BANKS & EXCHANGING SERVICES

In İzmir, banks and exchange offices are clustered in the Alsancak and Konak neighborhoods. In resort towns they are often located in the town's square or main shopping area or near the bus terminal. Banks are open weekdays and often offer better exchange rates (and don't take commissions). Exchange offices are usually open daily.

EMERGENCIES

When you call emergency numbers in Turkey, the person who answers the telephone is unlikely to speak English. Your best bet is to ask a Turkish speaker to place the call for you.

🚨 Emergencies **Ambulance** ☎ 112. **Fire** ☎ 110. **Gendarme (rural areas only)** ☎ 156. **Police** ☎ 155.

🏥 Hospitals **Bodrum State Hospital** ✉ Kıbrıs Şehitler ☎ 252/313–1421. **Çeşme Alper Cizgekanat State Hospital** ✉ Izmir Cevreyolu, off the Izmir interstate before the Boyalik Hotel ☎ 232/712–0777. **İzmir Public Hospital** ✉ Ali Çetinkaya Bul. ☎ 232/463–2121. **Kuşadası State Hospital** ☎ 256/618–2414.

INTERNET, MAIL & SHIPPING

Internet cafés are available in all coastal towns, even some of the smaller ones. Some public areas have Wi-Fi.

Post offices are identified by the letters PTT in black on a yellow background. Post offices in busy resort towns often keep very late hours in summer, and are open 8:30–5:30 in the off-season.

🖪 Internet Cafés **İzmir** ⊠ Plevne Bul. 21/2 ☎ 232/244–2347. **Java Internet Café (Kuşadası)** ⊠ Riza Sarac Cad. No. 21. **Palmiye** ⊠ Neyzin Tevfik Cad. 196, Bodrum ☎ 252/317–0022.

🖪 Post offices **Bodrum** ⊠ Cevat Şakir. **Çeşme** ⊠ On the waterfront, north of the ferry dock. **İzmir** ⊠ Cumhuriyet Meydanı. **Kuşadası** ⊠ Barbaros Hayrettin Bul.

MEDIA

Kuşadası's only English publication is the *Kuşadası Guide,* which tends to have a few feature articles and a lot of advertisements. Bodrum has a fare share of English newspapers, including the *Bodrum Observer,* which has well-written, informative articles and good coverage of the peninsula with a focus on current events in Bodrum. The *Aegean Sun* provides listings of ongoing/upcoming festivals and concerts. *Caria News* is more like a visitor's guide than a newspaper and does have some helpful tidbits and listings. *Bodrum News* is another free guide focusing on activities in Bodrum.

TOUR OPTIONS

Travel agencies in all major towns organize tours of the historical sites. Selçuk also has many tour operators that organize these kinds of excursions (refer to Selçuk, in main chapter above).

In İzmir, Setur Travel is very reliable. In Kuşadası, try Akdeniz Turizm, as well as travel agencies along Teyyare Cad., to arrange escorted tours to Ephesus; to Priene, Miletus, and Didyma; and to Aphrodisias and Pamukkale. In Bodrum, Sun Travel Agency offers a wide variety of outdoor excursions (horseback riding, surfing, trekking, off-roading), as well as historical/cultural tours to Didyma, Milas, and Çomakdăı.

🖪 **Akdeniz Turizm** ⊠ Atatürk Bul. 26, Kuşadası ☎ 256/614–1140. **Setur Travel** ⊠ Atatürk Cad. 194/A, İzmir ☎ 232/463–6100. **Sun Travel Agency** ⊠ Kaynak Sok. No. 20 ☎ 252/363–7556.

VISITOR INFORMATION

Visitor Information offices are generally open daily from 8:30–12:30 and 1:30–5.

🖪 **Bodrum** ⊠ Barış Meydanı ☎ 252/316–1091 🖳 Bodrum bus station ☎ 252/316–2637. **Çeşme** ⊠ Iskele Meydanı ☎ 232/712–6653. **Didyma** ⊠ Eski Kaymakanlık Binası ☎ 256/811–4529. **İzmir** ⊠ Akdeniz Mah., 1344 Sok., No. 2, Pasaport ☎ 232/483–5117. **Kuşadası** ⊠ Liman Cad. No.13 ☎ 256/614–1103. **Milas** ⊠ Belediye Cad. ☎ 252/513–7770. **Selçuk** ⊠ Atatürk Mah., Agora Çarşısı No. 35 ☎ 232/892–6945.

The Turquoise Riviera

WORD OF MOUTH

"Near Antalya are some of the most beautiful beaches in the Mediterranean as well as historical sights such as Phaselis . . . You should also visit Kekova, which has an ancient city buried in the sea; you travel over it with a boat, and you may actually swim there surrounded with tombs rising from the sea and houses below you."

—JeuneTurC

WELCOME TO THE TURQUOISE RIVIERA

TOP REASONS TO GO

★ **Take a Blue Cruise**
Sail into the turquoise waters of remote and pristine bays on your own chartered Blue Cruise yacht.

★ **Trek the Lycian Way**
Choose a one-day or multi-day hike along this long-distance trail that runs parallel to much of the Turquoise coast, from the coastal mountain forests to untouched beaches.

★ **See spectacular ruins**
Explore the ruins of some of the most spectacular ancient cities in the world—from mountaintop Termessos, to overgrown Olympos, and the extraordinarily intact Roman theater at Aspendos.

★ **Golf** Hit some balls on the immaculate links laid out under the umbrella pines of upmarket Belek.

★ **Luxuriate in gorgeous lodgings** Relax in a beautifully restored Ottoman mansion-turned-hotel on the wild and rugged Datça peninsula.

Apollon Temple, Side

1 The Datça Peninsula. A yacht chartered in Marmaris or Bodrum is the best way to visit the craggy hills and ancient coves of one of Turkey's most unspoiled stretches of coastline.

2 The Lycian Coast. Rent a car from Dalaman or Antalya and slowly explore the charming ports, boutique hotels, uncrowded beaches, and ancient ruins along the little-developed coastal circuit.

Altinyayla
Korkuteli
[D 350] [D 650]
Termessos◆
Imecik
50
Elmali
Gonuk
[D 400]
Perge◆
Aspendos◆
○Antalya
Side○ Manavgat
[D 695]
Phaselis
Altinyaka
Antalya Körfezi
Cyanae **Myra**◆
[D 400]
Kumluca
Finike Körfezi
[D 400]
Alara Han◆
Alanya○

e a

3 Antalya. This vibrant city is a good place to base yourself for taking in the ancient sites of Aspendos, Perge, Termessos, and Phaselis.

4 Pamphylia. The area from Antalya to Alanya, including the sites of Termessos, Perge, Aspendos, and Alara Han is considered historic Pamphylia. The newly spruced-up centers of Side and Alanya have recovered some of their former charm and benefit from warm spring and autumn seasons.

GETTING ORIENTED

The area known as the Turquoise Riviera stretches along the Mediterranean coast from the rugged and unspoiled Datça peninsula on Turkey's southwestern tip to the resort hotels springing up along the Antalya-Alanya strip. The fir-clad mountains rising behind the coastline are punctuated by the ruins of splendid ancient Greek and Roman cities, through which passed the likes of Alexander the Great, Julius Caesar, and St. Paul.

Olüdeniz Beach

TURQUOISE RIVIERA PLANNER

Getting Here & Around

It makes the most sense to fly to the Turquoise Coast if you're coming from Istanbul or elsewhere on the Aegean. The main airports here are in Dalaman and Antalya. Once here, you'll find renting a car allows you to get around with the most ease; many of the sights you'll want to see are off the main road, and the area is filled with beautiful coastal drives.

Blue Cruising

A yacht charter in a *gulet*, a wooden motor boat or sailing boat, is the quintessential relaxing way to explore Turkey's coast, especially along the Mediterranean, with its tranquil waters, secluded inlets, beautiful beaches, and craggy coastline. For the full effect, plan at least four days and at best a week (perhaps from Antalya to Fethiye, or a tour of the Datça peninsula from Marmaris).

How Much Time Do You Need?

If you just have a weekend or so on the Turquoise Riviera and want to see ancient sites, base yourself in Antalya and drive out to great classical sites nearby like Termessos, Perge, or Aspendos. If you want to taste the grandeur of the area, stay in Göcek and hire a yacht for a day.

A road trip around the Lycian coast—a total of some 10 hours' driving, which can start in either Antalya or Dalaman—is beautiful, and full of the ruins of ancient Lycian cities like Xanthos, Pinara, and Patara. There are many unspoiled small towns and lovely hotels to stay in en route. Such a tour could take as little as three days, but would be more relaxed if you spend five to seven.

This six-day tour allows you to tack on an extra day if you wanted to stay longer somewhere. On Day 1, leave Antalya and visit Termessos. Overnight in the mountains above the limpid lagoon of Ölüdeniz. On Day 2, visit Ölüdeniz, the ghost town of Kaya, and Fethiye; overnight in the same hotel. On Day 3, visit the ancient Lycian cities of Pinara, Xanthos, and Letoön, finishing up with a swim in Patara. Overnight in Kalkan. On Day 4, head to Kaş and take a day boat trip to Kekova. Overnight in Kaş. On Day 5, visit St. Nicholas's Basilica in Demre, have lunch in Finike, and visit Arycanda in the afternoon. Overnight in Çıralı and see the burning Chimera. On Day 6, visit Phaselis, then return to Antalya.

Top Swimming Spots

- Mermerli Beach on Antalya harbor wall.
- Amid the harbor ruins of Phaselis.
- The beach ringed by mountains in Çirali/Olympos.
- In remote Adrasan or Patara.
- In the warm sandy lagoon of Ölüdeniz.
- Off the long sand reaches of Dalyan.
- Diving off a boat almost anywhere.

When to Go

The ideal months on the Turquoise Riviera are May, June, and September. Summers can be hot, especially in July and August, and that's also when the beaches tend to be fuller and waterfront discos pump out their most egregious levels of noise.

Winters very rarely drop below freezing on the coast but few establishments bother with central heating, so bring a thick sweater if you're visiting between mid-December and March.

Alanya and Side stay warmest longest. They're also best visited when charter tourists are least likely to be about, before or after the high season.

Along the Lycian coast, expect thunderstorms after mid-October and an average 12 days of rain per month in December and January. Snow graces mountain peaks well into May.

About the Local Food

Regional specialties along the coast include mussels stuffed with rice, pine nuts, and currants (one of the many stuffed dishes that fall under the general heading *dolma*); *ahtopot salatası*, a cold octopus salad, tossed in olive oil, vinegar, and parsley; and grilled fish—*çupra* (sea bream), *levrek* (sea bass), and *alabalık* (trout). Unless otherwise advertised, these are almost all farmed fish–if you want the open sea version, ask if this is *deniz levreği* (sea bass "from the sea"). Most of Turkey's tomatoes, cucumbers, eggplants, zucchinis, and peppers are grown along the coast, so fresh salads are delicious. In Lycia, a local home-cooking speciality is stewed eggplant with basil—wonderful if you're offered it. *Semiz otu* (cow parsley) is a refreshing appetizer in a garlic yogurt sauce.

For More Information on the Area

For a detailed guide to all sites between Antalya and Fethiye, it's worth picking up *Lycia*, by Cevdet Bayburtluòlu (always on sale at the Suna & Inan Kiraç Museum, Antalya). There is also an excellent interactive history on ⊕ www.lycianturkey.com.

Booking a Local Tour

On the whole, if you want to find out what local tours are available–from boat tours, trekking tours, or other local special-interest tours–it's most effective to wander through the center of town that you are in. Choose a local travel agency that looks well kept, and chat with the owner. Don't hesitate to move politely on to another one if you feel hassled or inadequately served. Another option is to ask at your hotel, but they are likely to add a surcharge for commission.

WHAT IT COSTS

	$$$$	$$$	$$	$	¢
Restaurants	over $25	$16–25	$11–15	$5–10	under $5
Hotels	over $250	$151–250	$76–150	$51–75	under $50

Restaurant prices are for one main course at dinner or for two mezes (small dishes). Hotel prices are for two people in a double room in high season, including taxes.

Updated by
Hugh Pope

The Turquoise Riviera is just as stunning as the name suggests, with luminous blue-green ocean waves lapping at isolated coves and beaches that range from multicolored polished marble pebbles to miles of yellow sand. Spectacular archaeological ruins are never far away.

THE DATÇA PENINSULA & MARMARIS

Modernity confronts antiquity in the westernmost portion of the Mediterranean coast. The beaches are gorgeous and the mood is laid back, if you don't stay in the resort areas of Datça or Marmaris proper. Datça is quieter than Marmaris, but Eski Datça and Reshadiye are lovely little villages where you can appreciate a calmer way of life. The timeless stone alleys of Eski Datça give a sense of being in another, less stressful world. The ancient ruins of Knydos and Loryma, both best reached by boat, are some of the loneliest and most evocative sites along the whole coast.

Datça Peninsula

❶ *Datça town is 76 km (47 mi) west of Marmaris and 167 km (104 mi) west of Dalaman on Rte. 400.*

★ If you make it all the way to the **Datça Peninsula,** you may never want to leave. Winds keep pine forests to sheltered hollows, and habitations are few and far between. Driving along the thin neck of land between the Aegean Sea to the north and the Mediterranean to the south feels like you are entering the gateway to another, older world. This is not somewhere to drop by for a day or two: you need at least three days to savor in full the uncluttered joys of this unique destination—it's a place with few pressures, as well as wide horizons and more than 50 little beaches for inner contemplation. The best time to visit is in spring, when the hills are carpeted in poppies, daisies, and wildflowers, and restaurants offer dishes concocted with wild thyme, rosemary, and other herbs that flourish in the hills and by the sea.

Datça is a small, little-developed port town with some characterstics of a resort. In itself it's not the best place to stay—Eski Datça and Reşadiye are older and have more charm—but if you're here, it's pleasant to spend an evening wandering around the harbor and sipping a drink at one of the quayside cafés. The weekly market is on Saturday, which is what attracts Greek islanders from nearby Symi. It's also the best place to arrange a boat trip to Knydos, a trip that takes six hours at sea but is a more charming day out than the 40-minute ride from Datça to Knydos by car. A lovely day out and meal at an unspoiled beach can also be had at **Kargı Koyu,** 3 km (2 mi) east of central Datça.

LOCAL HERBS

Don't miss trying the local herb Kaya Koruğu, if you have the opportunity. It grows on the coast and is sometimes translated as sea cow parsley, which doesn't sound as appetizing in English, but it's said to "lift" the palate with a taste between watercress and aniseed.

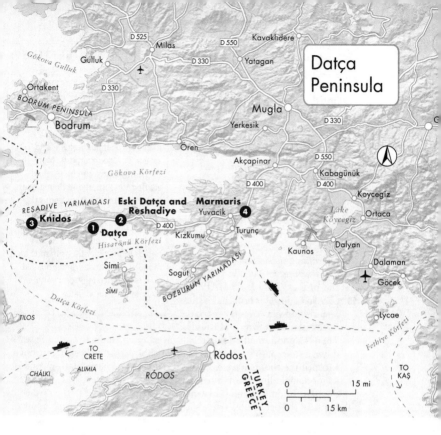

Where to Stay & Eat

$ ✕**Emek Restaurant.** Everything is made on the premises in the spotless kitchens of this excellent eatery, the best of the bunch overlooking Datça harbor. The owner and chief chef Seyyar Kantarlı says her secret is real olive oil and all fresh ingredients. The fried squid is delicious, and wild Datça herbs make menus interesting in spring. The homemade bread is some of the best on the coast. Call in the morning to reserve a window-side table. ⊠ *Yat Limanı Datça* ☎ *252/712–3375* ▭ *MC, V* ⊗ *Nov.–Feb.*

$ ✕**Yeşim Bar Restaurant.** One of only two buildings on the pleasant beach at Kargı Koyu, Yeşim offers sunbeds, umbrellas, and showers at no extra cost to visitors ready to buy at least a glass of tea. A lawn, with trees shading a bar, makes this a cool respite from sun worshipping. The menu includes pizzas, fish, and meat. Sometimes there's live music, too. ⊠ *Follow the southernmost coast road for 3 km (2 mi) east of Datça; stop at the beach where the tarmac ends* ☎ *252/712–8399* ▭ *MC, V.*

☖ $$$$ ▥**Perili Köşk.** This charming, British-dominated resort is a village of fairy-tale buildings (the name means "fairy castle") and lovely gardens tucked away on a deserted corner of coastline on the southern side of the Datça peninsula. It's geared toward teaching people how to sail small yachts, but if sailing isn't your thing, other options include tennis, mountain biking, or relaxing at the beach. Some think the resort is overpriced, especially since most activities cost extra, but booking through the British sailing tour operator Sunsail (www.sunsail.com) can save money. ⊠ *50 km (31m) west of Marmaris, or 20 km (13 mi) east of Datça, turn south on a dirt track at the Perili Köşk sign, then continue on 1 km (1 mi) to beach,* ☎ *252/723–3330* 🖶 *252/723–3768* ⊕ *www.sunsail. com* ⊃ *108 rooms* ⌂ *1 restaurant, 2 bars, 2 pools, refrigerators, dive shop, Wi-Fi, babysitting, tennis, fitness, sauna, beauty treatments, mountain bikes, billiards, boating, windsurfing* ⊟ *MC, V* ⊙ *Closed end of Oct.–May 1* ⏦ *MAP.*

$$ ⊞ **Villa Carla.** This hotel has a stunning clifftop view over the sea to the Greek islands of Symi and Rhodes. There's a good small pool in the terrace garden, and a five-minute walk down a steep path leads to the hotel's pebbly, crystal-clear private cove. Most of the rooms have a sea view. The hotel is particularly proud of its food, including hearty breakfasts, free afternoon tea, and 17 starters on offer for dinner, and the owner is a passionate guide to the rare wild fauna of the peninsula. There's a satellite TV in the comfortable, open-spaced lobby. ⊠ *From Datça harbor, head east along the coast, following the signs to Villa Carla* ☎ *252/712–2029* 🖶 *252/712–2890* ⊕ *www. villacarladatca.com* ⊃ *19 rooms* ⌂ *Some a/c, fans, Wi-Fi, bicycles, laundry facilities, pool* ⊟ *MC, V.*

$ ⊞ **Bora Hotel.** If you'd like to stay in town, this simple hotel right behind Datça harbor has clean, bright rooms. Service can be a bit sloppy now that the original owner has turned the business over to his children, however, and the double glazing on the windows may not keep out all the street noise during the high season. ⊠ *Just above yacht harbor,* ☎ *252/712–2040* 🖶 *252/712–0080* ⊕ *www.borahoteldatca.com* ⊃ *18 rooms* ⌂ *in-room safes* ⊟ *MC, V* ⊙ *Oct.–May.*

Nightlife

Nurs (⊠ 200 m east from harbor ☎ 532/512–0406) has a poolside bar where live music from acoustic guitars or the piano can be enjoyed most nights from June to September. The **Sounds Gallus** club just east of the port is the main discothèque for Datça, right next to Nurs. Doors open after midnight.

Eski Datça and Reshadiye

❷ ★ Turkish satirical poet and polemical left-wing social critic Can Yücel retired to a modest old stone house in Eski Datça, setting an artistic tone

---

BEST WAYS OF GETTING TO DATÇA

By air, the least time-consuming route is to fly to Dalaman Airport and make the three-hour drive west to Datça. There are flights to Dalaman from Istanbul, Ankara, and several European airports. More pleasantly, Datça can be reached via Bodrum Airport and then a two-hour car-ferry ride from Bodrum Port to Datça's Körmen Port. In the June–September season, these boats run from both ports at 9 AM and 5 PM. In winter they run only on Monday, Wednesday, and Friday at 9 AM from Datça to Bodrum and at 5 PM from Bodrum to Datça.

for this pretty backwater and nearby Reshadiye. The formerly Greek-populated village, 3 km (2 mi) from Datça harbor, is one of the few in Turkey that has survived intact. It is now experiencing fine restoration efforts that have produced several lovely small houses to rent. Nobody hurries through the stone-paved alleys, and the local **Datça Sofrası** restaurant hosts an open literary evening every Thursday.

Where to Stay & Eat

$ ✕ **Datça Sofrası.** This is an ideal lunch spot for visitors to Eski Datça, with a vine-covered terrace and traditional Turkish braised meats emerging from under a brass-hooded charcoal brazier. The menu is also rich in vegetarian dishes and starters concocted from local wild herbs. In the hottest summer months, guests can also take refuge in a cool cellar. ⊠ *Hurma Cad. 16, Eski Datça* ☎ *252/712–4188* ▤ *no credit cards.*

$$$–$$$$ ▥ **Mehmet Ali Ağa Konağı.** A stay in this restored mansion, opened in
Fodor'sChoice 2004 after a multimillion-dollar restoration, offers the unique chance
★ to experience the lifestyle and surroundings of a 19th-century Ottoman nobleman. The owners have lovingly re-created five rooms in the main mansion that are works of art in themselves, fitting excellent modern bathrooms behind the original woodwork, restoring old wall paintings, and choosing fine antiques to match. Standard rooms are large and situated around a lovely garden. Fragrant cedarwood has been used throughout, and the details are faultless, right down to the use of nearly one million custom-made iron nails. The hotel's Elaki Restaurant is a gourmet's delight. Specialties include Mediterranean and Ottoman dishes. At breakfast, the homemade jams are so good you'll be tempted to eat them right out of the little bowls. Reserve at least one month in advance in July and August. The hotel also arranges hikes and trips to ancient sites. ⊠ *Reshadiye, Datça,* ☎ *252/712–9257* ▤ *252/712–9256* ⊕ *www.kocaev.com* ⇋ *13 rooms, 2 suites* ⌂ *Some fans, some a/c, pool, 2 bars, minibars, Internet room, meeting room, Turkish bath, massage, bicycles, shop* ▤ *MC, DC, V* ⊗ *Nov.–mid-Apr.* ⑩ *BP.*

$$ ▥ **Dede Pansiyon.** This comfortable stone pansiyon is swathed in bougainvilleas and decorated with curiosities like concrete flagstones set with old bathroom fittings. The rooms have kitchenettes and themes like "Picasso" or "Theater." It's a good option for its village-jumble layout and the large swimming pool, one of the few in Eski Datça. ⊠ *Can Yücel Cad.,* ☎ *252/712–3951* ▤ *252/712–3951* ⊕ *www.dedepansiyon.com* ⇋ *6 rooms* ⌂ *bar* ▤ *no cards.*

$ ▥ **Yağhane Pansiyon.** If you are in search of help in channeling inner reflection, this comfortable stone-built hotel with a fine English lawn out front specializes in weeklong courses of yoga, meditation, Ayurvedic treatments, and "the search for your inner snake." The owners walked all the way from London until they found Eski Datça and stopped. Home-cooked vegetarian meals are served on a pleasant terrace. Even the locally made forged-iron gates feature the symbols of yin and yang. Reserve well in advance. ⊠ *Eski Datça,* ☎ *252/712–2287* ▤ *252/712–4580* ⊕ *www.suryaturkey.com* ⇋ *4 rooms* ⌂ *Shared bathrooms, fans in rooms, yoga terrace, café, guided walks* ▤ *no credit cards* ⑩ *CP.*

¢ ▥ **Doğa Pansiyon Apart.** Excellent for long- as well as short-term stays, this quiet hotel and boarding house set in olive groves offers unusually large rooms and open views. The establishment has its own one-acre garden with almond, mandarin, orange, and lemon trees. ⊠ *On the outer edge of Eski Datça,* ☎ *252/712–2178* ⊕ *www.dogapansiyon.com* ⤶ *10 rooms* ⚭ *Bar, restaurant, refrigerators; no a/c.*

Knidos

❸ *38 km (24 mi) west of Datça*

Windswept Knidos sits on a headland at the very end of the Datça Peninsula, at the point where the Aegean meets the Mediterranean. A primitive site, its ruins are scattered amid olive groves and few hints of modern civilization. The city was founded in the 7th century BC by Dorian Greeks and prospered because of its excellent location on shipping routes between Egypt, Rhodes, Ephesus, the Greek mainland, and other major ports. Its main claim to fame was a temple to Aphrodite that housed a 4th-century BC statue of the goddess by Praxiteles, a realistic nude that the historian Pliny called the finest statue in the world. The statue became a tourist attraction, drawing travelers from afar, among them Cicero and Julius Caesar. Carried off to Constantinople by the Byzantines, it was believed lost in a palace fire, although excavations in 1970 turned up a piece of white marble apparently signed by Praxiteles that could have been part of it. To see the foundations of the unusual **circular temple** that housed the statue of Aphrodite, make your way to the restaurants by the harbor and follow the path leading uphill to the right.

Back by the harbor, there is a small **odeon,** or concert hall. On the promontory with the lighthouse is the rectangular, stone **Lion Tomb.** The sad-eyed lion is in remembrance of a victory over Sparta. The original is now on display in the British Museum with another famous relic from Knidos, a statue of the goddess Demeter. Her **sanctuary,** however, is up the original stairway that leads to the upper portion of the town.

Knidos is most romantic when reached by sea, as the ancients did. Boats leave regularly from Datça in season, although the trip takes three hours each way. The drive from Datça takes 45 minutes.

OFF THE BEATEN PATH

★

LORYMA – Large, immaculately cut stones form the walls of a castle that stands guard over lonely Bozuk Bay, making Loryma one of the most beautiful spots on the coast. The citadel dates from Hellenistic times—the late 3rd through 1st centuries BC. Loryma can be reached by road from Bozburun, but approaching from the sea (by boat from Marmaris or Kızkumu) is all the more dramatic. ⊠ *20 km (12 mi) west of Marmaris, turn south on local road signposted Bozburun and continue to follow signposts to Loryma.*

$$$ 🏨 **SABRINA'S HAUS** – This hotel just outside the shipbuilding harbor of Bozburun can be a base for visiting **Loryma** and is a lovely getaway in any event, especially since it can only be reached by boat or via a 15-minute hike. It's right on the water, and has a gorgeous splash of gardens and palm trees amid the stony mountains of Bozburun Bay. Rooms vary from the basic to the spectacular, so make sure you know which you are getting. This is a wonderful get-away-from-the-rest-of-the-

world kind of place. It's a bit of a journey, too, so plan to spend at least two nights. ✉ *Follow the coast about 1 km (mi) east of Bozburun until the road ends, then call for the hotel boat.,* ☎ *252/456–2456* 🖷 *252/456–2470* ⊕ *www.sabrinashaus.de* ⇥ *13 rooms* ⚹ *Restaurant, bar, dive shop, windsurfing, boating; no TV, no room phones.* ▭ *MC, V* ⊗ *Mid-Nov.–mid Apr.* ⦿⧵ *MAP.*

Marmaris

❹ *91 km (56 mi) west of the international airport at Dalaman*

The big, brash resort city Marmaris has two faces, and they're hard to reconcile. From the sea, a thick line of resort hotels stretches around the northern edge of a great bay, the whole encircled by a magical necklace of pine-clad mountains. Behind those same hotels, however, the city has been overwhelmed by boxy concrete development and streets lined with a hundred generically named eateries. An annual horde of European tourists descends on these workaday establishments, but for the international traveler, there is little special about Marmaris that cannot be savored elsewhere in Turkey. The only reasons most come here are to meet a yacht, to travel on to the Greek island of Rhodes, or perhaps to take up an unbeatable deal at one of the best resort hotels, some of which are spectacular worlds unto themselves (which is just fine given that you probably won't want to see much else here).

If you're in Marmaris, though, don't miss the city's best achievement, a 10-km **seafront promenade** that stretches all the way from the easternmost marina known as Netsal, past the old fortress, along the palm-lined main boulevard of town, and then out between the beach and the fancy hotels that line the coast, all the way to the outlying resort of **Içmeler.** Along the way there are any number of cafés at which to pause for refreshment or to take in fine views of sea and mountains. For $5, the footsore can ride back on one of the shared water taxis that run up and down the coast in season (usually Apr.–Nov.).

There are a few historic sites in what was until a few decades ago a small, sleepy fishing port. These include a modest 16th-century **citadel,** first built by Süleyman the Magnificent, shelled to bits by the French in the First World War and rebuilt in the 1980s. There is a small museum inside (both are closed on Mondays).

Good day outings from Marmaris include a boat trip from the harbor to **Turunç** on a visit easily arranged by yourself, your hotel, or any of the many travel agencies. Another fine destination is **Sedir Island** (Cedar Island). This will likely involve a bus ride north to the gulf of Gökova and then a boat. Sedir harbors one of the most perfect beaches in the world—if only one could have it to oneself. The sand is made up of tiny egg-shaped pearls of a luminous white marble, making the water brilliantly clear as you swim before the impressive escarpments of Mt. Kavak over the sea to the north. An hour's bus ride from Marmaris will also take you to the refreshing sulfurous mud baths near **Lake Köyeceğiz** or, on a long but doable day trip, to the town of **Dalyan** and the ruins of ancient Kaunos.

Marmaris Bay is also home to some of Turkey's biggest and busiest marinas, and is one of the main bases from which sailing yachts and wooden gulets can be chartered for Blue Cruises. For **scuba diving,** walk down the line of diving boats near the municipal information center on Iskele Meydanı and choose the boat that seems the most professional and best equipped.

A 60-minute catamaran service to the Greek island of **Rhodes** leaves Marmaris harbor every day at 9 AM, returning at 4 PM, with a single or day return ticket costing $26. For ticket information, contact Yeşil Marmaris Tourism (252/412–2290. It's worth considering spending the night in Rhodes, since Greek island life typically grinds to a halt during the midday hours.

> ### THE GULET
>
> Blue Cruise charter boats come in three main types: most are *gulets,* wooden motorized sailing yachts with a pointed bow and stern. These days, they're built for comfortable cruising, and many have amenities such as air-conditioning, and can accommodate up to about eighteen guests. Boats with a pointed bow and a flat stern, often with windows like a mediaeval galleon, are known as *aynalı kıç,* or mirror-bottom. The prettiest are boats with a pointed prow and a rounded stern that are known as *tirandil* (or nut-shell).

Where to Stay & Eat

Some city blocks in Marmaris appear to be made up entirely of restaurants with a pavement-to-pavement profusion of tables and menus that seem like a catalog of world food. The most striking views can be had from café tables where the seafront promenade curves into the bay around the citadel, and these attract the tourists. The locals, however, prefer the slightly better-prepared food in restaurants that look out onto the Netsel yacht marina just to the east.

$-$$ ✕**Antique.** Right next to Pineapple, this establishment is similarly favored by the Turkish residents of the city. It offers a free shuttle to the restaurant from any hotel and has a side specialty in Chinese dishes. The food is fine, but service is somewhat brusque—unusual in Turkey. ⊠ *Netsel Marina* ☎ *252/413–2955* ▤ *MC, V.*

$$ ✕**Yat Marina Restaurant.** Far from Marmaris's madding crowds, this is where to catch a flavor of the life of international yacht folk. The chefs don't go in for the omnibus menus common in town, preferring to concentrate their considerable talents on getting favorite Turkish dishes just right. It's fun to walk around the busy marina where huge rigs pull millionaires' luxury motor cruisers from the water as European pensioners scrub the hulls of their much smaller "pocket" yachts. ⊠ *Follow the coast road 8 km (5 mi) east out of Marmaris and park outside the marina gate* ☎ *252/422–0022* ▤ *MC, V.*

★ **$-$$** ✕**Pineapple.** The menu is eclectic but mainly Italian-themed at this international restaurant in the Netsel marina. The house specialty is roast lamb, but the chef also prepares pasta and pizza. Above Pineapple is its sister restaurant, My Marina English Pub—not as generic as the name might suggest, and with quite nice views out large windows. ⊠ *Netsel Marina* ☎ *252/412–0976* ▤ *AE, DC, MC, V.*

CLOSE UP

Blue Cruising

THE MOST CHARMING WAY to visit the Turquoise Riviera, or the Aegean Coast, is on a Blue Cruise, in a *gulet*— a wooden motor yacht or sailboat. Time has done remarkably little to spoil the crystal-clear waters, pine-clad inlets, and limpid lagoons. This will be one of the most unforgettable holidays you've ever had, but there is some organization necessary.

How much will it cost? *Gulets* come in all shapes and sizes, the majority with between 4 to 12 two-person cabins. To hire your own boat, prices work out to between $80 to $150 per person per day in July and August, perhaps half that in April or October. Most charter on terms that cover all but food and drink. After a discussion with the boat's cook, you and a member of the crew go to the local supermarket and load up. Cabin charters—when you join a group of strangers—are generally on an all-inclusive basis, and start at about $300 per week.

When to go? May is pretty, uncrowded, and charters are cheap, but the water is cooler. June is warm and still not too busy. July and August are hotter, busier, and more expensive. September and early October are often perfect at sea, but the mountainsides are less green.

Other things to consider are how long you have and which port is closest to the sites you want to see. Fethiye is a major jumping-off point, as are Bodrum, Marmaris, and Göcek. Ideally, two weeks are needed to see the whole coast from Bodrum to Antalya, but most travelers only have a week. There are cruises of a few days and even day cruises.

Look for a boat with a large area for relaxing in the stern and a good flat space on the foredeck for sleeping outside in hot weather. Don't accept anything too squashed: eight cabins in a boat under 80 feet is too much. If you're out in July and August, look for air-conditioning and enough power-generation capacity for it. Ask about extras like a windsurfer or kayaks.

The captain is important, too. Make sure you can communicate, and if you're arranging the cruise from abroad, insist on a telephone conversation before sending your deposit (usually 30%-40% of the total). Look for someone who listens to your wishes, and be wary if you are met with a patronizing "leave-it-all-to-me" attitude. If you want to sail rather than motor, you need to be doubly sure you have the right vessel. And when you get to the boat, check the captain's license, insist on seeing life vests, and test emergency equipment like radios.

If you're hiring a boat after you've arrived in Turkey, you can walk down to the quayside and haggle, but this can be risky in high season. Most people book months ahead. Look for operators registered with both the Turkish Association of Travel Agencies (TURSAB) and the Chamber of Shipping.

On the Internet there are sites for individual boats and large agencies operating from major ports. For Marmaris, try www.yesilmarmaris. com. Fethiye is popular, with www.albatrosyachting.com, www. bethereyachting.com, www. compassyachting.com, www. fethiyeyachting.com, or www. alestayachting.com. Antalya is served by www.olymposyachting.com.

4

$$$ ▣ **Martı Resort.** There's not always much to differentiate between the big resort hotels in Marmaris, but the well-established Martı manages to avoid the often brutal architectural profile of the big hotels. Low, Ottoman-style tiled roofs with tall chimneys, sweeping pools, and a gorgeous view over a sandy beach toward the mountains of Marmaris Bay make this resort hotel popular among international travelers and Turkish vacationers. Rooms are pleasant, and the food is good, too.

> **FRANKINCENSE**
>
> The area around Marmaris is known for its frankincense forests. On the water's edge, between the city and the Pupa Yacht Hotel, is a lovely national park. In Marmaris market you can buy the frankincense, which is the dried sap of the trees. As incense it's known to be quite soothing.

✉ *İçmeler, Marmaris,* ☎ *252/455–3440* 📠 *252/455–3448* ⊕ *www. marti.com.tr* ➯ *270 rooms, 2 suites* ⚭ *3 restaurants, 5 bars, Internet room, tennis courts, 2 pools, gym, dive shop, in-room safes, meeting rooms* ▤ *AE, MC, V* ¶◎¶ *MAP.*

$$ ▣ **Ibero Star Grand Azur.** This international resort is one of the few places with real architectural style in Marmaris. Its sleek, curving profile overlooks lush tropical gardens, and the whole is a 15-minute walk to the central restaurants and bars. If you're going to stay in central Marmaris, this is probably the best you'll find. The rooms are on the generic side, but the staff is polite and the beach well maintained. The concierge will arrange boat tours to Turunç. ✉ *Kenan Evren Bulv. 13* ☎ *252/417–4050* 📠 *252/417–4060* ➯ *257 rooms, 30 suites* ⚭ *2 restaurants, 3 bars, room service, minibars, 1 outdoor pool, 1 indoor pool, 3 tennis courts, gym, massage, sauna, beach, shops, baby-sitting, dry cleaning, water sports, meeting rooms, billiards; no-smoking rooms* ▤ *AE, DC, MC, V* ¶◎¶ *MAP* ⊕ *www.hotelgrandazur.com.*

¢ ▣ **Pupa Yacht Hotel.** This clean, simple hotel east of Marmaris is one of the rare establishments left in Turkey that is peaceful and right on its own little beach. It overlooks its own yacht jetty and the unspoiled, pine-clad mountains beyond. Watching the sun rise over the water from the balcony of your room is what a holiday should be all about. A modest restaurant and bar mean you can enjoy a quiet evening by a lawn that leads to a pebbly beach. The rooms are small and pretty basic—but they're not the main reason to come here. As the hotel's name implies, it is an extension of a yacht-charter business, and is popular with the European sea-going crowd, so reserve a month in advance in season. ✉ *Follow the coast road east of Marmaris for 5 mi, and watch for* PUPA YAT *signs.,* ☎ *252/413–3566* 📠 *252/413–8487* ⊕ *www.pupa.com.tr* ➯ *19 rooms* ⚭ *restaurant, bar, bicycles, boating, dive shop, public Internet, beach* ▤ *AE, MC, V* ¶◎¶ *BP.*

Nightlife

Marmaris comes alive at night with a wide selection of bars and dance clubs. European charter tourists display the art of serious drinking on **Bar Street** in the old town and its four solid blocks of drinking establishments. The major clubs here offer seething dance floors, and it's generally an opportunity for excess. The largest open-air club is **Back Street Garden Bar** (⌧ Marmaris Bar Street, Old Town ☎ 252/412–4048). Another busy club is the **Crazy Daisy.** The party goes on farther west, toward İçmeler, at the restaurant-bar **Malibu Beach** (⌧ Uzunyalı 248 Sok. No. 9 ☎ 252/412–6778). At İçmeler beach itself are dance clubs and karaoke bars with raucous crowds partying into the night.

For a more upmarket scene, try the **Marmaris Palace Beach Club** (⌧ Marmaris Palace Hotel, Pamucak Mevkii, İçmeler ☎ 252/455–5555), out on a jetty between Marmaris and Içmeler. It has a restaurant and DJs offering a medley of house, chillout, and trance music.

THE LYCIAN COAST

4

Lycia is the heart of the Turquoise Coast. It's a beautiful, little-developed area with charming port cities, unique hotels, and uncrowded beaches, not to mention some of Turkey's most fascinating ancient ruins: Xanthos, Pinara, Patara, Olympos, and Phaselis.

Dalyan

❺ *25 km (16 mi) west of Dalaman Airport on Rte. 400 and local roads (follow signs).*

Dalyan is a lovely place for a three-day break, especially for those who prefer a quiet vacation in an environment that's been developed in a way that is sensitive to the natural surroundings and the native flora and fauna. The city is on the winding, reed-flanked banks of the Dalyan River, between the great expanse of Lake Köyeceğiz and the lovely beach of İstuzu. The town is known for its Carian tombs, which are carved into the cliff that rises behind the 15-foot high reeds fringing the undeveloped west bank of the river—an especially fine sight when floodlit at night. Boats lined up along the quayside in the center of town—they're all part of the Dalyan Kooperatifi and fares are regulated; there is no bargaining unless there are many idle boats—will take you on expeditions to the beach, to sulfur baths, on explorations of the lake, to the ruins of the ancient city of Kaunos, and to the pretty bay of Ekincik. If your hotel is on the river, the boatmen will pick you up from there, too. Trekking and footpaths are developing fast, and include walks to Ekincik and elsewhere. Birdwatchers love the lake, where 180 species of bird have been logged. Local markets are also colorful: there's one in Dalyan on Saturdays and one at the local center of Ortaca on Fridays. Dalyan doesn't have much nightlife, and its main-street shops are now no longer rug dealers but estate agents hoping to cash in on the villa-buying boom by British and other European visitors.

★ ☯ The unspoiled sands of **İztuzu Beach** stretch for 8 km (5 mi), with the Mediterranean on one side and a freshwater lagoon on the other. In June and July *Caretta caretta* sea turtles lay their eggs here. This is a conservation area, and signs along the beach mark possible nesting places and warn you not to stick umbrellas in the sand or behave in other ways that could disturb the turtles.

The
Lycian Coast

KEY
Beaches
Ferries

The ancient ruins at **Kaunos** (about 15–30 minutes by boat from Dalyan) include the rock tombs, a crumbling Byzantine basilica, a massive Roman bath restored as a site museum, and a well-preserved semicircular theater cut into the hillside in the Greek style. Most date from the 4th century BC, and were carved by a people called the Carians, who dominated the region west of here. The style, however, is that of ancient Lycia, the neighboring region to the east.

Where to Stay & Eat

★ $–$$ ✕ **Riverside Restaurant.** The menu at this excellent eatery on the banks of the Dalyan River overlooking the tombs of Kaunos focuses on fish. Starters include delicious items such as olives with walnuts and garlic; baked eggplant mashed with yogurt, garlic, raisins, pine nuts, and dill; or purslane in a mayonnaise and lemon sauce. ⊠ *Sağlık Cad., Maraş District. Follow the Dalyan River bankside walkway 500 m south from the main Sq.* ☎ *252/284–3166* ⊟ *AE, DC, MC, V.*

★ $$ ✕⌂ **Dalyan Resort.** This beautifully built hotel opened in 2005 on a bend in the Dalyan River. A bit farther out of Dalyan town center than most other hotels, and more sophisticated, the grounds include wide, well-tended gardens, a tennis court, a large pool, and a bright, well-designed restaurant where even the bread is made in-house. ⊠ *Kaunos Cad. No.*

50, Maraş, Dalyan—drive south along the river from Dalyan town square and follow the many signs, ☎ *252/284–5499* 🖷 *252/284–5498* ⊕ *www.dalyanresort.com* ➷ *16 standard rooms, 24 suites, 18 junior suites* ⚲ *TV, pool, in-room safes, minibars, 3 bars, restaurant, shop, meeting room, Internet room, Turkish bath, massage* ▤ *AE, MC, V* ⭗ *BP.*

$ ▦ **Asur Hotel.** With a large swimming pool and gardens overlooking the Dalyan River, this one-story hotel is a good option. The rooms are clean and pleasant, and free use of bicycles cuts the time taken to cover the kilometer (½ mile) to the center of town. ☎ *252/284–3232* 🖷 *252/284–3244* ⊕ *www.asurotel.com* ➷ *34 rooms, 10 suites* ⚲ *In-room safes, restaurant, café, snack bar, room service, minibars, pool, bar, bicycles, Internet room, Turkish bath, sauna, fitness center, billiards* ▤ *AE, DC, MC, V* ⭗ *Closed Oct.–May* ⭗ *BP.*

⭗ **$** ▦ **Beyaz Gül.** This curious hotel is run by an old-fashioned Turkish lady, and staying here is like living in a fairy-tale cottage. Kids love the rooms decorated with bears, woolen socks, and other knick-knacks. A little oasis on the riverfront south of the town center, it has a direct view of the tombs from its garden café and restaurant. ⊠ *Balikhane Cad. 92/93, Maraş,* ☎ *252/284–2304* 🖷 *252/284–2207* ⊕ *www.beyazgul.info* ➷ *5 rooms* ⚲ *restaurant, bar* ▤ *No credit cards.*

$ ▦ **Happy Caretta.** This small hotel is in a shady garden on the banks of the Dalyan River opposite the Kaunos tombs. The rooms are attractively decorated in wood, terra-cotta-style tiles, and white stucco. Guests can swim in the river off a small jetty in front of a splendid row of cypress trees, or wait for a boat to take them to the beach. ⊠ *Kaunos Cad. No. 26, Maraş District; drive south down the Dalyan River and follow the signs* ☎ *252/284–2109* 🖷 *252/284–2109* ⊕ *www.happycaretta.com* ➷ *10 rooms, 4 suites* ⚲ *Restaurant, bar, Wi-Fi* ▤ *MC, V* ⭗ *BP.*

Fodor'sChoice
★

Göcek

❻ *22 km (14 mi) east of Dalaman Airport on Rte. 400.*

For the visitor who wants a taste of the grandeur of the Turquoise Riviera, but has little time to spare, Göcek is perfect. The yachting resort town is just a 20-minute drive over the mountains from Dalaman Airport, enjoys gorgeous vistas of sea and mountains, has easy access to the sea, and offers good, upmarket places to eat, sleep, and shop. Three marinas and an annual regatta make this a major center for Turkey's yachting world, and weekends see it awash with Istanbul *sosyete* (essentially the rich, frequently spoiled, and occasionally glamorous children of the upper classes) on parade. From Göcek, an hour's drive reaches the natural beauties of Dalyan, the sights around Fethiye/Ölüdeniz, or great Lycian sites like Tlos and Xanthos. There is only one private beach in Göcek itself, so hop on one of the several wooden tour boats that head out each morning to explore elsewhere. The best swimming and snorkelling are around the beaches or in the coves of the **Twelve Islands,** strung out like a necklace across the mouth of the bay.

Göcek is in prime Blue Cruise territory, so you can rent a yacht or a *gulet*, for as much time and money as you have to spare. The most popular anchorages include Tersane, Kapı Creek, Cleopatra's Bay, the obscure ruins at Lydae, Tomb Bay, or the lovely island of Katrancı.

The **Sundowner Beach** run privately by Swissotel at the eastern end of Port Göcek marina (☎ 252/645–2760) is one of the most spectacular—and expensive—on the Turquoise Riviera. It costs $26 for guests. For some this is a small price to pay for an excellently maintained beach and bar establishment, and a completely unspoiled, wraparound view of the bay and mountains. The beach is open 10 AM to 6 PM, later if anyone wants to stay; the bar is open in the evening and dinner is served after 7 PM.

Where to Stay & Eat

$$$–$$$$ ✕ **Verandah Restaurant.** This open wooden chalet with a great view over the masts of Port Göcek marina to the mountains beyond is where the visiting yachting elite gathers. Run by the Swissotel in town, it's expensive and has immaculate standards to match. You'll need to have identification with you to get past the gate to the port. ⊠ *Walk east out of town, restaurant is 100 yards after entrance to Port Göcek* ☎ *252/645–2760* ▤ *AE, DC, MC, V.*

$–$$ ✕ **Can.** This busy harborside fish restaurant is popular with Göcek natives because the large interior space is open all year round—and wireless Internet access is free. In summer, it also has seating around a seawater pool. The restaurant offers typical specialities like fish baked in salt, and prides itself on a selection of 30 starters including tuna with onion sauce and cheese, served with arugula salad. ⊠ *Western edge of municipal harbor* ☎ *252/645–1507* ▤ *MC, V.*

★ $–$$ ✕ **Özcan.** Cushioned bamboo chairs, attentive waitstaff, and the best grilled octopus you've ever tasted await you at Özcan, a fish restaurant on the wide esplanade that makes up Göcek's main public harborside. Starters include unusual mushrooms from the mountains out back, fresh seaweed dishes, and squid in garlic, oil, and lemon. An unusual—and delicious—fish is the big-eyed mullet, found in few other places than these waters. ⊠ *Middle of municipal yacht harbor* ☎ *252/645–2593* ▤ *MC, V* ☉ *Nov.–Apr.*

¢–$ ✕ **Limon Restaurant Bar.** This traditional Turkish meat restaurant is the locals' choice, since the prices are half that of the seafront establishments. There's no view except of the concrete-built hinterland of Göcek, but the Turkish kebabs, *pide*, and pizzas are excellent. ⊠ *Head north from Yapi Kredi Bank on the main shopping street, Limon is opposite the belediye (city hall)* ☎ *252/645–1898* ▤ *MC, V.*

★ $$ ✕▤ **Hotel Forest Gate.** This quiet cluster of white two-story villas surrounded by pine trees on the edge of the forest has generous rooms, a pool shaded by a great carob tree, and a friendly atmosphere. It's a good base for exploring the surrounding area, but the 10-minute walk back from the center of town is uneven and dark at night. Breakfast is basic but dinners are cooked fresh on demand. ⊠ *From the main road, turn into Göcek at the gas station at the entrance of town and follow signs east,* ☎ *252/645–2629* ▤ *252/645–2432* ⊕ *www.hotelforestgate.com* ⋍ *20 rooms, 4 suites* ⚭ *Restaurant, pool, bar* ▤ *MC, V,* ⵏ⃝ *BP.*

$$ ▤ **The Inn Swissotel Göcek.** The Inn gives all the luxury and excellent service you'd expect from an international chain and this is probably the

IF YOU LIKE DIVING

Scuba diving is good along most of Turkey's southwestern coastline, thanks to crystal-clear waters, a large number of islands, and steeply rocky coastlines plunging deep into the sea. The warm, placid bays along the coast are ideal, and many big beach resorts have snorkeling and diving gear. There is no blaze of colorful tropical reef life, but there are many sunken archaeological sites, where the ocean floor is littered with ancient columns and bits of stairways and tombs (but note that it is prohibited to go diving around certain sites). You can spend a peaceful day out with plenty of Mediterranean fish and underwater flora, exploring sunken wrecks and broken amphorae.

You can usually arrange a day's diving by wandering along the harborfront of any of the main towns, especially in Antalya, Kaş, Fethiye, Marmaris, and Bodrum. Dive operators and their contact information tend to change

annually so, again, your best bet is simply to go down to the harbor and see what looks good. Diveboat operators like to tie up alongside each other so you can quickly work out who'll suit you.

A word of warning: there are many amateurish dive operators in Turkey and the industry is very lightly regulated, so check qualifying documents and pay close attention to the state of the equipment, especially if you're joining a very touristy, crowded boat.

The governmental **Turkish Diving Federation** (⊠ Ulus İşhane, A. Blok. 303–304, Ulus, Ankara ☎ 312/310–4136 and 312/309–5076)can provide information on the permits you need for diving independently. If you are going to take a diving course, make sure the school is recognized by one or both international diving organizations, CMAS and PADI, and has instructors who speak English.

best place in town to stay. That said, make sure you get one of the nonattic rooms: fitting into Göcek's low-rise building codes means that the attic rooms really are just that, with low ceilings. Some rooms have walk-out access to the pool, across the lawn—few, however, have a real sea view. An additional advantage of staying here is a free on-demand shuttle to Göcek's spectacular but expensive Sundowner Beach. Wi-Fi is available, but access will cost you a whopping $29 per day. ⊠ *Cumhuriyet District, Göcek, 48310* ☎ *252/645–2760* 🖷 *252/645–2767* ⊕ *www. gocek.swissotel.com* 🛏 *57 rooms* ⚹ *Cable TV, in-room safes, minibars, pool, restaurant, shop, sauna, spa, fitness room, meeting room, Wi-Fi* ▤ *AE, MC, V* ☉ *Nov.–mid Apr.* ⏋ *BP.*

$$ ▨ **Villa Danlin.** On Göcek's main shopping street, this is a good small hotel with rooms shielded from most noise. The location is ideal for access to the harbor and restaurants—and of course the shops. ⊠ *Çarşı İçi, Göcek 48310* ☎ *252/645–1521* 🖷 *252/645–2686* ⊕ *www.villadanlin. com* 🛏 *13 rooms* ⚹ *TV, minibars, pool, laundry, Wi-Fi* ▤ *MC, V* ☉ *May–Oct.* ⏋ *BP.*

If you get overheated on the main road between Göcek and Fethiye, and need an antidote to the relentless fashionability of Göcek, follow the brown sign south to **GUNLÜKLÜ BEACH** (⊠ About 10 km from Göcek, 17 km from Fethiye. ✆ $4 per car) – It's a good place to stop for a picnic in a forest of small chestnut trees or to take a swim from a dark sand beach in the unspoiled bay. In season, a shop down by the beach sells basic food. Be forewarned, though: the beach tends to get crowded on weekends with Turkish day-trippers from Fethiye, and the facilities can be a bit rough and ready.

Fethiye

❼ *50 km (31 mi) east of Dalaman Airport on Rte. 400.*

This busy port town is a good base for exploring the ruins of ancient Lycia in the mountains that rise to the east. Fethiye was known in antiquity as Telmessus (not to be confused with Termessos, near Antalya), and was the principal port of Lycia from the Roman period onward. In front of the town hall is one of the finest of several tombs found throughout the city: this one represents a two-story Lycian house, with reliefs of warriors on both sides of its lid.

The small original town was once called Mekri and populated mainly by Greeks before the Greek-Turkish population exchange in 1924. It was renamed in 1934, after an Ottoman pilot called Fethi Bey. He was killed when he crashed in the mountains of Lebanon while attempting a historic flight that was to link all the Middle Eastern provinces of the Ottoman Empire on the eve of the First World War in 1914. Today's town is quite modern, having been substantially rebuilt after an earthquake in 1957. Strolling along the seafront promenade is a pleasant evening outing, and scuba diving enthusiasts can choose between half a dozen dive boats that collect in the harbor. The town is most fun on Tuesdays, when village folk flock into Fethiye for the weekly market. The harbor has many yachts available for Blue Cruising.

The **Fethiye Museum** (Fethiye Müzesi) has some fine statues and jewelry from the glory days of Telmessus, and the labels are in English. ⊠ *Off Atatürk Cad. (look for signs)* ✆ *$3* ☉ *Tues.–Sun. 8:30–5.*

Impressive ancient Lycian **rock tombs** are carved into the cliff that looms above town. The largest is the **Tomb of Amyntas**, presumably the burial place of a 4th-century BC ruler or nobleman. Inside are the slabs where corpses were laid out. To reach the tombs, you'll have to climb many steps—the stairway starts at Kaya Caddesi, near the bus station—but your effort will be well rewarded, particularly at dusk, when the cliffs take on a reddish glow.

Along the crest of the hill overlooking the old town are the battlements of a **castle**, whose foundations date back to antiquity and were later built up by the 12th-century crusader Knights of St. John and the Ottoman Empire. The main road around the central harbor square of Fethiye also runs past the stage of the antique **theater** of Telmessus, a recent chance rediscovery that gives a sense of history to the modern buildings all around. The rest of the ancient town remains under its urban tomb.

Gemiler Island is a scenic must, surrounded by an amphitheater of mountains and scattered with Byzantine remains dating from the 7th to the 9th centuries AD. There are also some Lycian tombs from the 2nd century BC, as well as a 19th-century Greek church with some intact mosaics dedicated to St. Nicholas.

The 16th-century **Hamam** (⊠ Hamam Cad., close to the main harbor Sq. ☎ 252/614–9318 ⊕ www.oldturkishbath.com) is still in use. It's a fine way to scrub off the barnacles after a long voyage, and full of atmosphere with 14 domes and six arches.

Where to Stay & Eat

$$ ✕ **Meğri Restaurant.** Hidden in a sidestreet of the bazaar, the permanent part of this restaurant has stone walls, high wood ceilings, and decorative kilims. In summer, most of this large, upscale restaurant spills out into a large courtyard in the middle of the bazaar. A vast menu mixes dishes from Asia, France, Turkey, and the Mediterranean. Portions are large and the food is quite good. ⊠ *Eski Cami Geçidi Likya Sok. 8–9* ☎ *252/614–4046* 🖷 *252/612–0446* ▤ *MC, V.*

$–$$ ✕ **Carpe Diem.** This glass-fronted, pleasingly modern café-restaurant on the harbor-front walkway has a determinedly German flavor: bratwurst, liverwurst, and *weissbier* (wheat beer) are all on offer. With an unimpeded view of the harbor and bay, it's also a great place just to stop in for an evening drink. ⊠ *Ece Marina, Karagözler* ☎ *252/614–3986* ▤ *MC, V.*

$–$$ ✕ **Lafiore.** This Italian restaurant in the bazaar was set up by the Meğri "chain," and provides a rare and welcome change from the "Costa del Kebab." It offers a full Italian experience, replete with faux Italian-villa al fresco—with Turkish grace notes, of course. Just remember, you're not in Italy, so don't expect too much. ⊠ *Eski Cami Ceçidi Likya Cad.* ☎ *252/612–4046* ▤ *MC, V.*

$–$$ ✕ **Meğri Lokanta.** The Meğris pretty much rule the restaurant market in Fethiye, but it's a well-deserved hierarchy, at least for now, as their food is quite consistently the best in town. This excellent, straightforward Turkish meat restaurant is on the western edge of the bazaar and much favored by local inhabitants. The lentil soup is a knockout. ⊠ *Western edge of the bazaar* ☎ *252/614–4047* ▤ *MC, V.*

$$$ 🏨 **Ece Saray.** Modeled on the grand hotels of the French Riviera, this is an excellent luxury hotel in a lovely location on the harbor front. Part of the Ece Marina complex, all rooms have full sea views and the fitness center and health spa are particularly impressive. Opened in 2002, its cheaply built plaster-stone façade has crumbled in places, but otherwise the hotel is hard to fault. ⊠ *Ece Marina, Karagözler* ☎ *252/612–5005* 🖷 *252/614–7205* ⊕ *www.ecesaray.net* ⌁ *34 rooms, 14 suites* ⚹ *2 restaurants, 2 bars, in-room safes, minibars, cable TV, pool, dive shop, Wi-Fi, hair salon, sauna, health club, spa, Turkish bath, massage* ▤ *AE, MC, V* ⍾ *BP.*

$ 🏨 **Yacht Plaza.** This fine medium-sized hotel directly on the seafront has its own yacht jetty, waterside bar, and pool. Probably the best of the line of hotels east of the harbor, it's owned by the same family as the older Yacht Hotel (worth considering if the Yacht Plaza is full) nearby. Rooms are clean and simple with tile floors, but make sure you're getting a sea view. Note that some signs refer to this as Yeni Yacht ⊠ *Karagöller, just east of the Ece Marina,* ☎ *252/612–5067* 🖷 *252/ 612–5068* ⊕ *www.yachtplazahotel.com* ↝ *31 rooms* ⚭ *Restaurant, bar, cable TV, pool, some Wi-Fi, airport shuttle* ▭ *No credit cards* ¶⃝ *BP.*

Nightlife

Fethiye has a strip of cheaper, less appealing hotels along Çalış Beach that stretches west of town—this is where the package tours from northern Europe tend to stay and there are plenty of bars. It's a long way to go for a drink if you're staying in town, but the scene has an appeal for the younger crowd.

During the week, nightclubs are busiest in Hisarönü—one of the string of also not-so-appealing resorts that lie due south of Fethiye, halfway to Ölüdeniz. On weekends the action moves to clubs off Hamam Street in the center of Fethiye. A small indoor dance club, sometimes featuring live Turkish music, is **Mango Bar** (⊠ 29 Hamam Cad. ☎ 252/614–4681).

Sports and the Outdoors

You can take one of the boats or water taxis in Fethiye's harbors on a variety of **boat tours,** some including meals, to Göcek, the Twelve Islands, Gemiler Island, or Ölüdeniz. Itineraries are posted, and there are people on hand to answer questions. Be sure to shop around, as packages vary widely. Costs range from around $20 to $30 per person. Ask to inspect the boat before booking: in theory, for instance, all boats should carry a spare outboard motor in the case of breakdown, yet few do. If Ölüdeniz is your destination, be aware that windy weather can make for heavy waves. Most tours leave about 10 AM, returning about 6 PM.

Ölüdeniz

★ ❽ *60 km (38 mi) east of Dalaman Airport; 9 km (6 mi) from Fethiye.*

Ölüdeniz (it means "dead sea") is one of Turkey's great natural wonders, an azure lagoon rimmed by white sand and pebble beaches. The area, the picture-perfect scene most often featured in Turkish tourism promotion posters, can be reached by day cruise from Fethiye or other ports, by car, or by *dolmuş.* One inland route is through Ovacık (it's the shorter option if you're coming from outside Fethiye) but a prettier one leads past the ruined town of **Kaya,** climbing steeply from a point 1 km west of the harbor.

The water of Ölüdeniz is warm and the setting entirely delightful, even with the crowds. The view is even more splendid from the air, and this is one of Turkey's premier locations for paragliding. Travel agencies in town will organize jeep safaris into the high mountain pastures and villages in the mountains all around for about $40 for the day, with lunch.

If you want to bathe at the iconic sandbar that lies across the mouth of the lagoon, then you must enter **Ölüdeniz Natural Park**—go down to the seafront, turn west, then left at the fork where you can see the toll booth (🖮 $7 per car or $2 per person on foot). There's a capacious car park, but even from here, it can be a hot trek of a several hundred yards. The crowds love it here, and the setting is absolutely beautiful, but the beach is still just a beach. Lounge chairs ($3) and umbrellas ($3) can be rented, and there are changing rooms, toilets, and a modest snack restaurant. Just around the corner a concession rents out pedalos and kayaks for $11–$13 per hour.

Another sand beach can be found behind the park in the shallow, warm waters of the lagoon. Although theoretically public property with free access to all, in practice this beach is run by the campsites and restaurants that line the shore. Use of their facilities, however, is unlikely to be much more expensive than those in the park itself.

The Lycian Way starts in the hills above Ölüdeniz, and one of its most pleasant sections is the 3–5-day walk to Patara.

Where to Stay & Eat

After two decades of building, the many hotels behind the Ölüdeniz seafront are settled into a relatively pleasant harmony of Mediterranean tiled roofs, growing trees, restaurants, and poolside bars. They're decent enough and all pretty similar—rooms tend to be smallish, having essentially been purpose-built for package tours, but many are block-booked in advance by European agencies for the entire season. Some keep rooms back, and a full list can be seen at ⊕ www.oludeniztourism.org. All the following are reasonably near the sea front and offer pools and air-conditioned rooms. Addresses aren't really necessary: all the hotels are signposted, and it's hard to recommend one of these over another anyway. **Hotel Karbel Sun** (⊠ Ölüdeniz ☎ 252/617–0173 ⊕ www.karbelsun.com); the **Flying Dutchman Hotel** (⊠ Ölüdeniz ☎ 252/617–0441), which also has a popular restaurant; or the **Magic Tulip Hotel** (⊠ ☎ 252/617–0074 ⊕ www.magictulip. com). For a much more enjoyable experience, try one of the hotel/resorts off the beach, listed below.

$$$ ▦ **Meri Hotel.** Built in 1973, this hotel was the first—and last—to be allowed by the government to set up shop on the famed Ölüdeniz lagoon. Built on a steep incline amid terraced gardens and overlooking one of Turkey's most beautiful bays, the site is a delight. Rooms are another story: although clean enough, they're small and somewhat down-at-the-heel, overpriced, and some don't have a sea view. To reach many of them involves riding up a rickety furnicular lift. There's not much else nearby, though. ⊠ *Ölüdeniz, well-signposted* ☎ *252/617–0001* ☎ *252/617–0010* ⋫ *70 standard rooms, 24 family rooms* ⌂ *3 restaurants, bar, cable TV, minibars, beach, 2 pools* ▤ *MC, V* ⭐️ *AP* ⊕ *www.hotelmeri.com.*

$$ ▦ **Montana Pine Resort.** Though it's a long way from Montana, this hotel is also in a splendid mountain setting. It's 3 km (2 mi) above Ölüdeniz, with fine views over pine clad slopes. The Sundowner Bar has a wonderful vista of the sea. Rooms are airy and have balconies. Up above the coast, the air is cooler here but there's a daily shuttle service to the Ölüdeniz beach. This is the place to kick your feet back and celebrate when you've finished the Lycian Way, which officially ends (or starts) close by the Sundowner Bar. ⊠ *Ölüdeniz* ☎ *252/616–7108 or 252/616–6366* ☎ *252/616–6366* ⋫ *149 rooms with bath, 5 suites* ⌂ *2 restaurants, 5 bars, cable TV, in-room safes, minibars, 3 pools, health club,*

hot tub, sauna, miniature golf, shops, airport shuttle ⊟ *AE, DC, MC, V* ⊘ *Closed Nov.–May.* ⊕ *www.montanapine.com.*

★ **$–$$** ⊞ **Ocakköy Holiday Village.** Built in an abandoned Greek village of stone houses, this 6-acre spread is a delightful retreat. The predominantly English clientele keep coming back for the rural atmosphere and easy access to the sites of the Fethiye region. Many more of their compatriots, however, are buying apartments and villas that are beginning to disfigure the Ovacık valley below. Luckily, the hotel's trees and gardens keep this development at bay. Helpful staff make a stay here especially pleasurable, and suites have kitchenettes. There is a daily shuttle to Ölüdeniz, 7 km (5 mi) away, and the hotel can arrange paragliding, dive trips, and day-long boat excursions. ⊠ *4 km after the end of Fethiye on the Ölüdeniz road, a signpost shows the way at the first turning on the right. Keep right and head for the stone houses higher on the hill. Ocakköy, Fethiye* ☎ *252/616–6156 or 252/616–6157* 🖷 *252/616–6158* ⊕ *www.ocakkoey.de* 🖙 *8 rooms, 6 studios, 32 cottages* ♿ *restaurant, 2 bars, refrigerators, 2 pools, shop, massage, library, broadband, Internet; no TVs, no room phones* ⊟ *AE, DC, MC, V.*

Sports & the Outdoors

A good day out on a boat can be arranged by the skippers of **Ölüdeniz Kooperatif,** who work out of a kiosk halfway between the main body of hotels and the beach. Between May and November, their 15 boats will take groups out to coves with catchy names like Blue Cave, Butterfly Valley, Aquarium Bay, St. Nicholas Island, Cold Water Spring, Camel Beach, and Turquoise Bay. Trips usually run from 11 AM to 6 PM, and cost about $15 per person with lunch (beer and cold drinks extra).

Paragliding is a busy industry in Ölüdeniz, and experienced pilots can soar aloft for up to five hours in near-ideal conditions in the summer. The launch point is about 1,700 yards up Mt. Baba, some 20 km (13 mi) by forest tracks from Ölüdeniz—the tour operators drive you up from town. Tourists flying tandem (it will cost around $120) with a pilot generally stay up for 30-40 minutes before landing gently on the beach. Full training to internationally recognized certificates in solo piloting is available. Most travel agencies can arrange a flight; in town try **Eftelya Tourism** (⊠ On main road close to Ölüdeniz Beach ☎ 252/617–0014).

Nightlife

On weeknights, the nightlife at Hisarönü, Ölüdeniz, is livelier than in Fethiye itself. Main streets bustle with real estate agents, restaurants, and shops selling jewelry and clothing. After complaints, most of the discotheques have soundproofed their walls although the bass still seeps out. Most operate only in the season between May to October and marquees to look for are **Grand Boozey Bar,** which specializes in satellite TV transmissions of British soccer matches, or the **Club Barrumba,** which whips up a foam party on Wednesday nights.

Kaya

9 *5 km east of Fethiye, either from the road west of the harbor or through Ovacık and Hisarönü.*

Atmospheric Kaya is a ruin of a different order from others along the Mediterranean Coast. It was a thriving Greek community until 1923, when all the village's residents were sent to Greece following a population-exchange agreement between the two countries. Nowadays it's pretty much deserted, with some Turkish village settlement on the edges. Spread across three hills, Kaya is eerily quiet and slowly crumbling. You can wander through small cuboid houses reminiscent of those in the Greek Islands, some with a touch of bright Mediterranean blue or red on the walls. In the two basilicas the murals have been defaced, although Christ and the apostles are visible in one.

Where to Eat

★ $$–$$$ ✕ **Levissi Garden Wine House and Restaurant.** This fine restaurant is in what was once the house of a prosperous Greek merchant. The specialities are steaks and good Turkish wines. In the heat of summer, you can take refuge in a cool basement, or ponder the ingenious gutter system that diverts all rainwater from the roof into a 40-ton cistern. The restaurant floodlights the abandoned buildings all around it at night, making for a particularly evocative—or spooky, depending on your take—atmosphere. ⊠ *Kayaköy, Fethiye* ☎ *252/618–0108* ▤ *MC, V.*

$ ✕ **Oba Kebab Evi.** Set in a pleasant and spacious garden on the plain a few hundred yards from the main slope of Kaya, this is a traditional Turkish meat restaurant where you order your meat, then cook it yourself on a charcoal brazier supplied by the establishment. There are basic salads and appetizers to go with your main dish. ⊠ *near Kaya's main slope* ☎ *252/618-0222* ▤ *V, MC.*

Tlos

⑩ *22 km (14 mi) east of Fethiye.*

A day expedition to Tlos, a spectacular ancient Lycian city high above the valley of the Xanthos River, can be arranged from any town on the coast from Göcek to Kaş. From the **acropolis** a fine view can be had to the west of the Xanthos Valley—then as now a rich agricultural area—and to the east of the mountains that cradle Tlos's Roman theater. The fortress at the summit is Turkish from the 18th century and was a popular haunt of the pirate Kanlı ("Bloody") Ali Ağa. Below the fortress, off a narrow path, is a cluster of rock tombs. Note the relief here of Bellerophon, son of King Glaucus of Corinth, mounted on Pegasus, his winged steed. The monster he faces is the dreaded Chimera—a fire-breathing creature with a lion's head, goat's body, and serpent's tail. (Famously, Bellerophon had been sent to the King of Lycia with a sealed message saying that he should be put to death on arrival. Unwilling to kill this noble figure outright, the Lycians set him apparently fatal tasks like fighting the Chimera. He survived them all with the aid of Pegasus and won half a kingdom.) If you have time, hike over to the theater you saw from the fortress; among the ruins are carved blocks depicting actors' masks. Nearby, the old baths provide more good views of the Xanthos Valley. ⊠ *From Fethiye take the exit to Rte. 400 and follow the local road east to Antalya, where a yel-*

low sign marks the right turn that leads southwest for 15 km (9 mi).
☞ *$3* ☉ *Daily 8:30–sunset.*

OFF THE
BEATEN
PATH

SAKLIKENT GORGE – Tlos is very close to this gorge, a popular spot for picnicking and a wonderful place to cool off on a hot summer's day. Children especially love wading up the walkway through the cold stream at the bottom of a deep rock crevasse. There are several places to eat: In the nearby village of Yaka Köyü (signposted) is the vast but peaceful **Yaka Park Restaurant** (☎ 252/638–2011). On the site of a now-demolished windmill, it has its own trout farm, guaranteeing the fish will always be fresh.

Pınara

⓫ *40 km (24 mi) southeast of Fethiye; 40 km (25 mi) north of Kalkan, look for sign on Rte. 400*

Pınara (it means "something round" in Lycian) is a romantic ruin around a great circular outcrop backed by high cliffs, reachable from most holiday spots in western Lycia. It was probably founded as early as the 5th century BC, and it eventually became one of Lycia's most important cities. You need time and determination to explore as it's widely scattered, largely unexcavated, and overgrown with plane, fig, and olive trees. Park down in the village of **Minare** and make the half-hour hike up the clearly marked trail. At the top of a steep dirt track, the site steward will collect your admission and point you in the right direction—there are no descriptive signs or good site maps.

The spectacular **Greek theater,** which has overlooked these peaceful hills and fields for thousands of years, is one of the finest in Turkey. It's perfectly proportioned, and unlike that of most other theaters in Turkey, its stage building is still standing. The site also contains groups of rock **tombs** with unusual reliefs, one showing a cityscape, and a cliff wall honeycombed with hundreds of crude rectangular "pigeonholes" which are believed to have been either tombs or food storage receptacles. Nearby villagers volunteer to show tourists this site; it's not a bad idea to accept the offer as they know the highlights. A tip is customary. ☞ *$2* ☉ *Daily 8:30–sunset.*

Letoön

⓬ *63 km (39 mi) southeast of Fethiye; 17 km (11 mi) north of Kalkan on Rte. 400; follow the signposts west.*

This site was not a city but a Lycian national religious center and political meeting point for the Lycian League, the world's first democratic federation. It can be reached on day tours from western Lycia's main centers—Fethiye, Ölüdeniz, Kaş, or Kalkan. It is a magical site best visited in the late afternoon, perhaps after a visit to nearby Xanthos, which administered the temples in ancient times. Excavations have revealed three temples in Letoön. The first, closest to the parking area, dates from the 2nd century BC and was dedicated to Leto (hence the name, Letoön), the mother of Apollo and Artemis. The middle temple, the oldest, is ded-

Ancient Cultures of Lycia & Its Neighbors

TURKEY'S MEDITERRANEAN COAST is steeped in five thousand years of history—so much so that in Side, the hotels, restaurants, and night clubs are literally built into the ruins of the Greco-Roman city.

Broadly speaking, the geographic divisions of the coastline of ancient times survive today. The westernmost area from from Datça to Dalyan was part of Caria, an ancient Hellenistic kingdom based in nearby Bodrum/ Halicarnassus. Caria reached the height of its power in the 4th century BC, and the tomb of its most famous ruler, Mausolus, was such a wonder of the world that it coined the word *mausoleum*. From Dalyan to Phaselis the coast is thought of as Lycia, after a people of very ancient but uncertain origin, some of whom possibly colonized this section of the Anatolian coast from Crete. It now hosts small-scale hotels and harmonious yachting ports. From Antalya to Alanya is the area called Pamphilia, thought to mean mean "the land of the tribes," much of which is now quite built up and commercial.

Caria, Lycia, and Pamphilia share much the same, rather obscure, history. Museums exhibit relics from Bronze Age mountain settlements that date back to 3000 BC, the best being in Antalya. From early times, dwellers on this coast supplied traders plying by ship between richer parts of the Mediterranean. When nearby empires weakened, local pirates preyed on shipping instead.

Neither of Caria, Lycia, nor Pamphilia ever became centers of great independent civilizations. They flourished when protected as remote provinces by strong Greek, Roman, and Persian leagues or empires and suffered in times of war and turbulence.

Our knowledge of indigenous cultures is patchy, but notable in many ways. In Homer's epic, Lycia's Sarpedon memorably declaims that the privileges of the elite must be earned by the elite's readiness to fight for their people. And while not a matriarchal society, Lycians are thought to have been matrilineal and gave women a more equal place than, say, ancient Greece. Some locals were fiercely independent. The people of Xanthos committed mass suicide rather than submit to the first Persian conquest, and later burned their city (again) rather than pay extra taxes to Rome's Brutus. In addition, the democratic, federal basis of the Lycian League is acknowledged as one source of the U.S. constitution.

Great cities like Termessos have names that go back at least 3,000 years and populations that rarely had much to do with outside conquerors. The buildings of most of the archaeological sites visited today, however, date from Greek and Roman times, when the prosperity of the coast attracted St. Paul on his way to the even greater city Ephesus.

Overall, the population of this whole area has long been a mixture of waves of new arrivals, from Greek colonists to Persian administrators, retired Roman legionaries and Turkic shepherds, to today's sun-seekers. Despite wars, plagues, and population exchanges, however, there is some degree of continuity: genetic tests discovered that all two dozen of the local workers on a site north of Antalya were related to the bones that they had just dug out from 1,300-year-old graves.

icated to Artemis and dates from the 5th or 4th century BC. The last, dating from the 1st century BC, belongs to Apollo and contains a rare Lycian mosaic depicting a bow and arrow (a symbol of Artemis) and a sun and lyre (Apollo's emblems). These are the three Gods most closely associated with Lycia.Compare the first and last temples: The former is Ionic, topped by a simple, triangular pediment and columns with scroll-shape capitals. The latter is Doric, with an ornate pediment with scenic friezes and detailing, and its columns have undecorated capitals. Reerection of some columns of the Temple of Leto has made the site more photogenic. 🖃 *$1* 🕙 *Daily 8:30–sunset.*

Xanthos

★ ⓭ *61 km (48 mi) southeast of Fethiye; 17 km (10 mi) north of Kalkan on Rte. 400.*

Xanthos, perhaps the greatest city of ancient Lycia, is famed for tombs rising on high, thick, rectangular pillars. Xanthos also earned the region its reputation for fierceness in battle. Determined not to be subjugated by superior forces, the men of Xanthos twice set fire to their own city, with their women and children inside, and fought to the death. The first occasion was against the Persians in 542 BC, the second against Brutus and the Romans in the 1st century BC. Though the site was excavated and stripped by the British in 1838 and most finds are now in London's British Museum, the remains are worth inspecting. Allow at least three hours and expect some company: Unlike the other Lycian cities, Xanthos is on the main tour-bus route.

You can start your exploration across from the parking area, at the 2nd-century AD **theater,** built by Lycians in the Roman style. Inscriptions indicate it was a gift from a wealthy Lycian named Opromoas of Rhodiapolis, who helped restore many Lycian buildings after the great earthquake of 141 AD. Alongside the theater are two much-photographed pillar **tombs.** The more famous of the pair is called the Harpy Tomb—not after what's inside, but because of the half-bird, half-woman figures carved onto the north and south sides. Other reliefs show a seated figure receiving various gifts, including a bird, a pomegranate, and a helmet. This tomb has been dated to 470 BC, although the reliefs are plaster casts of originals in the British Museum. The other tomb consists of a sarcophagus atop a pillar—a rather unusual arrangement. The pillar section is probably as old as the Harpy Tomb, the sarcophagus added later. On the side of the theater, opposite the Harpy Tomb and past the agora (the ancient meeting place), is the Inscribed Pillar of Xanthos, a tomb dating from about 400 BC and etched with a 250-line inscription that recounts the heroic deeds of a champion wrestler and celebrated soldier named Kerei.

Across the road and past the parking area is the large Byzantine **basilica** with its abstract mosaics. Along a path up the hill are several sarcophagi and a good collection of rock-cut house tombs, as well as a welcome spot of shade. Xanthos's center was up on the acropolis behind the theater, accessible by a trail. 🖃 *$4* 🕙 *Daily 8:30–sunset.*

The Lycian Way

UNTIL THE 1950S, the only way to reach the Lycian Coast was by boat or by bone-rattling trips through the mountains in antiquated motor vehicles. Even the main roads of today date only from the 1970s. This is why the stretch of the Turquoise Riviera between Antalya and Fethiye remains remarkably unspoiled. And it's also why it was the perfect place to site Turkey's first and most famous long-distance trekking route, the Lycian Way.

The footpath runs for over 300 miles, marked by red-and-white painted blazes every 50–100 yards, along tractor tracks by the sea, following ancient Roman roads, and sometimes clambering up barely visible goat tracks to peaks that rise to nearly 6,500 feet at Mt. Tahtalı, one of many high mountains known as Mt. Olympos in antiquity. The upsides include breathtaking views, discovering innumerable ancient ruins, and a chance to accept hospitality in villages little touched by tourism or time. The downside is that backpacks can get heavy and skills with a compass or satellite positioning devices are essential to avoid becoming lost in regions where few people pass by. Despite government support, the track has no legal status and is subject to adjustments due to landslides and fencing by landowners. If you lose the trail of red-and-white flashes, go back to the last one you saw and try again. Be aware, too, that the yellow-and-green Lycian Way signposts are not maintained by their original sponsor, an Istanbul bank, and can be misleading.

It would take a month to walk the Lycian Way from end to end, so most people choose to do a section at a time, camping on high pastures, bathing in remote coves, or relaxing in pansiyons on the way. A few sections are for more serious trekkers, but Kate Clow, the Englishwoman who first designed and mapped the Lycian Way in 2000, recommends several popular day walks near Olympos, including one between Adrasan and Olympos over Mt. Musa; one between Olympos and Tekirova, over the high mountains between Beycik and Gedelme; and one from Karaöz or Adrasan to the lighthouse on Taşlık Point. Finding a starting point is easy with Clow's handbook to the trail, or if you spot one of trail markers. Clow's book *The Lycian Way* is the only guide and source of good maps of the route, and the Web site ⊕ www.lycianway.com has updates and satellite grid references. As a trekking agent and mule organizer, Clow recommends **Middle Earth Travel** (⊠ Gaferli Mah., Cevizler Sok. No. 20 Göreme, Nevşehir 50180 ☎ 384/271-2558 or 384/271-2559 🖷 384/271-2562 ⊕ www.middleearthtravel.com).

The best times to trek are in February to mid-March (sometimes rainy but always fresh), early May to mid-July (when spring flowers are out), or September to mid-November (when the sea water is warm and the weather cooler). And when you've finished the Lycian Way, you can try Clow's new project, the St. Paul Trail, which tracks the apostle's journey from Perge/Aspendos north through the canyons of the Toros mountains to Antioch in Pisidia.

Patara

⓯ *70 km (44 mi) southeast of Fethiye; 20 km (13 mi) north of Kalkan, off Rte. 400.*

Patara was once Lycia's principal port. Cosmopolitan in its heyday—Hannibal, St. Paul, and the emperor Hadrian all visited, and St. Nicholas, the man who would be Santa Claus, is said to have been born here—the port eventually silted up. The dunes at the edge of the site are now part of one of Turkey's longest and completely unspoiled sand beaches. From here, too, runs one of the best sections of the Lycian Way, a three-to five-day walk to Ölüdeniz.

The **ruins** you'll find today are scattered among marshes and sand dunes. The city was famous for a time for its oracle and its temple of Apollo. Herodotus wrote that the oracle worked only part-time, as Apollo spent summers away in Delos (probably to escape the heat!). The heavy stones that make up the front of the monumental **bathhouse** are impressive, and a **triple arch** built by a Roman governor in 100 AD seems a tenth of its age. Patara has never been excavated, and Apollo's temple is assumed to await excavation under the sands. 🖭 *$2.*

Although the sight of the 2,000-year-old theater half-buried in sand is unique, one good reason to come here is **Patara Beach,** a superb 11-km (7-mi) sweep of sand dunes popular with Turkish families yet never so crowded you need to walk far to find solitude. Umbrellas should only be planted within 20 yards of the sea to prevent disturbance to the nests of *Caretta caretta* turtles. There is a wooden café on the beach that has toilets, changing huts, umbrellas, loungers, drinks, and food.

Where to Stay & Eat

$ ✕ **Tlos Restaurant.** This little restaurant by the side of the road is keenly kept by a chef from the town of Bolu, legendarily the hometown of Turkey's best cooks. Individual attention is assured, and alcoholic drinks can be brought over from the Lumière Hotel opposite. ⊠ *On the right on the main street leading to the ruins through the village of Patara* ☎252/843–5135 ▤ *MC, V* ☉ *Nov.–Apr.*

$ ⌂ **Hotel Lumière.** Surrounded by trees and plants, this is a pleasant place to rest after a day's sightseeing has gone on too long to reach the major centers on the coast. Good-sized rooms are decorated with old kilims, and mosquito nets are available if you ask. There is a small pool and the hotel's owner will run clients the 5 km down to the beach in her car. ⊠ *On left in village on way to Patara ruins* ☎ *242/843-5043* ⊕ *www. hotellumiere.com* ⤳ *16 rooms* ⚐ *fans, safe in reception, pool, laundry, Wi-Fi; no a/c* ▤ *MC, V* ⵁⵁ *BP.*

Kalkan

⓰ *80 km (50 mi) southeast of Fethiye; 27 km (17 mi) west of Kaş, on Rte. 400.*

Kalkan used to be the poor relation to other resorts on the Lycian coast, but has recently emerged as a top-notch destination, with fine restaurants and excellent hotels to match its superb, steep views of the Mediterranean Sea. The ranks of villas spreading up the mountainsides all around ensure that tourism seasons are growing longer and more prosperous. The old stone alleways are now positively sleek with whitewash and the small port is crowded with yachts in summer.

Without much archaeology of its own, despite the great Lycian sites nearby, Kalkan is trying hard to develop its own tourism offerings. It's an excellent base for touring the area and the surrounding sites. Agencies in town like **Kalamus Travel** (⊠ Yalıboyu, also doing business as Mavi Real Estate ☎ 242/844–2456) can arrange paragliding, diving, horseback riding, jeep safaris, village visits, mountain walks, and guided trips to Lycian ruins.

Where to Stay & Eat

$$–$$$ ✕ **Paprika Bistro and Restaurant.** Set up by two Turkish couples from Istanbul in 2001, Paprika has a cosmopolitan atmosphere and an interesting array of food all made on the premises. Mouthwatering combinations include hot chick peas with buttered pastrami; leg of lamb with laurel, onion, and wine; a melting hot chocolate pudding; and a pudding of figs and dates. Even the menu is handmade, and there's live jazz on Tuesday and Friday evenings in the high season. ⊠ *Ikizevler 12/B, Yaliboyu* ☎ *242/844–1136* 🖃 *MC, V.*

$–$$$ ✕ **Gironda.** This gourmet restaurant is designed like a rich villa with sump-
FodorśChoice tuous sofas and plaster-of-paris statuary, and the excellent food alone
★ merits a stay in Kalkan. The fare is outstandingly fresh and the dishes are well thought-out: even a humble lamb pie topped with filo pastry pops with tastes of baby onion, sesame, and mushrooms. Other specialities are pan-seared fish, eggplant with cheese, and fish baked in parchment, as well as a wide variety of pastas. Tables on the terrace upstairs enjoy great views of Kalkan Bay. ⊠ *Two streets up from the harbor in the old town* ☎ *242/844–3136* 🖎 *Reservations essential* 🖃 *MC, V* 🕐 *Nov.–Apr.*

★ $–$$ ✕ **Aubergine.** This restaurant is an exception to the general rule of avoiding harbor-front eateries. The menu is adventurous and well explained, and includes salmon *en croute,* stuffed sea bass with bacon, extra large steaks, and occasionally wild boar shot in the mountains. All the desserts are homemade. ⊠ *On the harbor front* ☎ *242/844–3332* 🖃 *MC, V.*

$–$$ ✕ **Çatı.** At this midmarket Turkish meat restaurant on the slopes above Kalkan, a freshly baked long *lavash* bread is brought to the table when you're seated, along with starters of walnuts and hard white cheese matured in goatskin. The restaurant prides itself on its *acılı ezme,* an appetizer of finely chopped hot chile, tomato, and onion, and the meats that follow are delicious. Thick Turkish *pide* and paper-thin *lahmacun* mincemeat pizzas are also available. ⊠ *Şehitler Cad. 55, Menteşe* ☎ 242/844–3069 ▤ *MC, V.*

$$$
Fodor'sChoice
★
🏨 **Hotel Villa Mahal.** Clinging to a cliff face with a wraparound view of Kalkan Bay, this immaculate establishment is one of Turkey's most spectacular hotels. A gorgeous pool juts out into the air, making swimming feel like flying, and the beach club at the bottom of the cliff offers sea access and many water sports. A hotel boat will run you five minutes across the bay to Kalkan harbor if you want an evening in town. Be ready, however, for the 181 steps from top to bottom, and be aware that a hotel walkway passes in front of the picture windows of the standard double rooms. If there is anywhere in the world to splash out on a great room, this is it—try the Sunset Suite with its spacious layout and blue mosaic hot tub and enjoy a second honeymoon. ⊠ *Patara Evler Yani, about 2 km east of Kalkan. Take care on the precipitous last approach,* ☎ 242/844–3268 🖷 242/844–2122 ⊕ *www.villamahal.com* ⇥ *4 rooms and 2 suites* ⋄ *3 restaurants, minibars, 4 bars, Internet room, water skiing, in-room safes, massage; no children under nine* ▤ *MC, V* ⊙ *Nov.–Apr.* ⦿ *BP.*

$$
🏨 **Hotel Pirat.** This 1986 concrete hotel lacks personality and shows its age in poor design, but the location is great: right on the harbor, and the three pools have superb views over the bay. The hotel is divided into two; the rooms in Pirat II are somewhat better than in Pirat I. Check that your balcony overlooks the water, not the villa sprawl climbing the slopes above town. ⊠ *Kalkan harbor* ☎ 242/844–3178 🖷 242/844–3183 ⊕ *www.hotelpirat.net* ⇥ *126 rooms, 10 suites* ⋄ *2 restaurants, 2 bars, cable TV, safe in reception, 3 pools, meeting room, beach* ▤ *MC, V.*

★ **$$**
🏨 **Harpy Hotel.** Despite its unimaginative concrete block architecture, this is an attractive hotel and an unusually good value. Set against wild olive shrubs on the slopes around Kalamar Bay, the views are stunning. The rooms are bigger than most, with terracotta-style floors and large balconies. An ambitious U.S.-trained manager was hired in 2005 and is improving the already high standards of service in the hotel and its gourmet restaurant. A shuttle is available to get into Kalkan proper ⊠ *Head east of Kalkan to Kalamar Bay, turn left as you come over the ridge and follow the signs* ☎ 242/844–1133 🖷 242/844–1132 ⊕ *www.harpy.com.tr* ⋄ *2 restaurants, 2 bars, cable TVs, DVD on request, safes, minibars, shops, meeting room, fitness room, sauna, hot tub, massage, Wi-Fi* ▤ *V, MC.*

$
🏨 **Kleo.** Clean, central, and airy, this modest pansiyon with pleasant split-level rooms has everything most holidayers could need. Top-floor rooms and the breakfast terrace enjoy a sea view. ⊠ *First street above the northwestern corner of the harbor, behind Pirat Hotel* ☎ 242/844–3776 ⇥ *5 rooms* ⋄ *safe in reception, laundry* ▤ *No credit cards* ⦿ *BP.*

Kaş

16 *107 km (67 mi) southeast of Fethiye via Rte 400; 180 km (112 mi) from Antalya via Korkuteli mountain road.*

In the 1980s, Kaş was the main tourist destination on the Lycian coast, but it has since fallen somewhat by the wayside. Perhaps it was just too laid back; there doesn't seem to be any rush about anything here. Its central location makes it a reasonable choice, however, as a base for exploring the ruins of Lycia. Villa building has sensibly been shunted onto the Çukurbağ Peninsula, meaning that the town retains the feel of the a small fishing village.

Kaş has a few ruins, including a monumental **sarcophagus** under a massive plane tree, up the sloping street that rises behind the tourist office. The tomb has four regal lion's heads carved onto the lid. In 1842, a British naval officer counted more than 100 sarcophagi in Kaş—then called Antiphellus—but most have been destroyed over the years as locals nabbed the flat side pieces to use in new construction.

A few hundred yards west of the main square, along Hastane Caddesi, is a small, well-preserved antique **theater,** and next to the district prefect's office east of the harbor is an old wooden barn of the type once universally used as granaries in Lycian villages—and still clearly modeled on old Lycian architectural forms. Even more unusually, ask at Meis discotheque to see their 3rd-century BC cistern, carved from the solid rock. Kaş makes a good base for boat excursions, and a profusion of scuba diving boats shows the growing demand for the areas rich underwater sights.

The hour-long boat ride to the Greek island **Kastellorizon** (the name of the island is Meis in Turkish—like the Kaş disco) gives you a taste both of Greece and what Kaş must have been like before the 1924 population exchange, when it was mostly populated by Greeks. Since a day trip only allows one to see the island during exactly the hours most Greeks are having their midday siesta, it's worth trying to arrange to stay the night; there are several hotels and a few pansiyons. The island has an impressive 12th- to 16th-century crusader castle with crenellated graystone walls, a large cave with fine stalactites, and the 1835 church of St. Konstantine and Eleni, which reused granite columns taken from the Temple of Apollo at Letoön in Lycia.

Other excursion options include Simena and Kekova Sound; Demre, site of the old church of St. Nicholas of Christmas fame; or Patara and Patara Beach. Be aware that high winds can make for a very rough ride, particularly round the cape to Kekova.

Where to Stay & Eat

★ **$–$$$** ✕**Chez Evy.** No place in Kaş has more character than this delightful restaurant. Prices might be high, but that's because Evy has a tendency to serve portions that are double the size of those anywhere else. Dining is in an intimate garden around the back in summer, where shared tables and Evy's big-hearted solicitousness create an atmosphere where everybody is soon talking to everybody else. A *digéstif* is a special treat in the cozy bar that's decorated with eveything from a vast golden French empire clock to Evy's dancing, cappucino-drinking red parrot. Don't believe rival restaurateurs nearby who claim Evy's has closed. In the November–April off-season, call for a reservation. ⊠ *Terzi Sok. 2, in a small street be-*

hind the Red Point bar. ☎ *242/836–1253* ⌣ *Reservations essential Nov.–Apr.* ▤ *MC, V.*

$–$$ ✕ **Mama's Kitchen Bi Lokma.** Mum runs the kitchen in this good family restaurant on the hill road rising east from the harbor. Big spring rolls mix mince, chicken, and cheese, and another speciality is *hünkar beğendi*, or "his majesty liked it," a mix of puréed baked eggplant and yogurt. ⊠ *Hükümet Cad. No. 2* ☎ *242/836–3942* ▤ *MC, V.*

$ ✕ **Bahçe.** This courtyard restaurant serves delightful Turkish dishes in a quiet garden setting, just opposite Kaş's iconic 4th- century BC King's Tomb. The waitstaff is one large family—each taking part in the preparation and serving of food. The starters are famous in Kaş. Especially tasty options are grated carrot with yogurt, mashed walnut, cold spinach, fish balls, and the *arnavut ciğeri*, cold fried liver prepared with chopped nuts. ⊠ *Anıt Mezar Karşisi 31* ☎ *242/836–2370* ▤ *MC, V.*

⟳ $$$ ▦ **Aquapark Hotel.** On the tip of the long peninsula west of Kaş, the Aquapark is a resort hotel with a long-standing reputation for excellent food. Light winds in summer mean that there is less humidity here than elsewhere in Lycia, and grassy terraces under the olive trees beckon anyone who wants to relax, read, or watch the boats go by. Children love the pair of seawater slides into one pool. There's no beach, but access to the sea is possible from a platform on the rocky point. There is also a disco. ⊠ *Take the road out of Kaş to the Çukurbağ Peninsula, drive 2 km (1 mi) to the farthest point on the road that does a circuit around the point* ☎ *242/836–1902* 🖷 *242/836–1992* ⊕ *www.aquapark.org* ➬ *81 rooms, 42 suites* ⚭ *cable TV, minibars, miniature golf* ▤ *MC, V* ⊘ *Closed Nov.–Apr.* ⦿ *MAP.*

$$ ▦ **Hadrian Hotel.** This is a beautifully designed and immaculately kept

Fodor'sChoice hotel on the peninsula outside Kaş. There are plenty of hideaways on

★ the property for guests looking for a few days of privacy—if you can get a room. A platform on the rocks below gives access to the sea, and a rare luxury is a generous-sized seawater swimming pool. The only drawback is that the hotel is 500 yards down a steep hill from the main road, so a rental car is vital if you plan to do much sightseeing in the area. Reserve well in advance. ⊠ *Dog an Kaşaroğlu Cad. 10, Çukurbağ Peninsula. Well signposted once on the peninsula,* ☎ *242/836–2856* 🖷 *242/836–1387* ⊕ *www.hotel-hadrian.de* ➬ *10 rooms, 4 suites* ⚭ *Inroom safes, minibars, bar, 2 restaurants, dive shop, cable TV, public broadband Internet, laundry* ▤ *MC, V* ⊘ *Closed Nov. 15–Apr. 15* ⦿ *MAP.*

$$ ▦ **Hera Hotel.** Nobody can miss the yard-wide, solid stone columns bearing the temple-like façade of this hotel. As at the other establishments on Küçük Çakıl east of the harbor, the view is tremendous and sea swimming is available from the rocks in front. Rooms are adequate, but the hotel layout is something of a jumble. ⊠ *Küçük Çakıl 69,* ☎ *242/836–3062* 🖷 *242/836–3063* ⊕ *www.herahotel.net* ➬ *40 rooms, 6 suites* ⚭ *Cable TV, minibars, pool, gym, Turkish bath, sauna, hot tub* ▤ *MC, V* ⦿ *MAP.*

★ $ ✕▦ **Medusa Hotel.** This is probably the best-run of the generally good hotels that line the seafront road east of the harbor. Rooms are small, but most have lovely views and are well-maintained. The hotel has direct access to local diving schools and its own beach with rock platforms from which to swim in the sea. Managed since 2006 by a lively archaeologist from Belgium and his Turkish wife, whose parents own the hotel, you can count on the very best advice on which ancient sites to see. The restaurant is worth a visit in its own right, being reasonably priced and serving unusual Turkish-Ottoman food like fish baked in parchment, lamb fillet with cheese sauce, and lamb wrapped in filo pastry in garlic sauce. ⊠ *Küçük Çakıl 62,* ☎ *242/836–1440* 🖷 *242/836–1441* ⊕ *www.medusahotels.com* ⇄ *36 rooms, 1 suite* ⚭ *Cable TV, in-room safes, minibars, pool, restaurant, dive shop, Wi-Fi* ▤ *AE, MC, V* ☾ *Nov.–Apr.* ⃝ *BP.*

Nightlife

The **Meis Disco Bar** is a well-run discotheque and venue for live Turkish music performances. This is probably also the only night club in the world to boast a 3rd-century BC basement cistern carved out of solid rock, now laid out with tables, and quieter than upstairs. The ancient basement roof of solid stone slabs is held up by crude pillars and, according to the owner, sophisticated French glue. The cistern was discovered by chance when the original building—a high-doored former stable for camels, which were the main means of transport in Lycia until just a few decades ago—was being extended. (⊠ On eastern edge of harbor)

Simena and Kekova Sound

⑰ *30 km (19 mi) east of Kaş*

Simena (now known in Turkish as Kaleköy), Kekova Island, and its surrounding coastline are some of the most enchanted spots in Turkey, especially as the reflection of the full moon slowly traces its way across Kekova Sound. Most local transportation is by water, but a new road to nearby Üçağız, off Route 400, has eased the overland journey, which has magnificent views.

Kekova Island stands slightly off a shoreline notched with little bays, whose many inlets create a series of lagoons. Anchoring many are small fishing communities. The apse of a Byzantine church backs one beach known as Tersane, whose bay is a favorite swimming spot. The village of Üçağız has small pansiyons and waterside restaurants.

Simena, reached by a 10-minute boat ride or half-hour walk from Üçağız, is a pleasing jumble of boxy houses built up a steep rocky crag alongside layers of history: Lycian tombs, a tiny Greek amphitheater, and the medieval ruins of Simena Castle atop the rocky hill. As you cruise the waters between the villages, look overboard to see ancient Roman and Greek columns, buildings, stairways, and the ubiquitous Lycian tombs, a few up to their waists in water—the sunken remains of a succession of ancient cities. To go diving, you must obtain a permit in advance, but you don't need official papers to swim in the crystal-clear water of the bays while your boatman naps. Accommodation in Simena is basic and the restaurants are wildly overpriced, so, if you trust your boatman's galley, it's best to eat on board after your walk around the sites.

$ ▦ **Ankh Pansiyon.** This simple but overpriced hotel is the place to choose if you want to escape from the world and soak up the otherworldliness of Kekova Sound. Rooms are clean, and the family establishment has a small restaurant and a bar. The hotel has a charming jetty on which to sunbathe or from which to dive into the crystal clear water. Reserve well in advance. A motorboat is will pick guests up from nearby Üçağız; be prepared for a little spray. ⊠ *Ankh is the easternmost of the buildings along the Kekova seafront* ☎ *242/874–2171 or 532/431–9171* ⊕ *www.ankhpansion.com* ⇥ *8 rooms* ⚲ *public Internet,* ▤ *MC, V* ⊙ *Closed Nov.10–Apr.* �ⓘ *BP.*

Demre (Kale)

⓲ *37 km (23 mi) east of Kaş, 140 km southwest of Antalya on Rte. 400.*

Demre is where Saint Nicholas, who later became known as Father Christmas, made his reputation as bishop of the Graeco-Roman diocese of Myra in the first half of the 4th century. Among his good deeds, St. Nicholas is said to have carried out nocturnal visits to the houses of local children to leave gifts, including gold coins as dowries for poor village girls; if a window was closed, said the storytellers, he would drop the gifts down the chimney.

The monuments of ancient Myra are set against a hillside to the north; in the city, visitors can see the remains of the Byzantine basilica. Demre is, however, primarily an agricultural region, and even the Roman Emperor Hadrian built one of his great stone granaries in the little harbor of nearby Andriake. Today vegetables from the area reach Europe by refrigerated truck, but it's still possible to arrange boat tours to Simena and Kekova Sound from the harbor here.

A church was built around the tomb of St. Nicholas in the 6th century, but it was later destroyed in an Arab raid. In 1043 the **St. Nicholas Basilica** was rebuilt with the aid of the Byzantine emperor Constantine IX and the empress Zoë. It now stands near the center of Demre, a couple blocks from the square. St. Nicholas's remains, however, were stolen and taken to Bari, Italy, in 1087, where the church of San Nicola di Bari was built to house them. A few bones remained, so the story goes, and these can be seen in the Antalya Museum. The church in Kale today is mainly the result of restoration work financed by 19th-century Russian noblemen. It's difficult to distinguish between the original church, parts of which may date back to the 5th century, and the restorations, although the bell tower and upper story are clearly late additions. A service is held in the church every year on December 6, the feast day of St. Nicholas, as part of the annual symposium and festival organized by the Father Christmas and Call to World Peace Foundation. ☜ *$3* ⊙ *Daily 8:30–5:30.*

The monuments of ancient **Myra**— a striking Roman theater and a cliff face full of Lycian rock tombs— are about 2 km (1 mi) north of Kale, poorly marked by signs. The theater dates from the 2nd century AD and for a time was used for glad-

A NOTE ON NAMES

Demre is also known in Turkish as Kale, not to be confused with Kale, the Turkish name for Simena in nearby Kekova Sound. "Kale" is also Turkish for "castle."

iator spectacles involving wild animals. There are some good reliefs on the tombs (a stairway leads to a raised viewing platform so you can see them up close) and on the bits of pediments and statuary scattered about the grounds of the site. ⌒ *$3* ☉ *Daily 8:30–5 or 5:30.*

Where to Stay & Eat

$ ✕ **Ipek Restaurant.** It doesn't look like much and the waiters can be surly, but the kitchen cooks up excellent meat dishes that make this the restaurant of choice for many a native of Demre today. ⌂ *As you exit St. Nicholas Basilica, turn left along the pedestrian street. Ipek is 100 yards down, on the left* ☎ *242/871–5150* ▤ *MC, V.*

$ ✕ **Nur Pastaneleri.** After paying your respects to St. Nick, repair here to enjoy properly arctic air-conditioning and a cold drink or tea accompanied by some of Turkey's freshest *baklava,* the diamond-cut honeyed pastry with nuts. Until early afternoon the café also serves *su böreği,* a salty pastry flavored with feta cheese or mincemeat. ⌂ *As you exit the St. Nicholas basilica, look south over the square to a two-story modern shopping center with slim pillars down the façade; Nur Pastaneleri is on the corner* ☎ *242/871–6310* ▤ *MC, V.*

¢ ⌂ **Hotel Demre.** This family-run hotel looks like an Ottoman warehouse, but its vast restaurant/reception area is actually the legacy of a failed project to build a discotheque. The guest rooms upstairs are bright, clean, and well furnished. Several—unusually—have double beds and big picture windows. The hotel is just across the road from the beach and also has a pool. Demre is no beauty spot but this is good value and more atmospheric than the commercial hotels in town. The hotel has its own scuba diving boat. ⌂ *Kömürlük Beach. At the main Demre intersection on Rte. 400, turn south at the sign for Sülüklü Plaji, and continue as straight as possible for 2 km (1 mi).* ☎ *242/871–6525* 🖷 *242/871–6526* ⊕ *www.hotel-demre.com* ⤳ *26 rooms* ⌂ *Restaurant, bar, minibars, laundry* ▤ *MC, V* ☉ *Closed Nov.–Apr.* ⌂ *BP.*

Finike and Arycanda

⑲ *111 km (70 mi) southwest of Antalya along Rte. 400*

Finike is a good spot to stop for lunch or a jumping-off point for Arycanda and a series of less glamorous Lycian sites that dot the citrus- and vegetable-growing coastal plain. The small port town is friendly, helpful, and inexpensive—and a somewhat unexciting place to stay. A yacht marina harbors many European boats, but Finike, which makes most of its money from unglamorous hothouses for growing vegetables, seems to take their presence unfussily in its stride. A colorful town market is held every Sunday.

⑳ The well-preserved walls and lovely location of **Arycanda,** high in a mountain valley above Finike, make this ancient Lycian town one of the most beautiful and least crowded archaeological sites on the Turquoise Riviera. A parking area and an easy-to-follow trail leads up to the acropolis. First it passes the monumental **Roman baths,** perhaps Turkey's best-preserved bathhouse, with intact mosaic floors, standing walls, and windows framing the valley. The tombs, farther east along the trail, are more properly Roman rather than Lycian. North of the baths, toward the cliff face, is the sunken agora, a market with arcades on three sides. The middle gate leads into an intimate odeon—a small concert hall topped by a Greek-style theater with a breathtaking view of the valley and mountains often capped with snow. Paved streets, mosaics, and an old church are scattered among these structures. To reach Arycanda, drive 35 km (22 mi) north of Finike towards Elmalı, and watch for the Arycanda sign to the right.

Where to Stay & Eat

★ $ ✕ **Altın Sofra.** This restaurant in the marina is famed for its lamb and lambs' liver, but it serves a full menu including fish. There is a pleasant garden shaded by plane trees and acacias. Everything here is so fresh the chef refuses to add anything but olive oil and salt to flavor his meats. ⊠ *Inside the yacht marina, about 100 yards east of the entrance* ☎ *242/855–1281* ▤ *MC, V.*

★ ¢–$ ✕ **Anfora Balı Restaurant.** This unassuming-looking restaurant in a cool basement cavern set into the hillside by the main road offers fine seafood and excellent value. Specialities include pots of cooked squid, octopus, and shrimp. The fried squid is famously fresh. ⊠ *100 yards west of the marina entrance on Kordon Cad. (Rte. 400)* ☎ *242/855–3888* ▤ *MC, V.*

$ ▥ **Arikandos Hotel.** A bright and well-furnished commercial hotel just opposite the yacht harbor, the Arikandos is an excellent and inexpensive place to stay, if somewhat unromantic. The hotel has no pool, but a good public beach is a five-minute drive to the west. ⊠ *Center of town opposite yacht marina entrance* ☎ *242/855–5805* 🖷 *242/855–5809* ⊕ *www.arikandos.com* ↝ *52 rooms, 4 suites* ⌂ *Restaurant, 2 bars, cable TV, in-room safes, Wi-Fi* ▤ *MC, V* ⚋❘ *BP.*

Kumluca

㉑ *100 km southwest of Antalya on Rte. 400*

There is nothing touristy about the prosaic market town of Kumluca, and herein lies its charm. This is an honest working town of a type that can't be experienced elsewhere on the Turquoise Riviera. The main crossroads are decorated with the source of the town's fortunes: great plaster representations of eggplant, peppers, tomatoes, zucchini, and cucumbers. The eastern entrance of town is even more dramatic: a great archway of a tomato plant. Choose one of the pleasant upmarket cafés on the main square, and you'll be sipping your beverage alongside a genuine cross-section of weather-beaten yeoman farmers. Friday is the big day in Kumluca, when villagers from tens of miles around come to town to settle debts and shop at the sprawling market, the biggest in the region.

Where to Eat

¢–$ ✕ **Mithat Restaurant.** Mithat is the only good restaurant in the center of Kumluca that serves alcohol. Dishes include all the usual kebabs, along with some stews. The municipality has been promising to demolish Mithat and build a multistory car park for so long that nobody believes it anymore, and even if it does, the owners will simply set up shop nearby when that happens. ✉ *On Özer St., the first turning on the right as you head south from the vegetable-decorated main intersection* ☎ *242/887–1405* 💳 *MC, V.*

¢ ✕ **Öz Karadeniz Pide ve Pizza.** One of the better establishments on the little square behind the municipal building, Karadeniz has a row of chairs and tables outside under the shade of a roof. Its Turkish-style pizzas overflow with cheese and are an excellent recharge after an hour or two browsing Kumluca's Friday market. ✉ *Behind the municipal building, 50 yards northeast of the vegetable-decorated main intersection* ☎ *242/887–4387* 💳 *MC, V.*

Olympos

4

㉒ *89 km southwest of Antalya from Rte. 400; Read signposts carefully—don't take the turning to "Olympos Plaj" which in fact leads to Çıralı.*

Olympos and its "sister" towns Çıralı and Adrasan are places unique on the Turquoise Riviera for their natural beauty, ancient ruins, low-rise development, and an easygoing culture that mixes international backpackers, ecologically sensitive Turks, and European intellectuals. All three are right next to some of the best day walks on the Lycian Way, though the Olympos ruins are the main event in the area.

The ancient city of Olympos is named after a nearby peak that towers above the mountain range behind the beach. A lovely 500-yard walk through the overgrown site gives access to one end of the long sand-and-pebble beach, still completely unspoiled and backed by an amazing amphitheater of mountains. The sights can be seen in a day, but the natural beauty and laid-back atmosphere can prove addictive. One of the hotels has a slogan: "Come for a day, stay for a week," and it's surprising how often that happens.

The ruins of the ancient city of **Olympos** have never been excavated and, as a result, are wonderfully atmospheric. Because the ruins are next to a river and shaded by tall firs, flowering oleander bushes, and a mountain gorge, they are also delightfully cool in summer, the perfect time to explore.

Olympos was once a top-voting member of the 2nd-century BC Lycian League, but most of the buildings viewable today date from Roman times. Roman-era building started in earnest after officers—including the young Julius Caesar—crushed a two-year-long occupation of the city by invading rebels in about 70 BC. Many tombs are scattered around the ancient city, which is reached by two parallel paths that continue down to the beach.

> ## TIME IS OF THE ESSENCE
>
> The word is that you should visit Olympos soon! Rumor has it that one of Turkey's big industrial holding companies has plans to clear, excavate, and restore the site—and change forever one of the most romantic places in Turkey, a major archaeological ruin that can still be experienced just as 19th-century explorers rediscovered it.

The northern one offers access to a fine 18-foot-high gate, dedicated to Marcus Aurelius in 171 AD and mistakenly referred to by signs as a temple. Note how some walls around the site have clearly been rebuilt in later centuries with narrow arrow slits in the windows as if the city suddenly had to fortify itself. At the beach exit is a poetic inscription on a sarcophagus in memory of an ancient ship's captain, along with a carving of his beached boat—not that different from today's *gulets*. From here you can also climb to a small acropolis and some mediaeval fortifications where ancients would keep a lookout for ships and pirates.

The southern side of the ancient city is best reached by crossing the riverbed (dry in summer) by the land-side ticket office and heading east toward the beach along a well-beaten path that starts with a remarkable row of tombs with their sliding-stone windows still in place. Farther along are shipping quays, warehouses, a gorgeously overgrown amphitheater, a great bathhouse, and a temple whose two great rows of granite columns have collapsed inward and now lie half-buried in what feels like the floor of a tropical jungle. Farther south along the beach are the walls of a medieval castle variously occupied and improved by crusaders and also used as an outpost of Italian city states. ☎ $3.

The *pansiyon*-style hotels in the gorge that leads from the main road to the land-side entrance of the ancient ruins are all considered to be "in" Olympos and generally consist of wooden cabins and treehouses—sheltered platforms or rooms built around pine trees, sometimes several yards up the trunk. These "treehouses" are often the cheapest places to lodge.

The atmosphere in Olympos is mainly set by international backpackers, and many are on long journeys from Morocco to Thailand, so the place has a certain buzz. That buzz can, however, turn to loud noise and raucous partying at times, even though the Orange discotheque is set well away from most hotels in a side-gorge across the river. Also, because the wooden pansiyon structures are built on the ancient town, no proper sewage system has been put in place, which causes some worries about the sanitary situation. A calmer, better organized atmosphere prevails in the lodgings outside the gorge, but these are too far away to comfortably walk to the ruins and beach.

Where to Stay

$$ 🏨 **Daphne House.** This attractive hotel outside Olympos gorge opens directly onto the edge of a pine forest. Owners Bülent and Refiye will lend bikes and, at the guests' own risk, a couple of veteran cars to get to Olympos and the beach. Outside the heat of summer, Bülent is often happy to act as a free guide for local Lycian Way walks. Some rooms are small, and accessed by a difficult spiral staircase. ⌂ *50 yards after the last turning to Olympos, opposite the forest-fire fighters station* ☎ *242/ 892–1133* ⊕ *www.olimpos.org* ⌸ *10 rooms* ⌂ *Bar, restaurant, free broadband Internet, fans; no a/c* ▭ *MC, V* ⊙ *Closed Nov.–Apr.* ⍾ *BP.*

$$ 🏨 **Kekik Han.** This well-designed hotel in a garden with a lawn outside the gorge is one of the nicest outside the Olympos strip. You'll enjoy your stay more if you have your own car, although the owner will run you down to the ruins of Olympos for the walk to the beach. There's a bar in the garden for guests. ✉ *As you descend from Rte. 400, look for the sign down a dirt track about 500 yards before you reach a river ford and the final turn for Olympos itself,* ☎ *242/892–1158* 🖷 *242/892–1151* ⊕ *www.kekikhan.com* 🛏 *6 rooms* ⚒ *Restaurant, bar, broadband Internet* ⊟ *No credit cards* ⊘ *Closed Oct. 15–May 15* †○† *MAP.*

$ ✕⊞ **Bayrams.** Bayram is the name of the owner of this extraordinary institution, a central player in the Olympos scene. Some come for a beer and stay for a month, although few would say the ample evening buffet-service food is anything more than adequate. Tea is free, the music always seems to be appropriate, a fire pit keeps things warm when nights are cool, and somehow everyone meets and chats until late on the wooden platforms under the orange and mulberry trees. As with many other pansiyons in the Olympos gorge, it offers roofed platforms in the trees, which are the cheapest form of accommodation. The big, air-conditioned Internet room is a haven on a hot summer's day. There's no pool, but the staff happily hoses guests down as they water the orange trees. Some rooms have shared bathrooms. ✉ *About 200 yards from the entrance to the Olympos ruins,* ☎ *242/892–1243* 🖷 *242/892–1399* ⊕ *www.bayrams.com* 🛏 *80 rooms* ⚒ *Bar, restaurant; some a/c* ⊟ *AE, MC, V* †○† *MAP.*

$ ⊞ **Pirate's Land.** This is probably the best among the dozens of wooden pansiyons in the Olympos gorge, because its cabins are not crowded on top of each other and there is shade from the orange trees. It's also some distance from the noisier backpacker establishments. It has its own generator, useful since power cuts are not uncommon. ✉ *About 300 yards from the entrance to Olympos ruins,* ☎ *242/892–1172* 🖷 *242/892–1178* ⊕ *www.pirateslandhotel.com* 🛏 *24 rooms* ⚒ *Bar, restaurant* ⊟ *MC, V* †○† *MAP.*

Çiralı

㉓ *85km (65 mi) southwest of Antalya; down the beach from Olympos.*

The long beach at Çiralı is one of the wonders of Turkey—not least for how it has managed to escape the ravages of industrial tourism. The beach is mostly smooth white and multicolored marble pebbles mixed with some light gray sand. Float out on your back and marvel at the 5 km sweep of beach, the line of fir trees behind it, and the surrounding amphitheater of mountains that includes the 8,000-foot peak of Mt. Olympos. Several restaurants along the beach front make great places to eat and while away an evening.

A half-hour evening scramble up a sometimes steep path will bring you to the **Chimaera,** named after the ferocious fire-breathing beast of legend. Flames can still be seen rising from cracks in the rock, apparently also burning the gas deep below, since they reignite even if covered. In times past, the flames were apparently more vigorous, even visi-

> **WORD OF MOUTH**
>
> "Çirali is a great spot and a hidden treasure, a great getaway from the crowds and the touristy areas. It's near the ancient city of Olympos and the flames of the Chimaera."
>
> –brenda66

ble by sailors offshore. If you're staying in Olympos it's a 7-km (5-mi) walk, so it's best to drive to the bottom of the hill. Most hotels in the area will arrange a tour. Bring a flashlight.

Where to Stay

$$$ ⊞ **Olympos Lodge.** This is the grand pioneer of Çiralı's upmarket pansiyons, and it has a loyal clientele. Rooms are in white wooden cabins in a garden-orchard. This hotel is one of the closest to the beach, and has the shortest walk to the ruins at Olympos. Still, the restaurant is not as stellar as it once was, and a similar experience can be had for half the price not much farther down the beach. Reserve at least one month in advance. ⊠ *Drive down to Çiralı, turn right on the dirt track directly after the bridge over the river and follow the signs,* ☎ *242/825-7171* 🖷 *242/825-7173* ⊕ *www.olymposlodge.com.tr* ⤴ *12 rooms, 1 suite* ⋄ ⊟ *No credit cards* ⊘ *Closed Nov. 15–Apr. 15* ¦⊙¦ *BP.*

$$ ⊞ **Doğa Hotel.** If you want four relatively square walls and a solid roof, the Doğa hotel, owned by a Turkish parliamentarian, is one of the best-built. The building is in a large garden-orchard, and it's about 100 yards from the rooms to the beach. Excellent breakfasts on the lawn are a high point, and the restaurant does not overcharge for its delicious food. ⊠ *off Çiralı beach* ☎ *242/825-7366* 🖷 *242/825-7369* ⤴ *15 rooms* ⋄ *restaurant; no room phones* ⊟ *MC, V* ¦⊙¦ *BP.*

> **NEED A BREAK?**
>
> Midway between Kumluca and Kemer, not far from Olympos and Çirali, Rte. 400 passes by the great high spring of Ulupinar, which supplies water to much of this part of the Tekke peninsula. This is a lovely spot to stop and eat under cool high trees. One of the best of the restaurants here is the **Tropik** (☎ 242/825-0098), where you can dine on a platform over the river or even at a table with your feet right in the cold spring water. Specialities include a delicious oven-roasted lamb or, if you give some advance warning, an entire lamb roasted on a spit.

Adrasan

 94 km (59 mi) southwest of Antalya, follow Rte. 400 and then signs to Olympos, Çavuşköy, and Adrasan; 10 km from Olympos.

Adrasan has a good beach that is mostly sand and, like the Olympos-Çiralı beach, is rarely crowded. A line of unobtrusive small restaurants and hotels stands well back from the sea. Boat tours that take you to swim in local coves set off from the beach each morning at about 10 and cost about $25 including lunch.

A long, wonderful, and mostly forest-shaded day's walk along the Lycian Way will take you through shaded forests over Mt. Musa to Olympos; another walk will take you to the lighthouse at the point of the Tekke Peninsula. Take the official Lycian Way guide book (it comes with a map), adequate water, and preferably a guide for the often lonely pathways.

> **BEYOND OLYMPOS**
>
> Why go to Adrasan if you've seen Olympos, you might ask. It's one of Turkey's last quiet, basic, and locally run beachfront holiday spots. Hotels are also up to a third cheaper than those in Çiralı.

Where to Stay

$ ✕⚏ **Ceneviz Hotel and Restaurant.** This restaurant set back from the beach has good Turkish and international food served in large portions. Rooms are modest and clean. ⊠ *Deniz Mahallesi, Adrasan (halfway along Adrasan Beach),* ☎ *242/883–1030* 🖷 *242/883–1031* 🛏 *18 rooms* ⚴ *Restaurant, bar* ☰ *MC, V* ⦿ *BP* ⊗ *Closed Nov–Apr.*

$ ⚏ **Ford Hotel.** This basic but small and comfortable hotel lies between the sea and a mountain on the southern end of the beach. It has some of the best views in the area. ⊠ *Sahil Cad. No. 220* ☎ *242/883–1098* 🖷 *242/883–1026* ⊕ *www.fordhotel.net* 🛏 *27 rooms, 2 suites* ⚴ *Restaurant, bar, pool* ☰ *MC, V* ⦿ *BP.*

Phaselis

★ ㉕ *60 km (37 mi) southwest of Antalya on Rte. 400*

The ruins of Phaselis, the ancient port city majestically located at the edge of three smalls bays, are as romantic as the reputation of its ancient inhabitants was appalling: Demosthenes the Greek called them unsavory and Roman statesman Cicero called them rapacious pirates. Since the first Greek colonists from Rhodes bought the land from a local shepherd in the 7th century BC for a load of dried fish, classical literature is replete with the expression "a present from the Phaselians," meaning a cheap gift. Still, the setting is beautiful and Alexander the Great spent a whole winter here before marching on to conquer the east. A broad main street, flanked by some remarkably well-preserved buildings, cuts through the half-standing walls of the Roman **agora**. At each end of this main street is a different bay, both with translucent water ideal for swimming. A third bay, to the north, has great harbor stones carved by the ancients, and is less likely to be disturbed by tour boats.

A small **theater** with trees growing among the seats has a majestic view of Mt. Olympos, and fine **sarcophagi** are scattered throughout a necropolis in the pine woods that surround the three bays. The ruins are poetic and impressive, ideal for a picnic or a day at the beach, but weekends and high season days can be crowded and downright depressing when tour yachts from Antalya arrive with loudspeakers blaring. For some reason the refreshment stands at Phaselis are in a legal limbo, so today's pirates of Phaselis are the men selling overpriced drinks under the trees. ⚏ *$7 per person* ⊗ *June–Sept., 8:30 AM–7 PM, Oct.–May 8:30–5 PM.*

Kemer

㉖ *42 km (26 mi) southwest of Antalya on Rte. 400; 15 km (9mi) north of Phaselis on Rte. 400.*

Kemer is a center of intensive package-tourism development, with restaurants, bars, shops, a well-equipped marina, and dozens of resort hotels that can make you forget you're in Turkey. The new culture of all-inclusive tour packages is starving local restaurants of custom and quality. The town is, however, famous for its hard-driving nightlife, and if you're drawn here, the pleasantly landscaped area around the marina has some appeal. A five-minute walk south of the marina is Moonlight

Beach, managed by the local Türkiz Hotel, where you'll find one of Turkey's only dolphinariums—dolphin shows are at 3 PM every day but Sunday ($15 for adults, $8 for children). There is also a pool with slides (entrance to the pool is about $8).

Where to Stay

$$$$ 🏨 **Türkiz Hotel.** Kemer has lodgings to suit all the package-tour budgets. The Türkiz is one of the best—and more expensive—but you can sometimes find a cheaper booking through an online agency. Under U.S.-trained management for the past five years, this smoothly functioning luxury hotel offers a full range of services, including its own large, beachside watersports facilities. In the basement is the amazing Thalassa Center, 16,000 square feet of indoor seawater pools and spa therapy rooms with the latest in massage techniques. Note that the fourth-floor rooms have low ceilings, and that standard rooms are aesthetically more pleasing than the awkwardly laid out suites. ⊠ *Yalı Cad. 3, 07980* ☎ *242/814–4100* 🖷 *242/814–2833* 🛏 *146 rooms, 18 suites* ♨ *2 restaurants, 7 bars, cable TV, minibars, 2 pools, gym, sauna, Turkish bath, beach, dance club, nightclub, shops, meeting room, hair salon, Wi-Fi (fee)* ⊟ *AE, DC, MC, V* ⊕ *www.turkiz.com.tr.*

Nightlife

After a full refurbishment in 2006, the custom-made speakers of the **Türkiz Club Aura Moonlight Disco** (⊠ Moonlight Bay Beach ☎ 536/551–2748) are ready to crank volumes to previously unimagined heights—while promising that somehow the sound will all stay within the confines of the open-air arena. With a capacity of 4,000, it hopes to maintain its status as the leading light in the Kemer nightlife scene. The disco is managed by the luxury Türkiz Hotel five minutes' walk away. Otherwise, Kemer's nightlife is conveniently packaged into Disco Street and Bar Street. In the latter, **Prima** can be noisy and crowded; the **Sherlock Holmes** offers occasional live music.

OFF THE BEATEN PATH

For a cool, memorable day's hiking if you're near Kemer, pack a picnic and trek up the **GÖYNÜK GORGE.** Drive 15 minutes south from Kemer to the corner of the coast where Beldibi ends and Göynük begins, a point clearly marked by blue "city limits" signs at the bridge over a riverbed. Turn inland onto the unmarked tarmac and dirt track on the northern bank of the river and follow sporadic signs to the "wasserfall" into the gorge. When you no longer feel comfortable with the rockiness of the track, park by the side of the road and walk up. Having a guide with you is handy but not essential—red-painted signs from a local café will keep you on the right path, or just keep asking the way. There are usually a number of rafting tours from the resort hotels trekking up the gorge. Take note: when the motor road definitively ends, take the path up the left hand gorge, following the main river and a forest track carved into the side of the mountain, not the steeper right-hand one. Nearly an hour from the last car park, the road turns into a path, and you can take a refreshing swim where the cold, clear river flows through a long, deep crevasse carved by the water through the rock. Take your own drinking water, since there are no vendors anywhere near here.

★ ☾ A small jewel lies hidden in the orange groves behind the unexceptional resort town of Tekirova: a zoo that pays homage to all species of reptile, particularly the snake. Take the main Tekirova turning from Rte. 400, about 20 km (13 mi) south of Kemer. Turn left after 100 yards, following signs for the **EkoPark.** Neatly laid out rows of cages show all the local species, and plenty of others as well, along with cacti and the region's homeopathic herbs. English-language tours are available. Afterward, you can drive down to Tekirova Beach for a dip. Because of all the big charter tour hotels, the only public access route to the beach runs along the right bank of the dried-out river, through a car park and then to the beach. Waterskiing, paragliding, and other mechanized watersports are easy to organize here. ⊠ *Phaselis Cad. 1015 No. 14* ☎ *242/821–5138* ⊕ *www.ekopark.com.tr* ☒ *$15* ▭ *No credit cards* ☾ *June–Sept., 9:30 AM–7 PM.*

PAMPHYLIA

When the Greeks migrated from central Turkey to the Mediterranean coast, around the 12th century BC, the area east of Antalya became known as Pamphylia, the land of the tribes, reflecting the mixed origins of the new inhabitants. The area was remote because the coast was cut off from the main trade routes by the mountains.

Antalya is just one of several good options as a base for excursions to the region's major archaeological sites: Termessos, Perge, Aspendos, and Side. The other main options as a base are Belek, which has fancier resort-style hotels, and Side, which has a more intimate atmosphere and is less expensive.

Antalya

The tourist hub of Antalya is one of Turkey's fastest growing cities, and these days the international terminals of Antalya airport are busier even than in Istanbul. Most visitors are on package tours, but Antalya is also a popular destination among Turks. The enormous hotels east of Antalya are themed on Ottoman palaces or the great sights of European capitals and attract increasing numbers of conferences, too.

Antalya has variety, sophistication, and the attraction of having one of Turkey's best museums. It is also very big. You can happily stay within the winding streets of the

ANTALYA ORANGE BLOSSOMS

Antalya is famous for being the center of the intense glasshouse cultivation of vegetables and cut flowers for Europe. As early as 1671, Ottoman traveler Evliya Çelebi wrote that Antalya was celebrated for the growing of oranges, olives, figs, and pomegranates—all of which remain in production today, with some groves still not far from the city center giving a slight fragrance of orange blossom in the spring. By 1812 when the English sea captain Francis Beaufort passed by, nearly 8,000 people lived here, and he reported the population to be two-thirds Muslim. He saw "trees heavy with fruit" and wrote that "you could not choose a more beautiful place to establish a city."

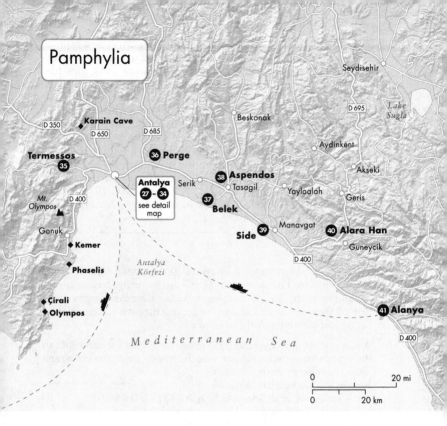

Pamphylia

atmospheric harbor and old city, known as the Kaleiçi—where there are small houses, restaurants, *pansiyons,* and Mermerli Beach—and hardly notice the big urban conglomeration all around. On the hilltop above the harbor are tea gardens and bars with views that extend south to the Bey Mountains right and around to the Taurus Mountains to the north.

Antalya has a tram service that runs every half-hour along the Antalya sea front, circles the old city, and goes out to the Antalya Museum; it costs $1 and departure times are posted at the stops.

What to See

❸❹ The first-rate collection at the **Antalya Müzesi** (Antalya Museum) in-
FodorśChoice cludes Turkish crafts, costumes, and artifacts from the Greek and Roman
★ eras (including notable statues of the gods, from Aphrodite to Zeus, in
the Gods Gallery), with bits of Byzantine iconography and some prehistoric fossils thrown in. Seven fine Roman sarcophagi from the 2nd century AD include a wonderful one illustrating the labors of a steadily aging
Hercules. Don't miss the remains of prehistoric man and the Seljuks, the
children's and ethnographic sections, and the fabulous open-air sculpture gallery. There is a reasonably priced, good cafeteria and a gift shop.
If you have the time, walk to the museum from the center of town along

the clifftop promenade, which has a fine sea view. ⊠ *Konyaaltı Cad.,
heading west out of town* ☎ *242/241–4528* 🖃 *$5* ⊙ *Tues.–Sun. 9–6.*

❸❸ Shady **Karaalioğlan Parkı** (⊠ Agustos Cad. at Atatürk Cad.) is a traditional park with trees, grass, and benches, as well as a view of the
Mediterranean. At the northwest end is a stone tower 49 feet tall, called
Hıdırlık Külesi. It dates from the 2nd century AD, and though no one
knows for sure what it is, the best guess is that it was a combined lighthouse and fort. At sunset, sip a drink at the Castle Bar next door to enjoy
an unforgettable panorama of the Bey Mountains. There is a path from
here down to the old harbor in the heart of the old town but it's steep
and not well lit, so probably best avoided if the Castle Bar has persuaded
you to have one drink too many.

Inside the Kaleiçi (Old Town)

The old town of Antalya lies within the fortified city wall; it's an excellent example of a traditional Ottoman neighborhood. A restoration project launched in the 1980s saved hundreds of houses, dating mostly
from the 19th century. Most of these were converted into pansiyons,
rug shops, restaurants, and art galleries.

★ **❸❶** One way to enter the old town is via **Hadrian's Gate,** a short walk from
Karalioğlan Park along the pleasant palm-lined Atatürk Caddesi outside the eastern edge of the old town walls. The gate was constructed
in honor of a visit by the Roman emperor in AD 130, and has three arches,
each with coffered ceilings decorated with rosettes. Ruts in the marble
road show where carts once trundled through.

★ **❷❼** Another way to enter the old city is via the **old harbor,** now filled with
yachts, fishing vessels, and tourist-excursion boats. If you're in a car,
follow the signs to the *yat liman,* (harbor) and you'll find a convenient,
free parking lot behind the quaysides. From here you can head up any
of the lanes leading north and east out of the harbor to get to the heart
of the old town.

Several of the old town's cobbled lanes lead north from the harbor to
❷❾ the old stone **Saat Kulesi** (Clock Tower), at the junction known to An-
talyans as Kalekapısı, one of the interfaces between the old town and
the new. Just next door you can have your face laser-carved into crystal by Looxis (242/242–4333).

★ **❸⓿** Behind the clock tower, the **Tekeli Mehmet Paşa Cami,** a mosque believed
to have been built around the end of the 16th century, is one of the finest
surviving Ottoman mosques in the region.

★ **❸❷** Fifty yards inside Hadrian's gate, turn left for the **Suna & Inan Kiraç Museum** (⊠ Hadrian's Gate), a little oasis in a group of restored buildings
decorated with an unlikely-looking painted exterior that researchers say
was the way most Antalya houses looked in Ottoman times. The museum has an excellent library of books on the region around Antalya—
although these are accessible only with special permission—and a good
range of guidebooks are on sale in the museum shop. The main display
rooms have interesting pictures of Old Antalya and a couple of rooms
with waxworks displaying a re-creation of Ottoman wedding scenes.

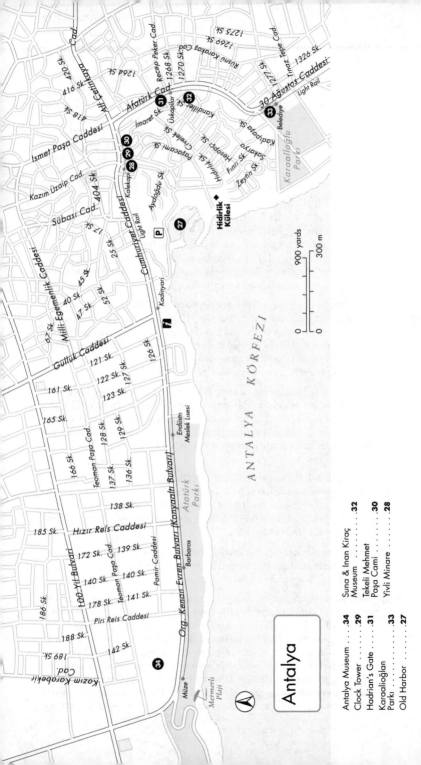

Antalya

Antalya Museum **34**
Clock Tower **29**
Hadrian's Gate **31**
Karaalioğlan
Parkı **33**
Old Harbor **27**

Suna & Inan Kiraç
Museum **32**
Tekeli Mehmet
Paşa Cami **30**
Yivli Minare **28**

The best part of the museum is the restored church in the garden, where there is a delightful display of historical kitsch from the potteries of the late Ottoman period.

28 Dark blue and turquoise tiles decorate the **Yivli Minare** (Fluted Minaret), a graceful 13th-century cylinder commissioned by the Seljuk sultan Alaaddin Keykubat I. The adjoining mosque, named for the sultan, was originally a Byzantine church. Within the complex are two attractive *türbes* (tombs) and an 18th-century *tekke* (monastery), which once housed a community of whirling dervishes. The monastery is now used as an unremarkable art gallery. The Nigar Hatun Türbe (Tomb of Lady Nigar), next to the monastery, though built in Seljuk style, is a 15th-century copy. The *medrese* (theological school) adjacent to the Fluted Minaret has now been glassed in under a bus-station-style roof and is a tourist-oriented shopping center. On offer is the standard tourist fare throughout Turkey—pottery, copperwork, carpets, and tiles—but the prices are better than at most other resorts along the coast. ⊠ *Cumhuriyet Cad., south side of Kalekapısı Mey.*

Where to Stay & Eat

★ $$–$$$ ✕ **Club Arma.** You can't miss this restaurant, which has a spectacular location halfway up the main road from the old harbor. Inside, airy stone arches give it elegant style despite the fact that this was once the port's petroleum depot. Club Arma is Antalya's most luxurious restaurant, serving octopus carpaccio, local *grida* or grouper, lobster, duck, chocolate soufflé, chestnut parfait, and fresh cheesecake, along with a full range of foreign spirits and cigars from a humidor. At 11 PM, the dance club alongside swings into action. ⊠ *Kaleiçi Yatlımanı No. 42* ☎ *242/244–9710* ⊟ *MC, V.*

★ $–$$ ✕ **Ekici Restaurant.** This is the most reputable of the harbor-front restaurants, with a spotless kitchen, good service, and excellent food. Typical specialities are fish stew and fish baked in salt. Even here, though, make sure you've agreed on the price of the fish before you order. ⊠ *Kaleiçi Yatlımanı No. 38* ☎ *242/247–8190* ⊟ *MC, V.*

$–$$ ✕ **Parlak Restaurant.** If shopping in the jewelry bazaar behind the clock tower has tired you out, try this long-time Antalya institution. The main speciality is chicken roasted over a long open pit of charcoal, but there's also a full range of fish, meat, and mezes to choose from as well. When challenged over the run-down state of the decor, the management insists that's the way their Turkish customers like it. ⊠ *Zincirli Han, Kazım Özalp Cad. No. 7* ☎ *242/241–9160* ⊟ *MC, V.*

$ ✕ **Mermerli Restaurant.** This restaurant enjoys an excellent view from its terrace well above the eastern end of the harbor, and the prices are better than on the waterfront itself. The menu is wide-ranging and they serve breakfast all day. It's a good spot for a meal if you want to relax at Mermerli Beach, down the steps from the restaurant, which controls access to the bathing spot. ⊠ *Banyo Cad. 25* ☎ *242/248–5484* ⊟ *MC, V.*

¢–$ ✕ **St. Paul's Place.** A club-like retreat on the first floor of a Christian religious center on the eastern edge of the old city, St. Paul's Place serves great coffee, American cakes, and home-cooked lunches (it's open only until 5:30 PM). It also has a library of exchange books and a garden with children's playground. The center also organizes religion-oriented tours. ⊠ *Yenikapı Cad.; turn into old city between Karaalioğlan Park and Hadrian's Gate, 100 yards on right* ☎ 242/247–6857 ⊟ *No credit cards* ⊘ *Closed the last week of Aug.*

¢ ✕ **Tophane.** This tea garden overlooks Antalya's harbor and serves inexpensive drinks and snacks along with its priceless views. If you don't feel like walking from here to the museum, you could splurge on a horse-drawn carriage from the top of the harbor road nearby (not a cheap method of transportation though). Otherwise, the Antalya tramway leaves the terminus at each end every half hour, arriving at the halfway point in front of the clock tower near Tophane teahouse at about quarter past and quarter to the hour. ⊠ *Cumhuriyet Alanı* ☎ *No phone* ⊟ *No credit cards.*

$$$$ ▦ **Hillside Su.** This resort hotel is unforgettable for its all-white color scheme, from the room TVs to the floors, and it's popular with the weekend crowd that comes in from Istanbul. Everything is designed and run to high and exacting standards—though this might make some travelers feel a little trapped, like the ornamental goldfish in the relentless lines of bowls around the reception area. ⊠ *Dumlupınar Cad. Konyaaltı,* ☎ *242/249–0700* 🖷 *242/249–0707* ⊕ *www.hillside.com.tr* ⤶ *294 rooms* ⚏ *5 restaurants, cable TV, minibars, 1 indoor pool, 1 outdoor pool, beach,* ⊟ *A, MC, V* ¶◎¶ *MAP.*

★ $$$$ ✕▦ **Talya Hotel.** This prime property rises over the cliffs just to the east of Karaalioğlan Parkı, commanding spectacular views of the Bey Mountains (ask for a corner room; these have numbers that end in 17). The hotel has its own bathing platform at the foot of the cliff. The restaurants all have good views and excellent reputations. One serves international cuisine, the others traditional Turkish fare. ⊠ *Fevzi Cakmak Cad. 30* ☎ *242/248–6800* 🖷 *242/241–5400* ⊕ *www.divan.com* ⤶ *204 rooms* ⚏ *3 restaurants, 4 bars, cable TV, babysitting, Internet café, beauty center, 24-hour room service, minibars, tennis court, pool, health club, Turkish bath, convention center* ⊟ *AE, DC, MC, V.*

★ $$ ▦ **Doğan Hotel.** Every room is unique and tastefully done in this family-run establishment. The ceilings are somewhat low but the Ottoman-style wooden decorations help compensate. The best seven or eight rooms on the top floors, like Room 125, have good views of the harbor, but others, like excellent Room 141, have charming views of the gardens. The staff are intelligent, fun, and accommodating. The hotel is only a short walk from the old harbor and Mermerli Beach. There is a lovely pool, too. ⊠ *Mermerli Banyo Sok. 5.* ☎ *242/247–4654 or 241–8842* 🖷 *242/247–4006* ⤶ *41 rooms* ⚏ *2 restaurants, pool, 3 bars* ⊟ *MC, V* ⊕ *www.doganhotel.com.*

$$ ✕▦ **Marina Hotel.** Three vintage Ottoman houses of white stucco with bay windows and dark-wood trim were restored and connected to make this attractive hotel in the historic heart of Antalya. The staff is attentive, and the restaurant serves French-inspired food—no less a personage than former French prime minister François Mitterrand once praised the onion soup. Inside, there are old carpets and kilims, and the rooms, though on the small side, are done in the same attractive white and dark wood as the facade. A pianist accompanies diners at dinner, and the swimming pool is large. ⊠ *Mermeli Sok. 15* ☎ *242/247–5490* 🖷 *242/241–*

IF YOU LIKE SKIING

Turkey isn't exactly a ski destination, but in winter and spring, there are two modest ski resorts within reach of Antalya. The newest is at Davraz, high above three mountain lakes near Isparta, 100 km (74 mi) north of Antalya. You can stay at the luxurious, 123-room **Sirene Davras Ski Resort** (☎ 212/368−6666).

The older resort is Saklıkent, 50 km (32 mi) west of Antalya. Snow cover tends to be thin and it's not held in high esteem among serious skiers. If you're here, try the 13-room **Bakırlı Motel** (☎ 242/446-1330 🖷 242/242-0128). The larger, 75-bed **Saklıkent Motel** (☎ 242/446−1137 🖷 242/312−6656 ⊕ www. saklikent.com.tr.) is another option. Both establishments rent skis.

1765 🖙 *41 rooms* ⚏ *Restaurant, 2 bars café, cable TV, room service, minibars, pool* ▤ *AE, DC, MC, V* ⦿⏐ *BP.*

★ $ ✕⊡ **Türk Evi Hotelleri.** This good-value hotel is in a row of restored 120-year-old houses just inside the old city walls. The lobby is tastefully decorated with antiques, and the restaurant is good. Rooms are relatively big, with wooden floors and Turkish carpets. None face the sea, though at the back, some look out over a pretty little garden. The view of the ancient yacht harbor from the Fortress bar, at the rear of the hotel, is breathtaking. ⊠ *Mermerli Sok. 2* ☎ *242/248−6591* 🖷 *242/241−9419* ⊕ *www.turkeviotelleri.com* 🖙 *18 rooms, 1 suite* ⚏ *2 restaurants, bar, pool, sauna, minibar, safes in room* ▤ *AE, MC, V.*

¢ ⊡ **Atelya Art Hotel.** This is an inexpensive, friendly hotel with larger than usual rooms, in the old town. The art consists of paintings by the owner, hanging in many rooms and corridors. Off season it can seem somewhat dimly lit and musty. In season, book at least one week ahead. ⊠ *Kaleiçi Civelek Cad. No. 21; Near the Kesik Minare mosque,* ☎ *242/241−6416* 🖷 *242/241−2848* ⊕ *www.atelyahotel.com* 🖙 *30 rooms* ⚏ *Restaurant, bar* ▤ *no credit cards.*

Nightlife & the Arts

The perfect start to any evening out in Antalya starts by watching the sun set from the clifftop **Castle Café and Bar** (⊠ Hıdırlık Cad. 48/1; ☎ 242/242−3188), next to Hıdırlık Kulesi—you can accompany your drink with some of their sesame and garlic dip known as *hibeş*. Otherwise, Antalya's bars are centered in three main areas: in Kaleiçi; in the new part of town, on Barlar Caddesi (Bar Street), running off Cumhuriyet Caddesi; and in Atatürk Park. Most visitors prefer Kaleiçi, where a profusion of bars competes for your attention. For dancing, the smartest place in town is undoubtedly on the harbor road at **Club Arma** (⊠ Kaleiçi Yatlimanı No. 42 ☎ 242/244−9710)

The Atatürk Kulture Merkezi, also known as AKM, is a complex with an exhibition space and several theaters in a cliff-top park about 3 km west of the city center. There are concerts year round—look for fliers posted around the city—and an annual film festival.

Sports & the Outdoors

BEACHES If you didn't know that **Mermerli Beach** was there, you'd never guess it. This small strip of sand and pebbles outside the harbor wall is reached from the Mermerli Restaurant halfway up the hill east of the harbor. The $5 price of admission to this quiet oasis in the heart of town includes loungers and umbrellas. (☎ 242/248–5484)

For many Turks, Antalya is synonymous with the thick crowds of holidaymakers on **Konyaaltı Beach,** and in high season the pebble strand is a hot and somewhat off-putting sight. The city has worked hard to improve the quality of the beach experience, though, with especially impressive results on the 1-km (½-mi) section starting after the museum and ending under Su Hotel. Here, paying an admission charge gives access to a grassy park behind the beach, restaurants, and playgrounds.

RAFTING Rafting has become a major activity from the big hotels, with several agencies offering trips up to various canyons. To avoid the crowds, it's best to get up to the water in the early morning before the package tourists are out of bed. Most companies will pick you up at your hotel. Reputable operators inlcude **Medraft** (☎ 242/312–5770) and **TransNature** (☎ 242/247–8688).

Shopping

Thanks to its size—in 2006, about 800,000 people lived here—the shopping streets have more variety than anywhere else on the Turquoise Riviera, although the merchandise, in general, is the same sort of stuff you find all over Turkey. East and north of the old town walls are where the less expensive clothing shops are found, including some jewelry arcades. The Kenan Evren boulevard along the seafront cliffs toward the museum is where upmarket clothing shops are concentrated, as well as the offices of airlines that run shuttle buses to the airport. A short taxi ride to the west of town is Antalya's fanciest mall, the Migros Shopping Center, which has a large supermarket, eight cinemas, a large food court, and branches of almost all of Turkey's big clothing chains like Mavi Jeans, LCW for children's clothes, Derimod for upmarket leathers, Bisse and Abbate for shirts, Vakkorama and Boyner for general clothing, and all kinds of international brand-name shops like Swatch, Lacoste, and Tommy Hilfiger among its 100 shops.

EN ROUTE When driving east on Rte. 400 from Antalya toward Perge, Aspendos, Side, or Alanya, don't miss one of the region's great culinary experiences: a meal in the strip of restaurants by the highway in Aksu. Turks on business in Antalya will detour for miles just to eat here. Ease off the highway onto the feeder road when you see a pedestrian bridge about 6 km (4 mi) east of the Antalya airport intersection, then park where you can.

$ ✕ **Öz Şimşek.** Try the superb kumin-flavored *köfte* meatballs with baked garlic and mild peppers along with a plate of mind-blowingly fresh *piyaz,* white beans in a sauce with sesame paste, tomato, parsley, egg, and olive oil. ✉ *Berberoğlu Çarşısı, Çalkaya* ☎ *242/426–3920* ⊟ *MC, V* ⊙ *6 AM–11 PM.*

$ ✕ **Ramazan'ın Yeri.** At the southern foot of the pedestrian overpass, this restaurant was one of the first in the strip and offers a remarkable

Timeline of the Turquoise Riviera

3000 BC First Paleolithic dwellers leave remains in mountains behind Antalya.

1400 BC A shipwreck off Uluburun near Kaş, discovered in 1982, shows Lycia was a key transit route for multinational east Mediterranean trade.

700 BC First Greek colonists arrive in Phaselis.

546 BC Persians finalize conquest of Asia Minor at Battle of Magnesia, contested by Greek revolts and invasions for next two centuries.

520 BC First Lycian coins minted. Lycian culture and architecture flourish under loose Persian control, notably under Pericles of Limyra 380-360.

334 BC Alexander the Great conquers the Mediterranean coast and drives the remnants of Persian rule out of Asia Minor. Alexander and his successors accelerate a shift away from public use of Lycian language in favor of Greek. The sarcophagus comes into fashion, replacing the old rock-cut tombs.

205 BC Foundation of Lycian League, the world's first democratic federation and an inspiration of the U.S. constitution. Each of 36 member cities elected representatives to the league council with the votes of free males.

197 BC Roman legions start taking control of Asia Minor. Despite bouts of piracy, Roman civil wars, and outside invasions, many of the monuments surviving today, including granaries and roads, are built in the prosperity of the ensuing three centuries.

141 AD and 243 AD Massive earthquakes devastate Lycia, and coastal towns decline with waning Roman power.

395 Anatolia becomes Christian under Byzantine Empire, bringing substantial building over the next centuries that survives until today, especially near the pilgrimage center of Myra (Demre).

540–745 Repeated outbreaks of Bubonic plague cripple Anatolia.

1071 Seljuk Turks break the Byzantine armies at Malazgirt. Within the next five decades, they conquer all of the coast from Alanya to Marmaris. Four centuries later, power shifts to the Istanbul-based Ottoman Turks.

1916 In arguably the last military action seen on the coast, the French gunboat *Paris*—now a diving attraction—is sunk by First World War Turkish artillery off Kemer.

1923 The exchange of Christian and Muslim populations between Greece and Turkey at the foundation of republic sees removal of last "Greeks," although most in Antalya spoke Turkish and only wrote it in Greek characters.

1950s First roads are cut along Lycian Coast. The main coastal road follows in 1970s.

1980–83 A military coup regime creates a national park on the Bey Mountains coast southwest of Antalya, saving most of the pine-clad mountains and beaches from developers.

4

smorgasbord of all animal parts fit to eat. There is a full range of the normal kebabs and stews, but this is the place to experiment. The four daily soups include tripe and *paça*, normally boiled from the head of a calf. In the refrigerator you can select delicacies to follow: ribs, cutlets, liver, kidney, and heart. Calf's brain can be found among the cold appetizers. ☎ 242/426–3231 ▤ MC, V ☉ *Open 24 hours*.

Termessos

★ ㉟   *37 km (23 mi) northwest of Antalya; take E87 north toward Burdur, bear left at fork onto Rte. 350 toward Korkuteli and follow signs to Termessos.*

Writers in antiquity referred to Termessos as the Eagle's Nest. Visit the site, 4,500 feet high in the mountains west of Antalya, and you'll understand why. The city was impregnable and now offers stunning vistas over the beautiful scenery of Termessos National Park. The warlike and fiercely independent people who made their home here launched frequent raids on their coastal neighbors. They were not Greek but a native Asia Minor people who called themselves the Solymians, after ancient Mt. Solymus, which rises above the city. Termessos remained autonomous for much of its history and was quite wealthy by the 2nd century AD. Most of its remains date from this period.

The attractions in Termessos start right by the parking area, with a monumental **gate** dedicated to Hadrian. The steepness of the path that leads up to the craggy remains of the city walls soon makes it clear just why Alexander the Great declined to attack. Next are a **gymnasium,** a **colonnaded street** (half of whose many statue bases once supported likenesses of famed wrestlers), a **bath** complex built of dark gray stone blocks, and the 5,000-seat **theater,** whose perch at the edge of a sheer cliff has one of the most spectacular settings in Turkey. From this staggering height you can view the Pamphylian plain, Mt. Solymus, and the occasional mountain goat or ibex. Termessos has one more wonder: a vast **necropolis,** with nearly 1,000 tombs scattered willy-nilly on a rocky hill. To get there, head back to the main trail and make a left. Tours can be arranged by agencies in Antalya, or you can hire a car. A visit takes at least four hours, and there is no restaurant at the site, so pack water and lunch. Wear sturdy shoes. ▨ *$3* ☉ *Daily 8–7.*

One kilometer (½ mile) north of the Termessos turnoff from E87 is the **Karain Cave** (follow yellow signs for Karain). Archaeological digs since 1919 have already proved that it was inhabited as far back as the Paleolithic Age, making it one of the oldest settlements in Turkey. Later it seems to have become a religious center for primitive man. Many of the Karain finds—stone implements, bones of people and animals, and fossilized remains including those of hippopotamuses—are on display in Antalya Museum, but there is also a small museum on the edge of the high meadow where the cave is. Part of the cave itself is also electrically lighted and open to the public, but this is a small site and probably only worth stopping at if you have time after seeing Termessos. ▨ *$3* ☉ *Tues.–Sun. 8–5.*

Perge

36 *22 km (14 mi) from Antalya, east on Rte. 400 to turnoff north at Aksu.*

Perge suffers from comparison with the more dramatic Termessos, and its 14,000-seat theater, though in good shape, is no match for its counterpart in nearby Aspendos, but it's still quite breathtaking. The splendid theater amid the **Perge ruins,** is unfortunately closed for repairs, but the stadium is one of the best preserved in the ancient world, and beyond that, there are the city's sturdy 3rd-century BC garrison towers. The vaulted chambers under the stadium bleachers held shops; marble inscriptions record the proprietors' names and businesses.

The rest of the site is about 1 km (½ mi) north. You enter through the old gates, after parking just outside the old city walls. Directly ahead is a fine colonnaded avenue. The slender, sun-bleached columns lining the street once supported a covered porch filled with shops. You can still see floor mosaics in some places, and delicate reliefs of gods and famous citizens decorate the entablatures between some of the columns. The long grooves in the paving are ruts worn by chariot wheels; the channel running down the center carried water from a fountain at the far end. St. Paul, who sailed here from Cyprus, preached at the basilica near the end of the street, on the left. ☞ *$7* ☉ *Daily 8–7.*

Belek

37 *30 km (19 mi) east of Antalya.*

Belek is a relatively new resort town and one of the only places in Turkey where the infrastructure was actually planned before the hotels were built. Belek is also all about a Turkish attempt to break into the golf holiday business and, eight golf courses later, it has certainly succeeded. It also has wide sandy beaches, although they can feel hot and exposed in the height of summer. Forests filled with the region's signature umbrella pines would be a paradise for naturalists and ornithologists—but many are fenced off to protect golf courses and property limits. The hotels are all giant resorts—you won't find cheap lodging here—and don't look for standalone restaurants, either, though the resorts tend to include all, or most, meals. For nongolfers, Belek is a possible base for exploring the local sites, but you'll need a car. It also hosts an extraordinary addition to Turkey's modern religious landscape—a church, a synagogue, and a mosque, all built in the same style and same place, partly for tourists, partly for the wedding business, and partly to advertize a tolerance that is not always found in other places of worship in Turkey.

Where to Stay

$$$$ 🏨 **Rixos Premium Belek.** A huge hotel that has 1 km of beach and can lodge 1,700 people at once, Rixos is one of the leaders of the pack of superhotels springing up in the area. Just don't forget your suncreen in the room before setting out on the long march to the pool. The complex is also next to a major aquapark, a four-acre marvel that's themed on the Trojan wars (the aquapark is managed separately; entrance is $50).

Almost everything except the VIP helicopter transfer option is included in the price. ⊠, ⊕ *www.rixos.com/belek* ⇦ *605 rooms, 34 suites, 130 villas ⚭ 8 restaurants, 13 bars, children's programs, cable TV, Internet, spa, watersports, golf course, tennis courts* ⊟ *MC, V* ⏐◎⏐ *AP.*

$$$ ⊞ **Gloria Verde Resort & Spa.** Opened in 1997, this is one of the best of the resort hotel complexes in Belek. Its three golf course are immaculate, and filled with well-heeled European tourists. Rooms are large and modern, with touches of Turkish crafts and antiques; many have excellent views. Service can be somewhat haughty, however. ⊠ *Acısu Mevkii* ☎ *242/710–0500* 🖶 *242/715–2419* ⊕ *www.gloria.com* ⇦ *289 rooms, 59 suites ⚭ 2 restaurants, 3 bars, cable TV, snack bar, tennis courts, 2 pools, spa, massage, sauna, Turkish bath, beach, squash, shops* ⊟ *AE, DC, MC, V* ⏐◎⏐ *MAP.*

$$$ ⊞ **Tatbeach Golf Hotel.** From the unusually light and airy lobby and rooms to the colorful and well-manicured gardens, this is a splendid hotel. Service is friendly, and a variety of water sports, in addition to the 27-hole golf course, are available. ⊠ *Belek, Box 1* ☎ *242/725–4080* 🖶 *242/ 725–4099* ⇦ *269 rooms, 33 suites ⚭ 2 restaurants, snack bar, tennis courts, 2 pools, health club, sauna, beach, 6 bars, shops* ⊟ *MC, V* ⏐◎⏐ *MAP* ⊕ *www.tatbeach.com.tr.*

Sports & the Outdoors

It's pretty much all about golf in Belek, with the brilliant greens of eight golf courses laid out beneath the umbrella pines—a number that is set to grow. Many golfers try a different course every day.

GOLF   The 45-hole **Gloria Golf Resort** (☎ 242/710-0600) is the biggest and arguably the best, with its superb landscaping and immaculate clubhouse. Each of its courses is par 72 and about 7,000 yards long. This is one of the more expensive courses, and if you're not staying in the nearby Gloria Resort, it will run you about $90 for a round.

The courses at **Club Nobilis** (☎ 242/710–0300), **Tat Golf Club** (☎ 242/ 724–4076), and **National Golf Club** (☎ 242/725–4620) are all nearly as good, and others are opening every year. For more information, see ⊕ www.golfturkey.com

HORSEBACK   The Norwegian manager of **Bellis Horse Farm** (⊠ Taşlıburun, Belek;
RIDING   ☎ 242/725–5727) runs pleasant stables. A small petting zoo supplies entertainment for children.

Aspendos

★ ❸   *49 km (31 mi) east of Antalya on Rte. 400 (follow yellow signs).*

Most experts agree that the **theater** in Aspendos is the best preserved in Turkey; its quality rivals that of the Colosseum in Rome. A splendid Roman **aqueduct** that traverses the valley utilized the pressure of the water flowing from the mountains to supply the summit of the acropolis, another superior example of Roman engineering. The water tower dates from the 2nd century AD, and its stairway is still intact.

Pay your admission to the main site at what was once the actors' entrance to the theater. Built during the reign of Emperor Marcus Aurelius (ruled AD 161–180) by a local architect called Xenon, it is striking for the broad curve of seats, perfectly proportioned porticoes, and rich decoration. The Greeks liked open vistas behind their stages, but the Romans preferred enclosed spaces. The stage building you see today was once covered in marble tiles, and its niches were filled with statues, some now on view in the Antalya Museum. The only extant relief on site depicts Dionysus (Bacchus) watching over the theater. The acoustics are fine, and the theater is still in use—for concerts and for the Antalya International Opera and Ballet Festival, held every June/July, rather than for the wild-animal and gladiator spectacles as in Roman times. Aspendos is not just a Roman site—the Seljuks used it as an imperial palace in the 13th century, and one of the two towers they added to the structure remains standing. There are traces of the distinctive Seljuk red-and-yellow paint work here and there, too.

Seeing the remainder of the site requires a hike up the zigzagging trail behind the theater, a trek of perhaps an hour or more. The rewards are a tall **Nymphaion**—a sanctuary to the nymphs built around a fountain decorated with a marble dolphin—and the remains of a Byzantine **basilica** and **market hall.** ▢ *$7* ☉ *Daily 8–7.*

Side

39 *75 km east of Antalya on Rte. 400.*

Charter-tour hotels crowding along this stretch of coast threaten to overshadow Side, but at its heart this city's delightful mix of ancient ruins and modern amenities is an underestimated jewel. Sandy beaches run along each side of town, and the area between the harbor and the ruins feels like a real town, not an industrial resort. Side, like Antalya or Alanya, has all sorts of options, from late-night dancing to beach lazing, shopping, or kayaking in mountain canyons. It's also close to the major sites of Aspendos and Perge, and less than an hour from Antalya airport. Like it's bigger Pamphylian sisters, it's best visited out of the heat of the high season July and August, but weekends can be crowded, too. With the right hotel, it's still possible to experience how Side felt in the 1960s, when the city was off the beaten track, and the likes of dancer Rudolph Nureyev and French intellectual Simone de Beauvoir were visitors.

Follow signs in from Rte. 400 for *Antik Side* and resist any sense of disappointment—it will dissipate when you suddenly find yourself driving onto the little peninsula through the delightful ruins of the Greco-Roman city. Through a last arch and past a collonade behind the theatre, park your car or, if staying in a hotel inside the town, ask to be let through the barricade that protects the harbor area from traffic. Ruins are all around: there's a lovely theater, with city and sea views from the top row, and 2nd-century AD temples to Apollo and Athena a few blocks south, on the tip of the peninsula. The town was founded by early Greeks, minting coins from 500 BC, but Side only began to expand when Pompey cleared out the slave-trading pirates in 67 BC. Most of the ruins, laid bare by one of the only systematic excavations of a whole city, date from the prosperous Roman period. One notable feature of the site are the well-preserved Roman communal public latrines.

Side offers plenty of opportunities for shopping. The main street to the harbor is flanked by fancy jewelry shops keen to take in tourist currency. All kinds of souvenir shops abound, as do suppliers of winter furs and leathers. The nightlife is varied and exciting, and whereas some resorts have to invent plaster-of-paris columns to conjure up a little atmosphere, Side's bars and discos are often in real ancient temples.

★ The **Side Müzesi** (Side Museum) is near the theater, in the restored Roman baths. The collection of Roman statues is small but one of the best in Asia Minor: it includes a gorgeous group of the marble torsos of the Three Graces, various cherubs, a brilliant satyr, and a bust of Emperor Hadrian. The sculpture garden behind the museum is larger than the museum itself and overlooks the Mediterranean. ⊠ *Selimiye Köyü* ☎ *242/753–1006* 🖅 *$2.50* ☉ *Tues.–Sun. 8–noon and 1–5.*

Where to Stay & Eat

$$–$$$ ✕ **Orfoz.** If you want to eat in the harbor area, choose the best restaurant: The bamboo chairs are comfortable, the tables well spaced, there are trees for shade, and the food is excellent. Fresh seafood is the speciality, including a melt-in-the-mouth octopus dish, but there's something for everyone on the international menu. The view over the western beach is just right at sunset, the service is good, and if there's a chill in spring or autumn, attentive waiters bring blankets. ⊠ *Liman Cad. 58/ C* ☎ *242/753–1362* ⊕ *www.orfozrestaurant.com* ▤ *MC, V.*

$$ ✕ **Paşaköy Bar and Restaurant.** Paşaköy's has reasonable food, but what differentiates this pleasant restaurant is its weird and wonderfully kitsch garden, decked out with bizarre mock-classical statuary and stuffed animals. The grilled meat dishes are good, the waitstaff is friendly and attentive, and the bartender can make a cocktail with a kick. ⊠ *Liman Cad. 98* ☎ *242/753–3622* ▤ *AE, MC, V* ☉ *Closed Dec.–May.*

$$ ✕ **Soundwaves Restaurant.** This open-air restaurant on a pedestrian walk overlooking the sea is decked out like a pirate ship but, unlike its piratical neighbors in the harbor, has a long and reliable reputation. If walking from the harbor, head 500 yards southeast through the temple and around the promontory. Specialities include fish baked in salt, garlic prawns, and thanks to an Australian half-owner, a deep-fried seafood dish called Tasmanian Squid. ⊠ *Barbaros Cad.* ☎ *242/753–1607* ▤ *MC, V* ☉ *Closed Dec.–Apr.*

$ ✕ **Gama Restaurant.** A pretty seafront location and a garrulous head waiter in Ottoman fancy dress combine to give this restaurant and sundowner bar a sense of holiday fun. There's lobster to eat—at a great price—and the menu ranges from spaghetti to spiced-up kebabs. All meals come with *lavaş,* a long unleavened loaf hot out of the oven. ⊠ *Barbaros Cad. Follow Side promontory around to the southeast for 400 yards.* ☎ *242/ 753–4219* ▤ *MC, V.*

$$$ 🛏 **Hotel Acanthus.** This modest four-story hotel is done in Mediterranean style, with whitewashed walls, dark-wood trim and terraces, a red-tile roof, and direct access to a fine sand beach. Rooms are comfortable if unimpressive. The same family runs the slightly older Cennet Hotel (an option if you can't get a room at Acanthus), and the two share a garden. The owners also sponsor the Aspendos Opera and Bal-

let Festival in June, so you may find both hotels full of musicians at that time. ⊠ *Side Köyü, Box 55* ☎ *242/753–3050* 🖷 *242/753–1913* ⊕ *www. baruthotels.com.tr/acanthus/eng/* 🔊 *104 rooms* ⚫ *2 restaurants, 2 bars, safe, minibar, tennis court, 1 pools, beach, windsurfing, parasailing, watersports* ⊟ *MC, V.*

$$$ 🖳 **Sunrise Queen Hotel.** On its own beach about 3 km (2 miles) northwest from the town center, this is a large and attractive resort made up of one large main building and four additional "blocks." The meal-plan food is quite good here, too. The place is often filled with tour groups, though many Turks also stay here. Suites have whirlpool baths, and there is live music nightly. ⊠ *Bingeşi, Kumköy Cad., on main seafront boulevard west of city* ☎ *242/753–4783* 🖷 *242/753–4760* ⊕ *www. sunrisehotels.com* 🔊 *312 rooms, 35 suites* ⚫ *4 restaurants, 9 bars, nightclub, 7 tennis courts, 6 pools (one indoor), safes, minibars, hair salon, health club, fitness center, 9 bars* ⊟ *AE, MC, V* 🖭 *MAP.*

★ ☙ $ 🖳 **Beach House Hotel.** If you want a charmed few days on the Side seafront, this is the place to stay. The rooms are modest and not air conditioned, but the ceiling fans create a breeze. This is where Rudolph Nureyev and Simone de Beauvoir once stayed. The hotel is built on the grounds of a Byzantine villa, whose ruins are used for a garden with lawns and a trampoline. The restaurant overlooks the sea. ⊠ *Barbaros Cad., Side 07330* ☎ *242/753–1607* 🖷 *242/753–1804* ⊕ *www. beachhouse-hotel.com* 🔊 *23 rooms* ⚫ *Beach, restaurant, bar; no a/c* ⊟ *MC, V* 🍽 *BP.*

$ 🖳 **Kamer Motel.** This is a modest, clean hotel in a quiet part of town, with views of the sea. All rooms have balconies, bathrooms, televisions, and air-conditioning. The restaurant overlooks the sea, too. ⊠ *Barbaros Cad. No. 47, Side 07330* ☎ *242/753–1007* 🖷 *242/753–2660* ⊕ *www. kamermotel.com* 🔊 *26 rooms* ⚫ *restaurant, bar* ⊟ *V* 🍽 *BP.*

Nightlife

The evening action begins after sunset as places like the **Barracuda Café and Bar** (⊠ Barbaros Cad. ☎ 242/753–2724) and **Temple Bar** (☎ 242/ 753–1181) set up cocktail tables in the Temple of Apollo and Athena on the southeastern corner of the harbor. It moves on to dance floors in the ruins and, at the other end of the harbor, the open-air **Lighthouse** discotheque and bar. Farther afield, **Oxyd,** built like a sub-Saharan adobe palace with a futuristic interior, is a 3-km (2-mi) drive along the boulevard that serves the resort hotels east of Side.

Sports & the Outdoors

BOAT TRIPS Boat trips along the Manavgat River can be arranged either from the harbor at Side or from the town of Manavgat (on Rt. 400, 1 km [½ mi] east of the turnoff for Side). Prices vary widely according to the length of the trip and whether food is provided; you should definitely bargain. Times often change, but a boat also usually leaves each morning about 9 AM for Alanya—check the evening before at the sales desk (no phone) in the middle of the small Side harborfront. Boats stop to let you swim, and some arrange for activities such as jet skiing, waterskiing, or water parachuting; be warned, however, that not all the operators are properly licensed or insured, and serious accidents have occurred.

JEEP SAFARIS Jeep safaris are also popular and can be arranged from one of several travel agencies in Side. One good option is **Unser Tour** (☎ 532/413–8431).

Alara Han

③② *118 km (73 mi) east of Antalya or 43 km (26 mi) east of Side, turn north off Rte. 400 onto local road signposted Alara Han; the site is 9 km (6 mi) inland.*

The Seljuk Turks fostered the prosperity of their 11th–13th-century domains with trade protected by a network of kervansarays—"inns" where caravans stop for the night—known in Turkish as *hans*. One of the more romantic of these is Alara Han, built in the early 13th century and now beautifully restored with a fountain, prayer room, unusual lamp stands carved into the stone, and lions' heads on the base of the arches, and a majestic vaulted interior. In summer, the inland countryside location also provides welcome relief from the sweltering coast.

For the energetic ready to scramble with hands and feet, an unusual hand-carved tunnel leads up to the Seljuk fortress built on the crags above the *han*. Continue to the last stop on the road to the Alara Cennet Piknik restaurant (☎ 544/260–5520). A flashlight is essential to make the climb, but if you don't have one, Adem Birdoğan at the Cennet Piknik can lend you one. Ask him for directions across the vegetable fields to the tunnel entrance. Afterward he'll cook you freshly caught trout and you can relax with a cold drink on the river bank, enjoying a cool breeze from the crystal-clear snow-fed river.

Alanya

③③ *135 km (84 mi) east of Side on Rte. 400.*

Alanya is Turkey's hottest resort town—literally. Temperatures here are higher than almost anywhere else in Turkey, averaging 106°F (27°C) in July and August, and the waves lapping the long Mediterranean beaches that sweep toward Alanya's great rock citadel are only a degree or two cooler. This makes high summer in Alanya heaven for sun-starved, disco-loving, hard-drinking north Europeans but rather hellish for anyone seeking a quiet holiday surrounded by nature.

That said, Alanya is now home to one of Turkey's biggest year-round expatriate communities, and in spring and autumn it's a pleasantly warm and inexpensive choice for a few days of easily accessible swimming, historic sites, and good food. The city is cleaning up its act, so to speak: former wastelands of concrete-block apartments are now colorfully painted, Ottoman districts around the harbor are well on the way to being restored, and the new and old houses inside the magnificent red-walled citadel are an unspoiled, eclectic jumble. The best swimming place is known as Cleopatra's Beach—yet another accretion to the fables surrounding Mark Anthony's courtship of the Egyptian queen—and its yellow sands extend northwest from the rock citadel. Foreign influence has led to improvements like the beginnings of a bicycle culture, hundreds of restaurants that can bill in multiple currencies, and a microbrewery that serves what many to believe is the best beer in Turkey.

Alanya is famed for its sandy beaches, within walking distance of most hotels. Boats can be hired from the harbor for relaxing day tours to caves around the citadel rock and a view of the only surviving naval arsenal of the 12th and 13th century Seljuks. Alanya, captured in 1221 by the Seljuk sultan Alaaddin Keykubad, was the Turkish Seljuks' first stronghold on the Mediterranean in their centuries-long migration westward. Several amusing stories explain the Seljuk sultan Alaaddin Keykubad's conquest: One says he married the commander's daughter, another that he tied torches to the horns of thousands of goats and drove them up the hill in the dark of night, suggesting a great army was attacking. Most likely, he simply cut a deal; once settled, he renamed the place and built defensive walls to ensure he would never be dislodged.

> ## THE SELJUK TURKS AND THE MEDITERRANEAN COAST
>
> The empire of the Roman Seljuks was the first Muslim empire to extend into Anatolia, long before the Ottomans arrived. It reached its height in the 13th century, when the Seljuks established full control of Turkey's Mediterranean and Black Sea coasts. Their capital was at Konya (Iconium), in central Anatolia, where winters were bitterly cold. As a consequence, the Seljuks established Alanya as a secondary winter capital, and there are many Seljuk remains in the area, including the Alara Han.

What to See

It's worth dropping by the **Alanya Müzesi** (Alanya Museum) just to see the perfectly preserved Roman bronze statue of a gleaming, muscular Hercules from the 2nd century AD. Other bronze statues feature Hermes and a graceful woman. There is also a large collection of ancient ceramics and interesting limestone ossuaries and heads from the late Roman period. ⊠ *Azaklar Sok., south of Atatürk Cad., Sekerhane Mah.* ☎ *242/513–1228* ☜ *$3* ☉ *Tues.–Sun. 8.30–noon and 1:30–5:30.*

Views of the splendid **kale** (citadel)on a mighty crag surrounded on three sides by the sea dominate all roads into Alanya. The crenellated outer walls are 7 km (4 mi) long and include 146 towers. The road pierces these outer walls through a short tunnel, and this is followed by a second line of fortifications, the **İç Kale** (inner fortress) where you can park and strike out on foot into the old city's residential area.

In the center of town are the remains of the original *bedestan* (bazaar), whose old shops are now rooms in a lacklustre hotel (The Bedestan Hotel). Along a road to the top of the promontory, a third wall and a ticket office defends the **Keep.** Inside are the ruins of a Byzantine church, with some 6th-century frescoes of the evangelists. Keykubad probably also had a palace here, although discoveries by the McGhee Center of Georgetown University—itself in a beautiful old Ottoman mansion perched on the cliff-face between the first and second ring of walls—indicates that in times of peace the Seljuk elite probably preferred their pleasure gardens and their hunting and equestrian sports on the well-watered plain below. Steps ascend to the battlement on the summit. A viewing platform is built on the spot where condemned prisoners and women convicted of adultery were once cast to their deaths. ⚠ **Do not attempt to descend toward ruins including the remains of the monastery on the outer point of the rock, since the mountainside is very treacherous.** ☎ *242/512–3304* 🗺 *$3 for İç Kale and Byzantine church; admission free to other sites* ⏱ *Tues.–Sun. 9-7.*

A minor masterpiece of Mediterranean military architecture, the 100-foot-high **Kızıl Kule** (Red Tower) was built by the Seljuks in 1225 to defend Alanya harbor and the nearby shipyard known as the tersane (arsenal). Sophisticated technology for the time was imported in the form of an architect from Aleppo who was familiar with crusader castle building. The octagonal red brick structure includes finely judged angles of fire for archers manning the loopholes, cleverly designed stairs to cut attackers off, and a series of troughs to convey boiling tar and melted lead onto besieging forces. Nowadays the Red Tower houses a small but interesting ethnographic museum. A short walk south along the water—or along the castle walls, if you prefer—is another defensive tower rising above the tersane, which is made up of five workshops all under an arched roof. Ships could be pulled up under the vaulted stone arches for building or repairs, and the cover was likely also useful for storing war supplies. ⊠*Eastern harbor at south end of İskele Cad.*

Where to Stay & Eat

$$$ ✕ **Kaptan's Filika Restaurant.** Right on Cleopatra's Beach looking up to the citadel towering overhead, this fine restaurant is where real-estate agents take new customers before hustling them off to the close-packed fields of villas and apartment blocks mushrooming on the flanks of the mountains north of town. Special dishes include lamb with rosemary or, ironically, sprinkled with thyme like that which used to grow where the new developments now stand. ⊠ *Güzelyalı Cad.* ☎ *242/513–1094* 🖃 *MC, V.*

★ **$$** ✕ **Red Tower Restaurant.** This is one of Turkey's first microbreweries, and the beer here is some of the best you'll find in the country. You have the choice of a traditional Pilsner, a light and sweeter Helles, a dark Marzen ale, or a wheat beer. The food is more in the nature of bar snacks. Upstairs is the Kale Yolu Et Lokantaı Turkish meat restaurant, which serves classical Turkish food overlooking the Alanya harbor and the Red Tower fortifications. On other floors are a fish restaurant and an international restaurant. On the roof terrace is an open-air Skylounge Bar. All are owned and managed by the same company. ⊠ *Iskele Cad. 80* ☎ *242/513–6664* 🖃 *MC, V.*

$ ✕ **Özsüt Alanya.** This modern, air-conditioned cake shop is the best place in town for restoring lagging caffeine or blood sugar levels—perhaps before an assault on the citadel above. It's part of a modern chain that has expanded rapidly through Turkish cities thanks to the excellent cakes, pastries, and sweets. ⊠ *Çarşı Mah., Iskele Cad., Kamburoğlu Apt. No. 84, Alanya* ☎ *242/512–2202* 🖃 *AE, MC, V.*

$$ 🏨 **Grand Kaptan Hotel** For dependable service and facilities, this seafront hotel, 4 km (2 mi) east of town, is the grandest in Alanya. It's frequented by international tour groups as well as visiting Turkish executives, and the main restaurant is geared toward large numbers of people. The outdoor pool is large and has a swim-up bar. A tunnel takes visitors under the highway to a beach where a barbecue restaurant operates in the summer. The beach lacks natural shade—but there are plenty of beach and water sports to occupy guests, from volleyball to jet skiing, windsurfing, and waterskiing. The rooms are a bit gloomy, and a few don't have private bath. A shuttle operates between the hotel and the town center six times a day. ⊠ *Oba Göl Mevkii* ☎ *242/514–0101* 🖷 *242/514–0092* ⊕ *www.kaptanhotels.com* 📞 *412 rooms, including 8 suites, most with bath* ⚴ *3 restaurants, 4 bars, snack bar, tennis courts, pool, Turkish bath, sauna, beach, fitness center, dive shop, dance club, in-room broadband* 🖃 *AE, MC, V.*

☾ **$$** 🖭 **Iberostar Club Alantur Hotel.** With a white stucco decor theme, wood-panel rooms, and a beach front location 5 km (3 mi) from Alanya, Iberostar's pleasant design and 6.5-acre (16-acre) spread raise it above the standard charter tour hotel. There's even an open fire in the lobby for chilly days in the off season. The management promises a special effort to look after children, but at the other end of the spectrum, the discotheque, open until 1 AM, can be noisy. ⊠ *Dimçay Mevkii, Alanya 07400* ☎ *242/518–1740* 🖷 *242/518–1756* ⊕ *www.iberostar.com* 📞 *355 rooms* ⚴ *Turkish bath, 3 pools, laundry facilities, tennis courts, boating, windsurfing, dive shop, babysitting, hair salon, dance club; some in-room TVs* 🖃 *AE, MC, V* ⑩ *AP.*

¢ 🖭 **Elysée Beach Hotel.** This relatively quiet, clean and modest hotel is on Alanya's Cleopatra Beach, not far from the center of town. The nicest rooms are on the ends of the corridors, overlooking the sea. The air-conditioning only works between June 15 and Sept. 30. ⊠ *Saray Mah., Ataturk Cad. No.145, Alanya, 07400* ☎ *242/512–8791* 🖷 *242/512–8795* ⊕ *www.elyseehotels.com* 📞 *60 rooms* ⚴ *Sauna, Turkish bath, pool, massage, fitness center, hot tub, table tennis* 🖃 *MC, V* ⊗ *Closed Dec. 15–Mar. 1* ⑩ *MAP.*

Nightlife

Alanya's nightlife centers around its harbor and the explosive beat on İskele Caddesi—although there are a few large dance clubs in Dimçay, about 5 km (3mi) outside town. Bars often have extensive menus, and restaurants frequently have live music or turn into impromptu discos after dinner. The Sherwood forest–themed, three-floor **Robin Hood Bar** (⊠ *İskele Cad. 24* ☎ *242/511–7692*) is the biggest on the block; it's open all year round and tries to cater to all tastes. Underneath Robin Hood is the **Amalia Bar** (☎ *537/796–9289*), run by two Dutchmen. The **James Dean Bar** (⊠ İskele Cad. ☎ *242/512–3195*) is popular and less expensive than some of the other haunts on the strip. **Zapf Hahn** (⊠ İskele Cad. ☎ *242/513–8285*) is the spot to go if you like techno.

Near the seafront on the road to Antalya, the **Summer Garden** offers free transport to five people or more from Alanya to it and its sister **Fresco** restaurant, both part of the same complex. The two large bars among the palm trees have a dance floor cooled with outdoor air-conditioning (really!). Open from 6 PM, the music doesn't stop 'til about 4 AM ⊠ *Konaklı Kasabasi, Alanya* ☎ *242/565–0059 or 535/768–1326* ⊗ *Open mid-May–mid-Nov.*

Sports & the Outdoors

Alanya's main beach, also known as Cleopatra's Beach, remains relatively uncrowded except in the height of summer. It's also easy to reach other nearby beaches, coves, and caves by boat. Legend has it that buccaneers kept their most fetching maidens at **Korsanlar Mağarası** (Pirates' Cave) and **Aşıklar Mağarası** (Lovers' Cave), two favorite destinations. Tour boats usually charge from $10 to $20 per person; hiring a private boat, which you can do at the dock near the Red Tower, should cost less than $60—don't be afraid to bargain.

Organized sporting events are new for sweltering, night-life oriented Alanya, but the past few years have seen the advent of **Alanya International Triathlon** (⊕ *alanyatriathlon.anjoni.net*), in the cooler weather of late October. There is also beach volleyball, basketball, handball, and other sporting events, especially in summer. One source of information is the organizer of the triathlon, the Antalya Hoteliers Association, Altid (242/513–4900 www.altid.org).

THE TURQUOISE RIVIERA ESSENTIALS

Transportation

BY AIR

The main airports serving the Turquoise Riviera are in Dalaman and Antalya. Antalya is the busiest international airport in Turkey, serving the coast from Alanya to Kaş, including Side, Belek, Kemer, Olympos, and Finike. Dalaman Airport serves the coast from Kaş to Datça, including Kalkan, Fethiye, Göcek, Dalyan, and Marmaris.

Operators include Turkish Airlines, now facing increasing competition from private newcomers Atlas Jet, Onur Airlines, Pegasus Airlines, Sun Express, and Fly Air. Pegasus Airlines' direct flight from İzmir to Antalya is just one of a number of convenient connections to the south coast that do not transit through Istanbul. The best agency to find international tickets on charter flights from Antalya is Belmondo.

A host of car rental concessions operate at all airports, including all international agencies. Airport buses also link the two airports to major towns. Major hotels and travel agencies will arrange airport shuttles as well. Yellow airport taxis are somewhat expensive for individuals but are usually well regulated with a clear legal pricing system prominently displayed, and are a good option if you're sharing.

If you are traveling by charter, make certain you call to reconfirm your ticket a day or two before departure. Charter companies often change the times of flights by several hours, and do not refund tickets for missed flights.

Taking a bus from Antalya airport into Antalya costs $6 and departs when full, but that's not the case the other way round. Buses to the airport leave the Turkish Airlines building on Cumhuriyet Cad. (on the clifftop boulevard) once every hour or two. Another bus leaves from nearby **Wing Turizm** (☎ 242/244-2236) at even more irregular times.

Yet another option if you're leaving from Antalya main bus station is to take a bus down the highway east of Antalya, get out at the airport intersection, and take one of the taxis waiting there for the last 2 km (1 mi) into the airport itself, for which the taxi charges about $3—it's a bit of a hassle, but something to consider. A taxi to the airport from the center, by comparison, costs $20.

From Dalaman Airport, airport buses will take airline passengers east via Göcek to Fethiye harbor ($12) and west to Marmaris intercity bus terminal ($17). Theoretically, the buses will leave Marmaris three hours before any flight, and Fethiye 2½ hours before. For more precise information, call Havaş, the Dalaman operating representative.

🔲 Airport **Antalya Airport** ☎ 242/330-3234 (international terminal), 242/330-3233 (domestic terminal). **Bodrum Airport** ☎ 252/523-0129. **Dalaman Airport** ☎ 252/792-5291. 🔲 Airlines and other Contacts **Atlas Airlines** ☎ 216/444-3387 call center, 242/243-3040 in Antalya, 252/ ⊕ www.atlasjet.com. **Belmondo Travel** ☎ 242/243-4640 main office in Antalya, 242/330-3949 office in international terminal 1, 242/330-3650 office in international terminal 2 ⊕ www.belmondo.net. **Havaş** ☎ 535/725-9660. **Onur Airlines** ✉ ☎ 212/444-6687 call center (domestic), 212/233-3800 (international), 242/743-0564 in Antalya ⊕ www.onurair.com. **Pegasus Airlines** ✉ ☎ 212/444-0737 (domestic call center), 212/697-7777 (international). ⊕ www.flypgs.com. **Sun Express** ☎ 232/444-0797 call center (domestic), 232/298-7298 (international), 242/323-4047 in Antalya, 252/692-5334 in Dalaman ⊕ www.sunexpress.com.tr. **Turkish Airlines** ☎ 212/663-6363 in Istanbul, 242/243-4383 in Antalya, 252/792-5395 in Dalaman, 252/412-3752 in Marmaris, 252/317-1203 in Bodrum ⊕ www.thy.com.

BY BOAT & FERRY

There are no longer any long-distance ferries serving the southwestern Turkish coast, but a number of ferries link individual Turkish ports with Greek islands. In general, anyone with a U.S. or European passport can visit Greece. Note that you need to be at the boats at least an hour before departure time to complete passport formalities. Be aware that shops and museums on Greek islands usually close during the midday heat and do not reopen until late afternoon, so it's usually sensible to stay a night or two if you are going to take the trouble of making the journey. However, that usually means you will have to buy two separate round-trip tickets.

A weekly car ferry (two hours) links the Greek island of Rhodes with the Turkish port of Marmaris. A major Marmaris agent handling hydrofoil and car ferry tickets to Rhodes is Yesil Marmaris. A day return trip is about $35. Hydrofoils also link Rhodes with Marmaris (50 minutes) and Fethiye (90 minutes).

A car ferry (two hours) links the Bodrum port with Datça's Körmen port (Körmen is run by the Datça port authority but is several km on the other side of the peninsula. In the June–September season, the Bodrum–Datça boats run from both ports at 9 AM and 5 PM. In winter they run just Monday, Wednesday, and Friday, at 9 AM from Datça to Bodrum and at 5 PM from Bodrum to Datça. If taking a car, reserve in advance.

In the summer, a passenger boat leaves every Saturday at about 9 AM from the Greek island of Symi to Datça Harbor, returning at 3:30 PM. On the Turkish side, tickets are negotiated for cash on board, usually less than $30. Remember that if you take this boat over to Symi, you cannot come back the same way for another week.

Another passenger boat runs daily from Kaş to the Greek Island of Kastellorizon, known as Meis in Turkish. This and much else in Kaş can be arranged by Phellos Travel. Passports must be presented by 9 AM for a 10 AM start. The boat returns at about 2 PM. The price of a day return trip is $40.

🚩 **Bodrum Port** ☎ 252/316-0882. **Datça Harbor** ☎ 252/712-2226. **Fethiye Port** ☎ 252/612-3733. **Körmen Port (Datça)** ☎ 252/712-2143. **Marmaris Port** ☎ 252/412-1013. **Phellos Travel** ☎ 242/836-1981 ⊕ www.phellostravel.com. **Yesil Marmaris** ✉ ☎ 252/412 2290 ⊕ www.yesilmarmaris.com.

BY BUS

Intercity buses leave for major holiday resort towns from all over Turkey, and they're not expensive—about $40 one way for the 12-hour journey from Istanbul to Antalya. These days, though, that's only about half the price of flying, which takes a fraction of the time.

Buses and minibuses are a competitive and useful form of short-haul transport within and around the Turquoise Riviera. Every city has an intercity bus terminal, and buses to smaller destinations set off from there. The major ones are in Antalya, Fethiye, and Marmaris. From these hubs smaller minibuses fan out to smaller destinations. Most main roads will see relatively frequent bus traffic during daylight hours, typically charging about $3 per 100 km per person on commercial routes, and non-municipal buses will generally stop anywhere if asked to. Shorter touristic routes, like the 11-km (7-mi) segment from the main road to Olympos or Çiralı can cost double that.

Note that when the intercity bus terminal is outside the city center (as it is in Antalya), it is customary for bus companies to provide minibus service from their city center locations to the station. Ask for a *servis* (minibus transfer service from the city center to the bus station) when you book your ticket, and you'll be given a pickup time from your hotel or the company's downtown office. Otherwise, finding your own way to the terminal can be difficult and time consuming. The Varan Bus Company is more expensive than others, but it has better service, no-smoking buses, and its own privately owned and spotlessly clean rest stops.

🚩 **Antalya Bus Terminal** ☎ 242/331-1250. **Fethiye Bus Terminal** ☎ 256/614-3531. **Marmaris Bus Terminal** ☎ 252/412-3037. **Varan Bus Company** ☎ 212/551-7474 in Istanbul, 242/331-1111 in Antalya.

BY CAR

Although the highways between towns are well maintained, the smaller roads are usually unpaved and rough, and the twisty coastal roads require concentration. To estimate driving times, figure on about 70 km (43 mi) per hour. By car from Istanbul to Marmaris or Antalya is at least a 10-hour, 750-km (470-mile) trek.

Many roads on the south coast are currently being upgraded, which makes things even more dangerous for now. You will be lulled into a sense of false security on a fine four-lane highway, and then, just as you've turned your head to look at a castle, the road will, with almost no warning, divert onto a gravel feeder road. The speed limit is 90 km/h on most country roads—120 km/h on real highways—and for your own safety it's best to stick to it. The police do have radars and they do use them.

Although driving in Turkey can be challenging, there are lots of reasons for driving yourself. The Turquoise Riviera is full of beautiful drives, principally the sweeping mountain highway between Antalya and Fethiye, the coast road that links the same two towns but follows the Lycian coast line, and the drive from Fethiye to Datça. Also, many sites are well off the main road, so if you don't have your own car, you'll always be at the mercy of travel agents and other tourists.

All airports have several car rental associations to choose from, and many hotels can arrange car rentals. In general, the smaller and more remote the place, the cheaper the rental, but the more minimal the service.

BY TAXI AND DOLMUŞ
Provincial taxis are somewhat expensive, but as everywhere in Turkey, they are clearly marked by their bright yellow color and rooftop sign. Fares generally work out somewhere near $1 per km traveled. It's best to take a taxi from an established taxi stand, where you see several lined up, since the drivers there will be regulars and if you should have a dispute or lose something, it is much easier to retrace the car that way. It is normal, however, to hail taxis in the street. For longer journeys, you may both wish to settle a price in advance, but normally, within city limits, the taxi driver should automatically switch on the meter when you get in. If he doesn't, insist upon it—say the words "*saatınız, lütfen.*" If that doesn't work, then start taking down his number and tell him you're going to report him to the tourism police.

Tipping is not usual, beyond rounding up to the nearest lira. Drivers are not allowed to charge extra per passenger, and they're not supposed to charge per piece of luggage, but a pile of suitcases will usually inspire a request for a tip.

BY TRAIN
Other than the tram that runs every half-hour along the Antalya sea front between Lara and the Museum, there are no train services on the Turquoise Riviera.

Contacts & Resources

BANKS & EXCHANGING SERVICES
The currency of choice on the Turquoise Riviera is cash, either the New Turkish Lira, euros, or American dollars. Traveler's checks are not a good idea in most places, since banks and currency offices may charge up to 10% of the face value to change them into local currency.

Probably the cheapest and safest way of funding your holiday is to take a mix of a few hundred dollars in cash for emergencies and a debit card from a major bank that works internationally through a network like Cirrus. With this you can withdraw money directly from the many cash machines dotted through the larger towns in the region, and your bank will typically charge you about 1% of the total for the convenience. Note, however, that small towns and villages rarely have such machines.

American Express is disliked and not taken in much of the region since it charges a larger than usual cut from merchants. Visa and MasterCard are widely accepted, but be aware that both subject you, the cardholder, to charges of 3% or more for each foreign currency transaction. The merchant also pays a similar sum. If you use cash, this will almost always award you a 10% discount in shops.

Remember, too, that most waiters, rug merchants, and other shopkeepers will open the bidding in a bargaining session with their perception of what you seem able to afford, not what the intrinsic value of the item or service is.

In an emergency, money wired to you from the U.S. will generally reach a Turkish bank branch for you to pick up within 48 hours, and even faster to banks that work with the Western Union money transfer system (choose the nearest one with the signature black and yellow sign). You will, however, need ID to pick the money up.

EMERGENCIES
If you need the police, call 155. They should be able to patch you through to an English-speaking person, but it may be helpful to have a Turkish speaker nearby.

If you're feeling ill and need a doctor, the best option is to take a taxi and ask for the *hastane,* or hospital, in the nearest town, where doctors and specialists can be found. A *poliklinik,* essentially a group of doctors that can treat most ailments, will usually also deal with first aid. In an emergency, head for the ACIL SERVIS, or emergency service, entrance of the hospital or clinic. If you need an ambulance, call the hospital to send one of theirs or call 112, although these ambulances will take you to a state hospital (*Devlet Hastanesi*) and the preferred choice is, almost always, one of the many private hospitals that have sprung up in most towns, since they have higher standards and are more likely to have English speakers. A doctor will see you for a cost of between $40 and $70, plus medicines. The state hospitals are cheaper and basically competent, but doctors are harassed, and visiting the emergency ward can be like arriving in a war zone.

If you need more medicine for an existing condition, and know its exact name, it's good to know that written prescriptions are not as necessary in Turkey as elsewhere, and you may be able to buy it directly from the *eczane,* or pharmacy. These are usually found in town centers, and if closed, will note the nearest local on-duty pharmacy on a sign in the window. Once there, patiently ring on the duty pharmacy's door—the pharmacist is usually asleep in the back.

🖪 Emergency Contacts **Ambulance** ☎ 112. **Police** ☎ 155.

🖪 Hospitals **Alanya Özel Hayat Hastanesi** ✉ Şekerhane district ☎ 242/512–4251. **Interhospital Antalya International Hospital** ✉ 933rd Cad. Kızıltoprak, behind PTT ☎ 242/311–1500. **Özel Antalya Hayat Kalp Hastanesi (for heart specialists)** ✉ 325th

Cad. No. 8, Bayındır District ☎ 242/335–0000. **Datça Devlet Hastanesi** ☎ 252/712–3082. **Özel Esnaf Hospital (Fethiye)** ☎ 252/612–6400. **Kaş Devlet Hastanesi** ✉ In center of town ☎ 242/836–1185. **Kemer Anadolu Hastanesi** ✉ Atatürk Bulvaı ☎ 242/814–5970. **Kumluca Develet Hastanesi** ✉ on hill east of town ☎ 242/887–1480. **Ahu Hetman (Marmaris)** ☎ 252/413–8801. **Medicus (Side)** ✉ Kemer ☎ 242/753–1111.

INTERNET, MAIL & SHIPPING

Clearly marked Internet cafés can be found in town centers and in some hotels all along the Turquoise Riviera. Many of the better hotels are installing wireless connections as well. Broadband is becoming available even in surprisingly out-of-the-way places like Olympos. Nowhere are connection speeds blazingly fast.

Mail is sent through post offices marked with a yellow PTT sign. The service is not very reliable, though. If you want to be sure mail will arrive, send it registered mail, which is only slightly more expensive.
🖪 **Fedex** ✉ Şelale Cad. No. 12, off airport road in Sinan district, Antalya ☎ 242/444–0505. **DHL** ✉ Portakal Çiçeği Bulvari No. 27/A, Yeşilbahçe Mah., Antalya ☎ 242/444–0040.

TOUR OPTIONS

GENERAL INTEREST Overall, tours are best booked through your hotel's favored travel agency, assuming you trust your hotel. Otherwise take a walk round the center of the town or resort where you are, and you're sure to see at least five agencies. Chat with the ones you like the look of, then choose the one you like best; by then you'll have a good idea of what's on offer and what's being charged.

From Antalya, Belek, or Side, it's worth seeing the antique ruins of Termessos, Aspendos, Perge, and Side. These are some of the best preserved classical sites in Turkey. You can drive there in your own car, hire a guide, or join an organized tour.

A Blue Cruise by chartered yacht along any of the sections of coast is always delightful.

HISTORY AND RELIGION There is growing interest in the Christian history of the south coast of Turkey, particularly due to its association with **St. Paul,** who evangelized the area. A trekking route known as the **St. Paul Trail** has been laid out taking in some places he is known to have passed through. Kate Clow, the woman who pioneered the Lycian Way route, has now waymarked the wilder and more remote route of this 400-km (250-mi) trail. There isn't much organized travel on this trail—a guide isn't really necessary and the trekkers are usually independent—but Middle Earth Travel arranges tours. More traditional week-long bus tours look at Christian sites in the Antalya area and then go on to Ephesus, where St. Paul preached in the theater. More information can be had from Paul's Place in Antalya.

Another site of religious interest is the Basilica of St. Nicholas, the 4th-century AD bishop of Myra, now Demre, whose good works gave rise to the legends that became **Father Christmas.** It's a long day tour from

Antalya, involving a four-hour drive, but very popular with Russian Orthodox visitors. Tours are available from almost all town-center tour operators.
🚗 **Middle Earth Travel** ☎ 384/271-2528 🖷 384/271-2562 ⊕ www.middleearthtravel. com. **Paul's Place** ☎ 242/247-6857.

OUTDOOR
ACTIVITIES

Trekking opporunities abound in this part of Turkey. For serious walkers, the 530-km (331-mi) Lycian Way is the standing challenge. If you prefer to have guided company, tailor-made or as part of a group, a good specialized agency is Middle Earth Travel.

Other ways to enjoy the wonderful landscape of the Mediterranean hinterland is to go rafting or trekking in three main areas—around Fethiye and Ölüdeniz, in Köprülü National Park near Antalya, and along Alanya's Dimçay River. You'll pass through soaring canyons and under ancient Roman bridges.

The Alraft Rafting and Riding Club, in Alanya, arranges rafting trips, as well as horseback riding treks. Also in Antalya are Medraft and TransNature, both outdoor-sports specialists. In Fethiye, Aventura specializes in all kinds of activities, including paragliding from Mt. Babadağ. In Side, Get Wet can arrange all kinds of outdoor activities such as rafting, trekking, and mountaineering.
🚗 **Alraft Rafting and Riding Club** ☎ 242/513-9155. **Aventura** ☎ 252/616-6427. **Get Wet** ☎ 242/753-4071. **Medraft** ☎ 242/312-5770. **Middle Earth Travel** ☎ 384/271-2528 🖷 384/271-2562 ⊕ www.middleearthtravel.com. **TransNature** ☎ 242/247-8688.

VISITOR INFORMATION
Two provinces of Turkey straddle the Turquoise Riviera: Antalya in the east and Muğla in the west (the dividing line is between Fethiye and Kalkan). Visitor information offices work for these two provinces during normal office hours and vary greatly in the quality of help they can give you. A veteran official by the name of Ihsan Tarhan in Antalya, for instance, will share his encyclopedic knowledge of the province, and official Ayten Aydının Dalyan will photocopy her own handwritten synthesis of all available information. Others will at best load a visitor up with picture brochures that tell you only slightly more than the average guidebook. Exceptions to this are the good guide to the sites of Antalya province run by the provincial governorate on ⊕ www.antalya.gov.tr and the usefully detailed official guidebook to Muğla Province available in most tourism information offices in that Province.
🚗 Official tourist offices: **Alanya** ✉ Damlataş Cad. 1 ☎ 242/513-1240 🖷 242/513-5436. **Antalya** ✉ Cumhuriyet Cad., In little booth opposite former offices in tall white official building abandoned after road blasting operations cracked its columns ☎ 242/241-1747. **Dalaman** ✉ At airport ☎ 252/692-5220. **Dalyan** ✉ Cumhuriyet Mey., Maraş Cad. No. 15 ☎ 252/284-4235. **Datça** ✉ Hükümet Binası, İskele Mah. ☎ 252/712-3163 🖷 252/712-3546. **Fethiye** ✉İskele Karşısı 1 🖷🖷 252/614-1527. **Kaş** ✉ Cumhuriyet Meyd. 5 🖷🖷 242/836-1238. **Kemer** ✉ Under the belediye, or city hall ☎ 242/814-1112. **Köycegiz** ✉ Atatürk Kordonu ☎ 252/262-4703. **Marmaris** ✉ İskele Meyd. 2, by marina ☎ 252/412-1035 🖷 252/412-7277. **Side** ✉ Side Yolu Üzeri, Manavgat ☎ 242/753-1265 🖷 242/753-2657.

Central Anatolia: Cappadocia, Ankara & the Turkish Heartland

WORD OF MOUTH

"Our original plan didn't include Konya, but we ended up making a 1-day stop there, and were glad we did. Konya is no traditional tourist town, but a holy place for Muslims, where the great mystic Rumi lived and where the whirling dervishes originated."

–progol

WELCOME TO CENTRAL ANATOLIA

Göreme valley

TOP REASONS TO GO

★ **Hike the valleys of Cappadocia** Trails lead past fantastic rock formations and to cave entrances that open on ornately decorated churches.

★ **Balloon over Cappadocia** Dangling high above the forested, rock-littered valleys in a basket, you'll sail past rock cones and fairy chimneys.

★ **Explore underground cities** Kaymaklı, Derinkuyu, and the other subterranean complexes are vast, multi-storied, equipped with kitchens, sewage systems, and stables, and once housed tens of thousands of inhabitants.

★ **Luxuriate in a cave** Some of Cappadocia's finest hotels are tucked into elaborately appointed caves, where soft lighting, fireplaces, and even Jacuzzis are common amenities.

★ **See the dervishes whirl** In Konya dervishes whirl in graceful spinning dances as a way to fill themselves with love, the essence of the divine.

Pottery making in Avanos

1 Cappadocia The weirdest natural landscape you're ever likely to see is a giant outdoor sculpture garden of elaborate cones, needles, pillars, and pyramids. As if these natural phenomena weren't enticing enough, hundreds of caves harbor elaborately frescoed churches from the early days of Christianity.

2 Konya One of Turkey's most popular pilgrimage sites houses a shrine to the 13th-century philosopher Rumi and is home to the whirling dervishes. Elegant mosques and seminaries enhance the holiness of the place.

3 Ankara & the Hittite Cities. Turkey's capital is home to the enduring legacy of Atatürk, founding father of the secular Turkish Republic. On the barren dusty steppe beyond the city are scattered the ancient ruined sites of the once mighty Hittite Empire. North of Ankara is Safranbolu, one of the best-preserved Ottoman-era towns in Turkey.

GETTING ORIENTED

Central Anatolia stretches across a vast, arid plateau, littered with the ruins of ancient civilizations, slashed by ravines in places and rising to the peaks of extinct volcanoes in others. Think of the region as a triangle, with Ankara, Turkey's sprawling capital, to the northwest; Cappadocia, the land of surrealistic geological formations to the northeast; and Konya, the city where the dervishes whirl, to the south, en route to Antalya and the Mediterranean Coast.

5

The Anıtkabir (Ataturk's mausoleum) in Ankara

CENTRAL ANATOLIA PLANNER

Getting Here & Around

Cappadocia and Central Anatolia are well served by intercity buses, which are modern and quite comfortable, but the distances are long. Air travel isn't much more expensive, though, so flying to Ankara will save a lot of time. Once you're here, renting a car is a good idea since you'll probably be traveling around a lot.

Best Walks in Cappadocia

The most memorable experiences you're likely to have in Cappadocia are hikes through the valleys, clambering up tall, soft rock formations that rise in endlessly entertaining forms. Even guides profess that they never cease to be amazed by the strange, mystical beauty of the landscape. These are some favorites:

Rose Valley (Güllüdere), where cave entrances lead to multi-story, ornately decorated churches.

Love Valley (Aşk Vadisi), perhaps named for the preponderance of phallus-looking rock protrusions.

Ilhara Valley, with a cluster of fresco-decorated churches above a river valley.

Soğanlı Kaya Kiliseleri, where you'll likely be alone to explore hundreds of dwellings and churches cut into the cliffs.

When to Go

In Cappadocia especially you'll probably be spending most of your time outdoors, so weather is important. Much of Central Anatolia is blazing hot in summer, freezing cold and all but impossible in winter. The best time to visit is early spring (May) before the crowds and heat come, or early fall (September), when the crowds are gone and winter hasn't yet arrived. You'll also enjoy Ankara more at these times—a college and government town, it's more alive when school and parliament are in session; in summer, those who can get out of town do, sucking much of the life out of an already listless city.

How Much Time Do You Need?

In Cappadocia, you can see the open-air museums and major valleys in two days, but you may well want to spend several more days soaking in the enchanting landscapes and enjoying the region's comfortable lodgings.

Don't go out of your way to spend vacation time in Ankara, but if you do find yourself here, while away a day in the city's few worthwhile sights, most notably the highly regarded Archaeological Museum, repository of the best archaeological treasures found in Turkey, and Atatürk's Mausoleum, the Anıtkabir. The capital also provides a logical base for exploring the ancient ruined sites of the Hittite Empire, which are contained within a triangle in northeastern Central Anatolia bounded by Hattuşa, Yazılıkaya, and Alacahöyük.

All the Hittite cities can be seen in a day trip from Ankara if you have a car. You can see Konya's famous museums, mosques, and seminaries in half a day, and you may want to use the city as a stopping off point if you're traveling between Cappadocia and Antalya or elsewhere on the Mediterranean coast.

Anatolian Eating

Central Anatolia is the one region in Turkey that does not touch water, so fish has to be trucked or flown in. Be prepared for a lot of meat; that means kebabs and lamb, often with yogurt and tomato sauce. In Konya you'll encounter *etli ekmek*, flatbread topped with ground lamb and spices, and you'll find *lahmacum*, a kind of flatbread Turkish pizza, throughout the region. Main courses are usually preceded by a delicious array of mezes, which here often include hot humus and pastırma (Turkish pastrami). If your waiter doesn't speak English, ask for the *meze tepsisi* (may-zay tep-see-see) and a tray of fresh appetizers should apear post haste.

Restaurants that cater to tourists serve beer, wine (which is produced locally in Cappadocia, with questionable results—try the Kalecik Karası or the Öküzgüzü, both reds), and liquor (including rakı, the aniseed Turkish liqueur beloved by Atatürk). In Konya and other more conservative towns, though, you might be hard pressed to find a drink. Whatever you eat and drink, you'll find it easy to dine in atmospheric surroundings—restored kervansarays, caves, Ottoman mansions, white-washed courtyards. In many restaurants you'll sit on cushions on the floor, and your meal may well be accompanied by live music.

Dress is casual in all but a very few restaurants in Ankara, reservations are rarely required, and credit cards widely but not always accepted—American Express poses a particular problem. Have cash on hand.

WHAT IT COSTS

IN CENTRAL ANATOLIA OUTSIDE ANKARA

	$$$$	$$$	$$	$	¢
Restaurants	over $25	$16–25	$11–15	$5–10	under $5
Hotels	over $250	$151–250	$76–150	$51–75	under $50

IN ANKARA

	$$$$	$$$	$$	$	¢
Restaurants	over $30	$21–30	$13–20	$8–12	under $8
Hotels	over $250	$201–250	$151–200	$100–150	under $100

Restaurant prices are for one main course at dinner or for two mezes (small dishes). Hotel prices are for two people in a double room in high season, including taxes.

Shopping Tips

You'll have to bargain in Central Anatolia, but haggling is not difficult. The general rule is to take something home for about half of what a merchant offers. Do not buy anything when you're on a group tour, or even while one is around—merchants admit their prices shoot up to twice what they should be, because guides ask for big commissions.

Good souvenirs to bring home from the region include the following:

Pottery, especially in Avanos

Onyx, sold across Cappadocia

Rugs and kilms, available everywhere, with an especially good selection in Kayseri, where they're made

Hand-crafted jewelry, found in most towns

Bazaars, always fun places to shop; those in Kayseri and Konya are especially atmospheric.

Guide or No Guide?

Guides make themselves known at the entrances to mosques and museums throughout Central Anatolia and can add a lot to a visit. (Tourist offices and hotels can also recommend reputable guides; expect to pay about $25–$60 a day.) They can often explain the significance of what you encounter and are helpful in interpreting signs, often in Turkish only. Inevitably, they have a family member who just happens to run a carpet, pottery, or jewelry shop. Don't dismiss these opportunities out of hand—a visit to a relative's shop often provides a chance for some genuine communication.

If You Have 3 Days

If you have only a short time to visit Central Anatolia, limit your visit to **Cappadocia** and make the best use of your time while there. You'll probably be sorry you didn't allot more days for the trip, but you'll get a good taste for the wonders this part of the world has to offer and be eager to come back. Fly to **Kayseri** in the morning, pick up a car if you're going to drive (the easiest way to see the region), and head to your hotel. **Avanos, Ürgüp, Göreme,** and **Uçhisar** are all nice places to stay, with a selection of good hotels—some unique and wonderful places to stay—and within easy reach of the valleys and other sights. Have lunch in the town in which you're staying, then head off to see the **Open Air Museums at Göreme and Zelve.** Remember, you're trying to pack a lot into a few days, so save some strength and leave enough time to head into the **Rose Valley** from Göreme so you can be at Paşabağı, the amazing monastic settlement carved into fairy chimneys, around sunset. On day two, wake up early and take a half- or full-day guided walk through **Rose Valley, Love Valley,** or some of the other fairy chimney valleys—this trek will probably be the highlight of the trip, and a guide will

add a lot to the experience. If you have time, and try to make sure you do, check out the underground city at **Derinkuyu** before plopping down in a cave bar for a drink. On your last day, and it will be hard to believe your time here is over when there's so much more to see and do, take a ride in a hot-air balloon—that is, if you're willing to wake up in the predawn hours and part with a hefty hunk of change. Few who make these sacrifices regret the experience. Spend what remains of your time here climbing **Uçhisar Castle** or checking out **Avanos** and its pottery shops.

If You Have 7 Days

A week gives you a generous amount of time to see the region, but you'll still want to spend as much of this time as you can in Cappadocia. Depending on how you're approaching the region, you might want to stop briefly in **Ankara** or **Konya.** A visit to the capital, easily reached from Istanbul by plane, allows you to tour the **Ankara Museum of Anatolian Civilizations,** which will give you a good background for all the history you'll see in the fields later, and the **Anıtkabir, Atatürk's Mausoleum,** for a better understanding of modern Turkey. You can see both

in a day, and that's all the time you will want to spend in Ankara. On the second day, join a guided archaeological tour of the **Hittite cities,** then head off to Cappadocia. If you're coming to Central Anatolia from Antalya and the Mediterranean Coast or from Pamukkale and İzmir on the Aegean Coast, you will pass through **Konya.** You might not want to spend more than an afternoon in this rather unattractive and dull city, but you'll probably enjoy visiting the **Mevlâna Museum** and the city's notable mosques and museums. Once you reach Cappadocia, follow the three-day itinerary above. You'll have a little extra time and the chance to take it easy and simply enjoy the fantastic landscapes or just hang out in your cave. You may want to make the trip to **Soğanlı Kaya Kiliseleri,** where you're likely to be alone to explore hundreds of rock dwellings and churches cut into the cliffs, and also down to the **Ihlara Valley,** where churches are cut into a cliff face above a river. You may also find yourself with one day of leisure, and one of the best ways to spend a relaxing day in Cappadocia is to hike into a valley, do a little climbing and exploring, and enjoy a picnic.

Revised and
Updated by
Benjamin
Harvey

Across the vast and mostly featureless steppes, the reminders of Central Anatolia's tumultuous past are generally few and far between—an abandoned kervansaray on the side of a road, a crumbling Greek church in a Muslim town, a Bronze Age city's ruins scattered across a picturesque valley. But the treasures of the region—both in museums and in the open fields—point to great battles and fearsome sieges, civilizations rising and being laid low, to constant flux since the dawn of civilized man. Some of the oldest known human settlements were established on the dusty, mostly treeless hills and valleys of Central Anatolia. The region hosts the accumulated history of some 11,000 years of human inhabitation, a claim matched by few other places on earth.

Today Central Anatolia's primary attraction, though, is not a shrine to past civilizations but to the whimsy of nature. The outer-space landscape of Cappadocia is one of the world's unique delights, an odd and beautiful wonderland where some people still live in caves. You'll discover unimaginable rock formations, spectacular valleys, ancient cave churches, and underground cities. As a traveler with limited time in Central Anatolia, we recommend you head straight for Cappodocia. Few people leave uncharmed.

Ankara, the modern, secular capital city of the Turkish Republic, is not terribly attractive or alluring, but it is here that the secular identity of this 99 percent Muslim nation was fashioned and where its future—perhaps in the European Union—continues to be debated. Within driving distance from the capital are the Hittite cities around Hattuşaş, as well as countless villages that are uniquely Turkish in character and stuck in time in a way that only remote villages can be.

CAPPADOCIA

Cappadocia comprises the triangle of land formed by the towns of Neveshir to the west, Ürgüp to the east, and Avanos in the north. Inside this triangle is one of the weirdest natural landscapes you're ever likely to see. More than 10 million years ago, three volcanoes began a geological symphony in Cappadocia that dropped lava, mud, and ash all over the region. Over eons, the explosive products of Mt. Erciyes, Mt. Hasan, and Mt. Melendiz cooled and compressed to form tufa, a soft, porous rock easily worn by erosion. Water poured down, carving and separating giant ridges of rock. Wind whipped around the formations, further shaping them into elaborate cones, needles, pillars

WHAT CREATED CAPPADOCIA'S "FAIRY CHIMNEYS"?

The volcanoes that formed Cappadocia are inactive now, but the most recent of them may have erupted just 8,000 years ago; Neolithic humans depicted the eruption in cave dwellings at Çatal Höyük. Nature continues to sculpt the landscapes of Cappadocia. Several millennia from now, some of the formations you see will be ground to dust by wind and water, while others will be newly separated from the mountains.

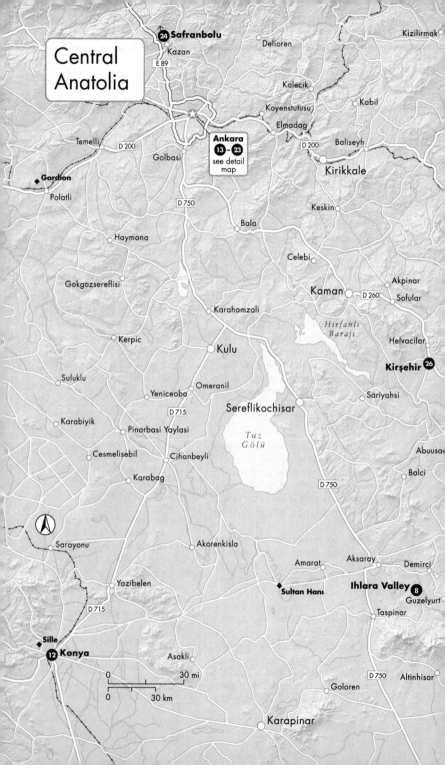

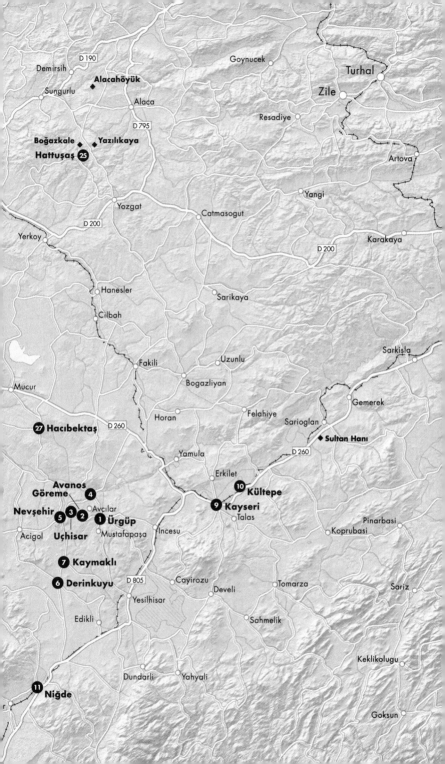

and pyramids. Harder layers of rock like basalt resisted erosion longer, and often ended up perfectly balanced, like hats, on top of a tall cone. Oxidation gave the formations color, and then humans began to do their own carving and shaping.

In effect, the region has become a giant outdoor sculpture garden. The valleys here are full of so-called "fairy chimneys," rock formations in improbable shapes of cones and enormous spires. Walks through these valleys are unforgettable; you might feel like you're wandering around on another planet. One of the great pleasures of being in Cappadocia is that you still often feel like you're a lone explorer here. Mystical experiences are not uncommon for those hiking across these valleys of wild geological formations.

Indeed, Cappadocia has an undeniable spiritual side, and its natural endowment is only part of the attraction. The region is thought to have been occupied by the Hittites, who worshipped sun gods and first came to power in Anatolia 4,000 years ago. Tiberius claimed Cappadocia as a province of Rome in AD 17, and the early Christians, who more than anyone else have left a human mark on Cappadocia, settled in the region about the same time.

The Christians who established secluded communities here apparently found the otherworldy landscape suitable both to their aesthetic tastes and to their need to hide from persecution. They sat on Cappadocia's rock pillars for years at a time in prayer and carved hundreds of churches into the inside of soft rocks, decorating them with beautiful frescoes. You can still explore these churches, and by the end of a trip you won't be surprised when you duck into a nondescript cave entrance and find carved columns, a domed roof, and vivid frescoes.

Arab raiders also came into the region in the seventh and eighth centuries, forcing the inhabitants into another burst of architectural creativity, this time digging entire cities underground for shelter. It's believed that many sprawling underground complexes have yet to be discovered, and the true extent of some of those that can be explored is still unknown.

Cappadocia remains an exotic place in other ways, too. You'll see local residents traveling between farms and shops in horse-drawn carts. Women drape their houses with strings of apricots and paprika for drying in the sun, and nomadic workers pitch their tents beside sunflower fields and cook on fires that send smoke billowing through the tent tops. In the distance, minarets pierce the sky. Even the hotels are exotic—many occupy caves, and are some of the most delightfully unusual lodgings in which you'll ever stay.

Ürgüp

 80 km(48 mi) west of Kayseri airport, 300 km (180 mi) south of Ankara, 725 km (435 mi) southeast of Istanbul.

Ürgüp is a logical base for exploring the surrounding towns, with a central location, a busy (for Cappadocia) town center, and several excellent hotels. The town is a fairly tacky jumble of buildings built up entirely for the tourism industry, though it's a good place place to find banks, money exchanges, travel agencies, trinket shops, and even a Turkish bath and a few nightclubs. In summer the streets are filled with tourists haggling in myriad languages over "antique" copper and "old" kilims (you're unlikely to find real antiques) or hanging out in cafés in the central square. Clustered around the outskirts of the dusty tourist town are beautiful old stone houses, many of which have

> ### SPEECHLESS IN CAPPADOCIA
>
> Travelers quickly find themselves running out of words to describe Cappadocia's landscapes. Here are some of the more common ones: bizarre, unreal, otherworldly, unique, weird, strange, comic, sublime, lunar, mystic, cosmic, alien, phallic, exhilarating, extraordinary. They're all true, as you'll see for yourself.

been converted into hotels with windows that open onto breathtaking vistas of serrated white cliffs dotted with manmade caves.

Ürgüp's **Turasan Winery,** one of the region's largest producers, offers free tours with wine tastings. Cappadocians have been making wine for thousands of years, though critics would say they're still not very good at it. Overall, as you'll soon learn, Cappadocia's wine is drinkable if not delicious, affordable and omnipresent—and vineyards add even more to the scenery. ⊠ *Cimenli Mevkii, Ürgüp* ☉ *Daily 8–5* ☎ *384/341–4961.*

Where to Stay & Eat

$ ✕ **Şömine.** Right on the main square, this welcoming lair takes its name from the fireplace that warms guests in winter; in summer, you can dine outside on the terrace. In any season, the typical Turkish cuisine is well prepared and well priced. ⊠ *On the main square, Cumhuriyet Meydani* ☎ *384/341–8442* ▭ *AE, MC, V.*

¢–$ ✕▦ **Old Greek House.** About 5 km (3 mi) outside Ürgüp in the little vil-
Fodor'sChoice   lage of Mustafapasa, the Old Greek House offers one of the best meals
★   and pleasant dining experiences in Cappadocia, with fresh, delicious home-cooked specialties served at a large round table with seating on floor cushions. Reservations are recommended. The lodgings are simple but comfortable. ⊠ *Sinasos, Mustafapasa* ☎ *384/353–5306* ⊟ *384-353–5141* ⊕ *www.oldgreekhouse.com* ⇗ *16 rooms* ⚑ *No a/c, no phones, no TVs, no elevator* ▭ *MC, V.*

★   ▦ **Esbelli Evi.** Owner Suha Ersoz started buying up a neighborhood of
$$ houses carved into a rocky hillside in 1987, and the inn he created from them consists of 10 standard rooms and 5 suites that are actually elegant little houses, with separate gardens and terraces, sitting rooms, and giant bathrooms with double-headed showers and clawfoot tubs. Suha encourages guests to linger in the stone- and vaulted-ceiling drawing room and on the breezy terraces and chat with one another, and he also welcomes children. ⊠ *Esbelli Sok. 8, P.O. Box 2, Ürgüp* ☎ *384/341–3395* ⊟ *384/341–8848* ⊕ *www.esbelli.com* ⇗ *10 rooms, 5 suites* ⚑ *Restaurant, no elevator* ▭ *AE, MC, V.*

Christianity in Cappadocia

CENTURIES AGO, the number one industry in large parts of Cappdocia was praying; it went along with hiding. A sizable Christian community had blossomed in Cappadocia within 200 years after the death of Jesus, and regional bishoprics were established in Kayseri and Malatya. The earliest Christians practiced their faith secretly, in cellars and caves, and even after the region was administered by the Christian emperors of the Eastern Roman, or Byzantine Empire, Cappadocia remained a frontier province subject to regular invasions by non-Christian armies and hordes. This forced the Christian communities here to hide their churches in hollowed-out caves and to build vast underground cities for shelter during times of hardship, leaving us some most fascinating and mysterious legacies of Cappadocia's past.

The oldest surviving churches date to the 6th century, but most churches were built between the 9th and 12th centuries, when Christian fresco art also flourished. St. Basil of Kayseri, St. Gregory of Nyssa, and St. George of Cappadocia, the patron saint of England, all lived and worshiped here. Basil was responsible for many of the monastic settlements in the region, as he established small, secluded communities of Christians far from the towns. From the 7th to the 10th centuries, the Christian Cappadocians were under near-constant siege from Arab raiders, and they are believed to have taken refuge in about 40 underground cities.

In other parts of Turkey, St. Peter, St. Paul, St. John, and St. Nicholas preached or set up churches. Letters to the Seven Churches of the Revelation were all addressed to religious communities in Turkey, and the first ecumenical councils were held in Nicea, present-day İznik. The Virgin Mary is also said to have traveled to Turkey with St. John and to have died somewhere near Ephesus.

$$–$$$ **Sacred House.** Each room in this 250-year-old Greek mansion con-
Fodor'sChoice   verted into a dark, Gothic-style castle hotel is like its own elegant mas-
★   ter chamber and feels like something a rich and debonair vampire might love. The owner says he likes to pick who gets to stay in his rooms, which are very comfortable but intense, with dark wood, lots of reds and deep browns, incense and candles, arched ceilings, fireplaces, and gorgeous Gothic-style carved doors; many baths are equipped with Jacuzzis. A little vial of cinnamon liqueur and shot glasses greet you upon arrival. ⊠ *Karahandere Mah. Barbaros Hayrettin Sok. 25* ☎ *384/341–7102* 🖷 *384/341–6986* ⊕ *www.sacred-house.com* 🛏 *7 rooms* ⌂ *Restaurant, bar; no elevator* ▤ *MC, V.*

$$ **Kilim Hotel.** This small, pleasant hotel is not as luxurious as some of its neighbors, but a central location, friendly staff, clean rooms, and large breakfast make it a good value. The best deals here are on the rooms in the front, with their spacious balconies. ⊠ *Dumlupinar Cad. 47* ☎ *384/341–3131* 🖷 *384/341–5058* ⊕ *www.hotelkilim.com* 🛏 *15 rooms* ⌂ *Restaurant, bar; no a/c, no elevator* ▤ *No credit cards.*

$$ ⬚ **Ürgüp Evi.** Soft lighting, fireplaces, and big, comfortable beds make these rooms in a cave extremely comfortable and pleasant, and the views from the hillside perch are extensive. The courtyard, lined with pillow-covered seats, is a fine place to enjoy a bottle of wine and watch the sunset. ⬚ *Esbelli Mah. 54* ☎ *384/341–3173* 🖷 *384/341–6269* ⊕ *www.urgupevi.com.tr* ⬚ *12 rooms, 2 suites* ⬚ *Restaurant, bar; no a/c, no elevator* ⊟ *AE, MC, V.*

★ ⬚ **Yunak Evleri.** A cave can really be quite luxurious, as the rooms with
$$–$$$ wood floors, antique furniture, and chairs covered by Turkish or Central Asian carpets, and very nice bathrooms at this hotel built into the side of a cliff prove; several open to terraces overlooking the town. Alcoholic drinks are available on the honor system, and meals can be served upon request in a private dining room. ⬚ *Yunak Mah.* ☎ *384/341–6920* 🖷 *384/341-6924* ⊕ *www.yunak.com* ⬚ *23 rooms, 6 suites* ⬚ *Restaurant, DVD; no a/c, no phones, no TVs, no elevator* ⊟ *AE, MC, V.*

Göreme

❷ *7 km (4 mi) northwest of Ürgüp.*

This bustling town with a cluster of restaurants and hotels is the most convenient base for exploring Cappadocia. Göreme is more or less inundated with backpackers, who find plenty of inexpensive lodgings, though some nicer hotels are in operation, too. There are Internet cafés in the main square, and a used book shop stocks a surprisingly good collection of foreign titles. You can live cheap and meet other travelers in Göreme, but the reason to be here is to see some of the most spectacular fairy chimney valleys in the region and the open air museums here and at nearby Zelve, both UNESCO World Heritage Sites.

One of the most rewarding walks from Göreme is through the **Rose Valley (Güllüdere),** where cave entrances lead to multistory, ornately decorated churches with columns that are two or three stories high. Roman graves, now unreachable, are adorned with Christian crosses and sit high upon eroded fairy chimneys. A hike through the valley often ends up at **Paşabağı,** the great monastic settlement of fairy chimneys (see the back of the Turkish 50-lira note for a picture). There are also spectacular hikes through **Love Valley (Aşk Vadisi),** perhaps named for the preponderance of phallus-looking rock protrusions.

The Open-Air Museums at Göreme and Zelve

These outdoor museums are the two requisite must-sees of Cappadocia and are normally packed with tourists. Göreme is a fairy-chimney valley famous for its spectacular cave churches. Zelve is a large cave community about 6 km (4 mi) away and provides a fascinating glimpse into how people lived in the rock-cut communities.

Göreme Açik Hava Müzesi (Göreme Open Air Museum). In summer get an early start to beat the heat and the crowds, who jam these fresco-filled spaces by midday. Or go after 5 PM, when it's cool and the crowds have thinned. The museum covers a large area with hundreds of caves, nooks, and crannies to explore, almost all of them easily reachable on paved paths.

The museum is a UNESCO World Heritage Site because of its spectacular landscape and the amazing collection of cave churches with Byzantine frescoes. The oldest rock church here dates from the 4th century. Frescoes first appeared around the 8th century, when the geometric designs directly applied to the rock face gradually gave way to scenes from the New Testament and the lives of the saints, all painted on plaster.

> ## "CAVE" DWELLINGS & CHURCHES
>
> Many of the sites you'll see in Cappadocia are man-made structures carved out of the soft rock. You'll commonly hear the structures called caves, because that's what they feel like. But a more accurate term is "rock-cut," which you'll also hear applied to churches, homes, and entire communities. This emphasizes that humans, not nature, hollowed out the amazing spaces you'll find inside the rocks.

The steep rock to your left as you enter housed a six-story **convent,** which had a kitchen and refectory on the lower levels and a chapel on the third; large millstones lay ready to block the narrow passages in times of danger. Opposite is a **monastery** on the same plan, close to the **Elmaı Kilise** (Church with the Apple), which has wonderfully preserved frescoes of biblical scenes.

Entrance to the **Karanlik Church** (**Darkness Church**), which was extensively restored by UNESCO, is an extra $3, but if you want to see frescoes, this is the place to do it. Vivid, beautiful color scenes decorate the walls and domed ceiling. There are also six rock-carved columns and a painting of Jesus on one of the domes. The **Çarıkı Kilise** (Church of the Sandal) was named after the footprint below the Ascension fresco; some experts believe it to be a cast of Jesus's own footprint.

You can still imagine the **kitchen/refectory,** with a huge counter table carved from the rock, packed at mealtime with priests and members of the early Christian community who lived here. The table could seat 40 to 50 people, and carved into the opposite wall is the place where they made their wine. ⊠ *About 1.5 km (1 mi) southeast of Göreme town center.* 🎫 *$7* ⊙ *Daily 8–7 in summer, 8–5 in winter.*

Zelve Açik Hava Müzesi (Zelve Open-Air Museum). While the prizes at Göreme are the fresco-decorated churches, the outdoor museum at Zelve provides a fascinating look at how people lived in fairy-chimney communities. Zelve was a center of Christian monastic life in the 9th through 13th centuries, and the town was inhabited until 1950, when erosion and cracking began causing slabs of rock to fall and villagers were transferred out of the hundreds

> ## LEAVE SOME DOORS UNOPENED
>
> You'll get frustrated if you try to duck into every open door in the open-air museums. Many of them lead only to basic hollowed-out rooms. The places worth seeing will be appropriately marked.

of cave dwellings. The site is only about 2,145-feet long, but there's plenty to explore. The community here is made up of several uneven, naturally carved rows of fairy chimneys. These and just about every spare rock face shelter hundreds of dwellings and worshiping places that vary in size—some are just simple cavelike openings and others are

> **DON'T LEAVE HOME WITHOUT IT**
>
> Take a flashlight, or better yet, a headlamp, to explore many of the rock-cut churches, underground cities, and cave dwellings.

multistory houses with rooms on several floors linked by stairs carved deep inside the rocks. Some of the structures have collapsed already, and giant pieces of carved ceiling lie upside down on the ground. Be prepared to climb around, and definitely bring a flashlight or you won't be able to explore some of the most interesting and extensive dwellings. You can probably see the whole place in a little over an hour, but you can easily spend more time if you're willing to climb around.

Just past the mosque, on the left, there's a tall set of stairs. Take a flashlight, go in, and explore the house. You'll go upstairs, twist around, and come out on the other side of the cliff. The **Carikli Church** here is said to be unusual in Cappadocia because it has scenes from the Way of the Cross. ⊠ *6 km (4 mi) northeast of the Göreme Open-Air Museum on the road to Avanos* ⌦ *$3.50* ☉ *Daily 8–7 in summer, 8–5 in winter.*

Where to Stay & Eat

★ ✕ **Alaturca.** The best restaurant in Göreme, and probably one of the best
$ in Central Anatolia, serves a delicious array of *mezes*, including garlic prawns, hot humus, *pastırma* (Turkish pastrami), and char-grilled calamari. Main courses are elegant renditions of such Turkish classics as *ali nazik* (grilled meat in yogurt and tomato sauce), but variations on steak, chicken, and seafood are all excellent. Reservations are recommended. ⊠ *Gefelli Mah.* ☎ *384/271–2882* 🖷 *384/271–2176* ⊟ *MC, V.*

$$ 🖭 **Ataman.** Rooms in the original section of this hotel, run by tourist guide Abbas and his wife, Şermin, are built into caves in the face of a rock; even the mazelike hallways are enticing and invite wandering. All rooms are individually decorated with kilims and handicrafts, and some have fireplaces. Room rates include breakfast and a dinner of excellent Turkish and international offerings. ⊠ *Uzundere Cad. 47* ☎ *384/271–2310* 🖷 *384/271–2313* ⊕ *www.atamanhotel.com* ⇐ *26 rooms* ⌂ *Restaurant, bar; no a/c, no elevator* ⊟ *No credit cards.*

¢–$$ 🖭 **Kelebek Hotel.** Comprising a backpacker-type pension and a rather posh hotel, the Kelebek offers rooms that range from basic cave rooms with communal baths to suites with large soaking tubs. The place has a young feel to it, and great views from the rooftop bar/restaurant. ⊠ *Avdinli Mah.* ☎ *384/271-2531* 🖷 *384/271-2763* ⊕ *www.kelebekhotel.com* ⇐ *19 rooms, 6 suites* ⌂ *Restaurant, bar; no a/c, no phones, no TV in some rooms, no elevator* ⊟ *No credit cards.*

¢ 🖭 **Ottoman House.** A cadre of regulars love this charming, longtime favorite for its friendly staff and clean, simple rooms decorated with beautiful carpets and embroideries. Not luxurious, but wonderfully

FodorsChoice
★

comfortable and atmospheric, and a perfect base for exploring the region. The cozy Harem Bar in the basement is a good place for an after-dinner drink. ⊠ *Uzundere Cad. 21* ☎ *384/271–2616* 🖷 *384/271–2351* 📱 *29 rooms, 3 suites* 🍴 *Restaurant, bar, pool, laundry service, Wi-Fi; no a/c, no TVs, no elevator* ▤ *MC, V.*

Uçhisar

❸ *3 km (2 mi) southwest of Göreme on the Avanos-Nevşehir road.*

A beautiful village on a hill, Uçhisar hosts some of the best places to stay in Cappadocia. The town is dominated by the Uçhisar Castle, the highest fairy chimney in all the land.

There are some carpet and rug shops here, but most of the town is residential, with clustered stone houses overlooking the valleys. Chickens peck along back streets and are tended to by women who live in nearby caves. From here, it's easy to take off for a walk down Pigeon Valley (Güvercinlik Vadisi), so named for the birds the villagers raise in distinctive-looking cotes lodged in the walls of the valley.

> **WORD OF MOUTH**
>
> "Cappadocia has great hikes, fantastic places to stay in Uçhisar, history with the underground cities and Byzantine murals, and warm friendly people. And the area isn't as built up as the coast. It's by far the most interesting place I've ever visited."   –christycruz

Uçhisar Kalesi (Uçhisar Castle) is not so much a castle as the highest fairy chimney in Cappadocia. This striking formation was once a settlement of rock-cut houses where people lived until erosion put everything in danger of collapse and residents moved to houses in the shadow of the giant rock. The hundreds of rooms lend the chimney a Swiss-cheese look. There's a great view of the town and the valleys at the top, but you'll have to walk a lot of stairs to get there. ⊠ *Near center of town* 🎫 *$3* ⏱ *Daily 8–sundown.*

Where to Stay & Eat

$ ✕ **Center Restaurant.** Locals say this is the best restaurant in Cappado-

Fodor'sChoice   cia. It's also inexpensive, accommodating (they'll make anything if you

★   ask ahead of time), and unpretentious. ⊠ *In the central Sq.* ☎ *384/219–3117* ▤ *MC, V.*

$ ✕ **Elai Restaurant.** An old coffee house on the lower slopes of Uçhisar Castle is now a luxury restaurant with a terrace and French flair. Specialties include fresh artichokes in olive oil and lamb chops. The same group also runs the Elai Houses, a few simple, elegantly appointed cave rooms nearby. ⊠ *Eski Göreme Cad.* ☎ *384/219–3181* 🖷 *384/219–3182* ▤ *AE, MC, V.*

$$–$$$$ 🏨 **Les Maisons de Cappadoce.** French architect Jacques Avizou has de-

Fodor'sChoice   signed some of the most beautiful living spaces in Cappadocia, and the

★   overall effect is one of calm and elegance. The services are few in comparison to a traditional hotel, but each house is fully equipped. Amphoras and giant clay pots are scattered about in perfect disarray, and flowers and plants everywhere set off the sparse, beautiful simplicity of the design. ⊠ *Belediye Meydani No. 24* ☎ *384/219–2813* 🖷 *384/219–2782* ⊕ *www.cappadoce.com* 🛏 *12 houses* ⚿ *Kitchens, no a/c, no phones, no TV, no elevator* ▤ *AE, MC, V.*

$$ 🖳 **Museum Hotel.** Rooms here maintain the contours of the original caves, but all are exquisitely designed and the bathrooms, most with stone walls, marble floors, and hot tubs, are gorgeous. The place also has the best terrace in Cappadocia, and the labyrinthine passages of the hotel are decorated with carpets and fine art. If you can afford it, stay in the Harem—it has an enormous king-size bed, beautiful art pieces, a bathroom as big as most hotel suites, and red and white wine flowing from taps. The Sultan and Elflatun suites are also honeymoon-worthy. ⊠ *Tekeli Mah. No. 1* ☎ *384/219–2220* 🖷 *384/219–2444* ⊕ *www.museum-hotel.com* 🛏 *14 rooms, 13 suites* ⚿ *Restaurant, bar, pool; no elevator* ▤ *AE, MC, V.*

Fodor's Choice ★

¢ 🖳 **Le Jardin des 1001 Nights.** These basic, small but clean rooms are suitable for travelers not looking to splurge. A treehouse lounge in the garden and a shady bar carved out of a pigeon house are delightful extras, as is the free minibus service to tourist sites. The staff is friendly and helpful. ⊠ *Tekeli Mah.* ☎ *384/219–2293* 🖷 *384/219–2505* 🛏 *10 rooms* ⚿ *Restaurant, bar; no a/c, no phones, no TV in some rooms, no elevator* ▤ *AE, MC, V.*

> ### BALLOONING OVER CAPPADOCIA
>
> The flights begin just after 5 AM, the safest time to fly because of the calm air, and usually last a little over an hour. A skilled pilot can take you right into a valley, sail through it so the rock cones loom on either side, then climb the edge of a tall fairy chimney. The flight usually ends with a champagne toast. Ballooning prices are wildly inflated in Cappadocia, because of a hotel-commission racket. A hotel owner can make $100 just for making a phone call to reserve a place for a guest, and this fee, of course, is tacked on to your bill.

5

Avanos

❹ *11 km north of Uçhisar, 10 km (6 mi) north of Göreme on the Nevşehir-Avanos road.*

A really fun little town on the banks of the Irmak River, Avanos is primarily known for its pottery, which vies for tourism as the biggest industry around. Avanos is a cool, relaxed place where the local potters specialize in Hittite shapes and designs inspired by pieces found in archaeological digs across Central Anatolia. Many potters also make ornate pieces in unusual shapes, as well as functional painted items such as wineglasses and tea sets. Pottery is a family affair in Avanos, and as you walk around and check out the local shops selling decorated clay pots and vases, you'll notice family members painting the pieces their fathers and grandfathers make. Almost all of the local potters will demonstrate for free how pottery was made in the old days—with a kick wheel and clay from the river.

Near the lively town square, a wobbly pedestrian bridge crosses the river, the banks of which are lined with cafés. Avanos is also famous for its underground tunnels, some of which may lead to as-yet-undiscovered underground cities or link up with larger ones in Kaymaklı and Derinkuyu. It seems there's a network of tunnels or secret passages underneath just about every house, which the residents probably once dug in case there was an urgent need to hide or escape. Ozkonak, discovered off a dirt road 20 km (12 mi) north of Avanos (not open to tourists), may be the largest underground city in Cappadocia, capable of sheltering up to 60,000 people for an extended period of time.

Where to Stay & Eat

$ ✕ **Bizim Ev Restaurant.** The fanciest restaurant in Avanos has a covered upstairs terrace and a shady, tavernish interior where local wines are displayed on huge racks. The house specialty is *Bostan Kebabı*, chicken or beef cooked with mushrooms, eggplant, onions and peppers, topped with cheese and served in a clay pot. Fresh vegetable appetizers in olive oil and heavy meat dishes dominate the rest of the menu. ⊠ *Orta Mah. Baklaci Sok 1* ☎ *384/511–5525* 🖷 *384/511–3336* ▤ *AE, MC, V.*

$ ✕ **Tafana Restaurant.** Tasty varieties of the local *lahmacum*, a kind of flatbread pizza, draw appreciative crowds. Tafana also serves soups and kebabs. ⊠ *Atatürk Cad. 31* ☎ *384/511–4862* ▤ *AE, MC, V.*

¢   ✕ **Kirkit Pension.** Four converted Ottoman houses comprise one of the FodorśChoice ★ best budget places in town to stay; clean rooms are decorated with carpets and Uzbek blankets from one of the many family businesses. The family also serves an excellent set-menu dinner, enjoyed outside in good weather and sometimes accompanied by live folk music. Owner Osman Diler also runs a travel agency and might be the best guy to know in all of Cappadocia. ⊠ *Atatürk Cad. 50* ☎ *384/511–3259* 🖷 *384/511–2135* ⊕ *www.kirkit.com* ⇋ *15 rooms* ⌂ *Restaurant, no a/c, no phones, no TV, no elevator* ▤ *AE, MC, V.*

¢   🏨 **Sofa Hotel.** Rooms are in a complex of 15 Ottoman houses built around a large central courtyard. Sitting areas, labyrinthine passages, and shady outdoor spaces with carpeted floors and long Ottoman-style benches abound. The owner is a collector of antique radios, carpets, and blacksmith tools that enhance the funky decor. Ask his son Erdinc, an enthu-

---

POTTERY & THE WORLD'S LARGEST HAIR COLLECTION

Galip Bey wears overalls caked with clay. "Do you want tea," he asks customers, "or wine?" Galip's pottery collection is outstanding, though pricey, and his gallery near the post office in the center of Avanos occupies a maze of caverns in the back of the store. Pieces include Hittite-style urns and pots, plates with semipornographic mythological scenes, and copies of famous museum pieces. Hanging from the walls in back is one of the weirdest displays you're likely to see in Turkey, or anywhere: what Galip says is the world's largest collection of human hair. Each lock (he estimates there are around 15,000 of them) is clipped to a card naming the woman who gave it to him.

siastic and helpful host who takes pride in his breakfasts, to show you the tunnels beneath the hotel. ⊠ *Orta Mah. 13* ☎ *384/511–5186* 📠 *384/511–4489* ⊕ *www.sofa-hotel.com* ⤳ *35 rooms* ⚄ *Restaurant; no a/c, no phones, no TV* ▭ *AE, MC, V.*

¢ ✕ **Venessa Pension.** Eight small but comfortable rooms occupy a cave atop a network of tunnels that have only been partially explored. The owner lives here, and is almost obsessively clean, not such a bad thing when you're staying in a cave. Some rooms have terraces. ⊠ *50500 Avanos* ☎ *384/511–3840* 📠 *384/ 511–5617* ⊕ *www.katpatuka.org/ venessa* ⤳ *6 rooms* ⚄ *No a/c, no phones, no TV, no restaurant* ▭ *MC, V.*

Shopping

The oldest, most famous and by far the funkiest of the pottery shops is **Chez Galip,** which you'll see up a hill in the center of town. **Chez Ferhat** (⊠ Center of town near the PTT post office ☎ 384/511—487158) has an excellent array of pieces and will usually let you go with a pretty good deal. **Chez Cengiz** (⊠ on the main road, left after the bridge) lacks the atmosphere of some of the bigger places, but is one of the many smaller guys who can make the same pottery pieces for a much lower price. The shops are generally open seven days a week during tourist season from 9 to around 6, depending on business.

> ### WHO DUG THE UNDERGROUND CITIES?
>
> No one really knows for sure, who, when, or why the underground cities were dug. What is certain is that some of these cities could house as many as tens of thousands of people safely underground for months at a time. The Hattis or Hittites may have dug the cities thousands of years ago, and it is known that early Christians fearful of Roman persecution used them as refuges. Enormous wheels weighing several tons are deep underground—they could be moved to block doors and keep invaders out. It's worth your money to hire a guide, who will give you insights into what life was actually like underground.

Nevşehir

❺ *17 km (11 mi) southwest of Avanos.*

Nevşehir is a dreadful little town that you should avoid. Known in ancient times as Nissa, it is primarily notable because it's on most of the signs in Cappadocia, and you'll have to at least know where it is to get around. It's enough to know that it's the biggest town around, and it's at the southwesternmost corner of Cappadocia. If you're not traveling around Cappadocia by car, you'll probably pass through the bus hub in town a few times as you visit the sights.

Derinkuyu and Kaymaklı

Derinkuyu is 30 km (19 mi) south of Nevşehir on Rte. 765, 9 km (6 mi) south of Kaymaklı on Rte. 765. Kaymaklı is 21 km (13 mi) south of Nevşehir on Rte. 765.

The underground cities of Cappadocia have excited the imaginations of travelers since the Greek mercenary leader/historian Xenophon wrote about them in the 5th century BC. Some of the cities are merely passages between different dwellings. Others really earn the title of "city." The impermeable tufa of Cappadocia kept the insides dry, and interior wells provided water. Some have a special feature—a space above the doorway that came in handy for pouring boiling oil onto would-be attackers. ❻ **Derinkuyu,** meaning "deep well," is the most extensive of the known underground cities that have been explored, though it's believed that Ozkonak, north of Avanos, might be even larger. Eight floors of about 18 in this subterranean labyrinth are open to the public. There are stables, wineries, trap doors, scores of rooms, a ventilation shaft, and as many as 600 entrances. In parts, you'll have to walk doubled over almost in half for a hundred meters through a cave corridor. ❼ **Kaymaklı,** about 9 km (6 mi) north, was discovered in 1950 and has been opened up to a depth of about 400 feet so far, and some believe it is connected to Derinkuyu. Sloping corridors and steps connect the floors, with cemeteries and kitchens on every other level. The ceilings are lower here and almost impossible for tall people to navigate. If you're only going to do one underground city, do Derinkuyu. ☎ 384/381–3194 💰 $6.50 for each city ☉ Daily 8–5.

Ihlara Valley

★ ❽ *About 110 km (66 mi) south of Nevşehir; take Rte. 300 west to Aksaray, then go 42 km [25 mi] southeast past Selime.*

The landscape changes dramatically when you head south through Cappadocia toward Ihlara. The dusty plains turn rich with vegetation, and the Melendiz River carves a rift into the sheer tufa cliffs, which rise up to 490 feet. If you have enough time to spend in Cappadocia, it may be refreshing to see green on a hike through the lush valley and explore some of the 20 churches hidden in nooks above the river. But apart from the churches, this terrain might not really seem like Cappadocia to you—there are no fairy chimneys. There are three other entrances to the 14-km-long (8½-mi-long) valley, and the most interesting section is the Ihlara Vadi Turistik Tesisleri, where a cluster of fresco-decorated churches are within walking distance of one another. You have to walk 426 steps down to get there.

Where to Stay & Eat

¢ ⌘ **Karballa Hotel.** A former Greek monastery on a nice piece of land offers basic rooms, among them some pleasant multilevel units that are good for families. A swimming pool is set in beautiful gardens. ✉ 68500 Guzelyurt ☎ 382/451–2103 🖷 382/451–2107 ⊕ www.kirkit.com ⇗ 20 rooms ⚹ Restaurant, bar, pool ⊟ AE, MC, V.

Kayseri

❾ *80 km (48 mi) east of Ürgüp.*

Kayseri is an old, socially conservative city famous for Seljuk mosques, an imposing 6th-century castle, and carpets. The city is now experiencing an industrial boom, which many believe is largely financed by companies with conservative Islamist roots. Hundreds of factories have been constructed here in recent years, and ambitious city plans show that planners expect the boom to continue.

Most visitors these days will see Kayseri only because its airport is the most convenient entrance to Cappadocia. If you've got a car and an hour or two to spare, take a whirl through the center of town; check out the castle, the mosques, and the simply impressive main square; then hit the road again. The long drive west out of Kayseri passes through an unattractive landscape that looks something like an abandoned construction site. Hints of more interesting landscapes begin to appear as you approach Ürgüp, when the landscape starts to explode into a surreal valley of giant phallic-like protrusions.

There's a tourism office in Kayseri's main square across from the castle and near the Hatun Hunat Cami, but don't expect it to be open when you go. The peak that overlooks the city, Mt. Erciyes, is covered with snow even at the hottest time of the year, and its eruption several million years ago helped to create the surreal landscape of Cappadocia.

Arkeoloji Müzesi (Archaeological Museum). The best pieces here are finds from Kültepe, site of the ancient Assyrian and Hittite city of Kaneş, including many cuneiform tablets. Greek and Roman artifacts are also exhibited. ⊠ *Kışla Cad. 2* ☎ *352/222–2149* 🖭 *$1.75* ☉ *Tues.–Sun. 8–5.*

Bedestan. Kayseri's 15th-century covered bazaar is noted for its carpets—and there are plenty of exceptional pieces from which to choose. Other necessities of Turkish life are also stocked in this jumble. A word on Kayseri and its carpet salesmen: In Turkish folklore the people of Kayseri are renowned for being cunning in business, so keep your wits about you during sales pitches. Accept the tea they offer; this gesture is a normal part of the pitch and carries no obligations. ⊠ *West of the Citadel.*

Çifte Medrese (Twin Seminaries). This complex in Mimar Sinan Park may be the oldest medical school in Europe. It is almost certainly the first in Anatolia, built in 1206 from money left by the daughter of a sultan, who is entombed on the right side of the courtyard. The two restored seminaries—the Giyasiye Medrese and Sifahiye Medrese—now hold a museum of Islamic medicine. Check out the ancient operating room, the carvings of snakes, and the very small rooms for mental patients for a glimpse into how the Seljuks healed their sick and wounded. ⊠ *Mimar Sinan Parkı* ☎ *352/231–3565* 🖭 *$1.25* ☉ *Wed.–Sun. 8–noon and 1–5.*

Hunat Hatun Cami, Medrese ve Türbe (Hunat Hatun Mosque Complex). The Hunat Hatun mosque complex is across from the citadel, and includes a bath, religious school, and tomb. The entrance is an ornate, conical half-dome typical of the Seljuks. Inside is a peaceful space with vaulted ceilings and carpeted floors, where usually a few men will be kneeling in prayer or reading from the Koran. The complex is named after Hunat Hatun, the wife of the greatest Seljuk Sultan, Alaadin Keykubat. She was a Georgian princess and is suspected to have poisoned her husband when he was about to disinherit their son from the throne. The *medrese* was constructed in 1237 after the death of her husband and rise of her son. Today, a bearded and smiling watchman may greet you and ask if you speak French. He may also ask if you've become a Muslim. If no, he smiles and welcomes you anyway. The mosque and its courtyard can hold some 10,000 people, and are usually full for Friday prayers. ⊠ *Talas Cad. at Cumhuriyet Meyd* ✆ *Free* ☉ *Daily 8–5.*

Kayseri Hisarı (Kayseri Fortress).Made of forbidding black volcanic stone, this 6th-century fortress is still the most salient, most menacing presence in Kayseri. The castle was built on the orders of the Byzantine Emperor Justinian and extensively repaired by the Seljuks in 1224. Inside its walls are loads of little bazaar shops, most selling goods that you're unlikely to feel impelled to buy—cheap belts, sandals, cell phone covers, spices, Turkish commando uniforms for toddlers. A small mosque inside was commissioned by the Ottoman conqueror of Constantinople, Fatih Sultan Mehmet.

Sahabiye Medrese (Sahabiye Seminary). Kayseri was an important center of learning for the Seljuks, and so has several ancient medreses, or Islamic schools. Sahabiye was built in 1267 and has an impressive gate and some of the finest carvings of the late Seljuk period. ⊠ *Facing the fortress.*

Ulu Cami (Ulu Mosque). Construction of the twin-domed "Great Mosque" was begun in 1135 and completed in 1205. It is near Düvenönü Square. ⊠ *Near Düvenönü Meyd. and the bazaar.*

Within **Atatürk Parkı** is the **Kurşunlu Cami**, built in 1585.

Kayseri is known for the **Seljuk tombs** that lie scattered about the town. The most interesting is the **Doner Kumbet,** or Revolving Tomb, on Talas Caddesi. All of its 12 panels have bas-reliefs, including one of the Tree of Life. ⊠ *Talas Cad., 1 km (½ mi) south of citadel.*

About 4 km (2½ mi) east of Kayseri is the **Çifte Kümbet** (Twin-Vaulted Mausoleum). This Seljuk octagonal tomb was built in 1243 for one of the wives of Keykubat I. ⊠ *Take Sivas Cad. east out of Kayseri.*

Mt. Erciyes. This is one of the three volcanoes whose enormous eruptions over a period of some 10 million years covered Cappadocia with lava and ash, the raw material that eventually gave rise to the region's distinct moonscape. At 12, 922 feet, Mt. Erciyes, 26 km (16 mi) south of Kayseri, is the tallest peak in central Anatolia. Even when it's blazing hot at the bottom of the ski lift in summer, the mountain summit is covered with snow. Erciyes is said to have decent skiing (for Turkey) from November to April. Treks to the top by foot can be treacherous and should be done with a guide. (Don't worry, they say the volcano is inactive.) The Dedeman Erciyes Kayak Merkezi (Ski Resort Dedeman Erciyes) is right at the base of the mountain, and has 5 ski lifts. The longest run is about 3.5 km (2 miles). There's also a disco across the street. ⊠ *Base of mountain* ☎ *352/342–2116.*

Where to Stay & Eat

$ ✕ **İskender Kebab Salonu.** You'll find a good range of standard Turkish fare at this place near the citadel. *İskender* kebap (of grilled lamb served with yogurt and a tomato sauce) is the specialty. ⊠ *Millet Cad. 5* ☎ *352/231–2769* 🖷 *352/232–7577* ⊟ *AE, DC, MC, V.*

★ ✕ **Beyaz Saray.** If you want to eat with the locals, stop by this inexpen-
¢ sive place where the specialty of the house is *oltu* kebap, a sandwich-like affair of spit-roasted meat. Also worth trying are the spicy chicken *pirzola* (finely ground, grilled meat), vegetable *köfte*, and divine chocolate baklava. ⊠ *Millet Cad. 8* ☎ *352/221–0444* ⊟ *AE, MC, V.*

$$$ 🏨 **Hilton Hotel.** This huge, curving, white presence overlooks the Hunat Hatun mosque and castle with a view to Mt. Erciyes. The only five-star hotel in the region provides all the modern comforts and is built above Kayseri's most modern shopping mall. ⊠ *Cumhuriyet Meydani Istasyon Cad. 1* ☎ *352/207–5000* 🖷 *352/207–5050* ⊕ *www.hilton.com.tr* 🛏 *212 rooms* ⚴ *Wi-Fi, restaurant, room service, bar, pool, gym, laundry service* ⊟ *AE, MC, V.*

★ 🏨 **Hotel Almer.** This hotel is modern and clean, with a fine bar and a restau-
$ rant serving local s pecialties. ⊠ *Osman Kavuncu Cad. 15, Düvenönü Meyd.* ☎ *352/320–7970* 🖷 *352/320–7974* ⊕ *www.almer.com.tr* 🛏 *63 rooms, 14 suites* ⚴ *Restaurant, bar; no elevator* ⊟ *AE, MC, V.*

OFF THE
BEATEN
PATH

You'll need your own transportation and some time to get to the magnificent **SOĞANLI KAYA KILISELERI, –** about 80 km (48 mi) southwest of Kayseri on Rte. 805 toward Niğde; look for the sign off the highway just after Yeşilhisar. You'll likely be alone to explore hundreds of rock dwellings and churches cut into the cliffs. A path follows a little stream past enormous, house-sized boulders and comes to churches with domed ceilings and hundreds of other dwellings and rooms that curve around a wooded canyon. It's completely quiet except for the birds chirping and the frogs croaking. Climb up the cliff face and look around from the top for an awesome experience.

Kültepe

🔟 *20 km (12 mi) northeast of Kayseri.*

Kültepe has all the charm of a minefield. The ruins—piles of rocks arranged in big rectangles—look like they might have been put there yesterday, and if there were poisonous snakes in Turkey, or zombies, they'd be here. A disreputable ending indeed for a once-mighty city—actually, two cities, called Kanesh and Karum and now known collectively as Kültepe. They comprised the most important trading colony in Anatolia under the Assyrians and were settled around 4000 BC. Merchants from all parts of the reachable world traded metals, foods, spices, and fabrics here. Kültepe has been a gold mine for information, and some 15,000 cuneiform tablets were unearthed here, including an Assyrian text mingled with Hittite words that is said to be the oldest written record of an Indo-European language. These texts have provided extremely valuable information about trade between the Assyrians and other Anatolian peoples, with descriptions of borrowing and lending, interest rates, marriages and divorces, slave trading and court decisions. If you must go, and unless you're a serious scholar of the period there's really no need to, you'll see such signs as WARSAMA'S PALACE, KING OF KANESH AND SON OF KING INAR and STAY OFF THE TRENCHES. There's a sign to KÜLTEPE KANIS KURUM just before the AKPET gas station. ⊠ *Rte. 260 toward Sivas* 🖭 *Free* ⊙ *Always open.*

Sultan Hani, another 30 km (18 mi) northeast on Rte. 260, is a remarkable, handsome kervansaray, built by Alaaddin Keykubat in 1236. Behind the thick, rectangular walls, travelers and their beasts found ample space for a rest. For a good view of the surroundings, take the stairway to the right of the main gate up to the roof. ⊠ *Rte. 260* 🖭 *$1.25* ⊙ *Daily 9–1 and 2–5.*

Niğde

⓫ *126 km (78 mi) southwest of Kayseri on Rte. 805.*

Niğde is a town with a lot of new factories and old farms, a lot of dust and not a whole lot that's worth seeing. The city flourished under the Seljuks in the 13th century. They built the triple-domed Alaadin Cami and the neighboring 11th-century fortress. The Ak Medrese, built in 1409, has stone carvings and a small museum and cultural center. A little outside of town is the Gümüşler Monastery, probably the only reason to come to Niğde as a traveler.

Gümüşler Manastiri (Gümüşler Monastery). The ticket man here says the 10th-century Eski Gümüşler church inside has the only picture of a smiling Virgin Mary in the world. Whether that's true or not, the frescoes inside are beautiful and amazingly well preserved. (The smiling Virgin Mary is in the back right corner of the church.) Parts of the monastery were carved as early as the 7th century but the frescoes, most from around the 10th century, were painted over by local Turkish Muslims, for whom depicting humans was a sin (idolatry). The pictures were cleaned and carefully recovered in the 1960s. The monastery also contains a little underground city, a kitchen, and lots of rock-carved rooms. The sign for the monastery will be one of the first things you'll see at the entrance to Niğde from Kayseri; it's about 3 km (2 mi) down the road from there. ⊠ *9 km (6 mi) northeast of Niğde, left off Rte. 805, in village of Gümüşler* 🖭 *$1.75* ⊙ *Daily 9–5; watchman will unlock bldg. for you.*

KONYA

⓬ *258 km (160 mi) south of Ankara; 142 km (88 mi) southwest of Ihara.*

Konya's mainly religious attractions are crowded with Muslims on pilgrimages, Turkish school children on trips, and foreign and local tourists. The city is experiencing a boom in popularity that coincides with the surging interest worldwide in the Sufi mystic poet Mevlâna Celaleddin

Mevlâna Celalledin Rumi

THE MUSEUM IN KONYA calls Rumi (also known as Jalal al-Din Muhammed Rumi or simply as "Mevlâna"), a "Turkish theosophic philosopher," though in reality he was born in Afghanistan and wrote his poetry in Persian. Born in the city of Balkh on Sept. 30, 1207, he came to Konya in 1228, when it was a part of the Seljuk Empire. By that time the young Rumi had already been deeply influenced by mystic readings and had taken the hajj to Mecca.

Rumi's transformative spiritual moment came in 1248, when his companion Shams Tabriz, who initiated Rumi into Islamic mysticism, mysteriously disappeared. Rumi's grief on the disappearance of his beloved friend, suspected to be a murder, sparked a prodigious outpouring of searching verse, music, dance, and poetry. After years of searching for his friend and teacher, Rumi found himself in Damascus, where he had a revelation that the universe was one and each person could be his own holy universe. He exclaimed:

"Why should I seek? I am the same as he.

His essence speaks through me.

I have been looking for myself!"

For the rest of his life, Rumi attributed much of his own poetry to Shams, and in a way that would become characteristic and controversial, mixed his love with his fellow man with his love for God and God's love for man. Rumi became known for his tolerance, his espousal of love, and his use of dance and song to reach spiritual enlightenment. Toward the end of his life, he spent 12 years dictating his master work, the *Masnavi*, to a companion. He died in 1273, and the Mevlevi order of dervishes, famous for their semas, or twirling dances, was founded after his death.

The central theme of Rumi's philosophy is a longing for unity—of men, of the universe, with God and with God's spirit. Rumi believed in the use of music, poetry, and dancing as facilitators for reaching God and for focusing on the divine. Through ecstatic dancing, singing, or chanting, Sufi worshippers believed they could negate their bodies and vain selves, becoming empty vessels to be filled with love, the essence of the divine. In Rumi's poetry, he talks of God as one might a lover, and the ecstatic states reached through dancing and singing sometimes border on the erotic. In recent years, Rumi's legacy has been revived, ensuring that his timeless teachings endure. His epitaph suggests he would have been happy with that:

"When we are dead, seek not our tomb in the earth, but find it in the hearts of men."

Rumi and the rise to power of a moderate Islamist government in Turkey.

At other times of the year, you're liable to see everything you want to see in what is in reality a pretty boring, very conservative town in about half a day; note that the dervishes do not dance regularly outside of festival time, and you're more likely to see them in Istanbul than in Konya.

The city's other main attractions are the Mevlâna Museum that holds Rumi's tomb and some notable mosques, most of them Seljuk in style.

What to See

Mevlâna Museum. When Rumi died in 1273, he was buried in Konya beside his father and a great shrine was erected above them. As Rumi's mystic teachings of love and tolerance, ecstatic joy and unity with God spread and his poetry gathered a greater following, his mausoleum drew pilgrims from all parts of the Islamic world. In 1927, four years after the establishment of the Turkish Republic, his shrine was declared a museum, though the Sufi order he founded was officially banned as part of the drastic secularization of Turkish society under Atatürk. Today the museum is one of the most visited sights in Turkey, attracting more than two million people a year, the majority of them local tourists. The Sufi dervishes have also been assigned a special status as "Turkish folk dancers," allowing them to perform their mystic twirling without the state overtly recognizing its undeniable religious basis.

The shrine is a holy site, and in line with Muslim traditions, women visiting it are required to cover their heads. Veils are available for free at the entrance to the museum. Inside is a well-lit room with music playing, unusual for a Muslim holy place and a further hint that Rumi was not a proponent of the traditional interpretations of Islam. The first thing you see are two gorgeous carpets at the entrance—one from the 17th century and the other from the 18th—then the dervish tombs, all of them with carved stone turbans that serve as headstones and beautifully decorated in ornate cloth. Rumi's tomb is the largest and at its head are two massive green turbans. The place is usually filled with Muslim pilgrims standing with their palms outward in prayer, and it is not uncommon to see men and women crying before Rumi's grave.

Rumi was famous for his inclusiveness and would have welcomed you here, no matter what your beliefs. He said:

"Come, come, whoever you are.
Wanderer, idolator, worshipper of fire,
Come even though you have broken your vows a thousand times.
Come, and come yet again.
Ours is not a caravan of despair."

The museum also has beautifully preserved prayer books and dervish clothing, including the iconic conical hats and the flowing white gowns the mystics wore while spinning in worshipful dance. ⊠ *Mevlâna Mahallesi* ☎ *332/351–1215* ⌦ *$7* ⊗ *Tues.—Sun., 8:30–5.*

Alaaddin Cami (Alaaddin Mosque). Completed in 1220 and recently restored, this graceful mosque crowning **Alaaddin Tpesi** (Alaaddin Hill) is in the Syrian style—unusual for Anatolia; the architect was Syrian. The pulpit stands in a forest of 42 columns taken from Roman temples. Most of the hill is devoted to a park, which contains a café. Below are the scanty remains of a Seljuk palace—two venerable stumps of walls. The city has for some reason deemed it expedient to throw an unsightly concrete shelter over them.

Büyük Karatay Medrese (Büyük Karatay Seminary). Emir Celaleddin Karatay founded this seminary in 1251. His tomb is in a small room to the left of the main hall. The medrese now houses a ceramics museum, the **Karatay Müzesi** (Karatay Museum), and it is easy to understand why this particular building was selected for that purpose. Its dome is lined with tiles, blue predominating on white, and the effect is dazzling. A frieze beneath the dome is in excellent condition, and the hunting scenes on the rare figurative tiles from the Kubadabat Palace in Beyşehir show the influence of Persia on Seljuk art. Included in the spectacular ceramics collection are figurines of humans and animals, with vine leaves highlighting them with shades of cobalt blue and turquoise. The soothing sound of a fountain spilling into a basin in the middle of the main hall sets just the right mood for meditation and study. ⊠ *Alaaddin Bul., at intersection with Ankara Cad.* 🖻 *$1.75* ⊙ *Tues.–Sun. 8:30–noon and 1:30–5:30.*

Etnoğrafya Müzesi (Ethnographic Museum). This small collection next to the Sahip Ata complex displays Islamic art, embroidery, carpets, and weapons. ⊠ *Larende Cad.* 🕾 *332/351–8958* 🖻 *$1.75* ⊙ *Tues.–Sun. 9–noon and 1:30–5:30.*

İnce Minare Medrese (Seminary of the Slender Minaret). The minaret at this 13th-century institution is bejeweled with glazed blue tiles. Unfortunately, it is now only half its original size, thanks to a bolt of lightning. Now a museum, the İnce Minare has a fine collection of stone and wood carvings. Note the ornate decoration of the building's entry portal. ⊠ *Alaaddin Bul., west side of Alaaddin Tepesi* 🖻 *$1.75* ⊙ *Daily 8:30–noon and 1:30–5:30.*

Sahip Ata. A magnificent portal marks the remains of this complex, a group of structures dating from 1283. Mosque buildings here have been converted into an **Arkeoloji Müzesi** (Archaeological Museum). Though the collection begins with items from the Bronze Age, its most important artifacts are Greek and Roman; the 3rd-century BC marble depicting the Twelve Labors of Hercules is outstanding. ⊠ *Larende Cad.* 🕾 *332/351–3207* 🖻 *$1.75* ⊙ *Tues.–Sun. 9–noon and 1:30–5:30.*

Selimiye Cami (Selim Mosque). Sultan Selim II started this mosque in 1558, when he was heir to the throne and governor of Konya, and the structure was completed after he had become Sultan Selim II. The style is reminiscent of that of the Fatih Cami in Istanbul, with soaring arches and windows surrounding the base of the dome. The

GIVE UP YOUR SOUL

The best time to visit is during the annual Mevlâna festival in mid-December, when the dervishes dance and there is a week of events dedicated to Rumi. Konya's Tourism Information Office (332/351-1074) can help you find tickets and make hotel reservations. Several of the staff speak English and are invariably delighted by foreign interest, but it is wise to call or fax several weeks in advance. Do not miss a show of the whirling dervishes if you get a chance to see it. It's beautiful, entrancing, and unique.

surrounding streets, which contain some shops, are full of character. ⊠ *Opposite Mevlâna Museum on Mevlâna Meyd.*

Sırçaı Medrese (Crystalline Seminary). Opened in 1242 as a school for Islamic jurisprudence and decorated with lavish tiles, the seminary provides a dignified home for the **Türbe Müzesi** (Museum of Funerary Monuments). The small Catholic church of St. Paul next door proves that Konya has remained as tolerant as it was in its Seljuk heyday. On the opposite side of the Sırçalı are Roman catacombs and a mosaic. ⊠ *Mimar Muzaffer Cad., south of Alaaddin Bul.* 🕮 *$1.75* 🕓 *Daily 9–5.*

Other mosques. On the way to Konya's ancient acropolis, the **Üçler Mezarığı**, heading west from Mevlâna Meydanı, are a few mosques on or just off Alaaddin Caddesi. **Şerefettin Cami**, built in 1636, was started by the Seljuks and completed by the Ottomans. The **Şemsi Tebrizi Cami and Türbe**, north of Şerefettin Cami, off Hükümet Alanı, is dedicated to Mevlâna's mentor and friend. Nearby is Konya's oldest mosque, the **İplikçi Cami** (Thread Dealer Mosque), which dates from 1202. **Aziziye Cami** (Sultan Abdül Aziz Mosque), dating from 1676, flanks the bazaar. Here, two short minarets rise above a loggia with a Florentine flavor.

Where to Stay & Eat

$$ ✕ **Horozlu Han Kervansaray.** This restored 700-year-old Seljuk kervansaray on the old Silk Road serves lunch, and the cavernous stone interior provides a cool refuge from the heat. Specialties include *ezo gelin* (lentil soup), *etli ekmek* (flat bread with ground lamb), and excellent fish, which vary according to the season. The menu is prix fixe. ⊠ *About 8 km (5 mi) north of Konya, Konya–Ankara Yolu Üzeri, TNP Yanı* ☎ *332/345–0538* ▤ *No credit cards.*

$ ✕ **Mevlevi Sofrasi.** At this welcoming place with an outdoor courtyard overlooking the Mevlâna Museum, the house specialty is *firin kebabı*, oven-cooked lamb served with a slice of onion, greasy but good. For desert, try the *saç arası*, a honey and nuts creation with a crispy crust. ⊠ *Nazimbey Caddesi No. 1A, Karatay* ☎ *332/353–3341* ▤ *332/353–4743* ▤ *MC, V.*

$ ✕ **Seyhzade Sofrasi Restaurant.** This spot with views of the Mevlâna Museum has good meat and *etli ekmek*, the Konya flatbread specialty topped with ground lamb. ⊠ *Right across from the museum* ☎ *332/353–9393.* ▤ *MC, V.*

¢ ✕ **Ali Baba Etli Ekmek 2.** For an authentic Turkish grease fix, this is the real deal. Here you'll commonly see a pair of Turkish businessmen share four-foot-long pieces of *etli ekmek*, the flatbread that's a Konya specialty, with miced meat and spices on top. ⊠ *Nisantasi mah (near the Afra mall)* ☎ *332/236–5218.* ▤ *MC, V.*

$$ ▥ **Rixos Hotel Konya.** The only five-star international hotel in Konya, the Rixos is a 25-story luxury hotel a little farther from the city center but within walking distance from the tram. It has many amenities, including an Olympic-size swim-

KONYA SPECIALTY

Make sure you try the local specialty, *etli ekmek*, while you're in Konya. It's flatbread topped with minced meat and spices.

ming pool and a haman, as well as nicely appointed rooms, and it's near a shopping mall. ☒ *Istanbul Yolu, Selçuklu* ☎ *332 / 221–5000* 🖷 *332/ 221–5050* ⊕ *www.rixos.com/konya* 🖥 *336 rooms, 19 suites* ⚭ *Restaurant, room service, bar, 2 tennis courts, 2 pools, gym, laundry service* 🖃 *AE, MC, V.*

$ 🏨 **Otel Selçuk.** Amenities at this large Western-style hotel include two in-house restaurants and a sauna. ☒ *Alaaddin Cad. 4* ☎ *332/353– 2525* 🖷 *332/353–2529* ⊕ *www.otelselcuk.com.tr* 🖥 *76 rooms, 6 suites* ⚭ *2 restaurants* 🖃 *MC, V.*

¢ 🏨 **Hotel Rumi.** Clean, comfortable rooms, friendly service, and an excellent location just a block away from Mevlâna's tomb make this one of the best places to stay in Konya. ☒ *Durakfaki Mah. Durakfaki Sok 5* ☎ *332/353–1121* 🖷 *332/353–5366* ⊕ *www.rumihotel.com* 🖥 *30 rooms, 3 suites* ⚭ *Restaurant, gym* 🖃 *AE, MC, V.*

¢ 🏨 **Şifa Otel.** At this comfortable, modern establishment only a few minutes' walk from the Mevlâna Museum, rooms are simply decorated and clean. The hotel management also runs the Şifa 1 restaurant next door. ☒ *Mevlâna Cad. 55* ☎ *332/350–4290* 🖷 *332/351–9251* 🖥 *32 rooms* ⚭ *No elevator* 🖃 *AE, MC, V.*

Shopping

Konya's **bazaar** was once known for its rug shops, but these now are more likely to be found around Alaaddin Caddesi. Meanwhile, the bazaar features an amazing array of ordinary goods. ☒ *Market district, near intersection of Selimiye Cad. and Karaman Cad.* ☉ *Mon.–Sat. during daylight hrs.*

Karavan Kilim Shop. At this treasure trove down the street from the Mevlâna Museum, thousands of carpets are piled up in a pleasant, dark wood old-fashioned showroom that feels like a rich man's bazaar. There are also copper pieces and antique furniture. ☒ *Mevlâna Caddasi No. 19/B* ☎ *332/351–0425* 🖃 *AE, MC, V.*

OFF THE BEATEN PATH

HOROZLU HAN AND SILLE – If you're heading out of Konya in the direction of Ankara, look for the fabulous Seljuk portal at the entrance to the ruined Horozlu Han, a former kervansaray near the four-lane beginning of Rte. 715. At Sille, 8 km (5 mi) northwest, St. Helena, mother of Constantine the Great, built a small church in AD 327. Nearby, frescoed rock chapels overlook the shores of a tiny artificial lake.

ANKARA & THE HITTITE CITIES

Ankara

258 km (160 mi) north of Konya, 454 km (281 mi) southeast of Istanbul.

As war raged elsewhere in Turkey, Ankara was made the capital, in part because it was in the middle of nowhere. The city still feels that way, despite being the center of Turkish political activity and having a large population of around four and a half million. A barren, dusty steppe city largely devoid of charm or personality, Ankara is exceptional mostly because it is home to the fascinating and enduring legacy of Mustafa Kemal, founding father of the secular Turkish Republic. The creation of the capital city is a monument to Atatürk's overpowering will.

But unless you've been invited to a cocktail reception by an ambassador—and even then if you have a choice, suggest the diplomatic summer residence in Istanbul—it won't be worth it to spend your vacation

> ### NOT A JOKING MATTER
>
> Be respectful in Turkey in all dealings concering the nation's founder. Insulting Atatürk is a crime here. A Turkish politician was recently charged with the offense—for chewing gum while he approached an Atatürk statue during a ceremony.

time in Ankara. For travelers looking to go to Cappadocia and other formerly hard-to-reach parts of Central Anatolia, the emergence of several low-cost airlines with direct flights to Kayseri means it is no longer necessary to spend a day in the capital if you don't want to.

If you do find yourself here, while away a day in the city's few worthwhile sights, most notably the highly regarded Archaeological Museum, repository of the best archaeological treasures found in Turkey, and Atatürk's Mausoleum, the Anıtkabir. The capital also provides a logical base for exploring the ancient ruined sites of the Hittite Empire, which are contained within a triangle in northeastern Central Anatolia bounded by Hattuşaş, Yazılıkaya, and Alacahöyük. All the Hittite cities can be seen in a day trip from Ankara if you have a car.

㉑ **The Anıtkabir** (Atatürk's Mausoleum). Atatürk's picture is on every single piece of Turkish currency, his visage hangs in just about every office and official building in the country, and his personality and ideas are the foundations of Turkish political thought. So his vast mausoleum, perched on a hilltop overlooking the capital city he built, is on a scale suitable to his stature in Turkey. A marble promenade flanked with Hittite-style lions leads to the mausoleum, where the sarcophagus under which the revered man's remains are interred lies beyond brilliant gold mosaics and a colonnade with inscriptions from his speeches. Soldiers march endlessly around the site, and nearly every important foreign dignitary who visits the capital goes to lay a wreath here in tribute of the man who, it is not an exaggeration to say, created modern Turkey. A museum with personal belongings from Atatürk's life, including his clothes and automobiles, is also here, as is a gift shop and an exhibit on the 1919–1922 War of Independence. An interesting map at the entrance to the war exhibit shows Turkey and the territorial claims various other nations were making on it at the time. ✉ *Anıt Cad., south end* ☎ *312/231–7975* ⊕ *www.tsk. mil.tr/anitkabir/index.html* ☞ *Free* ⊙ *Daily 9–5.*

 FodorsChoice ★

⑭ **Ankara Anadolu Medeniyetler Müzesi** (Museum of Anatolian Civilizations). Outside this museum is an impressive announcement—the Ankara Museum of Anatolian Civilizations was voted the European Museum of the Year. Never mind that this was in 1997. Despite the outdated plaudit, the museum is one of the two places that you really must visit if you're spending any time in Ankara (the other is Atatürk's Mausoleum, the Anıtkabir). Many of the best treasures uncovered from Turkey's ancient past

From Genghis Kahn to Atatürk

TAMERLANE, THE FEARSOME descendent of Genghis Khan, laid siege to Ankara in 1402 and wrested control of the city away from Beyazit, the Ottoman sultan. Then, perhaps bored with the landscape or seeking greater riches in the abundance of China, Tamerlane and his Mongol horde quickly gave the city back to the Ottomans and turned around and headed back east toward the Mongol plains. Tamerlane died a year later.

Tamerlane's victory in Ankara was but a later scene in the city's long history. Local legend attributes Ankara's foundation to the Amazons, the mythical female warriors, but many archaeologists have factually indentified it with Ankuwash, thought to have been founded around 1200 BC by the Hittites and then taken over by the Phrygians around 700 BC The city was known to the Greeks and Romans as Ancyra or Ankyra, and later as Angora, famed for its wool. Alexander the Great conquered Ankara centuries before Augustus Caesar annexed the city to Rome in 25 BC Over the coming millennia Ankara was attacked and

worn down by Persian, Arab, Seljuk, Mongol, and Ottoman invaders. By the early 20th century, Ankara was little more than a provincial town with nice goats and an illustrious past. In 1919, as World War I and the Turkish War of Independence raged, Mustafa Kemal Atatürk made Ankara the headquarters of his secular resistance movement. When Turkey was declared a republic four years later, Ankara was declared its capital. Atatürk mobilized the young nation's resources to make the city a symbol of a modern and secular Turkish city built on European lines. Tens of thousands of workers streamed in on foot to help build it, with designers intentionally abandoning Ottoman architecture in favor of a symbolic, stark modernism influenced by the Vienna cubist and German Bauhaus schools. As with most planned cities, Ankara today is mostly convenient and utterly characterless. Despite Atatürk's dreams, it never made a serious bid to overtake Istanbul as the country's cultural capital.

5

are housed here, including the best finds from the site of Çatal Höyük, one of the oldest human settlements ever discovered.

If you have a layover in Ankara, or even just a few hours to spare, the museum is a great place to start your trip to Turkey, providing a base of understanding for the incredible amount of history that has been played out in these lands. The museum is relatively small and has descriptions in English and Turkish, but a guide may be helpful in directing your attention to the most important pieces. Agree on a price in advance.

Particularly interesting are the Hatti and Hittite artifacts from the 2nd millennium BC, with their stylized stag and bull sculptures and drawings. There are also pieces from the Neolithic and Bronze ages, and from the Assyrian, Phrygian, Urartu, Hellenistic, and Roman eras. ⌂ *Gözcü Sok. 2* ☎ *312/324–3160* ⊕ *www.geocities.com/anadolu_muzesi/muze.* ⌨ *$4* ☾ *Sun.–Tues. 8:30–5.*

⓭ Ankara Hisarı (Ankara Citadel). Ankara's main historic sites are clustered around the Hisarı, also known as the citadel or castle, high on a hill overlooking the city. The plains on which Tamerlane defeated Beyazıt stretch to the northeast. There's not a lot to see at the crumbling Hisarı itself, as the city has grown around and even inside it. The inner walls date to the 7th century, and the best-preserved sections are around the Parmak Kapı. Ankara's oldest mosque, the 12th-century Alaaddin Cami, is also here, and the Ankara Museum of Anatolian Civilizations is within walking distance. ⊠ *Kireçli Sok. 6* ⊙ *Tues.—Sun. 10–6:30.*

㉓ Bakanıklar, the government district, fills the west side of Atatürk Bulvarı from Hürriyet Meydanı to the **Türkiye Büyük Millet Meclisi** (Grand National Assembly), the parliament building, at the intersection with Ismet İnönü Bulvarı. Within walking distance, in the Kavaklıdere neighborhood, is Embassy Row, with gardens, fine restaurants, and world-class hotels.

⓲ Cumhuriyet Müzesi (Museum of the Republic). You might think the Museum of the Republic would be one of the best places for a crash course on modern Turkish history. But the descriptions here are all in Turkish, so most non-Turks are confronted with a bunch of pictures of people they don't recognize and documents they can't understand. The museum is housed in Turkey's first parliament building, where politicians from 1925–1960 debated policies that would shape Turkey as a modern, secular nation. ⊠ *Cumhuriyet Bul. 22, off Ulus Meyd. (Nation Sq.)* ☎ *312/310–5361* 🕮 *$1.75* ⊙ *Tues.–Sun. 9–noon and 1:30–5.*

⓳ Etnoğrafya Müzesi (Ethnography Museum). Atatürk used this Ottoman Revival–style building as an office, and his body lay here for 15 years after his death while his enormous mausoleum was being built. The museum houses a rich collection of Turkish carpets, folk costumes, weapons, and Islamic calligraphy. ⊠ *Talat Paşa Cad., Opera* ☎ *312/311–3007* 🕮 *$1.75* ⊙ *Tues.–Sun. 8:30–12:30 and 1:30–5.*

⓯ Hacı Bayram Cami (Hacı Bayram Mosque). The 14th-century Hacı Bayram Cami is one of Ankara's most important sacred sites. Built of yellow stone and brick with glazed Kütahya tiles later placed in the interior, it is named after Hacı Bayram, the founder of the Bayramiye order of dervishes. Hacı Bayram's tomb is near the entrance to the mosque. If you want religious trinkets to take home, the area surrounding the mosque is a good place to get them. ⊠ *Bayram Cad., north of Hisarparkı Cad.* ☎ *312/310–8297* 🕮 *Free* ⊙ *Immediately after prayer times.*

⓱ Julyanus Sütünü (Column of Julian). Now surrounded by Turkish government buildings, the column was erected in honor of the Emperor Julian the Apostate (361–363), the last pagan Roman emperor. He won his epithet because he tried to reverse his father Constantine's decision to make Christianity the official religion of the empire. The column has 15 fluted drums and a Corinthian top that commemorates a visit by Julian in 362, as he passed through town on his way to death in battle with the Persians. ⊠ *Hükümet Meyd., just northeast of Ulus Meyd.*

㉒ Kocatepe Cami (Kocatepe Mosque). It took 20 years to built this gigantic mosque in the center of Turkey's secular capital. Officially opened

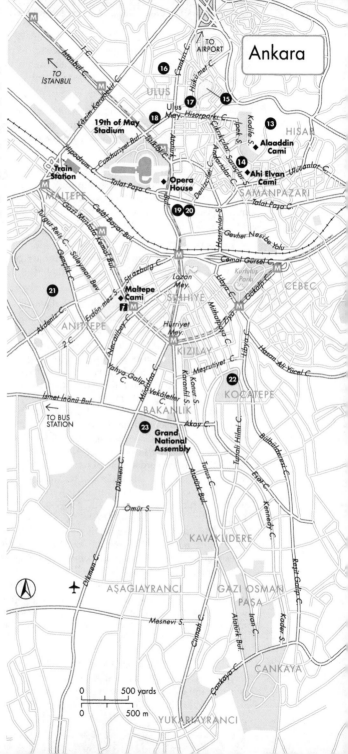

Ankara

in 1987, it is the site of most military and official funerals. The huge, illuminated mosque dominates the city skyline at night. The Kocatepe complex is one of Ankara's most prominent landmarks and also includes a supermarket and department store on its lower floors. ⊠ *On Mithat Paşa Cad.*

⑳ Resim ve Heykel Müzesi (Painting and Sculpture Museum). These galleries next door to the Ethnography Museum display works by contemporary Turkish artists. ⊠ *Talat Paşa Cad., Opera* ☎ 312/310–2094 ⌫ *Free* ☾ *Tues.–Sun. 9–noon and 1–5.*

⑯ Roma Hamamları (Roman Baths). You can't bathe at this third-century complex just north of Ulus Square, but you can see how the Romans did it. The bath system includes the frigidarium and caldarium (cold and hot rooms), as well as steam rooms with raised floors. ⊠ *Çankırı Cad. 43* ☎ 312/310–7280 ⌫ *$1.75* ☾ *Daily 8:30–12:30 and 1:30–5:30.*

Where to Stay & Eat

Be warned that prices in expensive Ankara are generally much higher than those elsewhere in Turkey, even Istanbul.

$$$$ ✕ **Kalbur.** Everything—yes, everything—at this excellent restaurant is made
Fodor'sChoice   of seafood. Like grilled meatballs, only the meat is shrimp. There are
★   Atatürk photos on the walls, no sign on the door, and you'll need to make reservations as much as a week in advance to get in. ⊠ *Or-An Sehri Carsi Merkezi C-3 Blok No. 23* ☎ 312/490–5001 ⌨ 312/490–5005 ▤ *No credit cards* ⌫ *Reservations essential* ☾ *Closed Mon.*

★   ✕ **Amisos.** In a restored old villa, this inviting restaurant serves Turk-
$$$ ish, Black Sea, and international fare, ranging from fish and caviar to soy chicken. One of Ankara's few fine-dining options that is open for both lunch and dinner, Amisos is a favorite with businesspeople for lunch and with an elite crowd for dinner. Ask for a table in the greenhouse. ⊠ *Filistin Sok. 28, Gazi Osman Paşa* ☎ 312/446–6098 ⌨ 312/446–8345 ⌫ *Reservations essential* ▤ *AE, DC, MC, V.*

$$$ ✕ **Washington Restaurant.** One of the oldest restaurants in Ankara, the Washington serves Russian dishes that were popular here in the past, including borscht, as well as Turkish traditionals. It's a little pricey, but popular with the diplomatic set. ⊠ *Nene Hatun Caddesi 97, Gazi Osman Paşa* ☎ 312 / 445-0212 ▤ *AE, DC, MC, V.*

$ ✕ **Ege Restaurant.** Black Sea fish is cooked in Aegean style here (Ege is the Turkish name for the Aegean Sea). Enjoy your meal with rakı and Greek music. Reservations are recommended. ⊠ *Büklüm Sokak, 54/B, Kavaklıdere* ☎ 312/428–2717 ☾ *Closed Sun.* ▤ *AE, DC, MC, V.*

★   ✕ **Göksu.** Black Sea cuisine is the specialty of Göksu (which means that
$ primarily seafood is served). The restaurant imports all its fish and cheese from the region, making it a popular hangout for people from that area. Rather incongruously, the walls are decorated with Hittite reliefs. ⊠ *Bayındır Sok. 22/A, Kızılay* ☎ 312/431–2219 ⌫ *Reservations essential* ▤ *AE, MC, V.*

$ ✕ **Segah.** Zenger Paşa Konağ near the citadel is often recommended for its food and view, but go to Segah, just down the road, instead. The food is better and cheaper, and the view is almost the same. But be prepared for the Turkish band—apparently they're trying to sound enthusiastically out of tune, and everyone sings along. And try the green beans. ⊠ *Kale Sok. No. 1, Ankara Kalesi* ☎ *312/309-8383* ▭ *AE, MC, V.*

$$$$ ▦ **Sheraton Ankara.** The best of the international hotels in Ankara is hard to miss; it's tall, white, and round. Rooms are big and comfortable, and service is professional. ⊠ *Noktalı Sok., Kavaklıdere* ☎ *312/468–5454* 🖷 *312/467–1136* ⊕ *www.sheratonankara.com* ⬃ *414 rooms, 12 suites* ⚏ *Wi-Fi, 3 restaurants, room service, bar, pool, gym, laundry service, fee parking* ▭ *AE, DC, MC, V.*

★ ▦ **Ankara Hilton SA.** This luxurious, 16-story building on Embassy Row
$$ with a view over the city provides everything you expect from a Hilton in an international capital. ⊠ *Tahran Cad. 12, Kavaklıdere* ☎ *312/468–2888* 🖷 *312/468–0909* ⊕ *www.hilton.com/worldwide/europe* ⬃ *324 rooms, 12 suites* ⚏ *2 restaurants, room service, 2 bars, pool, gym, laundry service, Wi-Fi, some DVDs, fee parking, no-smoking rooms* ▭ *AE, DC, MC, V.*

$$ ▦ **Grand Hotel Ankara/Büyük Ankara.** This high-rise across from the Grand National Assembly was long Ankara's poshest hotel and is still a good choice if you want a big hotel with a Turkish edge. ⊠ *Atatürk Bul. 183, Kavaklıdere* ☎ *312/425–6655* 🖷 *312/425–5070* ⬃ *192 rooms, 28 suites* ⚏ *2 restaurants, room service, pool, gym, laundry service, DVD, Wi-Fi,* ▭ *AE, DC, MC, V.*

★ ▦ **Angora House Hotel.** Inside the castle walls and within walking dis-
¢ tance of the Museum of Anatolian Civilizations, the Angora House has six rooms in a restored Ottoman house. The place has more personality than most hotels in Ankara do, but service is a bit rough and business travelers might not find this to be a good choice. ⊠ *Kale Kapısı Sok. 16, Kale İçi* ☎ *312/309–8380 or 311–1609* 🖷 *312/309–8381* 🖅 *angorabazar@e-kolay.net.tr* ⬃ *6 rooms* ⚏ *Room service, bar; no elevator* ☉ *Closed late Oct.–Apr.* ▭ *DC, MC, V.*

¢ ▦ **Hotel Almer.** This good budget option in Ulus is clean, modern, and provides a good base in Old Ankara. The modest bathrooms have showers only. ⊠ *Çankırı Cad. 17, Ulus* ☎ *312/309–0435* 🖷 *312/311–5677* ⬃ *81 rooms* ⚏ *Restaurant, bar* ▭ *DC, MC, V.*

★ ▦ **King Hotel.** On a quiet street near the American Embassy and the Turk-
¢ ish Grand National Assembly, the King Hotel is a favorite with perennial visitors to Ankara. The central location, the very helpful and friendly staff, the above-average restaurant, and the clean rooms all make this a great deal for the price (especially since a good breakfast is included). ⊠ *Güvenlik Cad. 13, Aşağıayrancı* ☎ *312/418–9099* 🖷 *312/417–0382* ⊕ *www.kinghotel.com.tr* ⬃ *36 rooms, 3 suites* ⚏ *Restaurant, room service, bar, pool; no elevator* ▭ *AE, DC, MC, V.*

Shopping

Down the hill south of the Hisar is an area known as **Samanpazarı,** where you can find rugs, crafts, antiques, and copper for sale. The **Gesav Sanat Evi** (Gesav Art House ⊠ Kireçli Sok. 6, Kale İçi) offers fine handicrafts without the pressure of bargaining. In the pedestrian area of the district of **Kızılay,** look for books and Turkish music, especially on Konur Sokak. There are also two good shopping malls in central Ankara—Karum and

Armada—where you can check out local Turkish brands. There's an antiques bazaar in Ayrancı on the first Sunday of every month.

Safranbolu

★ ⓤ *225 km (140 mi) north of Ankara.*

Tucked into the hills two hours north of Ankara is one of Turkey's loveliest treasures, a preserved slice of Ottoman past that has been designated a UNESCO World Heritage Site. Once a wealthy trading town, it was known for its golden saffron fields—from which the city derives its name. Safranbolu's merchants built stunning timber and stone mansions in the 18th and 19th centuries, a large number of which remain intact. Ignore the ugly new part of the city (and especially the big steel factory just outside town) and head to Safranbolu's historic center, hidden in a wide ravine, where cars are banned, artisans ply their crafts in open storefronts, and the old Ottoman houses line the cobblestone streets.

Some buildings in the historic center of town are open to the public, including the **Kaymakamlar Evi** (Governor's House), which has been restored with 200-year-old furnishings. ⊠ *Hıdrılı Yokuşu Cad.* ⓞ *Tues.—Sun. 9–noon and 1:30—5* 🖃 *$2.*

The nicely restored **Arasta** (Ottoman Market Hall) dates back to 1661 and used to house the small shops of shoemakers. Today it's filled with stores selling local handicrafts such as handmade cotton and linen clothes and other souvenirs.

If you're in the mood for a scrubdown, head to the historic **Cinci hamam**, where locals have been getting lathered up and massaged since the 16th century. ⊠ *near the main Sq.* ☎ *0370/712—2103* ⓞ *daily 6 AM–11 PM for men, 9 AM—10 PM for women* 🖃 *$8.*

Safranbolu's Bağlar district, on the slopes of a small mountain overlooking the city, was where wealthy locals had their summer homes in Ottoman times. Several of these old homes have been turned into hotels.

Where to Stay & Eat

$–$$ ✕ **Havuzlu Koşk.** To get away from the weekend crowds that sometimes descend on Safranbolu, head up to this restaurant in the mountainside Bağlar district, where the city's elite spent their summers during Ottoman times. The food, the usual assortment of kebabs and mezes, is very good, but the location—a 190-year-old house with a Safranbolu-style indoor pool for heating, and a very pleasant garden filled with fruit trees, is even better. ⊠ *Dibekönü Cad. 32* ☎ *0370/725–2168* 🖃 *MC, V.*

$ ✕ **Çevrikköprü Tesisleri.** A roadside parking lot overflowing with cars will let you know that you've arrived at this popular restaurant some 4 miles (6 km) east of Safranbolu, on the road to Kastamonu. By the side of a small stream, the rustic restaurant has outdoor tables

---

SAFRANBOLU SPECIALTIES

One of the local specialties worth trying in Safranbolu is *koyu* kebab: lamb baked in an earthenware dish.

set around a bubbling fountain, shaded by leafy vines. Meals start with a complimentary flatbread served with butter and honey. The house specialties are *koyu* kebab, and a very tasty local type of *pide* filled with spinach and ground meat. Do as the locals do, and order a pitcher of frothy *ayran*, a type of yogurt drink, to go with your meal. ⊠ *Kastamonu Yolu 6 Km.Safranbolu* ☎ *0370/737–2461* ⊟ *MC, V.*

$ ✕ **Kadıoğlu Şehzade Sofrası.** With low, round tables set around an enclosed courtyard shaded by grapevines, this restaurant is welcoming and laid back. On the menu are several tasty local specialties, including *Şehzade pilavı,* a dish of rice and mushrooms topped with a cheesy crust. Everything is served with freshly baked flat bread. ⊠ *Arasta Sok. 6, Safranbolu* ☎ *0370/712–5091* ⊟ *MC, V.*

¢ ✕ **Boncuk Arasta Kahvesi.** In the middle of the Arasta Bazaar this small café serves simple food, like stuffed grape leaves and the Turkish pancakes known as *gözleme.* Chairs and tables are set outside on the market's cobblestones, beneath drooping grapevines. The interior of the cafe is cozy, with lace curtains and tablecloths, and old wooden floors. Finish your light meal or snack with a expertly-made Turkish coffee, served in a long-stemmed copper urn with two pieces of Turkish delight on the side. ⊠ *Yeminiciler Arastası, Safranbolu* ☎ *0370/712–2065* ⊟ *no credit cards.*

$$ ⊡ **Gül Evi.** Opened in 2006 by a retired Istanbul architect and his wife,
Fodor'sChoice this restored Ottoman house has lots of style, deftly combining antique
★ and modern touches. The 120-year-old house has original, built-in divans that run along the walls—they've been upholstered in up-to-date fabrics and outfitted with funky pillows made of white felt. The original wood detailing and floors also remain, giving the place a warm feel. On the ground floor, where the stables used to be, is a cozy and inviting bar. ⊠ *Hükümet Sokak 46, Safranbolu* ☎ *0370/725–4645* ⊟ *0370/ 712–5051* ⊕ *www.canbulat.com.tr* ➷ *5 rooms* ⌂ *Restaurant, bar, café* ⊟ *AE, MC, V* ⏀ *BP.*

$$ ⊡ **Havuzlu Konağı.** In a typical affluent Ottoman-era Safranbolu house, this hotel has been meticulously restored. Painstaking attention has been given to detail, from the embroidered floral motifs on the blinds to the *havuz* (a traditional pool used not for swimming, but for cooling the house) in the breakfast room, from which the hotel takes its name. The excellent restaurant serves the Safranbolu kebab: grilled lamb, tomato sauce, and yogurt on pita bread, topped with cheese. ⊠ *Çelik Gülersoy Cad.* ☎ *0370-725–2883* ⊟ *372/712–3824* ⊕ *www.safranbolukonak. com* ➷ *23 rooms* ⌂ *Restaurant, café, no a/c, some TVs, Wi-Fi* ⊟ *AE, MC, V.*

$ ⊡ **Hotel Selvili Koşk.** Friendly and unassuming, this hotel is located in an impressive old house that's been painted light blue. Rooms have high ceilings, and small bathrooms are cleverly hidden inside old cupboards. There are large common areas with divans to lounge on and a large, pleasant garden where breakfast is served. ⊠ *Mescit Sok. 23, Safranbolu* ☎ *0370/712–8646* ⊟ *0370/725–2294* ⊕ *www.hotelselvilikosk. com* ➷ *26 rooms* ⊟ *no credit cards* ⏀ *BP.*

¢ ⊡ **Hacı Hüseyinler Konukevi.** An excellent budget option, this homey hotel is run by an elderly couple that live below the upstairs guest rooms and prepare breakfast in the morning. The 150-year-old Ottoman house has lots of old wooden details, while the rooms are simple—more like guest rooms in somebody's house than hotel rooms—but comfortable. There's a large garden where you can sit on divans and relax. ⊠ *Akçasu Mah., Ulukavak Sokak 16, Safranbolu* ☎ *0370/725–1048* ⌦ *4 rooms* ⋄ *no a/c* ▤ *no credit cards* �� *BP.*

¢ ⌂ **Raşitler Dağ Evi.** One of the most inviting of the restored homes that are now hotels in the Bağlar district, these rather elegant lodgings have antique furniture and lace curtains. The garden has pear and walnut trees and a vegetable patch that provides tomatoes for breakfast. The hosts, a retired air force colonel and his wife, are as friendly as can be. ⊠ *Değrmenbaşı 65, Safranbolu* ☎ *0370/725–1345* ⌦ *5 rooms* ⋄ *no a/c, Wi-Fi* ▤ *no credit cards* ⓘ *BP.*

Hattuşaş and the Other Hittite Cities

★ ㉕ *Hattuşaş is 158 km (98 mi) from Ankara, east on Rte. E88 and northeast on Rte. 190 until past Sungurlu; then follow road signs.*

The ancient ruined sites of the Hittite Empire are contained within a triangle in northeastern Central Anatolia bounded by Hattuşaş, Yazılıkaya, and Alacahöyük. All the Hittite cities can be seen in a day trip from Ankara if you have a car. Otherwise, you'd be best tagging along with a guided archaeological tour.

Hattuşaş, about 145 km (90 miles) east of Ankara in a loop of the Kizil Irmak River, was the capital of the Hittite Empire. In a beautiful setting of lush green valleys, with steep ravines and rocky hillsides, sheep graze among the ruins of a civilization that was already established here some 6,000 years ago. The entire site, with walls that are 7 km (4 mi) in circumference, was named a UNESCO World Heritage Site in 1986. Though picturesque, the site is extensive and there is little explanation.

Hattuşaş dates to the Bronze Age, and by 2300 BC a people called the Hatti were thriving here. The massive walls of the city surrounded a fortress, temples, large administrative buildings, houses, cemeteries, and decorated gateways and courtyards. Around 1800 BC, King Anitta of the as-yet-undiscovered city of Kushar formed an Anatolian confederacy and pronounced himself "Rabum Rabum," or King of Kings.

At about that time, however, a people called the Hittites wandered in. They claimed King Anitta's Hattuşaş as their capital and soon began to build their own empire around it. The Hittites, who like the Persians spoke an Indo-European language (unlike the Turks, whose language is Ural-Altaic), apparently entered Anatolia after crossing the Caucasus steppes beyond the Black Sea. They worshipped a storm god and a sun goddess, and had a well-ordered society with written laws. At their height, they conquered Babylon and battled the Egyptian pharaohs. Their reign came to an

GO WITH A GUIDE

When visiting the Hittite cities, guided trips will shed a great deal of light on otherwise unintelligible piles of rocks arranged in squares. The American Research Institute in Turkey, or ARIT, 312/427–2222, arranges periodic and highly praised guided excursions.

end after some 600 years, when tribes from the north sacked and burned Hattuşaş in 1200 BC The Phrygians then became the dominant people in the region.

One of the most famous finds in Hattuşaş is a copy of the Treaty of Kadesh, signed between the Hittite and Egyptian Empires after what might have been the largest chariot-battle ever fought. Some 5,000 chariots are believed to have been involved in one of the best-documented battles of the ancient world, between the Egyptian forces of Ramses II and the Hittite soldiers of Hattusili III. The treaty, written both in Egyptian hieroglyphs and in Akkadian using Cuneiform script, declares that both peoples and their gods want peace. It may be the world's first known peace treaty. An original can be seen at the Istanbul Archaeological Museum, and a copy hangs at the entrance to the Security Council chamber in the headquarters of the United Nations in New York.

Once at the site, ignore the awful reconstruction of a castle at the entrance, which looks like it was made out of Legos and covered with clay. The rest of the site consists mostly of huge blocks of ancient cut stones arrayed in rectangular patterns. The first ruins on the right are the **Temple of the Storm God** (Temple I). Inside there used to be statues of the storm god and sun goddess.

Continuing up the hill, you'll pass a series of gates in the city walls. The first is the **Aslankapı**, or Lion Gate. The lions there today are reproductions. Next is the very impressive **Yerkapı**, a long underground tunnel made of stones piled up and leaning into one another to form a triangle above you. Giant stones seem to hover overhead in an impressive display of ancient engineering. It was believed to have been a ceremonial entrance to the city. When the road forks, a left up the hill will take you to Büyükkale, said to be the royal residence of the Hittite kings with a view over the city.

Boğazkale is about 5 km (3 mi) north of Hattuşaş. There's not a lot to see there, though the village does have a pansiyon and a few restaurants. **Yazılıkaya,** about 2 km (1 mi) east of Hattuşaş, is thought to have served as the city's religious sanctuary; its name simply means "rock with writing." The walls here are covered with drawings of Hittite gods, goddesses, and kings from about 1200 BC. On the main shrine, 42 gods march from the left to meet 21 goddesses coming from the right. In the middle is the weather god Teshub with horns in his cap, and the goddess Hepatu riding a leopard. It's thought that funeral rights for kings were performed here.

The Hittite cities are about a two-hour drive east of Ankara. With

ROUGH GOING

If traveling from the Hittite cities to Cappadocia or vice-versa, be warned that the roads are almost criminally atrocious in places. Cars slide on a highway covered with a thick layer of dust, pebbles, and sand. Trucks coming from the other direction will expect you to get out of their way, no matter which side of the road they may be on.

your own car, you'll be able to do all three in the same day, as well as Alacahöyük. Most visitors will not feel the need to stay the night, though there are a couple of clean but unimpressive hotels around Boğazkale. ✉ *About $6 for all three cities* ☉ *Daily 8–noon and 1:30–5:30 (open later in summer)* ⊕ *www.hattuscha.de/eng/eng.html.*

Alacahöyük, about 25 km (15 mi) from Yazılıkaya, has evidence of human settlement dating back to 5000 BC All of the signs are in Turkish, but the site is impressive on its own and the small museum makes for a fun half hour or so. On display are bone arrows, some 7,000-year-old pitchers and pots that look like they could still be used, and a broken half-phallus with no explanation.

At the entrance to the site are a couple of sphinxes, a carved gate with scenes of men and animals, and some Early Bronze Age graves. The dead, the sign in Turkish says, were always buried in the northwest corner of the tomb, on their sides with their legs folded toward their chests, and facing south. Silver, gold, and weapons were found inside most of the graves. You'll likely be alone as you explore the site, with roosters crowing from the nearby village. ☎ *364/422–7011* ✉ *$1.75* ☉ *Daily 8–noon and 1:30–5:30.*

Kırşehir

26 *203 km (126 mi) from Ankara, east on Rte. E88 and south on Rtes. 765 and 260; 166 km (103 mi) from Boğazkale, west on Rte. E88 and south on Rtes. 785 and 260.*

Even the locals don't know where the major sites of Kırşehir are, so don't go out of your way to find them. There's a nice Seljuk mosque here and the place has a friendly village feel, but there's really no reason to stop unless you're an avid fan of Seljuk architecture. If so, you'll be interested in the Alaadin Cami and the Caca Bey Cami, both mosques built in the 13th century. If not, skip it. Caca Bey was also used as an astronomical observatory.

Hacıbektaş

27 *44 km (27 mi) south of Kırşehir, Rte. 260 to Rte. 765.*

You're likely to find Hacıbektaş a bit boring and unexceptional—un-

> ### THE SELJUKS
>
> A lot of what you'll see in the area east of Ankara was built by the Seljuks, members of a nomadic Turkic tribe that probably originated in or around Mongolia. The Seljuk Turks converted to Islam in the 10th century and began to push westward. They established their capital in Konya and would rule much of Anatolia from the 12th through 14th centuries, when the Mongols crushed them. Seljuk architecture is recognizable by its similarity to the Gothic architecture that was flourishing in Europe when the Seljuks dominated the Middle East. Many of the mosques, castles and kervansarays that brood over various Turkish villages were built in this style.

less you're there for the lively festival celebrating the town's spiritual namesake in late August. Hacı Bektaş Veli founded a Muslim sect here in the 13th century that was a synthesis of Sunni and Shii thought, blended with a touch of Christianity. He became the spiritual leader of the Jannissary warriors of the Ottoman Empire and gained a following of dervishes (Bektasis or Alevis) as well as some considerable political influence. The three-day festival celebrating him begins on August 16th of every year and is a colorful, popular affair with Sufi dancing and music in the streets. The souvenir shops sell trinkets with pictures of Atatürk, Hacı Bektaş, and the Imam Ali. Hacı Bektaş is buried in a tomb inside the **museum,** the main attraction in town. ⊠ *In the center of town* ⊕ *http://www.adiyamanli.org/hacibektas.html* ✉ *$1.75* ☉ *Tues.–Sun. 9–noon and 1–4:30.*

CENTRAL ANATOLIA ESSENTIALS

Transportation

BY AIR

Central Turkey is well served by Ankara's Esenboğa Airport, 30 km (19 mi) north of the city. There are direct flights from Europe and New York, as well as many domestic flights. Carriers include Delta Airlines and THY Turkish Airlines. THY also has daily direct flights from Istanbul to the airport at Kayseri, and that's by far the best option if time is short and you are planning only on visiting Cappadocia—Kayseri is within an hour's drive of most of the Cappadocian towns, and the THY shuttle will take you from the airport to any hotel in Cappadocia for $14. A low-cost airline was rumored to be planning flights directly to Nevsehir, but as of the writing of this edition, that had not yet happened.

A taxi into Ankara can cost as much as $25. More affordable shuttle buses, operated by Havaş, cost $3.50. Board them in front of the terminal shortly after flight arrivals, and you will be delivered to the train station or bus station.

🗂 **Delta Airlines** ☎ 312/468-7805, 800/241-4141 in the U.S. ⊕ www.delta.com. **Esenboğa Airport** ☎ 312/398-0100 ⊕ www.esenboga.com. **Havaş** ☎ 212/465-5656 ⊕ www.havas.com.tr. **THY Turkish Airlines** ☎ 312/419-2800

BY BUS

Few major towns or cities are not connected to Ankara by bus. The seven-hour trip from Istanbul costs about $22. There are many bus lines, and though there should always be seats available to major destinations, you may want to buy tickets in advance. The standard of buses is generally good, although some companies are better than others and cost a little more. Buses link most towns and cities within the region, and fares are reasonable (less than $12 from Ankara to most anywhere in Central Anatolia, for instance). You can also get to many of the major sights in Cappadocia by bus, but service is not frequent, so you'll find yourself often waiting for a ride, which can be excruciatingly uncomfortable in the summer heat.

The most comfortable long-distance bus lines and those with the best safety records are Varan Bus Company and Ulusoy. Ankara's Otogar bus station, called AŞTİ, is on Bahçelerarası Caddesi at Eskişehir Yolu. The

Ankara subway line from Kızılay district ends underneath the station. **Anakara Otogar** ☎ 312/224-1000. **Ulusoy** ☎ 312/419-4080 for Ankara, 212/471-7100 for Istanbul. **Varan Bus Company** ☎ 312/417-2525 for Ankara, 212/251-7474 for Istanbul.

BY CAR

Although most Turks and many tourists travel by bus, the independence provided by having a car in this region makes it a worthwhile expense, especially if time is short—you don't want to spend your short vacation waiting for buses. Renting cars and buying gas are expensive in Turkey, however, and you'll probably get a better rate through a tour company, especially if you purchase other services from them. The highways in Central Anatolia are generally well maintained and lead to all the major sights. Minor roads, however, are rough and full of potholes. On narrow, winding roads, look out for oncoming trucks, whose drivers often don't stay on their side of the road, and be especially careful at night, when animals and farm vehicles without proper running lights are likely to be on rural roads.

There are good roads between Istanbul and the main cities of Anatolia: Ankara, Konya, and Kayseri. Even so, truck traffic on the main highway from Istanbul to Ankara can be heavy. Two long stretches of toll road (*ücretli geçis*) linking Istanbul and Ankara—E80 to beyond Düzçe and E89 south from Gerede—provide some relief from the rigors of the other highways. You can also reach Central Anatolia on major highways from the Mediterranean coasts: From Ankara, E90 (also known as Rte. 200) leads southwest toward Sivrihisar; continue southwest on E96 to Afyon, where you can pick up highways going south to Antalya or west to İzmir. Rte. E88/200 leads east out of Ankara and eventually connects with highways to the Black Sea coast.

Ankara is a big city with chaotic traffic, so you'll save yourself a lot of grief if you park your car and get around by public transportation. The center of the city is relatively compact, and it is possible to walk to most places. A car is useful for excursions to the Hittite cities and to Cappadocia. Boğazkale and Hattuşaş are about 125 km (78 mi) east of Ankara, Konya is 261 km (162 mi) to the south, and Kayseri is 312 km (194 mi) southeast.

BY TAXI

Taxis are more expensive in Ankara than in Istanbul—a taxi from the airport, for instance, can cost you about $60. So take the Havaş bus service from the airport (runs every hour or half-hour), and once in the city, the subway is the best way to get around downtown. The cost of traveling by taxi to historic sites outside Ankara is usually reasonable ($30–$60), but always agree on the fare in advance. Cabs can be hailed, or ask your hotel to call one. You'll save money, though, if you travel in the capital by subway, bus, or dolmuş.

BY TRAIN

Regular rail service connects Ankara to both Istanbul and İzmir. The Ankara Express runs between Ankara and Istanbul; it leaves both places at 10:30 PM and arrives the next morning at 8. The price is about $35 for the sleeper bed and is by far the most comfortable train in the country. The Anadolu (Anatolia) Express also runs between Ankara and Istanbul, with simultaneous departures from both cities at 10 PM and with arrivals at 7 AM. There are no sleeper cars on this train, just regular seats that cost about $10. The final option between Istanbul and Ankara is the Başkent Express, which leaves Istanbul at 10 AM and arrives in Ankara at 4:50 PM, and leaves Ankara at 10:20 AM and arrives in Istanbul at 4:50 PM. The cost is about $13.

If you're traveling from the Mediterranean coast to Ankara by train, your choice is the İzmir Express, which travels between İzmir and Ankara and leaves both cities at 7 PM and arrives at 10 the next morning; the cost is about $10 per person. Another option is the İzmir Mavi, or Blue Train, which departs both cities at 6 PM and arrives at 8:30 AM; the cost is about $11.

There is very little train service between small towns in Central Anatolia. The one route that may be of use to tourists is Ankara–Kayseri, but it's generally much quicker to take a bus.

🚉 **Ankara train station** ⊠ Talat Paşa Cad., at Cumhuriyet Bul. ☎ 312/311-0620 for information, 312/311-4994 for reservations.

Contacts & Resources

BANKS & EXCHANGING SERVICES
It's easy to exchange money throughout Central Anatolia. Banks are open weekdays from about 8–2, and many currency exchanges in cities and tourist towns keep longer hours. Hotels will often cash traveler's checks. The easiest way to keep yourself stocked with Turkish lire is to use the ATM machines that you will find everywhere throughout the region, often even in the smallest towns.

EMERGENCIES
Your hotel is the best source of information on good hospitals, as well as on doctors and dentists.

🚑 **Ambulance** ☎ 112. **Police** ☎ 155.

INTERNET, MAIL & SHIPPING
Internet cafés abound in Cappadocia, especially in youthful Göreme and busy Ürgüp, but you'll find it's easy to go online just about anywhere. You'll also find Internet cafés throughout Ankara. Many hotels, even the most modest ones, now offer some form of Internet service. Some larger hotels are equipped with Wi-Fi, and many will have a computer in the lobby from which guests can check e-mail.

TOUR OPTIONS
TOURS FROM ANKARA Ankara travel agencies arrange bus tours to Cappadocia and Konya, as well as day trips within the city. Some also offer trips to the Hittite cities, and these tours are the best ways to see these places, since an informed guide can make sense of the rubble at your feet.

Setur Ankara ✉ Kavaklıdere Sok. 5/B ☏ 312/467-1165 🖷 312/467-8775. **T & T Tourism and Travel** ✉ Abdullah Cevdet Sok. 22/7, Çankaya ☏ 312/440-9234 🖷 312/440-2234. **Türk Ekspres** ✉ Cinnah Cad. 9, Çankaya ☏ 312/467-7334 🖷 312/467-2920.

TOURS IN
CAPPADOCIA

In Cappadocia, you might want to consider hiring a guide for at least one day of your visit. In general, guides here know the terrain well and can lead you to places you might not otherwise find, filling you in on fascinating details about the geology of the region, early Christians and other inhabitants, and other inside info; expect to pay about $25–$60 a day. Local tourist offices and hotels can make recommendations, or contact the companies below. Kirkit Voyage can arrange just about any activity in the region—horseback riding, hiking, rafting, or just sightseeing. Service is superb, managers are honest, and prices are reasonable.

Kirkit Voyage ☏ 384/511-3259 in Avanos. **Argonaut Escapades** ☏ 384/ 341-6255 in Ürgüp. **Otuken Travel** ☏ 384/271-2735 in Göreme. **Turtle Tour** ☏ 384/ 271-2388 in Göreme.

BALLOONING

One of the best ways to appreciate the expansiveness and diversity of Cappadocia's landscape is from a hot-air balloon. Before or after exploring the area on foot, invest in a morning ride with Kapadokya Balloons. Rides are offered from April through October and the cost is $230 per person.

Kapadokya Balloons ✉ Nevşehir Yolu 14/A, Göreme ☏ 384/271-2442.

VISITOR INFORMATION

Ministry of Tourism ✉ Gazi Mustafa Kemal Bul. 121 ☏ 312/229-2631 🖷 312/229-3661 ✉ Esenboğa Airport ☏ 312/398-0348. **Kayseri** ✉ Kağnı Pazarı 61, next to Hunat Hatun complex ☏ 352/222-3903 🖷 352/222-0879. **Konya** ✉ Mevlâna Cad. 21, by Mevlâna Museum ☏ 332/351-1074 🖷 332/350-6461. **Nevşehir** ✉ Atatürk Bul., next to hospital ☏ 384/213-3659. **Safanbolu** ✉ on the main Sq. ☏ 370/712-3863. **Ürgüp** ✉ Kayseri Cad. 37, inside park ☏ 384/341-4059.

Excursions to the Far East & the Black Sea Coast

WORD OF MOUTH

"What does it take to learn a couple words of Turkish? Not much! A simple 'merhaba' (hello) shows that you respect the country and culture. No one expects westerners to be fluent or literate in Turkish, but a little effort really goes a long way . . . You'll be pleasantly surprised at the positive reaction you will get with a little effort in the language department."

—jrlaw10

WELCOME TO THE FAR EAST

Church of the Holy Cross on the island of Akdamar

TOP REASONS TO GO

★ **Wandering the bustling bazaars of Şanliurfa and Gaziantep.** Craftsmen in these ancient cities still work the same way they have for centuries.

★ **Float in Lake Van** As in Israel's Dead Sea, the water is rich in minerals and very alkaline; you'll be remarkably buoyant in the startlingly blue water.

★ **Explore the ruins of Ani** Once the seat of a small Armenian kingdom, Ani is today pretty much a ghost town, filled with stunning ruins.

★ **Visit the cliffside monastery of Sümela** The climb up is fairly strenuous, but just seeing this remarkable sight is unforgettable.

★ **Journey up to Mt. Nemrut** The massive stone heads looking out over the horizon are an impressive sight to behold.

1 **The mountains of the Black Sea coast around Trabzon and the Sümela monastery:** This is the area least like the Turkey that visitors expect to see. With lush green valleys, snow-capped peaks, and small villages with chalet-like homes, it looks like a little piece of Switzerland.

2 **The region between Kars and Van:** This is Turkey's eastern frontier, filled with wide-open vistas, high mountain plateaus, and natural and manmade wonders, all offering a wonderful mix of adventure and history. Here you can see the haunting ancient city of Ani, the majestic Mt. Ararat, and the various sites around Lake Van, especially the island church of Akdamar.

3 **Around Diyarbakır and Mardin:** This area, part of ancient Mesopotamia, is steeped in history. The old cities are filled with honey-colored stone homes and small hillside villages surrounded by vineyards and look something like a Turkish Tuscany.

4 Gaziantep and Şanlıurfa:
Traveling around these cities
will give you the flavor of the
Middle East, from the bustling
bazaars where coppersmiths
bang away with hammers, to
the spicy local cuisine. This is
also the best spot to organize
a visit to the huge stone heads
atop Mt. Nemrut, also known
as Mt. Nimrod.

Climbing Mount Ararat,
Doğubeyazıt

GETTING ORIENTED

For the visitor who makes it to
Turkey's eastern regions, the rewards are plentiful: beautiful
scenery, wild nature, countless
historic sites, and ancient cities
where life has not changed
much over the centuries.
Turkey's eastern half is so vast
that it's possible to divide it into
separate regions, each offering
something different for travelers.

6

Mt. Nemrut

FAR EAST PLANNER

Getting Here

Getting to eastern Turkey once meant grueling bus rides that sometimes took more than a day. The arrival of budget air travel has changed this dramatically, and several domestic airlines now crisscross Turkey. And feeling the competition, Turkey's national carrier, Turkish Airlines, has started slashing fares on domestic routes. Best of all, Turkey's airlines don't penalize you for buying a one-way ticket, so it's possible to fly into one city and depart from another, which can save a lot of time.

When to Go

Spring and fall are generally the best times to visit these areas, with the exception of the Black Sea coast, which is usually less rainy during the summer but still quite cool compared to the rest of Turkey, which can be sweltering.

Hotels & Dining: With a few notable exceptions, the hotels in the east are basic, with little in the way of the upscale boutique hotels you might find along Turkey's coastline. Food in the Black Sea area relies on dishes made with dairy, corn flour, and seafood, especially *hamsi*, which is locally caught anchovy. Kebabs rule the rest of the east, although most restaurants will also offer a variety of stews and other ready-made hot dishes, usually meat-based.

Tips for the Excursions

TRABZON & THE BLACK SEA

■ Getting here: Fly to Trabzon from Istanbul.

■ How much time? Four to five days is enough to see the area. If you have extra time, spend another night in the Ayder area.

■ Getting around: We recommend flying here and renting a car, although it's possible to get around taking regional buses.

■ When to go: June-September is the best season. There is less rain, and the area, particularly the Kaçkar mountains, is blissfully cooler than the rest of Turkey.

■ Top sights: The Aya Sofia in Trabzon, the Sümela monastery complex, the high mountain summer villages around Ayder.

■ Tour by yourself or with a guide? It's easy to see most of the area by yourself, although touring the Kaçkar mountains is best done with a guide.

KARS, MT. ARARAT & LAKE VAN

■ Getting here: To save time, fly to Kars from Istanbul and then fly back from Van (or the other way around).

■ How much time? 4 or 5 days is enough. If you have extra time, stay an extra night in Van and do one of the sidetrips along Lake Van.

■ Getting around: Taking inter-city buses is good option in this region, although you might want to consider renting a car in Van to see the sights around Lake Van.

■ When to go: Winter is cold and dreary in Turkey's east, with many of the places you would want to visit inaccessible because of snow. Because of their altitude, Kars and Van are usually pleasant during the summer, although the sun can still be quite strong. May and June, when the area is especially green and covered with wild flowers, are good months to visit.

■ Top sights: The ruins of Ani, the fable-like Ishak Paş Sarayı in Doğubeyazıt, and the island church of Akdamar in Lake Van.

■ Tour by yourself or with a guide? You may want to consider hiring a guide for a visit to Ani as well as the area around Mt. Ararat and some of the sites around Lake Van.

DIYARBAKıR, MARDIN, MIDYAT & HASANKEYF

■ Getting here: Fly in and out of Diyarbakir from Istanbul.

■ How much time? 3-4 days will give you enough time to see this area. If you have extra time, spend another night in Mardin.

■ Getting around: Renting a car in Diyarbakir is the best option, although there are also inter-city buses.

■ When to go: Summer can be oppressively hot, with temperatures over 100 F, and winter is cold and damp, so the best time to visit is in spring (late April through early June) or fall (September to early November).

■ Top sights: the walls of Diyarbakir, the bazaar and side streets of Mardin, the exquisite stone homes of Midyat and the riverside ruins at Hasankeyf.

■ Tour by yourself or with a guide? Touring by yourself is a very good option, since distances are short and much of the excursion is really about walking around the area's old towns and soaking up the athmosphere.

GAZIANTEP, MT. NEMRUT & ŞANLıURFA (URFA)

■ Getting here: Fly in and out of Gaziantep from Istanbul.

■ How much time? Four or five days is enough time to see this area, if you have extra time, spend an extra night in Gaziantep to try another one of the city's great restaurants.

■ Getting around: We recommend flying and then renting a car, although inter-city buses are possible.

■ When to go: Summer can be oppressively hot, with temperatures over 100°F, and winter is cold and damp, so the best time to visit is in spring (late April through early June) and fall (September-early November).

■ Top sights: Mount Nemrut, the Gaziantep Museum, the bazaar in Gaziantep, the carp pools in Şanliurfa.

■ Tour by yourself or with a guide? It's easy to see this area by yourself, although you might want to consider taking a guided tour of Mt. Nemrut from Gaziantep.

Do You Need to Speak Turkish?

Because these areas are less touristed, finding English speakers can sometimes be a challenge, although many hotels in the area will usually have someone on staff who speaks some English.

How Careful Do You Need to Be?

During the 1980s and '90s, large parts of Turkey's east and southeast (but not the Black Sea area) were the scene of bitter fighting between the separatists of the Kurdistan Workers' Party and Turkish security forces. The fighting stopped, which allowed tourism in the region to get off the ground again, but there have been several isolated incidents in recent years, usually in remote areas where few tourists, let alone Turks, go.

6

TRABZON & THE BLACK SEA COAST

Revised and
updated by
Yigal Schleifer

Of all of Turkey's regions, the Black Sea coast least fits the bill of what most visitors imagine to be "Turkish." Instead of long, sandy beaches lined with resorts, the Black Sea's shores are rocky and backed by steep, lush mountains. And instead of sunny days, the area is often shrouded in mist. Culturally, the area has had as much Greek, Georgian, and Armenian influences as it has had Ottoman and Turkish. Although it is less visited than other parts of Turkey, the region is also one of the most rewarding. This excursion will take you to the Black Sea coast's most interesting destinations, from the historic seaside town of Trabzon and the nearby monastery complex of Sümela, clinging dramatically to the side of a cliff in a deep valley, to the Kaçkar mountains, whose 15,000-foot peaks tower over the area.

Trabzon, wedged between the Black Sea and the green mountains that rise behind it, is a city with a long historic pedigree that stretches back to Byzantine times. Today it is a modern city that, like many others in the region, is cursed with an overabundance of ugly concrete buildings. A little exploring, though, helps reveal the city's past, perhaps best represented by the magnificent Byzantine-era Aya Sofya church. Trabzon is also a good base for visiting the fascinating (though defunct) Orthodox monastery complex of Sümela. The monastery's location is breathtaking: hidden in a narrow valley and clinging to the side of a steep cliff. Although the monastery, which was functioning until the 1920s, and its beautiful frescoes have over the years been victims to vandalism, an extensive restoration project is under way.

As you head east from Trabzon, toward the border with Georgia, you will pass through Rize, Turkey's tea-growing capital, where hill after hill is covered with carefully laid out rows of dark green tea plants. From there you'll soon approach several valleys that lead up into the majestic Kaçkar mountains, dotted with small villages with wooden homes that evoke the Alps. Up in the Fırtına valley is Ayder, a mountain village that serves as a wonderful base for hiking and exploring the area's mountain trails and *yaylas,* which are fascinating high pasture summer villages where the rhythms of life seems to have changed little over the centuries.

TURKISH NUTS & TEA

Economic life on the Black Sea is dominated by two crops: hazelnuts and tea. Near Rize, the hills are covered in row after row of tea plants tended by villagers, who harvest the leaves in late spring. Every year, over 200,000 tons of tea are harvested in the area, most of it for domestic consumption. Turkey is also the globe's leading producer of hazelnuts, responsible for over 80 percent of the world's supply. Hazelnuts, often fresh off the tree and still in their shell, are easy to find in shops throughout the region, especially in late summer and early fall.

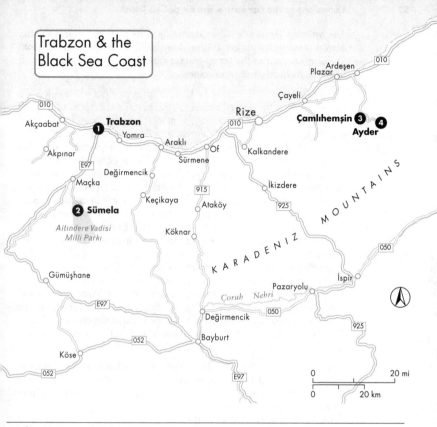

Trabzon & the Black Sea Coast

Trabzon

1 Trabzon has a dramatic location, perched on a hill overlooking the sea, with lush green mountains behind. Once the capital of the empire founded in 1204 by Alexius Comnene, grandson of a Byzantine emperor, the city was famed for its golden towers and glittering mosaics—probably built with family money diverted from the royal till before the fall of Constantinople.

Today's Trabzon seems far removed from that imperial past. The city is bustling and modern, with a busy port, crowded streets, and seemingly little to distinguish it from many other provincial Turkish towns. It only takes a little digging to get under the modern surface and reach the city's past. Byzantine-era churches, such as the lovely Aya Sofya, a smaller version of the similarly named church in Istanbul, can be found not far from modern apartment buildings. The city's old town, meanwhile, with its Ottoman-era houses, pedestrian-only streets, and lively bazaar offers a nice break from the concrete and crowds.

You can spend a day exploring the city, which is also a good base for a visit to the Sümela monastery. At night, have a fish dinner by the Black Sea or up in the hills overlooking the city.

The heart of Trabzon's social activity is in its pleasing central square, **Atatürk Alanı** (also called Taksim Meydanı), up İskele Caddesi from Trabzon's port. It's full of trees and tea gardens and surrounded by most of the city's hotels and restaurants.

The pedestrian-only Kunduracılar Caddesi leads west out of Atatürk Alanı into the maze of the **covered bazaar** (⊠ Just past Cumhuriyet Cad.), which includes a 16th-century *bedestan,* or market, that has been restored and now houses gift shops selling unremarkable trinkets and several cafés. Filled with clothing, housewares, and hardware shops, the bazaar also has a small but appealing section filled with coppersmiths, who make a variety of bowls, trays, and pots. The city's largest mosque, the **Çarşi Cami**, built in 1839, is joined to the market by an archway. Trabzon's Byzantine-era **citadel**, in between two ravines, is still imposing, though it's pretty much a ruin. Its ramparts were restored after the Ottoman conquest in 1461, although the remains of the Byzantine palace are insignificant. No army ever took Trabzon by force, though many tried. Inside the citadel walls is the 10th-century Church of **Panaghia Chrysokephalos** (the Virgin of the Golden Head), which was the city's most important church for several centuries until the Aya Sofya was built. The Ottomans converted it into a mosque, the **Ortahisar Cami,** in the 15th century. Not much is left of the building's Byzantine glory, although it's soaring basilica and massive columns are still impressive. ⊠ *Kale Cad.; from Hükümet Cad. (off Maraş Cad.), follow the Tabakhane Bridge over the gorge, turn left.*

You can get a good view of Trabzon from along **İç Kale Caddesi**, the street south of the citadel. From here you can also make out three other Byzantine monuments, all south of the Atatürk Alanı: the **Yeni Cuma Cami** (New Friday Mosque), built as the Church of St. Eugene in the early 13th century; the 13th-century **Teokephastos Convent,** on the other side of the hill; and the **Kudrettin Cami**, consecrated as the Church of St. Philip in the 14th century. Aya Sofya is visible about 3 km (2 mi) west of Atatürk Alanı.

★ Trabzon's best-known Byzantine monument, the 13th-century **Aya Sofya** (Church of the Holy Wisdom, or St. Sophia), sits on a romantic bluff overlooking the Black Sea. The ruined church, known in Greek as Hagia Sofia, has some of the finest Byzantine frescoes and mosaics in existence. It was converted into a mosque in Ottoman times and first opened to the public as a museum in 1963. The west porch houses the real masterpieces:

BLACK SEA SPECIALTIES

Size isn't everything, as the miniscule *hamsi* (Black Sea anchovy) proves. Although usually not much longer or fatter a finger on your hand, the *hamsi* is often called the "prince" of the Black Sea fish. In the Black Sea region, the little fish can be found in an almost endless amount of dishes: fried in a coating of corn meal, served in a fragrant pilaf, baked into bread, or thrown into an omelet (there have even been some attempts at making hamsi ice cream). Also try *muhallema* (a type of Black Sea cheese fondue) and honey made in the high mountain villages of the Kaçkars.

frescoes of Christ preaching in the Temple, the Annunciation, and the wedding at Cana, executed in a style that shows strong Italian influence. As at Istanbul's Aya Sofya, the artworks here were not destroyed by the Ottomans, only hidden under a hard layer of plaster. There's a shaded tea garden near the entrance. ⊠ *Kayakmeydan Cad.* ☎ *462/223–3043* ⊞ *$1* ⊘ *May–Sept., daily 9–6; Oct.–Apr., Tues.–Sun. 8–5.*

Atatürk Köşkü, Atatürk's summer villa (though he didn't actually spend much time here) is now a museum dedicated to the former leader. The attractive white gingerbread house, set in a small forest, is a pleasant place to visit and has a nice view of the city below. ⊠ *Soğuksu Cad., 7 km (4 mi) southwest of Trabzon's central Sq.* ☎ *462/231–0028* ⊞ *$1* ⊘ *May–Sept., daily 8–7; Oct.–Apr., daily 9–5.*

★ The **Trabzon Museum,** in a 1910 mansion built for a local banker, is intriguing because of the building itself, as well as for its collection. The main floor has incredibly ornate rooms that have been restored and filled with period furniture. The basement holds a variety of archaeological finds from the Trabzon region. ⊠ *Zeytinlik Cad. 10* ☎ *462/322–3822* ⊞ *$1* ⊘ *Tue.–Sun. 9–5.*

Where to Stay & Eat

$–$$ ✕ **Boztepe Aile Gazinosu.** Grilled meat and fish are the specialties at this restaurant with tables in a shady garden and on an outdoor terrace; it's a nice break from the bustle of downtown Trabzon. Above the city in the green Boztepe Park, the restaurant also has a lovely view of the Black Sea and Trabzon's harbor. Finish your meal with tea served in an old-fashioned samovar. ⊠ *Boztepe Mahalesi* ☎ *462/321–4536* ⊟ *MC, V.*

$ ✕ **Balıçı Dede.** On the western edge of Trabzon, this fish restaurant gets you as close to the water as possible. The sea and mountain views, and the sound of lapping water in the background, make the location a winner, especially at sunset. The fish, served grilled or fried, is fresh, and there is a full selection of well-made mezes to choose from. Alcohol is also served, unlike at many other restaurants in Trabzon. ⊠ *Merkez Akyazı Beldesi Devlet Karayolu Üzeri* ☎ *462/221–0398* ⊟ *MC, V.*

¢–$ ✕ **Brasserie Pera.** On a busy boulevard above Trabzon's main square, a string of cafés are trying to create something of a local hip scene. This one, with its striped awning and tables on the sidewalk, has a vaguely European feel to it and always seems to be the most crowded. The menu features sandwiches, salads, and pastas, along with a variety of cakes and ice cream, a nice break from kebabs. ⊠ *Yavuz Selim Bulvari 173* ☎ *462/326–4696* ⊟ *MC, V.*

¢–$ ✕ **Hürrem Sultan Sofrası.** Despite its budget prices, this eatery across from the Zorlu Grand Hotel has opted for a touch of class, with waiter service and tables draped with green tablecloths. The kebabs and döner, are good, if unexceptional, as is the assortment of meat and vegetable stews. ⊠ *Maraş Cad. 30* ☎ *462/322–2290* ⊟ *MC, V.*

¢ ✕ **Üstad Lokantası.** This homey restaurant on Atatürk Alanı is low on atmosphere, but it's hard to beat the well-made, very affordable food. A steam table at the entrance holds an assortment of dishes, including meat and vegetable stews baked in a large terra-cotta pot, stuffed cabbage, and Turkish-style meatballs. The rice pudding dessert is worth tasting. ✉ *Atatürk Alanı 18/B* ☎ *462/321–5406* ▤ *MC, V.*

¢ ✕ **Murat Balık Salonu.** Located on the north side of Atatürk Alanı, this small, no-nonsense restaurant offers Black Sea fish that's perfectly grilled and served with a slice of lemon, a hunk of raw onion, and grilled tomatoes and peppers. A glass case in the front holds the day's catch: red mullet, mackerel, anchovies, trout, or whatever else is in season. The small dining room, painted an electric green, is usually filled with local men who come in for a quick and unceremonious meal. ✉ *Park Karşısı* ☎ *462/322–3100* ▤ *No credit cards.*

$$$$ ▦ **Zorlu Grand Hotel.** With a marble-lined, atrium-like lobby topped by a stained-glass dome, this is certainly Trabzon's fanciest hotel, with prices to match. Rooms are large, elegant, and comfortably furnished. The staff is courteous and professional and the tranquil lobby, done up in an Art Deco meets Moorish style, is a nice refuge from the bustling streets outside. ✉ *Maraş Cad. 9, 61100* ☎ *462–326–8400* 🖷 *462/326–8458* ⊕ *www.zorlugrand.com* ⤴ *143 rooms, 14 suites ⌂ 2 restaurants, bar, cable TV, minibars, in-room safes, in-room dataports, indoor pool, gym, sauna, Turkish bath, laundry, dry cleaning, business services, parking* ▤ *AE, DC, MC, V* ¶⭕ *BP.*

$$ ▦ **Sağıoğlu.** Opened in 2003, this yellow-painted hotel is just off Trabzon's main square. The rooms are on the small side, but they are clean and comfortable, with small desks and beige-colored walls. It's a good fallback in case other hotels are booked up. ✉ *Taksim Işhanı Sok. 1, 61100* ☎ *462/323–2899* 🖷 *462/321–3703* ⊕ *www.sagirogluotel.com* ⤴ *20 rooms ⌂ Cable TV, minibars, Wi-Fi* ▤ *MC, V* ¶⭕ *BP.*

$$ ✕▦ **Usta Park Hotel.** Conveniently located off Atatürk Alanı, you can't miss the looming bright red Usta Park Hotel. Rooms are comfortable enough, if somewhat sparsely decorated, but gold-colored bedspreads add warmth. The rooftop restaurant, where breakfast is served, has a nice view of the sea, while the lobby has crystal chandeliers, brown leather lounge chairs, and Greek music playing in the background. ✉ *Iskenderpaşa Mah. 361100* ☎ *462/326–5700* 🖷 *462/322–3793* ⊕ *www. ustaparkhotel.com* ⤴ *114 rooms, 6 suites ⌂ Restaurant, bar, cable TV, minibars, in-room safes, exercise equipment, sauna, Turkish bath, meeting rooms* ▤ *AE, DC, MC, V* ¶⭕ *BP.*

★ $ ▦ **Horon Hotel.** One block off the main square, the Horon has spacious rooms done up in a slightly tacky peach and green motif. The professional staff is extremely helpful, though, and the parking and valet service are a blessing. On weekends be sure to ask for a room away from the rather loud bar. The rooftop restaurant, which offers a good-value prix-fixe menu, looks out over the sea and the rooftops below. ✉ *Sıramağazalar Cad. 125* ☎ *462/326–6455* 🖷 *462/321–6628* ⊕ *www. otelhoron.com* ⤴ *44 rooms ⌂ Restaurant, bar, cable TV, minibars, in-room safes, Wi-Fi, meeting rooms* ▤ *, MC, V* ¶⭕ *BP.*

¢ ▦ **Hotel Nur.** With a cheery staff and spotless rooms (though small and painted bright green), this is Trabzon's best budget option. Some of the front rooms on the higher floors even have a sea view. The hotel is conveniently located on a quiet side street just off Trabzon's main square. ✉ *Cami Sokak 15, 61100* ☎ *462/323–0445* 🖷 *462/323–0447* ⤴ *15 rooms ⌂ Cable TV, minibars* ▤ *MC, V* ¶⭕ *BP.*

Sümela/Mereyemana

② *47 km (29 mi) south of Trabzon on Rte. 885 to Maçka, and then east on road to Altındere National Park.*

Set in a dramatic valley and clinging to the side of a sheer cliff, the Sümela monastery (Mereyemana in Turkish) is a spectacular and unforgettable sight. The Orthodox monks who founded the retreat, also known as ★ the **Monastery of the Virgin,** in the 4th century carved their cells right from the rock. Built to house a miraculous icon of the Virgin painted by St. Luke, this shrine was later rebuilt and expanded by Alexius III, who was crowned here in 1340—an event depicted in the frescoes of the main church in the grotto. Where chunks of the frescoes have fallen off—or been chipped away or scribbled over by overly enthusiastic souvenir hunters and graffiti artists—three layers of plaster from repaintings done in the 14th and 18th centuries are clearly visible. Tolerant Ottoman sultans left the retreat alone, but after the Greeks were expelled from Turkey in 1922, the Turkish government permitted monks to transfer the Virgin icon itself to a new monastery in Greek Macedonia. The frescoes themselves are not as well preserved as those at Trabzon's Aya Sofya, but the setting—a labyrinth of courtyards, corridors, and chapels—is incredible. The monastery and its surrounding rooms are continually being restored, but there's not much hope the job will be finished soon. From the parking lot, you can pick up the well-worn trail that takes you on a rigorous 40-minute hike to the monastery—it's more than 820 ft above the valley floor and disappears completely when the clouds come down. If you're not up for the big hike, a 10-minute drive from the parking lot up a winding gravel road takes you to another trailhead, from where it's only about a 15-minute walk to the monastery. ⊠ *Altındere National Park* ☎ *No phone* 💰 *$3 per person, $4 for parking* ⊙ *Apr.–Oct., daily 9–6; Nov.–Mar., daily 9–4.*

Where to Stay & Eat

¢–$ ✕ **Sümer Restaurant.** With wooden gazebos set on the edge of a small river, this is a fine spot to have lunch or dinner after visiting Sümela, a 15-minute drive away. There is a wide selection of mezes, along with regional specialties such as *canlı alabalık* (fresh trout) baked in butter, and *kaygana,* an omlette made with Black Sea anchovies. On the weekends, the restaurant (formerly known as Sümela Ciftlik Restaurant) is filled with families from Trabzon on country outings. ⊠ *Maçka Sümela Manastırı Yolu Km 2* ☎ *462/512–1581* ▤ *MC, V.*

¢ ✕ **Sümela Sosyal Tesisleri.** Just below the Sümela monastery, this simple restaurant makes wonderful use of the stunning location—a series of open-air wood patios are spread out along a thunderous rushing stream. You can order köfte or kebabs, or choose from a few regional dishes, such as *kuymak,* the Black Sea version of cheese fondue. The cool air and shade make this is an excellent spot to rest after a visit to the monastery. ⊠ *Sümela Manastiri* ☎ *462/531–1207* ▤ *MC, V.*

$ ▥ **Coşandere Turistik Tesisleri.** Some 3 miles from the entrance to Sümela, this is an appealing option if you want to stay near the monastery. The hotel has several bungalows, but most of the rooms are in a four-story, chalet-like wooden building just opened in 2006. The cozy rooms have still-fragrant pine furniture and there are fluffy comforters on the bed. An open-air restaurant by the river serves trout baked in a terra-cotta dish, among other stomach-warming options. In addition to arranging visits to Sümela, the hotel can set up for day tours of nearby yaylas. ⊠ *Sümela Yolu, Maçka* ☎ *462/531–1190* 🖷 *462/531–1024* ⊕ *www. cosandere.com* 🛏 *40 rooms, 9 bungalows* ⚭ *Cable TV, minibars, shops* 🞸 *MC, V* ⊗ *Closed Oct.–Apr.* ⏇| *BP.*

¢ 🏠 **Kayalar Pansiyon.** Roughly 2 miles before you reach the admission booth to Sümela, this simple family-run pansiyon on the side of a grass-covered hill is the best option if you want to stay near the monastery. Run by the friendly Halit and Nereman Kaya (who also does the cooking), the rambling house has simple rooms with kilims covering the pine floors and walls painted white. Five of the rooms have balconies where you can catch a lovely breeze but only two of the rooms have en-suite bathrooms. ⊠ *Sümela Manastiri Yolu üzeri, Maçka* ☎ *462/531–1057* 🛏 *7 rooms* 🞸 *No credit cards* ⊗ *Closed Oct.—Apr.* ⏇| *BP.*

EN ROUTE Rize, 75 km (47 mi) east of Trabzon and the capital of the Black Sea's tea-growing region, sits above a small bay but below the foothills of the lush Pontic Mountains. There's not much else to do here but stop for a glass of the local brew in the hilltop **Zıraat Parkı,** a botanical garden near the town's western entrance. There's a small kiosk in the parking lot that sells gift packs of tea.

Morina Balı Lokantası—This unassuming restaurant on the coastal road halfway between Trabzon and Rize serves some of the best fish in the area. There's always a varied selection of freshly caught options—including meaty salmon steaks—cooked over hot coals or fried in a dusting of corn flour. The tomato-based fish chowder is also tasty. A pleasant garden is shaded by creeping vines. This is definitely worth a stop. ⊠ *22 miles out of Trabzon in the direction of Rize, Çamburn/Sürmene* ☎ *462/752–2023.*

Northeast of Rize, several forested valleys lead from the Black Sea into the towering and beautiful Kaçkar Mountains. Dotted with small villages, the cool mountains are a great place for hiking or just kicking back and checking out the alpine views. The mountains are also home to several yaylas, high pasture villages that are inhabited only during the summer and are accessible only by footpath.

Çamlıhemşin

❸ *124 km (77 mi) northeast of Trabzon; 22 km (14 mi) south of Ardeşen.*

The small village of Çamlıhemşin, at the junction of two rushing rivers, serves mainly as a gateway to mountain valleys above, particularly to the village of Ayder, but it's a pleasant and quiet overnight stop before heading up into the Kaçkars. There's not much to do here other than look out on the green mountains and listen to the river flowing by.

Where to Stay & Eat

¢ ✕ **Ibonun Yeri.** Run by friendly Ibrahim Uysal, this riverside restaurant on the road to Ayder serves grilled meats (the veal pan-fried in butter is delicious) and fresh trout. With pine walls and colorful local fabrics hanging from the ceiling, the restaurant is cozy and inviting. Ibrahim's wife works with him and is responsible for the flaky homemade baklava. ⊠ *Merkez Mah.* ☎ *464/651–7288* ▤ *No credit cards.*

$ ⌂ **Hemşin Houses.** Opened in 2006 by local guide Mehmet Demirci, this tranquil eco-lodge is the first and (currently) only proper place to stay in Çamlıhemşin—it's also a bit out of the way to get to, although only a few minutes' drive from the center of town. On a plot of wooded land that belonged to his grandfather, Demirci built four wooden cabins (each can sleep four) that look out over the forested mountains. An organic garden on-site grows berries, grapes, and vegetables, and a simple restaurant offers local foods. Getting to the lodge involves an easy 5-minute walk through the woods from the road. Your luggage will be ferried up the hillside in a metal basket pulled by a cable. ⊠ *Inönü Cad. 47, 53750* ☎ *464/651–7230* 📠 *464/651–7570* ⊕ *www.ecodanitap. com* ⇔ *4 cabins* ▤ *No credit cards.*

OFF THE BEATEN PATH — Most people take a left out of Çamlıhemşin and continue up to the mountain village of Ayder, but continuing straight on the road takes you up into the Fırtına valley, an often mist-shrouded place that sees few visitors and seems forgotten by time. Waterfalls and streams tumble out of the mountains, which are covered by thick stands of green pines. Small villages with peak-roofed two-story wooden houses cling to the mountainsides. As you drive along the road, you'll pass several examples of the elegant Ottoman-era humpback bridges that span the local rivers.

$ ⌂ **Fırtına Pansiyon.** The Firtina Pansiyon, in a converted schoolhouse, is the most inviting of the few places to stay in Firtina valley. Run by a local brother and sister, the pansiyon, which has six rooms and two bungalows, is nestled between the green mountains in a completely solitary spot. Rooms are small and have shared bathrooms, but the location is beautiful and a good spot for exploring the rest of the valley, which the owners can help you do. ⊠ *Şenyuva Köyü* ☎ *464/653–3111* 📠 *464-653-3111* ⊕ *www.firtinavadisi.com* ⇔ *6 rooms, 2 cabins* ⌂ *Sauna* ▤ *No credit cards* ⊙ *Closed Oct.–Mar.* ⏉ *MAP.*

Ayder

❹ *90 km (56 mi) northeast of Rize; 17 km (11 mi) southeast of Çamlıhemşin.*

At 4,000 ft and surrounded by snow-capped mountains and tumbling waterfalls, the mountain village of Ayder, with its wooden chalets and wandering cows, can seem like a piece of Switzerland transported to Turkey. Once a sleepy yayla, a high pasture village where locals would live in the summer, Ayder has become a popular destination for Turkish tourists and, increasingly, foreign ones. While a few years ago the village's bucolic nature was threatened by overdevelopment, local laws have now ordered all building to be done in the local style, with wooden exteriors and peaked roofs. Despite the summertime crowds that can sometimes fill the small village to capacity, the setting remains magnificent and the nights, when the stars put on a glorious show in the sky above, are still marvelously quiet. The village is also an excellent base for either day hikes or extended treks in the Kaçkars and for visiting some of the less accessible yaylas in the region to see a way of life that has changed little over the centuries.

Ayder has a grassy main square that during the summer frequently plays host to festivals celebrating local Hemşin culture, with music played on a local version of the bagpipe (known as the *bağlama*) and horon dancing, which has men and women dancing together in a big circle. Ayder is also known for its hot springs, which are reputed to cure all types of ailments. True or not, the **springs** (☎ 464/657–210 ☉ Mar.–Nov., daily 7–7; Dec.–Feb., daily 10–6 ☜ $3), housed in a modern, marble-lined building near the village's mosque, are good for a relaxing soak after a day of hiking. There are separate facilities for men and women, as well as private rooms for couples that want to bathe together.

The easiest yayla to visit from Ayder is Yukarı Kavron, about six miles from the village along a dirt road. A collection of squat stone houses, it's set on a high plateau surrounded by gorgeous mountains. There are several nice hikes leading out of the village. There is regular minivan service in the morning out of Ayder to the yayla, although it's best to check with your hotel or pansiyon about the exact schedule.

Where to Stay & Eat

¢ ✕ **Ayder Sofrası.** Run by the owners of the Haşimoğlu hotel, this large restaurant has a nice stone-lined terrace with wooden picnic tables that look over the mountains. The kitchen turns out trout and local dishes such as stuffed cabbage and *muhallama*, the local cheese fondue, and serves an open buffet breakfast every day. ⊠ *Ayder Kapalıcaları* ☎ *464/657–2037* ▤ *MC, V.*

¢ ✕ **Dört Mevsim.** This low-key restaurant has two things going for it: a great location that looks out on a magnificent waterfall and, a rarity for Ayder, a liquor license. You can drink your wine or beer along with mezes, kebabs, and *muhallama*. The outdoor terrace has a view of the waterfall; this is a good spot to rest your legs after a hike around Ayder. ⊠ *Şelale Karşısı* ☎ *464/657–2019* ▤ *No credit cards.*

¢ ✕ **Nazlı Cicek.** In a shaded ravine near the entrance to town, the family-run Nazlı Cicek serves tasty trout that is taken fresh from one of the cement pools on the premises. They also serve the usual assortment of grilled meats. You can eat inside the cozy restaurant, which has colorful Hemşin fabrics on the walls, or outside, near a running stream. ⊠ *Ayder Merkez* ☎ *464/657–2130* ▤ *MC, V.*

$ ▦ **Fora Pensiyon.** Run by local guide Mehmet Demirci and his wife (who also own the Hemşin Houses eco-lodge in Çamlıhemşin), this venerable Ayder pansiyon is located on the top of the hill at the entrance to the village. The wooden house has a rustic feel, with simple, cozy rooms lined with wide wooden paneling and shared bathrooms. A stone-lined outdoor terrace, where breakfast and dinner are served, looks out on the forested mountains and the village below. ⊠ *Ayder Kaplıcaları* ☎ *464-657-2153* 📠 *464-651-7570* ⊕ *www.turkutour.com* ⤳ *7 rooms, 1 bungalow* ▤ *No credit cards* ☉ *Closed Dec.–Apr.* ❖ *MAP.*

$ ▦ **Kuşpuni Dinlenme Evi.** Set on the edge of a green field, this wooden chalet has comfortable rooms that are larger than those in many of the other local pansiyons. With colorful rugs and kilims in the hallways, the place has a homey feel and the owners are very friendly. A nice restaurant with an outdoor terrace serves local specialties with wonderful views. ☒ *Yukarı Ambarlik* ☎ *464/657–2052* ✒ *15 rooms* ⚙ *Restaurant* ▤ *MC, V* ☺ *Closed Oct.–Apr.* ⧫ *BP.*

$ ⌂ **Otel Ayder Haşimoğlu.** Ayder's only full-service hotel is a large, wood-sheathed building near the hot springs. The rooms are comfortable; some have small balconies. The hotel has less charm than the pansiyons that dot Ayder, but the staff is professional and courteous. Because of its size, the hotel is popular with tour groups. ☒ *Ayder Kaplıcaları* ☎ *464/657–2037* 🖨 *464/657–2038* ⊕ *www.ayderhasimogluotel.com* ✒ *58 rooms, 7 cottages* ⚙ *Cable TV, minibars* ▤ *MC, V* ⧫ *BP.*

¢ ⌂ **Ahşap Pansiyon.** Up on a hillside looking over the village and the mountains, this wood chalet (*ahşap* means "made of timber" in Turkish) is a good choice. The small rooms are cozy, and the downstairs dining room has large windows with a nice view of Ayder and the mountains. ☒ *Yukarı Ambarlik* ☎ *464/657–2162* 🖨 *464/657–2212* ✒ *16 rooms* ⚙ *Cable TV, restaurant* ▤ *No credit cards* ☺ *Oct.–Apr.* ⧫ *BP.*

¢ ⌂ **Serender Pansiyon.** Owner Yusuf Mamuş was born in Ayder but went off to Istanbul to work. He came back in 2000 when he retired, and decided to open the friendly Serender Pansiyon, which is also where he and his wife live. The house, like most of the other pansiyons in Ayder, is made of wood. The rooms are simple, but have wonderful views of the mountains and waterfalls; there's the occasional sound of a cowbell in the distance. A lovely terrace where breakfast is served looks out on pastures and the mountains. ☒ *Yukarı Ambarlik* ☎ *464/657–2201* ✒ *14 rooms* ▤ *MC, V* ⧫ *BP.*

TRABZON & THE BLACK SEA COAST ESSENTIALS

Transportation

BY AIR

There are several daily flights to Trabzon from both Istanbul and Ankara. Fares are competitive, so check with the different airlines to see who has the best. The lowest are about $45–$60 one way.

BY BOAT & FERRY

The state-run ferry line between Istanbul and Trabzon, with stops in other Black Sea ports, has been discontinued. There has been talk of the line being revived under private ownership, so check with a travel agent or online for any developments. Even when it ran, though, the trip took 43 hours—not very practical.

BY BUS

The bus ride from Istanbul to Trabzon takes almost 20 hours, and at around $40, is not much cheaper than flying. There is daily service from Istanbul's Esenler bus terminal to the Trabzon bus terminal. There is also daily service from Ankara's AŞTİ bus terminal.

Bus service between towns runs frequently and is inexpensive. You can get schedules at the local tourist information office or directly from the bus station in Trabzon.

🛈**Ankara bus terminal** ☎ 312/224-1000. **Esenler terminal** ☎ 212/658-1010. **Trabzon bus terminal** ☎ 462/325-2397

BY CAR

Renting a car is the most convenient way of getting around the Black Sea area. The coast road from Trabzon eastward is currently in the process of being widened and turned into a proper highway, lessening travel time and making the driving experience much safer.

Avis has an office in downtown Trabzon, as well as one at the airport. There are also several local companies around Trabzon's main square (Atatürk Alanı). As elsewhere in Turkey, local companies may offer cheaper rates than international names, but not all companies include comprehensive insurance coverage in the price. Check the small print before agreeing on terms.

🛈**Avis** ☎ 462/322-3740 downtown, 462/325-5582 airport.

Contacts & Resources

EMERGENCIES

🛈**Police** ☎ 155. **Ambulance** ☎ 112.

GUIDED TOURS

Eyce Tours in Trabzon can help with arranging tours to Sümela and the region around Trabzon. Mehmet Demirci's Turku Turizm in Çamlıhemşin can help with arranging treks in the Kaçkar mountains and tours of the yaylas in the area.

🛈**Eyce** ☎ 462/326-7174 ⊕ www.eycetours.com.

VISITOR INFORMATION

🛈**Trabzon** ✉ Ali Naki Efendi Sok. 1/A (near Atatürk Alanı) ☎ 462/321-4659.

KARS, MT. ARARAT & LAKE VAN

Turkey's east is a region filled with stark contrasts: dusty plains and soaring mountains, simple villages and bustling cities. Near Turkey's border with Armenia and Iran, this remote region is also filled with natural and man-made wonders and, for the visitor, offers the chance to see a part of Turkey that has yet to be invaded by the tourist hordes. While this means that you may not find all the amenities and services available in western Turkey, the friendliness and hospitality of the area's predominantly Kurdish locals will very likely make up for it.

This excursion starts in Kars, which spent the early part of the 20th century under Russian occupation and still looks in places like a small Russian town. More than anything else, though, Kars serves as the base for exploring the haunting Ani, one of Turkey's most important historical sites. Once the capital of an Armenian kingdom that ruled the area more than a thousand years ago and that filled the city with stunning churches, Ani is today more like a ghost town, filled with ruins that still manage

Kars, Mt. Ararat & Lake Van

Erzurum
Tekman
Hinis
Varto
Yaygin
Kazanan
Mus
Akcosir
Heringok

Benliahmet
Pasinler
Horasan
Dellalhani
Tahir
Karacan
Binpinar
Bulanik
Nazik
Seyrantepe
Kavakbasi
Bitlis
Tosunlu

Kars 1
Pazarcik
Kurudere
Sarikamis
Kocakoy
Kagizman
Eleskirt
Karakose
Tutak
Patnos
Malazgirt
Kanahasan
Adilcevaz
Mt. Nemrut 8
Tatvan
Gevas

Ani 2
ARMENIA
Yerevan
Tuzluca
Igdir
Ahura
Diyadin
Mt. Ararat 4
Doğubeyazıt 3
Ercis
Muradiye
Muradiye Falls
Astvatsadsin
Takuriengiz
Ercek
Lake Van 5
Van 6
Orenburc
Akdamar 7
Gurpinar
Guzelsu

IRAN

0   30 mi
0   30 km

to evoke the city's former glory. Its location, at the edge of a windswept gorge with snowcapped mountains in the background and grassy fields stretching out to the horizon, only adds to Ani's mystique.

From Kars continue to Doğubeyazıt, a dusty town not far from the Iranian border. While the town isn't much to look at, it's blessed with being located almost at the foot of the mythical Mt. Ararat, the 16,850-foot peak that some believe is the resting place of Noah's ark. A perfect cone rising to the sky from the flat plains around it, Ararat is quite a sight to behold. Also in Doğubeyazıt is the Ishak Paşa Saray, an 18th-century palace in the hills above town which seems like it was transported straight out of a fairytale.

The next stop is Van, a modern and bustling city that is the economic capital of Turkey's east. Use this city as a base for exploring the area around the nearby Lake Van, one of Turkey's most fascinating natural wonders. Surrounded by mountains, the lake's blue-green waters are rich in minerals and very alkaline, meaning even the poorest swimmer will float with ease. The region around the lake is home to several intriguing historical sites, most importantly the magical island of Akdamar and its 10th-century Armenian church. It's an area that you could easily spend several days exploring.

Spotlight on the Armenians

ARMENIANS WERE ONCE an integral part of the ethnic mix in Turkey's east, although today none remain in the region. What happened to them is a topic of sensitive debate in Turkey.

There were various Armenian kingdoms in the region starting in the 3rd century BC and lasting until almost the 11th century AD. After that, the Armenians—who adopted Christianity in AD 301—became the subjects of a succession of rulers, from the Byzantines, to the Persians, and finally the Ottomans. Armenians ended up living in Eastern Turkey throughout the Ottoman Empire, with Istanbul eventually becoming one of their main cultural centers.

During World War I, when the Ottomans came under attack by Russia and the other allied powers, some Armenians in the east saw this as a chance for independence and rose up in revolt. The Ottoman response led to the death of hundreds of thousands (some claim even 1.5 million). The Turks, while admitting that large numbers of Armenians died at the time, say this was the result of war and disease, which also cost the lives of many others living in the region. Some 70,000 Armenians still live in Turkey, mostly in Istanbul.

Kars

The Kars airport is 4 miles out of town.

The setting for Turkish novelist Orhan Pamuk's somber novel *Snow*, Kars looks like the frontier town it is: forbidding and grayish, set on a 5,740-foot plateau and forever at the mercy of the winds. There are signs of a new breath of life all over the town, though, which is not far from Turkey's border with Armenia and Georgia. Some of Kars's Ottoman-era historic buildings are being beautifully restored as part of an ambitious project sponsored by the California-based Global Heritage Fund. The lifting of restrictions on visiting the ancient city of Ani—previously a closed military zone in the border area near Kars—has meant more tourists are coming through town, giving some locals the incentive to start upgrading what Kars has to offer. A sign of changing times was the opening, in 2006, of the city's first boutique hotel: the Kars Otel.

This minirevival would be only the latest twist of history in a city that has had at least its own share of ups and downs. Since AD 1064, Kars has been besieged over and over, by various and sundry invaders: from the Akkoyun to the Mongol warriors of Tamerlane. In the 19th century alone, it was attacked three times by czarist armies from Russia. The Turks retook the city in 1920, and Kars was formally ceded to Turkey after the war of independence in 1921. The Russian influence is still obvious in many buildings and in the rigid grid of streets that form the town's small center.

With its low buildings and compact town center, Kars has a relaxed, small-town feeling to it. The city has a reputation as being a liberal and secular-minded outpost, and it certainly has more bars and licensed restaurants than other towns in the conservative east. There is a sense of renewed optimism in Kars today, with locals hoping their position near the border might make the town something of a trade hub and that the tourist traffic to Ani in the summer and the nearby Sarıkamış ski resort in the winter will only increase, further stimulating the city's renewal. For now, though, Kars makes for a nice side dish to the main course that is the nearby mesmerizing site of Ani.

İç Kale (Kars Castle) overhangs the town from a high, rocky vantage point. Though it dates from the 10th century, most surviving fortifications were commissioned by Lala Mustafa Paşa in 1579—in 1386 Tamerlane swept violently through the region and razed the original structure. The castle has gone through some restoration in recent years, and the panoramic views of Kars merit the 10-minute walk uphill. ✉ *Kale Cad.* ☎ *No phone* 💲 *Free* ☉ *Daily 9 AM–sunset.*

The **Kümbet Cami** (Drum-Dome Mosque), at the foot of the hill by Kars River, is obviously not Turkish—originally the Armenian Church of the Twelve Apostles, it was built in the 10th century. You can still make out the Apostles on the exterior of the drum-shape cupola. The mosque is often locked, in which case the only view is through a rusty gate, but the exterior is architecturally interesting.

Just to the northwest of Kümbet Cami is the **Taşköprü,** also known as "the Stone Bridge," a bridge of Seljuk origin dating from the 1400s, built of volcanic rock. ✉ *Kale Cad., at foot of İç Kale* ☎ *No phone* 💲 *Free.*

On either side of the bridge you will be able to see some of the restoration projects being undertaken by the Global Heritage Fund. On the south side is the 300-year-old home of famed poet Nemik Kemal, which is being turned into a cultural center, while on the north side a row of Ottoman-era riverside timber and stone homes has been restored and painted. There are also plans to restore two ancient hamams near the bridge.

Kars Museum (Kars Müzesi), near the train station on the eastern edge of town, is difficult to find—you're best off taking a taxi—but it's well worth the trip. Two floors of displays cover Kars's many rulers—Roman, Greek, Seljuk, and Ottoman—and there are pieces of Armenian churches and a Russian church bell. You can also check out wall-size maps of Ani here, which will help you get your bearings in preparation for visiting the site. ✉ *485 Cumhuriyet Cad.* ☎ *474/212–2387* 💲 *$1* ☉ *Daily 8:30–5:30.*

Where to Stay & Eat

$ ✕ **Bistro Kar.** As the name implies, Bistro Kar, which opened in 2005, is trying to bring big-city style to provincial Kars. Set on a small bluff overlooking a park below, the restaurant is in a wooden structure that looks like a big gazebo; there are smaller gazebos for outdoor dining. The menu features classic mezes—stuffed eggplants and peppers stewed in olive oil, for example—along with grilled meats and fish. Roast goose is a local specialty, but you might want to call ahead to see if it's actually available. The restaurant serves alcohol and has a decent selection of wines. ⊠ *Resul Yıldız Cad. Buzhane Üstü* ☎ *474/212–8050* ▤ *MC, V.*

¢–$ ✕ **Fasıl Ocakbaşı.** On the second floor of a small shopping center in the middle of town, this kebab restaurant is a bit more relaxed than most other grill houses in town, with less hustle and bustle. It looks very 1970s, with wood paneling all around, but the food—mezes and grilled meat and fish—is well made. And unlike most kebab restaurants, this one has a liquor license. ⊠ *Faikbey Cad. 100, Yıl işhanı Kat 1* ☎ *474/212–1714* ▤ *MC, V.*

¢–$ ✕ **Kayabaşı.** This is the local attempt, mostly successful, at upgrading the city's dining scene. The food is the standard selection of kebabs, along with salads and *pide,* but the restaurant itself is set in a small park along a river and has a shady outdoor patio. The airy dining room has tables covered in pink and white tablecloths, and a large fireplace surrounded by comfy sofas. ⊠ *Şehit Hulusi Aytekin Cad., Mesut Yılmaz Parkı içi* ☎ *474/223–2065* ▤ *MC, V.*

¢–$ ✕ **Ocakbaşı Restoran.** The kebabs are simple and tasty but the restaurant itself has opted for a touch more class than elsewhere, with embroidered curtains, rust-colored tablecloths, and waiters in shiny vests. The lively dining room, which is dominated by a large copper grill, is usually filled with local men eating large meals and having animated conversations. ⊠ *Atatürk Cad. 276* ☎ *474/212–0056* ▤ *MC, V.*

¢–$ ✕ **Şirin Anadolu Mutfağı.** *Şirin* mean "charming" in Turkish and this humble restaurant certainly fits the bill. The walls are painted lime and the columns are pink, so it won't win any decor awards, but you'll be won over by the tasty food and friendly staff. Along with kebabs and an assortment of soups, the kitchen also turns out local specialties such as a lamb and chickpea stew called *piti.* Upstairs is a café with wicker chairs and colorful rugs where young locals spend hours chatting over tea and coffee. ⊠ *Karadağ Cad. 55* ☎ *474/212–3379* ▤ *MC, V.*

$$$ ▨ **Kar's otel.** Kars now has not just its first (and, so far, only) boutique hotel, but a very stylish one at that. In a wonderfully restored late-19th-century Russian-built mansion, the hotel has been done with a cool and minimalist white-and-gray color scheme. Original art on the walls depicts monuments in Kars. The top two floors of the three-story building have long balconies in the back with antique carved wood railings, where you can sit and order a drink from the hotel's bar. Breakfast is served in an open courtyard below, and there's a very appealing restaurant in the basement. ⊠ *Halitpaşa Cad. 79* ☎ *474/212–1616* 🖷 *474/212–5588*

KARS SPECIALTIES

Kars is famous throughout Turkey for its cheese and honey, and you'll see several shops throughout town with sheets of honeycomb and big wheels of the local cheese, known as kaşar, on display in their windows.

Büyük Zavotlar (Halitpaşa Cad. 220, 474/223–3138) is a particularly inviting shop that sells an aged *kaşar* that tastes much like an Italian pecorino. You can also do as the locals do and stop by in the morning for a takeout breakfast of delicious "*bal* and *kaymak*," honey with clotted cream.

⊕ *www.karsotel.com* ⌫ *5 rooms, 3 suites* � *Restaurant, cable TV, in-room broadband* ⊟ *AE, MC, V* ⌾❘ *BP.*

$$ ▦ **Hotel Karabağ.** Once one of Kars's top hotels, the Karabağ is looking a little frayed at the edges these days, with faded carpets and plastic plants in the lobby, but the rooms are good-sized and the staff friendly. It's on a busy main street, so be sure to ask for a room in the back. ⊠ *Faik Bey Cad. 184, at Atatürk Cad.* ☎ *474/212–3480* 🖷 *474/223–3089* ⌫ *45 rooms, 5 suites* ⚫ *Restaurant, bar, minibars, cable TV* ⊟ *MC, V* ⌾❘ *BP.*

$ ▦ **Kars Sim-Er Hotel.** On the edge of the city center, the seven-story Sim-Er is Kars's biggest hotel. The standard rooms are a bit shabby, though, with purple furniture, faded blue carpet, and tiny televisions—although many of them look out over the snow-capped mountains that surround Kars. The two-room suites, which have a pull-out couch and are decorated with more taste, are worth checking out. ⊠ *Sukapı Mevkii Erzurum Yolu* ☎ *474/212–7241* 🖷 *474/212–0168* ⊕ *www.simerhotel.com* ⌫ *146 rooms, 4 suites* ⚫ *Cable TV, minibars, sauna, meeting rooms, parking* ⊟ *AE, MC, V* ⌾❘ *BP.*

¢ ▦ **Güngören Oteli.** This is an excellent budget option. The rooms are comfortable (with full-size tubs, rare for budget hotels in this area) and were completely renovated in 2006—although, for some reason, someone decided that blue and neon green paint, with bedspreads to match, was a good idea. Located on a quiet side street, the friendly hotel also has a good restaurant, as well as a sauna and hamam in the basement. ⊠ *Millet Sok. 2* ☎ *474/212–6767* 🖷 *474/212–5630* ⌫ *40 rooms* ⚫ *Restaurant, cable TV, sauna, Turkish bath* ⊟ *MC, V* ⌾❘ *BP.*

Ani

❷ *42 km (26 mi) east of Kars on Rte. 36–07.*

Fodor'sChoice
★

The ruins at Ani are what draw most people to this remote area of Turkey. Until the Mongol invasion of 1236, Ani (also called Ocaklı) was the chief town of a medieval Armenian kingdom, with 100,000 inhabitants and "a thousand and one churches," according to historical sources. Although it was occupied by the Mongols, Ani still had a large Armenian population well into the 14th century. In 1319 the city was struck by a terrible earthquake, after which the townspeople began to leave. Today, scarcely a half-dozen churches remain, all in various states of disrepair, but even so, the sprawling site is breathtaking, with hundreds of stunning, weather-beaten ruins on a triangular promontory bounded on two sides by steep river gorges. Equally majestic is the surrounding countryside, a mix of severe mountains, tiny Kurdish settlements, and fields of wildflowers. There is a haunted, yet strangely meditative, feeling at the site, an open-air museum holding what are considered some of the finest examples of religious architecture of its period.

The ruins at Ani straddle the Alaçay River, which forms a natural border with Armenia. Until recent years Ani was a restricted military area, but the site is now open to visitors and requires no permits. There is a booth at the main gate where you must buy a ticket to visit the site. Ani has little shade and can get quite hot in the summer, so be sure to bring

6

a hat and water. You should plan on spending several hours at the site if you want to see the highlights, although, depending on your level of interest, you could spend an entire day exploring the various ruins.

Enter through the **Aslan Kapısı** (Lion's Gate), one of three principal portals in Ani's extensive city walls, which stretch for more than 8,200 ft. The 32-ft-tall walls were raised in AD 972 by the Armenian king Smbat II, though the lion relief itself was added by the Seljuk sultan Menuçehr in 1064. A small trail makes a circle through Ani; following it clockwise, the first major ruin you encounter is the **Keseli** (Church of the Redeemer), a huge quadrangular cathedral built in 1035. Its dome (1036) was hit by lightning in the 1950s, which cut the building neatly in half, leaving a surrealistic representation of an Armenian church with the rubble of its former half in the foreground. There are three churches in Ani dedicated to St. Gregory, the Armenian prince who converted his people to Christianity. The best preserved is the **Nakışlı**, built by an Armenian nobleman, Tigran Honentz, in 1215. Nakışlı is the most impressive ruin in Ani, not the least because it stands at the foot of a small ravine with a view over the Arpaçay River. Inside, note the remarkable cycle of murals depicting the Virgin Mary and St. Gregory. If you follow the path into the gorge, you will come to the striking **Kusanatz** (Convent of the Three Virgins), standing on a rocky outcrop.

The **Menuçehir Cami** (Menuçehir Mosque; 1072), which clings to the heights overlooking the Arpaçay River, but which is not difficult to get to, was originally an Armenian building, perhaps a palace. From here climb to the first citadel and continue to the second at the far edge of town, where the two gorges converge; you'll have a good view of the many cave dwellings in the walls of the western gorge, which once housed the city's poor. The **İç Kale** (Citadel), perched on a rocky plateau at the site's southeast end, is unfortunately off-limits. ☎ *No phone* ✉ *$3 for entire site* ⊙ *Daily 9–6.*

Doğubeyazıt & Mt. Ararat

Doğubeyazıt is 192 km (119 mi) southeast of Kars.

❸ The scrappy frontier town of Doğubeyazıt (doh-*oo*-bay-yah-zuht) is a good base from which to enjoy views of Turkey's highest and most famous mountain, the majestic Mt. Ararat (Ağrı Dağı). Not far from the Iranian border, the place seems neglected, if not downright forgotten, with dusty streets and crumbling buildings. But the pace here is laid-back and the locals are friendly. You'll share the town with sheep and Iranian travelers bringing in contraband cigarettes and other cheap goods from Iran. There aren't too many carpet and kilim shops here compared to tourist spots in western Turkey, so you can wander the main street, Çarşı Caddesi, without being bothered too much. A day is probably enough time to spend here, catching an early visit to the sites around Mt. Ararat and then the İshak Paşa Saray at sunset.

★ Doğubeyazıt's only sight, the enchanting **İshak Paşa Saray** (İshak Paşa Palace), is in the mountains southeast of town. The fortified palace was built in the late 18th century by local potentate Çolak Abdi Paşa and his son İshak. The interior of the building is extremely ornate, a fantastic mixture of Georgian, Persian, and Ottoman styles, though the gold-plated doors were carted off by Russian troops in 1917. Late afternoon is the best time to visit, when the sun casts a deep orange glow over the palace and the ruins of a citadel—carved into the opposite (and inaccessible) mountainside—whose foundations are Urartian but which was rebuilt several times through the centuries. There is a restaurant and teahouse above the palace, otherwise, the only hints of civilization are a cluster of Kurdish mud-brick houses and the occasional musician wandering from house to house in search of an audience. ⊠ *6 km (4 mi) southeast of town on road to Göller* ☎ *No phone* 🎫 *$3* ⏰ *daily 9–5.*

4 **Mt. Ararat** (Ağrı Dağı), an extinct volcano covered with snow even in summer, soars dramatically 16,850 ft. above the arid plateau surrounding it, dominating the landscape.

According to Genesis, after the Great Flood, "the waters were dried up from off the earth; and Noah removed the covering of the ark, and looked, and behold, the face of the ground was dry." The survivors, as the story goes, had just landed on top of Mt. Ararat. Many other ancient sources—Chaldean, Babylonian, Chinese, Assyrian—also tell of an all-destroying flood and of one man who heroically escaped its consequences. The mountain can be easily viewed from Doğubeyazıt, although actually climbing it requires a permit that can only be obtained several months in advance, and the trek must be done with a licensed agency. Local tour offices, though, will take you on a day trip that includes a visit to a village at the base of the mountain, which is the closest you can get to Ararat without a permit.

> ### HARK, THE ARK!
>
> Since medieval times the locals around Mt. Ararat have sold Christian pilgrims old planks reputedly from Noah's ark. Fragments of ancient timber, embedded in the ice, have been brought back by various ark-hunting expeditions, but radio-carbon dating tests have proved inconclusive. Satellite photos showed a "boat" embedded in a glacier at 12,500 feet, but examination proved it to be nothing more than a freak formation in the strata. Even so, expeditions by Christian groups constantly make new claims, and a second Noah's Ark was "discovered" in the 1980s on a hillside 20 km (12 mi) southeast of Ararat. Tours from Doğubeyazıt visit the site, but to most eyes, this "ark" is nothing more than a pile of rocks.

Where to Stay & Eat

¢–$ ✕ **Evin Restaurant.** A no-frills but friendly restaurant frequented by the locals—*evin* means "your home" in Turkish—this dining spot has a wide selection of prepared hot dishes including mantı (Turkish ravioli), roast lamb shank, and köfte. They also serve trout, kebabs, and döner. ⊠ *Abdullah Baydar Cad. 92* ☎ *472/312–6073* 🚫 *No credit cards.*

¢–$ ✕ **Murat Camping.** Despite the rustic name (there is a small campground on the premises), this restaurant is Doğubeyazıt's only option for a big night out. Located on a hillside just below the Ishakpaşa Sarayı, the large space has an outdoor terrace with a commanding view of Doğubeyazıt and the mountains around it. There is the usual selection of mezes and kebabs, live Turkish music in the evenings, and wine, beer, and rakı. ⊠ *Ishakpaşa Sarayı* ☎ *472/312–0367* ▤ *No credit cards.*

¢–$ ✗**Öz Urfa Kebap.** Looking something like a hunting lodge, with walls of rough wood boards and stools made out of tree stumps, this kebab restaurant has tons more atmosphere than most other places in town. There are several kinds of well-made kebabs on offer, as well as an assortment of *pides* cooked in the wood-burning oven. ⊠ *Ismail BeşikçI Cad. 34* ☎ *544/218–0418* ▤ *MC, V.*

¢ ✗**Kadın Destek Kooperatifi Lokantası.** Part of a local cooperative that helps women become financially independent, this is a good place to taste regional home cooking. Meals are simple and satisfying: you'll find options like chicken stewed in a tomato broth or meat sautéed with peppers and tomatoes. On Saturdays the women in the kitchen cook up a local specialty called *abigdor Koftesi,* a type of poached meatball made with lamb, onion, and various spices. The restaurant is in a somewhat drab and cavernous 2nd-floor space, but the tables are covered with purple tablecloths and the walls are hung with kilims made by members of the cooperative, which makes it a touch cosier. ⊠ *Ismail BeşikçI Cad., above the Bosch dealership* ☎ *472/312–4026* ▤ *No credit cards.*

$ ▥**Golden Hill Hotel.** Opened in 2004, this hotel at the entrance to town is hands-down Doğubeyazıt's best lodging option. The eight-story black-granite building has an atrium inside, with a fountain in the middle. The rooms are clean and new, with cream-colored walls and embroidered curtains. The suites have a separate room with a couch and a dining table, and are a good value. The rooftop restaurant, where breakfast is served, has a great view of Ararat. ⊠ *Çevreyolu Üzeri* ☎ *472/312–8717* ⊟ *472/312–5771* ⇙ *70 rooms, 20 suites* ⚿ *Restaurant, minbar, cable TV, in-room broadband, sauna, Turkish bath* ▤ *MC, V* ⭗ *BP.*

$ ▥**Hotel Nuh.** The Nuh has relatively large rooms that are a touch nicer than the other mid-level hotels in town. The furniture is dark wood and the bathrooms are clean, with newish tiles. The hotel's greatest asset is its large rooftop restaurant, which has a smashing view of Mt. Ararat. Most rooms also have a view of the mountain. ⊠ *Büyük Ağrı Cad. 65* ☎ *472/312–7232* ⊟ *472/312–6919* ⊕ *www.hotelnuh.8m.com* ⇙ *57 rooms* ⚿ *Restaurant, cable TV, meeting rooms* ▤ *MC, V* ⭗ *BP.*

¢ ▥**Sim-Er Doğubeyazıt Hotel.** About 5 km (3 mi) out of town on the way to the Iranian border, this large hotel, popular with groups, has rooms that are on the spartan side, and the small bathrooms have chipped tiles. The whole place, a two-story cement building painted a creamy off-pink, feels like it could use a good renovation. The location, though, means it has nice views of Ararat, and you can watch the sun set over the mountain from the garden filled with apricot, apple, and cherry trees. ⊠ *Iran Yolu* ☎ *472/312–4842* ⊟ *472/312–*

DOĞUBEYAZIT LODGING

If you're looking for a place to stay in Doğubeyazıt, there's not much to choose from. Narrow your decision with the knowledge that the Golden Hill is, undoubtedly, top choice. The only reason to stay somewhere else is if you can't get a room here. It might be slightly more expensive than the others, but it's still cheap by Western standards.

*5927 ⊕ www.simerhotel.com ⇆ 125 ⌂ Restaurant, cable TV ▤ MC,
V ⁐ BP.*

NEED A BREAK?	There's not much to see on the road from Doğubeyazıt to Van, so the lovely Muradiye waterfalls, some 83 km (51 mi) southwest of Doğubeyazıt, come as a welcome relief. From a small parking lot, a bouncy suspension bridge crosses a swiftly flowing stream and gives you a good view of the 20-ft falls. The area is filled with green poplar trees and local families who come here to picnic. A simple teahouse has a lovely view of the tumbling falls and is the perfect spot for taking a rest.

Lake Van & Environs

*171 km (106 mi) from Doğubeyazı, continuing past Muradiye to the
town of Van.*

❺ The landscape at **Lake Van** (Van Gölü) is eerily desolate, a result of winter flash floods and intense summertime heat—in August the average daytime temperature is 38°C (100°F). This is Turkey's largest and most unusual lake, though: 3,738 square km (1,443 square mi) of eerily blue water surrounded by mighty volcanic cones. Lake Van was formed when a volcano blew its top and blocked the course of a river, leaving the newly formed lake with no natural outlet; as a result the water is highly alkaline and full of sulfides and mineral salts, similar to the Dead Sea, though much less salty. Lake Van's only marine life is a small member of the carp family, the *darekh,* which has somehow adapted to the saline environment. Recreational water sports are limited, and beaches along the rocky shores are few and far between. Swimming in the soft, soapy water is pleasant, but try not to swallow any—it tastes terrible.

The towns of Adilcevaz and Ahlat, on Lake Van's north shore, are worth visiting only if you're in the area; you'll probably want to head instead to Van and the nearby island of Akdamar, along the lake's south shore.

❻ **Van.** As the commercial center of eastern Anatolia, Van has streets lined with modern shops and choked with traffic. There's a definite sense of bustle to the town, with restaurants and cafés filled with young people, many of them

A BITE TO EAT NEAR AKDAMAR

The Grand Deniz Turizm, in Gevaş, is a lovely place to eat after a visit to Akdamar. If you want, you can have the restaurant arrange for a boat to Akdamar (around $30 for a round-trip ride) from their dock, which can be followed by lunch or dinner when you return.

students from the local university. With its collection of rather uniform-looking cement buildings, what Van really lacks is a sense of history, which should not be surprising. The Van of today dates back to the early 20th century, when it was rebuilt some 5 km (3 mi) farther inland from Lake Van after being destroyed in battles with the Armenians and Russians during World War I. Old Van first appears in history 3,000 years ago, when it was the site of the Urartian capital of Tushpa, whose formidable fortress—built on a steep cliff rising from the lakeshore—dominated the countryside. What remains of old Van, in a grassy area near the lake, is a melancholy jumble of foundations that cannot be sorted out; only two vaguely restored mosques, one 13th-century, the other 16th-century, rise from the marshland.

One afternoon is enough to cover the main sights within Van, although the city serves as good base for exploring the sites around Lake Van.

Steps—considerably fewer than the 1,000 claimed in local tourist handouts—ascend to **Van Kalesi** (Van Castle), the sprawling Urartian fortress on the outskirts of town. A path branches right to Urartian tombs in the sheer south rock face; a cuneiform inscription here honors King Xerxes, whose Persian troops occupied the fortress early in the 5th century BC. The crumbling ramparts are still impressive, but as is true so often in these parts, it's the view from such a vantage point that makes the steep climb worthwhile. A taxi from the new town should cost no more than $6 one-way. Cheaper *dolmuşes* (shared taxis) depart regularly from Beş Yol, a large intersection two blocks west of the Büyük Urartu Hotel.

The new city's main attraction is the small but well-arranged archaeological and ethnographical **Van Müzesi** (Van Museum), which displays many Urartian artifacts: rich gold jewelry; belts and plates engraved with lions, bulls, and sphinxes; and a carved relief of the god Teshup, for whom their capital was named. The small solarium has a varied collection, ranging from prehistoric rock art to Urartian inventory markers to Turkish sarcophagi. If you're interested in local history and archaeology, the books for sale (some in English) are a wonderful source of information—and a bargain to boot. The museum underwent a complete renovation in the summer of 2006. ⌧ *Cengiz Cad., 1 block east of Cumhuriyet Cad.* ☎ *432/216–1139* 🖅 *$1* ⊙ *Daily 9–5.*

❼ On the tranquil, uninhabited islet of **Akdamar,** among the wild olive and almond trees, stand the scant remains of a monastery which includes the truly splendid **Church of the Holy Cross.** Built in AD 921 by an Armenian king, Gagik Artzruni of Vaspurakan, it is very much a cousin, architecturally, to the Armenian churches at Ani. Incredible high-relief carvings on the exterior make this church a work of art and one of the most enchanted spots in Turkey. Nearly the entire story of the Bible is told here, from Adam and Eve to David and Goliath. Along the top is a frieze of running animals; another frieze shows a vineyard where laborers work the fields and women dance with bears; and, of course, King Gagik is depicted, offering his church to Christ. The wall paintings in the interior of the church under-

DEAD SEAS

Like the Dead Sea in Israel, Lake Van is a novice swimmer's paradise. Though far from being as salty as the Dead Sea, owing to the various streams that flow into it and the large amount of rain and snowfall during the winter, Lake Van's alkaline water still keeps even the worst swimmer afloat. Don't expect the profusion of spas near the lake that you find in Israel, though; the water here is not as mineral rich and therapeutic.

went an extensive restoration in 2006. To reach Akdamar from Van, follow Rte. 300 to Gevaş, which is about 20 miles away. Entering Gevaş, you will spot ferries waiting at the landing (which is near the road and has a sign that says AKDAMAR) to collect the required number of passengers—between 10 and 15—for the 20-minute ride. Depending on how many people board the ferry, the cost is $3–$5 per person for a round-trip. If other tourists don't turn up, you must pay $25–$40 to charter the entire boat for a round trip—depending on your ability to bargain. ⊠ *Rte. 300, 56 km (35 mi) west of Van* ☎ *No phone* 🎫 *$1.25* ⊙ *Daily dawn–sunset.*

OFF THE
BEATEN
PATH

ÇAVUŞTEPE AND HOŞAP KALESI – From Van, drive 35 km (22 mi) south on the Hakkari road to Çavuştepe, where you can clamber around the stone foundations of the ruined 8th-century BC Urartian fortress-city Sardurihinli. Nearby are temple ruins and a 6th-century BC sacrificial altar. Admission to the citadel is $1, though it's sometimes difficult to find the caretaker. If you continue 15 km (9 mi) southeast on the same road, you'll reach Hoşap Castle, a dramatic fortress looming over a river chasm. The 17th-century complex, which was used as a base to "protect" (i.e., ransack) caravans, included a palace, two mosques, three baths, and a dungeon. The great gate, with its carved lions and an inscription in Farsi, is quite a show of strength; a tunnel carved through bedrock leads inside from here. Bring a flashlight, as there are no lights in the castle, which is open daily 9–5. Admission is $1.

❽ Across the lake from Van is one of Turkey's loveliest natural wonders, the beautiful and rarely visited crater lakes of **MOUNT NEMRUT** (Nemrut Dağı, which should not be confused with the more famous Mt. Nemrut farther west). From Tatvan, 146 km (91 mi) west of Van, a rutted road leads up the mountain to the 10,000-foot-high rim of what was once a mighty volcano. From the rim of the crater, you can see down to the two lakes below—a smaller one fed by hot springs and larger "cold" one. A loose dirt road leads down to the lakes, where very simple tea stands have been set up. The inside of the crater has an otherworldly feel to it, with its own ecosystem: stands of short, stunted trees and scrubby bushes, birds and turtles, and cool breezes. Few tourists make it to the lakes, and chances are your only company will be local shepards and their flocks.

Where to Stay & Eat

¢–$ ✕ **Anzaf Et Lokantaspı.** On the western edge of town, near the airport, this upscale (by Van standards) grilled meat restaurant serves good kebabs, as well as daily specials such as *kaburga,* roasted lamb stuffed with rice, and *sarma beyti,* kebab wrapped in a type of phyllo dough and then baked. The two-story restaurant has a breezy outdoor terrace with a view of the lake and the airplanes taking off and landing at the airport. ⊠ *Ipekyolu Havaalani Dağı, Van* ☎ *432/217–7872* ▤ *MC, V.*

¢–$ ✕ **Besse.** Van's previously rather basic dining scene has been shaken up in recent years by the arrival of several restaurants that offer the locals something classier. Besse, on the second floor above a shopping center, is one of the pioneers of this new trend, and it's a refuge from the bustling streets below, with walls painted a warm yellow, lights turned down low, and classical music playing in the background. The restaurant specializes in dishes (lamb, chicken, or trout) baked in terracotta pots and also makes a nice Ali Nazik, kebab served on top of yogurt that's been mixed with garlic and roasted eggplant. ⊠ *Melek ış Merkezi Kat: 1, Van* ☎ *432/215–0050* ▤ *MC, V.*

¢–$ ✕ **Grand Deniz Turizm.** This peaceful lakeside restaurant in Gevaş is a good spot for lunch or dinner after a visit to Akdamar. Tables are set on a pebbly beach near the water and have an open view of the lake and the mountains. The food, which includes local dishes such as kebabs and trout baked in a terracotta dish, is well made and delicious. ⊠ *Van-Tatvan Karayolu Km 40, Gevaş* ☎ *432/612–4038* ▤ *MC, V.*

> ### WHO WERE THE URARTIANS?
>
> Most visitors to Turkey have probably never heard of the the Urartians, but they're a big deal around Van, having left a significant imprint on the area. Most likely a confederation of local tribes, the kingdom of Urartu (known as Ararat in the Bible) first appeared in this region in the 13th century BC and by the mid-8th century BC ruled an empire extending from the Black Sea to the Caspian Sea. Known as expert builders, stonemasons, and jewelry makers, the Urartians created gold necklaces and bracelets, often with a distinctive lion's head motif, that are some of the most prized holdings in Turkish museums.

¢–$ ✕ **Kebabistan.** In a small alleyway filled with mustachioed men sitting on stools and sipping tea, this basic eatery serves the usual kebabs and hot prepared dishes, as well as good *pide* and *lahmacun,* a kind of flatbread topped with ground meat and baked in a wood-burning oven. The main dining room is a hive of activity, but upstairs is a comfortable and quiet dining room. ⊠ *Sinemalar Sokak, Van* ☎ *432/214–2273* ▤ *MC, V.*

¢ ✕ **Imsak Kahvaltı Salonu.** This cheery establishment with only a few tables has the same menu as its numerous competitors, but with its red and white checkered tablecloths and cozy athmosphere, it is particularly inviting. In addititon to the classic Van breakfast, they also serve *menemen,* eggs scrambled with tomatoes and green pepper, along with all the usual items you'd find in a Turkish restaurant. ⊠ *M. Fevzi Çakmak Cad. Bayram Oteli Altı, Van* ☎ *432/216–0921* ▤ *No credit cards.*

¢ ✕ **Saçı Beyaz.** Another of Van's new upscale restaurants, this place, just opened in 2006, serves delicious kebabs in a surprisingly elegant setting. The dining room, on a second floor overlooking a busy intersection, has tables covered in crisp white tablecloths and chairs of dark wood; the room's pillars are faced with the same wood. The courteous staff, dressed in white shirts and black ties, seem always poised to bring more plates of freshly baked flatbread to your table. Downstairs is the restaurant's pastry shop, which sells ice cream and good baklava. ⊠ *K. Karabekir Cad. Soydan Dağı, Van* ☎ *432/214–4016* ▤ *MC, V.*

¢ ✕ **Van Evi.** At the base of Van Castle, this is a good place to taste local dishes, among them *keledoş,* a stew made with meat, chickpeas, lentils, and butter, and *ekşili*, meat and spinach in a tangy sauce. Two long wooden pavilions with open sides serve as dining rooms and there is a large grassy area with tables and chairs for dining al fresco. ⊠ *At the entrance to Van Castle, Van* ☎ *0536/962–2832* ▤ *No credit cards.*

★ $$ ▥**Büyük Urartu.** This smoothly run hotel, one of the town's best, is also educational, with reproductions of Urartian art on the walls throughout. Guest rooms are small but pleasant, with gold-embroidered bedspreads and floral wallpaper; some face the noisy street—so ask for one in the rear. The whole hotel was spruced up in 2005, and it all looks fresh and clean. Celaleddin Başak, the friendly front-desk manager, can help arrange tours of the area. ⊠ *Cumhuriyet Cad. 60* ☎ *432/212–0660* 🖷 *432/212–1610* ⊕ *www.buyukurartuotel.com* ⇘ *72 rooms, 3 suites* ☖ *Restaurant, bar, minibars, cable TV, Wi-Fi, indoor pool, sauna, meeting rooms* ▤ *AE, DC, MC, V* ⁙⚬⁙ *BP.*

$$ ▥**Merit Şahmaran.** Head to this comfortable, well-run hotel if you want to stay on Lake Van itself. Located 12 km (7.5 mi) west of Van in the small town of Edremit, the Merit has large rooms with nice, modern bathrooms. Ask for one of the lakeside rooms, which have views of the lake and the mountains around it. There's an open-air terrace restaurant overlooking the water where you can watch the sunset and listen to the water lapping against the rocky shore. A stone pier juts out into the lake; from here you can take a dip in the water. ⊠ *Edremit Yolu Km 12, Edremit* ☎ *432-312-3060* 🖷 *432-312-2295* ⊕ *www.merithotels. com* ⇘ *90 rooms* ☖ *Restaurant, bar, in-room safes, minibars, cable TV, Wi-Fi, outdoor pool, sauna* ▤ *MC, V* ⁙⚬⁙ *BP.*

¢ ▥**Büyük Asur Oteli.** It might be a drab concrete building from the outside, but this is a good-value hotel, with tidy rooms painted lavender and beds with firm mattresses and crisp sheets. An "oriental"-style living room off the lobby is filled with pillows and kilims and you can kick back here and read a book or have a drink. The hotel's English-speaking owner, Remzi Bozbey, can help arrange tours around Lake Van. ⊠ *Turizm Sok. 5, Van* ☎ *432/216–8792* 🖷 *432/216–9461* ⊕ *www.buyukasur. com* ⇘ *48 rooms* ☖ *Bar, cable TV; no a/c* ▤ *MC, V* ⁙⚬⁙ *BP.*

¢ ▥**Otel Akdamar.** The squat Akdamar won't win any architectural prizes, but the rooms are comfortable and good sized, with walls painted white and beds draped in blue bedspreads. The hotel is located on Van's main drag, so ask for a room in the back. The hotel has one of the city's nicest bars, too, with comfortable lounge chairs. ⊠ *K. Karabekir Cad., Van* ☎ *432/ 214–9923* 🖷 *432/212–0868* ⇘ *69 rooms, 3 suites* ☖ *Restaurant, bar, minibars, cable TV, meeting rooms* ▤ *MC, V* ⁙⚬⁙ *BP.*

BREAKFAST IN VAN

Van is known for, among other things, its delicious local breakfasts—you'll get a hearty variety of locally-made cheeses, eggs (usually hard boiled) and, most importantly, *kaymak*, a delicious type of thick clotted cream that is eaten on bread with honey. The city is filled with small restaurants that serve breakfast all day long; Imsak Kahvaltı Salonu is particularly good. *Kahvaltı* is the Turkish word for breakfast.

KARS, MT. ARARAT & LAKE VAN ESSENTIALS

Transportation

BY AIR
Turkish Airlines has regularly scheduled flights from Istanbul to Kars or Van, as does Atlas Jet. Pegasus flies regularly from Istanbul to Van. The lowest one-way fares to Kars and Van are between $50 and $75.

BY BUS
There are daily buses from Istanbul and Ankara to cities in the east, although it's a long trip and not much cheaper than flying. Kars is about 18 hours from Ankara ($35), 22 hours from Istanbul ($45), and 10 hours from Trabzon ($20). Van is about 20 hours from Ankara ($30), 24 hours from Istanbul ($40), and 12 hours from Trabzon ($20). Van Seyahat makes the trip from Istanbul to Van. Kars Doğu takes passenger from Istanbul to Kars.

There is regular bus service from Kars to Doğubeyazıt and from there to Van.

Kars Doğu ☎ 212/658-1857. **Van Seyahat** ☎ 212/658-3365

BY CAR
Van is a long 1,644 km (1,021 mi) from Istanbul and Kars 1,435 km (891 mi) from Istanbul, only a short part of the road to either place along highways. Gas stations are plentiful, and roadside hotels and restaurants help break up the long, dusty, hot drives.

BY TRAIN
Not the best option, a train ride from Istanbul to Kars or Van (38 hours or more) is brutally slow. Per-person fares range from $22 (first class) to $40 (sleeper bunk).

Contacts & Resources

EMERGENCIES
Police ☎ 155. **Ambulance** ☎ 112.

GUIDED TOURS
Tour offices in Doğubeyazıt tend to go in and out of business every week, so if you need a guide, you're best off asking at your hotel and/or getting recommendations from other travelers.

The English-speaking guide Celil Ersözoğlu is a good option in Kars. He can arrange for trips to Ani and to some of the Armenian and Georgian monuments in the area.

The Ayanis travel agency in Van can help with travel arrangements and with organizing tours in the Lake Van area.

Ayanis ☎ 432/210-1515. **Celil Ersözoğlu** ☎ 532/226-3966 ⊕ celilani@hotmail.com.

VISITOR INFORMATION
Usually someone in the visitor centers knows at least a few words of English, but you would be advised to have a Turkish speaker on hand to help with translation.

Kars (⊠ Atatürk Cad. next to Süleyman Demirel Parkı, in Milli Eğitim Bldg. ☎ 474/223–2300 🖷 474/223–8452). **Van** (⊠ Cumhuriyet Cad. ☎ 432/216–2018 🖷 432/216–3675).

DIYARBAKIR, MARDIN, MIDYAT & HASANKEYF

To say that Turkey's southeast region has a rich history would be an understatement. This is, after all, part of the ancient area known as Mesopotamia: the land between the Tigris and the Euphrates rivers, where modern civilization got its start. This excursion takes you into the heart of this historic region, to cities that trace their past not over centuries, but over millennia and through landscapes that seem unchanged with time. This area is also the historic home of the Assyrian Christians, one of Christianity's oldest sects, and there are several fascinating Assyrian churches and monasteries that can be visited.

The excursion begins in Diyarbakır, which has long been the the region's commercial, cultural, and political center. Surrounded by a thick basalt wall that dates back to Roman times, Diyarbakır's old city has cobblestone lanes that lead to grand old homes hidden behind high stone walls—some of which are now open to visitors—intriguing old churches and mosques, and a lively bazaar that spreads out through a maze of narrow lanes.

From here you continue to Mardin, one of the most magical cities in Turkey. Sitting like a crown that looks down on a wide plain below, Mardin is a wonderful place to simply walk around and get lost. The narrow streets are lined with old stone homes, a collection of gorgeous mosques, and a bazaar where donkeys still carry most of the goods. Spend the day walking around and then relax in the evening at the terrace of one of the local restaurants or cafés and look out at the view below and the stars above. While you're there, be sure to visit Dayrul Zafran, an ancient Assyrian Christian monastery found in splendid isolation in the hills just outside of Mardin.

Midyat is one of the best-preserved small towns in Turkey. Once home to a sizable Assyrian Christian community, Midyat's old city is today mostly a ghost town, with many of its former residents now living in Europe. What they left behind is an incredible collection of honey-colored stone homes with exquisite carvings on their exteriors and several historic churches. As in Mardin, this is a wonderful place to spend a few hours walking around and soaking up the atmosphere. Mor Gabriel, another isolated Assyrian monastery, is nearby and worth visiting.

From Midyat, you can make the quick trip to Hasankeyf, a small town that sits in an enchanted spot on the banks of the Tigris River. Spend a few hours exploring Hasankeyf's cliff-top citadel, which dates back to Roman times, and a series of ancient cliff dwellings nearby, and then head down to the river, where you can eat lunch on a veranda that sits on stilts right over the Tigris's gently flowing waters. (Note: you might want to head here sooner than later—a dam project on the Tigris,

6

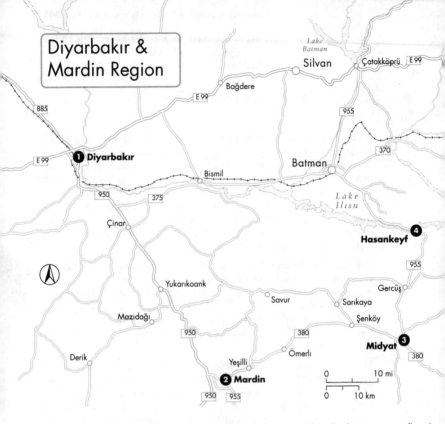

though still a long way from being completed, threatens to flood
Hasankeyf and its historic sites.)

Diyarbakır

① On a bluff above the Tigris River, the ancient city of Diyarbakır, one of
the oldest cities in the northernmost region of Mesopotamia (the area
between the Tigris and Euphrates rivers) is encircled by a 5.5-km (3-
mi) stretch of thick, impregnable black-basalt walls. Inside those walls
lie twisting alleyways, old stone homes, mosques, and a lively bazaar.
The city's long history has meant it's seen quite a succession of rulers,
from the Assyrians to the Urartians and Romans, and finally the Ottomans, who took control of the city in 1515. Diyarbakır has been an
important regional commercial and cultural center for centuries, and there
are some wonderful old houses, mosques, and churches in the cobblestone lanes of the old town.

In the 1980s and '90s, Diyarbakır was forced to absorb a large number of villagers fleeing the fighting in the countryside between Kurdish
militants and Turkish security forces, which taxed the city's poor infrastructure and social services and gave the city a grimey feel. In more recent years, though, the local municipality has embarked on several

CLOSE UP

Spotlight on the Kurds

THERE ARE AN estimated 20 million Kurds living in the mountainous region that covers parts of Iran, Iraq, Syria, and Turkey. Separated by ethnicity and language from their neighbors, the Kurds have for centuries found themselves the subjects of the area's various rulers.

Turkey has the region's largest Kurdish population, with an estimated 12 million, most of them living in the country's southeast region. When the new Turkish republic was founded in 1923, severe restrictions on Kurdish language and culture were put in place, part of a larger effort to unite the country's various ethnic groups under one national identity. During the 1980's, the Kurdistan Workers' Party (PKK), a militant Marxist group, began a bloody separatist war against the Turkish state that ended up costing the lives of more than 30,000 and caused great damage to social and economic life in the southeast. The PKK called for a ceasefire in 1999, after its leader was captured by Turkey, and its fighters retreated to the mountains of northern Iraq. In late 2004, though, it resumed its attacks on Turkish troops in the southeast, although the violence is, for the most part, restricted to remote parts of the region and is nowhere near the level of the 1980's and 90's. At the same time, as part of its efforts to join the European Union, Turkey has over the last few years passed legislation aimed at easing the cultural and political restrictions on the Kurds and has promised to revitalize the local economy, bringing a guarded sense of hope to the battlescarred region.

6

restoration and beautification projects, such as renovating historic homes in the old city and opening them up to visitors, which is helping bring the city's charm closer to the surface.

The Romans left a strong mark on Diyarbakır—not only did they lay the foundations for its famous **city walls**, but they created the basic layout of the old town: a rough rectangle with two main streets that cross and connect the four gates that are found at each compass point. The walls were reconstructed by the Byzantine Emperor Constantius in AD 349 and further restored by the Seljuks in 1088 and again 120 years later by Artakid Turcoman emir al Malik al-Salih Mahmud. On the whole, the walls remain in good shape along their entire length; indeed, if you feel like a bit of an adventure, the best way to appreciate these great walls is to wander along the top. Of the original 72 towers, 67 are still standing, decorated with myriad inscriptions in the language of every conqueror and with Seljuk reliefs of animals and men; you can also explore their inner chambers and corridors. To make a circuit of the city walls on foot, start at the **Mardin Kapısı** (Mardin Gate), on the south side near the Otel Büyük Kervansaray and take the wall-top path west toward the **Urfa Kapısı** (Urfa Gate), also called the Bab er-Rum. About halfway you will come to the twin bastions **Evli Beden Burcu** and **Yedi Kardeş Burcu**—the latter is also known as the Tower of Seven Brothers and was added to the fortifications in 1209. From here you can see the old Ottoman bridge over the Tigris, called **Dicle Köprüsü** (Tigris Bridge). Continue clockwise along the city wall, and you'll eventually reach another gate, the **Dağ Kapısı** (Mountain Gate), which divides Diyarbakır's old and new towns. Farther east, inside the ramparts, are the sad remains of the **Artakid Saray** (Artasid Palace), surrounded by a dry, octagonal pool known as the **Lion's Fountain**. Not long ago there were two carved lions here, now there's only one; what happened to the other is a mystery.

The ruins of the old town's **İç Kale** (Inner Fortress), a circular and heavily eroded section of the city walls, are notable for the 16th-century **Hazreti Süleymaniye Cami** (Prophet Süleyman Mosque), also known as the Citadel Mosque. It has a tall, graceful minaret and is striped with black basalt and pale sandstone, a favorite design of this city's medieval architects. Its courtyard fountain is fed by an underground spring that has probably supplied cold, clear water to the city for 5,000 years. ⊠ *İzzet Paşa Cad.* ☎ *No phone* ☉ *Daily dawn–sunset, except prayer times.*

In the center of the old city stands the **Ulu Cami** (Great Mosque), one of the oldest in Anatolia. Though its present form dates from the 12th century, in an older form it served as a Byzantine basilica; its colonnades and columns are made from bits and pieces of earlier Roman buildings. Note its Arabic-style flat-roofed and rectangular plan, which contrasts with the square-shaped and domed mosques common in Turkey. ⊠ *Gazi Cad., opposite Yapı Kredi Bank* ☎ *No phone* ☉ *Daily 10–sunset.*

Diyarbakır's **bazaar** encompasses the half-dozen streets surrounding Ulu Cami; most stalls are shrines to wrought metal—gates, picks, shovels, plumbing fixtures, plastic shoes, and other things you probably would not want to carry home in your luggage. Across the street from the mosque is the grand 16th-century **Hasan Paşa Hanı,** a photogenic kervansaray now mostly used by carpet and souvenir dealers and which was undergoing an extensive renovation in 2006.

Down a narrow alleyway near the Ulu Cami in the old city, the **Cahit Sıtkı Tarancı Müzesi** is a historic home dating back to 1734 that has been renovated and turned into an ethnographic museum, with rooms displaying scenes of life as it once was in Diyarbakır. The museum, which has a pleasant courtyard with a fountain, offers probably the best opportunity of seeing what an old Diybarbakır house looked like. ⊠ *Ziya Gökalp Sok. 3* ☎ *412/223–8958* ☉ *Daily 9–5* 🎫 *$1.*

Diybarbakır was once home to a large Christian population—Armenians, Chaldeans, and Assyrians—and several churches remain in the city, although the only one that still holds regular services is the Assyrian Orthodox **Meryem Ana Kilisesi,** on the western end of the old city. A peaceful oasis in the midst of the bustling city, the church, built on the site of what was a temple used by sun worshippers, has a large courtyard lined with basalt stones and a lovely chapel dating back to the 3rd century with an impressive wooden altar decorated with golden ornamentation. Services are held every Sunday at 8 AM, although only a few people usually show up. ⊠ *Ana Sok. 26* ☎ *No phone* ☉ *daily 9–5.*

Diyarbakır's **Arkeoloji Müzesi** (Archaeological Museum), where the exhibits cover 4,000 years of history, is located in the new city, a short walk from Dağ Kapı, the main entrance to the old town. In a somewhat rundown building, the exhibits include findings from excavations in the Diyarbakır area, from stone-age tools to Byzantine pottery and coins. ⊠ *Gazi Cad.* ☎ *412/223–8958* 🖃 *$1* ⊙ *Mon.–Sat. 8:30-4:30.*

The old town's most recognizable mosque is the **Kasım Padişah Cami** (1512), famous for its Dört Ayaklı Minare (Four-Legged Minaret), which appears to be suspended in the air—the minaret balances on four basalt columns, a marvel of medieval engineering. Legend has it that your wish will come true if you pass under the minaret seven times. ⊠ *Yenikapı Cad.* ☎ *No phone* ⊙ *Daily 10–sunset.*

OFF THE
BEATEN
PATH

If you need a break from Diyarbakır's heat and crowds, head to the **GAZI KOŞKU** – a restored stone house high above the Tigris River on the outskirts of town. The house is surrounded by shady trees and there is a flower-filled tea garden where you can cool off. It's a kilometer (.62 mi) south of the Mardin gate along the river road. ⊙ *9* AM*–midnight* 🖃 *35 cents.*

Where to Stay & Eat

$ ✕ **Asmin.** This is Diybarbakır's only real upscale restaurant, the place where well-to-do locals come for a break from kebabs and to have a more sophisticated dining experience—at least by local standards. The menu features such nonlocal items as schnitzel, beef Stroganoff, and filet mignon, and there's a surprisingly decent wine list. The food is well made and the softly lit dining room, with its comfortable armchairs and solicitous bow-tied waiters, is a nice change from the usual. ⊠ *Selahattin Yazıcıoğlu Cad.* ☎ *412/224–3197* 🖃 *MC, V.*

$ ✕ **Çarşı Konağı.** You have to pass through a small door off one of Diybarbakır's narrow old city lanes to get to this simple restaurant, in a restored historic stone home with a shaded courtyard—ask for directions. The small menu is made up of kebabs and delicious *sac tava,* chunks of beef sautéed in a woklike pan with tomatoes and green peppers; it's served right in the pan, with a mound of flatbread to soak up the tasty juices. This is also a very pleasant spot to cool off with a cup of coffee or tea. ⊠ *Gazi Caddesi Çarşı* ☎ *412/228–4673* 🖃 *No credit cards.*

★ $ ✕ **Selim Amcanın Sofra Salonu.** Diybarbakır's best-known restaurant is an excellent place to try the delicious regional specialty *kaburga,* lamb stuffed with a fragrant rice pilaf and slowly roasted. This labor-intensive dish usually needs to be ordered a day in advance, but SASS (as the restaurant is known) is one of the few restaurants that offers *kaburga* on demand, served with flair by waiters who divide the dish up tableside. With walls covered with mirrors and pink paint, the restaurant has a rather kitschy look; it's a local institution nonetheless. ⊠ *Ali Emiri Cad. 22/B* ☎ *412/224–4447* 🖃 *MC, V.*

¢–$ ✕ **Çemçe Diyarbakır Mutfağı.** Head here if you want to sample authentic local dishes, such as *perde pilaf,* chicken and rice baked inside a pastry shell, or for the more adventurous, *mumbar,* lamb intestines stuffed with rice and ground meat. The food, served buffet style, is well made and the setting—an old stone house with several small dining rooms decked out with rugs and antiques—is charming. ⊠ *Kuçuk Kavas Sok. (behind the Class Hotel)* ☎ *412/229–4345* 🖃 *MC, V.*

¢–$ ✕ **Emre Ocakbaşı.** Diyarbakır is filled with small grill stands that serve sizzling kebabs to hungry diners who polish them off sitting on stools at outdoor tables. This one, near the Dağ Kapı, the main access point to the old city, has both outdoor and indoor dining areas and serves excellent kebabs, including ones made with the local specialty, liver. Kebabs are served with flatbread, bulgur pilaf, and a tangy salad made with tomatoes, cucumber, parsley, and pomegranite molasses. ⊠ *Kıbrıs Cad. Çelenk Apt. Altı 1/A* ☎ *412/228–7238* ▭ *MC, V.*

¢   ✕ **Ka-Mer'in Mutfağı.** Good food for a good cause. This restaurant is run by a Diybarbakır-based organization that offers social services for local women and the proceeds help fund the group's activities. Staffed by the women the group helps, the kitchen turns out tasty and authentic local dishes, such as *içli köfte,* ground meat inside a bulgur shell; *mantı,* small dumplings that are the Turkish equivalent of ravioli; and a variety of stuffed vegetables. The dining room, which has simple wooden furniture and walls painted a soft yellow, is tranquil and pleasant. ⊠ *Ali Emiri Sok. 3r* ☎ *412/229–0459* ▭ *No credit cards.*

$$$ ▦ **Class Hotel.** Although somewhat characterless, the Class Hotel is certainly Diyarbakır's fanciest place to stay, with prices to match. Rooms are large and comfortable, all with desks and some with small couches. There's a Turkish bath in the basement, a small pool in the back, and a gym. ⊠ *Gazi Cad. 101* ☎ *412/229–5000* ▤ *412/229–2599* ⊕ *www. diyarbakirclasshotel.com* ⇔ *107 rooms, 7 suites* ⌂ *2 restaurants, bar, minibars, cable TV, pool, gym, sauna, Turkish bath, business services, meeting rooms* ▭ *AE, MC, V* �yO�yl *BP.*

★ $$ ▦ **Otel Büyük Kervansaray.** This attractive inn is inside a 16th-century kervansaray with sandstone walls, vaulted ceilings, and kilims that are used as curtains. Rooms are on the small side, but you're really paying for the atmosphere and the location, next to the Mardin Kapısı, inside the city walls. Rooms on the ground floor don't have air-conditioning, although they stay quite cool, even in summer. There is a lovely courtyard with a fountain where you can eat dinner or have a drink, and the hotel's pool is a welcome sight in Diyarbakır's heat. ⊠ *Gazi Cad.* ☎ *412/228–9606* ▤ *412/228–9606* ⊕ *www.dunyainsanlarininevi.com* ⇔ *31 rooms, 14 suites* ⌂ *Restaurant, pool, bar, minibars, cable TV, sauna, Turkish bath, meeting rooms* ▭ *AE, MC, V* �yO�yl *BP.*

¢   ▦ **D. Büyük Otel.** If it weren't in sun-baked eastern Turkey, the D. Büyük might be accused of being Art Deco, with its wood-panel lobby and modern couches. Rooms are pleasant, painted lavender and with dark wood furniture and sage-colored curtains. The staff is friendly and unpretentious and help make for a pleasant stay. ⊠ *İnönü Cad. 4* ☎ *412/228–1295* ▤ *412/224–4859* ⇔ *63 rooms* ⌂ *Restaurant, bar, minibars, cable TV* ▭ *AE, MC, V* ▸O◂ *BP.*

¢   ▦ **Hotel Birkent.** This budget hotel has surprisingly large rooms that are comfortable and well maintained. Walls are painted a light lavender, complemented by maroon carpets; bathrooms are small but spotless. The staff is friendly and helpful. ⊠ *İnönü Cad. 26* ☎ *412/228–7131* ▤ *412/ 228–7145* ⇔ *30 rooms* ⌂ *minibars, cable TV* ▭ *MC, V* ▸O◂ *BP.*

¢   ▦ **Turistik.** Once one of Diybarbakır's smartest hotels, the 1950s-era Turistik is somewhat the worse for wear, with stained carpets and ancient air-conditioning units. The hotel has two things going for it, though:

affordable rates and a nice pool and courtyard area, where you can cool off from the Mesopotamian heat. The rooms are a touch small, so a suite might be a better option, and still won't break the bank. ⊠ *Ziya Gökalp Bul. 7* ☎ *412/224–7550* 🖷 *412/224–4274* 💭 *57 rooms* ♨ *Restaurant, bar, outdoor pool* ▤ *MC, V* ⧦ *BP.*

Mardin

★ ❷ *96 km (60 mi) southeast of Diyarbakır.*

With historic stone houses clinging to a citadel-topped mountain that overlooks a vast plain below, Mardin has a magical setting. It was hit hard by the violence of the 1980s and '90s, and the city, which is populated by a mix of Arabic and Kurdish speakers, slid off Turkey's tourist map, but the return of calm to the region has meant that travelers are rediscovering this enchanted city's maze-like old town, intricately decorated homes, and lively bazaar. Mardin also now has two of the nicer hotels in the region, as well as one of the area's best restaurants.

Mardin was once the seat of a local dynasty, the Artukids, who ruled the area between the 13th and 14th centuries and left the city with several notable mosques and *medreses* (Islamic schools). The best of these are the the Lâtifiye Cami (Lâtifiye Mosque, 1371) and the Sultan İsa Medrese (Sultan İsa Seminary, 1385), the latter renowned for its exquisite stone carvings. The Seljuk Ulu Cami (Seljuk Ulu Mosque), which dates from the 12th century and has a ribbed dome that looks like an intricate lemon squeezer, is also worth a visit.

At the city's main square is the small **Mardin Museum,** set in a grand old stone house that used to be the home of an Assyrian Christian patriarch. The stone relief carvings on the exterior are quite exquisite. The museum's collection includes displays from archaeolgical digs around Mardin, with pieces from the Roman, Byzantine, Seljuk, and other periods. One floor has an ethnographic exhibit showing life in old Mardin. ⊠ *Cümhurriyet Meydanı* ☎ *482/212–1664* 🖾 *$1* ⊘ *Mon.–Sat. 8–5:30.*

Mardin was once home to a large Christian community and several churches still remain in the city, although only a few are functioning. The **Kirklar Kilisesi** (Church of the 40), an Assyrian Orthodox church, is usually open and worth visiting. It's down a narrow lane near the museum. The church dates back to the year 569 and has beautiful stone carvings and a shady courtyard. Neighborhood children will offer to take you there, which is probably a good idea, since it can be hard to find. ⊠ *217 Sağlik Sok. 8* ☎ *No phone* 🖾 *Free* ⊘ *Daily 8–5.*

Mardin's lively bazaar runs parallel to the old town's main street, Birinici Cad., and is refreshingly free of the stalls selling the usual tourist gifts. This is the place to come if you're looking to buy a new saddle for your donkey or a copper urn—or as is more likely, if you just want to get the feel of an authentic town bazaar. There are also spice shops, fruit and vegetable stands with produce piled high, and assorted other shops catering to local needs.

One of the big pleasures in Mardin is simply walking the old town's narrow cobblestone lanes and seeing what you come across. Although there are many ugly cement homes that have been built in recent years, there are enough historic homes remaining to give the city a great deal of charm. The stone used to build the old homes is the color of golden sand and looks especially beautiful at sunset.One of the best examples of an old Mardin home is the current **post office** (⊠ on Birinci Cad., across the street from an open-air teahouse, in the center of town).

OFF THE
BEATEN
PATH

Just 10 km (6 mi) southeast of Mardin is the Syrian **ORTHODOX DAYRUL ZAFRAN** (Saffron Monastery) – Dating to perhaps as early as the 6th century and partially restored in the 19th, the monastery is still in use. One of the brothers will give you a tour of the building, which sits like a golden jewel nestled in the scrubby hills around it, and perhaps introduce you to one of the *rahip* (priests) who still speak and teach Aramaic, the language of Christ. ⊠ *Off the road from Mardin to Nusaybin* ☎ No phone ⌷ *Free* ☉ *Daily 9–11:30 and 1–4:30.*

Where to Stay & Eat

$ ✕ **Cercis Murat Konağı.**This is certainly Mardin's best restaurant, if not
Fodor'sChoice one of the most outstanding places in the surrounding region. In a gorgeous old stone house that has been restored, maintaining the old details while adding a modern kitchen in the basement, the restaurant has several terraces with spectacular views of the plain that unfolds below Mardin. The dishes served are authentic local ones, such as lamb braised in a tangy green plum sauce. There is also a full spread of tantalizing cold and hot mezes, including tasty chickpea fritters and, owing to the Arab influence on Mardin, humus and falafel. ⊠ *Birinci Cad. 517* ☎ 482/213–6841 ▤ MC, V.

¢   ✕ **Erdoba Sofra Salonu.** Opened in the summer of 2006, this bright, comfortable eatery is on the second floor of a building on Mardin's main drag. Serving the usual kebabs along with prepared stews, the restaurant has lavender walls and tables with benches covered in colorful fabrics. If you order ahead of time, they can prepare the local specialty *kaburga,* lamb stuffed with rice. ⊠ *Birinci Cad. 233/A* ☎ 482/212–8849 ▤ *No credit cards.*

¢   ✕ **Kebabçı Yusuf Ustanın Yeri.** This outdoor restaurant in the heart of Mardin serves tasty kebabs and frothy *ayran,* a salted yogurt drink that's drunk with a ladle from metal bowls. The kebabs are served with fresh flatbread, so you can make your own wrap. It's across the street from the post office, one of the loveliest old buildings in Mardin. ⊠ *Birinci Cad. Üçyol Mevkii* ☎ 482/212–7985 ▤ *No credit cards.*

$$ ▤ **Artuklu Kervansarayi.** Entering this hotel, built inside a kervansaray that dates back to 1275, will make you feel like you're taking a trip back in time. The walls are made of thick stone and the narrow corridors seem like something out of a medieval castle. The hotel itself is decorated with colorful rugs and kilim-cloth saddlebags, as well as other antiques on the walls. The standard rooms, built in a new addition connected to the old structure, are on the small side, with unadorned stone walls and kilims on the floor. There is a terrace with a panoramic view and an "oriental"-style reading room with rugs and pillows where you can sit back and relax. ⊠ *Birinci Cad. 70* ☎ 482/213–7353 ☎ 482/213–7354

⊕ *www.artuklu.com* ↷*40 rooms, 3 suites* ⌂ *Restaurant, minibars, cable TV, Wi-Fi, meeting rooms* ⊟ *AE, MC, V* ⏇ *BP.*

$$ ⊞ **Büyük Mardin Oteli.** This modern hotel is built of local limestone; on the edge of Mardin, it has good views of the plain below and of the old city. Rooms are comfortable and the large beds have solid wood headboards. The floors are of black marble, and colorful kilims serve as curtains. The rooftop terrace has a wonderful view of Mardin, especially at sunset, when the whole city takes on a golden glow. ⊠ *Yeniyol Cad.* ☏ *482/213–1047* 📠 *482/213–1447* ⊕ *www.dunyainsanlarininevi.com* ↷ *43 rooms, 11 suites* ⌂ *Restaurant, cable TV, minibars, exercise equipment, Turkish bath* ⊟ *AE, MC, V* ⏇ *BP.*

★ **$$** ✕⊞ **Erdoba Konakları.** A series of historic homes that have been connected together, this hotel helped restart Mardin's tourism industry when it opened in 2001. The rooms have stone walls, beds with wrought-iron headboards, and smallish bathrooms with blue tiling. Some of the rooms are also small, so ask for one of larger ones. A breezy terrace has with wicker chairs where you can have a drink or a meal and take in the fine view. A good restaurant serves local dishes in a cavernous space below the hotel. ⊠ *Birinci Cad. 135* ☏ *482/212–7677* 📠 *482/213–7787* ⊕ *www.erdoba.com.tr* ↷ *45 rooms, 10 suites* ⌂ *Restaurant, minibars, cable TV, in-room dataports, Turkish bath* ⊟ *AE, MC, V* ⏇ *BP.*

Midyat

★ ➌ *67 km (42 mi) east of Mardin.*

Not far from Mardin, the lovely old town of Midyat is an architectural gem that has remained largely untouched by the blight of concrete—although the new part of the city is dismal. Formerly almost an exclusively Assyrian Christian town, old Midyat is filled with an astonishing number of beautiful homes built of stone the color of honey or golden sand. Walking through Midyat's narrow streets reveals house after beautiful house, many of them with gorgeous ornamental carving work on their exteriors. Many of Midyat's Christians left during the violence of the 1980s and '90s, leaving the place feeling a bit like a ghost town in certain areas, but the homes and churches remain, and now that a relative calm has returned to the region, some of them are even being renovated for use as summer homes by Assyrians who used to reside here but currently have the primary homes in Europe. You can spend a quiet day exploring Midyat and visiting some of the nearby Assyrian monasteries; this is also a good base for visiting the historical monuments at the nearby riverside town of Hasankeyf.

With their numbers dwindling, Midyat's Assyrian community rotates services throughout the old town's churches, so it's hard to know which one will be open. Your best bet is visiting the **Mor Barsaumo church,** open most afternoons. It has a beautiful chapel with distinctive locally made artwork and beautiful stonework. ⊠ *Şen Cad. 21* ☏ *No phone* 🖅*free.*

Twenty-five km (15.5 mi) southeast of Midyat is the **Mor Gabriel Monastery,** built on the site of a church that dates back to 387. The monastery is on the top of a hill in a desolate area, surrounded by fields and vineyards, a perfectly peaceful and tranquil setting. Reopened as a monastery in 1952 after having been closed for some time, the building is today home to 2 monks and 14 nuns, as well as the local patriarch, known as a Metropolitan. An old chapel and basement grotto hold the graves of monks who lived here throughout the centuries. There are usually English-speaking guides—young men who live there as students, who can show you around. ⊠ *25 km (15.5 mi) southeast of Midyat* ☎ *482/462–1425* ⚏ *Free* ⊙ *Daily 9–11:30 and 1–5.*

Where to Stay & Eat

¢–$ ✕ **Cihan Lokantaš.** This basic steam-table restaurant serves the usual variety of soups and stews, as well as *pide* and *döner.* The owners have tried to add some class by hanging white lace curtains and putting pots of plastic yellow flowers on the walls—your call if this is classy or tacky. Either way, the food is tasty, the staff are friendly, and the location, down the street from the Mor Barsaumo church, makes it one of the few decent options near Midyat's old town. ⊠ *Cizre Yolu Uzeri, Karakol Karş 52* ☎ *482/464–1566* ⊟ *No credit cards.*

¢ ✕ **Tarihi Midyat Gelüşke Hanı.** This grilled-meat restaurant is inside a beautifully restored *han,* which served as an inn for traveling traders and their animals, that is several hundred years old. You can eat outside by a gurgling fountain in the large courtyard or in one of the small private dining rooms, where you sit on rugs and eat from low tables, reclining on pillows when you're done. The kebabs here are very tasty and served with a tangy chopped tomato salad and a refreshing cold yogurt soup that has wheat berries in it. If you call a day in advance, they can prepare an Assyrian speciality called *dobo,* lamb stuffed with rice and pistachios. ⊠ *Eski Midyat Çarşısı* ☎ *482/464–1442* ⊟ *MC, V.*

$$ ▦ **Otel Matiat.** This swanky place on the outskirts of Midyat has large rooms with lounge chairs and spacious bathrooms and professional and courteous service. There is a large, inviting pool in front of the hotel, which opened in 2006 in a new structure built out of the local stone (the same used for the city's historic houses). ⊠ *Mardin Yolu Üzeri* ☎ *482/462–5920* 🖷 *482/462–6895* ⊕ *www.matiat.com.tr* ⤺ *52 rooms, 8 suites* ⚭ *Restaurant, bar, cable TV, Wi-Fi, exercise equipment, sauna, Turkish bath, meeting rooms* ⊟ *MC, V* ⦿ *BP.*

¢ ▦ **Midyat Konuk Evi.** Not officially a hotel, this exquisite old stone mansion on a narrow lane was beautifully restored and serves as a guest house run by the municipality. The building's six guest rooms are large, with high vaulted ceilings, big beds, beautiful dark-wood carved furniture, and suprisingly modern bathrooms. The three-story house is on a hill, and the terrace has a sweeping view of the old town of Midyat. It's a romantic place to stay, but don't expect much in the way of services beyond a cup of tea in the morning from the friendly attendant. ⊠ *Güher Sok.* ☎ *482/464–0719* 🖷 *482/464–2061* ⤺ *6 rooms* ⚭ *No a/c, no phones, no TV.*

Hasankeyf

❹ *43 km (27 mi) north of Midyat.*

Just a short drive from Midyat, Hasankeyf makes for a good half-day trip. Come, explore, have lunch by the Tigris River and then return to

Midyat, Mardin, or even Diyarbakır. This small town has a magical setting, with stone houses on the banks of the Tigris River, lorded over by a cliff topped with the remains of an ancient citadel.

The **citadel,** which dates back to Roman times, is at the top of a sheer cliff that rises 328 ft above the river. On the backside of the cliff, the citadel looks over a small canyon where several abandoned cave dwellings have been carved into the rock. What remains of the citadel is enough to give a sense of how grand it must have once been. The whole area is extremely atmospheric and worth exploring. ⊠ *No address; it's on a dirt road at the edge of town* ☎ *No phone* 🎫 *1$* ⏱ *Daily, 8:30–5:30.*

> ## THE TIGRIS DAM
>
> For the last several years a proposed dam project along the Tigris has put Hasankeyf in danger of being submerged. Although a vocal campaign by environmentalists and preservationists has been trying to keep that from happening, the Turkish government broke ground in August 2006 on the dam project, promising to move some of the town's monuments to higher ground. Several European governments are applying pressure on Turkey to hold off on the dam, but there are no guarantees that the town will be saved.

Just below the citadel, on the way into town, is the **Er Rizk Mosque,** which dates back to the 14th century and has a beautiful minaret that has intricate stone carvings on its exterior. ⊠ ☎ *No phone* 🎫 *Free* ⏱ *During daylight hours.*

Across the river from the citadel is another spot worth visiting, **Zeynelbey Turbesi,** a mausoleum built circa 1480 for a local nobleman. The stylized structure has an onion-dome top and is decorated with still-vivid turquoise-colored tiles set in calligraphy-like geometric patterns. ⊠ *On the Batman-Hasankeyf road, near the bridge* ☎ *No phone* 🎫 *Free* ⏱ *During daylight hours.*

Where to Eat

$ ✕ **Yolgeçen Hanı Dinlenme Tesisleri.** There are a number of simple restaurants along the riverside in Hasankeyf, but this one is located in a cool cave just back from the water, which makes it an inviting place for lunch during the hot summer. There are three levels inside the large cave, and the floors are covered in kilims and large, colorful pillows on which you can recline. The restaurant serves kebabs and a meaty and flavorful local river fish known as *şabot,* which is marinated in red pepper and oregano and grilled. ⊠ *Dicle Kıyısı* ☎ *488/381–2287* 💳 *No credit cards.*

¢ ✕ **Nehir Çardak.** Do you like dining by the water? How about virtually *in* the water? At this unique restaurant you'll be eating in small thatched-roof pavilions on stilts over the water of the Tigris River. The kitchen is actually in the water, with the cook standing in front of the grill with his pants rolled up so they won't get wet. The menu is very basic—either grilled fish or *köfte,*—but the rustic setting, the river flowing by, and the view of Hasankeyf's cliff are utterly relaxing and wonderful. ⊠ *Dicle Kıyısı* ☎ *No phone* 💳 *No credit cards.*

DIYARBAKIR, MARDIN, MIDYAT & HASANKEYF ESSENTIALS

Transportation

BY AIR

Turkish Airlines has regularly scheduled flights from Istanbul to Diyarbakır and to Mardin, as do Onur Air and Pegasus Airlines. Atlas Jet flies regularly to Mardin's small airport. The cheapest one-way flights cost $50–75.

BY BUS

There are daily buses from Istanbul to Diyarbakır and Mardin. The ride takes close to 20 hours and costs $38. From Diyarbakır, minivans leave regularly from Dag Kapı for the one-hour trip to Mardin and to Midyat.

BY CAR

The roads are mostly flat in this region and there have been significant improvements in road quality, especially between Diyarbakır and Mardin. Gas stations are plentiful.

BY TRAIN

Long but scenic, the train ride from Istanbul to Diyarbakır takes more than 35 hours. It's inexpensive—per-person fares range from $22 (first class) to $44 (sleeper bunk)—but time is money, and it's much easier to fly.

Contacts & Resources

EMERGENCIES

🚔 **Police** ☎ 155. **Ambulance** ☎ 112.

VISITOR INFORMATION

🚔 **Diyarbakır** ✉ Dağkapi Bureu Giriş Bölmü ☎ 412/221-2173 🖷 412/221-1189

GAZIANTEP, MT. NEMRUT & ŞANLIURFA

Forget about "George Washington slept here"; in this part of Turkey you're more likely to come across places that claim to have been paid a visit by the biblical patriarch Abraham. This area of southeast Turkey has such depth and richness of history that the cities and monuments trace their roots back to biblical times and beyond. Luckily for the traveler, much of that history hasn't been lost to the sands of time, and the ancient cities and historical sites that are part of this excursion are remarkably well preserved and visitor-friendly.

This excursion begins in Gaziantep, not far from Turkey's border with Syria; it's a vibrant and busy town with a fascinating and well-preserved old city and one of the Turkey's most authentic bazaars. Gaziantep also has a fantastic museum featuring a stunning collection of Roman-era mosaics from a nearby archaeological dig and is known among Turks as having some of Turkey's best food and certainly its best baklava: make sure to try some!

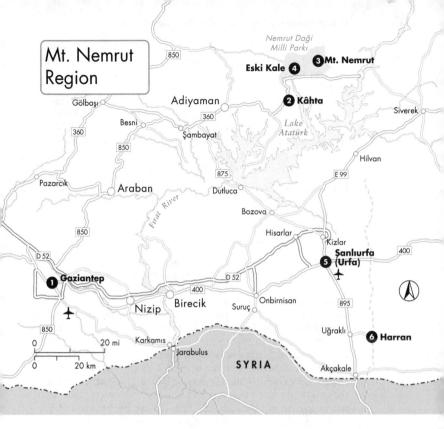

Mt. Nemrut
Region

From Gaziantep you will continue on to Mount Nemrut, a historical site that is something like a Turkish Stonehenge. The fascinating monument, dating back to the first century BC, improbably finds a collection of giant sculptures at the top of a lonely mountain—a lasting testament to the vanity of the ruler of a local dynasty.

Şanlıurfa is another of the area's ancient cities and a major pilgrimage site for Muslims in Turkey and from other countries in the area. There's a tranquil park with mosques and ponds with sacred fish built on the spot where many Muslims believe Abraham was born. (Abraham also figures prominently into the history of Harran, a fascinating historic site that's a quick side trip from Şanlıurfa.) Not far from the quiet of the park is the city's wonderful bazaar, where tailors work away on foot-driven sewing machines and the sound of coppersmiths hammering fills the air. The twisting lanes in the city's old neighborhoods are a wonderful place to wander and admire the beautiful old stone homes.

Gaziantep

❶ Gaziantep, the economic capital of Turkey's southeast, has an inviting mix of modern vitality and ancient tradition. Responsible for a good chunk of Turkey's industrial output, from bulgur wheat and pistachios to car parts and textiles, the city's modern part is lined with wide boulevards and ever-expanding housing tracts. At the literal and figurative heart of the city, however, lies a narrow-laned old town lined with graceful stone houses, a bustling bazaar filled with the sound of hammering coppersmiths, and a collection of restaurants and baklava bakeries that are considered among the best in Turkey. Only 65 km (40 mi) from the Syrian border, Gaziantep also has a distinctive Middle Eastern feel to it, from the historic homes with their large interior courtyards to the red-pepper paste and cumin used in the local dishes. You could easily spend two days exploring the city and its sites.

Like many cities in the region, Gaziantep's historic center is dominated by an ancient **citadel**, originally Roman but later further fortified by the Byzantines and the Selcuks. It's a pretty steep walk up, but the view from the top of the citadel over the Gaziantep bazaar district is fabulous. ⌦ *Free* ☉ *Open, Tues.-Sun. 8:30—4.*

Fodor'sChoice Not far from the citadel is the spiffy **Gaziantep Museum,** one of the city's ★ highlights. The collection used to be just the regular mix of antiquities from throughout the area's long history, but since 2005 it has also been host to a stunning collection of Roman-era mosaics rescued from a nearby archaeological site called Zeugma, which is slowly being submerged under the waters of a man-made lake. The intricate and beautiful mosaics, some portraying scenes from Roman mythology, others more artistic geometric designs, are clearly displayed and dazzling to behold. The fragment of a mosaic depicting a young woman with an enigmatic gaze (called "The Gypsy Girl") is quickly earning Mona Lisa–like iconic status in the area, with signs pointing visitors to her and with reproductions of the mosaic for sale throughout Gaziantep and even the rest of Turkey. ⌦ *Kamil Ocak Stat karşısı 1-2* ☎ *342/324–8809* ⌦ *$1.25* ☉ *May— Oct. daily 8:30–noon and 1–6; Nov.–Apr. 8:30–noon and 1–4:30.*

Hasan Suzer Ethnographic Museum, inside the warren of streets in the city's historic district, is a beautiful traditional Gaziantep house that's been restored and opened up to the public. The rooms of the house, which is built around a central courtyard, are done up with period furniture and somewhat stricken-looking mannequins dressed in traditional local costume. It's an excellent way to see the inside of a local old-style home, and the shady courtyard is a nice place to escape the Gaziantep sun. ⌦ *Hainfioğlu Sok. 64* ☎ *342/230—4721* ⌦ *$1.25* ☉ *Mon.–Sat., 8–noon and 1–5:30; closed Sun.*

You could spend a whole day losing yourself in Gaziantep's lively and sprawling **bazaar,** just south of the citadel. Gaziantep is known for copper work, and the sound of coppersmiths banging away is ubiquitous in the part of the market aptly known as the Coppersmiths' Bazaar. You'll also see saddle makers, woodworkers, spice vendors, and stalls selling everything from housewares and meat grinders to rugs with the image of Princess Diana on them! ☉ *Mon.–Sat. 9—6; closed Sun.*

Where to Stay & Eat

$ ✕ **Çavuşoğlu.** This place is a touch more refined than many of the other kebab houses in Gaziantep, with its comfortable chairs, beige walls with

Rediscovering Turkish Food in Gaziantep

Turks can be fiercely proud of the food in their region of the country, but even those from other places will easily admit that Gaziantep has perhaps Turkey's best food. Drawing on culinary influences from Turkish and Arab cooking, the earthy cuisine in Gaziantep is assertively spiced and flavorful. If you've grown tired of kebabs during your time in Turkey, be ready to rediscover them in Gaziantep, where kebab making is seen as both an art and a science. Among some of the best kinds of kebabs you can try here are *sebzeli kebab*, a skewer of lamb, tomato, green peppers, parsley, and garlic minced together, and *Ali Nazik*, cubes of grilled lamb taken off their skewer and served on a heavenly bed of smoky roasted eggplant and garlicky yogurt. Other specialties

include *mercimek koftesı*, small ovals made out of red lentils mixed with bulgur wheat, fresh herbs, red pepper paste, and spices and *yuvalama*, tiny dumplings made out of rice flour and ground meat, served in a yogurt broth.

Most of all, though, Gaziantep is famed for its flaky and buttery baklava, which incorporates with great success one of the area's leading crops, pistachios. It is, without a doubt, the preferred ending to any meal in Gaziantep. Gaziantep is rightfully known as Turkey's baklava capital and there are several shops incorporating the tongue-twister family name "Güllüoğlu," all of which vie for the title of being the city's best maker of the flaky sweet. One of the best is Baklavacı Güllüoğlu.

dark wood accents, and large photographs of local street scenes. The food is top-notch, with perfectly grilled kebabs and small *lahmacun*, round flatbreads topped with minced meat, and with just a touch of spicy heat. ⊠ *Eski Saray Cad. 11/B* ☎ *342/231–3069* ▤ *MC, V.*

$ ✕ **Imam Çağdaş.** Open since 1887, Imam Çağdaş is certainly doing FodorsChoice something right, and the crowds pack this restaurant in the bazaar dis-★ trict day and night. The food is earthy and sublime, from the Ali Nazik, minced meat kebab served on puree of roasted eggplant, garlic, and yogurt, to the *sebzeli* kebab, a skewer of lamb minced with garlic and parsley. Finish your meal with the restaurant's terrific syrupy baklava. ⊠ *Kale Civarı Uzun Çarşı* ☎ *342/220–4545* ▤ *MC, V.*

$ ✕ **Incilpinar Antep Sofrası.** Another of the city's top restaurants, this laid-back place is in the middle of a green park, and its several rooms are decked with kilims and low tables. There is also a shady courtyard. Along with very good kebabs, you can order various dishes that are baked in a terra-cotta pot. The restaurant also makes excellent *yuvalama*, a stew made with yogurt and small meat and rice flour dumplings. ⊠ *100. Yıl Atatürk Kültür Parkı Içi* ☎ *342/231–9816* ▤ *MC, V.*

★ **$** ✕ **Yörem.** Head here to take a break from kebabs and get a taste of classic Gaziantep home cooking. Run by a local woman who returned to Gaziantep after living in Europe for several years, Yörem is a cozy place. The menu rotates on a regular basis, but the food is consistently good. Among the dishes you might want to try are *yuvalama*, the meat and dumpling stew; *omaç,* a kind of patty made out of bread, tomato, onion, and parsley; and *kezan* kebab, eggplant stuffed with meat and poached. For desert try the local specialty *zerde sutlaç,* a rice pudding with a topping made from saffron. ⊠ *Incilpinar Mahallesi 3. Cad. 15. Sok.* ☎ *342/230–5000* ▭ *MC, V* ☉ *Closed Sun.*

¢ ✕ **Baklavacı Güllüoğlu.** This little shop, located inside a spice bazaar, is considered by many locals to have the best baklava in town. Run by a fifth-generation baklava maker, the humble store turns out a delicious version of the classic dessert, as well as other phyllo-and-nut-based sweets. ⊠ *Elmacı Pazarı 4* ☎ *342/231–2105* ▭ *No credit cards* ☉ *Closed Sun.*

¢ ✕ **Papirus Cafeteria.** The real attraction at this simple café that serves light fare such as pressed sandwiches and pizzas is the incredible old stone house it's located in. Down a narrow alleyway in one of Gaziantep's historic quarters, the building once belonged to an Armenian family. Its large courtyard is covered by leafy vines, while the interior of the house still has walls and ceilings covered with incredible fresco-like decorative painting. It's a nice place to cool off in the middle of the day. ⊠ *Noter Sok. 10* ☎ *342/220–3279* ▭ *MC, V.*

$$ 🏨 **Anadolu Evleri.** Down a narrow alleyway and behind a high wall hides
Fodor'sChoice this gem, a stylish but comfortable boutique hotel built into a historic
★ Gaziantep stone house. The rooms have been meticulously restored and are individually and charmingly decorated with quirky antiques like old radios and sewing machines, and there are antique telephones on the night tables. The central courtyard is delightful, with a loquat tree and tables shaded by umbrellas, as well as a covered seating area with a couch and comfortable chairs. Owner Tim Schindel, son of a Turkish mother and an American father, is extremely helpful and a good source of information about Gaziantep's cultural heritage. ⊠ *Şekeroğlu Sok. 6* ☎ *342/220–9525* 🖷 *342/220–9528* ⊕ *www.anadoluevleri.com* ↩ *10 rooms, 3 suites* ⚴ *Wi-Fi, TV in some rooms* ▭ *MC, V* ⚟ *BP.*

★ $ 🏨 **Antique Belkis Han.** Come to this charming, small hotel run by a local artist if you want to get a taste of what life used to be like in Gaziantep's old stone homes. Built in the 19th century, the gorgeous house has beautiful stone work and a lovely courtyard. Rooms are tastefully decorated with antique furniture and various knickknacks. The charming downstairs breakfast area has a long communal table, a stone floor, and is filled with more antiques. ⊠ *Kayacık Ara Sok. 16* ☎ *0342/221– 1228* 🖷 *0342/360–0880* ⊕ *www.belkishan.com* ↩ *6 rooms* ▭ *No credit cards* ⚟ *BP.*

$ 🏨 **Yesemek Otel.** It doesn't have much charm, but the mid-level Yesemek Otel does have spacious rooms with comfortable lounge chairs and good-sized bathrooms. Some rooms have balconies, which look out on a small park and an old mosque complex. The location, on a side street in the heart of town, is another plus. ⊠ *Isamil Say Sok. 4, 27010* ☎ *342/220–8888* 🖷 *342/220–8888* ⊕ ↩ *42 rooms* ⚴ *Restaurant, minibars, cable TV, in-room broadband* ▭ *MC, V* ⚟ *BP.*

¢ 🏨 **Hotel Katan.** With decent-sized rooms and bathrooms with tubs rather than just a shower, this seven-story hotel across the street from the museum is a good budget option. The front of the hotel faces a busy street, so ask for one of the quieter rooms in the back. ⊠ *Istasyon Cad. 58*

☎ 342/230–6969 ⓐ 342/220–8454 ⊕ ⇆ 42 rooms ⚭ Restaurant, minibars, cable TV, Wi-Fi ▤ MC, V � BP.

¢ ⊞ **Yunus Hotel.** On a quiet side street in the center of town, this well-run hotel with a friendly staff is an excellent budget option. The rooms are tidy, and bathrooms, though small, are lined with stylish, mosaic-like tiles. ⊠ Kayacık Sok. 16 ☎ 342/221–1722 ⓐ 342/221–1796 ⊕ ⇆ 28 rooms ⚭ Cable TV, minibars ▤ MC, V ıOı BP.

Kâhta

❷ 174 km (108 mi) from Gaziantep.

The quiet and dusty little town of Kâhta is really nothing more than a good base for exploring Mt. Nemrut, with a few good hotels and places to eat, but nothing else to see. The construction of the large Atatürk Dam and the resulting rising waters have meant that Kâhta is now a lakeside town, and a number of restaurants have taken advantage of this, opening up near the water, which makes for a pleasant place to have a meal.

Where to Stay & Eat

$ ✕ **Neşet'in Yeri.** This lakeside restaurant has an outdoor area shaded by an impressive grape arbor where you can eat trout or kebab while looking at the water. It's a nice spot to unwind after a visit to Nemrut. ⊠ Baraj Kenari ☎ 416/725–7675 ▤ MC, V.

¢–$ ✕ **Kahta Sofrası.** The pickings might be slim in Kâhta, but this place stands out for its friendly service and well-made food, including freshly baked *pide* as well as kebabs and prepared dishes like roast chicken and lamb stew. The restaurant is decorated with colorful rugs and is bright and open. ⊠ Mustafa Kemal cad. 15 ☎ 416/726–2055 ▤ MC, V.

$ ⊞ **Zeus Hotel.** With a pool and quiet garden, this well-run hotel is a good base for visiting Mt. Nemrut, something the friendly staff can help arrange. The rooms are spacious and comfortable—the color scheme is light purple with blue accents, and each has a small couch. ⊠ Mustafa Kemal Cad. 20 ☎ 416/725–5694 ⓐ 416/725–5696 ⊕ www.zeushotel. com.tr ⇆ 58 rooms, 8 suites ⚭ Restaurant, bar, pool, cable TV, minibars, sauna, Turkish bath ▤ MC, V ıOı BP.

¢ ⊞ **Hotel Nemrut.** Popular with tour groups, this hotel has clean, comfortable rooms, each with a small desk and extra pillows on the bed. The public areas are a bit dark and cheerless, though. The restaurant is on a shady terrace. The hotel can arrange for tours to Mt. Nemrut for around $10 per person. ⊠ Adıyaman Yolu ☎ 416/725–6881 ⓐ 416/725–6880 ⊕ www.hotelnemrut.com ⇆ 80 rooms, 4 suites ⚭ Restaurant, pool, minibars, cable TV, meeting rooms ▤ AE, MC, V ıOı BP.

Mt. Nemrut & Environs

228 km (142 miles) northeast of Gaziantep

❸ Mt. Nemrut (Nemrut Dağı), known as Mt. Nimrod in English, rises 7,052 ft above the Anatolian plain, a ruddy outcrop of rock and stunted trees that has become one of Turkey's most iconic historical sites. At the top of the ochre-pink, cone-shaped mountain is a stupendous spectacle: temples, each one a collection of remarkable-looking statues, stand on two

FodorśChoice
★

terraces—one facing the rising sun, the other the setting sun—with a man-made pyramid of small rocks, the **Tumulus of Antiochus,** between them. The man responsible for this fantastic project, King Antiochus I, is buried somewhere underneath—though they've tried, archaeologists have yet to find him: all attempts at excavation have caused cave-ins. From 64 BC to 32 BC, Antiochus was king of Commagene, a tiny Roman puppet state founded by his father, Mithridates the Great (it lasted until its annexation to Rome in AD 72). The kings of Commagene grandly claimed descent from Alexander the Great, and so young Antiochus reasoned that if Alexander was a god, he must be one, too. He set a veritable army of slaves to work building a suitable monument to himself. Enthroned on the two terraces are massive statues of gods, Antiochus seated among them as an equal.

Originally 26–30 ft high, the statues have been decapitated over the centuries by the forces of erosion and earthquakes; in 1926 a thunderstorm brought the last one—

> **WORD OF MOUTH**
>
> "My wife, my daughter, and I made the trip to Nemrut Daği . . . We had been told that the road from Kahta to Nemrut is extremely steep and a tough one, and when the van started its climb, I was very happy that I did not drive. It was absolutely wonderful to be up there, though, with the spectacular ruins."   –yakamozkar

Tyche, goddess of fortune—crashing down. Their gigantic heads were set upright by archaeologists in the 1950s on the ground around the tumulus; you can see how they combine the Greek harmony of features with Asian-looking headgear and hairstyles. On the east terrace, left to right, they are: Apollo, Tyche/Fortuna, Zeus (at center, with his pointed cap and bushy whiskers), Antiochus, and Heracles. The west terrace is a mirror image of the east, with the addition of some fine relief carvings portraying Antiochus shaking hands with Apollo, Zeus, and Heracles, all with smiles and dignity. Most of the inscriptions that are carved all over the site describe the Commagenes and their religious practices; the message on the throne of Antiochus reads, "I, Antiochus, caused this monument to be erected in commemoration of my own glory and of that of the gods." Follow the path that runs behind the statues to view the particularly fine inscriptions on the backs of the figures. Given the severe temperatures and strong winds at the summit, and the overall isolation of the site, one wonders why Antiochus didn't choose a more inviting location—a question best discussed over a steaming cup of tea at the small visitor center. ■ TIP➜ **Bring your own food and water for the excursion up the mountain.** ⊠ *Nemrut Daği* ☎ *416/737–1231* ✉ *$1* ☉ *May–late Oct., daily sunrise–sunset.*

Where to Stay

$ ⊞ **Hotel Euphrat.** This hotel on Mt. Nemrut, like the Otel Kervansary next door, is a low stone building with spartan but clean rooms. There is a restaurant decked out in kilims and rugs with a deck that has a spectacular view of the surrounding mountains and of the stars at night. The food is simple but tasty. The hotel also has a pleasant garden with

Basing Yourself to See Mt. Nemrut

KÂHTA IS THE EASIEST place to base yourself for a trip to Mount Nemrut, even though it's a 2 hour drive—you're best off signing up with a minibus tour from here , which will save you the driving up the mountain—the road is good, but windy and bumpy at times—and you'll get the benefit of a tour guide. ($15–$75, depending on the length of the tour and how many people share the minibus.) There are sunrise and sunset tours. Tour guides recommend setting out at 2 AM to reach the summit at sunrise. You can then return before the fierce midday heat. Sunset tours leave Kâhta at around 1 PM. ■ TIP→ The sunrise is lovely, but if you start later, you'll avoid the sunrise tourist rush and the coldest part of the morning.

If you're driving your own car and would like to catch the sunrise or sunset on Mount Nemrut without

having to start off too early in the morning or getting back too late in the day, you may want to consider spending the night in the small and tranquil village of Karadut, which is only five miles from the monument and has two decent places to stay and eat.

If you drive to the summit yourself, the trip from Kâhta takes a good two hours using the old road (from where you can stop at **Eski Kâhta** [Old Kâhta] on the way back) but half that using a newer road that goes through the village of Narince.

Because of severe winter weather conditions, the trip should be undertaken only between May and October—even then, when the sun is baking down on the plain, there are strong winds and a stiff morning chill at the summit.

6

---

cherry and quince trees. ⊠ *Nemrut Dağı, Karadut Köyü, 54 km (34 mi) from Kâhta, Karadut Köyu* ☎ *416/737–2175* 🖷 *416/737–2179* 🖘 *52 rooms* ⚄ *Restaurant, pool* ▤ *MC, V* ⑩ *MAP.*

★ $ 🏨 **Otel Kervansaray.** One of the few places to stop on Mt. Nemrut itself, the Kervansaray is in a low stone building near a waterfall 8 km (5 mi) from Mt. Nemrut's summit. The location is stunning, the rooms are basic but clean, and the food is simple but good. It's all wonderfully quiet. The pool is small and nothing fancy. ⊠ *Nemrut Dağı, Karadut Köyü, 54 km (34 mi) from Kâhta* ☎ *416/737–2190* 🖷 *416/737–2085* 🖘 *16 rooms* ⚄ *Restaurant, pool* ▤ *MC, V* ⑩ *MAP.*

OFF THE BEATEN PATH

Most people take the new road, for the shorter drive, but along the old road back from Mt. Nemrut to Kâhta, you'll pass more remarkable relics of Commagene in the small village of **ESKI KÂHTA** (Old Kâhta). ■ TIP→ Don't confuse Eski Kâhta, this historical site on the mountain slope, with Kâhta, where people stay. They're about 15 km apart. Cross the Kâhta ➍ River on the Seljuk Bridge to see Arsameia, now called **Eski Kale** (Old Castle), a former capital of the Commagene kingdom. Here, carved into the rock, is a stunning relief of Antiochus I's father, Mithridates, being greeted by Heracles. Higher up on the rock face are inscriptions proclaiming the glory of the Commagene dynasty; on the top of this peak stand the foundations of an ancient acropolis with colored floor mosaics.

A short distance down the road from the old castle is **Yeni Kale** (New Castle), built by the Mameluks over a smaller Commagene fortress. Recross the Kâhta via the **Cendere Köprü**, a single-span bridge with two tall columns on one end and one on the other, built by the Roman emperor Septimus Severus in the early 3rd century AD. Ten km (6 mi) before Kâhta is **Karakuş** (which means "black bird" in Turkish), named for the black eagle that guards, from atop a large column, the tombs of the royal ladies of Commagene.

Şanlıurfa (Urfa)

★ ❺ *143 km (89 mi) southeast of Kâhta on Rte. E99, or 135 km (84 mi) east of Gaziantep.*

With its golden-colored stone houses, religious shrines filled with visiting pilgrims, and a very authentic bazaar displaying mounds and mounds of the local specialty, crushed red pepper, in various shades and levels of spiciness, Şanlıurfa has a timeless quality to it. The city lies at the edge of the Syrian desert, not far from the border with Syria and, like Gaziantep, also has a strong Middle Eastern flavor—literally as well as figuratively, because the local food has a distinct Armenian influence. Formerly a sleepy and arid frontier town that underwent a huge boom due to GAP (the Güneydoğu Anadolu Projesi, or Southeast Anatolia Project, a large-scale damming and irrigation program undertaken by the Turkish government), Urfa is most famous as the supposed birthplace of the biblical patriarch Abraham. A half-dozen mosques crowd around the cave where many Muslims believe Abraham was born, and a pool near the cave is filled with what are believed to be sacred carp.

Şanlıurfa is more commonly called Urfa by Turks and in maps and tourism literature; *şanlı,* or "glorious," was added by an act of parliament to the city's name in 1984 to commemorate the city's resistance to the French military occupation of the area following World War I.

Urfa's old town, at the southern foot of Divan Caddesi, is a remarkable mix of Babylonian, Assyrian, Roman, Byzantine, and Ottoman architecture, albeit heavily eroded over the centuries. The **Urfa Kale** (Urfa Fortress) is a motley collection of pillars, upturned stones, and broken columns at the top of a wide staircase. It's impossible to detect any one architectural intent here, probably because the fortress has been razed and rebuilt at least a dozen times since the 2nd century BC. Climb to the summit for a fantastic view of the city. ✉ *Kale Cad.* ☏ *No phone* 🎟 *$1* ⏲ *Daily 9–6.*

Local legend has it that Abraham was born in the **Hazreti İbrahim Doğum Mağarası** (Prophet İbrahim's Birth Cave), a natural cave hidden behind the Hasan Paşa Mosque. Men and women enter through separate doorways. Most people huddled inside this small, dark cavern, darkened by 2,000 years of candle smoke, have come to pray, not to snap photos. There's not much to see, but the atmosphere is reverential. Tourists are welcome (many of the visitors inside are themselves from out of town), but remember that this is a shrine. ⊠ *Göl Cad.* ☎ *No phone* 🎫 *Free* ☉ *Daily, sunrise–sunset.*

Gölbaşı Parkı, home of the famed carp pools, is a shady oasis on hot days. According to legend, King Nimrod, angry at Abraham's condemnation of the king's Assyrian polytheism, set about immolating the patriarch. God awakened natural springs, dousing the fire and saving Abraham. Historically the story might not, well, hold water, but these springs remain, in the form of these sacred pools filled with carp—an incarnation, according to the myth, of the wood from Abraham's pyre. The place has a serene and distinctly spiritual feel to it, with groups of visiting pilgrims and families from Turkey and neighboring countries strolling about and feeding what are probably the most pampered fish in the world.

A short walk east from the park leads to Urfa's **bazaar,** where in summertime merchants wait patiently in the hot sun for the occasional tour group. The bazaar is a wonderful place to walk around, filled with small hans–a collection of stores and workshops built around a central courtyard–that have tailors, coppersmiths, and other artisans working away, using what seem like ancient machines and tools. At the literal heart of the bazaar is the wonderful *bedesten,* a large courtyard filled with chatting men playing backgammon or chess and sipping tea. Around the courtyard are the small workshops of tailors sewing inexpensive suits. Urfa's bazaar is a good place to shop for spices and copper items and you can usually find bargains, especially on carpets and kilims.

Urfa's old neighborhoods are filled with lovely stone homes covered with ornamental carving, and several hours exploring will be time well spent. One place worth seeking out is the old Assyrian church complex, **Il Özel Idaresi Vali Kemalettin Gazezoğlu Kultur ve Sanat Merkezi**—it's a mouthful, but neighborhood locals should be able to point you in the right direction—that has been restored and turned into a cultural center. The hours are unpredictable, but the walk there leads you through narrow alleyways and past several beautiful old houses. ⊠ *Kurtuluş Sok.* ☎ *No phone* 🎫 *Free* ☉ *irregular hours.*

Güzel Sanatlar Galerisi, the city's art gallery, right next to the post office, is another restored house that's worth visiting. The art may not be so impressive, but the stone mansion has delightful relief-carving work on its exterior and a lovely indoor courtyard. ⊠ *Sarayönü Cad.* ☎ *No phone* 🎫 *Free* ☉ *Mon.–Fri., 8:30–5, Sat. noon–4.*

Urfa also has a small but appealing **archaeological museum.** The displays are thoughtfully laid out and well lit, covering the area's long history. Especially interesting are a series of Hittite sculptures that were dug up in the area, and a collection of antique wooden doors with exquisite carving work. ⊠ *Çamlık Cad.* ☎ *414/313–1588* 🎫 *$1.25* ☉ *Mon.–Fri. 8–noon and 1–5:30,.*

Where to Stay & Eat

$ ✕ **Gülizar Konuk Evi.** One of the first restaurants in Urfa to open up inside one of the city's historic stone houses, this is also one of the best.

It serves the usual kebabs, along with some local specialties such as *çömlek*, a meat and vegetable stew slow-cooked in the oven, and *borani*, a stew made with lamb and spinach. Found down a winding lane, the old house also has a beautiful open-air courtyard with a fountain and a pomegranate tree. You can eat outdoors or in one of the "oriental"-style private dining rooms filled with rugs and pillows. ⊠ *Karameydanı Camii Yanı 22* ☎ *414/215–0505* ▤ *MC, V.*

$ ✕ **Urfa Sofrası.** This dining establishment is a bit more upscale than most of its competitors. An outdoor terrace overlooks a small park and the busy streets below. You can order kebabs, *pide*, and *lahmacun and kaburga*, lamb stuffed with rice. The dishes come served with a cold and refreshing yogurt soup made with chickpeas and wheat berries. Finish your meal with a small cup of bracing Arab-style bitter coffee, served by a roving waiter who pours the coffee from his copper urn. ⊠ *Karakoyun Işmerkezi Kat 1 No. 226* ☎ *414/315–6130* ▤ *MC, V.*

$ ✕ **Yıldız Sarayı Konukevi.** Set inside a large restored mansion, this restaurant has several private dining rooms decorated with rugs and pillows, as well as a breezy upstairs terrace. The kitchen turns out good kebabs and *içli kofte,* ground meat fried inside a bulgur shell, and tender lamb roasted in a red pepper sauce that tastes almost like American BBQ. ⊠ *Yorgancı Sok. 10* ☎ *414/216–9494* ▤ *MC, V.*

¢–$ ✕ **Altınşiş.** The combination of good food and friendly service makes this low-key restaurant especially appealing. There are kebabs and döner, along with *pide* and a large selection of prepared foods being kept warm on a steam table. The *güveç*, a meat and vegetable stew cooked in a large terra-cotta pot, is worth trying. The dining room is simple and cheery, with walls painted a light yellow and tables covered with blue cloths. ⊠ *Sarayönü Cad. 140* ☎ *414/216–0506* ▤ *MC, V.*

¢–$ ✕ **Çardaklı Köşk.** Another old Urfa stone house restored and turned into a restaurant, but this one looks out over the city's citadel and the fish-pool complex. Sit on the terrace or in one of the several *çardaks*, small private rooms where you can recline on pillows. The food, the usual mix of kebabs and *pides,* is unexciting, but the location makes up for it. ⊠ *Balıkgöl Civarı Tünel Çıkışı 1* ☎ *414/217–1080* ▤ *MC, V.*

★ $$ ⌂ **Hotel El-Ruha.** This sprawling hotel across the street from Urfa's fish pools is the city's top place to stay. Built of local stone, it has a comfortable lobby with leather couches and antique furniture, and the elevators are decorated with burled wood trim. Rooms are spacious and comfortable, with large beds, wood furniture, vaulted ceilings, and bathrooms with mosaic-like tiles; most have a view of the fish-pool complex. Service is attentive and professional. ⊠ *Balıklıgöl* ☎ *414/215–4411* 🖷 *414/215–9988* ⊕ *www.hotelelruha.com* ⋧ *71 rooms, 11 suites* ⌂ *2 restaurants, minibars, cable TV, gym, sauna, Turkish bath, business services, meeting rooms, parking* ▤ *MC, V* ⨾❘ *BP.*

$ ✕⌂ **Cevahir Konuk Evi.** Formerly a government guest house, this grand old stone home with a great view from its terrace is now in private hands. The hallways are lined with colorful rugs and antique furniture, while the rooms have high ceilings, stone walls, and white bedspreads embroidered with flowers. The tidy bathrooms have full tubs and fixtures with golden handles. There is a good restaurant with a large garden on the premises, although they often have live music at night, so be sure to ask for a room that doesn't face the courtyard. ⊠ *Byükyol Selahattin Eyyubi Camii Karşısı* ☎ *414/215–9377* 🖷 *414/216–1155* ⊕ *www. cevahirkonukevi.com* 🛏 *6 rooms, 1 suite* ⚭ *Restaurant, Cable TV, minibars, Wi-Fi* 🖃 *AE, MC, V* ⏐⏐⏐ *BP.*

$ ✕⌷ **Harran Hotel.** Once the city's best hotel, the Harran is looking a little aged but the rooms are spacious and comfortable and the bathrooms are decently sized. The hotel is centrally located and staffed by a phalanx of friendly employees, and there's a nice pool—a definite bonus during the hot Urfa summer. The restaurant on the top floor, where breakfast is served, has an unparalleled view of Urfa. ⊠ *Atatürk Bul.* ☎ *414/ 313–2860* 🖷 *414/313–4918* ⊕ *www.hotelharran.com* 🛏 *82 rooms* ⚭ *Restaurant, pool, minibars, cable TV, gym, sauna, Turkish bath, parking* 🖃 *AE, MC, V* ⏐⏐⏐ *BP.*

¢ ⌷ **Hotel Arte.** The owner of this little hotel studied architecture in France, and his schooling is reflected in the stylish interior, which feels more European than local—there's nary a kilim in sight. From outside the hotel looks like a glass-box office building; inside, though, it's comfortable and almost minimalist, with spacious rooms that have dark wood parquet floors, walls painted a stark white, and stylish wooden desks and nightstands. An upstairs lobby has comfortable leather couches and lounge chairs where you can sit back and watch the bustle of the streets below. ⊠ *Sinema Sok. 7* ☎ *414/314–7060* 🖷 *414/314–9010* ⊕ *www. otel-arte.com* 🛏 *33 rooms* ⚭ *Cable TV, minibars* 🖃 *MC, V* ⏐⏐⏐ *BP.*

Harran

❻ *50 km (31 mi) southeast of Urfa.*

A quick ride from Urfa, the ancient city of Harran is well worth a visit. The Urfa region is rife with dubious biblical legends, but there seems to be almost unanimous agreement that this Harran of modern Turkey is quite likely the Harran mentioned in the Old Testament as a place where Abraham spent some time before heading off to the promised land. True or not, today's Harran stands on the spot of a very ancient settlement, with crumbling fortifications surrounding what is now a simple village and the ruins of what was once the world's first Islamic university, built in the 8th century, just on the edge of town. Called the **Ulu Cami,** all that's left is a distinctive square minaret that can be seen from throughout Harran. Indeed, in Harran visitors get the sense that not much has changed here over the centuries, and some of the pastoral scenes around Harran, of shepherds driving their flocks of sheep along seem, well, almost biblical.

Harran's main claims to fame, besides playing host to Abraham, are its beehive-shaped houses, wondrous structures built of hay and mud, each topped with a conical roof. The small town is filled with them, although many are no longer family dwellings and are now used as stables or are in the process of collapsing. **The Harran Evi** is a good reconstruction of a traditional beehive home where you can take a tour of the inside living quarters and hear the guide extol the virtues—cool in summer, warm in winter—of its unique construction. After the tour, you can sit down for tea or a cold drink in the courtyard or in a rug-lined room inside the beehive house itself. ☒ *Ibni Teymiye Mah* ☏ *414/441–2020* ☑ *Free* ☉ *Daily, 8 AM–10 PM.*

The Geleneksel Konik Kubbeli Evi, just down the road from the Harran Evi is another reconstruction of a beehive house built by a rival local family. It's also worth visiting. The family that lives there is especially friendly and rather exuberant, literally running up to the entrance gate with broad smiles to greet visitors. ☒ *Çeşme Sok. 23* ☏ *542/337–8512* ☑ *Free* ☉ *Daily, 8 AM–10 PM.*

GAZIANTEP, MT. NEMRUT & ŞANLIURFA ESSENTIALS

Transportation

BY AIR

Turkish Airlines flies regularly to Gaziantep and Şanlıurfa. Onurair flies regularly to Gaziantep, and Atlas Jet has regular flights to Urfa and to Adiyaman, which is close to Kahta and Mt. Nemrut.

BY BUS

There are daily buses from Istanbul to Gaziantep and Urfa. The ride takes about 18 hours to either city and costs $30. There are regular minivans that make the quick run from Gaziantep to Urfa and from Urfa to Adiyaman, where you can catch a minivan to Kahta. There's an *otogar* (bus station) in each of the main towns.

Kamilkoc ⊕ www.kamilkoc.com.tr. **Ulusoy** ⊕ www.ulusoy.com.tr. **Varan** ⊕ www.varan.com.tr

BY CAR

With industry booming in the area around Gaziantep, the road leading to and from the city tends to be clogged with big trucks. There is a highway being built that will link Gaziantep and Urfa which should ease some of the congestion. It's expected to be finished in 2007.

Avis has an office in Gaziantep, near Şanlıurfa. Economy rates are $45–$55 per day with unlimited mileage; the drop-off fee is $100.

Avis ☏ 342/336-1194

BY TRAIN

The Toros Express leaves Istanbul three times a week on its long journey to Gaziantep. The trip takes close to 27 hours and tickets cost $22 for a first-class seat and $40 for a sleeper compartment.

Contacts & Resources

EMERGENCIES

Police ☏ 155. **Ambulance** ☏ 112.

GUIDED TOURS

The knowledgable Ayşe Nur Arun at Gaziantep's Arsan travel agency can arrange for tours in Gaziantep, around the region, and to Mt. Nemrut. Nemrut Tours in Kahta, which is connected to the Hotel Nemrut, arranges daily trips to Mt. Nemrut.

Harran-Nemrut tours in Urfa is run by the English-speaking Özcan Aslan, who is friendly and helpful. He can arrange trips to Harran and the surrounding region and also offers one and two-day tours to Mt. Nemrut from Urfa.

Arsan ☎ 342/220-6464 ⊕ www.arsan.com.tr. **Harran-Nemrut** ☎ 414/215-1575 ⊕ ozcan_aslant_teacher£hotmail.com. **Nemrut** ☎ 416-725-6881 ⊕ www.hotelnemrut. com.

VISITOR INFORMATION
Adıyaman ⊠ Atatürk Bul. 184 ☎ 416/216-1008. **Şanlıurfa** ⊠ Asfalt Cad. 4-D ☎ 414/ 215-2467.

UNDERSTANDING TURKEY

TURKEY AT A GLANCE

Fast Facts

Name in local language: Türkiye
Capital: Ankara
National anthem: İstiklal Marşı
Type of government: Republican Parliamentary Democracy
Administrative divisions: 81 provinces
Independence: October 29, 1923 (as successor state to the Ottoman Empire)
Constitution: November 7, 1982
Legal system: Civil, Penal, and Commercial Codes derived from various European continental systems
Suffrage: 18 years of age, universal
Legislature: Unicameral Parliament
Population: 72.8 million (December 2005 est.)
Population density: 228 per square mile
Median age: 28.1 years
Life expectancy: 72.6 years
Infant mortality rate: 39.7 per 1,000 live births

Literacy: 86.5%
Language: Turkish (official), also Kurdish and other minority languages
Ethnic groups: Turkish (est. 75–80%), Kurdish (est. 20–25%), Arab, Georgian (both est. 2–3%)
Religion: Muslim 99.8% (est. 75–80% Sunni, 15–20% Alevi), other 0.2%
Discoveries & Inventions: Smallpox vaccinations (in Ottoman times). The first mention of smallpox vaccinations in the West was probably in the diaries of Lady Mary Wortley Montague (1689–1762), who wrote about them in her letters home during a visit to the Ottoman Empire and subsequently introduced them into England.

"The Bosphorus with one key opens and closes two worlds, two seas."
–Pierre Gyllius, The Antiquities of Constantinople (1544–50)

Geography & Environment

Land area: 780,580 square kilometers (301,384 square miles)
Coastline: 7,200 kilometers (4,474 miles)
Terrain: High central plateau (Anatolia), narrow coastal plain, several mountain ranges
Islands: Several small islands off the Aegean and Mediterranean coasts and in the Sea of Marmara. There are too many islands to name them all, although most are islets and rocks, several of which are intensely disputed with Greece.
Natural resources: Coal, iron ore, copper, chromium, gold, borate, limestone, marble, arable land, hydropower
Natural hazards: Severe earthquakes, particularly along the north Anatolian fault line running from Istanbul to Van

Flora: More than 9,000 types of plants, of which 3,000 are indigenous
Fauna: 60,000 species including wolves, foxes, wild boars, wildcats, bears, deer, gazelles, and mountain goats. Domesticated animals include: water buffalos, Angora goats, camels, horses, donkeys, sheep, and cattle. There is also a large variety of indigenous and migratory bird species.
Environmental issues: Deforestation, rapid urbanization, air and water pollution, desertification, soil degradation through overuse of agricultural fertilizers, lack of biodiversity, dam building in southeast Turkey.

Economy

Turkey has a dynamic economy with a rapidly growing private sector although the state still plays a major role in banking and transportation. Its main sources of foreign currency are tourism, textiles, and the automotive industry. Agriculture accounts for 36% of total employment.

Currency: New Turkish Lira (YTL), introduced in 2005
Exchange rate: $1 = YTL1.58 (July 2006)
GDP: $362.5 billion
Per capita income: $5,062
Inflation: 10.1% in year to end (2006)
Unemployment: 11.9% (2006)
Work force: 24.4 million (2006)
Debt: 68% of GDP
Economic aid: ODA $635.8 million (2002)
Major industries: Automotives, textiles, food processing, electronics, steel, construction
Agricultural products: Tobacco, cotton, grain, olives, sugar beets, pulse, citrus, livestock

Exports: $73.4 billion (2005)
Major export products: Automotive products, apparel, textiles, foodstuffs, metal products
Export partners: Germany (13%), UK (8.2%), Italy (7%), U.S. (6.8%), France (5%), Spain (4.1%)
Imports: $116.5 billion (2005)
Major import products: Machinery, chemicals, semifinished goods, fuels, transport equipment
Import partners: Germany (13.6%), Russia (10.1%), Italy (6.9%), France (5.5%), China (4.4%), U.S. (4.1%)

"Come, Come whoever you are, wanderer, worshiper, lover of leaving. Ours is not a caravan of despair. Come even if you have broken your vows a thousand times, Come, come yet again."

—Rumi

Did You Know?

• The oldest known human settlement is in Çatalhöyük, in Turkey; it contains the earliest landscape painting. The earliest layers of the site are believed to date from around 7500 BC.

• Turks introduced coffee to Europe.

• Turkey is the world's largest exporter of hazelnuts.

• The world's first coins were minted at ancient Sardis in southwest Turkey in the seventh century BC.

• Istanbul is the only city in the world to straddle two continents.

• The English words *horde, kiosk, tulip,* and *yogurt* all come from Turkish.

• St. Nicholas, the original Santa Claus, was born in Demre in southern Turkey.

EATING OUT IN TURKEY

Where to Eat Out

Turkish people love to eat and there are several different types of dining establishments. The simplest, Turkey's fast-food joints, are the *kebapcı,* the *dönerci,* and the *pideci. Kebapcıs* specialize in kebabs—marinated cubes of meat (generally lamb), usually grilled along with vegetables on a skewer. *Dönercis* provide quick meals of spicy, spit-roasted sliced lamb, served either as a sandwich or with rice. At the *pideci* you'll find *pide,* a pizzalike snack made of flat bread topped with either butter, cheese, and egg or with ground lamb and baked in a wood-fired oven. These fast-food eateries are usually little more than counters at which you belly up to the bar for instant gratification.

Lokantas are unpretentious neighborhood spots that make up the vast majority of Turkish restaurants. In smaller cities there may well be three or four in a row, each with simple wooden chairs and tables and paper napkins. In towns, villages, and any city with a harbor, lokantas are often open-air, the better to take advantage of the waterfront and sky, or are surrounded by flower-filled trellises. Often you'll serve yourself cafeteria-style from large display cases full of hot and cold dishes—a relief if you don't speak Turkish. If there is no menu, it's usually because the chef only serves what is fresh, and that changes from day to day.

In the more upscale *restorans* (restaurants), you can expect tablecloths, menus, maybe even a wine list, and dishes drawn from the richer "palace" or "Ottoman" cuisine of Turkish royalty, often with continental touches. The best restorans are in Istanbul and Ankara, though others are scattered throughout the country.

Turkish Cuisine

Turkey is not just a geographic bridge between Europe, Asia, and the Middle East; it's a gastronomic one as well. Its cuisine reflects the long history of a people who emigrated from the borders of China to a land mass known as Asia Minor and built an empire that encompassed Arab, Asian, and European lands.

Turkish cuisine is full of vegetables, grains, fresh fish, and seemingly infinite varieties of lamb. Fish and meat are typically served grilled or roasted. The core group of seasonings and condiments is garlic, sage, oregano, cumin, mint, dill, lemon, and yogurt, always more yogurt. Turkish yogurt is among the tastiest in the world; and many travelers swear it helps keep their stomachs calm and stable while on the road.

There are now a small number of specialist vegetarian restaurants in Turkey, though they tend to be concentrated in Istanbul and Ankara. If in doubt, point to a dish and ask *"et var mı?"* ("Is there any meat in it?"). The answer will probably be "hayir" or "yok" (both meaning "no") or "evet" (meaning "yes").

This guide makes frequent references to "traditional Turkish cuisine." Here's what to expect.

Mezes are appetizers. Frequently a large tray is brought to the table and you point at what you want, or you can point at your selection from a display case. They're served with a basket of bread. Standard cold mezes include *patlıcan salatası* (roasted eggplant puree flavored with garlic and lemon), *haydari* (a thick yogurt dip made with garlic and dill), *dolma* (stuffed grape leaves, peppers, or mussels), *ezme* (a spicy paste of tomatoes, minced green pepper, onion, and parsley), *kızartma* (deep-fried eggplant, zucchini, or green pepper served with fresh yogurt), *cacık* (a garlicky cold yogurt "soup" with shredded cucumber, mint, or dill), *barbunya pilaki* (kidney beans, tomatoes, and onions cooked in olive oil), and *imam bayıldı* (slow-roasted baby eggplant topped with fried onions and tomatoes and seasoned with garlic). One taste of this last meze, and you'll understand how it got its name—which means, "The imam fainted with delight." Inevitably there will be other dishes based on eggplant, *patlıcan* in Turkish. Hot appetizers, usually called *ara sıcak,* include *börek* (a deep-fried or oven-baked pastry filled with cheese or meat), *kalamar* (deep-fried calamari served with a special sauce), and *midye tava* (deep-fried mussels).

Available almost any place you stop to eat, kebabs (*kebaps* in Turkish) come in many guises. Although the ingredient of choice for Turks is lamb, some kebabs are made with beef, chicken, or fish, usually grilled with vegetables on a skewer. *Adana kebaps* are spicy ground-lamb patties arranged on a layer of sautéed pita bread, topped with a zippy yogurt-and-garlic sauce. *İskender kebaps,* also known as *Bursa kebaps,* are sliced grilled lamb smothered in tomato sauce, hot butter, and yogurt. *Şiş kebaps* are the traditional skewered cubes of lamb, usually interspersed with peppers and onions. *Köfte kebaps* are meatballs made from minced lamb mixed with rice, bulgur, or bread crumbs, then threaded onto skewers.

Fresh fish, often a main course, is commonly served grilled and drizzled with olive oil and lemon. You will find *alabalık* (trout), *barbunya* (red mullet), *kalkan* (turbot), *kefal* (gray mullet), *kılıç* (swordfish, sometimes served as a kebab), *levrek* (sea bass), *lüfer* (bluefish), and *palamut* (bonito).

In the meat department there is *mantı,* a sort of Turkish ravioli served with garlicky yogurt that has a touch of mint. Grilled quail is most common inland; it's often marinated in tomatoes, yogurt, olive oil, and cinnamon. *Karışık ızgara,* a mixed grill, usually combines chicken breast, beef, a lamb chop, and spicy lamb patties, all served with rice pilaf and vegetables. *Tandır kebap,* lamb cooked in a pit, is a typical Anatolian dish.

For dessert you'll encounter several varieties of *baklava* (phyllo pastry with honey and chopped nuts) and *burma kadayıf* (shredded wheat in honey or syrup). Also popular are puddings—usually made of yogurt and eggs—as well as sweet rice or milk and rice flour.

Wine, Beer & Spirits

Alcohol is readily available and widely consumed, despite Turkey's predominantly Muslim culture. However, restaurants are required to have a special license to serve alcohol, which many of the smaller eateries don't have. Check before you sit down if this is a priority for you. In recent years there has been a rapid proliferation of new Turkish wines, including many made from foreign grapes. A limited selection of foreign wines is now also available, although they are relatively expensive. The longest-established—and still inexpensive and perfectly acceptable—local wines are Villa Doluca and Kavaklidere, both available in *beyaz* (white) and *kırmızı* (red). The most popular local beer is Efes Pilsen, your basic American-type pilsner. In late 1997 Efes began making a dark beer called, simply, Efes Dark. It also produces Beck's and Miller draught under license in Turkey. Other beers brewed under license in Turkey include Tuborg, Carlsberg, and Foster's. It's possible to find imported beers such as Budweiser, Heineken, and Grolsch. The national drink of Turkey is rakı, a relative of the Greek ouzo, made from grapes and aniseed. Usually it's mixed with water or ice, though many connoisseurs insist it's best drunk neat, and each sip of rakı followed immediately by a sip of cold water. People drink it throughout their meal or as an aperitif.

BOOKS & MOVIES

Books

Whether Homer's *Iliad* should be classified as fiction or nonfiction is up for debate, but it's still the most evocative reading on the Trojan War and the key players of Turkish antiquity. Perhaps it's best left as something unclassified.

Memoirs, Essays & Observations. The keenest insight into the ancient ruins that you may encounter on your trip comes from George Bean, author of *Aegean Turkey, Turkey Beyond the Meander, Lycian Turkey,* and *Turkey's Southern Shore.* John Julius Norwich's three-volume *Byzantium* chronicles the rise and fall of one of history's great empires, while Caroline Finkel's *Osman's Dream* provides a compehensive overview of the history of the Ottoman Empire.

Mary Lee Settle provides a vision of Turkey that is both panoramic and personal in *Turkish Reflections.* The book marks Settle's return to the country that was the setting for her novel *Blood Tie,* a 1978 National Book Award winner. Dame Freya Stark, one of the most remarkable travelers of our times, chronicles her visits to Turkey in *The Journey's Echo* and *Alexander's Path.* Only a piece of Mark Twain's *Innocents Abroad* is about Turkey, but it offers a witty glimpse of the country as it used to be. Hans Christian Andersen also wrote a memorable travelogue, *A Poet's Bazaar: A Journey to Greece, Turkey and up the Danube. The Letters and Works of Lady Mary Wortley Montagu* is a significant and entertaining book that delightfully documents life in 18th-century Ottoman Turkey—including its much-quoted passages about the harem—through the eyes of the wife of a British consul.

Irfan Orga's exquisite *Portrait of a Turkish Family* provides an evocative true-life memoir weaving personal history with modern politics as it addresses the impact of the upheavals of the early 20th century on his own family. Orhan Pamuk's *Istanbul: Memories of a City* interweaves the novelist's memories of his childhood and youth with black-and -white photographs and vignettes from the city's history; many think this nonfiction is much more readable than his fiction.

History. For modern Turkish history and politics, try *Turkey: A Modern History,* by Erik J. Zürcher, or *Turkey Unveiled,* an accessible, journalistic account of republican Turkish politics by Nicole and Hugh Pope.

More books have been written about Istanbul than about the rest of Turkey. Two of the finest portraits of the city are the excellent *Constantinople: City of the World's Desire 1453–1924,* by Philip Mansel, and *Istanbul: The Imperial City,* by John Freely.

Literature & Fiction. For an introduction to Turkish literature, track down a copy of *An Anthology of Turkish Literature,* by Kemal Silay. If you prefer to plunge into a complete novel, look out for *Anatolian Tales* or *Mehmet, My Hawk,* by Yaşar Kemal, one of the country's most famous modern novelists. Of the younger generation of Turkish writers, the best-known is Orhan Pamuk, whose dense melancholy prose means that his work is often more highly regarded than it is enjoyed. His novels include *My Name Is Red* and the acclaimed *Snow.* Louis de Bernieres's novel *Birds Without Wings* offers a portrayal of rural life in western Anatolia during the final years of the Ottoman Empire.

Agatha Christie's novel *Murder on the Orient Express* provides the proper atmosphere for a trip to Istanbul, and you can still visit Istanbul's Pera Palas Hotel, the terminus of the famous train, where Christie herself stayed. Harold Nicolson's *Sweet Waters* is usually billed as a thriller although it is more of a love story, and the detail draws heavily on the author's years as a junior diplomat in Istanbul in the years leading up to the outbreak of World

War I. If you love spy novels, *Istanbul Intrigues,* by Barry Rubin, paints a vivid picture of real cloak-and-dagger intrigues in the city during World War II.

Poetry. Poetry is notoriously difficult to translate, but *The Penguin Book of Turkish Verse* offers a good selection in English of leading Ottoman and Turkish poets. Nazım Hikmet (1901–1963) is generally regarded as Turkey's greatest, if still controversial, poet, and Randy Blasing and Mutlu Konuk have produced excellent English versions of Hikmet's most important poems in *Poems of Nazim Hikmet* and his extraordinary verse epic *Human Landscapes.* (The best English-language biography of Nazım Hikmet is *Romantic Communist* by Saime Göksu and Edward Timms.)

The poetry of the Muslim Sufi mystic Mevlana Celaleddin Mehmed Rumi (also known as "Rumi" or the "Mevlana") has few rivals in any language, whether for the beauty of his words or for his message of universal love and tolerance. There are several translations of his poetry: The best known include *Rumi: Poet And Mystic* by Reynold Nicholson, *The Essential Rumi* by Coleman Barks, and *Rumi: In the Arms of the Beloved* by Jonathan Star.

Movies

Western movies filmed in Turkey obviously tend to play up Turkey's exotic aspects, for better or worse. Director Joseph L. Mankiewicz's *Five Fingers* (1952), an Ankara-based spy thriller based on the book *Operation Cicero,* by C. L. Moyzisch, is noteworthy both for its action and for its clever dialogue ("Counter espionage is the highest form of gossip"). Peter Ustinov won an Academy Award for best supporting actor for his performance in the Jules Dassin–directed museum-heist film *Topkapi* (1964), which also stars Melina Mercouri and Maximilian Schell.

Alan Parker directed the film version of *Midnight Express* (1978), about Billy

Hayes's days in a Turkish prison following a drug conviction. The film's relentlessly horrific depiction of Hayes's experiences (some of which do not occur in his memoir) made the Turkish government exceedingly gun-shy about allowing Western moviemakers into the country. When *Midnight Express* was finally shown on Turkish TV in the mid-1990s, newscasters interviewed people in the street, who wept over the country's portrayal on-screen and the influence they feared the film may have had on perceptions of Turkey in the West.

Peter Weir's *Gallipoli* (1981) follows the exploits of two Australian soldiers preparing for and fighting in the historic battle in the Dardanelles during World War I. Critics generally praise the film, though some have noted a lack of sensitivity to the Turks.

Turkish cinema has a long history but it's only recently that Turkish movies have become more widely available to a foreign audience. Many reflect the dramatic social changes that Turkey has undergone in the last 50 years, but unfortunately, very few of the older movies are available with English subtitles.

Comic actor Kemal Sunal (1944–2000) remains one of the country's best-loved stars and made his reputation playing naive country boys who moved to the big city. Rarely a week goes by without at least one of Sunal's more than 80 movies being shown on Turkish national television. Some titles to watch out for include *Hababam Sinifi (Outrageous Class), Kapicilar Krali (King of Janitors), Salako (Moron), Inek Saban* (Shaban the Cow), and *Davaro.* His last movie was the comedy *Propaganda* (1999). Another name to look for is Yılmaz Güney (1937–84), the controversial leftist Kurdish filmmaker whose most famous movies include *Yol* (1982) and *Duvar* (1983).

In more recent years, Turkish cinema has undergone a renaissance. Turkish movies now regularly feature at international film festivals, and an increasing number are available on DVD (although most on sale in Turkey are Region 2, so you will need a multiregion DVD player to be able to play them in the U.S.). Notable ones include: Nuri Bilge Ceylan's *Uzak* (2000), a hauntingly beautiful depiction of loneliness, set in Istanbul, that manages to be simultaneously melancholic, humorous, and uplifting; Yılmaz Erdoğan and Ömer Faruk Sorak's *Vizontele* (2001), a charming and often hilarious portrayal of the effect of the arrival of electricity on a rural

community; and Fatih Akın's *Head-On* (*Gegen die Wand*) (2004), a stunning, if frequently brutal, love story of a couple who build a relationship out of their shattered lives. Turkey finally took revenge for *Midnight Express* with Serdar Akar and Sadullah Şentürk's *Valley of the Wolves: Iraq* (2006). Poorly scripted, anti-Semitic, and anti-American in tone, the movie nevertheless lays bare some of the many complexes and conspiracy theories that underpin popular Turkish conceptions of current events; it broke all box office records in Turkey on its release.

CHRONOLOGY

ca. 9000 BC   First agrarian settlements in the world are established in the area that is today southern Turkey and northern Iraq.

6500–5650 BC   Çatalhöyük, the largest early agricultural community yet discovered and the oldest known site with religious buildings, flourishes.

2371–16 BC   Reign of King Sargon of Akkad, whose empire reached from Mesopotamia to the southern parts of Anatolia (Asia Minor), the area that is now Turkey.

ca. 2200–1200 BC   Indo-European invaders include the Hittites, who establish an empire in Anatolia, pushing out the Mesopotamians.

1290 BC   The Battle of Kadesh, between the Egyptian and Hittite empires, halts Egyptian expansion and results in what is believed to be the world's first peace treaty.

ca. 1200 BC   New waves of invaders break up the Hittite empire.

1184 BC   The traditional date for the end of the legendary Trojan War, the accounts of which are believed to be based on a real conflict.

ca. 1000 BC   West coast of Asia Minor settled by Aeolians, Dorians, and Ionians from Greece.

ca. 657 BC   Foundation of Byzantium by Megarian colonists from Greece, according to legend, led by Byzas, for whom the city is named.

559–29 BC   Reign of Cyrus the Great, the founder of the Persian empire, who subdues the Greek cities of Asia Minor, defeats the Lydian king Croesus, reputedly the richest man in the world, and unifies Asia Minor under his rule.

334 BC   Alexander the Great conquers Asia Minor, ending Persian domination and extending his empire to the borders of India.

323 BC   Alexander the Great's sudden death creates a power vacuum, and his vast empire disintegrates into a number of petty kingdoms.

190 BC   The Seleucid monarch Antiochus III, defeated by the Romans at the battle of Magnesia, cedes his territory west of the Taurus Mountains to Rome.

133 BC   Rome consolidates its military and diplomatic gains in the region by creating the province of Asia Minor.

AD 284–305   Reign of the emperor Diocletian, who divides the Roman Empire into eastern and western administrative branches and shifts the focus of power eastward by establishing Nicomedia (İzmit) as a secondary, eastern capital.

325   The Ecumenical Council of Nicaea (İznik) meets in the first attempt to establish an orthodox Christian doctrine.

330   The emperor Constantine establishes Christianity as the state religion and moves the capital of the Roman Empire from Rome to the town of Byzantium, which is greatly enlarged and renamed Constantinople (City of Constantine).

527–63   Reign of Justinian I. The Byzantine empire reaches its military and cultural apogee. Aya Sofya, then known as Hagia Sophia, is rebuilt and rebuilt again.

674–78   Arab invaders sweep through the Byzantine empire and lay siege to Constantinople before being repulsed.

1037   The Seljuk Turks, nomadic tribes from central Asia recently converted to Islam, create their first state in the Middle East.

1071   The Byzantine emperor Romanos IV is defeated by the Seljuk sultan Alp Arslan at the Battle of Manzikert (Malazgirt), opening Anatolia to Turkish settlement.

1081–1118   Reign of Emperor Alexios I Commenus, who successfully deals with the threats of Venetians and crusaders. His daughter Anna chronicles the history of the time in the *Alexiad*.

1204   Constantinople is sacked by the Fourth Crusade, the Byzantine emperor is expelled, and the Latin Empire of Constantinople is established.

1243   The Seljuk sultan is defeated by Genghis Khan's Golden Horde at Kosedag, and the Seljuk Empire disintegrates into petty states.

1261   The Byzantine emperor Michael Palaeologus is restored to a greatly weakened throne.

1300   Traditional date of the foundation of the Ottoman Empire at Bursa under Osman I (1258–1326). Over the next century Osman and his sons conquer much of Anatolia and southeastern Europe.

1402   The Mongol leader Tamerlane (Timur) defeats the Ottoman emperor Bayezit near Ankara, leading to a decade of civil war among his sons.

1453   Constantinople, the remainder of the once mighty Byzantine Empire, falls to the Ottoman sultan Mehmet II.

1462   Mehmet II begins building a new palace at Topkapı.

1520–66   Reign of Süleyman the Magnificent, under whom the Ottoman Empire stretches from Iraq to Algeria. Ottoman culture reaches new heights, epitomized by the magnificent buildings of the architect Sinan.

1571   The defeat of the Ottoman fleet at Lepanto by an alliance of European states dents the legend of Turkish invulnerability.

1609   Work begins on the building of the Blue Mosque in Constantinople.

1683   The failure of the Ottoman siege of Vienna means that the high point of Turkish expansion into Europe has already been reached and marks the beginning of a decline. Over the next century most of eastern Europe is detached from the empire.

1774 The Treaty of Kuchuk Kainarji (Küçük Kaynarca) brings the Ottoman empire under the influence of Catherine the Great's Russia, and the Eastern question is posed for the first time: Who will get the Ottoman lands when the empire falls?

1807 Sultan Selim II is overthrown by the Janissaries, the Ottoman praetorian guard, whose influence has grown to dominate the imperial court.

1826 The sultan Mahmut II (1808–1839) massacres the Janissaries in the Hippodrome and attempts to introduce reforms, including compulsory male education; but the empire continues to disintegrate under the forces of nationalism.

1853–55 The Crimean War. Britain and France support "the sick man of Europe" in a successful bid to prevent Russian expansion into the Mediterranean. Florence Nightingale nurses the sick and wounded at Scutari (Üsküdar).

1876–1909 Reign of Sultan Abdül Hamid II, who begins as a constitutionally minded liberal and ends as a despot.

1877–78 The Western powers come to the aid of the Ottomans after they are defeated in another Russo-Turkish war, but most of the empire's territory in Europe is lost.

1889 Birth of Mustafa Kemal, who will become one of the most important men in modern Turkey.

1908 The revolution by the "Young Turks" compels Abdül Hamid to grant a new representative constitution.

1909 Abdül Hamid reneges on his reforms and is deposed by the Young Turks, who replace him with his brother, Mehmet V, the first constitutional sultan.

1911–13 The disastrous Balkan Wars discredit the movement, and a military government takes power under the triumvirate of Enver Pasha, Talat Pasha, and Cemal Pasha.

1914 The Ottoman Empire enters World War I on the side of the Central Powers.

1915 The Allies land at Gallipoli but are eventually repulsed with heavy losses.

1915–16 Armenians and many historians believe—and Turkey denies—that roughly one million Armenians die in eastern Anatolia, in a series of massacres and deportations instigated by the Ottoman authorities.

1918 The Ottoman armed forces are resoundingly defeated in WWI and forced to accept humiliating peace terms, including the occupation of Constantinople.

1919–22 Greek forces invade western Anatolia and are finally defeated by General Mustafa Kemal.

1922   The Mudanya armistice recognizes the territorial integrity of Anatolia. Under the leadership of Mustafa Kemal, the sultanate is abolished, and Mehmet VI, the last sultan, goes into exile.

1923   October 29: The Turkish Republic is proclaimed, with Ankara as its capital and Mustafa Kemal as its first president and leader of the sole political party, the Republican People's Party.

1924–34   Mustafa Kemal, soon to be renamed Atatürk (Father of the Turks), introduces sweeping reforms, including the secularization of the legal system, the banning of the fez and the veil, the enfranchisement of women, the introduction of a Latin alphabet and calendar, and the introduction of surnames.

1930   The name *Istanbul* is officially adopted.

1938   Atatürk dies.

1939–45   Turkey remains neutral throughout most of World War II, declaring war on Germany only in the final months in order to secure a seat at the new United Nations, of which the country becomes a founding member.

1950   In the first genuine multiparty elections in Turkey's history, Adnan Menderes is elected prime minister as leader of the Justice Party. The transition to democracy proves problematic, though, as mounting civil unrest prompts three military coups over the next 30 years.

1974   Turkey invades Cyprus in the wake of a failed, Greek-sponsored military coup, resulting in the island's partition.

1980   The republic's third military coup brings Chief of Staff Kenan Evren to power. Turgut Özal, a U.S.-educated engineer, takes control of the economy and introduces radical, Western-oriented free-market reforms.

1983   Turgut Özal is elected prime minister in the first postcoup elections.

1984   The Kurdistan Workers Party (PKK), led by Abdullah Ocalan, launches an armed campaign for greater political and cultural rights for Turkey's Kurds with the intent for eventual autonomy or full independence.

1987   Turkey applies for full membership in the European Union.

1993   Tansu Çiller is appointed as Turkey's first female prime minister.

1995   The pro-Islamic Welfare Party emerges as the largest party in December elections, but with only 21% of the vote, it is still far from a majority in Parliament.

1996   Turkey moves closer to economic integration with the European Union following a comprehensive free-trade agreement. The collapse of attempts by other parties to form a government allows the Welfare Party to take power at the head of a coalition with Tansu Çiller's True Path Party. Welfare Party chairman Necmettin Erbakan becomes Turkey's first avowedly Islamist prime minister, to the alarm of the country's staunchly secularist military.

1997 The Welfare Party–led coalition is forced to resign following behind-the-scenes pressure from the military. It's replaced by a three-party minority coalition.

1999 After being captured by Turkish agents on February 15, PKK leader Abdullah Ocalan announces an end to the PKK's 15 year-old armed struggle for Kurdish autonomy, which has cost an estimated 35,000 lives.

On August 17, an earthquake measuring 7.4 on the Richter scale hits the industrial town of İzmit just outside Istanbul, killing an estimated 25,000, leaving half a million homeless, and traumatizing the entire nation. On November 12, another earthquake, this time measuring 7.2 on the Richter scale, hits the northwestern provincial town of Düzce, killing another 1,000 people and leaving tens of thousands homeless.

2001 The Turkish Lira collapses, triggering a severe economic recession as the Turkish economy contracts by more than 9%.

2002 The moderately Islamist Justice and Development Party (JDP) wins a landslide victory in November elections.

2003 Turkish–United States relations plummet as the Turkish Parliament's failure in March to allow U.S. troops to transit through Turkey in the run-up to the war against Iraq is compounded by the U.S. seizure in July of Turkish special forces in northern Iraq.

2004 Frustrated by the slow pace of the easing of restrictions on the expression of a Kurdish identity, in June the PKK announces a resumption of its armed campaign, combining a rural insurgency in eastern Turkey with bombings in western Turkey.

2005 In October, Turkey officially opens membership negotiations with the EU. Criminal charges are levied against writer Orhan Pamuk, for statements said to be anti-Turkish, causing a huge international outcry; the charges are dropped at the end of the year.

2006 Orhan Pamuk wins the Nobel Prize for literature. Several terrorist bombings occur around the country: in Istanbul, Antalya, Marmaris, Adana, and Diyarbakir. Istanbul is named European Capital of Culture for 2010.

POLITICAL CLIMATE TODAY

IN THE GENERAL ELECTIONS OF November 2002, after more than a decade of economic crises, hyperinflation, and unstable fractious coalitions, the Turkish people finally wiped the slate clean, refusing to reelect any of the parties that had served in the previous Parliament and giving the largest share of the vote to the 15-month-old moderate Islamist Justice and Development Party (JDP). The JDP won 34% of the vote, giving it over two thirds of the seats in Parliament and enabling it to form the country's first single-party government since 1991.

The election of an Islamist government raised fears in the Turkish establishment—particularly the country's still powerful military—that it would attempt to erode almost 80 years of official secularism, but by Turkish standards, the JDP's first few years in office proved relatively trouble-free. The government oversaw an economic boom as the country recovered from a devastating recession in 2001, while pushing through a series of democratizing reforms in an attempt to edge Turkey closer to EU membership.

By mid-2006, however, there were signs that things were beginning to unravel. The economy was beginning to cool down and the JDP was coming under increasing pressure from its pious grassroots to ease restrictions on Islam in the public sphere (such as lifting the ban on the wearing of headscarves in universities and creating more state-run Islamic schools) at the same time as a changing of the guard in the military was bringing more assertive generals into positions of power.

Although the EU officially opened accession negotiations with Turkey in October 2005, it warned that full membership was at least 10 years away. By mid-2006 growing opposition to Turkish accession within the EU and Turkey's continuing refusal to open its ports and airports to ships and planes from the Republic of Cyprus (an EU member since May 2004) meant that even that date was looking extremely optimistic. The situation was complicated by international outcries against criminal charges brought retroactively against the writer Orhan Pamuk after he made statements deemed anti-Turkish in an interview with a Swiss publication in early 2005 (the charges were dismissed in December 2005).

Many EU–backed reforms have been enacted over the past few years—the death penalty has been abolished, measures have been taken against torture, and the Kurds have been given more rights and the government is paying more attention to their concerns. The idea of modern democracy has taken hold, and women have been given more rights—but politically, there is still a long way to go, in law and in ways of thinking.

TURKISH VOCABULARY

Words and Phrases

	English	Turkish	Pronunciation
Basics			
	Yes/no	Evet/hayır	**eh**-vet/**hi**-yer
	Please	Lütfen	**lewt**-fen
	Thank you	Teşekkür ederim	tay-shake-**kur** eh-day-**reem**
	You're welcome	Rica ederim	ree-**jah** eh-day-**reem** beer shay **day**-eel
	Bir şey değil		
	Sorry	Özür dilerim	oh-**zewr** deel-air-eem
	Sorry	Pardon	**pahr**-dohn
	Good morning	Günaydın	goon-eye-**den**
	Good day	İyi günler	ee-yee gewn-**lair**
	Good evening	İyi akşamlar	ee-yee ank-shahm-**lahr**
	Goodbye	Allahaısmarladık	**allah**-aw-ees-mar-law-deck
		Güle güle	**gew**-leh-**gew**-leh
	Mr. (Sir)	Bey	by, bay
	Mrs. Miss	Hanım	ha-nem
	Pleased to meet you	Memnun oldum	**mam**-noon ohl-doom
	How are you?	Nasılsınız?	**nah**-suhl-suh-nuhz

Numbers

	one half	büçük	byoo-**chook**
	one	bir	beer
	two	iki	ee-**kee**
	three	üc	ooch
	four	dört	doort
	five	beş	besh
	six	altı	ahl-tuh
	seven	yedi	yed-dee
	eight	sekiz	sek-**keez**
	nine	dokuz	doh-**kooz**

ten	on	**ohn**
eleven	onbir	**ohn**-beer
twelve	oniki	**ohn**-ee-kee
thirteen	onüç	**ohn-ooch**
fourteen	ondört	**ohn-doort**
fifteen	onbeş	**ohn**-besh
sixteen	onaltı	**ohn**-ahl-tuh
seventeen	onyedi	**ohn**-yed-dy
eighteen	onsekiz	**ohn-sek-keez**
nineteen	ondokuz	**ohn**-doh-**kooz**
twenty	yirmi	yeer-mee
twenty-one	yirmibir	**yeer**-mee-beer
thirty	otuz	oh-**tooz**
forty	kırk	kerk
fifty	elli	ehl-lee
sixty	altmış	**alt**-muhsh
seventy	yetmiş	**yeht**-meesh
eighty	seksen	sehk-san
ninety	doksan	dohk-**san**
one hundred	yüz	yewz
one thousand	bin	bean
one million	milyon	**mill**-ee-on

Colors

black	siyah	**see**-yah
blue	mavi	**mah**-vee
brown	kahverengi	**kah**-vay-**rain**-gee
green	yeşil	yay-sheel
orange	portakal rengi	poor-tah-kahl rain-gee
red	kırmızı	ker-muz-uh
white	beyaz	**bay**-ahz
yellow	sarı	sah-**ruh**

Days of the Week

Sunday	Pazar	pahz-**ahr**
Monday	Pazartesi	pahz-**ahr**-teh-see
Tuesday	Salı	sahl-luhl

Wednesday	Çarşamba	char-shahm-**bah**
Thursday	Perşembe	pair-shem-**beh**
Friday	Cuma	**joom**-ahz
Saturday	Cumartesi	joom-**ahr**-teh-see

Months

January	Ocak	oh-**jahk**
February	Şubat	shoo-**baht**
March	Mart	mart
April	Nisan	nee-**sahn**
May	Mayıs	my-us
June	Haziran	hah-zee-**rahn**
July	Temmuz	**tehm**-mooz
August	Ağustos	ah-oos-tohs
September	Eylül	ey-**lewl**
October	Ekim	eh-**keem**
November	Kasım	kah-suhm
December	Aralık	ah-rah-**luhk**

Useful Phrases

Do you speak English?	ingilizce biliyor musunuz?	in-**gee**-**leez**-jay bee-lee-**yohr**-moo-soo-nooz
I don't speak Turkish	Türkçe bilmiyorum	**tewrk**-cheh **beel**-mee-yohr-um
I don't understand	Anlamıyorum	ahn-**lah**-muh-yohr-um
I understand	Anlıyorum	ahn-**luh**-yohr-um
I don't know	Bilmiyorum	**beel**-meeh-yohr-um
I'm American/	Amerikalıyım	ahm-ay-**ree**-kah-luh-yuhm
I'm British	İngilizim	**een**-gee-leez-eem
What's your name?	İsminiz nedir?	ees-mee-niz nay-deer
My name is . . .	Benim adım . . .	bay-**neem** ah-duhm
What time is it?	Saat kaç?	sah-aht **kahch**
How?	Nasıl?	**nah**-suhl
When?	Ne zaman?	**nay** zah-mahn
Yesterday	Dün	dewn
Today	Bugün	**boo**-goon

Tomorrow	Yarın	**yah**-ruhn
This morning/ afternoon	Bu sabah/ ögleden sonra	**boo** sah-bah/ **ol-lay**-den sohn-rah
Tonight	Bu gece	**boo** ge-jeh
What?	Efendim?/Ne?	**eh**-fan-deem/neh
What is it?	Nedir?	**neh**-deer
Why?	Neden/Niçin?	**neh**-den/**nee**-chin
Who?	Kim?	keem
Where is . . .	Nerede . . .	**nayr**-deh
. . . the train station?	. . . tren istasyonu?	tee-**rehn** ees-**tah**-syohn-oo
. . . the subway station?	. . . metro durağı?	metro doo-**raw**-uh
. . . the bus stop?	. . . otobüs durağı?	oh-toh-**bewse** dor-**ah**-uh
. . . the terminal? (airport)	. . . hava alanı?	hah-**vah** **ah**-lah-nuh
. . . the post office?	. . . postane?	post-**ahn**-eh
. . . the bank?	. . . banka?	**bahn**-kah
. . . the hotel?	. . . oteli?	oh-**tel-lee**
. . . the museum?	. . . müzesi?	mew-zay-**see**
. . . the hospital?	. . . hastane?	hahs-**tah**-neh
. . . the elevator?	. . . asansör?	ah-**sewr**
. . . the telephone?	. . . telefon?	teh-leh-**fohn**
Where are the restrooms?	Tuvalet nerede?	twah-**let** nayr-deh
Here/there	Burası/Orası	**boo**-rah-suh/ **ohr**-rah-suh
Left/right	sağ/sol	sah-ah/sohl
Is it near/ far?	Yakın mı?/ Uzak mı?	yah-**kuhn** muh/ ooz-**ahk**muh
I'd like . . .	. . . istiyorum	**ees**-tee-yohr-ruhm
. . . a room	. . . bir oda	beer oh-**dah**
. . . the key	. . . anahtarı	**ahn**-ah-tahr-uh
. . . a newspaper	. . . bir gazete	beer **gahz**-teh
. . . a stamp	. . . pul	pool
I'd like to buy . . .	. . . almak istiyorum	ahl-**mahk** ees-tee-your-ruhm
. . . cigarettes	. . . sigara	see-**gahr**-rah
. . . matches	. . . kibrit	**keeb**-reet
. . . city map	. . . şehir planı	shay-**heer plah**-nuh
. . . road map	. . . karayolları haritası	**kah**-rah-yoh-lahr-**uh** hah-ree-tah-**suh**
. . . magazine	. . . dergi	dair-gee
. . . envelopes	. . . zarf	zahrf

. . . writing paper	. . . mektup kağıdı	**make**-toop **kah**-uh-duh
. . . postcard	. . . kartpostal	cart-poh-stahl
How much is it?	Fiyatı ne kadar?	fee-yaht-uh **neh** kah-dahr
It's expensive/cheap	pahalı/ucuz	pah-hah-**luh**/ oo-**jooz**
A little/a lot	Az/çok	ahz/choke
More/less	daha çok/daha az	da-ha choke/ da-ha ahz
Enough/too (much)	Yeter/çok fazla	**yay**-tehr/**choke** fahz-lah
I am ill/sick	Hastayım	**hahs**-tah-yum
Call a doctor	Doktor çağırın	dohk-toor **chah**-uh-run
Help!	İmdat!	eem-**daht**
Stop!	Durun!	doo-**roon**

Dining Out

A bottle of . . .	bir şişe . . .	**beer** shee-shay
A cup of . . .	bir fincan . . .	beer **feen**-jahn
A glass of . . .	bir bardak . . .	beer **bar**-dahk
Ashtray	kül tablası	kewl tah-blah-**suh**
Bill/check	hesap	heh-**sahp**
Bread	ekmek	ekmek
Breakfast	kahvaltı	**kah**-vahl-tuh
Butter	tereyağı	tay-**reh**-yah-uh
Cocktail/aperitif	kokteyl, içki	cocktail, **each**-key
Dinner	aksam yemeği	**ahk**-shahm yee-may-ee
Fixed-price menu	fiks menü	feex menu
Fork	çatal	**chah**-tahl
I am a vegetarian/ I don't eat meat	vejeteryenim/ et yemem	vegeterian-**eem**/ eht yeh-**mem**
I cannot eat . . .	. . . yiyemem	**yee**-yay-mem
I'd like to order . . .	. . . ısmarlamak isterim	us-mahr-lah-**mahk** ee-stair-eem
I'd like . . .	. . . isterim	ee-stair-**em**
I'm hungry/ thirsty	acıktım/ susadım	ah-**juck**-tum/ soo-sah-**dum**
Is service/the tip included?	servis fiyatı dahil mi?	sehr-rees **fee**-yah-tah dah-heel-**mee**

It's good/bad	güzel/güzel değil	gew-**zell**/gew-**zell** **day**-eel
It's hot/cold	sıcak/soğuk	suh-**jack**/soh-**uk**
Knife	bıçak	buh-**chahk**
Lunch	öğle yemeği	oi-leh **yeh**-may-ee
Menu	menü	meh-**noo**
Napkin	peçete	**peh**-cheh-teh
Pepper	karabiber	kah-**rah**-bee-behr
Plate	tabak	tah-**bahk**
Please give me . . .	lutfen bana . . . verirmisiniz	**loot**-fan bah-nah vair-**eer**-mee-see-niz
Salt	tuz	tooz
Spoon	kaşık	kah-**shuhk**

Basic Information on Traveling in Turkey, Savvy Tips to Make Your Trip a Breeze, and Companies and Organizations to Contact

There are planners and there are those who fly by the seat of their pants. We happily place ourselves among the planners. Our writers and editors try to anticipate all the issues you may face before and during any journey, and then they do their research. This section is the product of their efforts. Use it to get excited about your trip to Turkey, to inform your travel planning, or to guide you on the road should the seat of your pants start to feel threadbare.

AIR TRAVEL

CARRIERS

You'll probably find that THY/Turkish Airlines, the national flag carrier of Turkey, offers the most nonstops, though an international carrier based in your home country is more likely to have better connections to your hometown and serve a greater number of gateway cities. Third-country carriers (a foreign carrier based in a country other than your own or Turkey) sometimes offer the lowest fares.

The flying time to Istanbul is 10 hours from New York, 13 hours from Chicago, and 15 hours from Los Angeles. The flight from Toronto to Istanbul takes 11½ hours. Flying time from London is 4 hours.

Turkish Airlines operates an extensive domestic network, with 16 flights daily on weekdays between Istanbul and Ankara alone. In summer many flights to coastal resorts are added. **At provincial airports in particular it is often necessary for checked luggage to be identified by boarding passengers before it is put on the plane,** and all unidentified luggage is left behind and checked for bombs or firearms. If any luggage has not been identified, an announcement will be made on the plane before departure, based on the name on the label on the luggage, but attempts at the pronunciation of foreign names can mean that they are unrecognizable. Airline staff will announce whether you need to identify your luggage at some point before boarding but the messages may be difficult to hear or understand. If in doubt, ask the airline staff as they are checking your boarding pass and watch what the other passengers are doing.

Major Airlines From the U.S.: **Air Canada** ☏ 800/776–3000. **Air France** ☏ 800/237–2747. **American Airlines** ☏ 800/433–7300 ⊕ www.aa.com. **British Airways** ☏ 800/247–9297. **Continental Airlines** ☏ 800/523—3273 for U.S. and Mexico reservations, 800/231–0856 for international reservations ⊕ www.continental.com. **Delta Airlines** ☏ 800/221–1212 for U.S. reservations, 800/241–4141 for international reservations ⊕ www.delta.com. **Lufthansa** ☏ 800/645–3880. **Northwest Airlines** ☏ 800/225–2525 for U.S. reservations, 800/447–4747 for international destinations ⊕ www.nwa.com. **Olympic Airlines** ☏ 800/223–1226. **Onur Air** Onur ☏ 212/444–6687 in Istanbul for information and reservations for flights between Europe and Turkey ⊕ www.onurair.com. tr/onurairyeni/index.html. **Swissair** ☏ 800/221–4750. **TWA** ☏ 800/221–2000 in the U.S., 800/892–4141. **THY/Turkish Airlines** ☏ 212/339–9650, 800/874–8875, 212/444–0849 in Istanbul for reservations ⊕ www.thy.com/en-INT/. **United Airlines** ☏ 800/864–8331 for U.S. reservations, 800/538–2929 for international reservations ⊕ www.united.com. **USAirways** ☏ 800/428–4322 for U.S. and Canada reservations, 800/622–1015 for international reservations ⊕ www.usairways. com.

Within Turkey: **Atlas Jet** ☏ 212/444–3387 for information and reservations ⊕ www. atlasjet.com/en/default.asp. **Onur Air** ☏ 212/444–6687 for information and reservations ⊕ www.onurair.com.tr/ onurairyeni/index.html. **Pegasus Airlines** ☏ 212/444–0737 for call center and reservations ⊕ www.flypgs.com. **Turkish Airlines** THY ☏ 212/444–0849 for information and reservations ⊕ www.thy.com/en-INT/.

CHECK-IN & BOARDING
Double-check your flight times, especially if you made your reservations far in advance. Airlines change their schedules, and alerts may not reach you. Always **bring a government-issued photo I.D. to the airport** (even when it's not required, a passport is best), and **arrive when you need to and not before.** Check in usually at least an hour before domestic flights and two to three hours for international flights. But many airlines have more stringent advance check-in requirements at some busy airports. The TSA estimates the waiting time for security at most major airports and publishes the information on its Web site. Note that if you aren't at the gate at least 20 minutes before your flight is scheduled to take off (sometimes earlier), you won't be allowed to board. Extra security measures mean that you should be at the airport at least three and a half hours before your scheduled departure time if you are flying from Turkey to the U.S.

Minimize the time spent standing in line. Buy an e-ticket, check in at an electronic kiosk, or—even better—check in on your airline's Web site before you leave home. These days, most domestic airline tickets are electronic; international tickets may be either electronic or paper.

You usually pay a surcharge (up to $50) to get a paper ticket, and its sole advantage is that it may be easier to endorse over to another airline if your flight is canceled and the airline with which you booked can't accommodate you on another flight. With an e-ticket, the only thing you receive is an e-mailed receipt citing your itinerary and reservation and ticket numbers. Be sure to carry this with you as you'll need it to get past security. If you lose your receipt, though, you can print out another or ask the airline to do it for you at check-in.

Particularly during busy travel seasons and around holiday periods, if a flight is oversold, the gate agent will usually ask for volunteers and will offer some sort of compensation if you are willing to take a different flight. **Know your rights.** If you are bumped from a flight *involuntarily,* the airline must give you some kind of compensation if an alternate flight can't be found within one hour. If your flight is delayed because of something within the airline's control (so bad weather doesn't count), then the airline has a responsibility to get you to your destination on the same day, even if they have to book you on another airline and in an upgraded class if necessary. Read your airline's Contract of Carriage; it's usually buried somewhere on the airline's Web site.

Be prepared to quickly adjust your plans by programming a few numbers into your cell: your airline, an airport hotel or two, your destination hotel, your car service, and/or your travel agent.

At most airports you will be asked to **show your passport** before you are allowed to check in.

CUTTING COSTS

It's always good to **comparison shop.** Web sites (a.k.a. consolidators) and travel agents can have different arrangements with the airlines and offer different prices for exactly the same flight and day. Certain Web sites have tracking features that will e-mail you when good deals are posted. Other people prefer to stick with one or two frequent-flier programs, racking up free trips and accumulating perks that can make trips easier. On some airlines, perks include a special reservations number, early boarding, access to upgrades, and roomier economy-class seating.

Check early and often. Start looking for cheap fares up to a year in advance, and keep looking until you see something you can live with; you never know when a good deal may pop up. That said, **jump on the good deals.** Waiting even a few minutes might mean paying more. For most people, saving money is more important than flexibility, so the more affordable nonrefundable tickets work. Just remember that you'll pay dearly (often as much as $100) if you must change your travel plans. Check on prices for departures at different times of the day and to and from alternate airports, and look for departures on Tuesday, Wednesday, and Thursday, typically the cheapest days to travel. Remember to **weigh your options,** though. A cheaper flight might have a long layover rather than being nonstop, or landing at a secondary airport might substantially increase your ground transportation costs.

Note that many airline Web sites—and most ads—show prices *without* taxes and surcharges. Don't buy until you know the full price. Government taxes add up quickly. Also **watch those ticketing fees.** Surcharges are usually added when you buy your ticket anywhere but on an airline's own Web site. (By the way, that includes on the phone–even if you call the airline directly—and for paper tickets regardless of how you book).

Look into air passes. Many airlines, singly or in collaboration, offer discount air passes that allow foreigners to travel economically in a particular country or region. These visitor passes usually must be reserved and purchased before you leave home. Information about passes often can be found on most airlines' international Web pages, which tend to be aimed at travelers from outside the carrier's home country. Also, try typing the name of the pass into a search engine, or search for "pass" within the carrier's Web site.

Online Consolidators **AirlineConsolidator.com** ⊕ www.airlineconsolidator.com; for international tickets. **Best Fares** ⊕ www.bestfares.com; $59.90 annual membership. **Cheap Tickets** ⊕ www.cheaptickets.com. **Expedia** ⊕ www.expedia.com. **Hotwire** ⊕ www.hotwire.com is a discounter. **lastminute.com** ⊕ www.lastminute.com specializes in last-minute travel; the main site is for the UK, but it has a link to a U.S. site. **Luxury Link** ⊕ www.luxurylink.com has auctions (surprisingly good deals) as well as offers at the high-end side of travel. **Orbitz** ⊕ www.orbitz.com. **Onetravel.com** ⊕ www.onetravel.com. **Priceline.com** ⊕ www.priceline.com is a discounter that also allows bidding. **Travel.com** ⊕ www.travel.com allows you to compare its rates with those of other booking engines. **Travelocity** ⊕ www.travelocity.com charges a booking fee for airline tickets but promises good problem resolution.

ENJOYING THE FLIGHT

Get the seat you want. Avoid those on the aisle directly across from the lavatories. Most frequent fliers say those are even worse than the seats that don't recline (e.g., those in the back row and those in front of a bulkhead). For more legroom, you can request emergency-aisle seats, but only do so if you're capable of moving the 35- to 60-pound airplane exit door—a Federal Aviation Administration requirement of passengers in these seats. Seats behind a bulkhead also offer more legroom, but they don't have under-seat storage. Often, you can pick a seat when you buy your ticket on an airline's Web site. But it's not always a guarantee, particularly if the airline changes the plane after you book your ticket; check back before you leave. SeatGuru.com has more information about specific seat configurations, which vary by aircraft.

Fewer airlines are providing free food for passengers in economy class. **Don't go hungry.** If you're scheduled to fly during meal times, verify if your airline offers anything to eat; even when it does, be prepared to pay. If you have dietary concerns, request special meals. These can be vegetarian, low-cholesterol, or kosher, for example.

Ask the airline about its children's menus, activities, and fares. On some lines infants and toddlers fly for free if they sit on a parent's lap, and older children fly for half price in their own seats. Also inquire about policies involving car seats; having one may limit where you can sit. While you're at it, ask about seat belt extenders for car seats. And note that you can't count on a flight attendant to automatically produce an extender; you may have to inquire about it again when you board.

HOW TO COMPLAIN

If your baggage goes astray or your flight goes awry, complain right away. Most carriers require that you **file a claim immediately.** The Aviation Consumer Protection Division of the Department of Transportation publishes *Fly-Rights,* which discusses airlines and consumer issues and is available online. You can also find articles and information on mytravelrights.com, the Web site of the nonprofit Consumer Travel Rights Center.

Airline Complaints **Office of Aviation Enforcement and Proceedings** (Aviation Consumer Protection Division) ☎ 202/366–2220 ⊕ airconsumer.ost.dot.gov. **Federal Aviation**

Administration Consumer Hotline ☎ 866/835–5322 ⊕ www.faa.gov.

AIRPORTS

Turkey's major airport is Atatürk Airport, about 18 km (12 mi) from Istanbul. Adana, Adıyaman, Ağrı, Ankara, Antalya, Batman, Çanakkale, Dalaman, Denizli, Diyarbakır, Edremit, Elazığ, Erzincan, Erzurum, Eskişehir, Gaziantep, İsparta, İzmir, Kars, Kayseri, Konya, Malatya, Muş, Nevşehir, Samsun, Siirt, Sinop, Sivas, Şanlırfa, Tokat, Trabzon, Uşak, and Van all have smaller domestic airports, although flights in and out of many are infrequent. A new, and much larger, international terminal was opened at Istanbul's Atatürk Airport in January 2000, replacing its overstrained and rather shabby predecessor, which was converted into the new domestic terminal.

Sabiha Gökçen Airport now serves the Asian part of Istanbul although it is currently mainly used by international charters and some domestic flights. Almost all leading international airlines still arrive at Atatürk Airport.

Airlines & Airports **Airline and Airport Links.com** ⊕ www.airlineandairportlinks.com has links to many of the world's airlines and airports. **Atatürk Airport** ☎ 212/465-5555 ⊕ www.ataturkairport. com. **Sabiha Gökçen Airport** ☎ 216/585-5000 ⊕ www.sgairport.com.

Airline Security Issues **Transportation Security Administration** ⊕ www.tsa.gov/public has answers for almost every question that might come up.

GROUND TRANSPORTATION

In major destinations such as Adana, Ankara, Antalya, Bodrum, Dalaman, Istanbul, İzmir, Kayseri, Nevşehir, and Trabzon, there are shuttle buses to the airports run by the Havaş company. These run at regular intervals in the major cities and in the provinces are timed to coincide with incoming and outgoing flights. The other alternative is to take a taxi. In the provinces, it is sometimes possible to negotiate with a taxi driver for less than the metered fare. Many hotels will either arrange for a driver to collect you from the airport (and in Istanbul the more luxurious hotels even offer an extremely expensive helicopter shuttle) and for someone to take you to the airport. In the provinces, it is not unusual for hotels to offer to provide transportation free of charge, although the driver will still appreciate being tipped; typically YTL 10 for a 10-minute ride or YTL 20 for 20–25 minutes.

TRANSFERS BETWEEN AIRPORTS

The only city in Turkey with multiple airports is Istanbul, which has two: Atatürk Airport and Sabiha Gökçen Airport. There is no direct shuttle bus between them. It's theoretically possible to take a shuttle bus from one airport into the center of the city and then another shuttle out to the other airport, but this would be very time-consuming, and the only alternative, a taxi ride between the two, relatively expensive. If you have a connection between an international flight and a domestic flight, try to ensure that they both use the same airport in Istanbul, which would normally be Atatürk Airport. Domestic flights to Sabiha Gökçen Airport are usually cheaper than flights into Atatürk Airport (although prices to the latter vary considerably according to the time of day), but if you have a connecting international flight from Atatürk Airport, any saving would be more than offset by the time (and it could easily take two to three hours at a busy time of day) and expense of transferring between airports.

Havaş ☎ 212/465-5656 ⊕ www.havas.com.tr.

BOAT & FERRY TRAVEL

In some regions, particularly the Black Sea and greater Istanbul area, ferries are the most efficient means of getting around. On the Aegean and Mediterranean coasts, boats are used mostly for leisurely sightseeing and yachting.

The state-owned Turkish Maritime Lines used to operate car ferries and cruise ships from Istanbul to various points in the country. It was broken up and privatized, though, in the early 2000s and the new owners of its ships have only recently begun to operate them again. In mid-June 2006, the Cruise and Ferry Lines Deniz company, which is owned by the Turkish Chamber of Shipping, began operating one

cruise ship between Istanbul and İzmir, with ships leaving every other day. The journey takes 16-17 hours, arriving in İzmir in the early morning and returning to Istanbul that evening. It is expected that this line will operate from May through September. The one-way trip costs from $40 to $45 for a Pullman seat, $110 for a standard cabin, and $460 for a luxury four-berth cabin, plus $120 for a car. Tickets are available from Cruise and Ferry Lines Deniz or from travel agents that are members of the Association of Turkish Travel Agencies. At press time there were plans to add another ship on the same line later in the year, and other vessels to other destinations in 2007.

Yachting or sailing trips can be arranged in a number of ways: through tour operators in the U.S. with contacts and colleagues in Turkey, through tour operators in Turkey (⇨ Essentials Sections *in* individual chapters), or through private boat owners at the docks. No matter how you choose a sailing trip, make sure you have confidence in the people with whom you are working: The problem with simply finding someone at the dock is that you won't necessarily know anything about the crew, the boat, or the other passengers who will be on board.

FARES & SCHEDULES

All major credit cards and Turkish Lira (YTL) are acceptable forms of payment. In an emergency, a kindly ticket-seller may take dollars or Euros but you shouldn't rely on it.

Boat & Ferry Information **Cruise and Ferry Lines Deniz** ☎ 212/444-3369 for reservations and information ⊕ www.denizline.com.

BUS TRAVEL

In Turkey, buses are much faster than most trains and provide inexpensive service almost around the clock between all cities and towns; they're fairly comfortable and sometimes air-conditioned. All are run by private companies, each of which has its own fixed fares for different routes and, usually more significantly, their own standards of comfort. Most bus companies, such as Varan, Ulusoy, Kamil, Koç, and Pamukkale, which go between major cities and resort areas, can be counted on for comfortable air-conditioned service with snacks. There is often quite a close correlation between price and comfort, with the more expensive companies such as Varan also providing the most amenities. Most of the larger companies have their own terminals. In larger cities they run feeder shuttles from a number of different locations around the city to the main terminal. Contact details for only the larger companies is listed below.

Note that express buses running between major cities are significantly faster and more comfortable than local buses; look for one of these if you're traveling long distances.

By law, intercity buses are nonsmoking. The law is honored by larger companies, but sometimes ignored by the smaller ones—sometimes even by the driver.

For very short trips or for getting around within a city, take a minibus or a *dolmuş* (shared taxi). Both are inexpensive and comfortable.

FARES & SCHEDULES
The bus fare for Istanbul–Ankara costs about $10–$15 and for Istanbul–İzmir, from $12 to $18. With larger companies, fares usually include *su* (bottled water) and/or tea, as well as snacks on longer journeys. For smaller companies you may want to bring your own water in case beverages are not available.

PAYING
The larger companies have their own terminals and sales offices as well as Web sites and call centers offering e-tickets. For smaller companies, tickets are sold at stands in a town's *otogar* (central bus terminal); the usual procedure is to go to the bus station and **shop around for the best bus.** All seats are reserved. When buying your ticket, tell the ticket agent that you would like to sit on the shady side of the bus; even on air-conditioned buses the sun can feel oppressive on a long trip.

The larger companies will accept cash or major credit cards. Smaller companies will only accept cash. Travelers' checks are not normally accepted.

Bus Information Kamil Koç ☎ 444-0562, no code required ⊕ www.kamilkoc.com.tr. **Pamukkale** ☎ 444-3535, no code required ⊕ www. pamukkaleturizm.com.tr. **Ulusoy** ☎ 444-3535, no code required ⊕ www.ulusoy.com.tr. **Varan** ☎ 444-8999 for call center, no code required ⊕ www.varan.com.tr

BUSINESS HOURS
BANKS & OFFICES
Banks are normally open weekdays from 8:30 until noon or 12:30, depending on the bank, and then from 1:30 until 5. However, selected branches of some Turkish banks now remain open during the middle of the day, particularly in larger cities. Many banks throughout Turkey, even those in small towns, provide 24-hour service from ATM machines.

GAS STATIONS
Most gas stations are open from early morning until late evening, commonly from 6 AM to 10 PM, although there are no fixed rules and there can be considerable variation. In the larger cities and along major highways it is usually possible to find gas stations open 24 hours. Look for the sign 24 SAAT AÇIK.

MUSEUMS & SIGHTS
Museums are generally open Tuesday through Sunday from 9:30 AM until 5 or 5:30 PM and closed on Monday. Palaces are open the same hours but are generally closed Thursday. Many museums stop selling tickets 30 minutes before the actual closing time. Sometimes this is explicitly stated in the official times, but very often, particularly away from the major sites, it is unofficial and just a way for museum staffers to make sure they get away on time. To be on the safe side, try to ensure that you arrive at least 45 minutes before closing time.

PHARMACIES
Most pharmacies (*eczane* in Turkish) are open the same hours as shops, and as with

shops, there are variations according to the whim of the pharmacist. Typically, they are open 9:30 AM until 7 or 7:30 PM, Monday through Saturday. In larger cities, one pharmacy in each neighborhood is open 24/7 and is called the *nöbetçi eczane*. Even when a pharmacy is closed, there will be a sign in the window or door with details of the location of the nearest one. Your hotel will always be able to help you find the nearest *nöbetçi eczane*. If you are not close to your hotel, passersby will usually be able to help with directions.

SHOPS

Shops and bazaars are usually open Monday through Saturday from 9:30 to 7 and closed on Sunday. Smaller shops sometimes close for lunch between 1 and 2. In tourist areas, shops may stay open until 9 PM or even 10 PM and all day Sunday.

CAMERAS & PHOTOGRAPHY

Photography of what are deemed militarily sensitive sites is expressly forbidden in Turkey. Often you will see red signs with the silhouette of a soldier and a warning in Turkish, English, and German not to take photographs, but the definition of military sensitivity can be quite elastic. If in doubt, particularly when there are military personnel—such as guards—present, ask by gesturing with your camera before putting it to your eye. In rural areas, where children are usually falling over each other to have their picture taken, women may be reluctant. Again, ask permission before taking a picture.

The *Kodak Guide to Shooting Great Travel Pictures* (available at bookstores everywhere) is loaded with tips.

Photo Help **Kodak Information Center** ⊕ www. kodak.com.

EQUIPMENT PRECAUTIONS

Don't pack film or equipment in checked luggage, where it is much more susceptible to damage. X-ray machines used to view checked luggage are extremely powerful and therefore are likely to ruin your film. Try to ask for hand inspection of film, which becomes clouded after repeated exposure to airport X-ray machines, and keep videotapes and computer

disks away from metal detectors. Always keep film, tape, and computer disks out of the sun. Carry an extra supply of batteries, and be prepared to turn on your camera, camcorder, or laptop to prove to airport security personnel that the device is real.

FILM & DEVELOPING

All kinds of film and digital media (disks, cards, etc., for digital cameras) are widely available in Turkey. Prices will be higher in the little kiosks and stalls around the tourist sites.

VIDEOS AND DVDS

Most Turkish video players use VHS PAL (unlike U.S. players, which use NTSC). Most types of cassettes for camcorders (digital, VHS-C, 8 mm, etc.) are available in Turkey, but prices vary enormously.

For DVDs, Turkey is Region 2 (the same as Europe) while the U.S. is Region 1. As your DVD-player instructions will explain, DVDs for different regions can only be played on multiregion DVD players.

CAR RENTAL

Request car seats and extras such as GPS when you book, and make sure that a confirmed reservation guarantees you a car. Agencies sometimes overbook, particularly for busy weekends and holiday periods. Rates are sometimes—but not always—better if you book in advance or reserve through a rental agency's Web site. There are other reasons to book ahead, though: for popular destinations, during busy times of the year, or to ensure that you get a certain type of car (vans, SUVs, exotic sports cars).

Your driver's license may not be recognized outside your home country. You may not be able to rent a car without an International Driving Permit (IDP), which can be used only in conjunction with a valid driver's license and which translates your license into 10 languages. Check the AAA Web site for more info as well as for IDPs ($10) themselves.

Car rental rates in Istanbul begin at $40 a day and $250 a week for an economy car with unlimited mileage. Gas costs about $1.30 per liter. The majority of rental cars are stick shift, though it is possible to get an automatic with advance arrangements. Car seats for children are not compulsory and are often difficult to find, although offices of the multinational firms in larger cities may be able to provide them. Check when you make your reservation. A wide variety of mostly European car makes are available, ranging from the locally manufactured Tofaş (a subsidiary of Fiat) to Renault and Mercedes.

In many places, such as Cappadocia and the Turquoise Coast, you may want to rent a car so you can go exploring on your own instead of having to be part of a guided tour. When traveling long distances, however, you may find it easier to take public transportation (either a bus or plane)—unless you plan on sightseeing en route—and then renting a car when you arrive. For more information about driving in Turkey, *see* Car Travel, *below.*

Leave yourself enough time to return your rental when you have a plane to catch. It all depends on the airport and the location of the rental office. In provincial airports the rental offices are inside the terminal building and the procedure can be quite fast. In larger cities allow 30 minutes or more. Of course, it also depends on whether or not others are returning cars at the same time.

It's best to check the Web sites of the major multinationals listed below to see whether they have offices at your destination as no agency has complete national coverage. In the provinces there are also local agencies, some of which have offices at the local airport. Only the contacts for the major companies are listed below.

Hotels often either rent out cars themselves or have an informal relationship with a local agency—the latter also usually means that the local agency is anxious to keep the hotel happy by providing a good service; it's not unusual for the owner of the agency to be a relative of someone at the hotel. The rates for deals done through the hotel, which will include insurance etc., are often much cheaper than the multinationals.

CUTTING COSTS

Really weigh your options. Find out if a credit card you carry or organization or frequent-renter program to which you belong has a discount program. And check that such discounts really are the best deal. You can often do better with special weekend or weekly rates offered by a rental agency. (And even if you only want to rent for five or six days, ask if you can get the weekly rate; it may be cheaper than the daily rate for that period of time.)

Price local car-rental companies as well as the majors. Also investigate wholesalers, which don't own fleets but rent in bulk from those that do and often offer better rates (note you must usually pay for such rentals before leaving home). Consider adding a car rental onto your air/hotel vacation package; the cost will often be cheaper than if you had rented the car separately on your own.

When traveling abroad, **look for guaranteed exchange rates,** which protect you against a falling dollar. With your rate locked in, you won't pay more, even if the price goes up in the local currency. (Not the best thing if the dollar is surging rather than plunging.)

Beware of hidden charges. Those great rental rates may not be so great when you add in taxes, surcharges, cancellation penalties, taxes, drop-off charges (if you're planning to pick up the car in one city and leave it in another), and surchages (for being under or over a certain age, for additional drivers, or for driving over state or country borders or out of a specific radius from your point of rental).

Note that airport rental offices often add supplementary surcharges that you may avoid by renting from an agency whose office is just off airport property. Don't buy the tank of gas that's in the car when you rent it unless you plan to do a lot of driving. Avoid hefty refueling fees by filling the tank at a station well away from the rental agency (those nearby are often more expensive) just before you turn in the car.

Automobile Associations U.S.: American Automobile Association (AAA) ☎ 315/797-5000 ⊕ www.aaa.com; most contact with the organization is through state and regional members. **National Automobile Club** ☎ 650/294-7000 ⊕ www.thenac.com; membership is open to California residents only.

Major Agencies **Alamo** ☎ 800/522-9696 ⊕ www.alamo.com. **Avis** ☎ 800/331-1084 ⊕ www.avis.com. **Budget** ☎ 800/472-3325 ⊕ www.budget.com. **Hertz** ☎ 800/654-3001 ⊕ www.hertz.com. **National Car Rental** ☎ 800/227-7368 ⊕ www.nationalcar.com.

INSURANCE

Everyone who rents a car wonders about whether the insurance that the rental companies offer is worth the expense. No one—not even us—has a simple answer. This is particularly true abroad, where laws are different than at home.

If you own a car, your personal auto insurance may cover a rental to some degree, though not all policies protect you abroad; always read your policy's fine print. If you don't have auto insurance, then seriously consider buying the collision- or loss-damage waiver (CDW or LDW) from the car-rental company, which eliminates your liability for damage to the car. Some credit cards offer CDW coverage, but it's usually supplemental to your own insurance and rarely covers SUVs, minivans, luxury models, and the like. If your coverage is secondary, you may still be liable for loss-of-use costs from the car-rental company. But no credit-card insurance is valid unless you use that card for *all* transactions, from reserving to paying the final bill. All companies exclude car rental in some countries, so be sure to find out about the destination to which you are traveling.

Some countries require you to purchase CDW coverage or require car-rental companies to include it in quoted rates. Ask your rental company about issues like these in your destination. In most cases, it's cheaper to add a supplemental CDW plan to your comprehensive travel insurance policy (⇨ Insurance, below) than to purchase it from a rental company. That said, you don't want to pay for a supplement if you're required to buy insurance from the rental company.

Note that you can decline the insurance from the rental company and purchase it through a third-party provider such as Travel Guard (www.travelguard.com)—$9 per day for $35,000 of coverage. That's sometimes just under half the price of the CDW offered by some car-rental companies. Also, Diners Club offers primary CDW coverage on all rentals reserved and paid for with the card. This means that Diners Club's company—not your own car insurance—pays in case of an accident. It *doesn't* mean your car-insurance company won't raise your rates once it discovers you had an accident.

In Turkey, the rental agency will usually provide you with instructions about what to do if you have a breakdown or accident. They will also give you a contact number at which you can call them—usually the personal cell number of someone working at the agency. In most cases, they'll tell you that if you have a problem you should call them, tell them where you are, and they will come and find you. It's worth remembering that in the case of an accident, Turkish insurance companies usually refuse to pay until they have seen a police report of the accident. This is particularly important if another vehicle is involved, as the driver will need a police report in order to be able to file a claim with his or her insurance company or with your rental agency. In such a situation, call the contact number for your rental agency and allow them to handle all the procedures when they arrive.

CAR TRAVEL

In Turkey **a driver's license issued in most foreign countries is acceptable.**

Turkey has one of the world's highest auto accident rates. That said, having a car allows you the freedom that traveling by bus, train, or plane does not. The country has 40,000 km (25,000 mi) of paved and generally well-maintained highways, but off the intercity highways, surfaces are often poor and potholes frequent. Most major highways are two lanes, and cars pass each other with some frequency. Sometimes roads will have a third lane meant for passing; although the lane is usually labeled with which direction of traffic is meant to use it, drivers don't always follow this rule. So be extremely careful when passing. In general, always expect the unexpected. Don't, for example, always assume that one-way streets are one way in practice or that because you wouldn't do something, such as trying to pass in a dangerous situation, the other driver wouldn't either.

In some places it is possible to hire a driver together with a car. Unless you are feeling particularly intrepid, this is especially advisable if you're going to the more remote areas of eastern and southeastern Anatolia. Normally, the driver will be included in the package with the car and will either be the owner of the car or an employee of the agency renting it. If it's the latter and you're particularly happy with his performance, you may wish to give him a tip in addition to the price you pay to the agency. Around YTL 20 for a day's driving is reasonable.

Driving in Istanbul and other major cities is best avoided. Urban streets and highways are frequently jammed with vehicles operated by high-speed lunatics and drivers who constantly honk their horns. In Istanbul avoid the many small one-way streets—you never know when someone is going to barrel down one of them in the wrong direction. In cities, it's best to leave your car in a garage and use public transportation or take taxis. Parking is another problem in the cities and larger towns.

You should also avoid driving on highways after dusk because drivers often drive without turning their lights on. Vehicles may be stopped on the roads in complete darkness. In the countryside watch out for drivers passing on a curve or at the top of a hill, and beware of carts—very difficult to see at night—and motorcycles weaving in and out of traffic while carrying entire families.

Highways are numbered or specified by direction (e.g., the route to Antalya). Trans-European highways have a European number as well as a Turkish number (E6 is the European number for Turkish Route D100, for example). Note that route numbers may be inconsistent from map to map.

Note that **archaeological and historic sites are indicated by yellow signposts.**

EMERGENCY SERVICES

A road rescue service is available on some highways; before you embark on a journey, ask your car rental agency or hotel how to contact it in case of an emergency. Most major car manufacturers in Turkey (for example, Renault, Fiat, and Opel/General Motors) also have roaming 24-hour services. Most rental agencies will ask you to contact them before attempting to have any repairs done and will usually bring you a replacement car. They will almost certainly give you a cell number which you can call 24/7 in the case of any difficulty. If they don't, ask for one.

Turkish mechanics in the villages can usually manage to get you going again, at least until you reach a city, where you can have the car fully repaired. Most Turkish gas stations have at least one staff member with some knowledge of car mechanics who can diagnose problems and provide "first aid" or advice, such as directions to the nearest mechanic. If a gas station attendant fixes a minor problem, it is customary to give him a small tip of about $5–$10 depending on the time and effort expended.

In urban areas entire streets are given over to car-repair shops run by teams of experts—one specializes in radiators, another in electrical fittings, and another in steering columns. It's not expensive to have repairs done, but it's customary to give a small tip to the person who does the repairs. If you don't want to wait for the work to be done, **take all car documents with you when you leave the shop.**

Emergency Services There aren't any Turkey-wide emergency services for car trouble or theft. If you hire a car and have a problem, you should call the rental company. They will have given you a cell number to call in the event of an emergency.

GASOLINE

Shell, British Petroleum, Total, Elf, and two Turkish oil companies, Petrol Ofisi and Türkpetrol, operate stations in Turkey. Many of those on the main highways stay open around the clock, others from 6 AM to 10 PM. Almost all Turkish gas stations provide full service and have unleaded gas. Many attendants will clean your windows while the car's tank is being filled. Tipping is not obligatory though not uncommon if the attendant has been particularly attentive—YTL1 is usually enough. In the summer in western Turkey some gas stations have sprinklers which you can drive through slowly to get rid of dust. There may be long distances between gas stations in rural areas so, if you are heading off the beaten track, don't allow the tank to run too low. Most gas stations in towns and major highways take credit cards, although you will need cash in rural areas. Many gas stations also have small shops, or just a cooler, where you can buy chilled drinks such as bottled water.

ROAD CONDITIONS

Throughout Turkey signposts are few, lighting is scarce, rural roads are sometimes rough, and city traffic is chaotic, and the country's accident rate is one of the highest in the world. The top speed limit of 120 kilometers/hour (about 75 mph) is rarely enforced on major highways, although it is not unusual for the Turkish police to set speed traps on other roads. It is advisable to drive carefully and relatively slowly, and to be prepared for sudden changes in both road conditions and the behavior of other drivers.

RULES OF THE ROAD

In general, Turkish driving conforms to Mediterranean customs, with driving on the right and passing on the left, but be prepared for drivers to do anything. Seat belts are required for front-seat passengers and a good idea for those in back seats. Using a cell phone while driving is prohibited—but this law is seldom obeyed. Turning right on a red light is not permitted, but one is allowed through a flashing red light provided nothing is coming the other way. Speeding and other traffic violations are subject to on-the-spot fines. It is both illegal and inadvisable to drive under the influence of alcohol. Most rental companies do not allow you to cross international borders in a rented car.

ROAD MAPS

Road maps can often be found in tourist areas although the rental company will usually also provide you with one. Remember, though, signposting is erratic and maps often not very accurate.

CHILDREN IN TURKEY

Turkey is not the easiest place to travel with young children. There are long distances to cope with, lots of hiking around rock-strewn ruins, and few child-oriented facilities. Be sure to plan ahead and involve your youngsters as you outline your trip. When packing, include things to keep them busy en route.

With that in mind, Turkish people are often eager to be of assistance, especially with respect to children, and this can go a long way in offsetting frustrations at the absence of facilities. Restaurants are generally casual and accommodating to families, and diapers and baby food are easy to find in most towns. If you are renting a car, try to arrange for a car seat when you reserve, though it is not guaranteed that every agency will have one available.

COMPUTERS ON THE ROAD

Many of the better hotels have some means for guests to get online access. Ask when you make a reservation. In addition, larger post offices in major cities may have connection facilities. In an increasing number of places, especially larger cities and resorts, you may also be able to find a local Internet café. Contact your Internet provider before you go to find out if it has an access number in Turkey. If you have a GSM mobile, you should be able to plug it into your computer and access the Internet while in Turkey. There are some wireless hotspots in major cities, although most require online subscription. A few hotels, restaurants, and cafés offer free wireless connections over their own wireless modems; this is usually advertised with a sign in the window.

Although it is possible to find spare batteries for laptops, it's not easy, particularly outside the major cities; you're better off bringing one with you. If you have hardware problems with your computer while in Turkey, most major manufacturers have representatives in the major cities, although repair prices tend to be high and it is unusual for repairs to take less than one week.

Most important, remember that the Turkish electricity supply runs on 220 volts. Any equipment set up for U.S. voltage needs a good converter, and you are advised to bring one with you. Many laptops are equipped with built-in converters, but check with your computer dealer before you leave home to make sure you have what you need.

CRUISE TRAVEL

Cruise Lines Celebrity Cruises ☎ 305/539-6000 or 800/437-3111 ⊕ www.celebrity.com. Costa Cruises ☎ 954/266-5600 or 800/462-6782 ⊕ www.costacruise.com. Crystal Cruises ☎ 310/785-9300 or 800/446-6620 ⊕ www.crystalcruises.com. Cunard Line ☎ 661/753-1000 or 800/728-6273 ⊕ www.cunard.com. Holland America Line ☎ 206/281-3535 or 877/932-4259 ⊕ www.hollandamerica.com. Mediterranean Shipping Cruises ☎ 212/764-4800 or 800/666-9333 ⊕ www.msccruises.com. Norwegian Cruise Line ☎ 305/436-4000 or 800/327-7030 ⊕ www.ncl.com. Oceania Cruises ☎ 305/514-2300 or 800/531-5658 ⊕ www.oceaniacruises.com. Princess Cruises ☎ 661/753-0000 or 800/774-6237 ⊕ www.princess.com. Regent Seven Seas Cruises ☎ 954/776-6123 or 800/477-7500 ⊕ www.rssc.com. Royal Caribbean International ☎ 305/539-6000 or 800/327-6700 ⊕ www.royalcaribbean.com. Seabourn Cruise Line ☎ 305/463-3000 or 800/929-9391 ⊕ www.seabourn.com. SeaDream Yacht Club ☎ 305/631-6110 or 800/707-4911 ⊕ www.seadreamyachtclub.com. Silversea Cruises ☎ 954/522-4477 or 800/722-9955 ⊕ www.silversea.com. Star Clippers ☎ 305/442-0550 or 800/442-0551 ⊕ www.starclippers.com. Windstar Cruises ☎ 206/281-3535 or 800/258-7245 ⊕ www.windstarcruises.com.

CUSTOMS & DUTIES

You're always allowed to bring goods of a certain value back home without having to pay any duty or import tax. There's also a limit on the amount of tobacco and liquor you can bring back duty-free, and some countries have separate limits for perfumes; for exact figures, check with your customs department. The values of so-called "duty-free" goods are included in these amounts. When you shop abroad, save all your receipts, as customs inspectors may ask to see them as well as the items you purchased. If the total value of your goods is more than the duty-free limit, then you'll have to pay a tax (most often a flat percentage) on the value of everything beyond that limit.

Turkish customs officials rarely look through tourists' luggage on arrival. You are allowed to bring in 400 cigarettes, 50 cigars, 200 grams of tobacco, 1½ kilograms of instant coffee, 500 grams of tea, and 2½ liters of alcohol. Items in the duty-free shops in Turkish airports, for international arrivals, are usually less expensive than they are in European airports or in flight. Pets are allowed into the country provided that they have all the necessary documentation. Full details can be obtained from the Turkish diplomatic representative in your own country.

The export of antiquities from Turkey is expressly forbidden and the ban is rigorously enforced. If you buy a carpet or rug that looks old, make sure to obtain certification, usually from a local museum, that it is not antique. The seller will usually be able to help you. The ban on antiquities extends to historical artifacts, coins, and even pieces of masonry. There have been several recent cases where tourists, some of them children, have tried to take small pieces of stone home as souvenirs and been arrested at the airport on suspicion of trying to export parts of ancient monuments. A genuine mistake is not considered sufficient excuse. Even where the tourists have been ultimately acquitted, they have still had to spend many months either in detention or, more commonly, out on bail but denied permission to leave the country. Note, too, that Turkish antiquities laws apply to every piece of detritus, so **don't pick up anything off the ground at archaeological sites.**

Visit the Turkish embassy Web site in Washington, D.C., and the Web sites of the U.S.State Department and U.S. Embassy in Ankara for more information.

U.S. Information **U.S. Customs and Border Protection** ⊕ www.cbp.gov.**Turkish Embassy** ⊕ www.turkishembassy.org/.

EATING & DRINKING

For more information about traditional Turkish food, the availability of alcohol, and dining establishments in Turkey, *see* the Eating Out in Turkey section of the Understanding Turkey chapter. For information on food-related health issues *see* Health *below.*

The restaurants we list are the cream of the crop in each price category.

Prices on the restaurant chart (at the front of each chapter) are per main course, or 2 small dishes, at dinner. A service or "cover" charge (a charge just for sitting at the table, the bread, the water, etc.)of 10% to 15% is usually added to the bill but you should tip 10% on top of this. If a restaurant's menu has no prices listed, ask before you order—you'll avoid a surprise when the bill comes.

MEALS & MEALTIMES

Breakfast, usually eaten at your hotel, typically consists of *beyaz peynir* (goat cheese), sliced tomatoes, cucumbers, and olives, with a side order of fresh bread; the menu varies little, whether you stay in a simple pansiyon or an upscale hotel. Yogurt with honey and fresh fruit is generally available as well, as are tea and coffee.

Lunch is generally served from noon to 3, dinner from 7 to 10. You can find restaurants or cafés open almost any time of the day or night in cities; in villages getting a meal at odd hours can be a problem. Breakfast starts early, typically by 7. Most Turks fast during daylight hours during the Islamic holy month of Ramadan. During that time, many restaurants, particularly smaller ones outside the major cities, close during day and open at dusk.

Unless otherwise noted, the restaurants listed in this guide are open daily for lunch and dinner.

PAYING

Most relatively upscale restaurants, particularly those in western Turkey, take major credit cards. Smaller eateries will often accept only cash. For guidelines on tipping, *see* Tipping *below.*

RESERVATIONS & DRESS

Regardless of where you are, it's a good idea to make a reservation if you can. In some places it's expected. We only mention specifically when reservations are essential (there's no other way you'll ever get a table) or when they are not accepted. For popular restaurants, book as far ahead as you can (often 30 days), and reconfirm a day or two before the actual date of your reservation. (Large parties should always call ahead to check the reservations policy.) We mention dress only when men are required to wear a jacket or a jacket and tie.

Was the service stellar or not up to snuff? Did the food give you shivers of delight or leave you cold? Did the prices and portions make you happy or sad? Rate restaurants and write your own reviews in Travel Ratings or start a discussion about your favorite places in Travel Talk on www.fodors.com. Your comments might even appear in our books. Yes, you, too, can be a correspondent!

ELECTRICITY

Consider making a small investment in a universal adapter, which has several types of plugs in one lightweight, compact unit. Most laptops and mobile phone chargers are dual voltage (i.e., they operate equally well on 110 and 220 volts) and so require only an adapter. These days the same is true more of small appliances such as hair dryers. Always check labels and manufacturer instructions to be sure, though. Don't use 110-volt outlets marked FOR SHAVERS ONLY for high-wattage appliances such as hair dryers. The electrical current in Turkey is 220 volts, 50 cycles alternating current (AC); wall outlets take European-type plugs, with two or three round prongs.Make sure that you have a voltage and a plug converter if you're going to be using U.S. appliances.

Steve Kropla's Help for World Travelers ⊕ www.kropla.com has information on electrical and telephone plugs around the world. **Walkabout Travel Gear** ⊕ www.walkabouttravelgear.com has a good discussion about electricity under "adapters."

EMERGENCIES

If your passport is lost or stolen, contact the police and your embassy immediately (⇨ Embassies *below*). For information about food and staying healthy, *see* Health, *below.*

If you have an emergency, you're best off asking a Turk to call an emergency number for you because it's unlikely you'll find an English-speaking person. Even at the Tourism Police, the person answering the telephone is unlikely to speak English. So first, ask bystanders for help. They will almost invariably try their utmost to be of assistance and will usually know of nearby hospitals or doctors. The Turkish words for ambulance, doctor, and police—*ambulans, doktor,* and *polis,* respectively—all sound about the same as their English equivalents, as does *telefon* for telephone. Say whichever is appropriate, and you can feel fairly certain that you'll be understood when you use the words applicable to your emergency. Note that if you call an ambulance don't expect it to arrive immediately since traffic in the larger cities may cause delays

If you need a dentist, Turkish dentists, or *dişçi,* are unusually good for the developing world. Each works independently, so it's best to ask someone local you trust for the best one they know.

The British Embassy in Turkey maintains a full current list of hospitals on their Web site.

Embassies **British Embassy** ⊕ www. britishembassy.gov.uk. **Canadian Consulate (Istanbul)** ⊠ İstiklal Caddesi No. 373, Beyoğlu ☎ 212/251–9838. **U.S. Consulate (Istanbul)** ⊠ İstinye Mahallesi, Kaplıcalar Mevkii No.2,İstinye ☎ 212/335–9000 ⊕ http://istanbul.usconsulate. gov/. **U.S.Embassy (Ankara)** ⊠ 110 Atatürk Bul., Kavaklıdere ☎ 312/455–5555 ⊕ http://ankara. usembassy.gov/. **U.K. Consulate.** ⊠ Meşrutiyet Cad. 34, Tepebaşı, Beyoğlu ☎ 212/335–9000. General Emergency Contacts **Ambulance** ☎ 112. **Emergency (police, etc.)** ☎ 155. **Tourism Police (Istanbul)** ☎ 212/527–4503.

ENGLISH-LANGUAGE MEDIA

BOOKS

English-language books are now relatively easy to find in Turkey. In tourist areas they tend to be mainly books about Turkey or light novels, but several bookstores in the major cities, particularly in Istanbul, have a wide selection of English language books. Small outlets in tourist areas usually add a markup to the cover price which can vary from 10 to 50 percent. In larger bookstores, the prices are usually close to the Turkish Lira equivalent of the original cover price.

NEWSPAPERS & MAGAZINES

There are two English-language dailies in Turkey. The *Turkish Daily News* was established in 1961 by the Çevik family and is the oldest and best-established. It was bought by Aydın Doğan, Turkey's leading media tycoon, in 2000, and he subsequently fired the paper's editor, İlnur Çevik, who began publishing his own English-language daily in 2004 and called it the *New Anatolian.* Initially, the *New Anatolian* struggled but it has now overtaken the *Turkish Daily News* in terms of the quality and quantity of its news coverage. The *New Anatolian* lacks access to the Doğan Group's distribution network, though, and particularly outside Ankara and Istanbul, it can be hard to find. In the 1990s the *Turkish Daily News* was often able to use the de facto protection afforded by including virtually all of the foreign diplomatic community in Turkey in its readership to address controversial topics, such as the Kurdish issue, with a degree of freedom that Turkish-language newspapers could only envy. Its news content has thinned, however, in recent years and the paper has become reluctant to attract controversy, not least for fear that a critical stance would jeopardize other companies in the Doğan Group having access to state contracts. İlnur Çevik, the editor of the *New Anatolian,* is a member of the ruling Justice and Development Party (JDP) and thus only a reluctant critic of government policy. The other journalists on the paper, however, come from a variety of different backgrounds and it is not unusual for different columnists to express diametrically opposing viewpoints in the same edition of the paper. Both papers are also available online.

British newspapers such as the *Guardian* and the *Financial Times* have special editions are printed in Europe, as do the *Wall Street Journal* and the *International Herald Tribune*. In each case, the newspapers are more expensive than in their countries of origin but still reasonably priced. Other English-language European and U.S. newspapers can sometimes be found but, particularly for U.S. papers, are usually extremely expensive.

Foreign magazines such as *Time* and *Newsweek* are widely available in major cities and tourist resorts. *Time* and *Newsweek* sell for around $3. Other, more specialized foreign magazines can be found in some of the larger bookstores, although they may be several times more expensive than in their country of origin.

The Turkish Daily News ⊕ www.turkishdailynews. com.tr. **The New Anatolian** ⊕ www. thenewanatolian.com

RADIO & TELEVISION
There are no English-language television channels in Turkey although in the major cities most hotels have cable TV which includes foreign channels such as CNN International, BBC World, and BBC Prime. An increasing number of hotels have access to satellite television, which invariably includes some English language channels.

ETIQUETTE & BEHAVIOR
Turks set great store in politeness. No one will expect you to have mastered the intricacies of polite speech in Turkish, but a respectful attitude and tone of voice, combined with a readiness to smile, will often work wonders.

Although Turks are a very tactile people, particularly with friends of the same sex, this physical contact is like a language, full of pitfalls for the unwary. Be very careful about initiating physical contact, as misunderstandings are easy. Overt public physical displays of affection between the sexes are still not widespread and are likely to offend, particularly outside the major cities.

Turks shake hands as a greeting, although this is more common between men than between women. It is quite acceptable, and often very appreciated, if a foreign male initiates a handshake with another male when, for example, leaving a carpet shop. For handshakes between the sexes, unless the Turkish woman is obviously highly Westernized, a foreign male should leave it up to her to initiate any physical contact. It is usually best for foreign women to allow a Turkish man to initiate the handshake rather than trying to judge whether it is advisable or not. Occasionally, very religious Turkish males will pointedly avoid shaking a woman's hand.

A combination of simultaneously shaking hands and kissing on both cheeks is the usual form of greeting between male friends, while women friends more often kiss without shaking hands. However, the kiss is stylized (a cheek-to-cheek "air-kiss"), and it is unusual for the lips to make contact with the skin. On occasion, a Turk will actually kiss the cheek, but such a kiss is considered very forward when given to members of the opposite sex, particularly those of little acquaintance, and if you are a recipient, you should draw your conclusions accordingly. It is unusual for two people of the opposite sex to kiss cheeks at all, and you should be wary of kissing someone of the opposite sex in any manner unless you are confident it will not be misinterpreted.

Most Turks consider hospitality as both a duty and a source of pride. If you visit Turks in their homes, it is considered good manners to take off your shoes on entering. You will not be expected to bring gifts, particularly on a first visit, although a small token is always appreciated. Chances are the lady of the house will usually have gone to considerable trouble to prepare food if she has had prior knowledge of your arrival. So you, in turn, should go with an empty stomach and at least try the dishes that are offered to you. In appreciation, it is traditional to say *ellerinize sağlık* ("ell-lair-in-izeh sah-luk"), which translates literally as, "May your hands be healthy." No offense will be taken if you don't manage to say it, but it will be much appreciated if you do.

BUSINESS ETIQUETTE
Business etiquette is little different from everyday etiquette. In the major cities

many managers of larger companies will have worked or trained abroad, particularly in the United States, and will be familiar with the ways in which Western companies do business. Punctuality is appreciated, but chronic traffic congestion in Istanbul and Ankara means most business-people are used to people arriving a little late for appointments. A telephone call to warn of a late arrival is appreciated.

Business negotiations are usually conducted in a relaxed atmosphere, and the business of the day may be padded with polite conversation and the ubiquitous cups of tea. Provided you eventually get down to business, it is usually a good idea not to force the pace, as the preliminaries are a way for the parties to assess each other and establish mutual trust.

If you are taken out to dinner or on a sightseeing tour, you will be treated more as a guest than a prospective business partner, and your Turkish counterpart will insist on paying for everything. Spouses will usually be more than welcome on such occasions, although it is always advisable to check with your Turkish counterpart first.

MOSQUES

Turkey is comparatively lenient regarding the visiting of mosques—in many Muslim countries, non-Muslims are strictly forbidden to enter them at all. Most mosques in Turkey are open to the public during the day. Prayer sessions, called *namaz,* last from 30 to 40 minutes and are observed five times daily. These times are based on the position of the sun, so they vary throughout the seasons but are generally around sunrise (between 5 and 7), at lunchtime (around noon or 1, when the sun is directly overhead), in the afternoon (around 3 or 4), at sunset (usually between 5 and 7), and at bedtime (at 9 or 10)—a daily list of prayer times can be found in Turkish newspapers. During namaz it's best not to enter a mosque, and non-Muslims should **avoid visiting mosques midday on Friday,** when attendances are higher and it is the equivalent of Sunday morning for Christians or Saturday morning for Jews.

For women, **bare arms and legs are not acceptable inside a mosque.** Men should avoid wearing shorts as well. Women should not enter a mosque without first covering their heads with a scarf, though some guardians will overlook it when a female tourist does not cover her head.

Before entering a mosque, **shoes must be removed.** There is usually an attendant, and shoes are generally safe. If you feel uncomfortable about leaving them, you can always carry them in your backpack or handbag. It is considered offensive for a non-Muslim to sit down in a mosque (many tourists do sit down despite the signs requesting them not to). It is also advisable to show respect for both the sanctity of the mosque and the piety of those who might be praying in it by talking only in whispers. On no account should you try to take photographs inside the mosque, particularly of people praying.

A small donation is usually requested for the upkeep of the mosque. The equivalent of approximately $3 is appropriate. Some mosques heavily visited by tourists may also have a "shoe keeper," who will ask for a tip.

HEALTH

The most common types of illnesses are caused by contaminated food and water. Especially in developing countries, drink only bottled, boiled, or purified water and drinks; don't drink from public fountains or use ice. You should even consider using bottled water to brush your teeth. Make sure food has been thoroughly cooked and is served to you fresh and hot; avoid vegetables and fruits that you haven't washed (in bottled or purified water) or peeled yourself. If you have problems, mild cases of traveler's diarrhea may respond to Imodium (known generically as loperamide) or Pepto-Bismol. Be sure to drink plenty of fluids; if you can't keep fluids down, seek medical help immediately.

Infectious diseases can be airborne or passed via mosquitoes and ticks and through direct or indirect physical contact with animals or people. Some, including Norwalk-like viruses that affect your digestive tract, can be passed along through contaminated food. If you are traveling in an area where malaria is prevalent, use a repellant containing DEET and take malaria-prevention medication before, during, and after your trip as directed by your physician. Condoms can help prevent most sexually transmitted diseases, but aren't absolute and the quality of them varies from country to country. Speak with your physition and/or check the CDC or World Health Organization Web sites for health alerts, particularly if you're pregnant, traveling with children, or have a chronic illness.

No serious health risks are associated with travel to Turkey, although you should take precautions against malaria if you visit the far southeast. No vaccinations are required for entry. To avoid problems at customs, though, diabetics carrying needles and syringes should have a letter from their physician confirming their need for insulin injections. Travelers are advised to have vaccinations for hepatitis, cholera, and typhoid for trips to the southeast. Rabies can be a problem in Turkey, occasionally even in the large cities. If bitten or scratched by a dog or cat about which you have suspicions, go to the nearest pharmacy and ask for assistance.

Even in areas where there is no malaria, it's a good idea to use something to ward off mosquitoes. All pharmacies and most cornerstores and supermarkets stock a variety of oils and/or tablets to burn, as well as sprays and creams which you can apply to exposed skin; it's generally easy to identify these products as the packaging usually includes a picture of a mosquito. If you can't find what you want, try asking using the Turkish word for mosquito: *sinek*. It sometimes seems as though mosquitoes favor foreigners, particularly the fair-skinned, so a Turk's assurances that mosquitoes in a particular place are "not bad"" can be both sincere and misleading.

Given the high temperatures in summer, dehydration can be a problem in southern and eastern Turkey. Remember to keep sipping water throughout the day rather than waiting until you are very thirsty.

For minor problems, pharmacists can be helpful, and medical services are widely available. Doctors and dentists abound in major cities and can be found in all but the smallest towns; many are women. There are also *hastanes* (hospitals) and *kliniks* (clinics). Road signs marked with an H point the way to the nearest hospital. Even if they cannot converse fluently in English, most qualified doctors will have a working knowledge of the English for medical conditions.

FOOD & DRINK

Tap water is heavily chlorinated and supposedly safe to drink in cities and resorts. It's best to play it safe, however, and stick to *şişe suyu* (bottled still water), *maden suyu* (bottled sparkling mineral water), or *maden sodası* (carbonated mineral water), which are better tasting and inexpensive. Do not drink tap water in rural areas or in eastern Turkey. Turkish food is relatively safe, though you should still be careful, especially in more out-of-the-way areas.

OVER-THE-COUNTER REMEDIES

Many over-the-counter remedies available in Western countries can also be found in Turkish pharmacies, which are usually well stocked. Even a Turkish pharmacist who doesn't speak English will often be able to recognize a specific remedy—particularly if you write the name down—and be able to find an appropriate alternative if that medication is not available.

HOLIDAYS

The major Turkish holidays are as follows; schools and many offices will often close for a full or half day: January 1 (New Year's Day); April 23 (National Independence Day); May 19 (Atatürk's Commemoration Day, celebrating his birthday and the day he landed in Samsun, starting the independence movement); August 30 (Zafer Bayramı, or Victory Day, commemorating Turkish victories over Greek forces in 1922, during Turkey's War of Independence); October 29 (Cumhuriyet Bayramı, or Republic Day, celebrating Atatürk's proclamation of the Turkish republic in 1923—many businesses and government offices also close at midday, usually either 12:30 or 1, on the day before Republic Day); November 10 (the anniversary of Atatürk's death), is not a full-day public holiday but is commemorated by a nation-wide moment of silence at 9:05 AM). Many provincial towns also hold celebrations to mark the anniversary of the date that the Greeks were driven out of the area during the Turkish War of Liberation.

Turks also celebrate the two main Muslim religious holidays each year: the three-day Şeker Bayramı, marking the end of Ramadan and the four-day Kurban Bayramı, which honors Abraham's willingness to sacrifice his son to God. Because the Muslim year is based on the lunar calendar, the dates of the two holidays change every year, both moving forward by 11–12 days each time. The precise timing may vary slightly according to the sighting of the moon. Many businesses and government offices close at midday, usually either 12:30 or 1, on the day before the religious bayrams. In 2007 Şeker Bayramı is expected to start at midday on October 12th and last through until the evening of October 14th. In 2008 it is due to begin at midday on September 29th and last until the evening of October 2nd. In 2007 Kurban Bayramı will start at midday on December 19th and continue through the evening of December 23rd. In 2008 it will begin at midday on December 8th and continue through the evening of December 11th.

A word of note: If a religious holiday takes up three or four days of a working week, the government will often declare the rest of the week an official holiday as well. However, such decisions are usually made less than a month before the holiday actually begins.

INSURANCE

What kind of coverage do you honestly need? Do you even need trip insurance at all? Take a deep breath and read on.

We believe that comprehensive trip insurance is especially valuable if you're booking a very expensive or complicated trip (particularly to an isolated region) or if you're booking far in advance. Who knows what could happen six months down the road? But whether or not you get insurance has more to do with how comfortable you are assuming all that risk yourself.

Comprehensive travel policies typically cover trip cancellation and interruption, letting you cancel or cut your trip short because of a personal emergency, illness, or in some cases, acts of terrorism in your destination. Such policies also cover evacuation and medical care. Some also cover you for trip delays because of bad weather or mechanical problems as well as for lost or delayed baggage. Another type of coverage to look for is financial default—that is, when your trip is disrupted because a tour operator, airline, or cruise line goes out of business. Generally you must buy this when you book your trip or shortly thereafter, and it's available to you only if your operator isn't on a list of excluded companies.

If you're going abroad, consider buying medical-only coverage at the very least. Neither Medicare nor some private insurers cover medical expenses anywhere outside of the United States besides Mexico and Canada (including time aboard a cruise ship, even if it leaves from a U.S. port). Medical-only policies typically reimburse you for medical care (excluding that related to preexisting conditions) and hospitalization abroad and provide for evacuation. You still have to pay the bills and await reimbursement from the insurer, though.

Expect comprehensive travel insurance policies to cost about 4% to 7% of the total price of your trip (it's more like 12% if you're over age 70). A medical-only policy may or may not be cheaper than a comprehensive policy. Always read the fine print of your policy to make sure that you are covered for the risks that are of the most concern to you. Compare several policies to make sure you're getting the best price and range of coverage available.

Just as an aside: You know you can save a bundle on trips to warm-weather destinations by traveling in rainy season. But there's also a chance that a severe storm will disrupt your plans. The solution? Look for hotels and resorts that offer storm/hurricane guarantees. Although they rarely allow refunds, most guarantees do let you rebook later if a storm strikes.

Insurance Comparison Sites Insure My Trip.com ⊕ www.insuremytrip.com. **Square Mouth.com** ⊕ www.quotetravelinsurance.com.
Comprehensive Travel Insurers Access America ☎ 866/807-3982 ⊕ www.accessamerica.com. **CSA Travel Protection** ☎ 800/873-9855 ⊕ www.csatravelprotection.com. **HTH Worldwide** ☎ 610/254-8700 or 888/243-2358 ⊕ www.hthworldwide.com. **Travelex Insurance** ☎ 888/457-4602 ⊕ www.travelex-insurance.com. **Travel Guard International** ☎ 715/345-0505 or 800/826-4919 ⊕ www.travelguard.com. **Travel Insured International** ☎ 800/243-3174 ⊕ www.travelinsured.com.
Medical-Only Insurers Wallach & Company ☎ 800/237-6615 or 504/687-3166 ⊕ www.wallach.com. **International Medical Group** ☎ 800/628-4664 ⊕ www.imglobal.com. **International SOS** ☎ 215/942-8000 or 713/521-7611 ⊕ www.internationalsos.com.

LANGUAGE

In 1928, Atatürk launched sweeping language reforms that, over a period of six weeks, replaced Arabic script with the Latin-based alphabet and eliminated many Arabic and Persian words from the Turkish language.

English, German, and sometimes French are widely spoken in hotels, restaurants, and shops in cities and resorts. In villages and remote areas you may have a hard time finding anyone who speaks anything but Turkish, though rudimentary communications are still usually possible. Try learning a few basic Turkish words; it will be appreciated.

LODGING

Did the resort look as good in real life as it did in the photos? Did you sleep like a baby, or were the walls paper thin? Did you get your money's worth? Rate hotels and write your own reviews in Travel Ratings or start a discussion about your favorite places in Travel Talk on www.fodors.com. Your comments might even appear in our books. Yes, you, too, can be a correspondent!

Accommodations range from the international luxury chain hotels in Istanbul, Ankara, and İzmir to charming inns occupying historic Ottoman mansions and kerransarays to comfortable but basic family-run *pansiyons* (guest houses) in the countryside. It's advisable to **plan ahead if you'll be traveling in the peak season (April–October),** when resort hotels are often booked by tour companies.

Note that **reservations should be confirmed more than once,** particularly at hotels in popular destinations. Phone reservations are not always honored, so it's a good idea to e-mail the hotel and get written confirmation of your reservations, as well as to call again before you arrive. If you want air-conditioning, make sure to ask about it when you reserve.

Asking to see the room in advance is accepted practice. It will probably be much more basic than the well-decorated reception area. Check for noise, especially if the room faces a street or is anywhere near a nightclub or disco, and look for such amenities as window screens and mosquito coils—small, flat disks that, when lighted, emit an unscented vapor that keeps biting insects away.

Most hotels and other lodgings require you to give your credit card details before they will confirm your reservation. If you don't feel comfortable e-mailing this information, ask if you can fax it (some places even prefer faxes). However you book, get confirmation in writing and have a copy of it handy when you check in. If you book through an online travel agent, discounter, or wholesaler, you might even want to confirm your reservation with the hotel before leaving home—just to be sure everything was processed correctly.

Make sure you understand the hotel's cancellation policy. Some places allow you to cancel without any kind of penalty—even if you prepaid to secure a discounted rate—if you cancel at least 24 hours in advance. Others require you to cancel a week in advance or penalize you for the cost of one night. Small inns and B&Bs are most likely to require you to cancel far in advance. Most hotels allow children under a certain age to stay in their parents' room at no extra charge, but others charge for them as extra adults; find out the cutoff age for discounts.

Assume that hotels operate on the European Plan (**EP**, no meals) unless we specify that they use the Breakfast Plan (**BP**, with full breakfast), Continental Plan (**CP**, Continental breakfast), Full American Plan (**FAP**, all meals), Modified American Plan (**MAP**, breakfast and dinner), or are **all-inclusive** (AI, all meals and most activities).

The lodgings we list are the cream of the crop in each price category. We always list the facilities that are available—but we don't specify whether they cost extra: When pricing accommodations, always ask what's included and what costs extra. Properties indicated by an ✕⊡ are lodging establishments whose restaurant warrants a special trip.

Prices in the lodging charts found in each chapter are for two people in a standard double room in high season, including VAT and service charge. Private bathrooms, air-conditioning, room phones, and a TV are assumed unless otherwise noted. In the low season you should be able to negotiate discounts of at least 20% off the rack rate; it never hurts to try.

HOSTELS

Hostels offer barebones lodging at low, low prices—often in shared dorm rooms with shared baths—to people of all ages, though the primary market is young travelers, especially students. Most hostels serve breakfast; dinner and/or shared cooking facilities may also be available. In some hostels, you aren't allowed to be in your room during the day, and there may be a curfew at night. Nevertheless, hostels provide a sense of community, with public rooms where travelers often gather to share stories. Many hostels are affiliated with Hostelling International (HI), an umbrella group of hostel associations with some 4,500 member properties in more than 70 countries. Other hostels are completely independent and may be nothing more than a really cheap hotel.

Membership in any HI association, open to travelers of all ages, allows you to stay in HI-affiliated hostels at member rates.

One-year membership is about $28 for adults; hostels charge about $10–$30 per night. Members have priority if the hostel is full; they're also eligible for discounts around the world, even on rail and bus travel in some countries.

There are around 30 youth hostels in Istanbul. Student residences in Ankara, Bolu, Bursa, Çanakkale, İzmir, and Istanbul also serve as youth hostels. There has been an increase in the number of inexpensive hotels offering dormitory-style accommodation in recent years; they are aimed very much at young backpackers. Word of warning for families on a tight budget thinking about staying in a hostel: a cheap hotel is generally a better bet unless you want your children (and yourself) wakened at 3 AM by drunken students stumbling into the bunk above them.

Contacts Hostelling International–USA ☎ 301/495-1240 ⊕ www.hiusa.org.

HOTELS

Weigh all your options (we can't say this enough). Join "frequent guest" programs. You may get preferential treatment in room choice and/or upgrades in your favorite chains. Check general travel sites and hotel Web sites as not all chains are represented on all travel sites. Always research or inquire about special packages and corporate rates. If you prefer to book by phone, you can sometimes get a better price if you call the hotel's local toll-free number (if one is available) rather than the central reservations number.

If you're trying to book a stay right before or after Turkey's high season (April to October), you might save considerably by changing your dates by a week or two. Note, though, that many properties charge peak-season rates for your entire stay even if your travel dates straddle peak and non-peak seasons. High-end chains catering to businesspeople are often busy only on weekdays and drop rates dramatically on weekends to fill up rooms. **Ask when rates go down.**

Watch out for hidden costs, including resort fees, energy surcharges, and "convenience" fees for such things as unlimited local phone service you won't use and a free newspaper—possibly written in a language you can't read. Always verify whether local hotel taxes are or are not included in the rates you are quoted, so that you'll know the real price of your stay. In some places, taxes can add 20% or more to your bill. If you're traveling overseas **look for price guarantees,** which protect you against a falling dollar. With your rate locked in, you won't pay more, even if the price goes up in the local currency.

Hotels are officially classified in Turkey as HL (luxury), H1 to H5 (first- to fifth-class); motels, M1 to M2 (first- to second-class); and P (pansiyons—guest houses). These classifications can be misleading, however, as they're based on the quantity of facilities rather than the quality of the service and decor, and the lack of a restaurant or lounge automatically relegates the establishment to the bottom of the ratings. In practice, a lower-grade hotel may actually be far more charming and comfortable than one with a higher rating.

The major Western chains are represented in Turkey by Hilton, Sheraton, and the occasional Ramada and Hyatt. All tend to be in the higher price ranges.

The standard Turkish hotel room, which you will encounter endlessly throughout the country, is clean, with bare walls, low wood-frame beds (usually a single bed, twin beds, or, less often, a double), and industrial carpeting or kilims on the floor. However, less expensive properties will probably have plumbing and furnishings that leave much to be desired. If you want a real double bed (not two singles pushed together), go to a more expensive property, either Turkish or Western style; for the most part, there there is no distinction in Turkish between separate twin beds which are separate and those which are pushed together.

These are some Turkish words that will come in handy when you're making reservations: "air-conditioning" is *klima,* "private bath" is *banyo,* "tub" is *banyo küveti,* "shower" is *düş,* "double bed" is *iki kişilik yatak, and* "twin beds" is *iki tane tek kişilik yataklar* ("separate" is

ayrı; "pushed together" is *beraber).* There is no Turkish word for "queen bed," but they will probably use the English (a direct translation is *kraliçe yatağı).*The same is true for for "king bed" (they will probably use the English, though a direct translation is *kral yatağı.* The advice for noise-sensitive travelers is to ask for a quiet room.

Discount Hotel Rooms Accommodations Express
☎ 800/444-7666 or 800/277-1064. **Hotels.com**
☎ 800/219-4606 or 800/364-0291 ⊕ www.hotels.com. **International Marketing & Travel Concepts**
☎ 800/790-4682 ⊕ www.imtc-travel.com. **Steigenberger Reservation Service** ☎ 800/223-5652 ⊕ www.srs-worldhotels.com. **Turbotrip.com**
☎ 800/473-7829 ⊕ w3.turbotrip.com.

PANSIYONS

Outside the cities and resort areas, these small, family-run places will be your most common option. They range from charming old homes decorated in antiques to tiny, utilitarian rooms done in basic modern. As a rule, they are inexpensive and scrupulously clean. Private baths are common, though they are rudimentary—stall showers, toilets with sensitive plumbing. A simple breakfast is typically included.

MAIL & SHIPPING

The Turkish for "post office" is *postane.* Post offices are painted bright yellow and have PTT (Post, Telegraph, and Telephone) signs on the front. The central post offices in larger cities are open Monday through Saturday from 8 AM to 9 PM, Sunday from 9 to 7. Smaller ones are open Monday through Saturday between 8:30 and 5. Turks use franking machines in post offices rather than postage stamps. The latter are still available at post offices but are mainly sold to philatelists and nostalgists. Although you will occasionally see mailboxes away from post offices, these are often not in use. If you want to maximize the chances of your mail actually arriving, use only the boxes at the post offices themselves.

Mail sent from Turkey can take 3 to 10 days, or more, to reach its destination. The mail service is erratic, and you may arrive home before your postcards are received by friends and family.

Postage rates are frequently adjusted to keep pace with inflation. It generally costs about 50 cents to send a postcard from Turkey to the U.S. Shipping a 10-pound rug home via surface mail will cost about $25 and take from two to six months.

If you want to receive mail in Turkey and you're uncertain where you'll be staying, have mail sent to Poste Restante, Merkez Posthanesi (Central Post Office), in the town of your choice.

OVERNIGHT & EXPRESS SERVICES

There is no international overnight courier service to and from Turkey. The main couriers (DHL, Federal Express, etc.) have offices in Istanbul, but even they take three days from Turkey to the United States and United Kingdom.

An express postal service (Acele Posta Servisi -APS) operates from Turkey to 72 other countries for letters, documents and small packages.

SHIPPING PARCELS

In general it is not only much quicker but also much safer to carry your purchases with you, even if you have to pay for excess baggage, rather than entrusting them to the postal service. Most parcels from Turkey do eventually arrive at their destination, but be aware there is a risk they may become damaged or lost in transit. Other alternatives, such as courier services or shipping companies, are quicker and more reliable but often very expensive. Some stores and sellers in bazaars will offer to arrange to ship goods for you. However, where possible, it's still always better to carry your purchases home with you. If you do decide to have someone ship something for you, make sure it is a large and reputable store.

MONEY MATTERS

Turkey used to be the least expensive of the Mediterranean countries, but prices have risen in recent years as the Turkish Lira has appreciated by around 40 percent against major currencies such as the U.S. dollar. At press time, Istanbul was roughly equivalent to other cities in the Mediterranean in terms of cost, but in the countryside, and particularly away from the main tourist areas, prices are much lower—room and board are not likely to be much more than $50 per person per day.

Coffee can range from about $1 to $4 a cup, depending on whether it's the less-expensive Turkish coffee or American-style coffee, and whether it's served in a luxury hotel, a café, or an outlet of a multinational chain such as Starbucks or Gloria Jean's. Tea will cost you about 35¢–$1 a glass, rising to $1–$3 for a cup (the latter is larger). Local beer will be about $2–$6, depending on the type of establishment; soft drinks, $1–$3; lamb shish kebab, $3.50–$8; and a taxi, $1 for 1 km, about ½ mi (50% higher between midnight and 6 AM).

Banks rarely have every foreign currency on hand, and it may take as long as a week to order. If you're planning to exchange funds before leaving home, don't wait till the last minute.

Prices throughout this guide are given for adults. Substantially reduced fees are almost always available for children, students, and senior citizens. For information on taxes, *see* Taxes.

ATMS & BANKS

Your own bank will probably charge a fee for using ATMs abroad; the foreign bank you use may also charge a fee. Extracting funds as you need them is a safer option than carrying around a large amount of cash.

ATMs can be found even in some of the smallest Turkish towns. Many accept international credit cards or bank cards (a strip of logos is usually displayed above the ATM). Almost all ATMs have a language key that enables you to read the instructions in English. To use your card in Turkey, your PIN must be four digits long.

As elsewhere, using an ATM is one of the easiest ways to get money in Turkey. Generally the exchange rate is based on the Turkish Central Bank or the exchange rate according to your bank. The exchange rate is almost always better through an ATM than with traveler's checks, but not as good as when exchanging cash.

CREDIT CARDS

Throughout this guide, the following abbreviations are used: **AE,** American Express; **DC,** Diners Club; **MC,** MasterCard; and **V,** Visa.

It's a good idea to inform your credit card company before you travel, especially if you're going abroad and don't travel internationally very often. Otherwise, the credit card company might put a hold on your card owing to unusual activity—not a good thing halfway through your trip. Record all your credit card numbers—as well as the phone numbers to call if your cards are lost or stolen—in a safe place so you're prepared should something go wrong. Both MasterCard and Visa have general numbers you can call (collect if you're abroad) if your card is lost, but you're better off calling the number of your issuing bank since MasterCard and Visa usually just transfer you to your bank; your bank's number is usually printed on your card.

If you plan to use your credit card for cash advances, you'll need to apply for a PIN at least two weeks before your trip. Although it's usually cheaper (and safer) to use a credit card abroad for large purchases (so you can cancel payments or be reimbursed if there's a problem), note that some credit-card companies *and* the banks that issue them add substantial percentages to all foreign transactions, whether they're done in a foreign currency or not. Check on these fees before leaving home so that there won't be any surprises when you get the bill.

Before you charge something, ask the merchant whether or not he or she plans to do a dynamic currency conversion (DCC). In such a transaction the credit card *processor* (shop, restaurant, or hotel, not Visa or MasterCard) converts the currency and charges you in dollars. In most cases you'll pay the merchant a 3% fee for this service in addition to any credit-card-company and issuing-bank foreign-transaction surcharges.

DCC programs are becoming increasingly widespread. Merchants who participate in them are supposed to ask whether you want to be charged in dollars or the local currency, but they don't always do so. And even if they do offer you a choice, they may well avoid mentioning the additional surcharges. The good news is that you *do* have a choice. And if this practice really gets your goat, you can avoid it entirely thanks to American Express; with its cards, DCC simply isn't an option.

Credit cards are accepted throughout Turkey, especially in larger cities or towns, but many budget-oriented restaurants or hotels do not accept them.

Be warned that Turkey has one of the highest rates of credit-card fraud in Europe. Do not let your credit card out of your sight. Since March 2006 Turkey has started using "chip and PIN" as well as "swipe and sign." The chip-and-PIN system is a more secure method than swipe-and-sign and was introduced in parts of Europe several years ago but is only just now being used in the United States. It refers to the chip in the credit card, which contains identifying information. The card is inserted in the POS terminal. which reads the chip and sends the information down the line. The user is then asked to enter his/her PIN. and this information is also sent down the wire; if everything matches, the transaction is completed.

Reporting Lost Cards **American Express** ☎ 800/ 992-3404 in the U.S. or 336/393-1111 collect from abroad ⊕ www.americanexpress.com. **Diners Club** ☎ 800/234-6377 in the U.S. or 303/799-1504 collect from abroad ⊕ www.dinersclub.com. **MasterCard** ☎ 800/622-7747 in the U.S. or 636/722-7111 collect from abroad ⊕ www.mastercard.com. **Visa** ☎ 800/ 847-2911 in the U.S. or 410/581-9994 collect from abroad ⊕ www.visa.com.

CURRENCY & EXCHANGE

At the beginning of 2005, Turkey introduced a new currency, the New Turkish Lira (YTL) to replace the Turkish Lira (TL), which at the time was trading at an outrageous TL 1,350,000 to one U.S. dollar. The old Turkish Lira notes and coins were gradually phased out through 2005, although some still occasionally surface. In everyday conversation many Turks still refer to the old currency so it's not un-usual to be told that something is "one million," when it is actually YTL 1 or around 65 U.S. cents. The New Turkish Lira is divided into 100 New Kuruş, usu-ally referred to simply as "kuruş," and is issued in denominations of 1, 5, 10, 20, 50, and 100 YTL notes, and 1, 5, 10, 25, 50 kuruş, and 1 YTL coins.

To avoid lines at airport exchange booths, **get a bit of local currency before you leave home.** If you're taking a taxi from the air-port you will need Turkish currency.

Although fees charged for ATM transac-tions may be higher abroad than at home, Cirrus and Plus exchange rates are excel-lent because they are based on wholesale rates offered only by major banks. You won't do as well at exchange booths in airports or rail and bus stations, in hotels, in restaurants, or in stores, although you may find their hours more convenient.

Hotels and banks will change money, as will larger post offices, but in Turkey the rates are usually better at the foreign ex-change booths (look for signs saying FOREIGN EXCHANGE or DÖVIZ). Most are now connected online to the currency markets and there will be little difference between them.

Exchange bureaus are found only in big cities, usually in the center, so if you are heading to small towns make sure you change your money before leaving.

Bureaus in tourist areas often offer slightly less attractive rates—rarely more than 2–3 percent difference—than bureaus in other places. Almost all foreign exchange bu-reaus are open Monday–Saturday. Hours vary but are typically 9:30 AM–6:30 PM. In tourist areas it is sometimes possible to find a bureau that is open on a Sunday, but it will usually compensate for the inconve-nience by offering a rate 2–3 percent worse than those bureaus that close on Sundays.

İş Bankası, (İş Bank) is Turkey's largest bank, with many branches in the cities and at least one in each town, usually in the center of town.

Exchange Rate Information Yahoo Finance ⊕ http://finance.yahoo.com/currency. **Oanda.com**

⊕ www.oanda.com also allows you to print out a handy table with the current day's conversion rates. **XE.com** ⊕ www.xe.com.

TRAVELER'S CHECKS & CARDS

Some consider this the currency of the caveman, and it's true that fewer establish-ments accept traveler's checks these days. Nevertheless, they're a cheap and secure way to carry extra money, particularly on trips to urban areas. Both Citibank (under the Visa brand) and American Express issue traveler's checks in the United States, but Amex is better known and more widely accepted; you can also avoid hefty surcharges by cashing Amex checks at Amex offices. Whatever you do, keep track of all the serial numbers in case the checks are lost or stolen. Many places in Turkey, even in Istanbul, do not take trav-eler's checks, and even those that do in-variably offer better exchange rates for cash. You might find you have to go to a bank to exchange them. Lost or stolen checks, however, can usually be replaced within 24 hours, so you may want the added security of traveler's checks even if they prove a little more expensive.

American Express now offers a stored-value card called a Travelers Cheque Card, which you can use wherever American Ex-press credit cards are accepted, including ATMs. The card can carry a minimum of $300 and a maximum of $2,700, and it's a very safe way to carry your funds. Al-though you can get replacement funds in 24 hours if your card is lost or stolen, it doesn't really strike us as a very good deal. In addition to a high initial cost ($14.95 to set up the card, plus $5 each time you "reload"), you still have to pay a 2% fee for each purchase in a foreign currency (similar to that of any credit card). Fur-ther, each time you use the card in an ATM, you pay a transaction fee of $2.50 on top of the 2% transaction fee for the conversion—add it all up and it can be considerably more than you would pay for simply using your own ATM card. Regular traveler's checks are just as secure and cost less.

American Express ☎ 888/412-6945 in the U.S., 801/945-9450 collect outside of the U.S. to add

value or speak to customer service ⊕ www.
americanexpress.com.

PACKING

Why do some people travel with a convoy
of suitcases the size of large-screen TVs
and yet never have a thing to wear? How
do others pack a toaster-oven-size duffle
with a week's worth of outfits *and* supplies for every possible contingency? We
realize that packing is a matter of style—a
very personal thing—but there's a lot to be
said for traveling light. The tips in this section will help you win the battle of the
bulging bag.

Make a list. In a recent Fodor's survey,
29% of respondents said they make lists
(and often pack) at least a week before a
trip. Lists can be used at least twice—once
to pack and once to repack at the end of
your trip. You'll also have a record of the
contents of your suitcase, just in case it
disappears in transit.

Think it through. What's the weather like?
Is this a business trip or a cruise or a resort
vacation? Going abroad? In some places
and/or sights, traditions of dress may be
more or less conservative than you're used
to. As your itinerary comes together, jot
activities down and note possible outfits
next to each (don't forget those shoes and
accessories).

Edit your wardrobe. Plan to wear everything twice (better yet, thrice) and to do
laundry along the way. Stick to one basic
look—urban chic, sporty casual, etc. Build
around one or two neutrals and an accent
(e.g., black, white, and olive green).
Women can freshen looks by changing
scarves or jewelry. For a week's trip, you
can look smashing with three bottoms,
four or five tops, a sweater, and a jacket
you can wear alone or over the sweater.

Be practical. Put comfortable shoes at the
top of your list. (Did we need to tell you
this?) Pack items that are lightweight, wrinkle resistant, compact, and washable. (Or
this?) Stack and then roll your clothes when
packing; they'll wrinkle less. Unless you're
on a guided tour or a cruise, select luggage
that you can readily carry. Porters, like
good butlers, are hard to find these days.

Check weight and size limitations. In the
United States you may be charged extra for
checked bags weighing more than 50
pounds. Abroad some airlines don't allow
you to check bags weighing more than 60
to 70 pounds, or they charge outrageous
fees for every pound your luggage is over.
Carry-on size limitations can be stringent,
too. The standard for most foreign airlines
is 23 kilos, although in practice check-in
staff will usually turn a blind eye to an
extra 5 kilos (i.e., up to a total of 28 kilos).

Check carry-on restrictions. Research restrictions with the TSA. Rules vary
abroad, so check them with your airline if
you're traveling overseas on a foreign carrier. Consider packing all but essentials
(travel documents, prescription meds, wal-
let) in checked luggage. This leads to a
"pack only what you can afford to lose"
approach that might help you streamline.

Lock it up. If you must pack valuables, use
TSA-approved locks (about $10) that can
be unlocked by all U.S. security personnel
should they decide to search your bags.

Tag it. Always put tags on your luggage
with some kind of contact information;
use your business address if you don't
want people to know your home address.
Put the same information (and a copy of
your itinerary) inside your luggage, too.

Rethink valuables. On U.S. flights, airlines
are liableonly for about $2,800 per person
for bags. On international flights, the liability limit is around $635 per bag. But
items like computers, cameras, and jewelry
aren't covered, and as gadgetry regularly
goes on the list of carry-on no-nos, you
can't count on keeping things safe by
keeping them close. Although comprehensive travel policies may cover luggage, the
liability limit is often a pittance. Your
homeowner's policy may cover you suffi-
ciently when you travel—or not.

Report problems immediately. If your
bags—or things in them—are damaged or
go astray, file a written claim with your
airline *before you leave the airport*. If the
airline is at fault, it may give you money
for essentials until your luggage arrives.
Most lost bags are found within 48 hours,
so alert the airline about where you'll be.

If your bag was opened for security reasons in the United States and something is missing, file a claim with the TSA.

WHAT YOU'LL NEED IN TURKEY

Turkey is an informal country, so leave the fancy clothes at home. Men will find a jacket and tie appropriate only for top restaurants in Istanbul, Ankara, and İzmir; for more modest establishments a blazer will more than suffice. Women should avoid overly revealing outfits and short skirts. The general rule is: the smaller the town, the more casual and, at the same time, conservative the dress.

On the beaches along the Mediterranean, topless sunbathing is increasingly common—though it is still frowned upon. Shorts are acceptable for hiking through ruins but not for touring mosques. The importance of a sturdy, comfortable pair of shoes cannot be overemphasized. Istanbul's Topkapı Palace is incredibly large, and the ruins at Ephesus and elsewhere are both vast and dusty.

Light cottons are best for summer, particularly along the coast. If you're planning excursions into the interior or north of the country, you'll need sweaters in spring or fall and all-out cold-weather gear in winter. An umbrella is advisable on the Black Sea Coast, but as anywhere else in Turkey, as soon as rain begins to fall, people will appear almost magically on the streets to sell cheap umbrellas; so if you don't want to bring an umbrella with you, it's always possible to find one.

Sunscreen and sunglasses will come in handy. It's a good idea to carry some toilet paper with you at all times, especially outside the bigger cities and resort areas. You'll need mosquito repellent for eating outside from March through October, a flashlight for exploring in Cappadocia, and soap if you're staying in more moderately priced hotels. ■ TIP➜ Pack some moist wipes and a clothes-freshener spray to get rid of the smell of Turkish cigarettes.

PASSPORTS & VISAS

All U.S. citizens, even infants, need a valid passport and a visa to enter Turkey for stays of up to 90 days. Visas can be issued at the Turkish embassy or consulate before you go, or at the point of entry; the cost is $45 and must be paid in American dollars. If you do not have a visa and need to buy one at the point of entry, look for a sign saying VISAS usually just before passport control.

Even though visas are multiple entry and usually valid for 90 days, they cannot be issued for periods longer than the validity of the passport you present. If your passport has less than a month to run, you may not be given a visa at all. Check the validity of your passport before applying for the visa. Turkish officials may impose stiff fines for an overstay on your visa.

PASSPORTS

We're always surprised at how few Americans have passports—only 25% at this writing. This number is expected to grow in coming years, when it becomes impossible to reenter the United States from trips to neighboring Canada or Mexico without one. Remember this: A passport verifies both your identity and nationality—a great reason to have one.

U.S. passports are valid for 10 years. You must apply in person if you're getting a passport for the first time; if your previous passport was lost, stolen, or damaged; or if your previous passport has expired and was issued more than 15 years ago or when you were under 16. All children under 18 must appear in person to apply for or renew a passport. Both parents must accompany any child under 14 (or send a notarized statement with their permission) and provide proof of their relationship to the child.

There are 13 regional passport offices, as well as 7,000 passport acceptance facilities in post offices, public libraries, and other governmental offices. If you're renewing a passport, you can do so by mail. Forms are available at passport acceptance facilities and online.

The cost to apply for a new passport is $97 for adults, $82 for children under 16; renewals are $67. Allow six weeks to process the paperwork for either a new or renewed passport. For an expediting fee of $60, you can reduce the time to about two weeks. If your trip is less than two weeks away, you can get a passport even more rapidly by going to a passport office with the necessary documentation. Private expediters can get things done in as little as 48 hours but charge hefty fees for their services.

Before your trip, make two copies of your passport's data page (one for someone at home and another for you to carry separately). Or scan the page and e-mail it to someone at home and/or yourself.

VISAS

Visas are essentially formal permissions to travel to a country. They allow countries to keep track of you and other visitors and to generate revenue (from visa fees). You *always* need a visa to enter a foreign country; however, many countries routinely issue tourist visas on arrival, particularly to U.S. citizens. When your passport is stamped or scanned in the immigration line, you're actually being issued a visa. Sometimes you have to stand in a separate line and pay a small fee to get your stamp before going through immigration, but you can still do this at the airport on arrival. Getting a visa isn't always that easy. Some countries require you to arrange for one in advance of your trip. There's usually—but not always—a fee involved, and said fee may be nominal ($10 or less) or substantial ($100 or more).

If you must apply for a visa in advance, you can usually do it in person or by mail. When you apply by mail, you send your passport to a designated consulate, where your passport will be examined and the visa issued. Expediters—usually the same ones who handle expedited passport applications—can do all the work to obtain your visa for you; however, there's always an additional cost (often more than $50 per visa).

Most visas limit you to a single trip—basically during the actual dates of your planned vacation. Other visas allow you to visit as many times as you wish for a specific period of time. Remember that requirements change, sometimes at the drop of a hat, and the burden is on you to make sure that you have the appropriate visas. Otherwise, you'll be turned away at the airport or, worse, deported after you arrive in the country. No company or travel insurer gives refunds if your travel plans are disrupted because you didn't have the correct visa.

U.S. Passport Information U.S. Department of State ☎ 877/487-2778 ⊕ http://travel.state.gov/passport

U.S. Passport & Visa Expediters A. Briggs Passport & Visa Expeditors ☎ 800/806-0581 or 202/464-3000 ⊕ www.abriggs.com. American Passport Express ☎ 800/455-5166 or 603/559-9888 ⊕ www.americanpassport.com. Passport Express ☎ 800/362-8196 or 401/272-4612 ⊕ www.passportexpress.com. Travel Document Systems ☎ 800/874-5100 or 202/638-3800 ⊕ www.traveldocs.com. Travel the World Visas ☎ 866/886-8472 or 301/495-7700 ⊕ www.world-visa.com.

PHONES

The good news is that you can now make a direct-dial telephone call from virtually any point on earth. The bad news? You can't always do so cheaply. Calling from a hotel is almost always the most expensive option; hotels usually add huge surcharges to all calls, particularly international ones. In some countries, you can phone from call centers or even the post office. Calling cards usually keep costs to a minimum, but only if you purchase them locally. And then there are mobile phones ⇨ *below*, which are sometimes more prevalent—particularly in the developing world—than land lines; as expensive as mobile phone calls can be, they are still usually a much cheaper option than calling from your hotel.

Telephone numbers in Turkey have seven-digit local numbers preceded by a three-digit city code. Intercity lines are reached by dialing 0 before the area code and number. In Istanbul, European and Asian Istanbul have separate area codes: The code for much of European Istanbul is 212 (making the number look like it's in New York City—but it's not), and the code for Asian Istanbul (numbers beginning with 3 or 4) is 216. The country code for Turkey is 90.

CALLING WITHIN TURKEY

Inside Istanbul you don't need to dial the code for other numbers with the same code, but you need to dial the code (0212 or 0216) when calling from the European to the Asian side of the city or vice versa. All local cellular calls are classed as long distance, and you need to dial the city code for every number.

To call long-distance within Turkey, dial 131 if you need operator assistance; otherwise dial 0, then dial the city code and number.

The increase in the use of mobile phones in Turkey means that very few people now use pay phones, but it's still possible to find them. Most are the blue push-button models, although a few older telephones are still in use. Directions in English and other languages are often posted in phone booths. Most Turks do not use directory assistance, and even if you are lucky enough to find an English-speaking operator, you are unlikely to be able to find the number you want. Your best chance of success is to tell the staff at your hotel who or what you are trying to find and let them do the rest.

Public phones either use phone cards (particularly in major cities) or *jetons* (tokens), although the latter are gradually being phased out. Tokens are available in 7¢ and 30¢ denominations, while phone cards come in denominations of 30 (about $2), 60 (about $3.50), and 100 (about $5) units; buy a 60 or 100 for long-distance calls within Turkey, a 30 for local usage. Both tokens and phone cards can be purchased at post offices and, for a small markup, at some corner stores, newspaper vendors, and street stalls. Keep in mind that they can sometimes be difficult to find, so it's a good idea to buy one at the first opportunity. There are very few phones in Turkey which can be used with credit cards.

To make a local call, insert your phone card or deposit a 7¢ token, wait until the light at the top of the phone goes off, and then dial the number.

Some kiosks selling newspapers or small stores have phones which you can use to place calls. The cost is usually approximately the same as a standard pay phone. If you want to use one, say *"telefon"* (Turkish for telephone), and the proprietor will usually either produce a phone or show you where you can find one.

CALLING OUTSIDE TURKEY

The country code is 1 for the United States.

For international operator services, dial 115. Intercity telephone operators seldom speak English, although international operators usually have some basic English. If you need international dialing codes and assistance or phone books, you can also go to the nearest post office.

To make an international call from a public phone in Turkey, dial 00, then dial the country code, area or city code, and the number. Expect to pay about $3–$5 per minute.

Access Codes **AT&T Direct** ☏ 00/800-12277 in Turkey, followed by the area code and number. **MCI WorldPhone** ☏ 00/800-11177 in Turkey, followed by the area code and number. **Sprint International Access** ☏ 00/800-14477 in Turkey, followed by the area code and number.

MOBILE PHONES

If you have a multiband phone (some countries use different frequencies than what's used in the United States) and your service provider uses the world-standard GSM network (as do T-Mobile, Cingular, and Verizon), you can probably use your phone abroad. Roaming fees can be steep, though: 99¢ a minute is considered reasonable. And overseas, you normally pay the toll charges for incoming calls. It's almost always cheaper to send a text message than to make a call since text messages have a very low set fee (often less than 5¢).

If you just want to make local calls, consider buying a new SIM card (note that your provider may have to unlock your phone for you to use a different SIM card) and a prepaid service plan in the destination. You'll then have a local number and can make local calls at local rates. If your trip is extensive, you could also simply buy a new cell phone in your destination as the initial cost will be offset over time.

If you travel internationally frequently, save one of your old mobile phones or buy a cheap one on the Internet; ask your cell phone company to unlock it for you, and take it with you as a travel phone, buying a new SIM card with pay-as-you-go service in each destination.

Renting a phone in Turkey is very expensive, and it's not easy to find shops that rent. The best solution is to buy a SIM card and a pay-as-you-go service. There are three mobile phone providers in Turkey. The largest is Turkcell, followed by Telsim (which, at press time, had recently been bought by Vodafone and will change its name sometime in 2006 or 2007; they have yet to decide precisely when or to what— although it will include "Vodafone"), and Avea. Each has a network of stores, which are clearly marked, where it is possible to buy SIM cards and pay-as-you-go cards, although readers should take someone with them to translate.

Cellular Abroad ☎ 800/287-5072 ⊕ www. cellularabroad.com rents and sells GMS phones and sells SIM cards that work in many countries. **Mobal** ☎ 888/888-9162 ⊕ www.mobalrental.com rents mobiles and sells GSM phones (starting at $49) that will operate in 140 countries. Per-call rates vary throughout the world. **Planet Fone** ☎ 888/988-4777 ⊕ www.planetfone.com rents cell phones, but the per-minute rates are expensive.

RESTROOMS

Public facilities are common in the tourist areas of major cities and resorts and at archaeological sites and other attractions; in most, a custodian will ask you to pay a fee (ranging from 50 kuruş to YTL 2–3). In virtually all public facilities, including those in all but the fanciest restaurants, toilets are Turkish style (squatters) and toilet paper is often not provided (to cleanse themselves, Turks use a pitcher of water set next to the toilet). Sometimes it's possible to purchase toilet paper from the custodian, but you are well advised to carry a supply with you as part of your travel gear. Alas, standards of restroom cleanliness tend to be a bit low compared to those in Western Europe and America.

Many gas stations have restrooms. If you're away from tourist areas, look for a mosque, as many have restrooms as part of the complex of washing facilities for Muslims to perform their ablutions before performing their prayers. Standards of cleanliness at mosque restrooms are usually higher than at public facilities. Most, but not all, restaurants and cafés have restrooms but the standard is often extremely variable. In general, five-star hotels have the best facilities, and the staff rarely raise any objection if restrooms are used by foreigners not staying at the hotel.

The Bathroom Diaries is a Web site that's flush with unsanitized info on restrooms the world over—each one located, reviewed, and rated.

Find a Loo **The Bathroom Diaries** ⊕ www. thebathroomdiaries.com

SAFETY

Distribute your cash, credit cards, IDs, and other valuables between a deep front pocket, an inside jacket or vest pocket, and a hidden money pouch. Don't reach for the money pouch once you're in public.

Violent crime against strangers in Turkey has increased in recent years, but when compared with Western Europe or North America, it's still relatively rare. You should, nevertheless, watch your valuables, as pickpockets do operate in the major cities and tourist areas. Bag snatching has increased in recent years and women should be careful both when walking and when sitting at open-air cafés and restaurants. Bear in mind that organized gangs often use children to snatch bags.

In June 2004 the separatist Kurdish nationalists, the Kurdistan Workers Party (PKK), resumed its armed campaign after a five-year pause. It is currently conducting a two-front campaign: a rural insurgency in southeastern Turkey and a bombing campaign in the west of the country. One of the PKK's key targets is the tourism industry. There were bombings—and foreign fatalities—in 2005 and 2006. However, given that only two foreigners were killed in 2005 and three in 2006, out of the approximately 20 million tourists who visit the country each year, the danger is statistically very low. The situation is different in southeastern Turkey. While cities and major highways are relatively safe, you should be extremely cautious about visiting more out-of-the-way villages in the region, using unpaved roads or traveling after nightfall. Despite the country's proximity to Iraq, the ongoing insurgency there has had no noticeable impact on security inside Turkey. The U.S. occupation of Iraq remains deeply unpopular in Turkey and Turks will often have little hesitation in letting you know how they feel. However, they will invariably distinguish between the actions of the U.S. government and individual Americans. There have been no reports of any visiting Americans experiencing personal hostility or animosity. For an up-to-date report on the situation, check with the State Department Web site or hot line in Washington, D.C.

GOVERNMENT ADVISORIES

As different countries have different worldviews, look at travel advisories from a range of governments to get more of a sense of what's going on out there. And be sure to parse the language carefully. For example, a warning to "avoid all travel" carries more weight than one urging you to "avoid nonessential travel," and both are much stronger than a plea to "exercise caution." A U.S. government travel warning is more permanent (though not necessarily more serious) than a so-called public announcement, which carries an expiration date.

The U.S. Department of State's Web site has more than just travel warnings and advisories. The consular information sheets issued for every country have general safety tips, entry requirements (though be sure to verify these with the country's embassy), and other useful details.

Consider registering online with the State Department (https://travelregistration.state.gov/ibrs/), so the government will know to look for you should a crisis occur in the country you're visiting. If you travel frequently, also look into the Registered Traveler program of the Transportation Security Administration (TSA; www.tsa.gov). The program, which is still being tested in five U.S. airports, is designed to cut down on gridlock at security checkpoints by allowing prescreened travelers to pass quickly through kiosks that scan an iris and/or a fingerprint. How sci-fi is that?

General Information & Warnings Australian Department of Foreign Affairs & Trade ⊕ www.smartraveller.gov.au. **Consular Affairs Bureau of Canada** ⊕ www.voyage.gc.ca. **U.K. Foreign & Commonwealth Office** ⊕ www.fco.gov.uk/travel. **U.S. Department of State** ⊕ www.travel.state.gov.

LOCAL SCAMS

As Turkey has one of the highest credit card fraud rates in Europe, you should keep your credit cards within sight at all times to prevent them being copied. In many restaurants waiters will swipe your card at the table. If a waiter takes the card away, you should either ensure that it remains within eyesight or ask to accompany the waiter to the POS terminal (you can always manufacture an excuse such as telling the waiter that your bank sometimes asks for a PIN).

There have been a few cases of tourists traveling alone being given drugged drinks and then being robbed. The doctored drinks are usually soft drinks such as sodas. Turks are naturally anxious to ply guests with food and drink, and in the vast majority of cases, there should be no cause for alarm. However, if, for example, you are traveling alone and someone is particularly insistent on you having a cold soft drink and comes back with one already poured into a glass, treat it with extreme caution. If you have any doubts, do not consume it. Someone who is being genuinely hospitable will probably be confused and maybe a little hurt; both are better than your being robbed. If the drink is drugged, the person giving it to you will probably be suspiciously insistent that you drink it.

In crowded areas be aware of a common scam in which two men stage a fight or similar distraction while an accomplice picks the tourist's pocket.

WOMEN IN TURKEY

Turkey is a generally safe destination for women traveling alone, though in heavily touristed areas such as Istanbul, Antalya, and Marmaris, women unaccompanied by men are likely to be approached and sometimes followed. In rural towns, where visits from foreigners are less frequent, men are more respectful toward women traveling on their own. However, in the far east you should be particularly careful; women traveling alone have been known to be harassed in this region.

Some Turkish men are genuinely curious about women from other lands and really do want only to "practice their English." Still, be forewarned that the willingness to converse can easily be misconstrued as something more meaningful. If you are uncomfortable, seek assistance from a Turkish woman or move toward where there are other women present. When it comes to harassment by males, there really is safety in female solidarity. Young blond women will find they attract considerably more attention than brunettes. This is mainly because many Turkish men tend to associate anyone who fulfils their stereotypical image of a Russian with a sex worker. Women who are pregnant or have small children with them are generally treated with such respect as to be virtually immune from harassment.

As for clothing, Turkey is not the place for clothing that is short, tight, or bare, particularly away from the main tourist areas. Longer skirts and shirts and blouses with sleeves are what it takes here to look respectable. Though it may feel odd, covering your head with a scarf will make things easier on you (it's a good idea to have a scarf in your bag at all times). It also helps if you have the manager of the hotel where you are staying call ahead to the manager of your next hotel to announce your arrival—your next host will feel some responsibility to keep you out of harm's way.

As in any other country in the world, the best courses of action are simply to walk on if approached and to avoid potentially troublesome situations, such as deserted neighborhoods at night. Note that in Turkey, many hotels, restaurants, and other eating spots identify themselves as being for an *aile* (family) clientele, and many restaurants have special sections for women and children. How comfortable you are with being alone will affect whether you like these areas, which are away from the action—and you may prefer to take your chances in the main room (though some establishments will resist seating you there).

When traveling alone by bus, you should request a seat next to another woman.

TAXES

The value-added tax, in Turkey called Katma Değer Vergisi, or KDV, is 18% on most goods and services. Hotels typically combine it with a service charge of 10% to 15%, and restaurants usually add a 15% service charge.

Value-added tax is nearly always included in quoted prices. Certain shops are authorized to refund the tax (you must ask). Within a month of leaving Turkey, mail the stamped invoice back to the shop, and a check will be mailed to you—in theory if not always in practice.

When making a purchase, ask for a V.A.T. refund form and find out whether the merchant gives refunds—not all stores do, nor are they required to. Have the form stamped like any customs form by customs officials when you leave the country or, if you're visiting several European Union countries, when you leave the EU. After you're through passport control, take the form to a refund-service counter for an on-the-spot refund (which is usually the quickest and easiest option), or mail it to the address on the form (or the envelope with it) after you arrive home. You receive the total refund stated on the form, but the processing time can be long, especially if you request a credit card adjustment.

Global Refund is a Europe-wide service with 225,000 affiliated stores and more than 700 refund counters at major airports and border crossings. Its refund form, called a Tax Free Check, is the most common across the European continent. The service issues refunds in the form of cash, check, or credit card adjustment.

V.A.T. Refunds Global Refund ☎ 800/566-9828 in the U.S., 800/566-9828 in Canada ⊕ www. globalrefund.com.

TAXIS

Taxis in Turkey are yellow and very easy to spot. They cost about $1 for 1 km, or about ½ mi (50% higher between midnight and 6 AM). Make sure the meter says *gündüz* (day rate); otherwise, you'll be overcharged. Be aware that taxi drivers in tourist areas sometimes doctor their meters to charge more. Don't ride in a taxi in which the meter doesn't work. If you have doubts, ask at your hotel about how much a ride should cost. Many larger hotels will also find cabs for you, usually drivers or companies they know and trust. Note that saying the word *direkt* after giving your destination helps prevent you from getting an unplanned grand tour of town. Tipping is not required, though many taxi drivers expect tourists to round up the price of the ride to the nearest 50 kuruş. There are no extra charges for luggage. In Istanbul, if you cross one of the Bosphorus bridges, you will be expected to add the YTL3 cost of the toll to the bill regardless of which direction you are going (vehicles only pay going from West to East—the theory is that even if he does not have to pay to take you across, the taxi driver will have to pay to go back). In Ankara, taxi drivers are allowed to charge "night rates" (i.e. 50% higher) for trips to the airport because it's so isolated and often difficult for them to find a fare to bring back. Particularly in Istanbul and Ankara, taxi drivers often have a very limited knowledge of the city and will have to ask bystanders or other taxi drivers for directions. (⇨ Tipping, *below*).

TIME

Turkey is 2 hours ahead of London, 7 hours ahead of New York, 10 hours ahead of Los Angeles and Vancouver, 11 hours behind Auckland and 9 hours behind Sydney and Melbourne. Turkey uses daylight saving the same as North America and Europe.

TIPPING

In restaurants a 10%–15% charge is added to the bill in all but inexpensive fast-food spots. However, since this money does not necessarily find its way to your waiter, leave an additional 10% on the table. In top establishments waiters expect tips of 10%–15% in addition to the service charge. Although it's acceptable to include the tip on your bill in restaurants that accept credit cards, a small tip in cash is much appreciated.

Hotel porters expect about $2. Taxi drivers are becoming used to foreigners giving them something; round off the fare to the nearest 50 kuruş. At Turkish baths, staff members who attend to you expect to share a tip of 30%–35% of the bill. Don't worry about missing them—they'll be lined up expectantly on your departure.

Tour guides often expect a tip. Offer as much or (as little) as you feel the person deserves, usually $4–$5 per day if you were happy with the guide. If you've been with the guide for a number of days, tip more. Crews on chartered boats also expect tips.

Restroom attendants will not expect a tip in addition to the charge for using their facilities. If you visit a cinema, the usher will expect a small tip, typically YTL1–2.

TOURS & PACKAGES

GUIDED TOURS

Guided tours are a good option when you don't want to do it all yourself. You travel along with a group (sometimes large, sometimes small), stay in prebooked hotels, eat with your fellow travelers (sometimes included in the price of your tour, sometimes not), and follow a schedule. But not all guided tours are an *If This Is Tuesday, It Must Be Belgium* experience. A knowledgeable guide can take you places that you might never discover on your own, and you may be pushed to see more than you would have otherwise. Tours aren't for everyone, but they can be just the thing for trips to places where making travel arrangements is difficult or time-consuming (particularly when you don't speak the language). Whenever you book a guided tour, find out what's included and what isn't. A "land-only" tour includes all your travel (by bus, in most cases) in the destination, but not necessarily your flights to or even within it. Also, in most cases, prices in tour brochures don't include fees and taxes. And remember that you'll be expected to tip your guide (in cash) at the end of the tour.

New York-based Heritage Tours is highly recommended as a higher-end, full-service travel company. They can design a trip start to finish, including great hotels, private drivers, and tour guides. Pacha Tours is one of the top tour operators in Turkey.

Recommended Generalists Heritage Tours ☎ 800/378-4555 (U.S. and Canada) or 212/206-8400 ⊕ www.heritagetoursonline.com. **Pacha Tours** ☎ 800/722-4288 (U.S. and Canada) ⊕ www.pachatours.com. **Cappadoccia Tours** ☎ 384/341-7485 (in Turkey) ⊕ www.cappadociatours.com. **Credo Tours** ☎ 212/254-8175 (in Turkey) ⊕ www.credo.com.tr

VACATION PACKAGES

Packages *are not* guided tours. Packages combine airfare, accommodations, and perhaps a rental car or other extras (theater tickets, guided excursions, boat trips, reserved entry to popular museums, transit passes), but they let you do your own thing. During busy periods, packages may be your only option because flights and rooms may be otherwise sold out. Packages will definitely save you time. They can also save you money, particularly in peak seasons, but—and this is a really big "but"—you should price each part of the package separately to be sure. And be aware that prices advertised on Web sites and in newspapers rarely include service charges or taxes, which can up your costs by hundreds of dollars.

Note that local tourism boards can provide information about lesser-known and small-niche operators that sell packages to just a few destinations. And don't always assume that you can get the best deal by booking everything yourself. Some packages and cruises are sold only through travel agents.

Each year consumers are stranded or lose their money when packagers—even large ones with excellent reputations—go out of business. How can you protect yourself? First, always pay with a credit card; if you have a problem, your credit card company may help you resolve it. Second, buy trip insurance that covers default. Third, choose a company that belongs to the United States Tour Operators Association, whose members must set aside funds ($1 million) to cover defaults. Finally choose a company that also participates in the Tour Operator Program of the American Society of Travel Agents (ASTA), which will act as mediator in any disputes. You can also check on the tour operator's reputation among travelers by posting an inquiry on one of the Fodors.com forums.

The advantages of taking a package to Turkey are that they will be cheaper and less trouble than arranging everything for yourself. The main disadvantage is that the packages usually include one destination (i.e. Istanbul) and one, or at most two, hotels, so they don't work if you're planning to travel inside Turkey during your stay. You also have less flexibility in being able to choose your hotel.

Organizations American Society of Travel Agents (ASTA) ☎ 703/739-2782 or 800/965-2782 24-hour hotline ⊕ www.astanet.com. **United States Tour Operators Association** (USTOA) ☎ 212/599-6599 ⊕ www.ustoa.com.

TRAIN TRAVEL

The train routes in Turkey tend to meander, meaning that train travel is usually much slower than bus travel—sometimes as much as twice as long. Most travelers much prefer buses, which can be quite plush and comfortable, or flying. The term *express train* is a misnomer in Turkey. Although they exist, serving several long-distance routes, they tend to be slow. The overnight sleeper from Istanbul to Ankara (*Ankara Ekspres*) is the most comfortable and convenient of the trains, with private compartments, attentive service, and a candlelit dining car. There is also daytime service between Ankara and Istanbul. Trains also run between Istanbul and Edirne and between Ankara and İzmir. Turkish State Railways (Türkiye Cumhuriyeti Devlet Demiryolları) is the company that serves the country. The train trip from Istanbul to Ankara takes about 6½ hours nonstop, or roughly 10 hours overnight with stops along the way.

Seat61.com is a helpful Web site regarding train travel in Turkey.

Dining cars on trains between the major cities usually have waiter service and offer decent and inexpensive food. Overnight expresses have sleeping cars and bunk beds. The Istanbul–Ankara run costs $35, including tips; though advance reservations are a must, cancellations are frequent, so you can often get a space at the last minute.

Fares are lower for trains than for buses, and round-trips cost less than two one-way tickets. Student discounts are 10% (30% from December through April). Ticket windows in railroad stations are marked GIŞELERI. Some post offices and authorized travel agencies also sell train tickets. It's advisable to **book in advance, in person, for seats on the best trains and for sleeping quarters.** *See* Essential sections *in* individual chapters for more information on getting around the country by train.

There are no different classes on Turkish trains in the sense of first or second class. However, long-distance trains offer a number of options, such as pullman, compartments (with six seats in each), couchette, and sleeper.

In Turkish, pullman is *pulman,* compartment is *kompartmanlı,* couchette is *kuşetli,* and sleeper is *yataklı.*

Most train stations do not accept credit cards or foreign exchange, so be prepared to pay in Turkish lira.

Inter-Rail passes can be used in Turkey; Eurail passes cannot.

THE ORIENT EXPRESS

If you have the time—and money—consider the still-glamorous *Venice Simplon-Orient Express.* The route runs twice a year from Paris to Istanbul via Budapest and/or Bucharest.

Train Information **Venice Simplon-Orient Express** ✉ Sea Containers House, 20 Upper Ground, London SE1 9PF ☎ 020/7928-6000, 800/524-2420 in the U.S.

CONTACTS

seat61.com (w www.seat61.com/Turkey2.htm). **Turkish State Railways (Türkiye Cumhuriyeti De-** vlet Demiryolları) (☎ 312/311-0602 ⊕ www.tcdd. gov.tr).

Train Station Information **Ankara Tren İstasyonu** ☎ 312/311-0620. **Haydarpaşa Station** ☎ 216/336-0475. **Sirkeci Station** ☎ 212/527-0051.

TRANSPORTATION AROUND TURKEY

How you get around Turkey depends on your time and budget. The most common way to get around the country for both Turks and tourists is to travel by bus. If you have less time or are traveling very long distances, you may want to fly. Once you have arrived at your destination, you can get around by taxi, minibus, *dolmuş* (shared taxi), or rented car. Renting a car gives you more freedom to explore on your own but is more costly and can be more stressful.

TRAVEL AGENTS

If you use an agent—brick-and-mortar or virtual—you'll pay a fee for the service. And know that the service you get from some online agents isn't comprehensive. For example, Expedia or Travelocity don't search for prices on budget airlines or small foreign carriers. That said, some agents (online or not) *do* have access to fares that are difficult to find otherwise, and the savings can more than make up for any surcharge.

A knowledgeable brick-and-mortar travel agent can be a godsend if you're booking a cruise, a package trip that's not available to you directly, an air pass, or a complicated itinerary including several overseas flights. What's more, travel agents that specialize in a destination may have exclusive access to certain deals and insider information on things such as charter flights. Agents who specialize in types of travelers (senior citizens, gays and lesbians, naturists) or types of trips (cruises, luxury travel, safaris) can also be invaluable.

A top-notch agent planning your trip to Turkey will make sure you get the correct visa application and complete it on time; the one booking your cruise may get you a cabin upgrade or arrange to have bottle of champagne chilling in your cabin when you embark. And complain about the surcharges all you like, but when things don't work out the way you'd hoped, it's nice to have an agent to put things right.

Agent Resources American Society of Travel Agents ☎ 703/739-2782 ⊕ www.travelsense.org. **Online Agents Expedia** ⊕ www.expedia.com. **Onetravel.com** ⊕ www.onetravel.com. **Orbitz** ⊕ www.orbitz.com. **Priceline.com** ⊕ www.priceline.com. **Travelocity** ⊕ www.travelocity.com.

VISITOR INFORMATION

There are tourist information offices in most of the main cities in Turkey; check the Essentials section in each chapter. They can be helpful if you arrive in a destination without a hotel reservation, but you're better off trying to book something in advance.

New York Turkish Tourist Office ☎ 212/687-2194 ⊕ e-mail: ny£tourismturkey.org. **Washington D.C. Turkish Tourist Office** ☎ 202/612-6800 ⊕ e-mail: dc£tourismturkey.org.

WEB SITES

We're really proud of our Web site: Fodors.com is a great place to begin any journey. Scan Travel Wire for suggested itineraries, travel deals, restaurant and hotel openings, and other up-to-the-minute info. Check out Booking to research prices and book plane tickets, hotel rooms, rental cars, and vacation packages. Head to Talk for on-the-ground pointers from travelers who frequent our message boards. You can also link to loads of other travel-related resources.

After your trip, be sure to rate the places you visited and share your experiences and travel tips with us and other Fodorites in Travel Ratings and Talk on www.fodors.com.

All About Turkey There are, of course, hundreds of Web sites about Turkey; these are some of the standouts. **Antalya** ⊕ www.antalya2000.com ⊕ www.antalya-ws.com. **Fethiye** ⊕ www.fethiye-net.com. **Republic of Turkey** ⊕ www.turkey.org. **Travel in Turkey** ⊕ www.mersina.com ⊕ www.turkiye-online.com/ ⊕ www.exploreturkey.com. **Turkish Airlines** ⊕ www.turkishairlines.com. **Turkish Embassy in Washington DC** ⊕ www.turkishembassy.org or www.tourismturkey.org. **Turkish Ministry of Culture and Tourism** ⊕ www.goturkey.com. **Turkish Tourist Office** ⊕ www.turizm.gov.tr.

Currency Conversion Google ⊕ www.google.com does currency conversion. Just type in the amount you want to convert and an explanation of how you want it converted (e.g., "14 Swiss francs in dollars"), and then voilà. **Oanda.com** ⊕ www.oanda.com also allows you to print out a handy table with the current day's conversion rates. **XE.com** ⊕ www.xe.com is a good currency conversion Web site.

Time Zones Timeanddate.com ⊕ www.timeanddate.com/worldclock can help you figure out the correct time anywhere in the world.

Weather Accuweather.com ⊕ www.accuweather.com is an independent weather-forecasting service with especially good coverage of hurricanes. **Weather.com** ⊕ www.weather.com is the Web site for the Weather Channel.

Other Resources CIA World Factbook ⊕ www.odci.gov/cia/publications/factbook/index.html has profiles of every country in the world. It's a good source if you need some quick facts and figures.

INDEX

PHOTO CREDITS

ABOUT OUR WRITERS

Stephen Brewer first set foot in Turkey two decades ago and has been back many, many times since. He considers two of the world's all-time great travel experiences to be hiking through the valleys of Cappadocia and wandering the streets of Istanbul.

Evin Doğu was born in Baton Rouge, Louisiana, 26 years ago. Hoping to get in touch with her roots and fulfill her ever-present wanderlust, she moved to Istanbul in 2006 and has lived there ever since. When she's not traveling, Evin writes and translates for *Time Out Istanbul* and teaches English as a foreign language.

Benjamin Harvey was born in New York in 1979 and grew up in Alabama. He studied at Wesleyan and Columbia University and currently reports for the Associated Press from Istanbul, where he has lived on and off since late 2002.

Yeşim Erdem Holland grew up in İzmir, studied in Ankara, and lives in Istanbul. She's a journalist and writer who has worked for Turkish and foreign publications, including *Time Out* magazine and guidebook, the *Turkish Daily News,* and the Turkish daily national newspaper *Akşam.*

Gareth Jenkins was born and educated in Britain. After graduating from Durham University with a degree in Ancient Greek and Latin, he worked as an archaeologist and writer in Britain before setting off to travel and teach English in the Mediterranean. He spent five years in Egypt, Greece, and Israel before moving to Istanbul, where he has lived since 1989. He works as a freelance journalist and writer. He has published four books on Turkish history and politics.

Hugh Pope has lived in Turkey for 20 years and for most of them has been a correspondent for the *Wall Street Journal.* He is the author of *Turkey Unveiled: a History of Modern Turkey* and, most recently, of *Sons of the Conquerors: the Rise of the Turkic World,* a collection of reportage from China through Central Asia to the United States.

Yigal Schleifer is a freelance journalist based in Istanbul, where he writes for the *Christian Science Monitor* and the *Jerusalem Report,* among other publications. Living in Turkey since 2002, he has traveled extensively throughout the country, particularly in the Black Sea and southeast regions.